The Message of
A Course
In Miracles

A translation of the Text
in plain language

The Message of
A Course
In Miracles

A translation of the Text
in plain language

BOOKS

Winchester, UK
Washington, USA

First published by O-Books, 2010
O Books is an imprint of John Hunt Publishing Ltd., The Bothy, Deershot Lodge, Park Lane, Ropley,
Hants, SO24 0BE, UK
office1@o-books.net
www.o-books.com

For distributor details and how to order please visit the 'Ordering' section on our website.

Text copyright Elizabeth A. Cronkhite 2009

ISBN: 978 1 84694 319 5

A CIP catalogue record for this book is available from the British Library.

Design: Stuart Davies

Printed in the UK by CPI Antony Rowe
Printed in the USA by Offset Paperback Mfrs, Inc

We operate a distinctive and ethical publishing philosophy in all areas of
its business, from its global network of authors to production and
worldwide distribution.

CONTENTS

Preface

God is Formless, Infinite Being. Only God is Real.
You are Eternally One with God.
Forgetting this has given rise to a world of lack, limitation, and pain in
your mind.
Remembering this restores you to the natural Love, Peace, and Joy of your
Limitless Being in God.
The only purpose that the world that you perceive has for you is to be
forgiven your perception of separation from God.
Forgiving the world is how you remember that you are One with God.

This is the loving message of *A Course in Miracles,* a self-study course designed to help you undo all of your conscious and unconscious beliefs in separation from God so that you can return to an awareness of your Oneness with God. One of the *Course*'s stated purposes is to save you time on your return to God, but the *Course*'s style, especially in the essential Text, which lays out the theological foundation for the rest of the *Course,* presents time-consuming challenges. If you have tried to read the *Course* and found it too dense and difficult, you are not the only one. It *is* dense and difficult, even for experienced students. And if you are a student of the *Course,* you may feel that it is taking you too long to get its whole message.

The challenges presented by the *Course*'s style provide no benefit to the reader. Deciphering the *Course* is time-consuming, it leads to an intellectual struggle when practice is what is truly transformative, and it is simply not practical for the average student. This is why I have translated the Text of the *Course* into plain language through its central loving message of your Oneness with God.

I became a student of *A Course in Miracles* in 1984. My first sense was that on some level I had written it. It was familiar to me, but without my knowing what it was going to say. I felt that the *Course* was related to my purpose in the world and that one day I would do something more with it than just study it. I didn't know exactly how that would unfold, so I forged ahead with studying it with the Holy Spirit. Very soon I experienced Oneness through direct Revelations with God, and in the world through the miracle of the Holy relationship. My experiences of Oneness were not of the world, and they bore no resemblance to any experience I had had in the world, but they were far more familiar to me than anything in the world. Revelations taught me that only God is Real; the miracle of the Holy relationship made me aware that what I perceive is only in my mind, and that it is my choice whether I experience separation or Oneness.

After these experiences I felt, rightly or wrongly, that I was reading *A Course in Miracles* in a way that was different from other students. For one thing, the *Course* was not just theory for me because I was experiencing everything that it said on a level within myself I previously did not know existed. And no other student that I knew at the time was talking about experiencing Oneness with God, or with another in a Holy relationship. So no one was talking about the deep conflict experiencing Oneness brings to a mind that still values separation. I both needed my experiences validated, and feared that they would be validated. I felt that the experiences of Oneness I had were a total blessing, a source of pure Joy, and also a curse. I knew that I had experienced Truth, and I was grateful, but I was angry that the world that I loved was losing its value for me when I was only twenty years old, and I hadn't yet had a chance to pursue my dreams in it.

For many years I studied the *Course* only intellectually as a way to keep my experiences of Oneness at bay. I understood a little of the *Course* here, and a little of it there, but I couldn't see how it all fit together. Then, after fifteen years, I finally stopped resisting my experiences. As I read the *Course* through my openness to the Reality of my Oneness with God, the *Course*'s coherency began to emerge for me. This new clarity felt like a gift given to me, rather than something that I had attained. I read the Text again from the beginning, and I 'tested' this unified message as though it was the 'key' to the *Course*'s 'code'. This took me beyond the surface of the dense, difficult, and seemingly inconsistent words, and into the *Course*'s whole context. The more I accepted what my experiences of Oneness had revealed to me (that only God is Real), the crisper and simpler the Course's message became. I was finally experiencing what the *Course* says is another of its purposes: to help me sort out Truth from illusion.

With this consistent message of Oneness growing clearer in me, I got a nudge from the Holy Spirit to start teaching it to other students of the *Course*. I began by leading a study group, and after training as a life-coach I offered my services as a mentor to other students who wanted to save time and effort on their way to lasting Peace. I wrote blogs, a newsletter, and booklets to clarify the *Course*'s message, but I found that students were still confused, frustrated, and bogged down by the *Course*'s language in their day-to-day study.

In late 2007 I was prompted by the Holy Spirit to try putting the cohesive message I was reading in the Text into writing, paragraph by paragraph. I was surprised by this concept, and I tested it by translating the first few paragraphs of Part 2 in the first chapter. I immediately felt a satisfaction that I had not had in all my other attempts to clarify the *Course*. This was bringing clarity right where it was needed – directly to the reading of the Text itself. As I got to work translating the Text with the Holy Spirit, I realized that it was the culmination of my sense that the *Course* was my life's work, of the lessons of my experiences of Oneness, and of the sudden and amazing clarity that I had accepted after a decade and a half of study.

This translation has value not only as a study aid for students of the original *A Course in Miracles*, but as a spiritual teaching on its own. The loving message is the same in this translation as it is in the original, but here it is easier to access. You may choose to read it without ever reading the original. For that reason, what follows is a brief intro-duction to *A Course in Miracles*. However you use this book, I wish you peace on your return to God.

Liz Cronkhite
Las Vegas, Nevada, 2009

What is *A Course in Miracles*?

A Course in Miracles is one of many thousands of lesson plans designed to re-awaken you to the awareness that only God is Real, and that you are One with God. It is your choice to be separate from God – your True Being – that gives rise in your mind to a world of separation that is full of lack, pain, loneliness, attack, guilt, fear, and aimlessness. The *Course* comes from your True Self, the Christ in your Mind, the part of you that is Eternally Part of God, in answer to your call for Peace, and an end to suffering. Your free will means that you get to choose *when* you will learn what is taught in the *Course*, but whether the *Course*, or some other path, is the specific means for you to learn these lessons, is up to the Holy Spirit within you.

The *Course* has three parts: the *Text* (theory), the *Workbook* (practice), and the *Manual for Teachers* (path). There are also two supplements to the *Course*: *Psychotherapy: Purpose, Process and Practice*; and *The Song of Prayer: Prayer, Forgiveness, Healing*. They are written in a heavily figurative language that takes familiar everyday and religious terms, and gives them new, loving meaning. For example, *Christ* is not only Jesus, but the part of your mind that is eternally One with God. *Father* and *Son* mean God's Wholeness and Part of God's Wholeness. The *Course* also uses distinctions to clarify its meaning: *to create* means 'to be one with'; *to make* means 'to bring into existence'. God's *Creation*, then, is the Extension of God's Own Being, and you are Part of This in Truth. Everything else was made, not by God, but by your erroneous idea that What is All can have an opposite.

The *Course* teaches that there is no sin, because at no time can you make your perceived separation from God your reality. This perception is an error to be corrected, not punished. So the *Course* does not prescribe a lifestyle, because at no time is the world your reality, and what you do in the world has no effect on God. But, clearly, you think that you are in a world, and this is the source of all of your pain and sense of lack. The *Course* helps you to undo this by teaching you how to sort out Truth (God) from illusion (everything else) in your mind by teaching you to distinguish between the thought systems of the Holy

Spirit (your Christ Mind), and the ego (the personal mind). Under the Holy Spirit's guidance, your forgiving your perception that you are separate from God is the only purpose that the world has for you. By extending God's Love in your awareness (the miracle), you heal your sense of separation from God. When your forgiving is complete, your mind is healed, and it is prepared to accept the Wholeness of God again.

Every moment you are teaching yourself what you believe you are, and in the process of undoing your sense of separation from God, you are what the *Course* calls a 'teacher of God'.

Where *A Course in Miracles* Comes From

Starting in the mid-1960s, Dr Helen Schucman, a child psychologist, took down *A Course in Miracles* through a process of inner dictation. She identified the Voice in her mind speaking to her as Jesus. As the *Course* teaches, Jesus is now wholly identified with the Christ Mind and you can look at the Voice in the *Course* as the Christ, or Holy Spirit, in your mind, represented to Dr Schucman by the form of Jesus.

Dr Schucman considered herself the 'scribe' and Jesus the 'author' of the *Course*. She was assisted by a colleague, Dr Bill Thetford, who typed out the *Course* as she read from her notes. The whole process took around ten years, and *A Course in Miracles* was first published in 1975.

Translator's Introduction

This is a translation of the first edition Text of *A Course in Miracles*. It is written in plain, simple, everyday language to give you easy access to the *Course*'s message. But it is not simply a straight translation of the Text into more accessible language. It is an interpretation of the Text through its whole message, and through the translator's own experiences of Oneness through direct Revelation of God, and in a Holy relationship.

Besides the obvious undoing of the original Text's dense figurative language, this translation's content may seem on the surface to be very different from the original, but it really only provides a simplification of the original's content. For example, the original often seems to be speaking to you on two levels. It seems to straddle both your perception of the world as your reality, and the necessity of you recognizing that the world is only a perception in your mind, because God is your Reality. It provides a role for you in your relationships with others in your perception that you are in a world, and a superficial reading of it seems to imply that you are responsible for the salvation of others. But this translation takes you immediately to the deeper reading by bringing the *Course*'s whole context to the surface from the beginning, and throughout it speaks to you only on that level. It emphasizes your inward journey, so it deals only with your mind, which is where you must correct your perception of separation from God. It acknowledges that you think that you are in a world with others, but it always brings you back to the fact that the world and others are only in your perception. Because they are in your perception, they are in your mind, so you don't need to save *them*, but you need to save your mind from the belief that it is split between 'you' and a world that seems outside of you.

Since much of the original Text reads like a dialogue between Jesus and Dr Helen Schucman, who scribed it, and much of it addresses her specific experience, this translation attempts to generalize the Text's message as much as possible. Where necessary, many paragraphs in this translation offer clarifying elaborations that are not in the original. This means that some ideas are brought into focus earlier in this translation than they are in the original. Occasionally, to clarify an idea, examples not included in the original are offered in notes at the end of the book. But phrases like, 'You have not yet realized...' remain.

Because of the conversational tone of the Text, there are a few paragraphs and sections that veer off of the immediate topic. The translation of these passages is bracketed [] to delineate them from the surrounding context.

Dr Schucman experienced a Holy relationship with Dr Bill Thetford, who assisted her by typing out the manuscript as she read from her notes. A Holy relationship is an experience of Oneness with someone that you have perceived as outside of yourself. The lesson of the Holy relationship is that they are not separate from you, but a part of your Mind. While the *experience* of Oneness is always the same, each *expression* of the Holy relationship in the world is unique. Drs Schucman and Thetford were both aware of their Holy relationship, which resulted in a reciprocal experience where what one felt the other experienced as well. Many students do not have the opportunity to experience a Holy relationship with another who is experiencing it with them, so the passages in the original that deal with the specific aspects of the Holy relationship between Drs Schucman and Thetford have been generalized in this translation, and in a few cases whole phrases have been omitted. Where the omissions are significant, this is noted in a note at the end of the book.

Since the goal of the *Course* is to move you away from a personal identity, this translation has de-personalized God from a 'Who' to an 'It' as God is Everywhere. Male pronouns for God have been replaced by neutral pronouns.

In the original, it is not always clear when 'you' means you in your identification with a personal mind, as the decision-maker, or in your Oneness with God. In this translation, 'you' addresses the decision-maker. The decision-maker is your mind at the point where it seems to be split between God and a personal mind, so it is referred to in this translation as 'your split mind'. The decision-maker is the 'student' in your mind that decides from which 'teacher' you will learn what you are: the personal mind, which your split mind made, or the Holy Spirit,

Which you are, and Which is One with God. It is the level of your mind where your error of perceiving separation from God occurs, so it is the level where you must make correction.

References to Jesus have been limited to His specific role and most 'I' phrases have been translated as 'the Holy Spirit' or 'your Christ Mind'. Many Biblical, philosophical, and literary references have been omitted, and their meaning has been distilled as part of the whole paragraph in which they occur. An exception to this is where the *Course* gives an example of a correct reading of a Biblical passage.

Aspects and traits of God have been capitalized to clarify when the Text is referring to God, or to the experience of God.

To bring greater clarity, some terms have been changed or replaced. For example, this translation uses the term 'Real Perception' in place of 'real world'. The 'real world' is a change in your perception of the world that is brought about through miracles. A miracle is a shift in your perception away from separation, and toward the Oneness of your mind and all that it perceives. This can be either a shift in your internal experience alone or a shift in your physical world as well as in your experience. 'Real Perception' is used in this translation because 'perception' encompasses both what you perceive, and your interpretation of what you perceive.

This translation is based on the first edition Text of *A Course in Miracles*, because the first edition is in the public domain. The titles of chapters and sub-sections have been retained for ease of comparison to the original, even though they contain the figurative language that this translation undoes in the body of the Text. Since most students today study later editions, its sub-sections and paragraphs have been numbered for easier comparison to those editions. The sub-sections are numbered with Arabic numerals rather than in the Roman numerals of later editions, however, because the numbering system of later editions is copyrighted. A glossary of terms that compares terms in the original with this translation is included at the end.

Introduction

This is a course in miracles. You must learn the lessons in it, but you choose when you want to learn them. Free will does not mean that you choose what it is that you *need* to learn, but that you choose what you *want* to learn at any given time. This course does not teach you the meaning of God's Love, because that is beyond what you can be taught. But it does teach you how to remove your obstacles to God's Love, Which is your natural State of Being. Fear appears to be the opposite of God's Love, but God's Love is All that there is, and It has no opposite.

This course can be summed up in this way:

God cannot be changed.
Only God exists.
For you to know this is for you to have the Peace of God.

Chapter 1

The Meaning of Miracles

1. Principles of Miracles[1]

1. Miracles are extensions of God's Love in your awareness. They are
    always whole and complete, no matter their seeming form or size.
    Your every extension of God's Love is a miracle. Miracles do not
    always produce results that are visible to the body's eyes, and they
    may affect situations of which you are not aware.

2. Miracles are not spectacles to make others believe in God, or in
    your own power. They are the result of your true prayer, or
    communion, with God. Through prayer you receive God's Love;
    through the miracle you extend your experience of God's Love. The
    real miracle is God's Love; Its expression in the world that you
    perceive is not important. Your True Mind and Holy Spirit, Which
    are God's Love, are miracles.

3. Experiencing miracles is necessary for you as the means for you to
    remember that you are One with God. By extending God's Love
    you become aware that God's Love is within you. You receive the
    Love that you give, because you strengthen the awareness of God
    in your mind as you extend Love. All the miracles that you
    experience join in the plan of the Atonement, which is the complete
    correction of your perception of separation from God.

4. All of your fear and your sense of lack and limitation come from
    your belief that you are separate from God. Your experience of the
    miracle atones for, or corrects, your misperception by reminding
    you that you are One with God. By overcoming your fear, your
    experience of the miracle prepares you for direct Revelation of God,
    in Which you experience no fear.

5. Your experience of miracles comes from the Holy Spirit, the Voice
    for God in your mind. The Holy Spirit inspires and is in charge of
    miracles. It is the Holy Spirit in your mind that is really important,
    not the expression of the miracle. You cannot experience miracles in

the personal mind, which *is* separate from God. Attempts by you to manifest 'miracles' with the personal mind will lead you to a further sense of separation from God. Inspired by your Spiritual Mind, your experience of the miracle reminds you that you are One with God, and releases you from your belief that you are a personal self.

6.   God's Love is natural to you because you are One with God. When you do not experience miracles, it is because you are not open to God. You can always, without exception, experience miracles, but you must overcome your obstacles to God first.

7.   When you believe that what the body's eyes show you is reality, you fear God's Love, Which *is* Reality. You can have only one identity: the Holy Spirit or the personal self. Your experience of the miracle unifies your mind because it overlooks the appearance of separate personal selves, and looks only on God's Love.

8.   Because it comes from the Holy Spirit within you, your experience of the miracle reminds you that you are Spirit, not a body, healing your mind of its misidentification with a body. All forms of illness are the result of your identifying with a personal self in a body.

9.   As an expression of your Oneness with God, the miracle heals your guilt for perceiving that you separated yourself from God in the past, and it frees you from fear of future punishment for this. Your experience of a miracle comes to you from the Oneness of Eternity, and it overlooks separation and time. Your experiencing miracles is the only real purpose time has for you.

10. Gratitude is due to the miracle as an expression of your Real Identity. You can deny that you are One with God, but you cannot alter this Fact. You need to experience miracles as a means to remind you that you are One with God. When you return to full awareness of God, you will no longer need the miracle.

2. Revelation, Time and Miracles

1.   A Revelation is an experience of Oneness with God in Which you experience no doubt and no fear. In your perption that you are in a world, you often seek for this Oneness in physical relationships but they cannot achieve It. A Revelation unites you directly with God;

a miracle extends your awareness of God in your perception. You experience both the Revelation and the miracle in the individual mind, but they do not originate there. The individual mind induces action, but it does not inspire it. You are free to believe what you choose, and your actions attest to what you believe.

2.   The experience of the Revelation cannot be described. It is pure experience that is beyond words. Your experience of the miracle inspires you to action in your perception that you are in a world, and is more important in the early phase of your learning, because you must first learn to overcome your sense of separation from God in your mind's perception. God's Love as you experience it directly in Revelation transcends all perception.

3.   Because God is the Perfect Whole of Which you are a Perfect Part, it is appropriate for you to view God as greater than you, and therefore to look on the Revelation with wonder. Wonder is not an appropriate response to your experience of the miracle, which extends God's Love outward in your perception from the Holy Spirit in your mind. Wonderment is inappropriate toward Jesus, Who is not greater than you, but Who modeled the Christ Mind, Which is also in your mind. Jesus is due your love, respect, obedience, and devotion because He is a model for your complete awareness of God, which is still only a potential in you.

4.   Time is the only thing that seems to separate you from your Christ Mind, Which was modeled by Jesus. As you rise in your awareness of your Oneness with God, you will shift in your identification from the personal mind to the Christ Mind. It is necessary for you to attain the Christ Mind to prepare you for God. Christ is the Whole Truth in your mind. It is the part of you that is One with God.

5.   A direct Revelation of God comes to you through your Christ Mind when you are open to It. A Revelation reminds you that you are One with God, Which God has not forgotten, but you have.

6.   In time, it seems as though it will take forever for you to recognize the Oneness of your Mind. Your experience of the miracle saves you time by bringing Oneness to your mind now. It does not bring you to a full awareness of God, but each miracle you experience is a step

toward your full awareness of God.

3. Atonement and Miracles

1. Your Christ Mind is in charge of the plan of the Atonement, which is the full correction of your perception of separation from God. When you extend God's Love, you increase your own awareness of God's Love within you. By following only your Christ Mind, you will correct all of your perceptions of separation from God. This is your only purpose in your perception that you are in a world. When you have accepted complete correction, you will be Christ, Which *is* the correction.

2. Your split mind will become united again. The personal mind will give way to your Christ Mind, because your Christ Mind is Eternal. As a Part of God you are Love, and you must remember to think of yourself this way.

3. By accepting your Christ Mind as your Identity, you let go of, or forgive, your perceptions of personal selves in a world separate from God. This is the plan of the Atonement. Your experience of miracles, which are inspired by your Christ Mind, unite your mind and its perceptions in Oneness, and release you from your perception of separation from God.

4. Your Christ Mind is the awareness that you are One with God, and therefore your Christ Mind *is* the Atonement. Only the Christ in you can inspire your experience of miracles, which are extensions of God's Love. Your purpose is the Atonement, and you must put aside the personal mind, and be open to the guidance of your Christ Mind, to fulfill It. Experiencing miracles will lead you to be open to direct Revelation of God.

5. Your error in perceiving yourself as separate from God does not threaten God, but God does threaten your error. You are free to see yourself as a personal self separate from God, or to see the Truth that you are Spirit, Eternally loved by God in Oneness with God. The Atonement recognizes the latter, and undoes all of your fear. So when you are frightened by God, it is because you are defending a personal self as yourself. When you project the source of your fear onto the world of separation that you perceive, you

reinforce fear in your mind. But if you choose instead to extend God's Love in place of the world of separation, you undo fear in your mind.

6. Your behavior follows from your interpretations of the world that you perceive. To behave appropriately, you must learn to look out from the Holy Spirit in you to the Holy Spirit in all that your mind perceives.

7. Your Christ Mind extends God's Love even when you are not aware of It. You will experience the miracle when you are open to it, and overlook the personal mind and its perceptions, and unite with Christ in your perception. Your experience of the miracle reminds you that you are One with God, and extends Oneness to be all that you perceive.

8. Your experience of miracles always bless *you*, even if you cannot see a manifestation of them in the world. God's Love is always present, and your Christ Mind, not the personal mind, is in charge of any action that you should take. Only your Christ Mind is aware of what you need to correct your perception of separation from God.

9. You will experience miracles when you are ready for them. You accept as much of God's Love as you can at any given time, but your experience of the miracle does not really have a 'size' since God's Love is always Whole. When you accept God's Love for yourself, it is inevitable that you will extend It in your awareness.

4. The Escape from Darkness

1. Your denying that you are One with God does not change the fact that you are One with God. Your recognizing that you are in denial will threaten your identification with a personal self and make you fearful, but accepting that you are One with God will dispel all fear, since denying the Truth is the actual source of your fear. When you are no longer in denial, and you are willing to remember that you are One with God, you will naturally experience Peace and Joy.

2. Denying the Truth frightens you because on some level you are aware that you are deceiving yourself. This deception takes a lot of effort, and it results in a personal self that you work hard to make

14

real to you. As an extension of God's Love, your experience of the miracle reminds you that only God is Reality, and it corrects your perception of yourself as a personal self. Accepting this correction is your only real purpose, and it abolishes your fear by abolishing your denial of Truth that is the source of your fear.

3. Denying that you are One with God leads to your sense of lack, and to your making of a personal self to seek for the Wholeness that you gave away. In God you have Everything, and the purpose of the Atonement is to correct your perception of separation from God to remind you of this.

4. You overcome your fear and sense of lack, which are inspired by your denial of your Oneness with God, by forgiving, or overlooking, your error of perceiving yourself as a personal self. By extending God's Love, the miracle reminds you that Christ is your Reality, and it undoes all of your fear and lack. Jesus taught forgiveness by demonstrating the unreality of the personal self, and the Reality of Christ, by overcoming death. The idea that you should be punished for separating from God fails to acknowledge that your perception of separation from God is only an error. By allowing God's Love to be extended through you, you correct this error.

5. Wholeness and Spirit

1. Both the miracle and the body are temporary learning aids that you will put aside when you return to full awareness of your Oneness with God. The body is neutral, and it can be used by your mind to extend God's Love, or to perpetuate your sense of separation from God. You can put off your *awareness* of your Oneness with God, but you can never make your separation from God real. You can destroy the body, but you cannot destroy What you really are. You are One with God. Spirit

2. For you to be miracle-minded is for you to be open to the awareness that you are One with God *now*. Every miracle that you extend reduces the time that you need to fully remember that you are One with God. When you have remembered this, you will no longer need an individual self.

15

3.   When you have extended correction of your perception of separation from God to all that your mind perceives, you will be aware only of Oneness. If you perceive yourself as a personal self separate from God, you deny God's Oneness. You must accept that you are One with God to know yourself.

4.   Your mind *will* be healed of your sense of separation from God. Your experience of the miracle calls you to remember that you are One with God, even if you choose to deny this. God is One and Whole, and this is What Holiness *is.* God cannot be made un-whole. Your experiences of miracles affirm the Oneness of God.

5.   God is the Eternal Truth, and cannot change or be changed. God's Holy Spirit within you is Perfect, and cannot be changed. But you are free to choose if your mind will serve the Holy Spirit, or the personal self. In your perception of separation from God, these are the only choices available to you. If you choose to have your mind serve the Holy Spirit, you will become aware of your Oneness with God again, and you will be Limitless in your awareness. If you choose to have your mind serve the personal self, you will still be One with God, but denying This limits you, and introduces you to the perception of lack. To truly change your mind, you must open it to Truth.

6.   Your experience of the miracle is a sign that you are following your Christ Mind. This heals your sense of lack and limitation. Your identification with a personal self will not satisfy you, and the means that you have employed to make yourself feel whole again have not worked. As you let go of your identification with a personal self, you will be disoriented for a while, but the means that you have employed to feel whole have only increased your sense of lack and limitation.

6. The Illusion of Needs

1.   You can only be at Peace by completely forgiving, or releasing, your perception of separation from God. You will only learn how to do this when you accept that you need to do this, and when you want to do this. In God there is no lack, and therefore no needs. But by perceiving yourself as separate from God, you deprive yourself of

your sense of Wholeness, and you make lack and needs. You act according to the needs that you perceive, and this depends on how you perceive yourself.

2. The only lack that you need to correct is your sense of separation from God. By making a personal self, you seem to split your mind in two, and this leads to your sense of lack. Your sense of lack manifests as the personal self's many needs. Believing these needs are real, the personal mind orders them according to perceived importance, distracting you from recognizing that you really have only one need. Only by recognizing that you have only one need can you act in a way to truly correct it.

3. Your mind seems to be split into two levels: God and the personal self. Before you can recognize that your mind is not really split, and that only God is your Real Mind, you have to acknowledge that it is a mistake to believe in a split mind. Until you do, no real correction can occur. An error must be corrected on the level where it seems to occur.

4. Your perception of a world is the level of your mind where the error seems to occur. The personal mind is like God's Mind in that it believes in what is in it. You cannot find your own way out of a fearful world because you made it, and your belief in it makes it your 'reality'. But from the Holy Spirit's point of view, the purpose of the world that you perceive is to correct your perception of separation from God.

5. All forms of fear are not real, because they do not come from God. You correct your perception of separation from God by questioning whether what you believe in is One with God. This is how your experience of the miracle helps you sort out the false from the true:

God's Love undoes fear.
If you experience fear, then you are not experiencing God's Love.
And:
Only God's Love is Real.

If you experience fear, then you are experiencing an illusion.

17

You only need to accept this to be free of fear, lack, and limitation. Only God's Love can undo fear.

7. Distortions of Miracle Impulses

1. Your perception of yourself as a body makes it hard for you to be aware of God's Love within you. Your desire to physically 'love' another is a distortion of your desire to experience God's Oneness. You can experience Real Pleasure only by extending God's Love. When you don't extend God's Love, you deny that you are One with God, and you validate your illusion of a personal self that is separate from God. But your extending God's Love corrects this misperception. You will never be at Peace using a body to try to be whole.

2. Do not forget that you are One with God, and that only God can satisfy you. For a while you must extend God's Love through a body, because you are not yet aware enough of your Oneness with God to see beyond it. The only real use the body has is as a learning device through which you learn to remember that you are One with God.

3. Your perception of yourself as separate from God (a personal self in a body within a world) is a distortion of your mind; a fantasy. Your reactions and actions in your perception that you are in a world stem from your unawareness that it *is* a fantasy. This fantasy, which includes the fantasies that you have in the world and recognize as such, are attempts to satisfy the false needs that have arisen from your sense of separation from God. They are destructive in nature because they are your attempt to undo Reality, but they are real only to you who make them, and believe in them. If you extend God's Love instead of the fantasy of separation, the experience of the miracle will be real to you because you will believe in it. Your belief in it will strengthen God's Love in your total awareness. Your fantasies will fall away as the satisfying nature of God's Love will make fantasies unnecessary. God is lost to you as you try to make another reality and defend it. As long as you believe in personal selves and bodies, you will think that you are lost to God. Your only real goal is to extend God everywhere.

(Here, at the end of this first chapter, the Text diverges from its above topic to discuss the importance of these early concepts.)[1]

4.   This is a course in mind training, and it requires attention and study. It is important for you to carefully study the concepts in these earlier parts, because later parts will rest on them. These early concepts will imply things to you that will be expanded on later, but first you need an awareness of God's Love to undo your fear of what is to come.

5.   You have a tendency to fear God as something separate from you, rather than to know God as the Whole of Which you are Part. So it is important to lay down a solid foundation of trust so that you do not fear God. Your experience of God's Love undoes fear, because the miracle reminds you that you are One with God. Some later steps of this course will involve your direct approach to God, and you need the experience of miracles to prepare you for this. It is your awareness of your Oneness with God that heals your mind. This is what this course explains. You might occasionally experience this Oneness through direct Revelation with God, but to bring your Oneness with God into your full awareness, you need to experience the miracle.

Chapter 2

The Separation and the Atonement

1. The Origins of Separation

1. *Creation* is God's Being extending Infinitely and Eternally. God
    creates by extending God Everywhere, Always. Being One with
    God, you create in the same way, and you have the same Loving
    Will to extend God as God does. You are Whole and Perfect in your
    Oneness with God, and there is no lack in you, because there is no
    lack in God. Your ability to create, or to extend your mind, is not
    lost because you perceive yourself as separate from God. But this
    inappropriate use of your mind results in *projection*, which is what
    happens when you believe that you lack, and you make your own
    ideas to fill that lack. This process happens this way:

    > First, you believe that you can change God by separating off part
    > of God's Mind.
    > Second, you believe that this makes lack and imperfection real.
    > Third, you believe that you can make split-off, separate selves,
    > and that you have made a separate self for you.
    > Fourth, you believe that you are your own source, and that what
    > you are is your own choice.

2. This is the separation; the 'detour into fear'. This is not real. You are
    Eternally One with God, and wholly like God. Just as God extends
    only God, as Part of God, you too can only extend God. But because
    God's Will is Free, so is yours.

3. God is Whole. This is Truth. The separation introduced the idea of
    lack to you. Lack is untruth, or illusion. Believing in illusion is a
    choice, and it will disappear in an instant if you want it to, because it
    is only a misperception. Your perception of a world is like a dream
    from which you have to awaken. But you cannot do so as long as you
    project the source of the world that you perceive away from you. You

Eternally have within you the ability to extend God as God extends God. In Reality, extending God is your only choice, because God made your Will Free for your Joy in extending the Perfect.

4.   All of your fear comes from your belief that you have the power to change God. Of course you cannot, and you have not, really done this. Recognizing this is how you undo fear. The means for undoing fear is accepting correction of your perception that you have separated yourself from God. At first, because you are so used to being afraid, you may be fearful of correction, confusing it with the rest of your illusions. But once you have accepted that you are One with God, and that you have not changed this Fact, you will recognize this is the way out of fear. You will recognize that your Oneness with God has always been the Truth.

5.   The particular forms of your illusions do not matter; God's Love can overlook them all with equal ease. The purpose of you experiencing miracles is to make it clear to you that God's Love is Truth, and everything else is illusion. All expressions of God's Love, no matter their seeming form or size, are equal. In Reality, you are unaffected by all expressions of lack-of-love, whether they seem to come from within you, or from outside of you, because Peace is within you, and It does not come from outside of you. Your mind is sick when it seeks outside itself for wholeness. Your mind is healthy when it recognizes that it is Whole and is at Peace, untouched by any perceptions of lack-of-love. By extending God's Love, you correct your perception that *you* have problems because *others* seem to lack love.

2. The Atonement as Defense

1.   The experience of miracles is natural, corrective, healing, and available to you. They can do anything, but they cannot work if you are doubtful or afraid. Your fear endows what you fear with the power to hurt you. You believe in what you value, and when you are afraid you are valuing illusions. Truth and illusion then have equal power in your mind, and this destroys your Peace. The Peace of God comes from your recognizing that only God can bring you Peace. This Peace cannot be shaken by illusions. God does not

hurt, and anything that does not come from God cannot truly affect you. Your accepting this undoes your fear.

2. When you deny that you are One with God, you defend illusions, and your belief that you are a personal self. But denial can be used to defend Truth as well. You can, and should, deny that your illusions can hurt you. Your awareness of your Oneness with God depends on this. You are free to choose what you will defend, but your mind and will are only Truly Free when they serve Truth.

3. You automatically defend what you value. It will be easy for you to defend your awareness of your Oneness with God when you value it. In every situation you must learn to ask, *What do I really value?* You will save time by acknowledging that God offers you What you really want. When you do acknowledge this, the means for remembering God will be obvious to you.

4. The plan of the Atonement, which is the correction of your perception of separation from God, is the only defense that cannot be used to attack. You did not make it, so it is unlike the personal self's defenses, which can both protect and attack. The Idea behind the Atonement is God's Love. The Atonement Itself is an Act of Love. It is a plan for undoing the separation in your mind by using your perception of a world, which does not exist in God, but which you made in your mind. You can refuse the Atonement, but you cannot use It for the personal self's goal of separation from God. This is why the Atonement can only heal.

5. Since separation from God is only an illusory idea, it has an ending. The lessons of the plan of the Atonement are how this ending unfolds in your illusion of a world. The Atonement as the *full correction* of your perception of separation from God is the final lesson. Both learning and a world as your classroom have value only in time, because in God you have Everything, and you do not need to change anything. But in your perception of a world, you can learn to correct your perception of separation from God, bringing you closer and closer to full awareness of God. Only while you believe in separation is learning meaningful.

6. The personal mind makes you relive your sense of separation from God over and over so that nothing really changes, but the plan of

the Atonement truly undoes your erroneous belief that you are separate from God. The complete correction of your perception of separation from God ends your need for time. The plan of the Atonement uses your experience of the miracle to bring the end of time nearer by bringing God into your awareness *now*. Time's only value is the unfolding Atonement.

7. The Atonement requires that you give over your entire mind to correction. As long as you identify with a personal self, you will feel this total commitment to correction as loss. To the personal mind, all defenses of the Truth are attacks on it. But the strength of the Atonement is in that it does not attack; it simply undoes error. Your extending God's Love is not an attack; it is correction. This is how your experience of the miracle defends Truth. As you become more and more aware of your Identity in God, your awareness of Oneness will envelop your entire mind, and ensure your sense of security.

3. The Altar of God

1. Only in your mind can you recognize that you are One with God. The personal mind defends and maintains your sense of separation from God by protecting the body. The personal mind's fantasies about the perfect body come from the belief that you can heal your sense of loss through the body by perceiving it as a temple of the mind. This *does* recognize that the mind is where correction is needed, but it does not recognize that the body is only an idea in the mind, where your true Wholeness lies. The personal self's emphasis on beautiful bodies comes from your fear of real correction. The Holy Spirit in your mind, however, overlooks the body, recognizing that it is nothing, and that the mind is every-thing.

2. Only by total commitment of your mind to correcting your sense of separation from God will your mind be restored to Wholeness. There was no fear in your mind before the idea of separation from God. Both fear and separation are mistakes that must be undone for your mind to be healed, and for you to be fully aware of God again. Then you will not experience loss or fear.

3. Your mind *will* eventually be healed of its perception of separation

from God. You have Free Will to delay your awareness of your Oneness with God, but because Oneness is the Truth, you cannot make your perception of separation permanent. The pain caused by your perceiving separation from God is ultimately intolerable for you, and when you are truly willing to accept that there is a way out of pain, you will be willing to accept the Holy Spirit within you again. For a long while you will be conflicted as you alternate between the personal self and the Holy Spirit, but it is certain that you will return to full awareness of God.

4. The Holy Spirit cannot see error, and It only looks for correction, dissolving all solutions the personal mind seeks to make through the body. The Holy Spirit always looks within your mind, and It recognizes immediately when your mind is hurt and seeks to heal it. It does this by overlooking your perception of separation from God, and by looking to your Oneness with God. This brings your mind into the Holy Spirit's service, and makes it harder for you to accept the pain of delaying your full awareness of God. You will become less and less tolerant of even minor discomforts brought about by perceiving separation from God.

5. As Part of God your perfect trust in the Holy Spirit brings the Perfect Peace that is your natural State of Being. Until you achieve this trust, you are throwing away Oneness, and using inappropriate means to feel whole again. The real means to Wholeness are natural to you, and you do not have to make any effort for them. Because you are One with God, the correction of your perception of separation from God is the only gift worthy of your mind. You are Eternally One with God, and you have God's Peace within you. When you are not at Peace, you are deceiving yourself, and your mind is not open to the Holy Spirit. You must see the world that you perceive as a means of healing your sense of separation from God, and the plan of the Atonement is given to you to guarantee that you will succeed in remembering that you are One with God.

4. Healing as Release from Fear

1. Now physical healing will be addressed. The Atonement as the correction of your perception of separation from God is the *idea*

24

behind physical healing; your experience of the miracle, as the extension of God's Love, is the *means* of physical healing. Physical healing is the *result* of your accepting correction of your perceived separation from God. Physical healing is not a miracle in itself, but the *result* of your accepting God's Love. The form sickness takes is irrelevant, because all forms of perceived separation from God are corrected by accepting your Oneness with God. All physical healing is really release from the fear brought about by perceiving yourself as separate from God. To heal, you cannot be fearful, because in fear you do not perceive yourself as One with God.

2.   A major part of the plan of the Atonement is to undo your mistake of confusing the mind with the body. To be physically sick is to be not in your right mind, because it comes from your belief that you are in a body that you cannot control. Your experience of miracles corrects this mistake in your *mind*, which is where the mistake occurs. The body can only respond to your mind, and it can only manifest sickness when it is responding to an erroneous thought. Your belief that the body can be sick on its own is a belief in magic. Magic is the belief that physical matter has a power the mind cannot control. This mistake shows up as your belief that the body and mind are both real, and that each has a power that can affect the other. When you can accept that only the mind is real, you will no longer confuse yourself with a body and manifest sickness.

3.   Your Spirit is One with God, your mind can extend God's Love, and the body is a learning device for your mind while you perceive yourself in a world. The body is neutral, it has no power of its own, and it cannot introduce errors into your mind of itself. The worst that you can do with the body is to not use it to learn of God. The body is simply a part of your experience in your perception of a world. It is almost impossible for you to deny that you experience a body, and doing so you will also deny the power of your mind, which made it.

4.   The physical remedies that you apply to heal the body reinforce your belief in magic. Magical thinking teaches you that the body

makes its own illness; using physical remedies to heal it reinforces this mistake. But it is not evil to use them. Sometimes your belief in the illness is too strong for you to let in the awareness that healing is the result of correcting your perception of separation from God. When this is the case, it is better for you to temporarily believe in the physical remedies. When you are sick, you are already in a fearful state, and if you confuse God's Love with fear, then the experience of the miracle will only increase your fear.

5. The form that correction of your perception of separation from God takes is not important. It will come to you in a form that is helpful to you at the time. To be fully effective, God's Love must be experienced by you in a way that you can understand without fear. This does not mean that you experience It in Its purest form, but that you experience It in a form to which you are open right now. The goal of your experiences of miracles is to increase your awareness of your Oneness with God, not to limit it by making you more fearful.

5. The Function of the Miracle Worker

1. Before you can accept physical healing as an extension of God's Love, it is important that you understand your fear of release from your identification with a personal self. If you do not understand this fear, you will teach yourself that release from the personal self is loss. This idea supports the separation, and it arises from your fearful belief that you have succeeded in breaking off a part of God's Mind, and in limiting it to a personal self in a body. This is not real. Recognizing that this is not real corrects your mind where the error of separation occurs. Remember, only your mind has power, and correction must happen in your mind. Your Spirit is Eternally One with God, and the body is only a learning device for your mind. The body cannot make errors of its own, because it does not have the power to do so. Only your mind can give up its own mistakes, and doing so is the only application of its power that is meaningful in your perception of a world.

2. Magic is the misuse of the mind's power. Your belief in physical remedies is magical thinking, but you should not use the mind to

heal the body if you are afraid to do so. Fear and egocentricity go together, and fear makes you vulnerable to perceiving physical healing as coming from the power of the personal mind, rather than from the recognition that you are One with God. When you are afraid, it is actually better for you to accept physical remedies for healing the body, because you will not make the mistake of thinking they come from your personal power. As long as you are afraid, you should not attempt to accept the experience of the miracle for physical healing.

3. Your experiences of miracles are expressions of your mind when it is aligned with God. To accept a miracle, you cannot judge your mind, or what it perceives. To correct your perception of separation from God, you do not have to wait for what you perceive to change. In fact, your purpose is to be miracle-minded despite what is appearing to you. You must be open to God's Love, even if only briefly, in order to extend God's Love to what is appearing.

4. If you rely on your personal readiness to extend God's Love, you will be confused about where your experience of miracles comes from. Instead, trust the Holy Spirit, the Source of God's Love within you. When you don't extend God's Love, it is because you are afraid and confused about what is real, and you are refusing to accept correction of your perception of separation from God. When you do accept correction, you will recognize that healing is recognizing your Oneness with God.

5. *Your one responsibility is to accept for yourself correction of your perception that you are separate from God.* This means that you recognize the power of your mind, and that it is only your mind that needs correction. Once you accept this, your mind will only heal. By denying the separation and reinstating your awareness of your Oneness with God, you will be in a position to extend God's Love to all that you perceive. You will teach yourself that you are not separate from God, and that your perception of separation is not real. You will release your mind from valuing the body, and you will remember that you are mind.

6. The body has no power, and it cannot learn. It can only follow your mind, and if you endow it with power it does not have, it becomes

an obstacle to your learning. Only your mind can learn. Spirit is Whole and does not need learning, and the body is powerless and neutral. Your mind can bring the body into alignment with it by recognizing that the body is not the learner, and by looking past it to Spirit.

7. The learning that corrects your sense of separation from God turns you away from the body's sight, and turns you inward to your mind and Spirit. This often causes you fear, because you are afraid that spiritual sight will reveal that you are guilty of separation from God. This may make you uncomfortable, but the discomfort is only temporary. When the Holy Spirit sees your perception of separation from God, It only looks to correct this perception, not to punish you for it. The Holy Spirit only knows of your Oneness with God, and It disregards the idea of separation. The Holy Spirit does not inspire fear, and you should recognize that the discomfort that you feel is an indication that you need correction.

8. You fear healing because you are unwilling to totally accept that your mind needs to be healed. What the body's eyes see cannot heal, nor can anything physical heal your sense of separation from God. As long as you believe that what the body sees is real, your attempts at correction will be directed away from real healing. Real Perception looks inward at the mind, but in your identification with a personal self, you won't look inward because you believe that you will see your own guilt for separating from God. Yet, since you really do believe that you are separate from God, you cannot correct this belief without first looking inward at it.

9. The ability to heal wasn't necessary before your perception of separation from God, but as long as you believe in a world, healing is necessary as a means of keeping the Truth in your mind. True charity means that you look on the Holy Spirit in what you perceive, even when you cannot yet accept It in yourself. Like other true spiritual ideas, charity is needed only in the separation, and it is a dim reflection of the Oneness of God that you cannot conceive of yet. Charity is essential for you to be miracle-minded.

10. Charity means that you look past what is appearing to look on the Holy Spirit, even when you do not yet accept that the Holy Spirit is

in you. You would have no need of charity if you already knew that the Holy Spirit is within you. Through charity you acknowledge both that you need to see the Holy Spirit, and that you will accept the Holy Spirit. You need charity while you perceive yourself in a world, and extending God's Love, which expresses charity, lessens your need for a world. Only a direct Revelation of God transcends your perception of a world; your experience of miracles is needed to shorten your need for a world. Remember that when you extend God's Love, you are lessening your suffering by undoing guilt for separating from God in the past, and undoing fear of punishment for this in the future.

a. *Special Principles of Miracle Workers*

11. (1) When you extend God's Love, you do not have to be concerned with how or when it manifests in the world that you perceive. The Holy Spirit will arrange this.

12. (2) All healing rests on your understanding the distinction between God, and the world that was made in your mind to be separate from God. Correcting the confusion between the two heals you.

13. (3) If you respond to any manifestation of separation from God with anything but a desire to correct your perception of separation, you will be confused about what is real.

14. (4) Your experience of a miracle denies your separation from God, and affirms your Oneness with God. Only miracle-mindedness corrects in a real way. What cannot correct your perception of separation from God is not real. Since it isn't real, it is empty, and you must project meaning onto it.

15. (5) The miracle's correction of your perception of separation from God provides your perception for healing. Until you have accepted this correction, your forgiving is a means of judging rather than healing.

16. (6) True forgiving corrects your perception of separation from God. It does not judge what is appearing, which does not matter. It looks inward toward God to heal your mind of its perception of separation.

17. (7) Your cooperation with the Holy Spirit is essential for remem-

bering that you are One with God. Your perception of a world belongs to the Holy Spirit for correction, and Reality belongs to God. In Reality, you are One with God; the world that you perceive exists only for you to remember this.

18. (8) In any situation in which you perceive the need for healing, either in your mind or in what your mind perceives, think of it this way:

> 'I am here to heal by letting the Holy Spirit work through me.
> I do not have to worry about what to say or what to do, because the Holy Spirit will direct me.
> I am content to be wherever the Holy Spirit needs me to be, because I know the Holy Spirit is always with me.
> I will be healed as I let the Holy Spirit teach me to heal.'

6. Fear and Conflict

1. Fear, and the behavior that it inspires in you, seem to just happen to you, as though they are beyond your control. Yet only acts inspired by the Holy Spirit should be automatic to you. The Holy Spirit cannot control fear, but you can. If you choose, the Holy Spirit can take over everything that is not important, and can guide you in everything that is important. When you are afraid, it is because you are identifying with a body and a personal self. This makes it impossible for the Holy Spirit to reach you, because you are confused about what is real.

2. You have to choose to undo your confusion about reality, because the Holy Spirit is not responsible for this confusion. You do not excuse your own insane behavior by saying that it is beyond your control, yet you do condone your own insane thinking. There is a confusion here that you must look at. After the act, you take responsibility for what you did, but not for the thoughts that motivated your behavior. But you are responsible for what you think, because it is with the mind that you make choices. What you do follows what you think. You cannot make separation real by giving fearful behavior its own motivation apart from your mind. Your behavior will come under the control of the Holy Spirit as

soon as you give your mind to the Holy Spirit. Whenever you are afraid, you have believed in separation from God, and you have not been following the Holy Spirit's guidance.

3. Your controlling behavior that comes from your belief in separation from God cannot result in your healing. Fear is an indication that your mind has chosen separation, and this is why you feel guilty. Your mind, not your behavior, needs to be changed, and this is a matter of your willingness to change. Only at the level of your mind do you need guidance, because it is your mind that needs correction. A change of behavior means nothing, and does nothing, because your behavior follows your mind.

4. Letting go of fear is your responsibility. Do not ask for release from fear, but rather for release from the source of your fear: your perception of separation from God. You are too tolerant of, and too passive about, the thoughts that maintain this perception. How this misperception shows up is not important, but the misperception itself is crucial. Its correction is the same in every circumstance: Before you make any choice, ask for the Holy Spirit's guidance. Then you have no source for fear.

5. Your fear of God causes you strain, because it results in a conflict between your desire for your Wholeness in God, and your desire to maintain your perception of separation from God. This shows up in two ways: First, your conflicting goals show up as conflicting actions, either at the same time, or one after the other. This is intolerable to you, because then your mind is split, and part of it wants the other goal.[1] Second, you behave in a way that you think God wants you to, but without wholly wanting to yourself. While this produces consistent behavior, it causes great strain for you. In both cases, your mind and your behavior are in conflict, because you are not doing what you wholly want to do. This makes you feel coerced and angry, which results in you projecting the source of your anger onto someone else. Whenever you are afraid, it is because you have not wholly chosen God. Your mind is split, and therefore your behavior is inconsistent. Changing your behavior may shift your conflict from the first type of conflict to the second type of conflict, but it will not undo your fear.

31

6. It is possible for you to reach a point where you wholly give your mind over to the Holy Spirit automatically, but this implies a willingness that you have not yet attained. The Holy Spirit does not ask for more than you are willing to do right now. When you are wholly willing, the strength to *do* comes naturally. It is not hard to do God's Will when you recognize that you are One with God. The lesson here is simple: Only your mind makes fear, and it does so when you are conflicted between wanting God, and wanting separation from God. Your fear can be undone by your wanting only God.

7. To correct your perception of separation from God, know that the conflict that you experience comes from your fear of God. Remind yourself that you have chosen to be separate from God's Love, or you could not be afraid. From here, your process of correction is practical steps that are part of the larger process of your accepting full correction of your perception that you are separate from God. These are the steps:

> Acknowledge that you are feeling fear.
> Fear comes from your rejection of God's Love.
> The only remedy is to wholly accept God's Love.
> Only by extending God's Love can you correct your perception that you are separate from God, and undo your fear.

8. By extending God's Love, you demonstrate your acceptance of God's Love for yourself. It is a sign that you recognize the Holy Spirit in you by extending the Holy Spirit in your awareness. When you are afraid, you have put yourself in a position of needing to correct your perception of separation from God. You have made a choice without God's Love in your mind. Correcting this misperception is what the plan of the Atonement was made for. As long as you merely recognize that you need correction, you will be fearful. But when you accept God's Love, you will undo fear. This is healing.

9. You experience fear, but you rarely acknowledge the power of your mind. For you to be released from fear, there are some things that

32

you must wholly accept. Your mind is very powerful, and it is always extending itself. Your thoughts and beliefs can literally move mountains. You may think that acknowledging this about your mind is arrogant, but that's not why you won't accept it. You prefer to think of your thoughts as powerless, because you don't want to see that it is your thoughts that gave form to your desire to be separate from God. Denying your mind's power keeps guilt for the separation away from your awareness, but it also makes you believe that you are powerless, and that your thoughts don't deserve respect. You have no idle thoughts. All of your thinking produces form at some level.

7. Cause and Effect

1. You may complain about fear, but you are the one who makes yourself fearful. You cannot ask the Holy Spirit to release you from fear, because the Holy Spirit knows that the source of your fear is your perceived separation from God, which does not exist. But you believe that fear and separation are real, and if the Holy Spirit tried to change your thoughts, and the world that they've made for you, It would be interfering with cause and effect, the most fundamental Law of Mind that there is. It goes against the purpose of this course to depreciate the power of your mind, and it is more helpful to remind you that you do not discipline your thinking. You may think it will take a miracle for you to do this, and it will. You can, and must, be trained to be miracle-minded.

2. Your mind will not be able to serve the Holy Spirit until you learn to discipline your thoughts. To experience God's Love, you must fully accept the power of your thinking, otherwise you will continue to foster a sense of separation from God. In order to extend God's Love, you must genuinely respect the power of your mind, and accept that your thoughts lead to your perceptions and experiences.

3. Both miracles and fear are thoughts in your mind. If you were not free to choose one, you would not be free to choose the other. When you choose to extend God's Love, you reject fear, even if only temporarily. You are afraid of everyone, everything, God, and the

Truth in you, because you have made separation real to you, and you believe in the reality of a world that you made to replace God. This makes you unconsciously feel guilty, and fear punishment from God. You then perpetuate your perception of separation from God, because you are afraid to approach God. But you are not really afraid of God; you are afraid of your own thoughts about God. This is painful for you. The way out of pain is to accept that your own thoughts cause your perceptions and experiences. In Reality, there are no perceptions, and your experience is only God. So the fundamental conflict in your mind that is played out in your perception of a world, is between Reality and separation from Reality. All Love comes from your Oneness with God, and all fear comes from your perception of separation from God. The conflict in your mind is between your desire for both God, and separation from God.

4. You made fear, because you believe that you made separation from God real, and because you believe you made it, you believe in it. Your belief that the separation is real makes fear seem out of your control. Controlling fear will not undo it, because your belief that it needs to be controlled only gives it more power over you. Extending God's Love is the way for you to undo fear, because it undoes your perception of separation. Until you accept this, you will be conflicted, because you believe in the power of something that does not exist.

5. Your Oneness with God, and your separation from God, cannot both be true. Your belief in one is your denial of the other. Actually, God is Everything, and your perception of separation from God is nothing. Your perception of separation is undone when you accept this. But what you believe is true for you, and so the separation seems to have occurred for you. It is not helpful to deny that you believe you are separate from God. But focusing on this only perpetuates your sense of separation. First, you must acknowledge that you believe you are separate from God, but only because you have to acknowledge a mistake to accept that correction is needed. When you have done this, you can accept correction immediately. This seems to be a process that takes time, because you made time

to make separation from God real to you. But time can be used by the Holy Spirit to correct this misperception. From God's perspective, the purpose of the world that you perceive is to correct your perception of separation from God.

6.   God's Creation is God's Own Being, and It is only One. In your perception of separation from God, your mind perceives many separate beings, or personal selves, so you must overlook every perception of personal selves, and look to God. The Wholeness of your True Mind is greater than each corrected perception of separation that you make, so as long as you believe anything but God is true, you will not know this Wholeness. You cannot resolve your conflicted mind until you overlook *all* of separation, and then you will understand True Wholeness. As long as any part of the separation is true for you, you will believe in nothingness. The full correction of your perception of separation is the plan of the Atonement.

7.   Your willingness to undo fear, and your full acceptance of correction of your perception of separation from God, are not the same thing. Your willingness is a prerequisite for, and implies your desire to accept, correction, but this does not mean your desire is undivided. You will overcome fear by extending God's Love, but your willingness is only the beginning of fearlessness for you. You may think that it will take a long time to move from willingness to complete fearlessness, but remember your process is under the Holy Spirit's direction, not the personal mind's direction.

8. The Meaning of the Last Judgment

1.   You can correct any confusion that you may have over the personal mind's solutions to your perception of separation, and the real solution, which is your extension of God's Love, by remembering that you are not your own source. God only extends God, and when you remember that you are One with God, you will extend only God. The Extension of God is God's Will, and your Will. But when you are identified with a personal self, you inevitably believe in the solutions that it makes, and they will be real to you, but not to God. This distinction between God's Will, and what the personal

mind makes, leads to the real meaning of the Last Judgment.

2.   The concept of the Last Judgment is frightening to you because you do not realize that God cannot judge. You made judgment in the separation to reinforce the separation, but it can be used in the plan of the Atonement as a process of evaluation. The Last Judgment seems to be a long, long way off, but the experience of the miracle is offered to you as a way to bring God into your awareness *now*, to reduce the time that you need to remember your Oneness with God. You can quickly free yourself from all fear, to fully extend God's Love, and to bring Peace to your entire mind.

3.   The Last Judgment does not belong to God, but to you as a process of evaluation that you undertake with the Holy Spirit in your mind. In your mind, the Holy Spirit sorts out God from the illusion that a world is reality, so that you can wholly choose God. You will vacillate between God, and the world until you have fully sorted them out. The Last Judgment is your final healing, not a punishment. Punishment is an idea alien to God, and the goal of the Last Judgment is to restore you to God.

4.   To be free from the illusion that you are separate from God, you must accept that it *is* an illusion, and that God is Truth. This is a constructive process of separation. You will ultimately look on your Oneness with God, and be glad. This will inevitably result in your perception of a world falling away from you, because you will realize that it has no real value, and you will no longer believe in it.

5.   The term 'Last Judgment' is frightening to you not only because in your guilt you project vengeance onto God, but because you associate 'last' with death. But the Last Judgment is really the Doorway to Life, because fear is not Life, but death. You must judge everything that you have made, and remember only your extensions of God, which help you to remember that you are One with God. This is time's only real purpose for you. When all that you remember is God's Love, you will no longer be afraid. This is your part in the plan of the Atonement.

Chapter 3

The Innocent Perception

1. Atonement Without Sacrifice

1. To be sure that any left-over fear associated with miracles is undone in your mind, you must understand that the plan of the Atonement was set in motion by the *resurrection* of Jesus, not the crucifixion of Jesus. Only if you believe that separation from God is real can you believe that God would encourage Jesus to suffer because Jesus was good. This fearful concept of God arose from your perception that separation from God is real, that you are guilty for it, and that your punishment is justified for it. You should ask yourself if God, Which does not know separation, but only Oneness and Love, thinks in this way.

2. The personal mind justifies its own persecutions by teaching that God persecuted Jesus for the salvation of all. This is why it holds hard to this view of God. But again, can you believe that a Loving God would do this? It is very important to let go of the idea that Jesus was 'punished' because *you* are guilty. If you retain any belief in this idea, you will not understand the Loving Correction of the plan of the Atonement.

3. The idea of vengeance does not come from God, but is projected onto God from your guilty mind. Nothing in the world that you perceive has anything to do with God, because God did not make it, and God does not maintain it. Since God does not know the world, God does not hold anything that happens in it against you, or against Jesus. The idea that God rejected Adam, and ejected him from the Garden of Eden, is the same kind of error of projection from your guilty mind. Your guilt, and expectation of punishment, are why you sometimes will not trust the Holy Spirit.

4. The idea of sacrifice also does not come from God, but from your guilty belief that you need to be punished for separating from God. Sacrifice comes from your belief that separation from God is real,

and sacrifice is not Love, but vicious attack. Your belief in it inspires fear in you, and leads to your mind being closed to God's Love.

5. Jesus has been represented as a sacrificial lamb Whose bloody death washed away your sin. But it wasn't Jesus' death that undoes sin; it was His demonstrated awareness of His Oneness with God that undoes the concept of sin. Your guilt for separation from God is not undone by destruction. It is undone by your recognition that your Oneness with God is unchanged by your perception of separation. [Innocence is not weakness, but strength.]

6. When you are aware of your Oneness with God, you have Everything, and you don't need to sacrifice to get something to make you whole. You have no need to project a world for the same reason. In Oneness with God, you can only extend God's Love. Jesus' crucifixion is viewed by your split mind as reconciling God and man in a frightening 'atonement', that actually comes from your decision to not know God. But the Christ Mind manifested by Jesus is the State of awareness of Oneness with God to Which the real plan of the Atonement seeks to restore you.

7. The plan of the Atonement, which is the correction of your perception that you are separate from God, comes from the Truth in you, and it only blesses you. It could not bless you if it meant you harm. There is no evil, and in your Oneness with God, you can overcome the *idea* of evil. The resurrection of Jesus demonstrates that illusions cannot destroy Truth. This is the real meaning of Atonement, the Perfect Lesson, the one that demonstrates that Jesus represented Truth. If you can accept that illusions cannot destroy Truth, you will be released from your perception of separation from God.

8. In your Oneness with God you are Innocent, because there is no harm in God. You can only know God when you release yourself from all belief in guilt. When you accept this, you will know that correction, not sacrifice, is the appropriate gift for your mind, and your mind will extend only Truth.

2. Miracles as True Perception

1. Truth and illusion cannot be understood in degrees, or in

opposition to each other. Everything and nothing cannot co-exist. What is True cannot be false, and what is false cannot be True. Until you make a firm commitment to God, Which is Truth, your thinking will be inconsistent. You cannot make a firm commitment to illusion, because it is nothingness, and is not real. Whether you recognize it or not, you do experience God sometimes. You can never totally deny Everything, but you can totally let go of nothingness.

2. You cannot be partly Innocent and partly guilty, since they are mutually exclusive. To look out from your Innocence is True Perception, because It looks on your Oneness with God, and nothing else.

3. Whenever you are afraid of someone or something in the world that you perceive, you are making illusion real to you, and blocking God's Love. You are denying the corrective power of God's Love. In the experience of a miracle, you perceive illusion as illusion, and let it be, without judgment, knowing that only God exists, and that only God is Real. When you accept that you are Innocent, you will not perceive anything but God as Real.

4. You are afraid of God's Will because you have used your mind, which in Reality is One with God, to make a world apart from God. This makes it seem as though God is Something separate that wants to punish you for rejecting It. But you are holding back the Real Power of your mind, and making it seem as though your Will is imprisoned by God. Yet to be One with God is to be of One Mind and One Will with God. When you know that you are One with God, you are in Heaven.

5. Your trusting the Holy Spirit in you is how you remember that you are One with God. You and the Holy Spirit are One with God, and this Oneness is the Peace of God. But you can only see This by giving up all belief in guilt, and the attack on yourself that it fosters through your perception of a world of separation. Oneness means that your mind perceives only Oneness.

6. To correct your perception of separation from God, you must withdraw your belief in illusion, and invest in Truth instead. You cannot make illusions true, and if you are willing to overlook all

that the personal mind perceives to look on Truth instead, Truth will be reinforced in you. Your True Perception looks on Reality, and simultaneously erases misperceptions throughout your mind. This is the healing that the experience of the miracle brings to you.

3. Perception versus Knowledge

1. Because only God is Real, you can only be certain in God. This is Knowledge. In your perception that you are in a world, you can only perceive, and since perception can vary, it means that you are not certain. Your True Perception, however, can lead you back to God.

2. In your perception that you are in a world, you are not at Peace, because you do not know yourself, your mind's Wholeness, or God. You find the answer to your question, 'Who am I?' by extending God's Love. Your experience of the miracle, then, is your corrected, or True, Perception. You only need to correct *perception*, because in God there is no question and no perception, only an awareness of your Oneness with God.

3. [In your perception that you are in a world, you may ask, 'Who am I?' to keep God away by projecting the Answer in the future. If you think you already know who you are, you will not question, and you will keep your mind closed, because you are actually afraid of the Answer.]

4. ['Visions of God' would be miracles, not a direct Revelation of God, because they involve perception. They are corrected perception, however, and your natural Spiritual Vision.]

5. You can know yourself only in God. When you extend God's Love in your perception, you perceive that the Holy Spirit is Real, which ultimately leads to you knowing yourself in God. You must first *perceive* the Holy Spirit before you can transition to *knowing* God. While you still wonder what is real, it is clear that you do not know that you are One with God. [God is Pure Being, and a Revelation of God results only in *experience*. Perception is the level of your mind where *action* is taken. It is the level of miracles. Even your most corrected, spiritualized perception occurs at the level of the personal mind. God is Eternally within you, but for you to *perceive*

God's Love is not the same as you *knowing* only God.]

6.   Your perception must be corrected before you can be aware of your Oneness with God, which will bring you Complete Peace. You are not separate from God's Mind, and all that you perceive is not separate from your mind. God filled your mind before you made perception and a world to perceive, and God will fully replace them in your mind again, but your perceptions must be brought into alignment with God first.

7.   When you attack others in the world that you perceive, you make separation from God real to you, and you hurt yourself. You forget that your perceptions are only in your own mind, and you become afraid of others, because they seem like strangers, rather than your own projected perceptions. For you to perceive correctly is for you to overlook the personal mind's perceptions of others, and to extend God's Love so that you remember your Oneness with God. For you to think like God is for you to extend only God in your mind. God's Mind is Whole. When you look on separation as real, you do not remember God.

4. Error and the Ego

1.   The abilities and functions that your mind has in your identification with a personal self are only shadows or your real Power. The separation seems to have split your mind into two levels, God and the personal self, which conflict because they are meaningless to each other. You are not certain of anything in your perception that you are in a world , because the level of the personal mind is the level that replaced Certainty with choice. The choices that you make with the personal mind can also seem to split your split mind into further levels. You are free to make a loveless choice, which means you can choose to not know God. Only God is free from conflict, because God is One. From the point of view of the separation, God's Mind seems to be split into God and your Christ Mind/Holy Spirit, with your Christ Mind/Holy Spirit being the highest level of God-awareness that you can attain in your perception that you are in a world. But in God, there are no levels. From the point of view of God, God and God's Answers to the

separation (your Christ Mind/Holy Spirit) are One, because they are unified in purpose.

2. The first split in your mind that made you seem to be no longer One with God, was your introduction of *consciousness*: the personal mind, the level of perception and choice. The personal self is supposed to be your attempt to make yourself not-God, but you can only ever be One with God. The personal self will always be open to question; only in God can you be Certain of What you are.

3. When you identify with a personal self, you question yourself, but you will not accept the Real Answer to What you are, because this Answer will undo the personal self. In your split mind, you must always be afraid and confused, because you can never be certain, which means being One. You must be conflicted, because your mind is divided against itself. This internal insecurity you project outward onto a world that seems full of strangers ready to attack you. Your fear *is* justified when you perceive yourself as a personal self, and that is why the only way out of fear is to remember that you are not the self that you made; you are One with God. You can never make the self that you made True, and What you really are is unchanged by your misidentification with a personal self. This is why you will eventually choose to heal your mind of its perceived separation from God.

4. Your corrected split mind does correctly perceive your Oneness with God, but it should not be confused with God's Mind, because it can still make another choice. God's Mind knows only God, and there is no other choice in Oneness. But your corrected mind correctly perceives God's Love, and this is a miracle that corrects your misidentification with a personal self.

5. The personal mind is very active, because it chooses to be uncertain and to *perceive*, rather than to simply know God. Your only way out of uncertainty is consistent perception. Your decision to know God again, Which is the natural State of your mind, puts your mind in the service of the Holy Spirit. This corrects your perception. [You can never completely sever your mind from God. In fact, the world that you made and sustain in your mind, though an error, indirectly affirms that the power of your mind comes from God.]

6. You made the body as a means to *perceive,* because you must perceive *with* something. Your split mind identifies with a body in an attempt to escape its uncertainty about what it is. The Holy Spirit cannot join with a body because of the body's inherent emptiness as a thought apart from God, and your identifying with a body makes the Holy Spirit seem almost unreachable to your mind. Your split mind perceives the Holy Spirit as a threat, because It makes you aware that the body is not your Real Identity. But the Holy Spirit never attacks; It simply overcomes error because It is Truth. Even in its misidentification, your mind cannot help but to at least vaguely recognize this.

7. In Reality, you are One with God, and this is not changed because you have chosen to perceive separation from God as real. The Holy Spirit cannot undo your perceived separation from God as long as you want separation. Jesus was a man who remembered God, and Who corrected His perception of separation from God at the level of His mind where the separation seemed to be real. He showed that the mind, not the body, is real. He accepted God's Will as His own. The Holy Spirit cannot return you to God against your will, but, if you choose, you can put your mind under the Holy Spirit's guidance, and correct your perception of separation from God. Your misperceptions are your obstacles to God, and, if you let go of them, your perception will be corrected, and you will naturally choose God again. You are called to God, but you must make the choice to answer This Call. The Peace of God is your Reality.

5. Beyond Perception

1. To recap:

> The personal mind's abilities are only shadows of your real Power.
> Perception, which is judgmental, was introduced into your mind after the separation.
> Uncertainty is inherent in your perception that the world is real.
> The resurrection of Jesus demonstrated that the mind, not the body, is real, and this awareness is the corrected perception that

leads to God.

Jesus' resurrection was possible because He knew he was One with God.

These ideas highlight an important distinction:

2. Since the separation, you have confused God's Creation with the physical universe that you made to perceive separation from God. God's Creation is God's Formless Being extending Infinitely and Eternally. God's Being is Everywhere. The physical universe is finite, time-bound form. It is very concrete, limited, and specific. You made a world to fill the perceived lack in your mind brought about by your perception of separation from God, and anything made in your perception of this world is made for the same reason, and reaffirms separation. Ingenious and inventive thinking always give rise to concrete form. They do not come from God, because God is already Whole, and does not need to make anything.

3. God's Mind does not inspire action, only Being. What you have made of yourself makes it impossible for you to just *be* with God. God doesn't change, and, in God, *you* do not change. Yet change is part of your experience in your perception that you are in a world, so it is obvious that, if you perceive yourself in a world, you do not know that you are in God. You are free to make this choice, but clearly you do not make this choice from an awareness of your Oneness with God.

4. You should not direct the question, 'What am I?' toward the personal mind, which you made, and with which you identify. Your asking it implies that what you made knows the answer, and can supply you with the answer. But in the personal mind you cannot perceive yourself correctly, because in Reality you do not have an image to be perceived. An 'image' is only symbolic and can be changed, and so it is not unchanging as God is Unchanging.

5. You can know God *because* God does not change. Knowledge is not open to interpretation. But perceiving meaning is always open to mistakes, because interpretation can change. Confusing God with the world that you perceive is your attempt to be separate from God and One with God at the same time. This only confuses you

about yourself even further. The personal mind has become ingenious in its attempts to make separation from God real to you. But this is only wasted effort for your mind. Being Whole, God does not require ingenuity to make anything. Ingenuity will not help you to remember God, and, when you are willing, you can free yourself of the effort ingenuity requires.

6.   [Prayer is a way of asking, and prayer is the means through which you remember God's Love. The only meaningful prayer is to ask for help to forgive, or to let go of, your perception of separation from God, so that you can remember your Oneness with God. So true prayer is asking for help in remembering What you already have. When you have forgiven yourself your illusion of separation from God, you will remember that you have Everything. In your perception that you are in a world, you can resemble God only by extending God's Love, because you have forgotten that *you* are God's Love. God is your Source, and to extend God's Love is your only purpose.]

7.   God extends God, and God is All that is. But in your identification with a personal self, on every level you are evaluating and selecting from the myriad of choices presented by the.world that you perceive. Judgment is necessary for you in the personal mind, so that you can select what to value, and, by valuing it, make it real to you.

8.   There is no need for judgment when you know only Oneness. In your identification with a personal self, you seem cut off from your Source, you are always incomplete, and you can only perceive separation. God does not have separate parts. To know any Part of God is to know All of God, because God is One. When you remember What you really are, you will know God.

6. Judgment and the Authority Problem

1.   God has no need for judgment, because God is One. Judgment is used by the Holy Spirit only to help you sort out Truth from illusion. After the Last Judgment, which is your own final sorting out of Truth from illusion, you will have no use for judgment. Judgment is used by the personal mind to perceive fragmentation

in place of Oneness. When you judge with a personal mind, you make the world your reality.

2. You lose Peace when you choose to judge with a personal mind, because it makes real to you a world that is not real. For the personal mind to reject Oneness, it must perceive many different forms that are unlike each other, and then judge, or evaluate, them, so that it can reject some forms, and accept others. It accepts as real what it judges as valuable, and it rejects as unreal what it judges as less valuable. One of the illusions of the personal mind is that what it rejects is not real to it, but would you judge *against* something you did not believe is real? If the personal mind perceives it, it believes it is real. In the end, though, there really are no wrong or right judgments made by the personal mind, because what it judges is not real. Your judging in any form with the personal mind implies that it is up to you to decide what is real.

3. When you choose to look on yourself and the world in your mind without the personal mind's judgment, you will experience deep Peace. When you look on your Oneness with God, and extend God's Love in your awareness, you will realize that it is meaningless to judge a world that is not real. Your own meaning is lost to you when you judge with the personal mind, because you believe that the imperfect personal self is you, and that the world it is judging is real. All of your doubt comes from your belief that you need the personal mind's judgment to organize the life that you perceive that you are living in a world, and to define the personal self. But when you look only on your Oneness with God, the personal mind's judgment will be automatically replaced by your recognition of Truth.

4. [What you perceive, but reject, is fearful to you, because you believe that rejecting it means that you have lost control over it. It shows up in the dreams that you have when you sleep, because what you refuse to accept, you block from conscious awareness. What you reject is not dangerous to you, but your rejecting it makes it *seem* dangerous to you.]

5. When you are tired, it is because you have judged yourself capable of being tired. When you laugh at others, it is because you have

judged them as unworthy. When you laugh at yourself, you have to laugh more at others, because you cannot believe that you are more unworthy than they. All of this makes you feel tired, because it is depressing. The personal mind's constant judgment is almost intolerable. You cannot really be tired but you can wear yourself down with constant judgment. Yet you cherish such a debilitating ability because you want to be the one who decides what is real. You also fear judgment, because you are afraid it will be used against you. You believe this to the extent that you believe that judgment is valuable in establishing you as your own source.

6. God offers only Love. Extending God's Love is the way that you remember that you are One with God. True Justice means recognizing that the world is not real, and that only God is Real. This is judgment's only real use. You only need this judgment because you have forgotten that you are One with God.

7. The personal self manifests many problems in itself, and in its perceived 'life' in a world, but they all have one source: the belief that God is not real, and that the personal self is its own source. This is the 'authority problem'. God is your Source, or Author, but your mind is split between the personal self, and the Holy Spirit. In your identification with a personal self, you experience your mind as incomplete and conflicted, and anything it makes is also incomplete and conflicted. The personal self is not real, and its belief that it is real, and its own source, means that it can only make illusions. When you identify with a personal self, you believe its illusions are true.

8. When you reject God and identify with a personal self, you believe that you are only that personal self, and that you are your own source. This doesn't really make sense, and sometimes you may become so confused about your source that you wonder if you exist at all. So you project the delusion that you are your own source onto a world, so that it seems as though the world made you. You then battle with 'others' in the world that you perceive over who has the power to define you. This power struggle with others reflects the guilt and fear that you feel deep down, because you believe that you have stolen God's Power. None of this affects God,

because you cannot really make yourself separate from God. God offers you only a correction for this error in perception.

9. When you no longer want to reject God, you will know that God cannot reject you. You have not stolen God's Power, but you have given up your awareness of It as *your* Power. But you can give up judging an unreal world, and simply know that you are always in God.

10. Peace is the natural State of your Being in God. You can reject your natural State, but you cannot change What It is. Your only problem is that you do not accept God as your Source, and this denial is the reason for all of your fears. This is not offensive to God, but it is offensive to *you*. When you deny that God is your Source, you deny your own Peace. Your perception of a world that is real *is* your denial that God is your Source.

11. Your belief in a world that is real limits you, but you do not accept that it is your Free Will to believe in it, or to let it go. Judgment is the way that you limit yourself by making some parts of the world valuable, and, therefore, real to you. But your wishing that the world is real does not make it so. Only God is Real, and you can be at Peace only when you accept this.

7. Creating versus the Self-Image

1. Your thought system can either extend God's Love, or make something separate from God. These choices are alike in their power, but differ in their results. A thought system that is based on the lie that you can be separate from God is not weak, because it is made by your mind, which is One with God. You have to understand your Power so that you can undo what you have made.

2. Instead of accepting the Power of your mind to make a world that is the opposite of God in every way, you made the concept of the 'devil'. Even though what the 'devil' offers has no real value, it is still supposed to be powerful enough to attract you away from God. Does this make sense? You cannot overcome your confusion about your source by depreciating the power of your mind and projecting it onto a 'devil'. On some level, you know that you cannot weaken your mind anymore than you can weaken God, and

to think that you can is to deceive yourself.

3. Your decision to be separate from God makes a thought system that is real in your perception of a world, but is meaningless to God. It is real to you because you believe in it. The 'fall', or separation, did not occur because God tempted you to destroy yourself. God only knows God's Oneness, and any idea that God, or any Part of God, is capable of destruction, is an error.

4. You are One with God, except in the idea that separation from God is possible. The image you have of yourself as a personal self in a body does not exist in God, Where there are no images to perceive, only Oneness to know. You can make a concept of yourself that is separate from God, and you can believe in it ,but you cannot make it real. All of your defenses were made to protect you from the awareness that your concept of yourself is not real. While you believe that the concept that you have made is real, your mind will be split from the Holy Spirit, you will not know your Oneness with God, and you will be afraid for your self-concept.

5. Through belief your mind can make a world separate from God, make it seem very real and very fearful, and deny that God is its Source. In a sense, this belief *is* the 'devil'. The world that you have made to be separate from God is a lie, and it will disappear when you accept that God is Truth. Your Oneness with God is the only thing that cannot be changed, and, in Truth, you are still in Peace, though your mind seems conflicted. As you return to God, you will feel your undoing of the personal self's thought system as fear of death. But remember that there is no death, only a *belief* in death.

6. The thought system that you made *will* be undone. For you to fear this is for you to choose death, because God is Life, and separation from God, were it possible, would be death. You are not of a world; you are of God. You will leave the world, not by dying, but by accepting that only God is Truth, and letting go of the world. Only in your perception of a world does it make sense for you to believe that you are your own source. For you to believe that you can make both a world and God true, is for you to believe that God is not One, and free of conflict.

Chapter 4

The Illusions of the Ego

1. When you are truly devoted to extending God's Love, you will be motivated, because it is natural for you. For you to live from the Holy Spirit, then, is for you to be motivated. But it is not natural for you to live from a personal self, so this tires you. To live only from the Holy Spirit is to be enlightened.

2. In your perception that you are living a life in a world, you can live from the Holy Spirit within you, or from a personal self. To live from the Holy Spirit is to know that *God is*. When you live from a personal self, you are denying God. The personal self embarks on many useless journeys through the world, but the Holy Spirit's only journey is to God.

3. You can choose to put aside the personal self, and to remember your Oneness with God. Until then, though, your perception of yourself living a life in a world is wasted re-enacting the separation from God: loss of power, futile attempts to regain power, then death. This is the story that you will see replayed again and again in the world that you perceive by many seeming 'selves', until you voluntarily let go of the world. Do not make your life in a world about suffering, but rather about remembering that you are One with God. The Holy Spirit will take you on the journey to remembering God, and if you study these lessons carefully, they will prepare you for it.

1. Right Teaching and Right Learning

1. Ideas are clarified and strengthened in you by your extending, or *teaching*, them. You are both your own teacher and your own pupil. Your mind automatically extends what you believe. The Holy Spirit within you can only teach you that you are the Holy Spirit; the personal mind can only teach you that you are a personal self. To teach from the Holy Spirit, you not only have to believe in the Holy

Spirit, you have to believe that the Holy Spirit is within you.

2. Learning means change. The separation was the first change that you introduced into your mind, and it was painful, so you fear change, because you are afraid that change will bring you further pain. You think that by guarding the personal mind's thought system, and allowing no change to come into it, you will find Peace. But Peace is only possible from the Holy Spirit in your mind. The Holy Spirit and the personal mind are diametrically opposed, and cannot join. The Holy Spirit cannot make the personal mind stronger, or reduce its conflict. But your mind, which only *seems* separated from God, and believes in the personal self, can learn either that it is a personal self, or that it is One with God.

3. It is your split mind, not the Holy Spirit in your mind, that needs to be taught, and it is frightened, because what it needs to learn is how to relinquish the personal self that it believes it is. It perceives this as destruction, but the Holy Spirit does not attack. The Holy Spirit only shows you how your belief in the personal self arose so that you can let go of it. When the Holy Spirit reminds you of your Oneness with God, your split mind cannot help but be frightened.

4. Teaching that you are the Holy Spirit, and therefore learning that you are the Holy Spirit, is the only way that you are going to change your mind, and undo your perception of separation from God. Your merely accepting intellectually that the separation has not occurred is not going to undo it. The separation, and the world that it gave rise to in your mind, are very real to you, and you can only undo them by coming from the Holy Spirit in your mind. When you willingly give up the personal mind as guardian of your thought system and open your mind to the Holy Spirit, the Holy Spirit will gently correct your mind, and lead you back to God.

5. As God's Teacher, the Holy Spirit's goal is to no longer be needed by you because you have fully remembered that you are One with God. It is impossible for the personal mind to understand this, because in order to continue to exist for you, it needs to teach you forever that separation from God is real. It is natural for the

personal mind to do this for its own survival, but it is not natural for you to learn this from the personal mind. The personal mind cannot choose to undo itself, but you can choose to undo it, because it is not you.

6. The personal self that you think is you will conflict with other personal selves in any situation in your perception that you are in a world, but the Holy Spirit overlooks all personal selves, and sees only the Holy Spirit everywhere. In your perception that you are in a world, you teach from the personal self to glorify the personal self, so you see the Holy Spirit as a Teacher to be either rejected or exalted. If you think of the Holy Spirit as Something separate and superior, you *will* be afraid of It. The Holy Spirit could not teach you that you are One with God if It were separate from you, and you would not be able to teach yourself through the Holy Spirit if It were separate from you.

7. You do not have to do anything to establish your Worth. As Part of God, you are Inherently Worthy. Only in your delusions does the concept of your unworthiness have meaning. As long as you reject your Oneness with God, you will be frightened by the concepts of inferiority and superiority. The Holy Spirit is a patient Teacher Which will remind you of your Worthiness as Part of God, over and over, until you learn It. God does not threaten the personal self, because the personal self isn't real; God does not threaten the Holy Spirit, because the Holy Spirit is Part of God.

8. The personal mind that you believe you are exploits every situation to glorify itself, because it is insecure. It will exist for you as long as you believe in it, and it will always be insecure because it is incomplete and unreal. On some level, you know that it is not real, and you do not trust it. The only way out of its insecurity for you is for you to let go of it, and accept that only God is Real. When you are afraid, remember that only God is Real, and that you are One with God. The personal mind may dispute this, but the personal mind cannot know you as you are in Truth.

9. God did not make fear; you did when you chose to be separate from God. You are not at Peace when you are not aware that you are One with God. Your identifying with a personal self is your choice to be

afraid, instead of at Peace. When you know again that you are One with God, you will not be able to understand this choice. You do not have to believe in it now. All of your efforts to make separation real to you only put off your remembering your Oneness with God. God is inevitable for you, because you are One with God.

10. The personal mind with which you identify is afraid of the Joy that the Holy Spirit inspires in you, because when you experience Joy, you withdraw from the personal mind, and from fear. The personal mind likes you to be fearful, because fear attests to the reality of your separation from God. Let it go! You do not have to listen to the personal mind, or to protect it. You can listen to only God through God's Holy Spirit. The Holy Spirit cannot deceive you, because It *is* you. Let go of the personal self, which is a false picture of you, and is unworthy of you. Do not look out at a false and unworthy world and believe that it is your reality.

11. The personal mind is not worthy of you, and it cannot bring you Peace. Do not support it. Only God is worthy of you, even though you have chosen to leave God. But God is Eternal, and you are Eternally One with God, and you can choose to return to This awareness. Your doing so is the only thing that is certain. What is not Eternal is not part of God, and the personal self cannot make anything Eternal, or certain.

12. You cannot do anything real with a personal self, but with the Holy Spirit you can save yourself from your perception of separation from God. You must put aside the personal self and extend God's Love from the Holy Spirit within you in order to perceive yourself Truly. Only your perception of God's Love is a worthy Gift to give yourself.

13. You can give the personal self and the body to the Holy Spirit so that you can be free of concern for them, and the Holy Spirit will teach you of their unreality. The Holy Spirit understands your temptation to believe in them as real, and in order to heal your mind, It needs you to teach yourself through the Holy Spirit that they are not real. Jesus overcame the body and the personal self, and you can use Him as an example. When you are tempted to suffer, remember Him and be happy instead.

2. The Ego and False Autonomy

1.   How could your mind ever have made the personal self? It seems as though this happened in the past, but time isn't real, and it only *seems* as though it happened in the past, because the error is occurring now. [In God there is only God. This cannot be understood by the personal mind, which perceives many separate, specific, concrete forms as real.]

2.   You make a personal self for yourself that is very changeable, because it is not real. You also make a personal self for all of the bodies that you perceive, and your perceptions of them can also change. Your interaction with other personal selves can change both you and them in your mind, because they are not real. You don't even have to be physically close to another to change your mind about them. You can change your mind about them just by thinking about them, which proves that personal selves are nothing but thoughts in your mind.

3.   The personal self with which you identify is made by your denial of God. This is happening now, and this is how the personal self has happened all along. But your mind does not have to work this way.

4.   You love and protect the personal self, because you believe it is you. In this, your split mind resembles God, Which loves Itself. Your reactions to what you have made are not surprising, but as long as your origins are open to belief, you are looking at yourself from a split mind. God is beyond belief, and can only be *known*. Teaching and learning are necessary for you until you remember God. The truest belief that you can have is that there is another way to look at yourself, because, with this belief, you acknowledge that the personal self is not you.

5.   You perceive undoing the personal self's thought system as painful, even though it is not. In your identification with a personal self, you do not know what is truly helpful to you, and what is truly harmful to you. But though you may not recognize it, you have agreed to cooperate with the Holy Spirit to undo the personal self. You may be conflicted about this, which only means that you are still identifying with a personal self. This will not last. Be patient with yourself, and remember that it is inevitable that you

remember God.

6. You can only truly *give* Love from a place of knowing that you *have* Love. To the personal mind *giving* means sacrifice, because to it *giving* means *giving away*. The personal self only willingly gives when it believes it will get something greater than what it is giving. This is the personal self's law of 'giving to get', which it does as it evaluates itself in relation to other personal selves. The personal self is obsessed with the idea of lack, because it was made by your perceived separation from God, which *is* lack. It perceives other personal selves as real only to validate its own reality. 'Self-esteem' for the personal self means that it temporarily believes enough in its own reality to not need others to validate it. The personal self is always vulnerable to perceiving threats to its existence.

7. The personal self is always comparing itself to others, and it is incapable of perceiving Oneness. It was made from lack, and can only give from lack, and this is how the idea of 'getting' arose in your mind. The personal mind regards the body as its home, and all appetites and needs, whether they are physical or emotional, originate in the personal mind, and are the means of 'getting' something to confirm the personal self's existence to itself. But it is your mind that decides that this is possible, and it is your mind that is confused about what is real.

8. The personal self believes that it is its own source. This idea is meaningless and frightening, and so it tries to unite with other personal selves to validate its own existence, or to attack them to appear strong. It cannot, however, question its own origins, because the belief that it is independent is its very foundation. The personal self is your split mind's belief that it is isolated and alone. Your split mind tries to get the Holy Spirit to acknowledge the personal self to make it real, but the Holy Spirit is unaware of the personal self, because the Holy Spirit is Real, and the personal self is not. The personal mind is also unaware of the Holy Spirit, but it does perceive that within you it is being rejected by Something greater than itself. Self-esteem for the personal self can only be an illusion, because it is never wholly certain of its own existence. As Part of God, your illusion of the personal self is a myth, and not

part of you, though you can use the power of your mind to make myths seem real. But this does not make them real. [Mythical stories in the world that you perceive are not inspired by the Holy Spirit, are ambiguous, and tend to be good-and-evil in nature, so that even the most benign myths have fearful connotations.]

9. Your split mind comes up with many myths to explain the origin of the personal self, just as it uses magical thinking to give power to the physical world that you perceive. Most of these myths are concerned with 'the creation', meaning the physical world, and have an associated form of magical thinking. Evolution is one myth that your split mind has come up with to explain the personal self's origins. You associate the personal self with physical birth because, in your identification with it, it is hard for you to believe that the personal self is an idea that existed before the physical world. Some of the split mind's more 'religious' myths teach that an individual spirit, or 'soul', existed before the world and that it will continue after it temporarily experiences a personal self in the world. Some myths may even teach that the 'soul' will be punished for this lapse into a world separate from God. But it is not your Spirit that needs salvation.

10. Salvation is really the correction of your perception of separation from God. It is necessary before you can be restored to full awareness of your Oneness with God. Your corrected perception, being in total alignment with God's Love, undoes your split mind and your perception that the personal self is real, and leads to your awareness of your Oneness with God automatically.

11. It is important for you to understand that using the personal self to correct your perception of separation from God is only temporary. Your perceiving the personal self as real is a block to your awareness of your Oneness with God, but using the personal self to extend God's Love restores your Oneness with God to your awareness. Eventually, your corrected perception will lead you to the awareness that the personal self is not necessary at all. You might wonder how this is possible while you seem to be living in a world, but who is the 'you' that seems to be living in a world? As Part of God, your Spirit is Immortal and Unchanging. It is not a

continuum weaving in and out of mortality, nor does It need to experience a personal self to understand Itself in comparison. God is All, and God has no opposite to which It can be compared. That is how God is different from everything that your mind has made.

3. Love Without Conflict

1. The idea that you are One with God is not understandable to the personal mind, because it sees God as Something separate from you. That you are One with God is the Whole Lesson of the plan of the Atonement, which, by correcting your perception of separation from God, leads you beyond the plan itself to Oneness with God. Just as God extends only God, so do you. This has not stopped because of your split mind's illusion of the personal self. Your Extension continues as God's Extension continues, because you are One. The personal self and the Holy Spirit will never be One, but the Holy Spirit will always be One with God. You can be certain that your Oneness with God is unchanged.

   God is untouched by the personal self, and will not be undone by it. Amen.

2. This is a prayer that you can use when you are tempted to believe in separation from God. You need guidance because you have denied the Truth in yourself. The Holy Spirit's role is to make clear to you What is True, and what is false, so that you can overcome the obstacles to Truth that your split mind made. Unite your mind with the Holy Spirit within you, and you can overcome your split mind.

3. The personal mind regards the Holy Spirit as its enemy because the personal mind arose from the separation, and its existence is dependent on the separation continuing. As a reward for believing in it, the personal mind offers you a sense of temporary existence that is its own beginning and ending. When you identify with it, you believe this existence is your own. In comparison, the Holy Spirit offers you Eternal, Unchanging Being. When you experience a direct Revelation of God, you never wholly believe in the

personal self again. How could its temporary, insecure 'life' compare to God's Eternal, Stable Being?

4.   God's Love is Oneness. In your split mind, you cannot believe that you are One with God, and that God Loves you, because you are not One with the personal self that you made, and that you hate. Because it is the denial of Oneness, the personal self has no allegiance to you, its maker, either. You 'love' the personal self because you made it, but you also hate it because you project your decision to be separate from God onto it. All 'love' in the world that you perceive reflects this love/hate that you have for the personal self that you made, and that's why the Oneness of God's Love cannot be understood by the personal mind. But when you wholly want to experience God's Love, It will immediately enter your mind. The personal mind is not capable of wholly wanting anything because of its perception that lack is real, and wholeness is impossible.

5.   You can have an experience of Wholeness that is very different from what the personal self offers, and when you do so, you will never want to deny It again. The only reason God does not fill your entire mind is because of your belief in the personal mind. You must be open and willing for God to fill your awareness. This condition is set by your inherent Free Will as Part of God.

6.   No power other than your own True Will is strong and worthy enough to guide you. Your Will is as Free as God's Will. Through the Holy Spirit within you, you can remember God's Love for you, and your Love for God. This remembering is God's Will. When you call on the Holy Spirit, you will always be answered. You cannot call on any other god, because there is no other god.

7.   You must give up every thought that is an obstacle to God. You hold onto many little scraps of fear that prevent God from filling your mind. The Holy Spirit cannot destroy what you have made, but the Holy Spirit can help you undo it. You must look for, and find, all the obstacles that you have to God so that you can ask the Holy Spirit to help you undo them. The Holy Spirit will respect what you have made, but the Holy Spirit will not support it, unless it is aligned with Truth. The Holy Spirit is always with you, and It

will wait as long as it takes for you to turn to It. You must eventually turn to the Holy Spirit, because the Holy Spirit *is* you. You need only wholly want the Holy Spirit for the Holy Spirit to respond to your call.

8. Look at what you are really asking for, and be honest with yourself, and with the Holy Spirit. If you do this sincerely, the Holy Spirit will prepare your mind for God. Once you have experienced God, you will be ready to learn to extend God's Love without limit. How long do you want to deny to God What is One with God?

9. *In God you have Everything.* In this idea is your Freedom. It frightens the personal mind because it means it does not exist. In God, Where All is One, 'to have' and 'to be' are the same. In God, you *have* Everything and you *are* Everything. But in the world that you perceive, which not only *is* separation but *manifests* separation, you can 'have' things that are separate from what you 'are'. You lack in your identification with a personal self, so you constantly need to 'get' things or people to 'be' whole.

10. The Calm Being of God, Which extends Forever in your Whole Mind, is banished from the personal mind. But the personal mind is desperate, because its undoing is inevitable. You exert a lot of effort to protect this personal identity, and very little to remain aware of God. It is insane for you to believe what is not true, and to protect it at the cost of Truth.

4. This Need Not Be

1. When you do not hear the Holy Spirit it is because you are not listening to It. That you *do* listen to the personal mind is demonstrated by your fearful attitudes, feelings, and behavior. But this is what you want and you fight to maintain, and what you are desperate to save. In your identification with a personal self, you struggle to save its image, but you do not seek for Christ, Which is your Oneness with God. In the world of separation that you perceive, you see the dark mirror in which your split mind looks to maintain the illusion of the personal self's reality. But it is up to you where you will look to find yourself.

2. Remember, it is your mind, not your behavior, that needs to

change. Whenever you are not Joyous, it is because you have looked at the world, seen separation, and believed it is real. Instead, look past the world and remember God's Love, then extend It instead. This may seem hard, but your mind is One with God's Mind, and it is actually much easier for you to think *with* God than for you to think *against* God. Your denying this supports the personal self, but splits your mind.

3. When you are depressed, it is because you feel that you are deprived of something that you want and do not have. Remember that, as Part of God, you have Everything, and if you are not aware of This, it is because of your own choice. You can choose again.

4. When you are anxious, it is because of the personal self's inherent insecurity. You can put as much effort into extending God's Love in your awareness as you put into maintaining the personal self.

5. When you feel guilty, know that you have not violated God's Laws, and exchange the personal mind's perception of 'sins' for the Holy Spirit's correction of your perception of separation from God. Only the personal mind can experience guilt, and when you feel guilty, it is because you believe that a personal self is you. You will be released from guilt when you are willing to accept that the world and the personal self are not real, and that what you do in your perception that you are in a world has no effect on God.

6. Watch your mind for all the ways that you believe that the personal self is you. The personal self offers you nothing, and protecting it tires and depresses you. You must make an effort to detach yourself from your identification with it. When you voluntarily give up the personal self, your mind will be healed.

7. Staying aware of your Oneness with God and engaging with the Holy Spirit is easy when you think that you are worth the effort. Look to the Holy Spirit for your Real Worth, and do not be deceived by the personal mind's unworthy image of you. The Holy Spirit cannot reach you when you identify with a personal self.

8. Every situation is an opportunity for you to be Happy, but you have refused This. As Part of God, your Power is Limitless, but you can limit the expression of your Power. Through the Holy Spirit, you can release yourself from the limits of the personal mind, and

extend God's Love everywhere and always. Do not settle for less than this as your goal. Watch your mind for any obstacles to God, and let them go. You can judge how well you are doing by how you feel. This is the correct use of judgment. The personal mind *is* lacking, and it should be judged and found lacking. It cannot exist without your desire for it, and your protection of it. When you judge it truly, you will automatically withdraw your power from it.

9. God is in your mind. You only need to look at the personal mind and say, and mean, 'I know this is not true' and God will fill your entire mind again. Your identification with a personal self cannot keep God from your mind, but it can keep God from extending Itself through your mind, and making you aware of It.

10. Christ is the part of your mind that is One with God. The 'Second Coming of Christ' simply means the end of your perception of separation from God, and the healing of your mind. Jesus is just like you, and He calls you to join in the Second Coming. You may feel that you are unworthy, but that is only the personal mind's attempt to convince you that *it* is real, and that you are not One with God. Your awareness that you are One with God *is* Christ, and is the healing of your mind.

11. Christ is One with the Holy Spirit in your mind. They are your Oneness with God, just as the personal mind is your separation from God. They are with you even in your perception that you are separated from God. You *will* choose to let go of the personal mind and to join your mind with Them in extending God's Love. This will heal your mind. Jesus raised the dead knowing that only God is Real, and Jesus can serve as an inspiration for you, because He knew there was nothing that an awareness of God's Love cannot overcome. Because you are One, Christ's call to you, and your answer, are the same.

5. The Ego-Body Illusion

1. Everything in the world that you perceive can be used to help you to remember that you are One with God, but the personal mind wants to keep this from your awareness. The personal mind is concerned with control, not with wholeness. This makes sense

from its perspective, since it arose from your denial of Wholeness. You will inevitably recognize with your entire mind that the personal mind is not real, but the personal mind must keep this hidden from you in order to preserve itself.

2. The personal mind is threatened by both the body, which it sees as unworthy of it, and the Holy Spirit, Which will undo it. It cannot completely obliterate the Holy Spirit from your mind, though, so it distorts the Holy Spirit's Loving Thoughts into an 'unacceptable' physical impulse to 'love' another.[1] Seeing physical 'love' and the Holy Spirit's Love as one threat makes it easier for you to repress them both and to preserve the personal mind, because the Holy Spirit's Love *will* undo the personal mind.

3. It is insane for you to confuse God with the body, but this confusion is essential to the personal mind, which needs you to repress both. It *does* make sense that the personal mind is threatened by God, because your awareness of God *does* undo the personal mind. But it does not make sense for the personal mind to fear the body, because it identifies with it.

4. The body is the personal mind's chosen home. It feels safe in this identification because, when you identify with the personal mind, the body's vulnerability is 'proof' that you cannot be One with God. But the personal mind also hates the body because the body is not good enough for it. This is very confusing to you, because the personal mind simultaneously teaches you to look to the body for safety, and that the body cannot protect you. So when you ask, 'Where can I go to be safe?' the personal mind tells you to look to *it* for protection. But since the personal mind is identified with the body, this answer does not make sense either. Having no real answer for you, the personal mind suppresses your question. Though out of your awareness, the question of where you can go to be safe does remain in your subconscious, and it makes you uneasy. But you will not find an answer if you do not ask the question.

5. So you *must* ask the question, 'Where do I go to be safe?' To find the Answer, you must be consciously aware of the question, and not be unconsciously driven by it. You must keep the Goal in mind, because you learn best when you value what you are seeking. But

remember that the personal mind does not value a Lasting Answer.

6. The personal mind cannot give you a Lasting Answer, because the Eternal only comes from God. The personal mind, then, keeps you preoccupied, busy, and seeking for safety and comfort in the world that you perceive, without letting it rise to your conscious awareness that this is what you are seeking. The personal mind loves to present you with problems that you cannot solve. So, in every situation, you must learn to ask, 'What am I really seeking?' When you clarify that you are seeking for Eternal Safety, then the Means to find It will automatically come to you. When you decided that remembering God is your Purpose, you set the course for the rest of your life, and it will remain in effect unless you change your mind.

6. The Rewards of God

1. The personal mind cannot understand what threatens it, and when you identify with the personal mind, you do not understand what threatens you. Only your identification with the personal mind gives it any power over you. It is not a separate power, but a belief about yourself. This belief does not affect the Truth in you, Which goes on Unchanged, despite your attempts to separate from It.

2. In learning to escape from the illusion of separation from God, be grateful for the opportunities to extend God's Love that the world that you perceive offers to you. It is the same gratitude that is appropriate for you to extend to the Holy Spirit, because both are in your mind. Whenever you act from the personal mind, you perceive that separation from God is real, and you miss an opportunity to correct this misperception. You must overlook every perception of separation and extend God's Love instead, and then you will have come as far in your awareness of God as you can in your perception that you are in a world. From here you return to God easily.

3. You have little trust in the Holy Spirit, but this will change as you turn to the Holy Spirit for guidance more and more. The rewards of Peace and Joy will convince you that the Holy Spirit is the only sensible choice, because the personal mind brings chaos and

misery. You learn better through rewards than through pain, because pain is not real, and it only seems to happen in your perception that you are in a world. But God's Rewards are Eternal, and since *you* recognize Them and the personal mind cannot, it is obvious that you are not a personal self. As long as you feel that you must escape from the personal mind, you still believe in it. So you cannot escape from it by humbling, controlling, or punishing it.

4. The personal mind and the Holy Spirit cannot join in you. Your split mind maintains your perception of separation from God by dissociating your Christ Mind. It denies your natural impulse to extend God's Love. The personal mind does not do this, but your *identification with* the personal mind is the means that your split mind uses to maintain your belief that the separation is real. It is your decision to identify with the personal mind that allows this belief to continue.

5. You threw away your awareness of your Oneness with God because you did not value It. You have taught yourself that the personal mind is joy, and that God is misery. The Holy Spirit teaches you the Value of God by leading you to recognize how miserable you are without God, through experiences that bring the Joy of God closer to your awareness. You have Free Will to choose, but you will not value the 'rewards' of the personal mind in the Presence of the Rewards of God.

6. The Holy Spirit's trust in you is greater than your trust in It, but this is what you are learning to correct. Your mission is to learn to identify with the Holy Spirit instead of with the personal mind. The Holy Spirit is God within you, and your identification with It is the correction of your perception of separation from God.

7. Through the Holy Spirit your perception of separation from God is undone. Be grateful for the many opportunities to overlook a separate world filled with separate selves, and to look on God's Love instead. One experience of real recognition of the Presence of the Holy Spirit returns your mind to Wholeness for a moment. The Holy Spirit leads you back to your Oneness with God, because What has been dissociated by your split mind is still in your mind.

8. As you extend God's Love, you draw closer to the Holy Spirit; as you act from the personal mind, you withdraw from the Holy Spirit. You must join with the Holy Spirit to extend *only* God's Love, because your mind is One. You will remember that you are One with God *only* by extending God's Love. First, you must extend God's Love, and then you will be ready for God, because God's Love is God's Oneness.

7. Creation and Communication

1. The content of a personal self's 'life' in the world that you perceive does not matter. But correction of your perception of separation from God is only meaningful to you in the context of the individual 'life' that you perceive as yours. Though God's Mind is abstract, and is therefore everywhere, the personal mind with which you identify, being the opposite of God, is very concrete, and its illusions are very specific. Your split mind, which believes in a personal self as your reality, believes your existence is defined by separation.

2. The personal mind perceives many separate things that are whole in themselves, but never in One Being. It will join with other personal selves as long as their joining reinforces its separateness. If it perceives a threat to its separateness, it will break off the connection. Its reactions are always to specifics, and though it can generalize by noting similarities among others and among situations, it is not capable of real abstract thinking, which perceives Oneness. The closest that the personal mind comes to abstract thinking is responding to specific persons or situations as though they are *other* specific persons or situations which they resemble.

3. The Holy Spirit, on the other hand, sees only Oneness. It does not try to establish a reality apart from God. It knows it is One with you and with God. God is in your mind, and your Oneness with God is Everywhere and Always. It cannot be changed. Your Oneness with God is your only Purpose. You can distort this Purpose, and you can choose to be unaware of It, but you cannot change It.

4. The personal self's existence is dependent on relationships to

define it, but it is very specific about how, with what, and with whom it will relate. Your Being, however, is only One. It is Reality extending Everywhere, Forever. You limit your own sense of reality when you cut yourself off from your Being. You can only correct this by giving over your entire mind to the Reality of God. Do not shrink from this. Your Whole Mind in God is your Home, and your Real Identity.

5. Even in your perceived separated state you have not stopped being One with God's Being, in Which you have Everything, and in Which you extend God's Being to increase your Joy. God extends God Everywhere and Always, and this is how you are One with God. This is what Creation is. There is no 'how' or 'with what' or 'to whom' in Oneness. Remember, in God there is no difference between *having* and *being*. In God you give God always.

6. God does not need your worship, because God does not have a separate personal self that needs to be uplifted. But when you do not accept your Oneness with God, God's Oneness is blocked from extending Always and Everywhere. When you are cut off from your Joy, God's Joy is incomplete. If you were truly capable of separating from God, God would not be Whole.

7. Your Oneness with God is unchanged by your perception of separation from God, but you can only know God with your entire mind. Through Revelation, you can experience God directly for a moment, but you must bring your entire mind to God for all time. Revelation cannot be brought into the world that you perceive, but it can change your experience of that world's reality. Your perception of a world must be replaced by your awareness of your Oneness with God.

8. God's Love is extended whenever you choose to follow the Holy Spirit's guidance. You are secure when you follow the Holy Spirit, because only a personal self is vulnerable. You are One with God, and God is extended to you and through you, and this is God's Joy. Changing your mind about yourself is how you share in God's Joy. By following the Holy Spirit, you extend God's Love in your awareness. The Holy Spirit will guide you until you have returned to full awareness of your Oneness with God.

Chapter 5

Healing and Wholeness

1. Your healing results in you experiencing True Joy. If you are unhappy, you have refused healing. Joy is naturally extended from your Whole Mind. When you try to heal without coming from God's Joy, you will experience conflicting results.

2. Fear and Love cannot both be real. You cannot be wholly fearful and still be alive, so the only Whole and Real State of Being is Love. Love and Joy and Wholeness are the same. For you to heal is for you to make yourself aware of your Wholeness again, and so for you to be wholly Joyous. Every time you extend God's Love in your awareness you return to your Whole Mind.

3. Every Loving Thought blesses you, and heals your mind. Be thankful for the opportunities to heal by extending God's Love that the world that you perceive offers to you. You are worthy of God's Joy, because you are the Extension of God's Joy. You can extend God's Love, because you are One with God. This is your healing prayer:

Let me extend God's Love to know my Self.

1. The Invitation to the Holy Spirit

1. Your healing is your overlooking a world of separation, and your looking on God's Oneness instead. Then your Whole Mind will rejoice, and extend without limit. Only your healed mind can experience God Eternally. This is your Joy, and you cannot *have* Joy until you choose to *be* Joy, because in God having and being are the same. To the Holy Spirit, *getting* is meaningless, and *giving* is everything, because by *giving* the Holy Spirit extends Its awareness of What It is. This is how God creates. This is the opposite of how the personal mind thinks, because when you give a *thing* away you *do* lose it. But even the personal mind is aware that when you share

an *idea* you do not lose it. In fact, you strengthen it in your mind, particularly the more you extend it. If you can accept that the world is only an idea, then the personal mind's association with giving and losing will be gone from your mind.

2.   Your process for remembering God starts with these simple concepts:

   Ideas increase in your mind when you extend them.
   The more you extend them, the stronger they become in your
      mind.
   Everything is an idea.
   To extend, then, is to increase in your awareness.

3.   With these concepts in your mind, you can invite the Holy Spirit into your awareness. The Holy Spirit can only come into your awareness at your own invitation. The Holy Spirit is your Christ Mind, and It was the Mind in Jesus.

4.   The Holy Spirit is known by other names: Healer, Comforter, Guide, Universal Inspiration, Teacher, Correction, Voice for God. The Holy Spirit is as high in your awareness of God that you can go in your perception that you are in a world. God is Everywhere, and you can block your awareness of God, but you cannot lose God.

5.   The Holy Spirit *is* your Christ Mind, Which is aware of God. It is the part of your mind that has not left God. In your perception of yourself as separate from God, the Holy Spirit is the name given to the Part of your mind that is the Correction for this perception. It is the Part of your mind that calls you back to being aware of your Oneness with God. When your mind is Whole again in your awareness, you will no longer hear a Call, but the Holy Spirit is Eternally Part of your Whole Mind.

6.   God cannot change your perception of separation because you have Free Will. But God is still in your mind as the Holy Spirit, and you are free to choose the Perceptions of the Holy Spirit, Which almost reach God. When you wholly identify with the Holy Spirit, you will be so aware of your Oneness with God that you will easily return to God.

7. The Holy Spirit's Perception contains elements that are similar to God:

    > First, the Holy Spirit is aware of *only* the Holy Spirit, and It extends Itself to keep Itself in Its awareness.
    >
    > Second, It does not try to make a reality apart from God, and therefore It does not obstruct your awareness of God.
    >
    > Third, It points beyond the healing It brings to your mind to your Oneness with God. When you are fully aware of the Holy Spirit, enough of your mind will be in line with God to shift easily into being God.

2. The Voice for God

1. Your healing is not the same as your Oneness with God, but it *is* correction of your perception that you are separate from God. The Holy Spirit's Perception heals you by looking past your perception of a world to your Oneness with God. Like your experience of the miracle, the Holy Spirit's Perception undoes the time that you need to remember that you are One with God. The Holy Spirit is your decision to heal your mind *now* by letting go of separation from God. Time does not undo your Oneness with God, and the Holy Spirit, and your experience of the miracle, reflect your Oneness with God.

2. The Holy Spirit is your Joy. It calls you to return to God, and answering Its Call is your mind's only real purpose. The Holy Spirit is both the Correction and the Means by Which you correct your sense of separation from God.

3. The Holy Spirit has not left your split mind. When you listen to the Holy Spirit, the personal mind disappears for you. Your choice is always to hear either the Holy Spirit or the personal mind. The personal mind is not of God, but the Holy Spirit is the Voice for God. With great effort and willingness, you can learn to hear only the Holy Spirit. This is what Jesus ultimately learned, and He is an example for you to follow.

4. You are One with God, but you have let the idea of separation from God become real to you, so you need the Holy Spirit to guide you

back to God. Through the Holy Spirit, separation falls away from your mind, and you become aware again that you are One with God.

5.   God is your Wholeness. But in your perception of separation from God, you are not aware that you are Whole, and you need guidance to make the choices that will help you to remember God again. Your choosing the Holy Spirit is your choosing God. Your perception of separation blocks the full extension of God's Wholeness Everywhere, Always, and the Holy Spirit is the Voice for God within you that restores Wholeness to your awareness.

6.   The Holy Spirit teaches you to remember God and to forget the separation. In God, all is One, and there are no choices. But your perception of separation is your belief that opposites are possible, and so you must make choices in your perception of separation. Choosing is how you exercise your mind's power in your perception that you are living a 'life' in a world. The Holy Spirit is one choice; the personal mind the other. You may have chosen to leave God to believe that you are a personal self, but, through the Holy Spirit, God has not left you.

7.   The Voice of the Holy Spirit does not command, demand, or attack; It quietly reminds you of God, and It is compelling *because* It reminds you of God. It shows your mind the way to Peace even in the midst of the turmoil you make. Peace is stronger than conflict because It heals. Conflict divides and does not increase, so there is no gain in it. When you listen to the voice of the personal mind you lose *sight* of God, though you cannot lose God. God is lost to your awareness until you choose to be aware of God again.

8.   The Holy Spirit is your Guide for making choices that will lead you back to full awareness of God again. Both the world and God are in your mind, and the Holy Spirit is the Way in Which God's Will is expressed to you in your perception that you are in a world. The Holy Spirit comes from your Oneness with God, but you have been wanting to follow another guide. You must choose which guide you will follow. Which you follow is your judgment, because it is a decision based on which one offers what you value more.

9.   The Holy Spirit in Jesus is the same Holy Spirit in you. It was Jesus'

decision to follow only the Holy Spirit that gave Him all His power. He is a model for you, and He can help you to make the same decision, because He is One with you through the Holy Spirit. He showed that returning to God is a decision, and that you can make this decision.

10. Jesus let Christ in His Mind change Him, and you can let It change you. Your Christ Mind hears only God's Voice, and speaks with only God's Voice. The world is an idea that tires you, and the Holy Spirit is the Idea that brings you Rest. Your Joy is in answering the Holy Spirit's Call to you. You will be aware again that you are One with God when you let go of your perception of separation from God. It is your mind's only purpose to be restored to Wholeness again. Listen only to the Holy Spirit, and extend only God's Love to replace your perception of separation.

11. When you are tempted to listen to the personal mind, turn to the Holy Spirit to remember God. The more you extend God's Love, the more you will want to extend God's Love, and be restored to an awareness of your Oneness with God.

12. For you to behave like Jesus is for you to respond from only the Holy Spirit within you. This is how Jesus is a model for you. God is beyond belief, but returning to God is not beyond what you can accomplish. In God you have no limits. This is the message that you will extend from the Holy Spirit within you.

3. The Guide to Salvation

1. You can use your perception of others to heal your mind by perceiving the Holy Spirit instead of personal selves. Your Perception of the Holy Spirit is your Bridge to God; It is your corrected perception. The Holy Spirit is from God, and is in your mind.

2. The Holy Spirit is the Idea of healing, and It grows and is strengthened in you as you extend It. It calls you to God, and is the Idea of God in your mind. Since you are One with God, the Holy Spirit *is* you. As you see the Holy Spirit in place of personal selves, you increase your awareness of the Holy Spirit. Others do not have to be aware of the Holy Spirit for you to experience this miracle.

Your mind is healed as you replace your perception of separation with your awareness of the Holy Spirit.

3. *What* you perceive and *how* you perceive are both in your mind. There are two opposed ways of looking at others, also both in your mind. See separate personal selves as reality, and you will believe that you are a separate personal self apart from God. See the Holy Spirit in place of personal selves, and you will recognize the Holy Spirit in yourself. What you acknowledge as Truth, you strengthen in yourself.

4. The Voice of the Holy Spirit is weak in you, and this is why you must extend It. It must be strengthened in your awareness before you can hear It. The Holy Spirit is not weak, but your willingness to hear It is. If you look for the Holy Spirit in the personal mind with which you identify without extending the Holy Spirit in your perception, you will make the mistake of perceiving a limited personal self as you. This will frighten you, because you will be looking for What frightens the personal mind *with* the personal mind that you think you are.

5. [Time is a concept of your split mind, and delay is a device of the personal mind. Both are meaningless to God.] The Holy Spirit is the opposite of the personal mind, and Its Perceptions are the opposite of the personal mind's perceptions. The Holy Spirit's Purpose is to undo everything that your split mind has made. It undoes them where they are, at the level of the personal mind, so that you can understand the change.

6. [The Holy Spirit and the personal mind are not understandable to each other. Being Part of God, the Holy Spirit understands Eternity, Which is *timelessness*. The personal mind believes in time, which it does not question. *Now* is the only aspect of time that is Eternal.]

7. Using the personal mind's own language, the Holy Spirit mediates between the personal mind's beliefs and Truth. It looks beyond what your split mind has made, and looks toward God. It does not destroy, but reinterprets, what your split mind makes. The Holy Spirit's Purpose is therefore to reinterpret *you* on behalf of God.

8. You cannot understand yourself as a separate personal mind, because your mind is not limited to a personal self. Your Mind is

One with God, and It extends Everywhere. It is of This that the Holy Spirit reminds you, because This is What the Holy Spirit sees. Your awareness of the Holy Spirit extending everywhere is Peaceful, and this threatens the personal mind. Peace threatens the personal mind, because it was born in your internal conflict, and it depends on it continuing. The personal mind is strengthened in your internal conflict, and, when you believe in conflict, you attack because you feel threatened. The idea of conflict calls on the personal mind, just as Peace calls on the Holy Spirit. You will always experience conflict in time, just as you can only experience Peace in Eternity.

9. Your perceptions derive meaning for you from your identification with either the personal mind or the Holy Spirit. Which identification you accept is the foundation for your beliefs. Your perception of separation from God is another way of saying that you believe that your mind is split and conflicted. The personal mind is a symbol of this conflict, just as the Holy Spirit is a Symbol of your Wholeness and Peace, so how you perceive others is determined by what you want to strengthen in yourself. Through the personal mind you may perceive separation, but the Holy Spirit can reinterpret your perceptions.

10. The Holy Spirit is your Perfect Teacher, because It uses the perception that you made to teach you to use it differently. You cannot be wholly resistant to the Holy Spirit, because your mind is still One with God. The personal mind may deny this, but the Part of your mind that is Part of God is stronger than the personal mind. This is Where the Holy Spirit resides within you in Peace. As Part of God, you can only be at Home in Peace and Eternity.

11. The personal mind perceives the world as a place of separation from God, but the Holy Spirit can use your perception of a world as a means to remind you of God. Because your mind is split, the Holy Spirit must teach you through opposites. The Holy Spirit perceives time, and uses it to remind you of Eternity. Accept correction from the Holy Spirit, and learn what correction can teach you. Look and think with the Holy Spirit to remember God. The Holy Spirit is Part of God, and Part of you. It is your Guide

through time, and out of time. The Holy Spirit remembers God for you, and asks only that you extend your awareness of It to increase your Joy.

4. Teaching and Healing

1. In fear, you may hide the Holy Spirit, but It is still Part of you. Correcting your perception of separation from God is your way out of fear. The Holy Spirit will help you to reinterpret everything that you perceive as fearful as untrue, and It will teach you that only What comes from Love is True. You cannot destroy Truth, and you must accept It, because It is a Part of God, and of you. Nothing Loving is lost to you, because It comes from the Holy Spirit, the Voice for Oneness within you. What is not Loving cannot be saved for you, because it is not real. Correcting your perception of separation from God secures God in your awareness, and when your entire mind is healed of its perception of separation, it will be entirely safe from the personal mind's fearful perceptions. When you hear only the Holy Spirit, the personal mind will be undone.

2. The personal mind is weak because it is limited awareness. It does not really exist; it was never born, and it will not die. Your Real Mind continues into and beyond your perception of physical birth. Your Real Mind *is.* Your mind will expand as you return to the Holy Spirit the part of your mind that you gave to the perception of separation from God. The Holy Spirit is here to show you how to free your mind of its limited awareness. You cannot undo your perception of separation without the Holy Spirit, because the Holy Spirit *is* the Correction of your perception of separation. Extending the Holy Spirit in place of the world of separation in your mind is how you learn to perceive only the Holy Spirit. Your entire mind is One with God, and you cannot be limited to a personal self.

3. Every Loving Thought that you have is part of your Whole Mind, because Love is What your Whole Mind is. As Part of God, you create with God by extending God's Love Everywhere, Always. Your belief in the personal self can keep you from awareness of God, but in God this has no meaning. The Holy Spirit's awareness of your Oneness with God is always in your mind, extending

Everywhere, Always. The personal mind's thoughts cannot be extended, because its thoughts occur on many levels that can conflict, and can even oppose each other on the same level. Opposing thoughts cannot be extended, because they are not One. Since you are One with God, you can extend only God's Loving Thoughts, and this is Heaven. When you decide that you want to be without limitation, the Holy Spirit will 'purify' the part of your mind that you have given over to the perception of separation by reinterpreting its thoughts as unreal. Your decision to give it to the Holy Spirit *is* its purification.

4. Jesus heard only the Holy Spirit, because He understood that the Holy Spirit is the correction of separation from God. Your choosing to hear only the Holy Spirit implies your willingness to extend God in your awareness. The Christ Mind in you is compelled to extend Itself in place of your perception of a world because It is Whole. In Truth, you cannot be hurt, and when you demonstrate that you can be hurt by blaming others for your pain, you are hurting yourself. 'Turning the other cheek' means recognizing that nothing outside of your own thinking can hurt you.

5. You teach yourself by living what you believe. You can use teaching to heal by extending Loving Thoughts in the recognition that this strengthens Them in your mind. What you teach reinforces what you believe, and when you extend your Christ Mind in place of your perception of a world of separation, you return to Joy.

6. The Holy Spirit corrects your perception of separation from God by undoing the personal mind. By following the Holy Spirit, you return to God, and you can only do this completely by giving up all belief in the personal mind's perceptions, and giving your entire mind to the Holy Spirit. The Holy Spirit's correction is not complete until you experience only the Holy Spirit. You will learn what you teach yourself. The Holy Spirit is always with you, because the Holy Spirit is One with God. You reject God when you believe any of the personal mind's perceptions are real. You must learn that your entire mind belongs to God.

7. Correcting your perception of separation from God gives you the

power of a healed mind, but this is not the Power of God. When you have accepted that you need correction, you must devote yourself to forgiving, or letting go of, all of your perceptions of separation in order to heal your entire mind. As long as you hold back any part of your mind for the personal self, the full Power of God's Oneness is limited in your awareness. Only your complete mind can be One with God, because God is Whole. Only the Thoughts that you think with the Holy Spirit are not lacking.

8.   In your Wholeness, you cannot suffer. The Holy Spirit within you has saved all of your Loving Thoughts, and It purifies them of any limitations that keep them from extending everywhere, always. Peace is with you because you are One with God. Extend God's Love so that you will always remember It. You are pure enough to hold God's Love, and strong enough to extend God's Love. With the Holy Spirit to guide you, you have the Wisdom of God, Which is your Being. God's Loving Thoughts are always with you.

5. The Ego's Use of Guilt

1.   The personal mind's use of guilt needs to be clarified. The personal mind has a purpose, just as the Holy Spirit has a Purpose. The personal mind's purpose is fear, because fear and separation from God go together. The personal mind uses logic, just as the Holy Spirit does, and you choose which you will follow. Both are in you.

2.   There is no guilt in God, and you return to awareness of your Oneness with God through correction, not through punishment. The part of your mind that you have given over to the perception of separation will be restored to Oneness when you have undone this perception, and this will give rise to Joy and Peace in you. Guilt causes fear, not Peace, in you. Not only does your guilt not come from God, it is a symbol that your attack on God is real. This means nothing to God, but everything to the personal mind. All of your guilt stems from your belief that you have attacked God by success-fully separating from God.

3.   Your belief in the personal mind is your belief that you attacked God, and detached part of God. The personal mind teaches you that you, being *it*, stole God's Power. When you identify with the

personal mind, you unconsciously believe this, you feel guilty for it, and you fear punishment from God, Which you see as outside of you now that you are separate from It. This is the insane and delusional thinking of the personal mind.

4.   Your belief in the personal mind makes it 'reality' for you. In your Oneness with God, your Mind extends only God. This is the same ability that can make your illusions seem like reality to you. But for you to think with God, and like God, is for you to experience only Joy. Guilt is not natural to you, because it is your belief that your separation from God is reality. The personal mind perceives the separation as a real attack, a sin, not as merely a misperception that leads to your sense of lack. It must do this for its survival, because if you understand this lack as only a misperception, you will successfully take steps to undo it. This is 'death' to the personal mind, but freedom for you.

5.   Your guilt is the cause of all of your suffering. Illness is your attack on the body, which you identify with in your identification with a personal self, in an attempt to lessen God's punishment of you for separating from God. It is a form of magical solution for guilt. This is the personal mind's arrogance, because it first projects a punishing intent onto God, and then takes this intent as its own right. The personal mind tries to take all of the power it attributes to God, because it recognizes that it can only trust *you* if you totally believe only in *it*.

6.   You cannot go against God, even in your identification with a personal self, but you can *seem* to make a different reality. Every moment you are making a decision about what you want, and the decision's effects will automatically follow. You only have two choices: the Holy Spirit or the personal mind. You cannot undo the Holy Spirit, because It is One with God, but you can undo the personal mind, because you made it. What is One with God cannot be changed or undone, but what you have made can be changed and undone, because it is not real. You really cannot think apart from God, though you can seem to, and you can believe in what you think.

7.   Your Mind is One with God. Your guilt is an indication that you do

not know this, that you believe that you can make a mind apart from God, and that you want to. Every thought that you have with the personal mind comes from guilt, and is attended by guilt. You cannot escape guilt when you identify with the personal mind, which you believe you must follow. You will feel guilty for the separation, because you will feel responsible for it. By taking responsibility for the separation, you imply that it is real. If the separation were real, you *would* be responsible for it. But your only real responsibility is to accept correction of your *perception* of separation from God. By accepting correction instead, the symptoms of your guilt will disappear.

8.   As long as you continue to perceive yourself as separated from God, you will feel guilty. This will affect your behavior and your experience, because what you want you expect. Your mind does make your 'life' in the world, but, if you want, you can accept correction of your perception of separation from God instead. The moment that you fully accept correction, you will return to God. When you give up the personal mind, your Oneness with God will become apparent to you.

6. Time and Eternity

1.   God is not waiting for you, because God does not live in time. But the extension of God's Love is blocked while you wait to return to God. Your Christ Mind is waiting for the return of the part of It that you have given to perceive separation from God, just as the part that you gave away is waiting to be whole again. Delay does not matter to God, but it is painful for you. You choose to be in time, and therefore you believe that is where you are. But you do not belong in time, and you do have a choice. Your Place is in Eternity, Where you are One with God.

2.   Your guilt preserves time for you by inducing in you fear of punishment from God in the future. This ensures that the separation, which seemed to begin in the past, will continue into the future, because your fear will keep you from undoing the personal mind, and from approaching God. Guilt and fear are the personal mind's security and continuity. But God offers you True

Continuity in Eternity. When you choose God, you will exchange guilt for Joy, viciousness for Love, and pain for Peace. The Holy Spirit's Role is to unchain you from the personal mind. The personal mind will fight this in every way, at every moment. You know this, because you made the personal mind, and you give it its power.

3. Remember your Oneness with God ,and remember that This cannot be undone. Your Christ Mind extends everywhere, and you can let the Holy Spirit show you how to replace your perception of a world of separation with This awareness. The Holy Spirit and the personal mind simultaneously interpret you differently, though the personal mind always speaks first. You only need to be interpreted in the separation. In God you just *are*.

4. The personal mind judges, and it is always wrong, because its judgments are based on the error of perceiving you as separate from God, which they are made to uphold. The Holy Spirit undoes the personal mind's judgments. The personal mind cites Scripture for its own ends, and even interprets the Bible as a witness for itself. The Bible is a fearful thing in the personal mind's judgment, and you don't ask the Holy Spirit to guide your interpretations of the Bible, because you believe that It would judge against you.

5. There are many examples of how the personal mind's interpretations are misleading, but here are a few examples of how the Holy Spirit can reinterpret the Bible:

6. 'As ye sow, so shall ye reap' the Holy Spirit interprets to mean: You cultivate in yourself what you value. Your judgment of value is what gives something value to you.

7. 'Vengeance is mine, sayeth the Lord' means you should give the idea of vengeance to the Holy Spirit to undo for you, because it is not natural to your Real Mind.

8. 'I will visit the sins of the fathers unto the third and fourth generation' is interpreted by the personal mind as a guarantee of its own survival. The Holy Spirit interprets this as meaning It can reinterpret for you what earlier generations misunderstood, and therefore release you from fear.

9. 'The wicked shall perish' is a statement of correction for the Holy

Spirit, Which interprets 'perish' as 'be undone'. All thoughts that are not of God must be undone. The word 'undone' is threatening to the personal mind, which interprets it as 'destroyed'. But the personal self will not be destroyed, because it is an idea in your mind. You will reinterpret it as unreal, so that you can release yourself from fear. The part of your mind that you have given to the personal self will return to your Whole Mind in Oneness with God. You can delay this, but you can never make separation and fear real.

10. You do not need to fear that the Holy Spirit will condemn you; It will only dismiss the idea of separation from your mind. Because you are One with God, any belief in guilt in yourself is your belief that God is guilty. Bring all of your guilt to the Holy Spirit to undo it. No matter how guilty that you think that you are, the Holy Spirit knows it is not true. The Holy Spirit's Purpose is to remind you that you are One with God.

11. Where you look to find yourself is up to you: your Christ Mind or the personal mind. Be patient with yourself as you learn to let go of your illusion of separation from God. The Holy Spirit is Infinitely Patient, as God is Infinitely Patient.

12. You must learn that Infinite Patience brings Peace *now*, exchanging time for Eternity. Infinite Patience comes from the Infinite Love of God, Which you need to learn. Time is a learning device that has no use for you when you no longer need to learn. The Holy Spirit knows that time is meaningless, and this is what It reminds you of every moment as It leads you back to Eternity. The Holy Spirit is the only Blessing that you can truly give. You must extend the Holy Spirit in your awareness to know that you are the Holy Spirit.

7. The Decision for God

1. Do you really believe that you can make a mind that is separate from God, and that has its own thought system? Do you really believe that you can plan for your security and happiness better than God can? You do not have to be careful or careless; you only need to give all your cares to the Holy Spirit, Which Loves you because you are One with God. All hope is yours because the Holy

Spirit cares for you, and you cannot escape this. You can choose to accept the Holy Spirit's Care, and to extend the Holy Spirit to all that your mind perceives.

2. In your perception of a world, there are examples of many who have attempted to heal others without healing themselves. They did not overcome their perception of a world because they did not wholly trust that they could. While they could sometimes overcome sickness, their lack of belief in their Christ Mind meant that their results were inconsistent. Unless you accept full healing of your mind, you will believe that God's Love is incomplete. You are asked to return your entire mind to God, because God's Mind is Whole. Your knowing this is what heals you. The part of your mind that you have given to separation is yours to give back to God.

3. Why do you listen to the personal mind's demands to protect it when you know that the Holy Spirit is within you? God asks only that you extend the Holy Spirit to your entire mind, as the Holy Spirit was extended to you. God wants you in Perfect Peace, because you are One with God. When you do not accept correction of your perception of separation from God, it is because you identify with a personal self, and you believe its defense of its own existence is *your* own defense. It means you do not want to be healed.

4. The time for your healing is *now*. You are not asked to figure out for yourself how to undo your perception of separation from God, but to accept the Holy Spirit as the Correction. The Holy Spirit will make the undoing clear to you, and It will tell you what you need to do. God's Extension is incomplete as long as you believe that you are lost to God.

5. Whenever you are not completely Joyous, it is because you have believed that the world is real. Perceiving this as 'sin', you feel guilty, and you become defensive, because you expect God to attack you. This is your own decision, and you can undo it. You do not need to repent, because you are not guilty. When you feel guilty, you reinforce your belief that separation from God is real. Instead, you can let the Holy Spirit undo the separation for you.

6. Making a decision is not hard, and you will realize this if you accept that you are not Joyous by your own decision. The first step in undoing this decision is accepting that you made a decision that you can undo. Be consciously aware of your own thinking, and understand that the Holy Spirit provides the process of correction for your unhappy thinking. Your only part is to return to the thought where you made the error, and to give it to the Holy Spirit to undo. Say this to yourself, understanding that the Holy Spirit will come to you when your invitation is sincere:

> 'I am not at Peace, so I must have decided against Peace.
> I made this decision myself, and I can change it.
> I want to change it, because I want to be at Peace.
> I do not need to feel guilty, because the Holy Spirit will correct my decision.
> I choose to let the Holy Spirit decide for God for me.'

Chapter 6

The Lessons of Love

1. The relationship of anger to attack is obvious, but you do not always recognize the relationship of fear to anger. Your being angry always involves your projecting the cause of your sense of lack onto others in the world that you perceive. But *you* are responsible for your sense of lack, which is brought about by your belief in separation from God, and this is what you ultimately must accept. You are angry when you believe that you have been attacked by another, that attacking back to defend yourself is justified, and that you are not responsible for your perception of attack. These irrational premises lead you to the irrational conclusion that attacking back is more appropriate than extending God's Love. The way for you to undo this conclusion is to question the premises on which it rests. In fact, you can only be attacked by your own belief that you are a personal self in a hostile world, attacking others for your own belief is not justified and will not protect you, and you *are* responsible for what you believe.

2. You have been asked to take Jesus as a model, since an extreme example is a particularly helpful lesson for you. You teach yourself all the time, no matter if your thoughts are based in Truth or in illusions. You may believe in an error, but this can be corrected.

1. The Message of the Crucifixion

1. It is time to look at Jesus' crucifixion again. So far, this course has emphasized that it was not a form of punishment, but it does have a positive interpretation that is wholly benign if you properly understand it.

2. Jesus' crucifixion was nothing more than an extreme example, the value of which lies in the kind of teaching it facilitates. You have misunderstood it, because in the guilt of your split mind you perceive fearfully. Your Christ Mind is in you always, and you do

not have to be crucified to become aware of It. You become aware of Christ in your mind by extending It. While Jesus' resurrection was emphasized before, His crucifixion also offers you release from fear if you are willing to look at it without fear. It will help you to understand what you need to teach yourself.

3. In your identification with a personal self, you react as though you are being crucified. You project the source of your pain onto others in a world, instead of recognizing that it is only your own thoughts that hurt you. Your projection leads to anger, which fosters attack, and promotes more fear. The real lesson of Jesus' crucifixion lies in the *seeming* intensity of an attack on Him by others. If Jesus is to serve as a model for you, you must understand that attack is impossible.

4. Attack can only be made on a body, which isn't real. Nothing that is destructible is real, and so its seeming destruction should not inspire anger in you. If you believe anger is justified, then you are teaching yourself that separation from God is real. The purpose of Jesus' crucifixion was to show you that there is no reason to perceive attack in unfair treatment, because you cannot be unfairly treated. When you respond with anger, you are identifying with a body, and you are therefore teaching yourself that you are an illusion.

5. The Christ Mind in Jesus is the Christ Mind in you, and you can know this only by extending It in your awareness. You can choose to see yourself as unfairly treated, but when you do so, remember that Jesus was treated unfairly in the judgment of the personal mind, but that He did not share this judgment. He offered a different interpretation of attack which you can share. If you will believe it, you will teach yourself that you cannot be attacked.

6. You learn what you teach yourself. If you react as though you are being treated unfairly, you are teaching yourself that the personal self and unfair treatment are reality. This is not what you want to learn if you want to remember that you are One with God. Instead, teach yourself that you are One with God. and realize that God cannot be attacked. Do not defend yourself, because defense means that you believe that you can be attacked. You are not asked to be

crucified, but to follow Jesus' example in situations that are much less trying, and to not use them to justify anger. There is no justification for anger, so do not teach yourself that there is. Remember, what you believe you will teach yourself, and if you believe with Jesus, you will teach yourself as Jesus taught Himself.

7. Your resurrection, or rebirth, is remembering that you are One with God. Jesus is a model for remembering that God is already in your mind, because Jesus believed it was true for Himself. You must believe it is true for you to teach it to yourself, and to extend it in your awareness. [The Apostles slept during the so-called 'agony in the garden', but Jesus was not angry with them, because He knew that He was not a personal self that could be abandoned.]

8. You are weakened as a teacher and as a student when you do not listen only to the Holy Spirit. But you cannot really betray yourself, because the Holy Spirit is within you, even if you deny It. [It is wise for you to follow Jesus as a model, because He will save you pain.]

9. Jesus chose to demonstrate that the worst form of attack, as the personal mind judges it, was nothing. In the personal mind's perception, Jesus was betrayed, abandoned, beaten, torn, and killed. This did not come from God, or affect God in any way. It happened because personal minds projected guilt and fear onto Jesus, even though He taught only healing.

10. You do not have to have Jesus' experiences to learn from them. The Holy Spirit is happy to use them to teach you to remember God. When you learn from them, you understand how your Christ Mind is the Way, the Truth, and the Life. By your hearing only the Holy Spirit, you never have to sacrifice. By listening to the Holy Spirit, you can learn from the experiences of others without having the experiences directly yourself. This is because your mind is One, and you can choose to perceive the Holy Spirit. By extending the Holy Spirit, you will learn to hear It in everything.

11. In your Christ Mind, you cannot be unfairly treated, because It is One. You do not have to be crucified to know that you have the Holy Spirit with you. To learn from Jesus, you must share Jesus' perception of His experiences. The world that you perceive is constantly engaged in validating the separation. Jesus' one lesson

was that any perception that makes the separation real cannot be justified. Jesus did this with an extreme experience, because it would be a good lesson for you, who will not experience anything so extreme, to not give into perceptions of attack. God does not want you to suffer.

12. Jesus' crucifixion is the symbol of projection, and His resurrection is the symbol of correction. Your mind, and all of its perceptions, must be corrected, so that you can know your Oneness with God again.

13. This is the message of the crucifixion:

Teach only Love, because that is What you are.

14. If you interpret Jesus' crucifixion in any other way, you are using it for attack rather than for Peace. The Apostles misunderstood it because of their own projections and, out of fear, they spoke of the 'wrath of God'. Their sense of guilt made them angry about Jesus' crucifixion.

15. This is an example of the upside-down thinking in the New Testament, even though its gospel is really only a message of God's Love. If the Apostles had not felt guilty in their own sense of separation from God, they would never have quoted Jesus as saying, 'I come not to bring peace but a sword.' This was the opposite of everything Jesus taught. They also misunderstood Jesus' reactions to Judas. Jesus did not believe in betrayal, and this is what His crucifixion taught. He did not call for Judas to be punished, because, as Christ, Jesus could only extend God's Love in His Own awareness. Jesus was teaching that guilt is not possible, so He would not have called for condemnation.

16. When you read what the Apostles wrote, remember that Jesus said that there was much that they would understand later. They were not wholly ready to accept Christ Consciousness for themselves yet. Do not allow any fear to enter as you are guided toward Christ, because you are not asked to be a martyr, but a teacher of Truth. You cannot sin, and you cannot be punished for sin. The concept of punishment involves the projection of blame, and reinforces the

idea that blame is justified. Your behavior teaches you the beliefs that motivate it. Jesus' crucifixion was the result of the conflict in the split mind between the personal and the Christ. This conflict seems just as real to you now, and the lesson of Jesus' crucifixion is valuable to you now.

17. You need to learn to value God, because you need to learn to value your Self. Fear makes it impossible for you to value God, because, when you are afraid of What you are, you reject It. You therefore continue to teach yourself that rejection is real.

18. Your Power as Part of God is always present. You must extend your awareness of God in your perception to replace the world of separation to learn that rejection is meaningless. The separation is the idea that you rejected your True Self, and if you teach yourself this, you will believe that it is true. God does not reject God, and you must think like God to be One with God in your awareness again.

19. Remember that the Holy Spirit is the Bridge in your mind between God, and your perception of separation from God. When you listen to the Holy Spirit, you will know that you can neither hurt, nor be hurt. When you recognize that your perception of a world of separation only needs God's Love, you will have learned of the Holy Spirit, and you will be eager to extend God's Love in your perception instead.

2. The Alternative to Projection

1. Your mind seems to be split as it rejects God within it, and this is your perception of separation from God. God is Whole, and you cannot be One with God unless your mind is also whole. This is your only way to Peace. Your belief that the separation is real leads to your belief that God is something separate from you. Once you believe in the separation, projection becomes your mind's main defense of it, and the means which keeps it going in your mind.

2. What you project you do not believe is part of you. You, and what you project, are therefore different in your mind. Since you have rejected it, you have judged against it, and you continue to attack it to keep it separate from you. You do this unconsciously, keeping

from your awareness the fact that you have attacked and split your mind, and you think that this makes you safe.

3.   But projection always hurts you, because it reinforces your belief in your split mind, and its only purpose is to keep the separation going in your mind. It is your split mind's means for making another 'reality' where there is a world in which you have a personal self among other separate, different selves. The personal mind with which you identify also uses projection to evaluate your personal self as 'better' than other selves, further obscuring for you that your evaluation of them is only a projection that comes from your mind. Projection always goes with attack, because projection is your means for blaming others for your discomfort, and thereby justifying your attack on them. You cannot be angry unless you are projecting the source of your anger onto something else. Projection destroys your perception of yourself, and of what your mind perceives. It begins by you denying that God is in your mind, and then leads to you making a whole world, which you also deny is in your mind.

4.   You have an alternative to projection: *extension*. Both of these abilities are in your mind. The personal mind projects, and the Holy Spirit extends. Their goals are opposed, and so are their results.

5.   The Holy Spirit begins by perceiving you as God's Love, and, knowing that This is the Truth of your Mind in God, It extends God's Love to be all that your mind perceives. You can have no anger in extension, because in it All is One. This is the correction of your perception of separation from God, which is your only need. Your extending God's Love is the only way for you to be happy in your perception of a world, because it is your awareness that you are not in a world.

6.   You can only find Joy in the joyless by realizing that you are not really there. You are One with God, and God did not make a world. This cannot change, and it is forever true. This is a Fact, not a belief. What is One with God is True, and you are True because you are One with God. If you deny this, you deny God, since you cannot accept God without yourself, and you cannot accept yourself without God.

7. The Oneness that the Holy Spirit perceives reflects the Oneness of God, but what the personal mind perceives has no reflection in God. The Holy Spirit is your Bridge between the personal mind and God, and It teaches you to remember God by teaching you to see the reflection of God's Oneness everywhere. The personal mind will tell you that it is impossible for you to remember God, but the Holy Spirit guides *you*, not the personal mind. Perception began with idea of separation from God, and perception will end with the idea of separation from God. Your entire mind will return to God, because your Whole Mind *is* God.

8. God extends God, and God's Extension does not leave God's Mind. God's Mind is One, and so is yours. The Holy Spirit enables you to see this Oneness *now*. You are One with God, but you cannot extend God until you know only God again.

9. Your thoughts always stay in your mind. This is as true for your Thoughts of God as for your thoughts of separation. In the personal mind, you *perceive* – interpret, evaluate, choose. But perception cannot escape the basic Law of Mind that your thoughts do not leave your mind, though you can deny them through projection. Though perception is not real, it is in your mind. and the Holy Spirit can use it. The Holy Spirit can turn your perception toward God. This seems like something that will be fulfilled far in the future, only because you do not want it now.

10. The Holy Spirit does not believe in time, but It uses time to correct your perception of separation from God. The Holy Spirit knows only God is Real, and you can learn to know only God is Real, too. The Holy Spirit can only speak for God, and It tells you to return your entire mind to God, because it has never left God. All that you need to do to return to God is to correct your perception of separation from God, and this is your recognition that *the separation never occurred*. The personal mind cannot make the separation real, because the personal mind is not real.

11. The personal mind accepts the idea that your return to God is necessary, because it can make this seem difficult for you. The Holy Spirit, however, knows that you have never really left God, and that there is nothing difficult in being What you are. You must

learn to perceive with the Holy Spirit, and to see your mind, and all that it perceives, as One with God. There is no conflict in the Holy Spirit's Perceptions, because They are fixed only on God. Only the Holy Spirit can resolve your sense of conflict, because It perceives only Truth, and It extends only Truth.

12. The personal mind projects to deceive you through denial. The Holy Spirit extends to perceive Oneness, and there is no conflict, because What the Holy Spirit perceives is All the Same. The Holy Spirit only knows the Holy Spirit, and only extends the Holy Spirit, and this is the Peace of God within you. The Peace of God is in your mind Forever, and It must extend everywhere, always, for you to be aware of It.

13. The Holy Spirit is your Whole Mind, and only by extending the Holy Spirit to be all that you perceive can you recognize It. The personal mind projects legions of diverse personal selves, and it teaches you that they are real. But the Holy Spirit is One, and It teaches you to extend only the Holy Spirit. Your part is to undo your belief in separation from God, and to align your mind with the Holy Spirit, Which can replace the world in your mind, and fill your entire mind with God's Oneness.

3. The Relinquishment of Attack

1. Every idea that you have begins in your mind and extends from there, and you know yourself by *what* you extend. The Holy Spirit holds God in your mind, and It perceives only what is in accord with God. It does not attack anything so that God can extend without limit. God is never threatened, and your Mind in God can never be harmed. The personal mind is not a part of your Mind in God, but you can teach yourself through the personal mind what is not true. You *have* taught yourself to believe that you are something other than God, and by continuing to teach this, you strengthen this belief in your mind. What you teach you learn.

2. So to be free of conflict, you must teach yourself by the Holy Spirit, and therefore learn only from the Holy Spirit. You are only Love, but in denial you make yourself Something that you have to learn to remember. 'Teach only Love because that is What you are' is the

message of Jesus' crucifixion, and the One Perfect Lesson that you must learn by teaching It to yourself. You will believe that you are what you project through the personal mind, or What you extend through the Holy Spirit.

3.   Your sense of safety lies in extending the Holy Spirit, because as you perceive the Holy Spirit's Gentleness, your mind learns that it is Gentle. When you extend only the Holy Spirit, you will have no more thought of safety, because you will be aware that you are One with God. In God, you can only bless, because you are Blessed. Your sense of safety will come from your giving up your identification with a personal self, which is an attack on the Truth in you. Teach yourself attack in any form, and you will learn that attack is real, and you will be afraid. But attack is a lesson that does not come from God, and so you can unlearn it by not teaching it to yourself.

4.   Your salvation comes from teaching yourself the exact opposite of everything that the personal mind teaches. You will learn the Truth by extending It to be all that you perceive. The only way to have Peace is to teach It, and by teaching It you will learn that you have It. This is the only way for you to remember God. Any idea that you extend you must already have in your mind, and it is strengthened in your mind through the conviction of your teaching. Teach only Love to learn that you have Love, and that you are Love.

4. The Only Answer

1.   The Holy Spirit is the Answer to your question, 'What am I?' The personal mind always speaks first, but it does not mean you well, because it knows that you can withdraw your support from it at any moment. If the personal mind meant you well, it would be glad that you don't need it, just as the Holy Spirit will be glad when you fully remember God, and no longer need the Holy Spirit's guidance. But the personal mind does not think it is part of you, its maker. This is its primary mistake, and the foundation of its whole thought system.

2.   You are One with God, and this is why attack is impossible in God.

God is Love, but you made the personal mind without Love. You believe that you are separate from and outside of God, and the personal mind speaks for this belief. It does not love you. The first question ever asked by your split mind, 'What am I?' can never be correctly answered by the personal mind. You live in doubt in your identification with a personal self, and though the personal mind raises many questions, it cannot truly answer any of them. The busy-ness of the personal mind obscures your primary question, because you have the Answer within you, and *the personal mind is afraid of you.*

3.   You will understand your conflict when you understand that the personal mind can never be sure of anything, because it isn't real. The Holy Spirit may not speak first, *but It always answers.* You have called on It at one time or another, in one way or another, and you have been answered. Since the Holy Spirit comes from the Truth in you, you have the Answer to your primary question within you *now.*

4.   The personal mind cannot hear the Holy Spirit, but it does believe that part of its maker is against it. So it feels justified in attacking you. It believes the best defense is attack, and it wants you to believe this, too. When you do so, you are identifying with it. You can identify with a personal self, but you cannot be one with it. Because it perceives something against it in you, the personal mind then turns to the body as its ally, because the body is not part of you. The personal self/body alliance is based on your perceived separation from God. When you identify with a personal self/body, you are afraid, because you are siding with separation.

5.   The personal self uses the body to attack your mind, because it realizes that you can end it and the body merely by recognizing that they are not real. It tries to persuade you that the body is more real than the mind, and that the mind serves the personal self. In your Christ Mind, you cannot believe this.

6.   This is the one answer of the Holy Spirit to every question that your split mind raises: Only God is Real, and you are One with God. You have chosen to deny this, and to perceive a world of pain instead. But this is not real, and God calls to you to remember your Oneness

with God. There will be nothing of a world left in your mind when you wholly remember God. The personal mind's ideas confuse you, because you do not realize that they are not real. When you remember God, only God will be Real to you, because only God is the Truth.

7. In God, What you are is Perfectly Certain. The question 'What am I?' does not exist, because it is Eternally answered. In God's Being is Everything. There are no questions in God, as there are in the world that you perceive. You have God's Certainty within you, but the part of your mind that you have given to separation now only has the *ability* for Certainty.

8. In your split mind, *abilities*, which are only potentials, replaced what *is*, and left you uncertain. In God, you don't need any abilities, because you are Perfect. Perfect abilities are meaningless, because their potential has been met. Impossibly, in your mind it now seems that the Perfect must be perfected. But your belief in the impossible makes it seem possible.

9. God did not make abilities, but the kindest solution for the abilities that you have made is for them to be developed in a way that can get you out of your perception of separation from God. The Holy Spirit will help you to develop your abilities this way, but you are in charge of whether or not you accept this guidance. You are always in charge of remembering God, with the Holy Spirit as your Guide, and with Jesus as your model. You therefore remain empowered, which demonstrates that you are not powerless.

10. You are only in an impossible situation because you believe that it is possible to be in an impossible situation. If God shows you your Perfection before you are willing to see It, God would be proving that you are wrong. This would teach you that you are not Perfect, but lacking, and unable to bring yourself to the awareness of your Perfection. This is how the personal mind thinks of you, but God knows you are already Perfect. It is impossible for God to insult you, because you are One with God. Because this is Unchangeable, the personal mind's belief that it has insulted God is also impossible.

11. The Holy Spirit will never command you, because the Holy Spirit knows it *is* you. The extension of Oneness is the Law of God's Mind, and the Holy Spirit is faithful to this Law. You can be faithful to other laws, not because they are true, but because you made them. God cannot lose Its Own Certainty of you, and God would gain nothing by proving to you that your thinking is a mistake. You learn what you teach, and if God teaches you that you have sinned, then God is teaching God that God has sinned. If God confronts you with the Truth while you still believe God is Something separate, how could you not be afraid that God will punish you? Forcing you to look at your mistake before you are willing to do so would reinforce the separation in your mind, rather than help you find God in your Mind.

12. God doesn't teach, because God does not perceive lack. God is Whole, and has nothing to learn. Teaching's goal is change, and God is Changeless. You did not lose your Perfection in the seeming separation, only your *awareness* of It. Instead, you became aware of the harsh voice of the personal mind. It can never shatter the Peace of God, but it did shatter your *awareness* of Peace. God does not attack the personal mind, but, being questioned, God gave an Answer. The Answer is your Teacher, the Holy Spirit.

5. The Lessons of the Holy Spirit

1. The Holy Spirit knows more than you know in your identification with a personal self, but It is teaching you to be One with It. In your identification with the personal mind you believe that you are not Perfect, and you teach yourself incorrectly. God only knows your Mind as Whole, and It cannot teach you that your mind is split. What God does know is that Its full extension is blocked. God is still Complete, but you do not know this, and God wants you to know it again.

2. The Holy Spirit is a Kind Voice that will not frighten you, but It will remind you that fear is not real, and that God is Real. The Holy Spirit will not show you that the world that you believe in is not real, but It will remind you that you are with God *now*. Then the Holy Spirit can train your mind to know the difference between

God and the world that you perceive, so that you can learn that the world is not real. Then, when you are frightened by your belief in a world, you will know to turn to God to undo your fear.

3. The Holy Spirit teaches through approach rather than through avoidance. It teaches you what you need to learn to have Joy, not what you need to learn to avoid pain. It is simpler to say, 'Do only that!' because it is clear, easy to understand, and easy to remember.

4. You believe that a world is reality, and this is frightening to you. The Holy Spirit will always answer you in a form that is meaningful to you where you believe that you are, so as to gain your trust. But the Holy Spirit does not judge your life in your perception that you are in a world, because It knows it is not real. Knowing this is how It undoes fear. The world is only in your mind, and it will not last, but the Holy Spirit, Which comes from God, speaks only for What lasts Forever.

a. *To Have, Give All to All*

1. When you have let go of the body, the personal self, and the world, you will know that you are Eternal. You may think that this is accomplished through death, but nothing is accomplished through death, because death is nothing. Life is of the Mind of God, and in the Mind of God. The body does not contain you who are Life, and it neither lives nor dies. Jesus overcame the idea of death through His recognition of the Christ Mind in Himself, and you can overcome death by recognizing the Christ Mind in you. Death is an attempt by your split mind to undo its conflict by *not* deciding to be Whole again, and *this will not work.*

2. God did not make the body, which is destructible, and therefore not Eternal. The body is a separation device, a symbol of the personal self, and therefore it does not exist. But the Holy Spirit always takes what you have made and uses it as a learning device. It reinterprets what the personal mind uses as proof of separation into a demonstration that separation is not real. Your mind can heal the body, but the body cannot heal your mind, so the body must exist as an idea in your mind. You can demonstrate this when

95

you extend God's Love.

3. The Holy Spirit motivates you to extend God's Love. It will always teach you that only your mind is Real, because only your mind can be everywhere. But the body is a separate, specific thing, so it cannot be part of you. It is meaningful to be One Mind, but there is no such thing as one body, so by the Law of Mind, the body is meaningless.

4. From the Holy Spirit's perspective, God's Love can be extended everywhere, always, but you may not believe this yet, so you cannot use it. This idea is important, because it is the foundation of the thought system that you need to teach yourself through the Holy Spirit. You cannot extend God's Love without believing this, because believing it is the belief in One Mind. Only Total Love can be offered to your Complete Mind. If you understand this, then limiting Love is meaningless to you.

5. The Holy Spirit leads you to God by translating your *perception* of Oneness in your experience of a world to *actual* Oneness with God. The personal mind uses the body for attack, for pleasure, and for pride, and this perception is fearful to you, because it makes the separation real to you. The Holy Spirit recognizes that you think that you are a body, so It uses it to teach you to extend God's Love in your awareness. Love can be extended, but fear cannot be extended. Your fear comes from and promotes attack, which leads to separation, not Oneness. The personal mind, which *is* fear, may sometimes join with other selves, but always for what each one can get *separately*, not for Oneness. The Holy Spirit extends only What can be extended everywhere, to keep It in your awareness. The Holy Spirit's teaching begins with:

Give what you want everywhere, to keep it in your awareness.

6. Turning in this direction is your very first step in correcting your perception of separation from God, and the only part that you need to do without the Holy Spirit. Making this choice is exercising your Free Will, and it demonstrates that you are in charge of your correction. You are still very identified with a personal self, or you

would not have had to make this choice. So the personal mind will be threatened, and this may lead to you experiencing increased feelings of conflict. You may remain at this stage of acute conflict for a long time. You may even try to accept the conflict rather than continue on to its resolution. But now that you have made this choice, the Holy Spirit has come to help you. In fact, you cannot go on without the Holy Spirit, because your choice was the choice *for* the Holy Spirit.

b. *To Have Peace, Teach Peace to Learn It*

1. When you believe in separation from God, you fear abandonment and retaliation, because you believe rejection and attack are real. You perceive rejection and attack around you, and you teach yourself to reject and to attack. These are the results of denial and projection. You teach yourself what you believe you are, and it is apparent that you can teach yourself wrongly. You may believe that your Christ Mind is attacking you, because when you do not share the personal mind's thought system, you weaken it, and it perceives this as attack. You will identify with the thought system that you accept, because it teaches you what you believe that you are. If the thought system comes from Truth, only Truth extends from It; if the thought system is a lie, only deception proceeds from it.

2. The Holy Spirit knows that the only real change is a change of mind, but that is not where the Holy Spirit begins with you. You must be motivated to change, and strengthening your desire to change is the Holy Spirit's only goal. When you are motivated to change, then your change is guaranteed. Your desire for change is the change of mind that brings about real change.

3. The first step in undoing your perception of separation from God is undoing your concept that you need to 'get' things from outside of you to be whole. Remember, God is One, extending Everywhere, Always, so *having* is the same as *being*. So the Holy Spirit's first lesson was, 'Give what you want everywhere, to keep it in your awareness.' But when the world that you perceive is very real to you, this increases your conflict, because *giving* is equated with

giving away, not with *keeping*. So the first lesson seems to be a contradiction in your conflicted mind. Because your mind is conflicted, its motivation is conflicted, so you cannot learn consistently yet. Your projection of this internal conflict leads to your perception of a world that you do not trust, and where you do not give for fear of loss. This is why the first step is the hardest for you. Still very identified with a personal self, and responding to the world that you perceive as though it is reality, you feel that you are being asked to deny reality.

4.   To the personal mind, the first step does not make any sense. It must see it this way, because the only other alternative is for you to see that *it* does not make sense. But it *is* the personal mind that does not make sense, and real change can only come to you when you change your mind. For a while, you will be in conflict as you accept both the lessons of the personal mind, and the lessons of the Holy Spirit, but as the Holy Spirit's Voice becomes clearer to you, you will feel compelled to listen.

5.   The way out of conflict for you when you have accepted two opposing thought systems is to choose one, and to let go of the other. You identify with the thought system that you choose, and if you identify with two thought systems which are diametrically opposed, you cannot be at Peace. You will teach and learn conflict as long as you believe that both the personal mind and the Holy Spirit are real. But you *do* want Peace, because you have called for It, and God's Voice has answered. What the Holy Spirit teaches makes sense; conflict does not make sense.

6.   There is really no conflict between the Holy Spirit and the personal mind, because only one is real. The personal mind will try to tell you that it is up to you to decide what is real, but the Holy Spirit will teach you that only God is Real. Reality is not your decision. As you listen to the Holy Spirit, and you experience Its quiet Power, you will realize that you have been trying to undo your own Reality. That is why you must remember to allow the Holy Spirit to decide for God for you.

7.   You are not asked to make senseless decisions, but you can think that this is what you are being asked to do. But you must recognize

it makes no sense for you to decide what Reality is. The Holy Spirit perceives your conflict, and Its second lesson is:

To have Peace, teach Peace to learn It.

8. This is still only an early step for you, because you still don't recognize that *having* and *being* are the same. But it is more advanced than the first step, which only began your change of mind, because it is an affirmation of your desire to get out of conflict. However, as long as you see Peace as only *more* desirable rather than as the *only* thing that you want, it means that you still value the separation. You are not ready to make the ultimate decision yet, but this step is essential for it. You have not accepted that only God is Real, and so your wanting only God still seems difficult for you. Yet you are One with God, and it is not difficult for you to want What you are.

9. This second step is a huge step for you toward the perception of Oneness that reflects God. As you go in this direction, you are going toward the center of your mind, where real change will occur. Your progress will be intermittent, but the second step is easier than the first, because it follows naturally from it. Your realization that you really want Peace is the growing awareness that the Holy Spirit teaches you.

c. *Be Vigilant for God and His Kingdom*

1. The Holy Spirit sorts out what is True from what is false in your split mind by teaching you to judge everything in it according to God. The Holy Spirit keeps what is in accord with God, corrects what is partly in accord with God, and lets go of what is totally out of accord with God. This is how the Holy Spirit teaches you to remember Oneness. Remember, though, that what the Holy Spirit rejects, the personal mind believes is real. The Holy Spirit and the personal mind are in fundamental disagreement about everything, because they are in fundamental disagreement about what you are. The personal mind's beliefs about you vary, and this is why it fosters different moods in you. But the Holy Spirit knows you with

Certainty, and only engenders Joy in you. It rejects what cannot foster Joy, so only the Holy Spirit can keep you wholly Joyous.

2.   The Holy Spirit does not teach you to judge others, because It does not want you to teach yourself that your projections of separation are real. The Holy Spirit would not be consistent if It taught you to strengthen what you must release. In your mind, however, the Holy Spirit *does* use judgment, but only to remind you of Oneness, Which you can then perceive without judgment. This allows you to teach yourself to *be* without judgment. This undoing is necessary so you will extend God's Love rather than project separation. The Holy Spirit's third lesson is:

Extend only God's Love in your awareness.

3.   This is a step toward real change. It still acknowledges separation, because it implies that you can be aware of something else. But it has advanced far from the first lesson, which simply taught you how to change your mind, and from the second, which helped you identify Peace as more desirable than conflict. This step emphasizes the difference between Peace and conflict so that your Ultimate Choice is inevitable.

4.   While the first step engenders conflict in you, and the second step also entails some conflict, this is the step in which you learn to consistently turn away from conflict. You can choose to let go of the personal mind as much as you can choose to listen to it. This lesson teaches you that you *must* choose to let go of the personal mind. It does not concern itself with the many forms that the personal mind's resistance may take; instead it shows you where you should put your efforts. This lesson does not deny that the personal mind may tempt you, but it does tell you what to do without exception. Your consistency is called on despite the chaos of the personal mind. Chaos and consistency cannot coexist, and as long as you must make an effort of awareness, you will still believe that you have two realities from which to choose. But by teaching you What to choose, the Holy Spirit's third lesson will ultimately teach you that there is no choice at all, because only God is Real. This will free

your mind to return to God.

5. Choosing through the Holy Spirit will lead you back to God. You are One with God, but you must learn to remember this. The third step inherently helps you to remember What you are, because it contains the other two steps, and goes beyond them to Oneness. If you have in your mind only What God put there, then you are acknowledging that you are One with God. You are accepting your mind as it is, and since it is Whole, you are teaching Peace, because you believe that It is Real. In this third step, the Holy Spirit prepares you to return to God's Being.

6. First, you learn that knowing you *have* rests on *giving*, not on *getting*. Then you learn that you want Peace, and that you must teach yourself Peace if you want to learn It. Peace is of God, and you must identify with Peace to remember God. You have believed that you are separate from God, and you have therefore excluded yourself from God. So you must teach yourself that you are One with God, and exclude from your mind your belief that you are something else.

7. The third step protects your awareness of God from your illusion of separation, so that you will identify with God again. God's Love is an Experience, not a belief. The Holy Spirit speaks for This Experience, Which ultimately leads you to God's Being. As long as God is only a belief for you, you will have questions and doubts fostered by the personal mind. So you must go beyond belief to experiencing God's Love by extending only God's Love in your awareness. You cannot experience God until you give your entire mind to God.

8. For you to extend God's Love without exception, you must perceive your mind's Wholeness, or Oneness. You must keep this Oneness in your awareness, and not let any belief in separation teach you that your mind is not Whole. God's Wholeness does not depend on your perception, but your *awareness* of your Wholeness does. God cannot be changed, and only your awareness needs to be corrected. You cannot remember God while you are confused about what you are. This is why you must make an effort to be aware of only God. It is within you to know only God as God

Knows only you.

9.   God is Truth; everything else is illusion. When you reject God, it is as though you are without God, and when you make another reality to replace God, your mind is no longer One. Your mind contains a perception of a world in which you seem to exist in separation from God, and from everything in the world that you perceive. This world that you have made seems to imprison your will, and your belief in its reality means that your mind needs to be healed. The way to heal your mind is to extend God's Love to replace the world of separation in your mind. When your mind is healed, you will teach yourself only Wholeness. This makes you a teacher as Jesus was a teacher. Jesus had to make an effort to be aware of only God's Love, just as you do.

10.   The third step is a statement of what you want, and it demonstrates your willingness to let go of everything else. If you follow the Holy Spirit, you will take this step. Your effort to be aware of only God is the signal that you *want* to follow the Holy Spirit. Your effort is required only until you realize that being aware of God is natural to you, and does not require effort. You have put a lot of effort into maintaining a personal self and the world, because they are not true. Now you need to turn your effort against them. Only this effort will end all effort for you as you return to God's Being, Which is both what you *are*, and what you *have*. There is no effort for you to make in God, because, in God, you don't have to make God Truth, and you don't have to protect God. In God, All is One and Limitless.

Chapter 7

The Gifts of the Kingdom

1. The Last Step

1. In your split mind, part of your mind *seems* to be separate from God, but your mind is always really One with God. As an Extension of God you are as Limitless as God, but you extend God, God does not extend you. This is the only difference between your mind and God's Mind.

2. God is your Source and you extend God, but you cannot be God's source. God is not limited to your God-like Mind, but for God to extend everywhere, God must extend *through* your God-like Mind. This is your Oneness with God. When you extend only God's Love in your awareness, you will remember that you are One with God.

3. The Love that you extend is Part of you, as you are Part of God. Love cannot be contained, and It must extend Everywhere to be What It is. Love is Limitless, and It extends Forever in Eternity with God, Where It has always been, as God has always been. The Love that you extend is God's Love, and It is Eternal because you are.

4. The personal self is competitive and demanding, not Loving. It does not understand Oneness, but it bargains with others to be sure that what it gets is equal to or greater than what it gives. But to really gain, you must give what you want to keep it in your awareness. When you bargain with others, you imply that you must get something outside of you to be whole, and this is not of God. To be Whole like God is to extend God as God does. God does not limit What God gives, because God is not limited.

5. Jesus gave only God's Love, because That was What He believed He was. What you believe you are determines what you give, and if you believe that you are One with God, then you must extend God as God extends God. Joy and Eternity are the same. God

extends without limits and beyond time, and as you are One with God, you extend God's Love without limits and Eternally. You are Eternal; in Peace and Joy Forever.

6.   For you to think like God is for you to be certain of What you are, and for you to extend like God is for you to extend God's Love as God extends Love to you. This is where the Holy Spirit leads you, so that your Joy will be complete as you recognize that you are Whole. The last step in your remembering God is your knowing *only* God again. This is hard to explain, because Truth is beyond explanation. But the Holy Spirit can transform the ideas that you have made into something useful, and can clarify the idea of the 'last step':

7.   God does not take steps, because God is already Whole. God does not teach, because God does not change. God does nothing *last*, because God is the Beginning in that God is the Source of All, and because God does not live in time, but in Eternity. The 'last step' that God takes, then, is not a step. When you let go of what has never been, What has Forever been is not changed, but continues as It always has. God does not hide This from you, because it is God's Will to share It with you. It has never been withheld from you.

2. The Law of the Kingdom

1.   Your healing is the only kind of thinking in your perception that you are in a world that resembles God's Thoughts, and that can easily transfer to God. When you perceive sickness as real, in you or in another, you believe it is possible to be in need. Separation then becomes real to you. God does not make sickness or separation, and you cannot know that you are One with God when what is not of God is real to you.

2.   To heal, you correct your perception by choosing to see the Holy Spirit as Real, instead of separate selves as real. This restores God in your perception, so that you know that you are Whole again. Your extension of Oneness reflects the Oneness of God. It is the unchanging Law of Mind, in your perception of a world and in God, that what you project or extend is real to you. But the thoughts of the personal mind, which govern your perception of a

world for you, are different from God's Thoughts. So in your perception of a world where you have the choice to listen to either the personal mind or the Holy Spirit, your thoughts can result in diametrically opposed experiences for you.

3. In God, the Law of Mind extends God because God is Reality. In your perception of a world, the Law is adapted to 'You project what you believe is true.' This is the teaching form of the Law, because outside of God you lack, and so you have to learn. You therefore teach yourself what you are, and you learn what you are, from what you project onto your perceptions of others and the world. There is no teaching and learning in God, because God is Whole and Certain. God extending God is the Law of Creation by which you were created, and by which you create in your Oneness with God.

4. In a form that you can understand in your perception of a world, the Holy Spirit teaches you that the Law of Mind and Creation is Oneness. The form does not alter the meaning of Oneness, but makes It understandable to you. The personal mind cannot teach this to you, because Oneness is not meaningful to you in your perception of separation as reality. The personal mind would have to change the meaning of Oneness to hold onto a form of separation.

5. To the Holy Spirit, the *form* that the lesson of Oneness takes never matters, but its *meaning* always matters. The meaning of every lesson is always the same for the Holy Spirit. [God does not extend God to convince you of your Oneness with God, but God extending God is What God *is*. You are One with God, and you only have to *learn* this because you perceive yourself as separate from God.]

6. The Holy Spirit teaches you to remember God, and to forget the personal mind. You will not understand the Holy Spirit's lessons in Oneness while you still listen to two teachers in your mind. You will only learn to be consistent by learning of one Teacher, and forgetting the other.

7. The Perfect Consistency of God's Oneness cannot mean anything to you while you are confused about what is real. Your confusion

interferes with the Meaning of God's Oneness. There is only One Meaning in God, and the Meaning of God *is* God. It is also you, who are One with God, and who extend God as God extends God. God doesn't need to be explained, but extended. In God, All is One; only God exists in God. This is Reality, and nothing can change It.

3. The Reality of the Kingdom

1.   The Holy Spirit teaches only God's Oneness, and It applies It everywhere, always. Because there is no conflict in the Holy Spirit, Its every effort and every result is maximal. By teaching you the Power of God's Oneness *through* you, the Holy Spirit teaches you that God's Power is yours. The situation it is applied to does not matter. Your awareness of God's Power does not establish It as yours, because you are already One with God, but your awareness of It does enable you to use It. Your Christ Mind is with you always, so *you* are the Way, the Truth, and the Life. You do not make God's Power anymore than Jesus did. It is Everywhere, Always, and you cannot understand It as belonging only to some of what you perceive. This perception of God's Power makes It meaningless to you by limiting the Unlimited.

2.   God's Meaning is in God's Oneness. Time does not touch It, but you belong with It. You are God's Meaning, though you think that you are separate from It. Seeing yourself as separate from your Meaning, you experience yourself as something unreal. The personal mind teaches you that you are *not* What you *are*. This is really impossible, so you cannot really teach it and learn it. And since your Christ Mind is always teaching Itself What It is, What It is teaching is unknown to the personal mind. So the personal mind is suspicious of *you*, because you cannot be fully committed to *it*. Your Christ Mind is committed to Peace, and this threatens the personal mind, so the personal mind's 'enemy' is therefore *your* Ally.

3.   The personal mind is not part of you, because it perceives itself at war. It looks outward to others for allies. But the personal mind's allies are *your* enemies, because the personal mind only sees its own projections. *You* are not at war, and you must look only on the Holy

Spirit to be at Peace. When you look only on the Holy Spirit you have no conflict, but when you look on the personal mind's projections of others, conflict enters your mind. You must put consistent effort into looking only on the Holy Spirit, or you will believe that conflict is true. Conflict is impossible, and your believing in it is the same as your perceiving yourself as something unreal.

4.   For you to be One with God is for you to be aware of *only* God. As long as you believe that you can be aware of what is not real, you are choosing conflict. But is it a choice? It seems to be, but seeming and Reality are not the same. In your Oneness with God, there is no *seeming*. Reality is yours because you *are* Reality. Learning this is how *having* and *being* come together in your mind. The Holy Spirit is the only Reality in your mind, and Its Thoughts are clear, because They reflect God. The Holy Spirit sees only the Holy Spirit, because It can only see Itself.

5.   God is in your Mind, because God is What your Mind *is*. This is beyond doubt, and when you question it, the Holy Spirit answers by showing you that to question Reality is to question meaninglessly. The Holy Spirit's only Purpose is to undo your questions and lead you to Certainty. When you are Certain, you are perfectly calm because you have no doubt, and you extend your Serenity because It is What you are.

4. Healing as the Recognition of Truth

1.   You *can* remember Truth again, and this is your only need. God Knows you because you are One with God, and the Holy Spirit inspires your awareness of Oneness. Both this Knowledge and the Holy Spirit come from God, but the healing of your mind does not come directly from God. God knows that you are Whole, as God is Whole. Healing your mind is simply the *result* of you allowing this awareness into a state of mind where you do not know that you are One with God. God is unaware of your belief in separation, so separation does not exist, but your belief in it makes you unaware of God.

2.   The Holy Spirit teaches *through* you so that you learn that It is *in* you. This process leads you to the knowledge that you are One

with God. You can extend God's Love everywhere without exception, because your mind is One with God. This is God's Law, and the Holy Spirit reminds you of It. Your mind is healed by your remembering God's Law of Oneness, and by your forgetting the personal mind's law of separation. When used by the Holy Spirit, forgetting becomes a means for you to remember better, rather than to deny Truth.

3. The personal mind does not teach you that you are everywhere, because that would defeat the purpose of separation. So in your identification with a personal mind you do not really *learn*, because all that can really be taught is the Law of Mind that the mind can only see itself. But the Holy Spirit teaches you to use what the personal mind makes to teach yourself the opposite of separation. It does not matter what kind of learning, or learning ability, is used. All that you need to do is make an effort to learn from the Holy Spirit, and the Holy Spirit's One Goal will unify your efforts and abilities. To contribute to One Result, the Holy Spirit emphasizes what is the same in your efforts and abilities, rather than what is different.

4. Give all of your abilities over to the Holy Spirit to use for healing your mind, because the Holy Spirit knows your mind is Whole. You heal your mind by remembering your Wholeness, which means remembering God. You have forgotten God, but the Holy Spirit uses your means of forgetting as a means of remembering.

5. The personal mind's use of your efforts and abilities is also unified in its goal of separation, and this is why it can never be reconciled with the Holy Spirit's Goal of Oneness. The personal mind seeks to divide and separate your mind, and the Holy Spirit seeks to unify and heal your mind. As you teach healing, you are healed, because your mind is One. Through healing you undo your belief in the differences projected by the personal mind, and you extend your awareness of Oneness instead. Even in a state where your mind is out of accord with God, this Perception is in accord with God's Law. The strength of this corrected perception is so great that it brings your mind into alignment with God's Mind by serving the Holy Spirit, Which your mind can perceive everywhere.

6. You are delusional if you think that you can oppose God's Will. The personal mind thinks it can, and it offers you its 'will' as a gift. *You do not want it.* It is not a gift; it is nothing at all. What you *have* and *are* is God's Gift to you, and by forgetting It, you forget yourself. Healing your mind, then, is the way for you to approach God by extending God's Love everywhere in accordance with God's Law of Oneness. If you do not extend God's Love everywhere, the Law of Oneness will be meaningless to you. But all meaning is contained by This Law, and in This Law.

7. Seek only God, because God is the Truth. There is nothing else. God is All Being, and your Being is God's Being. When you heal your mind, you let go of your sense of vulnerability, which is caused by your identification with a personal self. You perceive your mind's Oneness instead of perceiving the personal mind, in yourself, or in others. This strengthens the Holy Spirit in your awareness, because it denies fear. Your choice of Oneness is the only invitation that God's Love needs, and It comes to your entire mind, because Love is What your Whole Mind *is*. You will forget what you are *not* by becoming aware of What you *are*, and this is how you will fully remember What you are.

5. Healing and the Changelessness of Mind

1. The body is only a framework for you to develop abilities. What those abilities are used for is your decision. It is obvious what the personal mind's decision has led to, but the Holy Spirit's use of the body only for healing your mind does need to be clarified. When you attempt to heal the world that you perceive without accepting healing for your mind, you do not understand what you are called to do.

2. Only minds can join, and the part of your mind that seems split off must join with your God-like Mind to heal your entire mind. Since the personal mind cannot undo your desire to be One again, it teaches you that the body is real, and that it can join with other bodies to be whole, so that it does not need your mind. It gives to the body your mind's ability to think independently of God. But your behavior does not teach or learn since you can behave in ways

that conflict with your beliefs. Believing that the body has the attributes of your mind weakens you as a teacher/learner, because you always teach yourself what you do believe. If you teach yourself that both sickness (body) and healing (mind) are real, you are teaching yourself inconsistently, and you will hardly learn what you teach yourself inconsistently.

3. You must teach healing to learn healing. The Holy Spirit heals your mind by joining with the part of it that you have projected onto a world, by extending God's Love there instead. The Holy Spirit does not confuse your mind with a body. Your mind cannot hurt, but a body in the service of the personal mind can hurt other bodies. You will only believe that you have been hurt by others, or that you have hurt others, if you confuse yourself with a body. Your recognition that you are mind and not a body can be used for either true healing, or for magical thinking. Magical thinking always involves your belief that the world is real, and it indicates that you fear the true healing that will return your mind to the Oneness of God. This is why it does not work.

4. True healing strengthens your awareness of your Oneness with God; magical thinking weakens this awareness in you. True healing comes from your recognition that the Oneness of your mind is everywhere; magical thinking is a way of seeing your mind as a healer with special gifts that can be offered to those who do not have this gift. As a magical healer, you might think that this gift comes from God, but if you think that God's Gifts are for you alone, then you limit your awareness of God to a personal self, and you do not know that God is Everywhere.

5. Healing that is of the Holy Spirit always works, so unless you teach yourself healing through the Holy Spirit, your results will vary. Real healing is always consistent and whole, because it is conflict-free. When you make exceptions to healing, you teach yourself that conflict is real. God does not make exceptions. What is of God is Everywhere, Always. Only your fear of Oneness makes the idea of exceptions meaningful to you, and it makes you afraid of the exceptions that you make, because you think that they keep you from Oneness. A 'fearful healer' is a contradiction that only a conflicted

mind can perceive as meaningful.

6.   Fear will not make you happy; healing your mind always will. Fear always makes exceptions; healing your mind never does. Fear causes you to perceive separation from God, because it comes from denying part of yourself; your healing causes you Peace, because it comes from your awareness of Oneness. Your healing is predictable, and you can depend on it, because it comes from God, and only God is Real. Your healing is inspired by the Holy Spirit, and it is in accord with God's Law of Oneness. God is Consistent, and you can only understand healing consistently, because to be consistent is to be One. Your Whole Meaning comes from God, and you cannot be out of accord with God,,because God cannot be out of accord with God. You cannot separate yourself from God, because God's Being is your Being.

7.   As an unhealed healer, you may try to heal others to receive their gratitude, instead of extending God's Love to be aware of God's Love within you. You will then receive so little, because you will have limited your awareness to a personal self. This is a lesson in sickness, not in healing. But the True Lesson is constantly available to you, and It is so powerful that you can recognize your Oneness with God in one instant, and change your entire perception in the next instant. When you change your mind, you are using the only power that you have for change. This does not contradict the Changelessness of God's Mind. You think that you have changed God's Mind as long as you try to learn through the personal mind. This puts you in a seemingly contradictory position: You must learn to change your mind *about* your mind. Only by learning to do this can you learn that your mind *is* Changeless.

8.   When you heal, the Changelessness of Mind is exactly what you are learning. You perceive the Holy Spirit's Reality, instead of the varied and changing world of bodies and personal selves. Only the Holy Spirit never changes Its Mind. But when you perceive sickness as real, you think that you can change God's Mind, and then you don't know What you are. When you see only the Changeless, you are not changing anything, because It is Real. By changing your mind about the world's reality, you undo the

changes that your split mind thinks it has made.

9. You hear two voices, so you perceive in two ways. The personal mind shows you images and idols to worship out of fear, but that you can never love or understand or appreciate, because they are not part of you. The Holy Spirit shows you only the Truth, Which you love and understand and appreciate, because you are One with It. You are One with God in Love, Understanding, and Appreciation. The personal mind cannot understand this, because it does not understand, love, or appreciate what it makes. The personal mind joins with others to take something away from them, believing that whenever it deprives another of something it has increased itself. But God increases by extending God, as you increase God by extending God. The Glory and Joy of God are yours to give. Do you want to?

10. You cannot forget God, because the Christ Mind is within you, and It is One with God. For you to forget Christ is for you to forget your True Self, so it is for you to forget God. Your belief in a world is your forgetting of God. This is why you must remember your Christ Mind, Which is One with God. By remembering your Christ Mind as you extend It to replace the world of separation that you perceive, you change your mind about yourself. Your Mind is powerful enough to let go of its perception of a world, and to become aware of only God again. Jesus shares the Christ Mind, not His body, in communion with you, because the body is an illusion. Perceive only your Christ Mind in everything, everywhere; encompassing all things. You are blessed when you perceive only This, because only This is True.

11. Learn of the Truth in you through Christ in your Mind. As you extend Christ to replace the world of separation in your mind, you will heal your mind. Be grateful to the world that you perceive for this opportunity, because as you extend Christ, Christ will return to your full awareness, which is your gift to God. God will accept this gift, and give it back to you in Oneness. Your true communion with the Holy Spirit is extending God everywhere, always. You can love and appreciate and understand God only as One. This is the Law of Creation, and It governs all Real Thoughts.

6. From Vigilance to Peace

1. Although you can love your mind only as One, you can perceive it as fragmented. However, you cannot see something in part of it that you do not believe is all of it. This is why you must give up your perception of separation entirely, or you have not given it up at all. Your total perception will be affected by your thoughts, whether they are projections of fear from the personal mind, or extensions of God's Love from the Holy Spirit. Your thoughts make reality for you, and you will not know God is Reality if you project fear, but you will know God is Reality when you extend God's Love.

2. When you accept that separation from God is real, you cannot love, because your belief in separation is your belief that Love has been destroyed. This is your misunderstanding of What Love is, so you do not perceive yourself as Loving. God's Love is God's Being, and yours. When you are unaware of this, you believe that you are something unreal, and this is confusing to you. Your thinking is powerful enough to do this, but it is also powerful enough to accept correction of this, because its Power is of God. You have the power to direct your thinking as you choose, and if you do not think that you do, you are denying your power, and believing that you are powerless.

3. The ingenuity that the personal mind employs to preserve itself derives from the very Power of your Mind Which the personal mind denies. Its denial is an attack on the Power that is preserving it, and this results in extreme anxiety for you, who identify with it. So the personal mind denies what it is doing, which is logical for its survival, but insane for you. The personal mind relies on the one Power that negates its existence *for* its existence. Afraid of its Source's Power, the personal mind must depreciate this Power, but if its Source is powerless, its own existence is threatened. This is intolerable for the personal mind, so it projects nonexistence onto your Being in God instead. This is meant to guarantee that it will continue, because you will identify with *it* in the absence of your Real Identity.

4. The personal mind does not believe in wholeness, because it was

made from fragmentation, and it is faithful to it. Mind always reproduces as it was produced, and the personal mind reproduces fear because it was produced out of fear. This is its allegiance, and because you are God's Love, Which *is* Wholeness, the personal mind is vicious to *you*. God's Love is your Power, and the personal mind must deny It, because It gives you everything that you need. When you know you have Everything you will not want the personal mind. The personal mind's own maker, then, does not want it. You will reject it as soon as you remember God. And when you recognize the Holy Spirit anywhere, you do remember God.

5.   The personal mind opposes all Love, all recognition of the Holy Spirit, all corrected perception, and God. It perceives Their threat, because it senses that the commitments that your mind makes are total. Forced to detach from you, the personal mind will attach to anything else. But since there is nothing else, it makes up illusions to believe in.

6.   The Holy Spirit does not perceive illusions, so It does not attack them. Illusions do not exist for the Holy Spirit, and It resolves the conflict in you that is engendered by your belief in illusions by teaching you to perceive conflict as meaningless because only God is Real. The Holy Spirit does not want you to understand conflict, because the meaningless cannot be understood. You can understand God only because only God is Real.

7.   If you keep in mind What the Holy Spirit offers to you, you will make an effort to remember only God . You may find this hard to believe, because you believe in something other than God. Belief does not require effort unless it is conflicted. Effort has no place in Peace, and it is only necessary for you when you have beliefs that are not true. The Holy Spirit only inspires your effort to believe in What is True, because you have believed in what is not true. What you believe in is true for you. When you do not believe that God is the Only Reality, you seem to have thoughts that contradict, and therefore attack, God.

8.   The personal mind believes that it can attack God, and it tries to persuade you that you have done this. Since the mind cannot attack, the personal mind logically proceeds to the belief that you

are a body. Because it does not see you, its maker, as you really are in God, the personal mind can see itself any way it wants to. Aware that it is weak, it wants your allegiance, but not as you really are in God. It wants to engage you only in its own delusional thought system, because otherwise your God-like Mind will undo it. It wants no part of God, since only God is Real, and it does not really exist. Your commitment to either God or the personal mind must be total, or your mind will be split between them. Since they cannot coexist in Peace, if you want Peace, you must give up conflict by giving up the personal mind entirely, and for all time. This requires your effort to be aware of only God for as long as you still believe that the personal mind is also real. While you believe that two contradictory thoughts systems are both true, you will need to make an effort to be aware of only Truth.

9. Your mind seems to be divided between the personal mind and the Holy Spirit, so it is not totally committed to either. Your Identity in God is beyond question, except by you when you are identifying with a personal self. What you are is not established by what you perceive, or touched by it at all. Your identity confusion is not a problem of fact, but of understanding, because you think that what you are is up to you to decide. This is what the personal mind believes totally, and it is fully committed to it, but this is not true. The personal mind is totally committed to untruth, because its perceptions totally contradict the Holy Spirit's Perceptions, and God's Reality.

10. Only the Holy Spirit can perceive your Meaning, because your Meaning is the Knowledge of God. Any belief that you accept apart from This will obscure the Holy Spirit in you, and will therefore obscure God to you. Unless you perceive yourself Truly, you cannot know God, because you are One with God. Your Oneness with God is your Wholeness, your Sanity, and your Limitless Power. This Power is God's Gift to you, because This is What you are. If you separate your mind from the only Power that there is, you will perceive yourself as weak.

11. Perceiving yourself without God's Power, and therefore as weak, you attack. But the attack is blind, because there is nothing to

attack. So you project illusory images onto an illusory world, perceive them as unworthy, and attack them because they are unworthy. This is all that the personal mind's world is: nothing. It has no meaning; it does not exist. If you try to understand it, it will be real to you. Making the meaningless meaningful is an insane effort.

12. The idea of separation from God has entered your mind because you have judged that God is not wholly desirable. You want something else, so you have made something else, but it will attack your Real Mind, and divide your efforts. You can extend only Peace, but you cannot extend Peace with a conflicted mind. You must put your efforts only into being aware of God, because extending God is your Joy. If you do not extend God, you are not thinking with God, or like God.

13. The Holy Spirit gently reminds you that you are sad and depressed because you are not fulfilling your Function as Part of God, and you are therefore depriving yourself of Joy. This is your choice, not God's. If it was possible for you to make a will separate from God's, then what is meaningless would be real. But God cannot be changed, and conflict is not really possible. This is what the Holy Spirit teaches consistently. Your Will is One with God's Will, and anything that opposes This is meaningless. Being Perfect, your Whole Mind can only extend God's Joy in Oneness with God.

7. The Totality of the Kingdom

1. Whenever you fail to extend God's Love, you will feel deprived, because denial is as total as Love. It is as impossible for you to deny part of your mind, as it is for you to love it partially. Total commitment means you are committed all the time. Your mind is powerful, and when you use it to deny Reality, Reality is gone for you. Deny any part of Reality, and you will lose your awareness of all of It. But denial is a defense, and you can use it *for* Reality as well as against It. Use denial against Reality, and it is an attack on your mind, but give it to the Holy Spirit, and denial can be used to undo the personal mind's illusions so that you can recognize Reality. For you to recognize Part of Reality is for you to appreciate All of It,

because It is One. Your Real Mind is too powerful to be excluded. and you will never be able to completely exclude your True Self from your thoughts.

2. Whenever you look on the insanity of the world that you perceive, whether on individuals or collectively, you are given an opportunity to be blessed. You can only receive blessing by extending blessing. This is the Law of God's Mind, and It has no exceptions. You will feel that you lack Love when you refuse to extend Love, not because you are really without It, but because by denying It you are not aware that you have It. Your response in every situation is determined by what you think that you are, and what you want *is* what you think that you are. What you want to be, then, determines every response you make.

3. You have God's Blessing Eternally, but you do need *your* blessing to know that you have God's Blessing. The personal mind's concept of you is that you are deprived, unloving, and vulnerable. You cannot love this self, but you can let it go. You are not a personal self. When you believe that the personal selves that your mind perceives in a world are reality, you believe that you, too, are a personal self. All of your illusions are made together, and dispelled together. Do not teach yourself what you do not want to be. What you perceive is the mirror in which you see yourself: either a personal self, or One with God. Perception will last until all that you perceive is that you are One with God. You made perception, and it will last as long as you want it.

4. Illusions will last for you as long as you value them. Your values shift, but they are powerful, because they are judgments of your mind. The way to dispel your illusions is to recognize that they do not have value for you, and so to put them out of your mind. While they are in your mind, you give life to them, but there is really nothing there to receive your gift.

5. The Gift of Life is yours to give, because God gives Life to you. You are not aware that you have It because you do not extend It. You cannot really make nothing 'live'. You both *are* and *have* Life, but in your illusions, you are not extending Life, and you have forgotten your Being. All of your confusion comes from your not extending

Life, because extending Life is God's Will. You cannot do anything Real apart from God, and what you do apart from God is not real. To remember yourself, give God as God gives God. Honor yourself by extending only God's Love.

6.   Honor and appreciation are due only to the Extension of God's Oneness, Which God Honors and Appreciates. You cannot be apart from God's Extension, because in your Oneness with God, *you* are God's Extension. Rest in God's Love, and keep Peace in your awareness by extending God's Love. But extend God's Love to be all that your mind perceives, or you will not know that you both *have* and *are* God's Peace. You will not know that you are Perfect until you honor everything your mind perceives.

7.   The Part of your mind that is Part of God is the only Teacher worthy to teach the part of your mind that thinks it is separate from God. The Holy Spirit is with you everywhere, and It teaches you the same lesson everywhere. It teaches you the Inestimable Worth of your Mind, with the Infinite Patience born of the Infinite Love of God. Your every perception of separation is an attack you make on yourself, and it is a call for the Holy Spirit's Patience, Which translates the attack into a blessing. You attack others, or you perceive an attack on yourself from others, when you feel deprived, and do not know that you are blessed. Give a blessing from the Abundance of God's Love within you in place of attack to teach yourself that you are blessed. Do not join with an illusion of lack, or you will perceive yourself as lacking.

8.   You will not attack others when you perceive them as attacking you, unless you think that they were depriving you of the experience of Wholeness that you can only have in God. But you cannot lose Wholeness unless you do not value It and you do not want It. Your rejection of Wholeness makes you feel deprived, and you project this rejection onto others, blaming them for your sense of deprivation. Ultimately, you are afraid of others because you believe that they are attacking you to take from you the Wholeness that you can only experience in God. Your own rejection of God is the basis for all of your projections onto others from the personal mind.

9. In your identification with a personal self you cannot trust, because you believe that you are alone. You do not take responsibility for making yourself alone, and you have no allegiance to God, Which will undo the personal mind. Believing that you have separated from God, you project the cause of separation onto others, and teach yourself that they are out to take God from you. Though nothing can cause you to be separate from God, whenever you attack another, your underlying belief is that they can. Through projection you see in others what you wish for. If you want to be separate from God, you will believe that others are making you separate from God.

10. You *are* the Will of God, so do not accept anything else as your will, or you deny What you are. When you deny What you are, you will attack others, because you will believe that you have been attacked. But see God's Love within you, and you will see It everywhere, because It *is* everywhere. Perceive God's Love in place of separate personal selves, and you will know that your mind is One with God. You are incomplete without God, as God is incomplete without you. Your understanding this is the Peace of God. Your only way out of the personal mind's thinking is to accept your Oneness with God, just as the only way into the personal mind's thinking is to believe that you are separate from God. You will have Total Understanding when you understand God's Totality.

11. You will have correctly evaluated the personal mind's thought system when you perceive it as wholly insane, wholly delusional, and wholly undesirable. This correction allows you to perceive your Oneness with God as wholly Real, wholly Perfect, and wholly Desirable. When you only want to be One with God, God will be All that you have, All that you give, and All that you are. What you give to the personal self is a sacrifice, but What you give to God are Gifts to yourself. God treasures what you give to yourself, because giving to yourself is giving to God. All Power and Glory are yours, because you are One with God.

8. The Unbelievable Belief

1. You cannot experience anger without projecting it, and you cannot

119

experience Love without extending It. This statement reflects how the Law of Mind always works. The Law of Extension of Oneness, by Which God created you, and by Which you create, is how God keeps God in God's Mind. For the personal mind, this Law is the Means by Which you project away from yourself what you do not want to keep. For the Holy Spirit, this Law is the Means by Which you give what you value to keep it in your awareness. For the Holy Spirit, It is the Law of Extension; for the personal mind, It is the Law of deprivation. How you apply the Law determines whether It produces Abundance or scarcity in your awareness. This choice is up to you, but it is not up to you whether or not you use this Law. Your mind must project or extend, because this is Life.

2. To undo the association of projection and anger, you must fully understand how the personal mind uses projection. The personal mind always seeks to preserve your perception of separation from God, although it devises ingenious ways to reduce the conflict this causes in your mind so that the conflict does not become so intolerable that you give it up. It tries to persuade you that *it* can get rid of the conflict so you don't try to free yourself of it by undoing your perception of separation. Warping the Law of Mind to defeat the Mind's Real Purpose of Oneness, the personal mind projects the source of your separation from God onto others in the world that you perceive to persuade you that the conflict is not in you.

3. There are two major errors in this attempt. First, projection is a distorted form of extension, and only a unified thought can be extended. Conflicting thoughts are not unified, but opposed. You cannot teach yourself that both God and not-God are real. And since your thoughts do not leave your mind, it does not make sense for you to think that you can keep one of these ideas and project the other idea away. Second, giving an idea away is the way that you *keep* it in your awareness. It is a total distortion of extension for you to believe that you can exclude from your mind the cause of your separation from God by seeing it outside of you. This means that you must work hard to keep out of your awareness the thoughts that are the source of what you project. You know on some level that the thoughts that you project are still buried in your mind, and

that they may creep back up to your awareness. Since the thoughts that you project never really leave your mind, then, you must keep your mind occupied so that you do not recognize them.

4. You cannot project illusions without believing that you are an illusion yourself. There is no way to escape this Law of Mind, because Mind cannot be fragmented. Mind cannot be attacked and broken into pieces. But the personal mind believes that It can, so it uses projection to make it seem as though this has really happened. The personal mind does not understand that your Mind is One, so it does not understand What you really are. But the personal mind's existence is dependent on you, because it is made by your belief. The personal mind is your error in identification, and it does not have a consistent model, so it does not develop consistently. It is the result of your misapplication of the Law of God by your distorted mind misusing its power.

5. *Do not be afraid of the personal mind.* It depends on your mind, you made it by believing in it, and you can undo it by withdrawing your belief in it. If you project responsibility for your belief onto others, you will maintain it. But when you accept sole responsibility for the personal mind, you will lay aside all anger and attack, because they come from your projecting responsibility for your separation from God onto others. Once you accept responsibility for your separation from God, give it over to the Holy Spirit to undo it completely so that all of its effects will vanish from your mind.

6. The Holy Spirit will teach you to perceive Truth, Which is beyond belief. You can forget the personal self at any time, because it is unbelievable. The more that you learn about it, the more that you will realize that you cannot believe in it. It is apparent that what you perceive with the unbelievable is meaningless, but you may not recognize it as unbelievable, because it is made *by* your belief.

7. The purpose of this course is to teach you that the personal self is unbelievable, now and Forever. You who made it cannot make this judgment *from* it. By accepting the Holy Spirit, you are deciding against your belief that you are a personal self, and you are correcting your perception that you are separate from God. Your

True Identity is in your Oneness with God. This Identity is beyond doubt, and beyond belief. Your Wholeness has no limits, because It is Infinite.

9. The Extension of the Kingdom

1. Only you can limit the Power that God gave to you, because God's Will is that your Power is Limitless. God does not will you to deprive yourself of your Extension of God anymore than God wills to be apart from Its Extension of Itself. Do not withhold your Extension of God, or you withhold yourself from God. The personal mind is selfish, but the Holy Spirit is Self-full. The Holy Spirit mediates between the personal mind and your God-like Mind, and always chooses your God-like Mind. To the personal mind this is partiality, and an attack on it. To the Holy Spirit this is Truth, because in Its Self-fullness It cannot exclude you.

2. The Holy Spirit knows that the part of your mind that you have given to separation is included in the Holy Spirit, just as the Holy Spirit is included in God. The Power of Its Whole Mind, and of God, is the Holy Spirit's own Fullness, and Its Extension of God is Whole and Perfect. The personal mind cannot prevail against God's Wholeness, and only God is Whole. God's Extension is given all of God's Power, because It is God's Being. Extending is the opposite of loss, as blessing is the opposite of sacrifice. Being must be extended because that is how It knows Itself. The Holy Spirit yearns to extend its Being, as God extends God. Being God's Extension, the Holy Spirit wills to extend, not to contain, God.

3. Extending God is the Holy Spirit's only Function. The Holy Spirit's Fullness cannot be contained anymore than God's Fullness can be contained. Fullness *is* extension. The personal mind's thought system blocks the Holy Spirit's extension, so it blocks your only Function and Joy, and leaves you feeling unfulfilled. When you do not extend God, you *are* unfulfilled, but God cannot be unfulfilled, so you *must* extend God. You may not be aware of your Extension of God, but this cannot interfere with your Extension's Reality, anymore than your unawareness of the Holy Spirit can interfere with the Holy Spirit's Being.

4.   God's Oneness extends Forever, because It is the Mind of God. You are not Joyous because you do not know your own Self-fullness. Look on the world that you perceive as reality, and you will not feel whole. Your mind will be split, and not know its Fullness. You will need to experience a miracle to make yourself aware of your mind's Wholeness, and to heal it. Your awareness of Wholeness is your awareness of God's Oneness. The Self-fullness of the Holy Spirit makes the selfishness of the personal mind impossible, and your extension of God inevitable. God's Oneness is always Perfect Peace, because the Holy Spirit is fulfilling Its Function, and Complete Fulfillment *is* Peace.

5.   Your Extension of God is unchanged, and the Holy Spirit knows It and can bring It into your awareness whenever you are willing. It is Part of your Being and Fulfillment. All of God's Extension is yours because It is Everywhere, being extended to your Mind from God.

6.   You have not failed to extend God's Oneness, and you have not lost It for yourself. It is God's Will that you be One with God Forever, *and you are*. It is not possible for you to disobey God's Will; this idea has no meaning. Your Self-fullness is as Boundless as God's Fullness, and It extends Forever in Perfect Peace. It extends in Perfect Joy, and only the Whole can ever extend from Its Wholeness.

7.   You have not lost your Identity or Its Extension, Which maintains your Identity in Wholeness and in Peace. Your experiences of miracles are expressions of your awareness of this. They reflect your corrected perception by replacing the world of separation in your mind, and your awareness of this correct perception is maintained by your extending God's Love. Your experience of the miracle is your lesson in totally corrected perception, because any time that your mind perceives correctly, you perceive the Wholeness of your Mind.

10. The Confusion of Pain and Joy

1.   Your Oneness with God is the result of Ideas inherent to God, just as your perception of a world of separation is the result of ideas

inherent to the personal mind. Taken to their logical conclusion, the personal mind's inherent ideas are total confusion. If you really saw this, you would not want it. The only reason that you do want it is because you do not see all of it. You are willing to look at the personal mind's inherent ideas, but not at their logical outcome. You have not looked at the logical outcome of God's Inherent Ideas, either. Your Extension of God is the logical outcome of your Oneness with God. This is established by God. and is happening in your God-like Mind. But your state of mind, and what you see in your mind, depends on what you believe about your mind. Whatever your beliefs may be, they determine what you accept into your mind.

2.   It is obvious by now that you can accept into your mind what is *not* there, and that you can deny What *is* there. Though you can deny the Function that God gave to your Mind, Its Function cannot be prevented. This is the logical outcome of your Oneness with God. To see this logical outcome, you must be willing, but its Truth has nothing to do with your willingness. Truth is God's Will and yours. Deny that God's Will is your Will, and you deny God and yourself.

3.   The Holy Spirit directs you to avoid pain, and if you recognized this, you would not resist the Holy Spirit. The problem is not whether or not what the Holy Spirit says is true, but whether or not you want to listen to the Holy Spirit. You do not recognize what is truly painful or Truly Joyful, and you confuse the two. The Holy Spirit's Function is to teach you to tell them apart. What brings you Joy is painful to the personal mind, and as long as you confuse yourself with a personal mind, you will confuse pain and Joy. This confusion leads you to feel that you are being called on to sacrifice. Follow the Holy Spirit and you *will* give up the personal self, but this is not a sacrifice, because the personal self is nothing. In fact, you will gain Everything. When you believe this, you will no longer be conflicted.

4.   You need to demonstrate to yourself that God's Will *will* bring you Joy, because this is not obvious to you, and you believe that doing the opposite of God's Will is better for you. You also believe that it is possible to *do* the opposite of God's Will, so you believe that an

impossible choice that is both fearful and desirable is open to you. But God *Wills*; God does not *wish*, which is all that the personal mind can do. Your Will is as Powerful as God's Will, because your Will *is* God's Will. But the personal mind's wishes do not mean anything, because they are wishes for the impossible. You can wish for the impossible, but you can Will only with God. This is why the personal mind is weak and you are strong.

5. The Holy Spirit sides with the Will of God, Which is your Strength. As long as you avoid the Holy Spirit in any way, you want to be weak. And since weakness is frightening, it means that you have decided to be afraid. The Holy Spirit never asks you to sacrifice, but the personal mind always asks you to sacrifice your True Identity. When you are confused about which asks you to sacrifice it is because you project the personal mind's motivation onto the Holy Spirit. Your trust in the Holy Spirit is then impossible, and you are not going to follow a Guide that you do not trust. But this does not mean that the Holy Spirit is untrustworthy; it means that you are untrustworthy, because you are projecting the personal mind's motivation onto the Holy Spirit. But this is only a matter of your belief. You believe that you can betray, so you believe that everything can betray you. This is only because you have chosen to follow false guidance, which you cannot follow without fear. Because you associate guidance with fear, you will not follow any guidance at all. It is no surprise that you are confused about the Holy Spirit!

6. The Holy Spirit is Perfectly Trustworthy, as you are. God Trusts you, therefore your Trustworthiness is beyond question. It is Forever beyond question, though you may question It. You are the Will of God, and God's Will is not an idle wish. Your Identification with God's Will is not optional since It is What you are. Your sharing God's Will with the Holy Spirit is not really open to your choice, though you may think that it is. Your thinking so is the error that is your whole sense of separation from God. Your only way out of this error is to decide that you do not have to decide anything. Everything is already yours by God's Decision. This is God's Will, and you cannot undo It.

7. Giving up a decision that was never yours to make in the first place, but which the personal mind guards jealously, is not accomplished by your wish. It has already been decided for you by the Will of God, Which has not left you without Guidance. The Holy Spirit will teach you how to tell the difference between pain and Joy, and so lead you out of the confusion that you have made. You experience no confusion in your Oneness with God, Which is God's Will.

8. Your experience of the miracle is in accord with God's Will, Which you have forgotten, because you are confused about what *you* will, which means that you are confused about what you *are*. You are God's Will, and by not accepting this you are denying yourself Joy. Your experience of the miracle is a lesson in Joy. It is a lesson in extending, which is a lesson in Love, which *is* Joy. Every miracle that you experience is a lesson in Truth, and by extending Truth in your awareness, you learn the difference between pain and Joy.

11. The State of Grace

1. The Holy Spirit guides you truly, because your Joy is Its Joy. This is Its Will everywhere, because It speaks for God's Oneness, Which *is* Joy. Following the Holy Spirit is the most natural and easy thing for you to do in your perception that you are in a world, because the Holy Spirit is not *of* the world, and *neither are you*. The world that you perceive goes against your True Nature, because it is not in accord with God's Law of Oneness. In your perception of a world you perceive various degrees of difficulty in what you do, because you do not want anything wholly. But by extending God's Love everywhere without exception, you will learn that in your Natural State of Oneness there is no difficulty, because Oneness is a State of Grace.

2. Grace is your Natural State of Being in God. When you are not in a State of Grace, you are out of your Natural Environment, and you do not function well. Then everything is a strain because you are in an environment that you made apart from God. You cannot adapt to it or it to you, and there is no point in trying. You can be happy only in God. God is Where you belong, so you do not experience any strain in God. God is also the only Environment that is Worthy

of you, because your Worth is beyond what you have made.

3. Look at the world that you have made in your mind, and judge its worth fairly. Is it worthy of you who are One with God? Does it protect your Peace and shine Love upon you? Does it keep away fear and allow you to give always, without any sense of loss? Does it teach you that extending God is Joy, and that God thanks you for extending God? The only Environment in Which you can be happy is One Where you say 'yes' to all of these questions. You cannot make this Environment any more than you can make yourself. It is God's Oneness. God watches over you and denies you nothing. But when you deny God, you do not know this, because you are denying yourself Everything. You who could extend God's Love everywhere are literally denying yourself Heaven.

4. You are called upon to teach only God's Oneness to What is One with God. You can make no exception to teaching this Lesson, because this is a Lesson in lack of exceptions. When you return to God's Oneness through this Lesson, you will have healed your mind, and you will be thankful to God. You will have become the Perfect Teacher, because you will have learned this lesson from the Holy Spirit within you.

5. When your mind has only God, it knows only God. It extends God everywhere, undoing your every thought of separation from God, and transforms your entire mind into Greatness. The Greatness of God is here for you to recognize, to appreciate, and to know. Your recognizing God's Greatness in place of a world of separation is your accepting What is yours. God gives God everywhere, and if you recognize God anywhere, you acknowledge What God has given to you. The Truth is the easiest Thing for you to recognize, and It is immediate, clear, and natural. You have trained your mind to not recognize Truth, and this has been difficult for you.

6. Truth is your Natural Environment, and out of your Natural Environment it is natural for you to ask what Truth is. You do not know yourself, because you do not know God. You do not know that you extend God, because you have blocked your awareness of this with a world of separation. Only your Whole Mind is One with God, because only your Whole Mind can extend God as God

127

extends God. Whenever you extend God's Love instead of project separation, you heal your mind, and you acknowledge God's Creation. Your perception of a world cannot have undone What you can recognize in its place, and the Glory that you perceive in place of the world must be in your mind. The part of your mind that you have given to separation is One with your Mind and with God. Deny the Power of this part of your mind and you deny your Power and God's Power.

7.   You cannot deny part of Truth and know Truth. You do not know that you extend God, because you do not know that you are One with God. You do not know yourself, because you do not know God. Your extending God does not make you Real, any more than you as God's Extension make God Real. You can *know* both yourself as God's Extension, and your own Extension of God. God's Being is *known*, not *made*, by extending. Because God Extends God to you, you can know God. But God's Extension must fill your entire mind for you to know God. Without God, you do not know What you are. God's Oneness is the Boundless Extension of God. Know, then, the Extension of God with your entire mind, and you will know God.

Chapter 8

The Journey Back

1. The Direction of the Curriculum

1. Peace, not knowing God, is your motivation for learning this course. You are not at Peace as long as you are conflicted, and Peace is required before you can know God again, because Peace is the State of God's Being. Your acquiring Peace is not a condition set by God for your return to God, but it is required, because you have made an imaginary will apart from God's Will that is unlike God's Peaceful State. It is God's Will that you know God, and, if you are opposing God, you cannot know God. You do not yet find God wholly desirable, because, if you did, you would not be so ready to throw God away when the personal mind wants your attention.

2. The personal mind may seem to distract you from learning Peace, but the personal mind does not have the power to distract you unless you want it to. The personal mind's voice is not real, but you cannot expect it to say, 'I am not real.' You are not asked to dispel this voice without the Holy Spirit's Voice to replace it. You *are* asked to evaluate the personal mind's ideas in terms of their results to you. When you do not want them because they deprive you of Peace, you will let them go.

3. Every time that you respond to the personal mind you will experience conflict, and you will lack Peace. But this is a conflict with no opponent, and you must recognize this to be at Peace. The part of your mind that you have given to perceiving a world that is attacking you is part of your Peace, and you are giving up your Peace to interpret this world as real. You cannot have the Peace that you give up; you keep Peace *in* your awareness only by extending It *from* your awareness. When you give up Peace you are excluding yourself from It, and you do not remember that you have It. This state is so alien to God's Oneness that you cannot understand the Peace of God.

4. What you have learned through the personal mind has not made you happy, so there must be something wrong with its lessons. On this basis alone you should question its lessons. The goal of learning is change. Are you satisfied with the changes your past learning has brought to you? If you are not satisfied with what you have learned, then you must not have gotten what you wanted from the lessons.

5. The Holy Spirit's lesson plan is the opposite of the lesson plan that you have made for yourself through the personal mind, and so is its outcome. If the outcome of your plan has made you unhappy, and you want another outcome, then you must change to the Holy Spirit's lesson plan. Your first change must be a total change in the Holy Spirit's direction, because a meaningful lesson plan must be consistent. You have been following two teachers with diametrically opposed lesson plans that cannot be integrated and that interfere with each other. You have experienced vacillation but not change, because you have not made a choice of teacher, and you are reluctant to give up one for the other, even though the personal mind is not real. Your conflicted lesson plan teaches you that both the personal mind and the Holy Spirit are real, leaving you with no rational basis for real choice.

6. You must fully recognize the senselessness of your lesson plan before you will be willing to make a change in direction. You cannot learn simultaneously from two teachers that totally disagree about everything. It *is* possible to learn entirely different things in entirely different ways about entirely different things, but you are learning about *yourself*. Your Reality is not affected by either the personal mind or the Holy Spirit, but, by listening to both, your mind is split about what your reality is.

2. The Difference Between Imprisonment and Freedom

1. The rational basis for your choosing which teacher to follow is which teacher knows your reality, and that is the Holy Spirit. The lesson you must learn is how to remove your obstacles to God, and you can only learn this from the Holy Spirit. The personal mind does not know what it is trying to teach, because it is trying to teach

you what you are, and it does not know What you are. It is only an expert in confusion, and this is what it teaches. Even if you could totally disregard the Holy Spirit, which is impossible, you would learn nothing from the personal mind, because it knows nothing.

2.   There is no reason for you to choose the personal mind as your teacher, and your total disregard of what it teaches is the only thing that makes sense. The personal mind is not the teacher that will teach you that you are One with God. The personal mind has never given you a sensible answer to anything, and your own experience with it should disqualify it as your teacher. Learning is Joyful for you when it leads you along your Natural Path and develops your awareness of What you already have. When you are taught against your Nature, you lose yourself, and you limit your Will. But your Will is in your Nature, and It cannot go against your Nature.

3.   When your Will is Free you don't learn from the personal mind, because it does not exist for you. That is why the personal mind is a denial of your Free Will. God never coerces you, because God's Will is your Will. The Holy Spirit teaches only in accordance with God's Will, but God's Will is not a lesson; It is What you *are*. The Holy Spirit's lesson is that your Will and God's Will are One. This undoes everything that the personal mind tries to teach you. Not only does the direction of the lesson plan have to be consistent, but the content of the lesson plan must be consistent as well.

4.   Through the personal mind you teach yourself that you want to oppose God's Will. This is an impossible lesson that is unnatural to you, and your trying to learn it limits your Will. It makes you afraid of your Free Will, because your Free Will will undo the limits that you are trying to learn. The Holy Spirit opposes any limits on your Will, because It knows that your Will is God's Will. The Holy Spirit leads you along a path to your Free Will, and teaches you how to disregard everything that the personal mind uses to hold you back.

5.   The Holy Spirit teaches you the difference between pain and Joy, which is the same thing as saying It teaches you the difference between limitation and Freedom. You cannot make this distinction

without the Holy Spirit, because you have taught yourself through the personal mind that limitation *is* freedom. You believe them to be the same, and you cannot tell them apart. You cannot ask the part of your mind that taught you that they are the same to teach you that they are different.

6.   The Holy Spirit's direction is your freedom from limitations, and Its Goal is God. The Holy Spirit cannot conceive of God without you, because it is not God's Will to be without you. When you learn that your Will is God's Will, you will understand that you cannot will to be without God any more than God can will to be without you. This is your Freedom and Joy. Deny this, and you deny God's Wholeness, because you are Part of God.

7.   God's Will is Limitless, and all Power and Glory lie within It. Its Strength and Love and Peace are Boundless. There are no boundaries in God's Will, because It extends Everywhere, and It encompasses Everything, because It is One. Being One with Everything, Everything is Part of God's Will. Because God extends only God, you are like God. You are Part of God, Which is all Power and Glory, and, therefore, you are as Limitless as God.

8.   The Holy Spirit appeals to the Power and Glory within you to restore God's Oneness to your awareness. Its appeal, then, is to Oneness to acknowledge that It is One. When you acknowledge Oneness, you automatically bring this acknowledgment to all that your mind perceives, because you have acknowledged your Whole Mind. By this recognition, you extend your awareness of Oneness in place of the world of separation. The awareness of God runs easily and happily through your entire mind in answer to the Holy Spirit's Call for God. This is your natural response to the Holy Spirit, because the Holy Spirit is the Voice for you and for your Extension of God.

3. The Holy Encounter

1.   Glory to God and to you, because you are One with God. Ask for Glory and It is yours, because you already have It. Ask to know God, and you will learn that you are One with God. If you want to know God, you will learn how to accept God, because your

decision to learn of God is your decision to listen to the Holy Spirit, Which comes from God, and can therefore teach you how to accept God. There are no real limits on your mind, so there are no limits on your ability to learn of God. There is no limit on the Holy Spirit's teaching, because the Holy Spirit's Purpose is to teach you. This is the Holy Spirit's Joy and your Joy.

2.   Only your fulfilling God's Will perfectly will bring you total Peace and Joy. Fulfilling God's Will is the only experience that you can fully experience, because the only Experience in God is God. But your wish for other experiences blocks God's Will from your awareness. God's Will cannot be forced on you, because It is an Experience that you must be totally willing to accept. The Holy Spirit understands how to teach you this, but the personal mind does not. That is why you need the Holy Spirit, and why God gave the Holy Spirit to you. Only the Holy Spirit's Teaching will free your will to unite with God's Will and the Power and Glory that are yours in Oneness with God. Power and Glory are the natural outcome of your Being in God.

3.   God's Will and your Will are One through extension. Oneness results in the extension of Itself through the Will to be One. This is Creation. For God to extend God, God must give you the ability to extend God. You are One with God, and It is your Holy Function to extend God without limit. Only the Holy Spirit, Which is of God, can teach you how to do this.

4.   In every encounter with others in your perception that you are in a world, remember to extend God's Love to make it a holy encounter. Your perception of, behavior toward, and thoughts about others reflect what you believe about yourself. Do not forget that in others you will find yourself or lose yourself based on whether or not you extend God's Love in place of the personal mind's projections. Whenever you meet others in the world that you perceive, you are given another chance to remember that you are One with God, so do not leave them without extending God's Love to receive God's Love. The Holy Spirit is always with you so you can remember What you really are.

5.   Whether you are listening to the Holy Spirit or the personal mind,

the goal of the lesson is always, 'Know yourself.' There is nothing else for you to seek, and you are always looking for the Power and the Glory that you think that you have lost. Whenever you are with others, you have the opportunity to reclaim your Power and Glory by extending God's Love in place of the personal mind's projections. The personal mind will tell you that your Power and Glory are in the personal mind alone, but the Holy Spirit teaches you that everything that you perceive is in your mind. When you are with others, you are teaching yourself what you are. You will experience pain or Joy, limitation or Freedom, depending on whether you are following the personal mind or the Holy Spirit. Your responsibility to yourself is to remember that you are One with God.

6. God's Oneness is not limited to the personal mind, and you cannot find yourself in the isolation of the personal mind. To find yourself, you cannot listen to the personal mind, because its purpose is to defeat its own goal of finding you. But the personal mind does not realize this is what it is doing, because it does not know anything. But *you* can know this is what it is doing by looking at the limits that the personal mind places on you. This is your one responsibility, because once you do look at what the personal mind is doing, you will accept correction of your perception of separation from God. You will look on your error of believing that when you look on others you are seeing something outside your mind, and you will make it a holy encounter with your Self instead by extending God's Love in place of the personal mind's projections.

7. God is Whole, and you who are One with God can only encounter part of yourself. God's Power and Glory are Everywhere and you are not excluded from Them. The personal mind teaches that your strength is in a personal self alone, but the Holy Spirit teaches that all Strength is in God, and, *therefore*, It is in you. God does not Will that you suffer for an error, so God gave you the Holy Spirit to undo your error. Through God's Power and Glory within you, your mistaken decisions are undone completely, releasing you from every limiting thought anywhere. Your mistaken decisions do not have power because they are not true, and the limitations they seem to produce are no more real than they are.

8. Power and Glory belong to God alone, and so do you. God extends What belongs to God, and What belongs to God is God. God is Everything. Extending yourself in your Oneness with God is the Function that God extends to you. By fulfilling your Function perfectly you will remember both What you *have* and What you *are* in God. You cannot be powerless to extend God, because extending God *is* your Power. Glory is God's gift to you, because Glory is What God is. Remember What you are by seeing God's Glory everywhere.

4. The Gift of Freedom

1. God's Will for you is complete Peace and Joy, and when you are not experiencing Them,, it is because you are refusing God's Will. God's Will is Forever Changeless. When you are not at Peace it is because you do not believe that you are in God. But God is All. God's Peace is Complete and you are included in It. God's Law governs you, and you cannot exempt yourself from It, though you can choose to not follow It. But when you do make this choice, you feel lonely and helpless, because you are denying yourself Everything.

2. Your split mind denies itself Everything by separating from Everything, so the Holy Spirit comes into your mind to bring Everything to your awareness again. The personal mind is your illusion of isolation, maintained by your fear of the very loneliness that is the result of your identifying with a personal mind. The Holy Spirit is with you always, even to the end of your perception of a world, and that is why your loneliness is actually gone. The Holy Spirit's purpose is to undo your perception of a world of separation, not by attack, but just by being What the Holy Spirit is. Since the Holy Spirit is with you everywhere you perceive yourself, you can undo the world in your mind. Your remembering the Holy Spirit is your remembering your True Self and God, Which sends you the Holy Spirit.

3. God's Will is done completely whenever you extend God completely. Jesus united with God's Will by completely extending God in His awareness. This is what He modeled, and your problem

in accepting this is your desire that the world be real. Undoing the world in your mind is your salvation, so the Christ in your Mind is your salvation. The world is the idea that Love is impossible, and, to maintain the world's reality, the personal mind must despise and reject your Christ Mind. But when you accept the Christ within you, you deny that the world is real, and you accept that only God is Real. Christ's Will is God's Will, and your decision to follow your Christ Mind is your decision to hear the Holy Spirit and to follow God's Will. God sent you the Holy Spirit so that you can extend Peace and Oneness in your awareness.

4.   The part of your mind that perceives a world of separation needs Peace, and, if you want Peace, you must extend Peace in your perception to know that you have Peace. Your healing comes only from the guidance of the Holy Spirit within you. You must want Its guidance, or Its guidance will be meaningless to you. Your healing is the joining of the Holy Spirit to all that you perceive. Only if you believe that the Holy Spirit knows what you need to do will you give your split mind to the Holy Spirit. If you don't choose to follow the Holy Spirit, you are deciding for separation from God, and you will not heal your mind.

5.   Your healing is the joining of your will with God's Will, because your perception of separation from God is overcome by your Oneness with God. Your decision to join your will with God's Will must be undivided, or it will not be whole. Your mind is the mechanism of decision. and it determines whether you will separate and suffer, or join and be Joyous. The Holy Spirit cannot force on you the decision to join, because the part of your mind that you have given to separation is equal in strength to the Holy Spirit within you. Even in separation your will is free, and God Itself cannot limit it, so the Holy Spirit cannot limit it. The Holy Spirit's Strength can make yours invincible, but It cannot oppose your decision to be separate without competing with you and undoing God's Oneness.

6.   Nothing can oppose your decision, because God gave your will its power, and the Holy Spirit can only acknowledge this. If you want to be like the Holy Spirit, the Holy Spirit will help you, but if you

want to be different from the Holy Spirit, the Holy Spirit can only wait for you to change your mind. The Holy Spirit can teach you, but you must choose to follow Its teaching. This is your freedom, and you will not learn Freedom through tyranny. You will not understand God's Oneness by one Part of It having power over another Part of It. Being the Will of God, your mind is One, and this is all that the Holy Spirit teaches.

7. Your Will is the Holy Spirit's Will, Which is God's Will. If this were not so, your will would be limited, not free. With a personal self you can do nothing, because the personal self *is* nothing. The Holy Spirit is nothing without God, and you are nothing without the Holy Spirit, because, by denying God, you deny your Self. The Holy Spirit remembers What you are for you, and when you remember the Holy Spirit, you remember God. This is your Freedom, because you can only be Free in God's Limitlessness. Praise God and yourself who are One with God, and give this gift in gratitude. God extends your Praise and Gratitude Everywhere, Always, and by extending Freedom, you will be Free.

8. Freedom from limitations is the only gift that you can offer to the part of your mind that you perceive as separated from you, because, in Reality, it is Whole as God is Whole. Freedom is Creation, because it is the Extension of God's Love. When you seek to limit your awareness of yourself to a personal self among other personal selves in a world separate from God, you cannot extend God's Love, and you lose your Identification with God and the Holy Spirit. [Your Identification is with the entire Holy Trinity (God, Christ, and the Holy Spirit), because They are One. You cannot identify with One without the Others. If you exclude yourself from Them, you perceive Them as separated. You are included in the Holy Trinity, because It is Everything. You *will* fulfill your Function, or the Holy Trinity would be incomplete. No Part of It can be limited for you to understand What It is.]

5. The Undivided Will of the Sonship

1. You cannot be separate from your True Identity and be at Peace. Your perception of separation from God is a delusion, not a

solution. When you are delusional, you feel that the Truth will attack you, and you do not recognize that the Truth is True, because you want the delusion. Not wanting Truth, you perceive illusions, which block God from your mind. You can undo this by extending God's Love to all that your mind perceives, just as the Holy Spirit extends God's Love to you. Your mind is nothing in the isolation of a personal self, but unite your mind and its perceptions into Wholeness, and its power will be greater than its separate parts. The Mind of God is yours, and this Mind is invincible, because It is Whole.

2.   The undivided Will of your Whole Mind extends God perfectly, being God's Will and being like God. You must include yourself in God's Will to understand What It is and What you are. By believing your will is separate from the Holy Spirit's Will, you exclude yourself from God's Will, Which *is* your True Self. But to heal is to make whole, so to heal your mind is to unite the Holy Spirit with all that your mind perceives by recognizing that God, not a world of separation, is in your mind. Your Perfection is only in God, and you can only know this by recognizing that God is in your entire mind. Your recognition of God is your recognition of your True Self, because there is no separation between God and What is One with God. You will realize this when you recognize that there is no difference between your will and the Holy Spirit's Will. Let God's Love shine on your acceptance of the Holy Spirit, because Its Reality is yours and God's. When you join your mind with the Holy Spirit, you are signaling your awareness that God's Will is One.

3.   God's Oneness encompasses your Oneness with the Holy Spirit. When you join with the Holy Spirit, you restore God's Power to yourself. The Holy Spirit offers you only your awareness of God's Power in you, and in that lies all Truth. As you unite with the Holy Spirit, you unite with God. Glory to the Oneness of God! All Glory lies in God's Oneness. because It is united. The Love of God that you extend bears witness to God's Will for you and to your Joy in uniting with God's Will.

4.   When you unite with the Holy Spirit, you are uniting without the personal mind, because the Holy Spirit is not limited to the

personal mind. Your uniting with the Holy Spirit is the way for you to renounce the personal mind and to go beyond it to Truth. Your success in transcending the personal mind is guaranteed by God, and the Holy Spirit shares this confidence. The Holy Spirit brings God's Peace back to your mind, because It received It from God for you. Nothing can prevail against your will united with the Holy Spirit, because nothing can prevail against God's Will.

5.   If you want to know the Will of God for you, ask It of the Holy Spirit, Which knows It for you, and you will find It. The Holy Spirit will not deny you anything, because God does not deny the Holy Spirit anything. Your journey with the Holy Spirit is simply your journey back to your Home in God. Whenever you are afraid it is because the personal mind has tried to join the journey, and it cannot do so. Feeling defeated and angry, the personal mind feels rejected and attacks. But you are not vulnerable to its attacks when you remember that the Holy Spirit is in you. You have chosen the Holy Spirit instead of the personal mind as your Companion on this journey. If you try to hold onto both, you will vacillate between different directions, and you will lose your way.

6.   The personal mind's direction is not the Holy Spirit's Direction, so it is not yours. The Holy Spirit has one Direction for your mind, and It is the same Direction It taught Jesus. Only your illusions of another direction can obscure the Holy Spirit's Direction for you. Do not give the personal mind the power to block you on your journey, because it has no power of its own, and your journey is to Truth. Reach beyond the personal mind's attempts to hold you back and reach for the Holy Spirit, Which goes before you and beyond the personal mind. The Holy Spirit's Strength will never falter, and you can choose to share It. The Holy Spirit gives Its Strength willingly and gladly, because the Holy Spirit needs you as much as you need It.

6. The Treasure of God

1.   Your *seemingly* separate will joined with the Holy Spirit's Will is your Wholeness. Your journey to God begins with this joining, and it continues as you extend God's Love to be all that you perceive.

Every strengthening of your awareness of God strengthens your entire mind. God's Welcome awaits your entire mind, as the Holy Spirit welcomes your joining with It. Do not forget God's Oneness for anything that the world that you perceive has to offer.

2. The world that you perceive can add nothing to God or to your Oneness with God, but your belief in its reality can blind you to God. You cannot perceive the world as real and know God, because only God is Real. The choice of what is Truth is not yours to make. If it were, you would have destroyed yourself when you chose to be separate from God. God does not Will your destruction, because your Oneness with God is Eternal. God's Will saves you *from* your illusion of the personal self by saving you *for* your True Self in God.

3. Glorify God, Which the personal mind wants to deny. The world that you perceive has no power over God's Oneness. You can find Joy only in the Eternal, not because It is All that there is, but because nothing else is worthy of you. What you extend with God is Eternal, and only this is your Joy.

4. Learn what is God's treasure and your treasure from this story of the prodigal son: The son of a loving father left his home, and he gave away all that he had for something he thought had greater value. But he learned that it had no value. He thought that this hurt his father, and he was ashamed to return to him. But when he did go home, his father welcomed him with joy, because the son was the father's treasure, and his father wanted nothing else.

5. God wants only you, because you are God's Treasure, and your Extension of God is your Treasure. Your Extension of God is your Gift to God, extended in gratitude to God for extending God to you. Your Extension of God does not leave you any more than you leave God as God's Extension, but It extends your *Oneness* with God as God extends God to you. As Part of God, you cannot take Joy in the unreal, and only God's Extension is Real. Your extending God returns Love to you, as God's extending you returns Love to God. This is the only Gift that is Eternal and True. You cannot accept anything else, or give anything else, and expect Joy to return to you. What else but Joy do you want? You did not make yourself or your Function, but you made the decision to be unworthy of both.

Yet you cannot really make yourself unworthy, because you are God's Treasure and What God values is Truly Valuable. There is no question of your Value, because your Value lies in God's extension of God to you, and this establishes your Value Forever.

6.   Your Function is to add to God's Treasure by extending God. And this is *your* Treasure. God's Will *to* you is God's Will *for* you. God cannot withhold Its extension from you, because God's Joy is in extending God. You can find Joy only as God does.and extending God is how you are like God. You do not understand this, because you do not understand God. When you do not accept your Function, you do not know What It is, and you will not accept your Function until you know What you are. Extending God is the Will of God. God's Will is extended to you for you to extend God. Your Will is not separate from God's Will, so you must will as God wills.

7.   When you think that you do not will with God, you are not thinking at all, because God's Will *is* Thought, and It cannot be contradicted *by* thought. God does not contradict God, and you who are One with God cannot contradict yourself by contradicting God. But your thoughts are so powerful that you can limit your mind if you choose. This does seem to make your Function unknown to you, but It is never unknown to God. And because It is known to God, It is Forever knowable by you.

8.   The only question that you need to ask yourself is: 'Do I want to know God's Will for me?' God will not hide Its Will. God revealed Its Will to Jesus, Who asked It of God, and Who learned What God had already given Him. Your Function is to join with the Holy Spirit within you, because, apart from It, you cannot function at all. The Whole Power of God's Oneness lies in your entire mind, not alone in the personal mind. God does not want you to be un-whole, because God does not want to be un-whole. That is why God extends God to you, and God gives you the Power to extend God. Your Extension of God is as Holy as you who are One with God. By extending God, you extend your Love and increase your Joy. You do not understand this, because you who are God's Treasure do not think that you are Valuable. With this belief you cannot understand anything.

9. The Holy Spirit knows the Value that God puts upon you. Knowing both God and you, the Holy Spirit's devotion to you comes from God. You cannot be separated from the Holy Spirit, because All of God's Mind is One, and God is your Life and your Being. Your journey to God is the reawakening of your knowledge that you are Forever One with God. It is a journey without distance to a Goal that has never changed. God cannot be described or explained, but you can experience God directly. The Holy Spirit can prepare you for the Experience of God, but God will dawn on you of Itself.

10. What God wills for you *is* yours. God has given Its Will to you who are God's Treasure, and God's Will is *your* Treasure. You are Beloved of God and Wholly Blessed. Learn this of the Holy Spirit, and set your Holy Will totally free by extending God's Blessing.

7. The Body as a Means of Communication

1. Your identification with a personal self in a body is how your split mind thinks it has attacked God. So you attack when you think attack can get you something, just as the personal mind thinks it has gotten something by attacking God. Attack always involves body-identification, whether the attack is physical or not. Attack would not appeal to you if you didn't think it could get you something, and you only think this when you identify with a personal self in a body. You will always be depressed when you identify with a body, because you who are One with God are belittling yourself when you limit yourself to a body. It is the same when you look on your perceptions of other bodies as reality. When you perceive other bodies as reality, you believe that you are a body, and you cut yourself off from salvation.

2. The Holy Spirit interprets everything that you have made in light of Its own purpose, and since the Holy Spirit is the Communication Link between you and God, It interprets the body as a means of communicating Itself to you. The personal mind uses your body-identification to make you seem separate from God, but the Holy Spirit reaches *through* your body-identification to join your mind. The Holy Spirit uses your perceptions of other bodies in the world that you perceive as opportunities to extend God's Love in place of

the personal mind's projections. The body has no value of its own, and the Holy Spirit's interpretation of it will entirely change your mind about its value.

3. If you use the body to attack yourself by making it real to you, it will seem to harm you. But if you extend God's Love *through* the body to teach yourself that the body is not real, you will understand the Power of your Mind. If you use the body only for the extension of Love, you cannot use it for attack. In the service of uniting your mind with the Holy Spirit, the body becomes a beautiful lesson in communion, until you are again aware of your Communion with God. This is how God makes you aware of your Unlimited Mind, Which you want to limit to a body. The Holy Spirit knows that the only reality of anything in the world that you perceive is the service that it renders God on behalf of your function of extending Oneness.

4. Communicating the Holy Spirit to your mind ends your sense of separation from God; making the body real to you, and therefore attacking yourself with it, promotes your sense of separation from God. The body is beautiful or ugly, peaceful or savage, helpful or harmful, depending on whether you use it for communicating the Holy Spirit to your mind or for separation from God. The way that you perceive *other* bodies reflects how *you* use the body. If you give the body to the Holy Spirit to use as a means of uniting your mind, you will see the physical world is nothing. Use the body for Truth, and you will see it truly. But use it for separation, and you will not understand its real purpose, because you will have misused it. Interpret anything in the world that you perceive apart from the Holy Spirit and you will mistrust it, hate it, attack it, and lose your Peace.

5. All of your sense of loss comes from your not understanding that loss is impossible. When you look on bodies as real, your Power and Glory are lost to your awareness. This is an attack on yourself, and you project this attack onto a world that you perceive outside of you. Do not look on the physical world as real; for your own salvation, extend God's Love instead. Do not belittle yourself by limiting your awareness to a physical world, but free your mind by

extending God's Love everywhere. The part of your mind in which you have projected a world is as Holy as your Christ Mind. For you to extend God's Love to it is for you to reach to God through your Oneness with the Holy Spirit.

6. Rejoice that you did not make yourself, and that you can do nothing real with the personal self. You are One with God, and God wills you the Power and Glory to accomplish God's Will when you accept It for yourself. God has not withdrawn Its Gifts from you, but you believe you have taken Them from God when you believe the separation is real. For God's sake, do not let any part of your mind remain hidden from God, because you are One with God.

7. The Bible says, 'The Word (or thought) was made flesh.' This is not possible, since your Mind is Real, but material form is not. It only seems as though there are two realities, just as it seems that every miracle manifests differently. Thought is not physical, and you can only *believe* it can make flesh. But thought *is* communication, and communication is the only natural use to which you can put the body. If you use the body for any other purpose, you forget the Holy Spirit's Purpose of extending God, and you are confused about the Holy Spirit's lesson plan.

8. A lesson plan that you cannot learn is frustrating and depressing, and this is why your perception of a world is depressing. The Holy Spirit's lesson plan is never depressing, because it is a Plan of Joy. Whenever you are depressed it is because you have forgotten the Goal of the Holy Spirit's lesson.

9. In your identification with a personal self you do not even perceive the body as whole. Its purpose is fragmented into many functions with little or no relationship to each other, so that it appears to be ruled by chaos. When you are guided by the personal mind, the body *is* ruled by chaos. But, when you are guided by the Holy Spirit, the body becomes the means by which the part of your mind that you tried to separate *from* the Holy Spirit through projection is returned *to* the Holy Spirit through the extension of God's Love. The personal self's temple thus becomes the Holy Spirit's temple, and *only* in this way is the body a temple to God. The Holy Spirit abides in the body by directing the use to which it is put.

10. When you use the body only to overlook it, and to communicate the Holy Spirit to your mind, the body is healed. This is the body's natural use, and, since it is natural, it makes the body whole. Your Mind is Whole, and your belief that part of it is physical, or not-Mind, is fragmented and sick. Your Mind cannot be made physical, but It can be made manifest *through* the physical if your Mind uses the body to go beyond it to extend Itself. If your Mind stops at the body, It is blocked in Its Purpose of extension, and It has attacked Itself.

11. Removing your blocks to your Mind's extension is the only way to guarantee a healed body. A healed body is the natural result when your Mind is working *through* it, but not *in* it. The goal of the personal mind's lesson plan is to teach you that you are a body. This blocks the extension of your Mind *through* the body by teaching you that you are *in* a body. This results in your distorted perception of the body, which fosters your belief in separation and manifests as illness. Your perception of the body as a separate entity with its own power must foster illness, because it is not true. The body is then useless for communicating the Holy Spirit to you, because it has become a means of attacking you. This is an obvious confusion of the body's purpose.

12. To communicate is to join, and to attack is to separate. If you try to do both simultaneously with the body, you will suffer. Your perception of the body can only be whole when it has only one purpose for you. By choosing one purpose, you will perceive the body only one way. Your confusing the body with the Goal of the lesson plan that you need to learn blocks your understanding of both the body and God. Your learning must lead beyond the body to re-establish the Power of your Mind that *seems* to be in it. This can only be accomplished if your Mind is free to extend Itself without limit, and so to be Whole. Limiting your Mind to a body is the cause of all illness in the body, because extension is your Mind's Function.

13. Depression is the opposite of Joy. When what you learn promotes depression instead of Joy, you are not listening to the Joyous Holy Spirit or following Its lessons. For you to see the body as anything

but a means of communicating the Holy Spirit to you is for you to limit your Mind and hurt yourself. Health is the result of a united purpose. If the body is brought under the Purpose of your Mind, it becomes whole, because your Mind's Purpose is One. Attack can only *seem* to be the body's purpose, because the body has no purpose apart from your Mind.

14. You are not limited by a body, and thought cannot be made flesh. But your Mind can be manifested *through* a body if It does not limit Itself *to* a body but goes beyond it. Whenever you look on *any* body as a real limitation on your Mind's extension of God's Love, you are limiting *yourself* to a body. But your whole purpose is to escape from all limitations. For you to perceive the body as a means of attack, and for you to believe that attack can bring you Joy, is for you to not learn of the Holy Spirit. Then your goal is in contradiction to the Holy Spirit's unified lesson plan, and it interferes with your ability to accept the Holy Spirit's Goal as your own.

15. Only God has a Unified Purpose, and It is Joy. When your purpose is unified, it will be God's Purpose. When you believe that you can interfere with God's Purpose, you believe that you need salvation. You have condemned yourself, but condemnation is not of God, so it is not Truth, and its results are not Truth. When you look on any body as a real limitation on your Mind's extension, you are condemning yourself. But all condemnation is unreal, since it is a form of attack, and it can have no real results.

16. Do not suffer from the imagined results of what is not true. Your freedom lies in the complete impossibility of the not-true having any real results. You are freed from illusions only by not believing in them. There is no attack, but there is Unlimited Communication, and therefore Unlimited Power and Wholeness. The Power of Wholeness is in Its extension. Do not limit your mind to a body in a world, and you will open your mind to God's Oneness.

8. The Body as Means or End

1. In your identification with a personal mind, your attitudes toward the body are attitudes toward attack, because the personal mind defines everything based on what it is using it *for*, rather than on

what the thing *is*. To the personal mind, the purpose of the body is to attack *with*, and because it equates you with the body, it teaches you that *you* are to attack with. The body is not the source of its own health, then, but its condition is the result of how you interpret its function. [*Your* Function is Part of your Being, because It comes from your Being, but the relationship is not reciprocal. The Whole defines the Part, but the Part does not define the Whole. In God, Which is One, to know Part is to Know the Whole, because God is All the Same and Unchanging. But in your perception of separation, whole things are made up of parts that can separate and reassemble into different wholes. Only at the level of perception of a world is *partly-whole* meaningful, because change is possible. In God, there is no difference between the Part and the Whole.]

2. The body seems to exist in a seeming world that contains two voices vying for its possession. Because you shift allegiance back and forth from the Holy Spirit to the personal mind, both the body's health and its sickness seem to be real to you. The body is a means of communication, not an end in itself, but the personal mind's goal for you is to perceive yourself as a body. Yet the personal mind has no real use for the body, because the body is not an end; it is nothing. The outstanding characteristic of all of the personal mind's goals is that *they have not satisfied you*. So the personal mind shifts ceaselessly from one goal to another, so that you will continue to hope that it has something to offer to you.

3. It is difficult for you to overcome the personal mind's goal that you identify with a body, because this is the same as its goal that you believe that you have attacked and separated from God. This belief is the personal mind's whole foundation. The personal mind has a profound investment in the body's sickness, because, if it is sick, it proves that *you* are vulnerable and cannot be of God. This argument appeals to the personal mind, because it obscures the source of the body's sickness, which is your attack on yourself by identifying with a personal self in a body. If you recognized this and stopped attacking yourself with your identification with a personal self, you would not give false witness to the separation

through a sick body.

4.   You do not recognize that the body's sickness is a false witness, because you have not wholly realized that you do not want the separation from God that the body's sickness seems to witness to. If you honestly look at the body's sickness, you will see that it is not such a strong witness to the personal self's reality. But because you want the personal self, you have chosen to use sickness as proof that it is real. The personal mind does not call upon witnesses that disagree with it, and neither does the Holy Spirit. The Holy Spirit's Function is to judge everything in the Light of God's Reality; the personal mind's judgment is biased toward its own reality.

5.   The body has no function of itself, because it is not real. But the personal mind makes the body real to you to obscure the Holy Spirit's function of communication for the body. The personal mind gives a purpose to everything that obscures your function of extending God. A sick body does not make any sense, because sickness is not what the body is for in the Holy Spirit's Perception. A sick body is meaningful only if you believe that the body is for attack, and that you are a body. Without these beliefs, the body's sickness has no purpose for you.

6.   The body's sickness is 'proof' that you can be hurt. It witnesses to your frailty, vulnerability, and your need for external guidance. The personal mind uses the body's sickness as an argument that you need *its* guidance, and it dictates endless prescriptions for avoiding catastrophe. The Holy Spirit recognizes that sickness is an error, and It does not bother to analyze its form, because it is meaningless. The Holy Spirit's Function is to extend Truth instead. *Any* way in which you handle sickness is meaningless, because it is nothing. The more complicated the sickness that results from error, the harder it is for you to recognize that it is nothing. But you do not have to examine all possible outcomes of error to judge it as nothing.

7.   The body is a learning device, not a teacher. It cannot tell you how you feel. You do not know how you feel, because you have accepted the personal mind's lesson that you are a body, and you believe that the body can tell you how you feel. The body's sickness is an

example of your insistence in asking the guidance of a teacher who does not know the answer to your question, 'What am I?' The personal mind itself cannot know how you feel. The only wholly true thing that you can say about the personal mind is that it does not know anything. Since it does not know anything, it has no reality.

8. The voice of the personal mind, which does not even exist, is so insistent in you, because you want it. It is an example of the power of your wanting, which can distort your perception even when what you want is not real. The personal mind has great skill in building illusions, and you will listen to it until you want only Truth. When you lay aside your desire for separation from God, the personal mind will be gone for you. The Holy Spirit's Voice is as loud as your willingness to listen to It. It cannot be louder than your willingness, because the Holy Spirit seeks to restore your freedom of choice, not to undermine it.

9. The Holy Spirit teaches you to use the body only as a means to extend God's Love in place of the world that your mind perceives so that you will teach yourself that only God's Love is Real. This will heal your mind. Anything that you use in accordance with the Holy Spirit's interpretation of its function cannot be sick; anything used for any other purpose *is* sick. Do not allow the body to mirror your split mind, or to be an image of your own perception of limitedness. Health is the natural state of everything when it is interpreted by the Holy Spirit, and it is the result of your giving up all love-less uses of the body. Health is the beginning of your proper perception of Life under the guidance of the Holy Spirit, Which is the Voice for Life Itself.

9. Healing as Corrected Perception

1. The Holy Spirit is the Answer to your question, 'What am I?' It is the Answer to everything, because the question 'What am I?' is the real question behind every question that you ask. The personal mind asks many questions, but it does not know what a real question is. You learn this as you begin to question the value of the personal mind, and to look at its questions. When the personal

mind tempts you to sickness, do not ask the Holy Spirit to heal the body, which is not the source of sickness. Ask instead that the Holy Spirit show you the correct *perception* of the body, because sickness is caused by your distorted perception of the body's purpose. Only perception can be sick or mistaken.

2. Wrong perception is your wish that God be different from What God is. Total Harmlessness is God's natural State of Being. Total Harmlessness is also the condition for your awareness of God. You do not have to seek for God, because God will dawn on your mind when you are Totally Harmless. Harmlessness is Part of What God is, and attaining Harmlessness is the only part of attaining God that is up to you. You need to do so little, because your part is so powerful that it will bring the Whole of God to your awareness. Accept your little part to know God again.

3. Wholeness is of the Mind, and only your Whole Mind heals. All forms of sickness, even unto death, are physical expressions of your fear of God. They are attempts to reinforce in your mind the reality of your separation from God. They are a pathetic attempt to make spiritual awareness ineffective by shutting it off. 'Rest in peace' is a blessing for the Living, not for the dead, because rest comes from being aware of God, not from denying God. [The dreams that you have when you sleep are illusions of joining, because they reflect the personal mind's distorted ideas of what joining is. But the Holy Spirit can use dreams to make you aware of God, if you turn them over to the Holy Spirit.

4. How you wake up after sleeping is how you have used sleep. Did you give your sleep to the Holy Spirit ,or to the personal mind? Whenever you awaken dispiritedly you did not give your rest to the Holy Spirit, because, if you had, you would have awoken Joyously. If you use sleep on behalf of sickness it *can* leave you stupefied and un-rested. Sleep is not a form of death anymore than death is a form of unconsciousness. Your mind can never be completely unconscious.] You can rest in Peace only when you are aware of God.

5. Healing happens to you when you decide to be aware of God, and to let go of your fear of God. Your decision to be aware of God

reflects your Will to Love, since all healing replaces fear with Love. The Holy Spirit does not distinguish between degrees of error. If the Holy Spirit taught you that one form of sickness is more serious than another, then the Holy Spirit would be teaching you that one form of sickness is more real than another. The Holy Spirit only distinguishes Truth from illusion, and It replaces illusion with Truth.

6. The personal mind always wants to weaken your True Mind. It tries to separate the body from your mind, which would destroy the body, because the True Power of your mind is the source of the thoughts that give rise to the body. But the personal mind thinks it is actually protecting the body by doing this. It projects its attack on you onto your True Mind, and it teaches you that your True Mind is attacking the body, and that removing you from your True Mind would heal the body. But your True Mind cannot be removed from you because It is of God. The personal mind despises weakness even though it tries to induce it in you. It always wants what it hates, because it wants to attack, believing that attack is the source of its power.

7. The Bible asks you to be perfect, to correct all errors, to have no thought of the body as separate from your mind, and to accomplish all things in the name of Jesus Christ. But Christ is not Jesus' Name alone, because you share the Christ Identity. The Name of Christ is One, and you are asked to do the works of Love, because your Mind is One and Whole. When you are sick, you are withdrawing from your Christ Mind. And when you withdraw from your Christ Mind, you withdraw from your Self.

8. This is a practical course that means exactly what it says. The Holy Spirit does not ask you to do what you cannot do, and it is impossible for the Holy Spirit to do what *you* cannot do. Nothing can prevent you from doing what the Holy Spirit asks, and everything argues *for* your doing it. The Holy Spirit cannot limit you, because God does not limit you. When you limit yourself you are not of One Mind, and that is sickness. Sickness is of your mind, not of the body. All forms of sickness signal that your mind is split, and that you do not accept One Purpose.

9. One Purpose, then, is the Holy Spirit's way of healing you. Healing only has meaning at the level of your mind, and re-establishing Meaning in the chaotic thought system that you made is the only way to heal your mind. Meaning is of God, and your only part is to meet the conditions of Meaning. Your return to Meaning is essential to God's Meaning, because your Meaning is Part of God's Meaning. Your healing is part of God's Wholeness. God cannot lose Its Wholeness, but you can forget It. Yet Wholeness is still God's Will for you, and God's Will is Forever and Everywhere.

Chapter 9

The Acceptance of the Atonement

1. The Acceptance of Reality

1. Fear of the Will of God is the strangest belief that you have ever made with the personal mind. It could only happen because your mind is split and has become afraid of What It really is. Reality only threatens *illusions*, because Reality only upholds Truth. The Will of God is What you are, and your fear of It means that you are afraid of What you are. It is *your* True Will that you are afraid of.

2. Your True Will is not the personal mind's will, and that is why the personal mind is against you. Your fear of God is your fear of your own Reality. You cannot learn anything consistently in a state of panic. The purpose of this course is to help you remember What you are, and if you believe that What you are is frightening, then you will not learn this course. But the reason *for* this course is that you do not know What you are.

3. Since you don't know your Reality, why are you so sure It is frightening? Associating Truth with fear is inappropriate when you do not know what Truth is. You are arbitrarily judging against Something that you don't know, and then you are deciding against It. You can only get out of this strange situation with a Guide Which *does* know your Reality. This Guide's Purpose is simply to remind you of What you want. The Holy Spirit is not trying to impose an alien will on you, but, within the limits that you put on It, to bring your own Will to your awareness.

4. You have pushed your True Will out of your awareness, and though It still exists, It cannot help you. To sort out Truth from illusion, the Holy Spirit looks at What you are denying, and finds the Will of God. The Holy Spirit is in your mind, so Its recognition of God's Will brings your Reality to your mind, and reminds you of What you are. Your only fear in this process is your fear of losing the personal self. But only What the Holy Spirit sees can possibly

be What you really have.

5.   The Holy Spirit does not ask you to sacrifice, but, if you ask
      yourself to sacrifice Reality, the Holy Spirit will remind you that
      this is not God's Will or yours. There is no difference between your
      Will and God's Will. Your mind is split, so you do not recognize that
      sharing God's Will is your salvation because It is Oneness.

6.   You cannot be aware of your Oneness with God when you want to
      be separate from God. You and God are One, and this is your Joint
      Will. But a divided mind cannot be One in its own awareness,
      because each part is different from the other, and this leads to
      confusion and loss of meaning. Only Oneness makes sense
      throughout your mind *because* it is One. It does not make sense for
      you to ask for what you do not want, but, as long as you are afraid
      of your True Will, that is what you are asking for.

7.   You may think that the Holy Spirit does not answer you, but
      consider what you are asking for. You do not ask for only your True
      Will, Which is All that you really want. This is because you are
      afraid that you will find out What your True Will is – and you will.
      So you persist in asking the personal mind to show you your will,
      but it cannot possibly know. This seems safe to you. Yet you cannot
      be safe *from* Truth, only safe *in* Truth. Only Reality is Safety. Your
      Will is your salvation because it is God's Will. Your perception of
      separation from God is only your belief that your will is different
      from God's Will.

8.   But you cannot believe that your will is *stronger* than God's Will, so
      you must believe that it is *different* from God's Will. This leaves you
      believing, like an atheist, that there is no God, or, like a martyr, that
      God's Will is frightening because It demands sacrifices. Either of
      these beliefs will make you panic, because you will believe either
      that you are alone, or that God is crucifying you. You may seek to
      be lonely or punished, but you cannot really want either of these.
      So you cannot ask the Holy Spirit for these 'gifts' and really expect
      to get them. The Holy Spirit cannot give you what you do not really
      want, because it is not Real. It is not Real because it is not *your* True
      Will for you.

9.   You will ultimately remember God, because you will ultimately

recognize your True Self. This Recognition is your realization that your Will and God's Will are One. In God's Presence there are no atheists or martyrs. In the Security of God's Reality fear is meaningless. Denying the Truth can only *seem* frightening to you. Fear is not real because it is without a cause; God is the only Cause. God is Love, and you *do* want God. This *is* your True Will. Ask for This and you will be answered, because you will be asking for What belongs to you.

10. When you ask the Holy Spirit for what will hurt you It cannot answer, because nothing can hurt you, so you are asking for nothing. Any wish that you have that comes from the personal mind is a wish for nothing, and it is really your denial of God in the form of a request. But the Holy Spirit is not concerned with form, only meaning, and the personal mind cannot ask the Holy Spirit for anything, because they cannot join. *You* can ask for Everything of the Holy Spirit, because your real requests come from your awareness of your Oneness with the Holy Spirit. The Holy Spirit cannot deny the Will of God or fail to recognize God's Will in you.

11. You do not see how much energy you waste denying God. You persist in attempting the impossible – separation from God – and you believe that achieving it would be success. You believe that you must have the impossible to be happy, and this conflicts with your Oneness with God. God does not Will that you be happy with what you can never have. God is Love, and this is a Fact that does not require your belief but your acceptance. You can deny Fact, but you cannot change It. If you hold your hands over your eyes you will not see, because you are interfering with the law of seeing. By the same token, if you deny Love you will not know that It is Truth, because your knowing It is the Law of Its Being. You cannot change Laws that you did not make, and the Law of Happiness comes from God, not from you.

12. It is frightening to deny What *is*, and your strong denial of It makes you panic. Only God is Real, and as Part of God you can want only God. But you can *seem* to persist in making the impossible goal of willing against Reality, and you can *seem* to devote your mind to

what you do not want. But your devotion cannot be real. Since what you want is not One with God, it is not Real; it is nothing. You cannot really devote yourself to nothing.

13. God is devoted to you, and in your Oneness with God you are devoted to God, or you would not be Whole. God is Everything and Reality, and you have Everything because you are Real. You cannot make the un-Real, because to lack Reality is frightening, and you cannot be One with lack and fear. As long as you believe fear is real, you will not extend God. Your concept of opposing realities makes God meaningless to you, but God's Reality *is* Meaning.

14. God's Will is All that will ever be. If you accept This, you accept Reality. You cannot make a different reality and know What Reality is. When you do believe that something other than God is real, you experience anxiety, depression, and panic, because you seem to be making yourself un-Real. When you feel these things, remember that the Truth is in you:

'Christ is in me, and Christ is in God.'

2. The Answer to Prayer

1. You may have experienced what seems to be failure when you have used prayer, not only in connection with things that are harmful to you, but also with requests that are in line with this course. You may incorrectly interpret this as 'proof' that this course is misleading. But you must remember that this course's purpose is to teach you to escape from fear.

2. If you ask the Holy Spirit for something that you want but that you fear, then your attainment of it would not really be what you want. Sometimes you don't achieve specific *forms* of healing, even when you have changed your mind enough to call on the Holy Spirit. For example, you may ask for physical healing because you are afraid of physical pain and discomfort. But in your identification with a personal self physical healing that comes from the Holy Spirit may be more threatening to you than the physical discomfort that you are experiencing. In this case, you are not really asking for release from fear, which is true healing, but from release from the *symptoms*

of fear that you have chosen.

3.   The Bible says that all prayers are answered, and this is true. When you ask the Holy Spirit you will be answered, but the answer will never be one that increases your fear. You may not hear the Holy Spirit's answer, but the answer will not be lost. You have received many answers that you have not heard, and they are waiting for you to hear them.

4.   If you want to know that your prayers are answered, never doubt your Christ Mind. Your faith in Christ is your faith in yourself. If you want to know God and the Holy Spirit, believe in your Christ Mind, Which has complete faith in you. You cannot call on the Holy Spirit and doubt the Christ in you. Extend the Holy Spirit to replace the world of separation in your mind, and hear only the Truth. As you listen only to your extension of the Holy Spirit, you will learn of the Christ in you. Listening for the Truth is the only way that you can hear Truth and know that you have It.

5.   The message that you receive from others is determined by whether you project separation onto them or extend God's Love to them. Remember to replace the personal mind's projections with the Holy Spirit, and you will hear the Holy Spirit. Your Holy extension of the Holy Spirit can tell you only of Truth. The personal mind's projections onto others may seem to be real to you, but the Holy Spirit is always present, and you can learn to listen for It instead. This is the Holy Spirit's Answer to your prayers if your faith in It is strong enough to hear It.

6.   You cannot pray for a personal self any more than you can find joy in a personal self. True prayer restates your Oneness with God through the Holy Spirit's awareness of It. Your salvation comes from you extending the Holy Spirit to replace the personal mind's projections, and the Holy Spirit is the Answer to your prayers. You cannot hear the Holy Spirit in the personal mind, because the personal mind is not What you are, and the Holy Spirit's *is* What you are. You will not know that your Christ Mind trusts you unless you extend this Trust by trusting the Holy Spirit. You will not trust the Holy Spirit's guidance, or believe that it is for you, unless you extend the Holy Spirit to replace the personal mind's projections

onto others. The Holy Spirit must be for what you perceive *because* it is for you. God did not give you the Holy Spirit for you to limit It to the personal mind, but as the Answer for your entire mind. Do not be deceived by the seeming reality of a world, but extend your Christ Mind in place of it.

7.   The Christ in you loves the Truth in you, as God does. You can believe in the deceptions of the split mind, but you cannot deceive the Christ in you, because It knows you are Christ. The Christ in you only hears the Holy Spirit in you. If you want to hear the Christ in you, hear the Holy Spirit in your in mind where you perceive a world. The Holy Spirit is the Answer to all of your prayers. Your prayers will be answered as you hear the Answer everywhere. Do not listen to anything else, because only the Holy Spirit is the Truth.

8.   You will learn that the belief your Christ Mind has in you is justified when you extend It in place of the personal mind's projections. Believe in your Christ Mind *by* extending It in place of the world of separation that you perceive, and your prayers will be answered with the Truth. Extend blessing to learn that you are blessed by God. When you do this, you are seeking the Truth in you, and you are not going beyond yourself, but toward yourself. Hear only the Holy Spirit in place of the personal mind's projections, and your prayers will be answered.

9.   The personal mind teaches you that what you don't believe in you side against and attack, and what you do believe in you accept and side with. But it also teaches you that to believe in God is to be gullible. But belief means to accept and to appreciate. When you don't believe in God, you don't appreciate God, because you cannot be grateful for what you do not value. Judgment of value sets a price, and as you set the price you will pay it.

10.   If you view giving God's Love as a means of getting something for the personal self, you will give little while hoping for a high return of what you seek. But, as with any payment, what you give attests to the value that you have put on what you are getting. If you understand that extending God's Love will strengthen your awareness of It within your own mind, you will extend God's Love

everywhere. When you limit your extension of God's Love to giving It to get something, you lose sight of the value of God's Love. Not valuing It, you will not appreciate It or want It.

11. You decide how much you value God's Love, and you extend God's Love to the extent that you value It, because extending It is how you keep It in your awareness. For you to believe that you can limit your extension of God and still become fully aware of God, is for you to believe that you can bargain with God to hold some of your mind back for the personal self. But God's Law is fair and perfectly consistent: *What you extend you accept as part of you.* It is impossible for you to not have God's Love, but it is possible for you to be *unaware* that you have It. When you recognize What you have, you will be willing to extend It, and only by this willingness to extend It will you recognize that you have It. You extend God's Love to the extent that you value and want It.

12. You ask the Holy Spirit to answer your prayers by extending the Holy Spirit to replace the world of separation that you perceive. If you recognize that the Holy Spirit is everywhere because your mind is everywhere, you will be asking the Holy Spirit for Everything, and you will be receiving Everything. The Holy Spirit cannot deny you anything, unless you deny the Presence of the Holy Spirit. The Holy Spirit's Answer to your prayers is all that you can ask for and receive. So say everywhere:

'Because I am willing to know myself, I choose to perceive the Holy Spirit.'

3. The Correction of Error

1. The personal mind in you is alert to the errors of other personal selves in the world that you perceive, but this is not the type of awareness that the Holy Spirit wants you to maintain. The personal mind has its own ideas of what is sensible, and it criticizes other personal selves that do not seem to agree with it. This makes sense to the personal mind. but not to the Holy Spirit.

2. To the personal mind, it is kind and right and good to point out errors in other personal selves and 'correct' them. But the personal

mind is unaware of what actual error is, and it is unaware of how to correct it. Your identification with a personal self is an error. and anything that the personal mind projects is an error. The way to let go of errors, then, is to let go of the personal self. When you correct another personal self, you are making error real to you by making the personal mind's projections real to you. But it is your job to overlook the personal mind's projections, and to look only on the Holy Spirit. You do not have to say anything to others; you only withdraw the personal mind's projections, and extend the Holy Spirit in your mind. No matter what the personal mind projects onto another, it is always an error.

3. When you point out errors in other personal selves, you are looking at the personal mind's projections of separation, because the Holy Spirit in you does not perceive errors. There is no communication between the personal mind and the Holy Spirit, and since the personal mind does not make any sense to the Holy Spirit, the Holy Spirit does not try to understand anything that it projects. The Holy Spirit does not judge what comes from the personal mind. because It knows that the personal mind is nothing.

4. When you react to the personal mind's projections onto others, you are not listening to the Holy Spirit. The Holy Spirit merely overlooks the personal mind's projections, and if you look on them as real, you will not hear the Holy Spirit. When you do not hear the Holy Spirit, you are listening to the personal mind, and making as little sense as the errors that you perceive in others. This is not correction. But this is more than not correction in others; it is not correction in yourself.

5. When another's behavior disturbs you, you can heal your mind only by perceiving the Holy Spirit instead. When you see error in others, you are accepting your own error of identifying with a personal self, and projecting it onto them. If you want to give over your error to the Holy Spirit, you must give over all error that you project anywhere, and replace it with a perception of the Holy Spirit. This is the one way to handle all errors and undo them. What you teach you learn. The Holy Spirit is everywhere, but if you look on the personal mind's projections as real, you are making an error,

and believing that you are guilty of separating from God.

6. The personal mind cannot correct error in you or in its projections onto others. But you can extend the Holy Spirit in place of the personal mind's projections, and perceive the Truth in you instead. Do not try to change others, but accept them as they are. The errors that you perceive in them do not come from the Holy Spirit, and only the Holy Spirit is Real in you and in your perceptions. Any error that you see anywhere cannot change this, and error can have no effect on the Holy Spirit at all. When you react to error in others, you make error real to you, and you lose your way, not because you are being punished, but because you are following the wrong guide.

7. Errors that you see in yourself or that you project onto others do not come from the Truth in you. Accept error as real anywhere and you attack yourself. If you want to find your way back to God, see that only the Truth is with you. The Holy Spirit in you forgives all seeming error in you and in your perception. Forgiving one is forgiving the other, because your mind is not really split. Correction cannot come to only one part of your mind, because it comes from Love, Which is Oneness. When you attempt to correct another, it is the arrogance of the personal mind, which mistakenly thinks it has the power to correct. True Correction comes from God.

8. The Holy Spirit corrects every error of separation in your mind, because your mind is really One with God. Do not try to correct from the personal mind, or you will forget that your function is healing your mind of your mistaken belief in the personal self's reality. Healing is your only function in time, and healing is all that time is for. In Eternity, your Function is to extend God. You do not need to learn this, but only to want this. That is the only purpose that the Holy Spirit gives to learning, an ability that you do not need in God, but that you made. Give learning to the Holy Spirit, because you do not really know how to use it. The Holy Spirit will teach you how to see yourself without guilt by teaching you how to perceive without guilt. Guilt will then lose reality for you, and you will forgive your errors.

4. The Holy Spirit's Plan of Forgiveness

1. Correction encompasses your entire mind, because it is the way that you undo your belief that part of your mind is separate and outside of you. To forgive is to overlook, so overlook the error of your perception of separation, because otherwise you will believe what you perceive. Accept that only the Holy Spirit is Real if you want to know yourself. But perceive the personal mind and its projections as real, and you will not know What you are. Remember that your Identity is One, and Its Reality is that It is Everywhere.

2. You have a part to play in the plan of the Atonement, Which is the total correction of your perception of separation from God. The plan does not come from the personal mind, because from the personal mind you do not know how to overlook your perception of separation from God, or you would not make it real to you. It would be only another error for you to believe that you do not make the perception of separation, or that you can correct it without the Holy Spirit. If you do not follow the Holy Spirit, your errors will not be corrected. The plan does not come from your identification with a personal self, because this limited identity is the error from which all of your other errors arise. But the plan is *for* you.

3. The plan of the Atonement is a Lesson in extending Oneness, which you have forgotten how to do. The Holy Spirit reminds you of the natural use of the abilities that you have made for separation by reinterpreting them into abilities that will extend God's Oneness in your awareness. If you want to use these abilities through the Holy Spirit, you cannot judge them as the personal mind does. The personal mind judges your abilities as a means to make separation from God real to you; the Holy Spirit judges your abilities as a means to remind you that you are One with God.

4. Because you ask for forgiveness, the personal mind also has a plan of forgiveness. The personal mind's plan, of course, makes no sense, and it will not work. The personal mind's plan is to make separation from God real to you first, and then to have you overlook it. But you cannot overlook what is real to you. So in its religions, your split mind resorts to meaningless 'mysteries' that

are supposed to save you, but that you are not supposed to be able to comprehend. This is sometimes done in Jesus' name, forgetting that Jesus' words are inspired by God, and that they are clear, because they speak of Ideas that are Eternal.

5. The forgiving that you learn from your Christ Mind does not use your fear of the unknown to undo fear, nor does it make what isn't real, real to you before destroying it. Your forgiving through the Holy Spirit overlooks from the beginning your belief in separation from God, therefore it never makes the personal self real to you. If you let any belief in the realness of the personal self enter your mind, you will also believe that you must undo it to be forgiven. But what has no effect does not exist, and, to the Holy Spirit, the personal self has no effects. By steadily and consistently canceling out all of the seeming effects of your identification with a personal self everywhere, the Holy Spirit proves to you that the personal self does not exist.

6. Teaching you forgiveness is the Holy Spirit's function, and the Holy Spirit knows how to wholly fulfill Its function. Extending God's Love is natural to you, and when you do not extend God's Love, something has gone wrong. Your extension of God's Love is merely a sign of your willingness to follow the Holy Spirit's plan of salvation, because, in your identification with a personal self, you do not know how. Only if you can accept that correction is the Holy Spirit's function and not the personal mind's function, can you learn that *accepting* correction is *your* function.

7. It is typical of the personal mind to confuse its function with the Holy Spirit's function. The personal mind believes that all functions belong to it, even when it does not know what they are for. In your identification with the personal mind this leads you to self-importance, and a confusion that makes you likely to attack anyone and anything for no reason. In your identification with the personal mind you are unpredictable in your responses, because you never know what is really happening.

8. If you do not understand what is happening, you will not respond appropriately. Regardless of how often you can find an explanation for how you respond through the personal mind, you should ask

yourself if the personal mind's unpredictability makes it the best guide for you. The personal mind's qualifications as a guide are questionable, and it is a poor teacher of salvation. It is not sound, and you have to be unsound yourself to follow it. It isn't true that you do not recognize that it is unsound, because your Christ Mind knows it is unsound, and your Christ Mind is within you.

9. The personal self lives on borrowed time, because its 'life' is borrowed from your Eternity. Do not fear the Last Judgment, but welcome It as you do the Second Coming of Christ, which is only your return to sense. This is not fearful.

10. Only illusions are frightening, and you only turn to illusions when you despair of finding satisfaction in Reality. But you will never find satisfaction in illusions, so you must change your mind about Reality. Only if you are mistaken in your decision to make Reality fearful is God right about What you are. You have been mistaken about God, because you do not know yourself. If you knew yourself, you could not have been wrong about God anymore than God could be wrong about God.

11. The impossible can happen only in illusions, and when you search for Real Meaning in them, you will not find It. The many signs of separation from God that you see are interpretations of the personal mind, so do not look for Real Meaning in them. The signs themselves have no more meaning than the illusion of separation into which they have been woven. Illusions can be pleasant or fearful, but never true. You may believe in them, and while you do they are true for you. But Reality is not gone. When you remember Reality, illusions will disappear. The Second Coming of Christ is not the return of Reality, but merely your awareness that It is always here.

12. For you who are One with God, Reality is here. It belongs to you and God, and It is Perfectly Satisfying. This is the awareness that heals you, because it is your awareness of Truth.

5. The Unhealed Healer

1. The personal mind's plan for forgiveness is what you teach yourself in your percepton that you are in a world, because you are an

unhealed healer. By definition, an unhealed healer tries to give forgiveness without having accepted forgiveness for their self. If you are religious, you may teach: 'I am a miserable sinner, and so are you.' If your approach is psychological, you make separation from God real for you by teaching that the individual personal self's story is reality, and that God does not matter in the healing process.

2. Each personal self has its own separate story, so personal minds cannot be One, and therefore they are not Reality. Uncovering your individual beliefs about a personal 'life' in psychotherapy is not going to turn this story into Reality. When you seek for truth in your illusions you must be unhealed, because you don't know where to look for Truth, and you don't know that only Truth heals.

3. There *is* an advantage in looking at your hidden beliefs, but only to learn that they are not real, and that they are meaningless. But if you are an unhealed healer you won't do this, because you won't believe it, and you'll follow the personal mind's plan of forgiveness in one form or another. If you are religious, you are likely to feel guilty for separating from God, to teach that guilt is real, and to advocate a form of payment or punishment to absolve your guilt. The personal mind *does* condemn you, and when you identify with it, you will project its condemnation of you onto God. You will believe that God is going to retaliate against you, and you will fear God's retribution. It is understandable if you have revolted against this concept of God, but revolting against it means that you believe in it.

4. Psychotherapy is one of the newer forms of the personal mind's plan of forgiveness, but the content remains the same. In psychotherapy, a personal self's story is reinforced as your reality. Since the personal identity is validated as real, the Power of your Mind is denied. For example, you may interpret the symbols in a nightmare that you have while sleeping as representing something bad that 'really' happened in the personal self's past. Now that this event is real to you, you then must deny the role that your mind plays in *choosing* what is real to you. This can lead to healing if you

realize that it is the personal mind that made this event real to you, and that it is as unreal as the event it has imagined. But if you identify with the personal mind and deny the role your mind plays in deciding what is real to you, you will deny the Holy Spirit's ability to correct your mind. Even in its confusion the personal mind recognizes the contradiction in attempting to heal the mind while diminishing its importance.

5. Even the personal mind will not grow strong if you counteract fear by reducing the importance of the mind. This inconsistency explains why nothing really happens in the personal mind's version of psychotherapy. If the therapist is an unhealed healer, he or she must learn from what they teach, and they are teaching nothing real. They are in the relationship with the patient to get something, but they don't know to extend God's Love, therefore they are not working correctively for themselves through their perception of the patient. The therapist attempts to teach their patient what is real without knowing Reality for themselves.

6. God has given you the ability to understand Truth. You cannot understand Truth by analyzing illusions like the psychotherapist. Nor, like the religious teacher, can you understand that Truth is in you by seeing sin in yourself, and looking to a distant God to remove it. Healing is not mysterious. Nothing will change until you understand Truth. If you could really be a 'miserable sinner' or an 'unimportant mind,' then you *could* only be healed by something outside of you.

7. Both forms of the personal mind's forgiveness will arrive at the characteristic irresolvable situation that the personal mind always leads to. An unhealed therapist or religious teacher may help someone see that where they are heading is not healthy, but they will not help another heal since they cannot show them how to change direction. A healer is one who has allowed their own direction to be changed for them by the Holy Spirit, and who no longer believes in separation from God. You are a healer when you extend God's Love in place of the personal mind's projections, and you learn that God's Love is within you. This is how your split mind is returned to Oneness. Extend God's Love continually, and

accept that It is here, and the Peace that this brings will assure you that It *is* here.

8.   A healer does not heal 'others' but recognizes that *healing is here*. Healing does not come from the personal mind, but it is within you, and you must extend it in your mind where you perceive a world. The Holy Spirit is the only Therapist, and It heals in any situation in which you let It guide you. Your part is only to put the personal mind aside, and let the Holy Spirit fulfill Its Function. You will be told exactly what to do or say in every encounter to teach yourself. You choose which guide you will follow; the personal mind will not help you, but the Holy Spirit always will. Trust the Holy Spirit, because helping you is the Holy Spirit's function, and the Holy Spirit comes from God. As you extend the Holy Spirit in place of the personal mind's projections, you will understand that you are not obeying the laws of the world that you perceive, but you are obeying Laws that work.

9.   This course provides you with a very direct and simple lesson plan, and it provides you with an awareness of the Teacher Which can tell you what to do. If you do what you are told, you will see that this plan works, and its results will be more convincing than this course's words. In fact, only the results will convince you that these words are true. By following the Holy Spirit you will learn this simple lesson:

Extend God's Love, and you will know yourself by your results.

6. The Acceptance of Your Brother

1.   You become increasingly aware of the Holy Spirit in you by Its Effects within your mind. You cannot see the Holy Spirit with the body's eyes, or hear It with the body's ears. If you perceive Joy even if you are not experiencing Joy yourself, there must be Something in you that is producing It. Then, if you are not experiencing Joy, it is because you are separating yourself from It.

2.   If it seems to you that the Holy Spirit does not consistently produce Joy in you, it is because you do not consistently extend Joy. You evaluate the Holy Spirit's consistency by your awareness of your

extensions of Joy, so if you are inconsistent it seems to you that the Holy Spirit is inconsistent. You can only be aware of Joy by extending It from the Holy Spirit within you, so the Holy Spirit cannot extend more Joy to you than you are willing to accept for yourself by extending It. The Holy Spirit's extension of Joy is unlimited. but you decide how much Joy you will accept by how much Joy you are willing to extend.

3.   The world is in your mind, but will you accept this? Only what you perceive can teach you what you are, because what you learn is determined by what you project or extend. What you call upon to perceive you call upon in yourself, and, by your perceiving it, it becomes real to you. God is One and knows your Mind as One. Only God is more than your Whole Mind, but your Whole Mind is not less than God. As what your mind perceives, what you project or extend affects your awareness of your Christ Mind. This is Oneness. Every part of your mind is part of you and Part of God, and shares in God's Glory. God's Glory is God's, so it is also yours. You cannot be less Glorious than God.

4.   God is only more than you because God is your Source and you are God's Extension, but God does not keep Itself from you. You extend God as God extends God to you, and not even your choice to perceive yourself as separate from God can change this. You remember your Oneness with God every time that you extend God's Love in place of the personal mind's projections. Your every extension of God's Love is whole and adds to your sense of wholeness, but you will not fully understand your Wholeness until you extend God's Love every-where. You can know yourself only in your Oneness with God. When you fully remember God, you will know your Limitlessness by accepting God's Limitlessness as your own. But in your perception that you are in a world, you will judge yourself as limited by the limits that you put on extending God's Love.

5.   You will learn how to fully remember God as you learn from the Holy Spirit how to extend God's Love everywhere to replace the personal mind's projections. As you learn the value of the effects of this, you will be filled with gratitude and appreciation. Your extension of God in your mind where you perceive a world will

witness to your Reality, as in Heaven your Extension of God witnesses to God's Reality. When in your awareness your Mind is Whole and One again, you will know It by Its Extension of God, Which will witness to your Reality and to God's Reality.

6. You don't need to experience miracles in Eternity, because they are healing. But while you still need healing, miracles are the witnesses to your Reality. You cannot extend miracles from a personal mind, because miracles are a way of giving God's Love to receive God's Love. In time, giving comes first, but in Eternity, giving and receiving are simultaneous, because All is One. When you have learned this, you will no longer need time.

7. Eternity is timelessness; It is 'always'. You will not understand this until you remember God's Limitless Mind. Like God, you are 'always'; in God's Mind and with a Mind like God's. In your Limitless Mind is your Extension of God, with Which you are One, and Which you fully understand. If only once you are fully aware of extending God, you will not want to perceive the world anymore, because you will see that it is meaningless. God's Meaning is incomplete without you, and you are incomplete without your Extension of God. Extend God's Love to replace the world in your mind and accept nothing else, and you will find your Extension of God and know your Oneness. You will never know that you are One with God until you learn that what your mind perceives is One with you.

7. The Two Evaluations

1. God's Will is your salvation, and God has given you the Means to find salvation easily. The Holy Spirit is everywhere in your mind, so you do not have to seek far for salvation. Every second gives you a chance to save yourself, and when you do not use these chances, you delay Joy for yourself. God's Will for you is Perfect Happiness right now. This is your Will, and the Will of your mind where you perceive a world, because your entire mind is One.

2. Your mind is united only in this Joint Will and in nothing else. This is Where your Peace is, and you will abide in Peace when you decide to accept correction of your perception that separation from

169

God is real. Correction is your only way to Peace. The reason is simple and obvious, but you overlook it. The personal mind is threatened by the obvious, because Reality is obvious. But you cannot overlook Reality unless you *choose to not look at It.*

3. Obviously, if the Holy Spirit looks with Love on you, It looks with Love on all that It perceives. The Holy Spirit knows What you are, so It evaluates you Truly. This evaluation is in your mind, because the Holy Spirit is in your mind, but so is your perception of separation from God, because you have accepted it there. The personal mind's evaluation of you is the exact opposite of the Holy Spirit's, because the personal mind does not love you. It does not know What you are, and it distrusts everything it sees, because its perceptions are constantly shifting. The personal mind is at best suspicious and at worst vicious. It cannot exceed this range because of its uncertainty, and it can never go beyond this range, because it can never *be* certain.

4. So you have two conflicting evaluations of yourself in your mind, and they cannot both be true. But you do not realize how completely different these evaluations of you are, because you do not under-stand how Exalted is the Holy Spirit's evaluation of you. The Holy Spirit is never deceived by what you do in your perception that you are in a world, and It never forgets What you are. The personal mind is always deceived by what you do, and most especially when it is confused by your response to the Holy Spirit. The personal mind is most likely to attack you when you respond Lovingly, because its evaluation of you is that you are un-Loving. Whenever your motives are out of accord with its perception of you, the personal mind will attack them, shifting abruptly from suspiciousness to viciousness in its uncertainty. But it does not make sense for you to attack the personal mind in return, because then you are accepting its evalu-ation of you as un-Loving.

5. You will not be happy if you choose to see yourself as un-Loving. If you do, you will limit yourself and regard yourself as inadequate. Don't turn to the personal mind to escape from your sense of inade-quacy, because it produced it, and it must maintain it for its own existence. You cannot escape the personal mind's evaluation of you

by using the methods it uses for keeping this image of you intact.

6.   You cannot escape the personal mind's belief system from within it, but you can go beyond it to the Holy Spirit and look back at the contrast. Only in this contrast can you see that the personal mind makes no sense. With the Limitlessness of God within you, you have chosen to be limited to a personal mind, and to whine about it. But you never ask who limited you, because for you to do so would open up the personal mind's whole thought system to question for you.

7.   The personal mind does not know what a real question is, because it doesn't really want to know the Truth. For you to not question your sense of limitedness is for you to deny Truth so that you can keep the personal mind's thought system intact. You can only question the personal mind's thought system at its source, which is your belief that your separation from God is real. This must be done from outside of the personal mind's thought system, because you are not within it. The Holy Spirit judges against the reality of the personal mind's thought system, because it knows that its source is not true. Since it is not true, anything that arises from it means nothing. The Holy Spirit judges everything from its source, and if its Source is God, then It knows that it is True, but if its source is not God, then It knows that it is meaningless.

8.   Whenever you question your value say:

'I am One with God.'

If you remember this when the personal mind speaks, you will not hear the personal mind. The Truth about you is so Exalted that only What is worthy of God is worthy of you. Choose what you want in these terms, and accept only What you would offer to God as wholly appropriate for God. You do not want anything else. Return yourself to God, and God will give you All of God in exchange for the return of you who completes God.

8. Grandeur versus Grandiosity

1.   God is Limitless, therefore so are you. Whenever you become even

dimly aware of your Limitlessness you automatically let go of the personal self, because you see how limited it is in comparison. The personal mind perceives this as an attack on it, and offers you 'gifts' to return to its 'protection'. Personal self-inflation is the only offer that it can make to you, and this is its alternative to God's Limitless Being. Which will you choose?

2. Personal self-inflation is always a cover for your despair over your sense of limitedness in your identification with a personal self, and it is hopeless for you to think that it can bring you relief, because it is not real. But when you identify with a personal self, your limitedness *is* real to you. If you didn't believe that you were limited, then personal self-inflation would be meaningless to you, and you wouldn't want it. Personal self-inflation is an attack on you, because a limited personal identity is an attack on you, and puffing up this identity only competes further with the Limitless Truth in you. It is your delusional attempt to *outdo* the Truth, but it will not *undo* the pain caused by your sense of separation from God. The personal mind is only suspicious of you as long as you despair over your limitedness, but it becomes vicious toward you when you decide that you will no longer tolerate it and seek for relief in Truth. Then it attacks you with personal self-inflation as a 'solution'.

3. The personal mind does not understand that there is a difference between its own self-inflation and God's Limitlessness, because it perceives both as forms of attack. When you abandon it to experience God's Limitlessness, it experiences this as an attack, and it attacks you back by grabbing your attention with self-inflation. It also cannot distinguish between sources of threat. It experiences both your Natural Impulse to extend God's Love and its own fearful perceptions of God as the same threat to its existence, even though one is a real threat, and the other is not. Perceiving threat and feeling vulnerable, it attacks you. Its only decision is whether to attack you now or withdraw to attack you later. If you accept its offer of personal self-inflation, it will attack you with it immediately; if you do not, it will wait.

4. The limited personal self is put out of your mind when you are aware of God's Limitlessness, because in God you are Free. Just a

hint of your Reality drives the personal self out of your mind, because you do not really want it. God's Limitlessness is without illusions, and It is compelling because It is Real. But your certainty of God's Reality will not stay with you if you allow the personal mind to attack you. If you let it, the personal mind will recover and mobilize against your release. It will tell you that you are insane and argue that God's Limitlessness cannot be within you, because you are limited. But your Limitlessness is not insane, because you did not make It. You made personal self-inflation, and you are afraid of it, because it is a form of attack on God. But your Limitlessness is from God and was given to you out of Love.

5. Your Limitlessness can only bless you, because It is your Abundance. By extending blessing, you hold your Limitlessness in your mind, protecting your mind from illusions, and keeping yourself in the Mind of God. You can only ever be in the Mind of God. When you forget this, you will despair and you will attack.

6. The personal mind relies on your willingness to tolerate it. If you look upon your Limitlessness you will not despair, and you will not want the personal mind. Your Limitlessness is God's Answer to the personal mind, because It is True and the personal mind is not. The personal self, inflated or not, cannot coexist with Limitlessness. And you cannot really alternate between them, because they are not both real. But your sense of limitedness and personal self-inflation *do* alternate, because they are extremes on the same level of constantly shifting illusions.

7. Truth and limitedness deny each other, because Truth is Limitless. Truth is always True, and It cannot vacillate. When you lose sight of your Limitlessness it is because you have replaced It with a personal self. It does not matter if the personal self feels small or inflated, it is never you. Your Limitlessness will never deceive you, but your illusions always will. You will not triumph over the personal self, but you *will* rise above its limits. In your Limitlessness you can only extend the Limitless and rejoice.

8. It is easy to distinguish the Grandeur of God's Limitlessness from the pride of the puffed-up personal self, because God's Love can be extended from you, but pride cannot. Pride does not produce an

173

awareness of God's Love, so it deprives you of the experience of the miracle, which witnesses to your Reality. Truth is not hidden, and Its obviousness lies in the Joy you extend from It and that returns to you. Your experience of miracles attests to the Grandeur of your Limitlessness but not to pride, because pride is limited to the personal self and cannot be extended. God wants you to look only on God's Extension, because It is God's Joy.

9. The Grandeur of your Limitlessness is not arrogance, because God witnesses to It, and only What God witnesses to is Real. Nothing Good can come of what you cannot share with God, and the Holy Spirit only has use for what is Good. What the Holy Spirit cannot translate into the Will of God does not exist. Personal self-inflation is delusional, because you use it to replace your Limitlessness, and What is Part of God cannot be replaced. God is incomplete without you, because God's Limitlessness encompasses Everything, and that means you.

10. You are irreplaceable in the Mind of God. Nothing can fill your Part in God, and, while you leave It empty, your Eternal Place merely waits for your return. Through the Holy Spirit, God reminds you of your Place in God, and keeps your Extension of God safe within It. You will not know your Extension of God until you return to It. You cannot replace God or yourself, because God values you and does not want it so. Your Value is in God's Mind, therefore not in the personal mind. For you to accept yourself as God created you is not arrogance, but it does deny the arrogance of the personal mind. To accept yourself as limited *is* arrogance, because it means that you believe that your evaluation of yourself is truer than God's evaluation of you.

11. Truth cannot be divided up, so your Evaluation of yourself must be God's Evaluation of you. You did not establish your Value, and It does not need to be defended. Nothing can attack It or prevail against It, and It does not vary; It merely *is*. Ask the Holy Spirit of your Value and you will be answered, but do not be afraid of the Answer, because It comes from God. It is a *Limitless* Answer because It comes from God. Listen, and do not question What you hear, because God does not deceive. To your question, 'What am I?'

God wants you to replace the personal mind's limitedness with Its Own Limitless Answer, so that you can stop questioning and know What you are.

Chapter 10

The Idols of Sickness

1.   Nothing beyond you can make you fearful or Loving, because nothing *is* beyond you. Time and Eternity are both in your mind, and they will conflict until you perceive time only as a means for regaining your awareness of Eternity. You cannot do this as long as you believe that anything that happens to you is caused by forces outside of you. Time is yours to use as you want, and nothing in the world that you perceive can take this responsibility from you. You can imagine that you have violated God's Law of Oneness, but you cannot escape from It. It was established for you, and It is as unchanged as you are secure in God.

2.   God extends God to you, and nothing but you exists, because you are One with God. *Only God exists.* Nothing beyond God can happen, because only God is Real. As you extend God you add to God, but nothing is added to God that is not God, because God has always been. Only what is temporary can upset you, but the temporary is not real, because you are God's only Extension, and God extends you Eternally. But your powerful mind determines what happens to you by choosing what to perceive, and how to respond to what you perceive.

3.   God cannot change Its Mind about you, because God is not uncertain about God. What God knows can be known by you, because God does not limit Its Knowledge. God extended God to you for God's sake, and gave you the power to extend God so that you are like God. That is why your Mind is Holy. Nothing can exceed the Love of God or your Will. Nothing can reach you from beyond God, because, being in God, you encompass Everything. Believe this and you will realize how much is up to you. When your Peace of mind is threatened, ask yourself, 'Has God changed Its Mind about me?' Then accept God's Decision, Which is Changeless, and refuse to change your mind about yourself. God cannot decide

against you, because God cannot side against God.

1. At Home in God

1. You do not know your Extension of God, because, as long as your mind is split, you are deciding against It. But you cannot attack your Extension of God, just as it is also impossible for God to attack you, because you are God's Extension. The Law of Creation is that you Love your Extension of God, because It is One with you. God's Extension is perfectly safe, then, being protected by God's Love. Any part of your mind that does not know this has banished itself from God, because it is not willing to know God. This could only have been done by you. You can recognize this gladly, because this recognition means that you have not been banished by God, therefore banishment does not exist.

2. You are at Home in God dreaming of exile, but you are perfectly capable of awakening to Reality if you so decide. In your perception that you are in a world, what you see in dreams at night you think is real while you are sleeping, but the moment that you wake up you realize that everything that happened in the dream did not really happen. You don't think this is strange, even though all the laws of the waking world were violated while you were sleeping. And so it will be when you awaken to God. [When you waken from sleep in the world, you are merely shifting to another dream of separation from God.]

3. You wouldn't bother to reconcile what happens in conflicting dreams if you recognized that neither one is Reality. You do not remember being awake in God. When you hear the Holy Spirit you may feel relief, because it seems as though Love is possible, but you do not remember that once you knew that Love is All that there is. And remembering Love is how you will know that this can be so in your awareness again. Only Love is possible, even though It does not seem to have been accomplished in your mind where you perceive a world. Yet Love was once so and is now, because It is Eternal. When you remember Love, you will remember that It is Eternal, and that therefore It is *now*.

4. You will remember God the moment that you wholly desire God.

For you to wholly desire God is for you to extend God, and this wills away your perception of separation from God, returning your mind to God, and to your own Extension of God. Knowing Both you will not wish to sleep, but to be awake in God and Happy. Dreams will be impossible because you will want only Truth, and Truth will be yours, because It is your Will.

2. The Decision to Forget

1.   You must first know God to choose to deny God, so your perception of separation from God is nothing more than your decision to forget God. This makes God seem fearful to you, because you feel that your decision to be separate from God is your attack on God. You are afraid *because* you have forgotten God and replaced God with illusions. So you are really afraid of your forgetting, not of God. When you accept God, you will no longer be afraid of God.

2.   When you decide to stop denying God, you will do more than merely undo fear. Your decision will return Peace and Joy and Oneness to your awareness. Offer the Holy Spirit only your willingness to remember God, because the Holy Spirit is waiting for your acceptance of God. God is in your memory, so give up everything that stands in the way of your remembering God. The Holy Spirit will tell you that you are part of God when you are willing to know your own Reality again. Do not let your belief in a world delay your remembrance of God, because, when you remember God, you remember yourself.

3.   To remember is to restore to your mind *what is already here*. You do not make what you remember. Remembering is accepting what is here, but that you have denied. Your remembering God by extending God in your mind where you perceive a world is a reflection of your Infinite extension of God in God. God will do Its Part when you are willing to exchange perception of a world for Knowledge of God. Nothing is beyond God's Will for you. Just be willing to remember God, and God will give you Everything.

4.   When you attack others in the world that you perceive, you are coming from the personal self, and denying your True Self in God.

You are teaching yourself that you are what you are not. When you deny Reality, you cannot accept God's Gift of Everything, because you have accepted something else in Its place. If you understand that this is always an attack on God, you will understand why attack is always frightening for you. If you further recognize that you are One with God, you will understand that you always attack yourself before you lash out at another.

5. All attack is an attack on yourself. It cannot be anything else, because it comes from your own decision to not be yourself, and to deny your True Identity. Attack is then the way that you lose your True Identity, because, when you attack, you must forget What you are. Your Reality is God's Reality, and when you attack, you are forgetting God. But God is not gone because you actively decided to forget God.

6. You would not make such an insane decision if you saw how it robs you of your Peace. You make this decision because you believe that it can get you something that you want. So what you want, then, must not be Peace of mind. But what could you want then? The logical conclusion of your decision to forget your True Identity is that you must put great effort into denying God. It is just this effort that makes you afraid of God.

3. The God of Sickness

1. You have not attacked God, and you *do* love God. You cannot change your Reality. You cannot will to destroy yourself, and when you think that you are attacking yourself, it is because you hate what you *think* that you are. Only the personal self can be attacked by you, because only the personal self can be hateful, and what this strange image of you makes you do can seem to be destructive. But the destruction is no more real than the image. You may worship the personal self as an idol, but idols are nothing, and your worship of them is a form of sickness. God wants you to be healed of this sickness and fully returned to God's Mind. God puts no limits on your ability to do this. Do not be afraid, because this is your salvation.

2. Extending the Holy Spirit is the only comfort for you in your

sickness of perceived separation from God. Remember, it does not matter what projection you exchange for an extension of the Holy Spirit. Whenever you accept the Holy Spirit, you remember God for your entire mind. Heal your mind by accepting God in your mind where you perceive a world. Your mind is not split into 'you' and a world outside of you, and the Holy Spirit is God's One Channel of healing, because your mind is One. The Holy Spirit is the Communication Link that joins your mind in Oneness, and joins your mind with God. For you to be aware of this is for you to heal your mind, because it is your awareness that your separation from God is not real, and so sickness of any kind is not real.

3. For you to believe in sickness in any form is for you to believe that Part of God can suffer. But Love does not suffer, because It does not attack and bring suffering to Its Mind. Remembering God's Love makes you invulnerable. Do not believe in a projection of the personal mind, no matter how real it seems, but remember the Presence of God's Love instead. Your recognition of God's Presence reminds you of the Truth in you, Which you had been denying. If you strengthen your denial of God, you will lose sight of yourself. Remind yourself of your Wholeness, and remember God.

4. When you look on sickness in any form as real, you worship an idol. You are One with God in Love, not idolatry. All forms of idolatry are distortions of God's Oneness taught by your sick and divided mind, which cannot understand that Love is Oneness, not power-over. Sickness is a form of idolatry, because it is your belief that power can be taken from you. But this is impossible, because you are One with God, Which is All Power. In your identification with a personal self, you have made an image of a sick god: self-created, self-sufficient, vicious, and vulnerable. This is the idol that you worship as yourself and that you project onto others in your identification with a personal mind. This is the idol that you put so much effort into saving and that you are afraid of losing.

5. Look calmly at what the personal self is offering you, and ask yourself if this is what you really want. To attain this, you are willing to attack the Divinity of your mind by perceiving part of your mind as a separate world outside of you, therefore losing sight

of your Divinity. You hide your Divinity to protect this idol, which you think will save you from the very dangers it brings, but which do not really exist.

6. There is no idolatry in God, but there is Great Appreciation, because All is One in God. You cannot be One with idols, but you are One with God. In your perception that you are in a world, health is the counterpart of valuing yourself in Heaven. Your Christ Mind does not make you worthy of God, but It brings you God's Love, because you do not value yourself. When you do not value yourself, you become sick, but your Christ Mind can heal you, because It can make you aware of your Value. Peace comes from God to you through your Christ Mind. It is always here for you, though you may not ask for It.

7. When you are sick, you are not asking for Peace, and you do not know that you have It. Your acceptance of Peace denies illusions, and sickness *is* an illusion. You have the power to deny illusions that you perceive anywhere in the world, merely by denying that *you* are an illusion. Your Christ Mind can heal you, because it knows your Value for you, and it is this Value that makes you Whole. A whole mind has no idols or conflicting laws. Your Christ Mind heals you, because It has only one Message, and this Message is the Truth. You will be Whole again when you have faith in the Message and in your Christ Mind.

8. Your Christ Mind does not deceive you about God, and you will learn this as you learn that you receive as much as you are willing to accept. Because you can hear the Holy Spirit, you can accept Peace now for your entire mind, and be free of all illusions. But if you have any other gods before God, you will not hear the Holy Spirit. God is not jealous of the gods that you made, but you are jealous *for* them. You save and serve the projections of the personal mind, because you believe that they make you. You made them to replace God, but you deny this, and you project onto them the frightening idea that *they* have replaced God so that you can believe that they, not God, are *your* source. Yet when your projections seem to tell you what you are, remember that nothing can replace God, and the replacements that you have attempted are nothing.

9. Very simply, you think that you are afraid of being turned into nothing by God, but you are really afraid of the nothingness that you made. In this awareness you are healed. You will hear the god to which you listen. You made the god of sickness, and, because you made it, you can hear it. This is not Oneness, because this is not the Will of God. Your god is not Eternal, and it will be unmade for you the moment that you indicate that you are willing to accept only the Eternal.

10. There is only One God, and you share Reality with God because Oneness is not divided. For you to place other gods before God is for you to place other images of yourself before you. You do not realize how much you listen to your gods, and how much effort you put into preserving them. They only exist because you honor them. But honor God instead and Peace will be yours, because It comes to you from your real Source. You cannot make God, and the god that you made cannot make you. When you honor illusions, you honor nothing. But you don't need to fear them, either, because they are nothing. You have chosen to fear Love, because It is Perfectly Harmless, and you have made yourself unlike It. Because of this fear, you have been willing to give up the Help of the Holy Spirit.

11. You will only find Peace in God within you. The Holy Spirit calls you to return to God, and you will hear It when you place no other gods before God. You must give up the god of sickness that you project onto a world to give up the god of sickness for yourself. If you see the god of sickness anywhere and believe it, you have accepted it as real. Having accepted it, you will worship it, because you made it to replace God. The god of sickness is your belief that you can choose which god is real. While it is clear that this has nothing to do with Reality, it is equally clear that this has everything to do with what you think is real.

4. The End of Sickness

1. Your attempt to reconcile illusion with Truth is magical thinking. Your true spiritual thinking recognizes that illusion and Truth cannot be reconciled. You cannot reconcile sickness and Perfection. In God you are Perfect, and if you believe that you are sick, then

you have placed another god before God. God is not at war with the god of sickness that you made, but you are. The god of sickness symbolizes your decision to separate from God, and it makes you feel guilty and afraid, because you cannot reconcile it with God's Will. If you attack the god of sickness, you will make it real to you, but if you let it go in whatever form it appears to you, wherever it appears to you, it will disappear into the nothingness out of which you made it.

2. Reality can only dawn on your clear mind. It is always here to be accepted by you, but you must be willing to have It to accept It. For you to remember Reality you must be willing to judge unreality as the nothing that it is. For you to overlook nothingness is for you to judge it correctly and to let it go. God cannot dawn on your mind when it is full of illusions, because you cannot reconcile Truth and illusion. Truth is Whole, and you can only know It can with your entire mind.

3. God's Oneness cannot be partly sick, and for you to perceive It that way is for you to not perceive It at all. Oneness cannot be divided and still be One. If you perceive gods other than God, your mind is split. You cannot limit the split, because you have removed part of your mind from God's Will, so it is out of control and cannot be ordered in a rational manner. When you misunderstand your mind, you perceive it functioning incorrectly.

4. God's Law of Oneness keeps your mind at Peace, because Peace is God's Will, and God's Law is *for* Peace. God's Law sets you free, but the personal mind's law limits you. Limitlessness and limitedness are irreconcilable; you cannot understand them together. Only God's Law is Real, and only God's Law works for you. Anything else is lawless and chaotic. Yet God protects you with Its Law of Oneness, and any other seeming law does not exist. A 'Law of Chaos' is a contradictory term. God is One, and chaos is without God, therefore it has no meaning. You may have given your Peace to these other gods that you made, but there is nothing to take your Peace from you, and you cannot really give your Peace away.

5. You cannot give up your Freedom, but you can deny It. You cannot do what God does not intend to do, because what God does not

intend does not happen. Your gods do not bring chaos, but you endow them with chaos, and then you accept it of them. But none of this has ever been. You are One with God, and God's Will and you extend God as God extends God. What you have made is unworthy of you, and you would not want it if you saw it as the nothing that it is. When you look on what you have made honestly, you will automatically look beyond it to What is in you and all around you. God cannot break through the obstacles that you make to God, but God will envelop you completely when you let your obstacles go.

6.   When you have experienced the Security of God, you will find it inconceivable to make idols to replace God. God's Mind holds no strange images of you, and what is not in God's Mind cannot be in yours, because your Mind *is* God's Mind. God's Oneness is Everywhere, and What is so for God is so for you. No false gods that you want to put between you and God affect God at all. Peace is yours, because you are One with God, and only God's Oneness exists.

7.   You will extend God's Love in your mind where you perceive a world when you lay aside all false gods. Your extension of the miracle is your act of faith, because by it you recognize that the Holy Spirit is here no matter what is appearing. It calls on the Holy Spirit to join your mind with what it perceives, and to strengthen it by joining. When you hear the Holy Spirit instead of the world, you strengthen your awareness of the Holy Spirit in you, and you weaken your belief in sickness. The Power of your Mind can shine on all that your mind perceives and undo the world, because your mind is One. Your Mind is Everywhere, and It is Eternal.

8.   God may be obscured to you by your perception of a world, but God remains in your Whole Mind and can never be completely forgotten by you. If you extend your awareness of God to replace the world of separation that you perceive, you will learn that God fills your Whole Mind. Your perceiving God will heal your mind, and when you know completely that God fills your mind, you will return to being God. But to return to this, you first have to acknowledge that God *can* be All that you perceive, because your perception of

separation from God was a shift from Limitlessness to limitedness in your awareness. Now you must shift back. God is still in your entire mind, even though you perceive a world, and God is calling to you. Put your faith in God, and God will answer you.

5. The Denial of God

1.   The god of sickness' rituals are strange and very demanding. Joy is not permitted, and depression is a sign of allegiance to this god, because it means that you have denied God. You may be afraid of committing blasphemy, but do you understand what blasphemy really means? For you to deny God is for you to deny your own Identity, and in this sense the 'wages of sin' *is* death, because for you to deny Life is for you to perceive death as real. You cannot really do this, but you can think that you can, and you believe that you have.

2.   When you deny God, you inevitably project the cause of your sense of separation from God onto others. You receive the messages that you project onto others, because they are the messages that you want to receive. You may believe that you judge others by the messages that they give to you, but you really judge them by the messages that you have projected onto them. Do not blame others for your lack of Joy, or you will not see God's Love in place of your projections and be Joyous. Denying that God's Love is here is what depresses you. Whenever you look on your projections as real, you are denying God.

3.   The personal mind's religion is allegiance to the denial of God. The god of sickness obviously demands the denial of health, because health is in opposition to its survival. What this means for you is that unless you are sick, you cannot keep the gods you made, because you could only want them in sickness. Blasphemy, then, is *self*-destructive not God-destructive, because it means that you are willing to not know yourself in order to be sick. Self-destruction is the offering your god demands of you, because, having made this god out of the insane desire to be not as you are, this god is an insane idea. But though it takes many different forms, it is one idea: your denial of God.

4. Sickness and death seemed to enter your mind against your will. The 'attack on God' makes you think that you are isolated and without a Source, and in your depression you make a god of depression. This is your alternative to Joy, because in your wanting to be separate from God, you cannot accept that God is your Source. But you *are* helpless without God, because God alone is the Help that you need.

5. Of the personal mind you can do nothing because you are not *of* the personal mind. If you were, then the personal self would be true, and you would not be able to undo it. It is because you did not make yourself that you do not need to be troubled over anything. Your gods are nothing, because God did not make them. You cannot make real anything unlike God, anymore than God can be One with anything unlike God. God extends God, and God cannot extend what is unlike God. God can only extend What *is*. Your depression comes from your perception of separation from God; it cannot come from the Oneness of God.

6. You who are One with God have not sinned, but you have been much mistaken. But this can be corrected, and God will help you, because God knows that you cannot sin against God. You denied God because you loved God, and you knew that if you recognized your love for God, you could not separate from God. Your denial, then, affirms your love for God and your knowledge that God loves you. What you deny you must once have known, and since you can accept denial, you can accept its undoing.

7. God has not denied you, and God does not retaliate, but God *does* call to you to return to God. When you think God has not answered your call, it is because you have not answered God's Call. God calls to you from beyond every projection that you make in your mind where you perceive a world, because God loves your entire mind. If you listen for God beyond your projections, you will be answered. The Love of God fills your entire mind, which is everywhere. Make Peace all that you perceive, and God will come rushing into your mind in gratitude for your gift to God.

8. Do not look to the god of sickness for your healing, but only to the God of Love, because healing is your acknowledgment of God.

When you acknowledge God, you will know that God has never failed to acknowledge you, and that God's Acknowledgment of you lies in your shared Being. You are not sick, and you cannot die, but you can confuse yourself with things that do. This confusion is blasphemy, because it means that you are looking on God and yourself without Love. God cannot be separate from you, and as you see one of you, you will see the other.

9.   You can love only the Eternal, because Love does not die. What is of God is God's Forever, and you are of God. God will not allow God, to suffer and God will not offer you anything that is not acceptable to God. If you accept that you are One with God, you will be incapable of suffering. But to do this, you must acknowledge that God is your Source, not because you will be punished if you do not, but because your acknowledging God is your acknowledgement of you as you are. In God you are wholly without sin, wholly without pain, and wholly without suffering of any kind. But when you deny God you bring sin, pain, and suffering into your own mind, because your mind has the Power God gave to it. Your mind is capable of making a world, but it can also deny the world that it made, because it is free.

10.   You have denied yourself so much, and God in God's Love for you does not want it so. But God cannot interfere with you, because God does not know you if you are not free. God would be attacking God if God interfered with you, and God is not insane. When you deny God, *you* are insane. God will never cease to love you, and you will never cease to love God, because that is the Condition of your Oneness with God, Which is fixed in God's Mind Forever. For you to know this is Sanity; for you to deny this is insanity. God extends God to you, and God's Gift is Eternal. Do you want to deny God the gift of yourself?

11.   Out of your gift of yourself to God, God's Wholeness will be restored to your awareness. You removed yourself from God's Gift by refusing Oneness with God and your own Extension of God. Heaven waits for your return, because It is your Home. You are not at home anywhere else or in any other condition. Do not deny yourself the Joy of your Oneness with God to have the misery that

you have made for yourself. God has given you the Means to undo what you have made. Listen to the Holy Spirit, and you will learn how to remember What you are.

12. God knows you are wholly sinless, so it is blasphemous for you to perceive guilt anywhere; God knows you wholly without pain, so it is blasphemous for you to perceive suffering anywhere; God knows you to be Wholly Joyous, so it is blasphemous for you to be depressed about anything. All forms of blasphemy are your refusals to accept that your mind is Whole, as it is in God. In God, your Whole Mind is Perfect, and you must learn to see Perfection everywhere to learn of your Reality and Perfection.

13. When you perceive what is not of God, you are denying God. God is the only Creator, and you can extend God only because God extends God to you. The 'gifts' of the personal self are meaningless, but your gift of God's extension is like God's extension of God to you, because It is given in God's Name. You must acknowledge God as your Source to know yourself in God. You believe that the sick things that you have made are real, because you believe that the sick images that you project are part of God. Only if you accept God as your Source will you have anything Real, because God has given you Everything. That is why for you to deny God is for you to deny yourself.

14. Arrogance denies Love, because Love extends and arrogance withholds. As long as you want both Love and arrogance, the concept of choice, which is not of God, will remain with you. Choice does not exist in Eternity but in time, so while you believe in time, you will believe in choice. Your belief in time is a choice in itself. To remember Eternity, look only on the Eternal. When you are preoccupied with the world that you perceive, you think that you are living in time. Your choice is determined by what you value. Time and Eternity cannot both be real, because they contradict each other. If you accept only the Timeless as Real, you will begin to understand Eternity and make It yours.

Chapter 11

God or the Ego

1. Either God or the personal mind is insane, and, if you examine them both fairly, you will realize that this is true. Both thought systems are whole and consistent within themselves, but they are diametrically opposed to each other, so your allegiance must be to one *or* the other. Their results, too, are as different as their foundations, and you cannot reconcile them by vacillating between them. Everything has a source but God, Which is *the* Source of Everything. Your decision as to whether God or the personal mind is insane is your answer to your question 'What is my source?' and you will be faithful to the source that you choose.

2. It does not make sense that the answer to your question 'What is my source?' involves conflict. You made the personal mind, so how could it have made you? The source of all of your conflict, then, is that the personal mind was made out of your wish to replace God with your own god. The personal mind is a delusional thought system in which you made your own source. Looked upon with perfect honesty, the personal mind is clearly insane, but the personal mind never looks on anything with perfect honesty. Its insane premise is buried in the dark foundation of its thought system, and either you accept that the personal mind, which you made, is your source, or its whole thought system will crumble for you.

3. The personal mind makes a world seem real through projection, but God extends God Infinitely, and this is Reality. You are God's Extension, and as you approach the Foundation of God's Thought System, your mind becomes clearer. But the closer you get to the foundation of the personal mind's thought system, the more unclear and confused your mind becomes. But God is always with you, and you must bring your awareness of God with you as you look at the foundation of the personal mind's thought system and

judge it honestly. Look at the terror at the center of the personal mind's thought system, and see that it rests on the meaningless idea that you have replaced God, so all of your fears rest on nothing.

4. In your Christ Mind, you are One with God, and when you have at last looked at the personal mind's thought system without fear, you will find the foundation of God's Thought System, Which it seemed to hide. Christ within you is of God, and It offers you Everything. Do not deny Christ to keep the personal mind's dark foundation hidden from you, because protecting it will not save you. With your Christ Mind, look closely at the personal mind, and Christ will lead you to God to be Whole again in your awareness. Answer the Call of your Christ Mind with Joy.

1. The Gifts of Fatherhood

1. You have learned of your need of healing, and you must bring healing to your entire mind to be healed. In this lies the beginning of your return to God, and it is the foundation on which God's Thought System will be rebuilt within your awareness again. God blesses every thought of healing that you have, because you are restoring yourself to Oneness with God. Whenever you extend God's Love in your mind where you perceive a world, you restore yourself to God's Oneness. You live in the Mind of God with your entire mind, because God wills to be Whole.

2. For you to be limited to a personal mind is for you to be separated from Infinity, but how can you be limited when Infinity has no limits? You cannot be *beyond* the Limitless, because What has no limits is Everywhere. God has no beginning and no ending, so God's Universe is God. You cannot exclude yourself from the Universe, because the Universe *is* God. You are One with God in your Christ Mind. Part of God cannot be missing or lost to God.

3. If you are not One with God, God's Will is not One. God's Mind cannot contain nothing; without you there would be an empty place in God's Mind. God's Extension cannot be blocked, and It has no voids. It continues Forever, even though you deny It. Your denial of God's Extension stops It in time, but not in Eternity, and

that is why your Extension of God continues and waits for your return to God.

4. You can wait in time, but time has no meaning. You made delay, but you can leave all time behind by realizing that what has a beginning and an ending is not of God. God places no limits on Its Own extension to you and through you. You do not know this, because you have tried to limit God's Oneness, so you believe that God is limited. You cannot know your own Extension of God by denying Infinity.

5. There is no contradiction in God's Universe. What is true for God is true for you. If you believe that you are separate from God, you will believe that God is separate from you. Infinity is meaningless without you, and you are meaningless without God. God's Oneness has no end, and this *is* the Universe. God is not incomplete and God extends Everywhere. Because God does not will to be separate from Infinity, God extends God Infinitely. Do not deny God Its Extension, because denying God as your Source denies your own Extension of God. God's Extension is God's Oneness, and your Extension of God honors God's Oneness. The Universe of Love does not stop because you do not see It, nor does your denial of It mean that you cannot know It. Look on the Glory of God's Oneness, and you will learn What God has kept for you.

6. Your Place in God's Mind is yours Forever. You can keep It in your awareness only by extending It as It was extended to you. You cannot be limited in God, because God extends God to you so that God will not be limited. God's Mind cannot be lessened, but it can be increased, because All of God extends Infinitely. Love does not limit, and What It extends is not limited. Your extending God without limit is God's Will for you, because only this will bring you God's Joy. Your Love is as Boundless as God's Love, because your Love *is* God's Love.

7. No Part of God can be without God's Love, and no Part of God's Love can be contained. God is your Legacy, because God's One Gift to you is God. You must extend God as God extends God to you to know God's Gift to you. Extend God without limit and without end to learn how much God has given to you. Your willingness to

accept God is demonstrated by your willingness to extend God as God extends God. God and your Extension of God are One. God Wills to extend God, and your Will is God's Will.

8. In your identification with a personal self you do not know your Will, because you deny It, and your denial means that you refuse to acknowledge Its existence. Your Oneness with God is God's Will, and by denying this you deny your own Will, therefore you do not know What it is. You must learn to ask what is God's Will in every-thing, because It is your Will. You do not know what It is in your identification with a personal self, but the Holy Spirit in you remembers It for you. Ask the Holy Spirit what is God's Will for you and the Holy Spirit will tell you *your* Will. Whenever it feels like the Holy Spirit is coercing you, it is only because you have not recognized your Will.

9. The personal mind projects God's Will outside of you so that it seems as though It is not *your* Will. This makes it seem possible for your will to conflict with God's Will, for God to demand of you what you do not want to give, and for God to deprive you of what you do want. But God only wants your shared Will, and God is not capable of demanding or depriving. Your Will is God's Life, Which God has extended to you. Even in time you cannot live apart from God. Denial is not death, and while you can deny you cannot die. Immortality is God's Will for you and your Will for yourself. You cannot will death for yourself, because God is Life and you are One with God. Oneness with God is your Will *because* it is God's Will.

10. You will not be happy unless you do what you Truly Will. You cannot change this, because it is unchangeable by God's Will and your Will; otherwise God's Will will not be extended. You are afraid of God's Will, because you believe that It is not yours. This belief is your whole sickness, and all of your fear and your every symptom of sickness and fear comes from this belief, because it makes you *want* to deny God. Believing that God's Will is not yours, you hide from God, and deny that God is within you.

11. You are asked to trust the Holy Spirit, because the Holy Spirit speaks for you. The Holy Spirit is the Voice for God, but remember that God does not Will to be limited, so God extends Itself *to* you

but does not thrust Itself *on* you. What God extends is still One with God, so nothing can contradict God. You who share God's Life must extend It to know It, because extending It is the way for you to know that you are One with It. You are blessed when you learn that to hear God's Will is to know your own Will. It is your Will to be One with God, as It is God's Will to be One with you. Your healing is the beginning of your recognition that your Will is God's Will.

2. The Invitation to Healing

1. Your perception of separation from God is sickness, and your decision to be healed is your first step toward recognizing that you truly want God. Your every perception of separation that you believe in is an attack that is a step away from healing, and your every extension of God's Love is a step toward your full healing. You *have* God and God's Extension, because you *are* God and God's Extension. Your Will is God's Will, because God wills you God. In Truth, you Will yourself to God because, understanding God perfectly, you know there is only One Will. But when you attack your mind with any perception of separation, you attack God's Oneness, you do not understand God, and the Peace that you really want is lost to you.

2. Your healing, then, is a lesson in understanding God, and the more that you practice it, the better a teacher and learner you become. When you have denied God, what better Witness is there to God's Reality than your own extension of God's Love? But It must be extended *from* you, not projected *away* from you for you to be healed. Every miracle that you extend reminds you that God is your Source. Every healing thought that you accept within your mind and through your extensions teaches you that you are One with God. In every hurtful thought, wherever you perceive it, lies your denial of God and of your Oneness with God.

3. Denial is as total as Love. You cannot deny that the world is in your mind, and that everything in the world is in your mind, or your Christ Mind will also seem to be separate and without meaning, and you will not understand any of your mind. You can only heal

yourself, because only you need healing. You need it because you do not understand yourself, and therefore you do not know what you do. Having forgotten your Will, you do not know what you want.

4.   Your willingness to heal is a sign that you want to be whole, and it opens you to the Holy Spirit's Message of Wholeness. With Its Own Complete Will, the Holy Spirit takes you far beyond your own small willingness to be whole to make your will Whole again. What can you not accomplish with God within you? But you must allow God into your awareness, because what you allow into your awareness is what is real to you.

5.   If you do not welcome the Holy Spirit, you will not hear the Holy Spirit. The Holy Spirit is always within you, but you cannot hear It when you choose to listen to the personal mind. Your effort to hear the Holy Spirit is the sign that you want the Holy Spirit. Think like the Holy Spirit just slightly, and the Holy Spirit will fill your mind. But whenever you turn to the personal mind, you lessen your awareness of the Holy Spirit, because you have turned away from It. Wherever you go and whatever you do, the Holy Spirit goes with you and waits for you to turn back to It. You can trust Its Patience, because It cannot leave a Part of God. But you need more than patience.

6.   You will not rest until you know your Function and fulfill It, because this is your Joint Will with God. To have God is to be like God, and God has given God to you to have. God's Function, then, is your Function. Invite knowledge of this into your mind again, and do not let anything obscure it. The Holy Spirit will teach you how to do this if you are even a little aware of God, and you are willing to let this awareness grow. Your willingness does not need to be perfect, because the Holy Spirit's is. Offer the Holy Spirit even a little place in your mind and you will be so relieved that you will offer It even more. As your awareness of the Holy Spirit increases, you will begin to remember your Oneness with God.

7.   You can be limited by the personal mind or Limitless in God, and you will accept whichever is your choice. You are free to listen to either and to determine how long you will listen. But this is not real

freedom, because you are choosing between What is Real and what is not. The Holy Spirit is always within you, but It cannot help you unless you are open to It. And the personal mind is always nothing, whether you are open to it or not. Your real freedom means your welcoming Reality, and only the Holy Spirit is Real. You do not need imaginary comforters, because the Comforter from God is already within you.

3. From Darkness to Light

1. Whenever you are weary, it is because you have attacked yourself. The Holy Spirit will rest you. The personal mind cannot rest you, because if it knew how, you would never have grown weary. You cannot suffer unless you hurt yourself, because suffering is not God's Will for you. Pain is not of God because God does not attack, and God's Peace surrounds you Silently. God is very Quiet, because there is no conflict in God. Your conflict is the root of all perceived 'evil', because it attacks blindly and does not see what it attacks. But it always attacks you in your Oneness with God.

2. You are indeed in need of comfort, because you know not what you do, and you believe that your True Will is not your will. At Home in God, you wander homeless and isolated in your denial. God does not let this be Real, because God is One with you. Your Will is God's Will, so it cannot be true of you, because it is not true of God.

3. If you knew What God wills for you, your Joy would be complete. What God Wills is always True. When the Truth dawns on you and you say, 'God's Will is mine' you will see such Beauty that you will know that It does not come from the personal mind. Out of your Joy, you will extend this Beauty in God, because your Joy cannot be contained anymore than God's Joy can be contained. The bleak little world will vanish, and you will be so filled with Joy that you will leap into Heaven and into the Presence of God. You cannot be told what this is lik,e and you are not yet ready. But you can remember often that What God wills for God, God wills for you, and What God wills for you is yours.

4. The way to God is not hard, but it is very *different* from the way of the personal mind. The way of the personal mind is the way of pain,

which God does not know. It is hard and lonely and filled with fear and grief. But this is not the way for you who are One with God. Walk to God, and do not see the hard way, because it is not fit for you who are One with God. God always surrounds you and extends through you. You cannot see the hard way when you walk to God, but if you do, it is because you are denying God. Deny the hard way instead, because God is with you and your way is clear.

5. God hides nothing from you, even though you want to hide yourself from God. But you cannot hide your Glory, because God wills you to be Glorious. You will never lose your way, because God leads you, and when you wander you go nowhere. The hard way is an illusion. Turn toward God, and the Part of you that is One with God will sweep you out of illusions Forever. God is your Source, and you are like God.

6. You who are One with God cannot live in illusion, because what is not real is not in you. Do not be deceived by the illusions of the personal mind, and do not let them enter your mind, because they have no place in What is One with God. When you are tempted to deny God, remember that there are no gods to place before God, and accept that God's Will for you is Peace. Peace is the only way for you to accept God's Will.

7. Only the Holy Spirit can comfort you. In the Quiet Place within you Where It abides, the Holy Spirit waits to give you the Peace that is yours. Extend this Peace to enter this Quiet Place, and find your Peace. Only from the Holy Spirit can you enter the Presence of God, because what is unlike God cannot enter God's Mind. What is not God's Thought does not belong to God, and your mind must be as pure as God's Mind to know What belongs to you. Be careful to keep the Holy Spirit in your awareness, because God dwells There in Peace. You cannot enter God's Presence with illusions in any part of your mind, because your mind must be whole to enter God's Presence. You cannot understand Wholeness until your mind is whole, and nothing that your mind perceives can be excluded from your wholeness if you want to know the Wholeness of God.

8. In your mind you can accept God's Oneness and bless It with God's Blessing. Then you will be ready to dwell in Quiet with God,

because it is your Will to be One with God. God blesses you Forever. If you extend God's Blessing in time, you will be in Eternity. Time cannot separate you from God if you use it on behalf of Eternity.

4. The Inheritance of God's Son

1. Do not forget that your Mind's Wholeness is your salvation, because It is your True Self. Being One with God, It is yours, and belonging to you, It belongs to God. Your True Self does not need salvation, but your split mind needs to learn what salvation is. You are not saved *from* anything but *for* Glory. Glory is given to you by God to extend It. But if you hate a perception in your mind you hate your True Self, and you do not understand your True Self, because you are looking on What is One with God without Love. And in doing so, you deny God Its Place in your Mind.

2. If you try to make God Homeless by denying God in your mind where you perceive a world, you will not know that you are Home in God. You cannot reject God without believing that God rejects you. God's Law keeps you safe, even in your denial of God, because God cannot intervene against your Will or lessen your Power. So look only to the Power that God gave to you to save you, and remember that It is yours *because* It is God's, and unite your entire mind in God's Peace.

3. Your Peace lies in the Limitlessness of Peace. If you limit the Peace that you extend you will not know your True Self. Every extension of God that you make is part of you, because it is Part of God. Do not fail to replace every projection of the personal mind with an extension of the Love of God that is yours. If you do this, you will know that God's Love is yours. As you make this exchange, you will return to God. That is God's Law for your Wholeness.

4. *Only you can deprive yourself of anything.* Your realizing this is the beginning of your reawakening to God. Your denial of this takes many forms, and you must learn to recognize every form of denial and to undo it without exception. In the beginning, this reversal in your thinking can be painful, because as you withdraw blame from others, you may turn it inward on yourself. But these are exactly

the same thing, because there is no difference between the mind that you project outward and the mind that you see within.

5.   Your projections onto others are part of your mind, so when you blame others for your sense of deprivation, you are still holding blame in your mind. And even when you blame yourself alone, you will not be able to avoid perceiving guilt in some form in the world that your mind perceives. Everything that you perceive is in your mind, and what is in your mind you will perceive, and that is why you must undo blame altogether, not shift it around your mind. All blame comes from the personal mind, so when you blame you cannot know yourself. Blaming yourself and blaming others are both forms of identifying with and defending the reality of the personal self. *You cannot enter God's Presence when you attack yourself by identifying with a personal self.* When you value God, you will hear the Holy Spirit. But you cannot value God without yourself, because your Glory is shared with God.

6.   Your Christ Mind waits within you to welcome you. You must come to your Christ Mind without guilt in your mind, or you will believe that you are barred from Christ. But it is impossible for you to be barred from Where God wants you to be. Love yourself with the Love of Christ as God loves you. You can refuse your Christ Mind, but you cannot be barred from your Christ Mind, Which is open to you Forever. God is Christ's Life and therefore yours, and God does not deny you anything.

7.   Within your mind, Christ waits to be restored to your awareness. God knows that you are as wholly blameless as God is blameless, and God is approached by you through your Christ Mind. Christ waits for your acceptance of Christ as your Self and of Christ's Wholeness as yours. Christ is One with God and lives in God and shines with God's Glory. Christ is the Extension of God's Love and Loveliness, as Perfect as God and at Peace in God.

8.   You are blessed as Part of God, and you will to extend God's Glory as God extends Its Glory to you. There is no guilt in you, because there is no guilt in God. Sharing God's Perfect Love, you must extend It to know both God and the Christ in you. Peace to you, who rest in God, and in whom your Whole Mind rests!

5. The 'Dynamics' of the Ego

1. You cannot escape illusions without looking at them, because your
    not looking at them is the way that they are protected. You do not
    need to shrink from your illusions, because they are not dangerous.
    When you realize that you do not want the personal mind, you are
    ready to look at its thought system more closely. The Holy Spirit is
    with you, and together you can dispel the personal mind's thought
    system. You can be calm in doing this, because you are only
    looking honestly for Truth. The 'dynamics' of the personal mind
    will be your lesson for a while, because you must look *at* it before
    you can look *beyond* it, because you have made it real to you. With
    the Holy Spirit you will undo error quietly, and then look beyond
    it to Truth.

2. Your healing is your removal of all that stands in the way of your
    awareness of Reality. You can only dispel illusions by not
    protecting them and looking directly at them. Do not be afraid,
    because you will be looking at the source of fear, and you are
    beginning to learn that fear is not real, because it does not come
    from Reality. You are also learning that you can dispel the effects of
    fear by recognizing that they do not affect Reality. The next step is
    for you to recognize that what does not affect Reality does not
    exist. What leads to nothing has not happened. You recognize
    Reality by Its extension, and what leads to nothing is not Real. Do
    not be afraid to look on fear, because there is nothing real there to
    be seen. Clarity undoes confusion, and Reality is clear, so when
    you look on illusions from Truth, It must dispel illusions for you.

3. Your lesson in the personal mind's 'dynamics' begins with your
    understanding that the personal mind has no 'dynamics'. The
    word implies a power to *do* something, and your whole illusion of
    separation from God lies in your mistaken belief that the personal
    mind has the power to do something real. The personal mind is
    fearful to you, because you believe it *has* done something real. But
    the Truth is very simple:

    All Power is of God.
    What is not of God does not have power to do anything real.

4. When you look at the personal mind, you are not considering dynamics, then, but *delusions*. You can regard a delusional thought system without fear, because it is not real, so its effects are not real. Fear becomes more obviously inappropriate when you recognize the personal mind's goal, which makes no sense, because it is diametrically opposed to the Reality of Oneness. The personal mind's goal is to be autonomous. Its purpose is to be separate, self-sufficient, and independent of any power but its own. This is why it is the symbol of your separation from God.

5. Everything that stems from the personal mind is the natural outcome of its central belief in separation, and the way for you to undo its results is for you to recognize that separation is not natural, because it is out of accord with your True Nature. To will in contradiction to God is not really *willing* but *wishing*. God's Will is One, because the Extension of God's Will is God. The underlying conflict that you experience in your identification with a personal self, then, is between the personal mind's idle wish to be separate from God and the Will of God, Which you share in Reality. This is not a real conflict.

6. You are Free in your Oneness with God, not in the limitedness of the personal mind. Your whole Function lies in your Oneness with God, because God's Function is yours. In God's Willingness to extend Its Function to you, God is One with you. Do not project onto God the personal mind's arrogant wish to be separate from God, because God's Will is Oneness, and you are included in God's Oneness. Freedom has no meaning for you apart from God, because God is your Reality. Your identification with the personal mind's limited separate self is costing you knowledge of your Oneness and Freedom in God. The personal mind sees all joining as threatening, and it twists even your longing for God into a means of establishing its own reality through religions that validate your perception of separation. But do not be deceived by its interpretations of your conflict.

7. The personal mind always attacks on behalf of separation from God. It believes it has the power to make separation from God real, and it does nothing else, because its goal of autonomy *is* separation.

The personal mind is totally wrong about what reality is, but it does not lose sight of its goal. It puts much more effort into its goal than you put into remembering God, because it is certain of its purpose, and you are confused, because you do not yet wholly recognize your Purpose.

8.   The last thing that the personal mind wants you to realize is that by identifying with it you are identifying with fear. If you do realize this, you will withdraw your identification and your power from it. But its one claim on you is that it teaches you that your identification with it gives power to you through the autonomy it offers. If you did not believe this, you would not listen to it at all. Its existence will not continue if you realize that, by identifying with it, you are limiting yourself, and depriving yourself of Real Power.

9.   The personal mind does allow you to see yourself in unflattering ways that isolate you from others and from God, but it does not let you see the guilt and fear behind these postures. It constantly minimizes your fear in ingenious ways, but it never undoes it. It can only teach you separation by teaching you to fear God, but you would not listen to it if you recognized what it was doing.

10.   The basic threat to the personal mind, then, is your recognition that all fear, in any form, is your fear of God, and that you only fear God because you identify with a personal self. The personal mind's illusion of autonomy is shaken to its foundation by your awareness of this, because, while you may tolerate a false idea of freedom by identifying with it, you will not accept fear if you recognize that it costs you God. And your awareness of God *is* the cost of fear, and the personal mind cannot minimize this. If you overlook God, you overlook yourself, and you fear your illusions, because they represent the attack on God that you believe is real. Believing attack is real, you feel guilty and afraid of your own Reality, and you do not want to find It, because you think It will retaliate against you.

11.   The personal mind's goal of separation can only be accomplished if God can be undone, and this is impossible. You will finally learn to distinguish the Possible from the impossible, and the True from the false, when you learn that all of your fear is fear of God, because

you mistakenly believe that you have attacked God and that God will punish you. According to the personal mind's teaching, only *its* purpose of separation can be accomplished, and God's Purpose of Eternal Oneness cannot. According to the Holy Spirit, only God's Purpose is possible, and It is always so.

12. You and God are One, and God's Freedom encompasses yours and would be incomplete without you. You can only be free in your Identification with God, and by fulfilling your Function in God. The personal mind believes that if you accomplish its goal of complete separation from God, you will be happy. But within you, you know God's Function is yours, and that you cannot find happiness apart from your Joint Will with God. If you recognize that the personal mind's goal of separation, which you have pursued so well, has only brought you fear, you will not be able to maintain that its goal is happiness. Since fear is the foundation of the personal mind, it needs you to believe that fear is happiness. Yet in your True Mind, you are not insane, and you can never believe this. Recognize what the personal mind is trying to do, and you will not accept it. Only through the insane personal mind do you choose fear in place of God's Love, and only through its insanity can you believe that you can gain Love by attacking God. In your True Mind, Which is Sane and completely protected by God's Love, you know that attacking God will only produce fear in you.

13. The personal mind analyzes; the Holy Spirit accepts. To analyze means to break down, or to separate out, but Wholeness can only be appreciated through acceptance. In its characteristically contradictory thinking, the personal mind attempts to understand totality by breaking it down into separate parts. The personal mind believes that power, understanding, and truth lie in separation, and, to establish this belief as real, it must attack to separate. It is unaware that separation cannot be made real, and it is obsessed with separation as salvation. So it attacks everything it perceives by breaking it into small, disconnected parts without meaningful relationships and therefore without any meaning at all. The personal mind will always substitute chaos for meaning, because to it separation is salvation, so harmony is a threat.

14. The personal mind's use of the Law of Perception that you perceive what you believe is real is the exact opposite of the Holy Spirit's use of the Law. The personal mind focuses on illusions and overlooks Reality. It makes real to itself every illusion that it perceives, and then, with circular reasoning, concludes that because what it sees is chaotic, Oneness is meaningless. And if Oneness is meaningless, then chaos must be real. Holding illusions in its mind, and protecting them because it has made them real, the personal mind concludes that chaos is reality, and Oneness is illusion.

15. The personal mind makes no attempt to understand this, because it is clearly not understandable, but it does make every attempt to demonstrate that chaos is real, and it does this constantly. It fragments your Mind, Which is One, into parts, and thereby loses the meaning of Oneness. It is left with a series of fragmented perceptions which it then unifies with a meaning it makes for itself. This, then, is the universe that it perceives, and then uses as a demonstration of its own reality.

16. Do not underestimate the personal mind's appeal to you, who want to listen to it. It selectively chooses its witnesses, and its witnesses are consistent. The case for separation is strong when you want to be separated. You cannot transcend the thought system that you choose, but a thought system without meaning cannot demonstrate anything real, and if you are convinced by it, you are deluded. The personal mind cannot teach What it denies, so it cannot teach you truly, because it overlooks Truth. Its witnesses attest to its denial, but not to What it denies. The personal mind looks straight at God and does not see God, because it is the denial that God is in you.

17. If you want to remember God, accept your Oneness with God, and you *will* remember God. Nothing can prove that you are unworthy of God, because nothing can prove a lie is true. The part of your mind that you perceive with the personal mind seems to demonstrate that God does not exist, but where God's Extension is, God must be. Extend God's Love in your mind where you perceive a world and your Extension will demonstrate the Truth. You witness to God by beholding God's Oneness, and in the Silence of your

Christ Mind, you don't need to demonstrate anything, because All is One.

18. In every relationship with others in the world that you perceive, you either project the personal mind's perception of separation or you extend God's Love, so that they witness either to the personal mind or to your Christ Mind. They convince you of the reality of the world or of God's Oneness, depending on which you want to perceive. Everything that you perceive is a witness to the thought system that you want to be true, and every relationship can set you free if you choose to extend to it God's Love instead of the personal mind's projections. Your relationship with another cannot witness to the reality of the personal mind unless you project the personal mind onto it. If you do not see your Christ Mind, it is because you have not extended your Christ Mind. You hear only your own voice, and if you teach yourself that you are Christ, you will hear only Christ.

6. Waking to Redemption

1. Not only do you believe what you see, but you see what you believe. Your perceptions are built on your experience, and your experience leads to your beliefs. When your beliefs are stabilized, your perceptions become stabilized. So what you believe you *do* see. When Jesus said, 'Blessed are ye who have not seen and still believe', he meant that those who believe in the resurrection of Christ will see it. The resurrection of Christ is the complete undoing of the personal mind by your Christ Mind, not by attack, but by transcendence. Christ *does* rise above the personal mind, and It lifts your mind to an awareness of its Oneness with God.

2. Do you want to join the resurrection or the crucifixion of Christ? Do you want to project separation or to extend God's Love? Do you want to transcend the limitations that you impose on yourself and be aware of God again? These questions are all the same and are answered together. The word 'perception' is used both for awareness and for interpretation, but you cannot be aware without interpretation, because what you perceive *is* your interpretation of yourself.

3. This course is perfectly clear, and if you do not see it clearly, it is because you are interpreting against it, and you do not believe it. Your belief determines your perception, so if you do not perceive what this course means, it is because you do not accept it. But different experiences lead you to different beliefs, therefore to different perceptions. Your perceptions are learned with beliefs that you learn from experience. Your Christ Mind is leading you to a new kind of experience that you will become less and less willing to deny. Learning from your Christ Mind is easy for you, because for you to perceive with Christ involves no strain, since Its Perceptions are your Natural Awareness. It is only the distortions in perception that you introduce through the personal mind that tire you. Let your Christ Mind interpret for you, and do not limit what you see by the limited beliefs that are unworthy of you as Part of God. Until you see Christ as your Self, you will believe that you are without God.

4. The Christ Mind manifested by Jesus is *your* resurrection and *your* Life. You live in Christ because you live in God. Everything that you see lives in you as you live in it. You cannot perceive unworthiness in your mind where you perceive a world and not perceive unworthiness in yourself. And if you perceive unworthiness in yourself, you perceive it in God. You can believe in the resurrection manifested by Jesus, because it has been accomplished *in* you. This is true now and always, because the resurrection of Jesus is the Will of God, Which does not know time or exceptions. Make no exceptions yourself, or you will not perceive what has been accomplished for you. Your mind rises in its Wholeness to God, as it was in the beginning, is now, and Forever will be, because Wholeness is your Nature in your Oneness with God.

5. Do not underestimate the power of your devotion to your god, the personal self, or the power that you have given it to have over you. You worship the god you choose: either the god you made or the God with Which you are One. Your limitation will be as complete as your Limitlessness, because you will obey the god that you accept. The god of crucifixion that you made demands that you crucify yourself and you obey, believing that power is yours

through sacrifice and pain. But the God of resurrection demands nothing, because It does not Will to take anything from you. God does not require obedience, because God does not require submission. God only wants you to learn of your Will and to follow It, not to sacrifice and submit, but to be Happy and Free.

6. Resurrection inspires your happy allegiance, because it is the symbol of Joy. It is compelling to you, because it represents what *you* want to be the Truth. The freedom to leave behind everything that hurts and humbles and frightens you cannot be forced on you, but it can be offered to you through the Grace of God. You can accept Freedom by God's Grace, because God Graciously accepts you as God's Own. Who is *your* own? God gives you All that is God's, and God Itself is yours in your Whole Mind. Guard your Whole Mind in your resurrection, because otherwise you will not be aware of God, and that you are safely surrounded by What is yours Forever.

7. You will not find Peace until you have removed the nails from your hands and taken the last thorn from your forehead by extending only God's Love in your mind where you perceive a world. The Love of God surrounds you whom the god of crucifixion condemns. Jesus did not die in vain, but He taught that Christ cannot die, and you must teach that Christ lives in you. Your redemption is the undoing of the crucifixion of Christ in you, and your every perception must be brought to it. God does not judge you who are guiltless, because God gives God to you.

8. In your identification with a personal self you have nailed yourself to a cross and placed a crown of thorns on your own head. But you cannot crucify the Christ within you, because God's Will cannot die. Christ has been redeemed from your crucifixion because you cannot kill What God has given Eternal Life. Your illusion of crucifixion may still hang heavy before your eyes, but it is not Reality. While you still perceive crucifixion, either for yourself or for others, you are perceiving illusion. You are beginning to be aware of Truth, but you still believe in illusions. You *will* forget illusions and become aware of the Christ in you as you let go of the illusions that you project onto others and extend God's Love in their place.

9. The Call to be aware of God is within you, and It comes *from* you. Christ is in you, but you must see Its extension of God's Love to know that It is there. Do not set limits on what you believe your Christ Mind can do *through* you, or you will not accept what It can do *in* you. It is done already, but you will not know this until you extend God's Love to be all that you see. You will recognize redemption only by extending it.

10. You *are* saved. Bring only this awareness with you everywhere in your perception that you are in a world, and your part in your redemption will belong to Christ. Your part must be Christ's part if you learn it of Christ. Your every extension of God's Love is equal to every other extension, because the Whole Power of God is in every part of your mind, and anything that contradicts God is nothing, because it does not exist. To God all things are possible, and in your Christ Mind you are like God.

7. The Condition of Reality

1. The 'reality' that you perceive as a world is not of God, because Reality is not as you see it with your split mind. What is of God is Eternal, and everything that the personal mind sees is perishable. So there must be another Reality that you do not see. The Bible speaks of a new Heaven and a new earth, but this cannot be literally true, because Heaven is Eternal and cannot be made again. To perceive anew is to perceive again, meaning that in the interval in between you did not perceive at all. What, then, is the Real Perception that awaits your being open to seeing It?

2. Every Loving Thought that you have ever had is Eternal. The only reality any of your perceptions has is when it extends Love. These are still *perceptions* because you still believe in your separation from God, but they are Eternal, because they are Loving. Being Loving they are like God and cannot die. You *can* attain Real Perception, and all that is necessary is your willingness to give up all other perception. But if you continue to perceive both Good and 'evil', you will believe that both Truth and illusion are real, and you will make no distinction between them.

3. The personal mind may see some good, but never *only* Good, and

that is why its perceptions are always variable. It cannot reject goodness entirely, because you would not accept that. But it always adds something that is not real, and therefore confuses illusions with reality. You cannot accept perceptions as partly true, so if you believe in both Truth and illusion, you will not be able to tell which is true. To establish the autonomy of the personal mind, you made a world unlike God, and you believed that what you made was real. But everything Real *is* like God. Through Real Perception you will be led to Heaven, because you will understand It.

4. Perceiving Goodness is not the same as knowing God, but accepting that only Goodness exists enables you to recognize a condition in which opposites do not exist, like the Condition of God. Accepting no opposite to God is the condition that you must meet to know God again. You have made many beliefs that you have placed between you and God, and these make up the world that you perceive with the personal mind. Truth is not absent in your perception of a world, but It is obscured. You do not know the difference between what you have made and God, so you do not know the difference between what you have made and your Extension of God. If you believe that you can attain Real Perception, then you believe that you can know yourself again. You can know God because it is God's Will that God be known by you. Your Real Perception is all that the Holy Spirit has saved for you out of the perception that you made. For you to use only Real Perception is your salvation, because it is your recognition that Reality is only What reflects Truth.

8. The Problem and the Answer

1. This is a very simple course. You may feel that you do not need a course which in the end teaches you that only Reality is True, but do you believe it? When you see What Real Perception can show you, you will recognize that you did not believe it. But the swiftness with which your new and only Real Perception will be translated into God will leave you only an instant to realize that only God is True. Then you will forget everything that you made – the good, the bad, the false, the true. As what your mind perceives comes to resemble

Heaven, even this Real Perception will vanish from your awareness. The end of the world is not its destruction but its translation into Heaven for you. This reinterpretation of the world leads to your corrected perception, which transfers easily to God.

2. The Bible tells you to be like a child, because children recognize that they do not understand what they perceive, so they ask about it. Do not believe that you understand what you perceive with a personal mind, because then the meaning of everything is lost to you. But the Holy Spirit has a real meaning for everything for you, and if you will let the Holy Spirit reinterpret your perceptions for you, It will restore to you What you have thrown away. But while you think that you know what anything means, you will not ask the Holy Spirit what anything means.

3. You do not know the meaning of anything that you perceive with the personal mind. Not one thought that you hold with it is wholly true. Recognizing this is your firm beginning. You are not misguided, because you have not accepted a real guide at all. Your greatest need is to be instructed through corrected perception, because you understand nothing. Recognize this, but don't accept it, because understanding is your Natural Right. Your perceptions are learned, and you have a Teacher within you. But your willingness to learn of the Holy Spirit depends on your willingness to question everything that you have taught yourself through the personal mind. You have taught yourself amiss, and you should not be your own teacher when you identify with a personal self.

4. You can withhold the Truth only from yourself. God does not refuse you the Answer to any problem that you perceive. Ask for the Answer that is yours, but that you did not make with the personal mind, and do not defend yourself against the Holy Spirit. You made the problem of perceiving separation, and God has answered with the Holy Spirit. Ask yourself this one simple question:

    'Do I want the problem or do I want the Answer?'

    Decide for the Answer, and you will have It, because It is already yours.

5.   You may complain that this course is not specific enough for you to understand and use, but perhaps you have not done what it specifically advocates. This is not a course in the play of ideas, but in the practical application of ideas. It is very specific to be told that if you ask you will receive the Answer. The Holy Spirit will answer every specific problem, as long as you believe that problems are specific. Its answer is both many and one, as long as you believe that the One is many. You may be afraid of the Holy Spirit's specific answers because you are afraid of what It will demand of you. But only by asking can you learn that What is of God does not demand anything of you. God gives; God does not take. When you refuse to ask the Holy Spirit, it is because you believe that asking is a form of taking something away from the Holy Spirit, rather than the opening of your awareness to the Holy Spirit.

6.   The Holy Spirit gives you only What is yours, and takes nothing in return. Everything *is* yours, and you share It with God. This is Reality. The Holy Spirit wills only to restore Reality to you, and It cannot misinterpret the question you must ask to have Reality restored to you. You *have* heard the Answer, but you misunderstood your own question. You believe that when you ask for guidance from the Holy Spirit, you are asking for deprivation.

7.   You who are One with God seem to not understand God. You believe that you can get by taking, so you believe in a world that takes, and you have lost sight of your Real Perception. You are afraid of the world that you see, but your Real Perception is still yours for the asking. Do not deny It to yourself, because It can set you free. Nothing of God will limit you who are One with God and whose Freedom is protected by God's Limitless Being. You are blessed when you are willing to ask the Truth of God without fear, because only then can you learn that God's Answer is your release from fear.

8.   You who are a Beautiful Part of God are asking only for what your Christ Mind promises you, and your Christ Mind will not deceive you. Heaven *is* within you. Believe that the Truth is in your Christ Mind, because your Christ Mind knows It is in you, and that your Mind is Whole in Truth. Extend God's Love in place of any of the

personal mind's projections and you have asked your Christ Mind for the Truth. You can see the Truth anywhere that you ask to see It.

9. Ask anything of your Christ Mind, and God will answer you, because your Christ Mind is not deceived in God, and God is not deceived in your Christ Mind. Do not, then, be deceived by the personal mind's projections onto others, and see only God's Love in their place, because you heal your mind by denying that it is split. Accept your entire mind as God accepts it, and heal your mind in Christ, because Christ is your healed mind. Christ is One with God, and Christ's every Thought is as Loving as the Thought by Which God holds Christ in Oneness. Do not be deceived by the personal mind's projections, because then you will be deceived in yourself. When you are deceived in yourself, you are deceived in God, and no deceit is possible in God.

10. In your Real Perception there is no sickness, because there is no separation and division. You recognize only Loving Thoughts, and the Help of God goes with you to extend everywhere. As you become willing to accept the Holy Spirit's Help by asking for It, you will extend It, because you will want to keep It in your awareness. Nothing will be beyond your power to heal, because the Holy Spirit will not deny your simple request. What problems will not disappear in the Presence of the Holy Spirit? Ask to learn of the Reality of the Holy Spirit by extending God's Love in place of the personal mind's projections, and you will see your Beauty reflected.

11. Do not accept the variable perceptions of the personal mind's projections, because it is your mind that you perceive, and you cannot accept healing without the part of your mind where you perceive. You extend your Real Perception as you extend Heaven, and this is how you heal your mind. To love yourself is to heal yourself, and you cannot perceive sickness as real and achieve your goal. Your Christ Mind and the part of your mind where you perceive a world are healed together, as they live together and love together. Do not be deceived by your perception of a world, because your mind is One, and it is One with God. Extend God's

Love in place of the world that you perceive and you will learn of God's Love for you.

12. If you are offended by another, pluck the offense from your own mind, because it is the personal mind's projection that you are seeing. When you are offended by the personal mind's projections, you are deceiving yourself, and denying your Christ Mind, in Which there is no offense, only healing. When you perceive offense you are doing it to yourself and condemning yourself, whom God does not condemn. Let the Holy Spirit remove all offenses in your mind, and perceive everything through the Holy Spirit, because the Holy Spirit wants to save you from your own condemnation. Accept the Holy Spirit's Healing Power, and extend It to everything that comes into your awareness, because the Holy Spirit Wills to heal you, in whom It is not deceived.

13. You are like a child that is terrified by his perception of ghosts, monsters, and dragons. And like a child, if you are willing to let go of your own interpretations and ask someone you trust for the meaning of what you perceive, you will be shown Reality, and your fears will go away. When a child is shown that the 'ghost' is a curtain, the 'monster' is a shadow, and the 'dragon' is a dream, he is no longer afraid and laughs at his own fear. And so the Holy Spirit can translate your misinterpretations into Reality, so that you can laugh at your fears.

14. You are afraid of the world that you perceive, of God, and of yourself. But you are merely deceived by your perceptions of these. Ask the Holy Spirit what they are, and you will laugh at your fears and replace them with Peace. Fear does not lie in Reality, but in your split mind, which does not understand What Reality is. Only your lack of understanding frightens you, and when you learn to perceive truly, you will be motivated to ask again for Truth when you are afraid. It is not the reality of the world, of God, and of yourself that frightens you. You perceive these as ghosts, monsters, and dragons. Ask the Holy Spirit for their reality, and It will tell you what it is. Because you are deceived by what you see, you need Reality to dispel your fears.

15. The exchange of your fears for Truth is yours for the asking. God is

not deceived in you, so you can only be deceived in yourself. But you can learn the Truth about yourself from the Holy Spirit, Which will teach you that, as Part of God, deceit in you is impossible. When you perceive yourself without deceit, you will accept your Real Perception in place of the false world that you made. And then God will raise you into Heaven.

Chapter 12

The Holy Spirit's Curriculum

1. The Judgment of the Holy Spirit

1. You have been told to not make your error of perceived separation from God real to you, and the way to do this is very simple, because if you want to make the error real to you, you have to *make* it real to you, since it is not true. But Truth is Real, and to believe Truth *you do not have to do anything.* Understand that you do not respond directly to anything, but you respond to your interpretation of it. Your interpretation then becomes the justification for your response. That is why you get lost analyzing the motives of others. If you decide that someone is really trying to attack you, desert you, or enslave you, you will respond as if they are really doing so, making separation real to you. When you interpret your error of perceived separation from God, you give it power and you overlook Truth.

2. For you to analyze the motivations of any personal self is very complicated, obscuring, and it always involves the personal mind in you. The whole process is your attempt to demonstrate the personal mind's ability to understand what you perceive, because you react to its interpretations as if they were fact. You may then control your behavior, but not your emotions, attacking your mind by splitting it again.

3. There is only one interpretation of motivation that makes any sense, and because it is the Holy Spirit's judgment, it requires no effort on your part: Your every extension of Love is True; everything else, no matter what form it takes in you or in others, is a projection of your split mind, therefore it is your call for healing. You are not justified in responding in anger to your call for healing. Your only appropriate response is a willingness to extend healing, because this is all that you are asking for. Offer anything else, and you assume the right to decide what is real with the personal

mind's interpretation. The danger to your mind is that if you interpret your appeal for healing as something else, your response will be to the personal mind's interpretation, not to heal your mind to return it to Reality.

4. There is nothing that prevents you from recognizing all of your calls for healing as exactly that, except for your own imagined need to attack Reality. It is only this that makes you willing to engage in endless 'battles' with Reality, in which you deny your real need for healing by making the need unreal. You would not do this except for your unwillingness to accept Reality as It is by denying It to yourself.

5. Do not judge with the personal mind What the personal mind cannot understand. Your investment in making the personal self real to you makes you an unreliable witness for Truth. You are unwilling to recognize your calll for healing, because you do not want to receive healing by extending it. For you to fail to recognize your call for healing is for you to refuse healing. When you refuse your call for healing it is because you want to maintain the illusion that you do not need healing, because only by answering the call can you be healed. Deny yourself an extension of healing and you will not recognize God's Answer to you. The Holy Spirit does not need your help in interpreting motivation, but you do need the Holy Spirit's help.

6. Only gratitude is an appropriate response from you to the world that you perceive, both for the Loving Thoughts that you extend there, and for the opportunities for healing that the personal mind's perceptions of separation give you there, because both bring Love into your awareness if you perceive them truly. All of your sense of strain comes from not perceiving truly. How simple is God's plan for your salvation! Gratitude is the one appropriate response to Perceptions that reflect Reality, because there is no conflict in Reality. There is only One Teacher of Reality, Which understands What Reality is, and Which does not change Its Mind about Reality, because Reality is Unchanging. In your identification with a personal mind, your interpretation of what reality is, is meaningless, but the Holy Spirit's Interpretation of Reality is

consistently True. The Holy Spirit gives this Interpretation to you, because it is *for* you. Do not attempt to heal the personal mind's projections of separation onto others in your way, because in your identification with a personal self, you do not know how to heal yourself. But instead, see your call for healing in the personal mind's projections, and you will recognize your own need for God.

7.   Your interpretation of the needs that you perceive in the world is your interpretation of *your* needs. By extending healing, you ask for healing, and, if you perceive that your one need is healing, you will be healed. You will recognize God's Answer as you want It to be, if you want It truly. Every appeal for healing that you answer by extending your Christ Mind brings God closer to your awareness. For the sake of your one need, then, hear every call for healing as what it is so God can answer you.

8.   By consistently applying the Holy Spirit's interpretation of the personal mind's projections of separation onto others as your own call for healing, you will gain an increasing awareness that the Holy Spirit's interpretation is equally applicable to the fear that you experience. It is necessary for you to recognize what is fear to demonstrate to you your need to escape from fear, but recognizing it is only the first step. The Holy Spirit still must translate fear into Truth, because if you were left with the fear, you would be taking a step away from Reality, not toward It. Your recognizing what is fear without disguise is crucial to undoing the personal mind, and the Holy Spirit's interpretations of the projections of the personal mind as your call for healing teaches you that fear itself is a call for healing. So the personal mind's perceptions of separation are what fear is. If you do not protect fear, the Holy Spirit will reinterpret it. The ultimate value of you learning to perceive your attack on God through the personal mind's perceptions of separation as your own call for Love is for you to recognize that your attack and the fear of God that it produces are not real. Fear *is* your call for Love in your unconscious recognition of the Love that you have denied

9.   Your fear is a symptom of your own deep sense of loss of God. When you perceive fear in the world that you perceive, and extend God's Love to heal your mind, the basic cause of your fear is

removed, and you teach yourself that fear does not exist in you. The Means for removing fear is in you, and you have demonstrated It by extending It. The only emotions you are capable of are fear and Love, and fear is false, because it was made out of your denial of God. But this denial depends on your belief in What is denied for its own existence. When you interpret fear correctly as an affirmation of your underlying belief in God, you will make fear useless to you. You will automatically discard defenses that do not work. If you look at What fear is supposed to conceal, fear will become meaningless to you. You will have denied its power to conceal Love from you, which was its only purpose, and the veil that you had drawn across your awareness of Love will disappear.

10. If you want to look on Love, Which is the Reality of your Whole Mind, recognize in your every defense against Love your underlying appeal *for* Love. Learn of Real Perception by answering your appeal for Love with Love. The Holy Spirit's interpretation of fear *does* dispel it in you, because you cannot deny your awareness of Truth. Reinterpreting fear is how the Holy Spirit replaces fear with Love and translates your error of perceiving separation from God into Truth. You will learn from the Holy Spirit how to replace your illusion of separation from God with the Fact of your Oneness with God. The separation that you perceive is only your denial of Oneness, and, correctly interpreted, it attests to your Eternal Knowledge that Oneness is True.

2. The Way to Remember God

1. Your experience of miracles translates your denial into Truth. To Love yourself is to heal yourself, and when you are sick you do not Love yourself. Sickness is your appeal for the Love that will heal you but that you are denying yourself. If you knew the Truth about yourself, you could not be sick. Your task as a miracle worker is to *deny the denial of Truth*. You must heal yourself, because the Truth is in you. But, having obscured It, your awareness of your Christ Mind must be extended in your perception, because Christ *is* here.

2. Christ is in your entire mind, no matter how dense are the illusions it seems to perceive. If you don't give power to illusions to obscure

Christ in your mind they have none, because the power of illusions comes from you. You must withdraw your power from illusions and remember all Power is of God. You can remember this throughout your entire mind, so do not allow the personal mind to make you forget it. You *must* remember God throughout your entire mind, and *this is what you have forgotten.* Your extension of healing to replace the personal mind's perceptions of separation is how you heal your mind and remember God. You forgot God when you perceived a world, and extending the Holy Spirit is the way to remember God.

3.   When you perceive that sickness in any form anywhere is real, it is *your* call for healing, so offer God's Love to heal you, because it is the only remedy that you need. You will be made whole as you extend wholeness, because for you to perceive in sickness your appeal for healing is for you to recognize in the personal mind's hatred of you your call for Love. For you to extend Love in place of the personal mind's perceptions of separation, which is all that you really want in any situation, is for you to extend Love to yourself. God Wills you to know your entire mind as yourself. Answer with Love any call for Love that you perceive, and your call for Love is answered. Your healing is the Love of Christ for God and for Itself.

4.   Your perceptions frighten you when you do not understand them. Your fears vanish when you ask the Holy Spirit for understanding, and you accept what It shows you. If you hide your fears, you will keep them. You can be helped if you accept that you do not understand what your perceptions mean in your identification with a personal self, but if you think that you *do* understand them, you will not open yourself to healing. You are hiding behind the heavy illusions that you have made and you are afraid, but, in your false certainty that you understand them, you are refusing to look at them with an open mind.

5.   Do not save your illusions, because they are not fit for Christ, so they are not fit for you. Look at what you are afraid of. Only your anticipation is frightening, because your illusions are nothing, so they are not frightening. Do not delay, because your illusions of hatred will not leave you without Help, and the Holy Spirit is here

now to help you. Learn to be quiet in the midst of the turmoil of the personal mind, because quietness is the end of strife and your Goal is Peace. Look straight at every illusion that rises to delay you, because your Goal is inevitable, since It is Eternal. The Goal of Love is your Right, and It belongs to you despite your illusions.

6. You still want What God Wills, and no illusions can defeat you who are One with God in your purpose. Your purpose was given to you by God, and you must accomplish It, because God Wills It. Remember your purpose, because it is your Will to do so. What has been accomplished for you is yours. Do not let the personal mind's hatred of you stand in the way of Love for you, because nothing can withstand the Love of Christ for God or God's Love for Christ.

7. Your Christ Mind is not hidden because *you* are hiding, and in a little while you will see Christ, because you will become aware of Christ within you as surely as Jesus became aware of the Christ Mind in Himself. His awareness was *for you*. In the resurrection of Jesus is your release, because your mission is to escape from crucifixion, not from correction. Trust in your Christ Mind, Which is with you as God is with your Christ Mind. Christ walks with God in Peace, and that means Peace goes with you on your way to God.

8. There is no fear in Perfect Love. Your way to God makes Perfect *to* you What is already Perfect *in* you. You do not fear the unknown but the Known. You will not fail in your mission, because Jesus did not fail in His. Trust Christ , Which trusts you completely, and you will easily accomplish the Goal of Perfect Love. Perfect Love *is*, and you cannot deny It. It is much harder for you to deny Perfect Love than it is for you to deny your denial of It, and what you can accomplish with your Christ Mind you will believe when you see It accomplished.

9. You've tried to banish Love, and you have not succeeded, but when you choose to banish fear, you *will* succeed. Christ is with you, but you do not know it. Christ lives within you in the Peace of God. Exchange awareness of this for your awareness of fear. When you have overcome fear with your Christ Mind – not by hiding fear, or minimizing it, or denying it in any way – Christ is What you will see. You cannot lay aside your obstacles to spiritual awareness

without looking at them, because you must look at them to judge against them and let them go. If you look at them, the Holy Spirit will judge them truly. The Holy Spirit cannot rid you of what you hide, because by hiding it you are not offering it to the Holy Spirit.

10. You are embarking on an organized, well-structured, and carefully planned program to learn how to offer to the Holy Spirit everything that you do not want. The Holy Spirit knows what to do, but, in your identification with a personal self, you do not understand how to use what the Holy Spirit knows. The Holy Spirit releases whatever you give to the Holy Spirit that is not of God. But you must be willing to look at everything yourself, because otherwise the Holy Spirit's knowledge is useless to you. The Holy Spirit will not fail to help you, because helping you is the Holy Spirit's only Purpose. You have more reason to fear the world that you perceive, which you made with fear, than to fear looking at the cause of your fear so that you can let go of fear Forever.

3. The Investment in Reality

1. Jesus once asked you to sell all that you have, give it to the poor, and follow Him. This is what He meant: You are poor when you have mistakenly invested in a world of separation, and if you have no investment in the world, then you can teach yourself and learn that God is your real Treasure. When you perceive any need in the world, you have the means to extend God's Love and supply the need, because the world is in your mind. You learn this lesson perfectly if you refuse to believe in poverty of any kind, because poverty is lack, and your only lack is God, so your only need is God.

2. When you insist on doing something or on not doing something in your perception that you are in a world it is because you believe that doing it or not doing it is your salvation, and this makes your separation from God real to you. Your *insistence* means your investment, and what you invest in is always related to your idea of salvation. The two questions you should ask yourself are: '*What* is to be saved?' and '*How* can it be saved?'

3. When you become angry for any reason, you believe that it is the

personal self that you need to save and that attack is the way to save it. Whether you feel attacked or you do the attacking, you are agreeing with this belief. *If you believe in attack you are poor.* Your perception of lack is your asking for Love, not for further lack. You can offer healing, but if you accept attack as real, you are making your lack of God real to you. If you did not invest in attack, you would not feel lack and need to overlook it.

4. When you are asked to do something in your perception that you are in a world that you consider outrageous in your identification with a personal self, *recognize that it does not matter what you do in the world* and do not insist on having your way. Your opposition makes the world matter to you and makes it real to you. But every request that you receive in the world that you perceive is really an opportunity for you to extend God's Love. When you deny yourself this opportunity, you deny that you are perceiving a call for salvation in the world because *you* are calling for salvation. Your sense of lack comes from the personal mind, never from God. You will not judge any request when you value only God and you no longer want anything from the world that you made.

5. It is your mind that must be saved, and it is saved through Peace. Your mind is the *only* thing that needs to be saved, and Peace is the *only* way for you to save it. Any response that you give to any perception in your mind that is not Love comes from your confusion of 'what' needs to be saved and 'how' it needs to be saved. The only answers are 'your mind' and 'Peace'. Do not lose sight of this or believe that there is another answer, or you will be poor and not know that you live in God's Abundance and that your salvation is here.

6. When you identify with a personal self you to attack yourself, make yourself poor, and make yourself feel deprived. You experience depression and anger because you exchange Self-Love for Self-hate, making you afraid of your True Self. You do not realize this, even if you are fully aware of anxiety. And not perceiving that the source of your anxiety is your own identification with a personal self, you try to handle anxiety with some sort of adjustment to the world that you perceive as outside of you.

In fact, it is crucial to your attempted adjustment to perceive the world as outside of you. To maintain your identification with a personal self, you must not realize that you make the world, and that there is no world outside of your own mind.

7. If the only Reality in the world that you perceive are the Loving Thoughts of your Christ Mind that you extend there through your Real Perception, then the world must be in your mind. Your insane thoughts are in your mind, too, but you will not acknowledge an internal conflict of this magnitude. It endangers your split mind, because your recognition that your mind encompasses completely opposed thought systems within itself is intolerable to you. So you must project outward the part of the split that opposes your mind's Reality. Everything that you perceive as the world outside of you is merely your attempt to maintain your identification with a personal self, because you believe that this identification is your salvation. The consequence of this is that you are in conflict with the world that you perceive, because you think that it is antagonistic toward you. This is necessary, because you must project on the world the antagonistic thoughts that you cannot tolerate within you. So to truly get rid of hatred, you must realize that any hatred that you perceive is in your mind and not outside of you. And you must get rid of hatred to see with your Real Perception.

8. God so loves you that God gives your perception of a world of separation to your Christ Mind to make it into Real Perception. Real Perception does not see the world of death; It sees only reflections of the Eternal. God gives you Real Perception in exchange for the world that you made to be separate from God, which is the symbol of death. If you could really separate yourself from God, you *would* die.

9. The world that you perceive with the personal mind is the world of separation. Maybe you are willing to accept even death to deny God, but God does not want it so, so it is not so. You cannot will against God, so you have no control over the world that you made, because it is not your *will* but your *wish* to be unlike God. The world that you made is totally chaotic, it is governed by arbitrary, senseless 'laws', and it is without meaning of any kind, because it

is made out of what you do not want projected from your mind out of fear. But it is only in your mind, and so is your salvation. Do not believe that the world is outside of your mind, because you can only gain control over it by recognizing where it is. You *do* have control over your *mind*, because your mind is where you make decisions.

10. If you recognize that all attack that you perceive in yourself or in the world is only in your own mind, you will recognize attack where it is, and you will be able to undo it. Your salvation is also in your mind, because Christ is in your mind. It is your mind, not the world that you perceive, that is the source of your erroneous sense of separation from God. But your Christ Mind is the Correction. Bring your perceptions of a world to your Christ Mind, because Christ is the Truth. From There, your perception will be changed. God and Christ dwell within you in Peace, and you will look out from Peace on your Real Perceptions. But to find this Peace, you must give up all investment in the world that you project from the personal mind and allow the Holy Spirit to extend your Real Perceptions from Christ within you.

4. Seeking and Finding

1. Love is Oneness, so the personal mind is certain that Love is dangerous, and this is its central teaching. It never says this openly, and when you identify with a personal self you will intensely engage in the search for Love. But the personal mind, though encouraging your search for Love very actively, makes one provision: do not find It. Its one rule can be summed up this way, then: 'Seek, but do *not* find.' This is the personal mind's one promise to you, and it will keep it. With you it pursues, with fanatic insistence, its goal of *not* finding Love, and, though its judgment is severely impaired, it is completely consistent.

2. Your search for Love under the guidance of a personal mind is therefore bound to end in defeat for you. The personal mind cannot Love, and in your search for Love, you are seeking for What it is afraid for you to find. But your search for Love is inevitable, because *you* want It. Because you are the personal mind's source, it

cannot be completely cut off from you, or you would not believe in it. It is your mind that gives it any existence at all. But it is also your mind that has the power to deny the personal mind's existence, and you will do so as soon as you recognize the futile journey on which the personal mind has set you.

3. Obviously, in your identification with a personal self, you do not want to find What will defeat this identification. The personal mind is totally unable to love, so it is totally inadequate in Love's Presence, because it cannot respond with Love at all. In the Presence of Love, you have to abandon the personal mind, because it is apparent that it does not teach you the response that you need to know Love. So the personal mind teaches you a distorted form of 'love' that calls forth the responses that the personal mind *can* teach. Follow its teachings, and you will search for Love, but you will not recognize Love.

4. The personal mind sets you on a journey that leads you to a sense of futility and depression. For you to seek and to not find is not joyous for you, and this is not the promise to yourself that you should keep. The Holy Spirit offers you another promise, one that will lead to your Joy: 'Seek for Love and you *will* find It.' Under the Holy Spirit's guidance, you will not be defeated in your Goal of Love. The Goal that the Holy Spirit sets for you is the Goal that the Holy Spirit will give to you. The Holy Spirit will never deceive you, whom It loves with God's Love.

5. You *will* undertake a journey because you are not at home in your perception that you are in a world, and you *will* seek for your Home, whether you realize It is within you or not. If you believe that your Home is outside of you, your search will be futile, because you will be seeking It where It is not. You do not remember how to look within, because you do not believe that your Home is there. But the Holy Spirit remembers It for you, and it is Its mission to guide you Home. As the Holy Spirit fulfills Its mission, It will teach you yours, because your mission is the same. By extending the Holy Spirit in your mind where you perceive a world, you are following the Holy Spirit Home.

6. Look upon the Guide that God has given to you to learn that you

have Eternal Life. Death is not God's Will or your will, because only Truth is God's Will. You do not pay a price for the Life given to you by God, but you do pay a heavy price for death. If death is what you want, you will sell Everything God has given to you to purchase it. And you believe that you have done this. But you cannot really sell What God has given to you, because What God gives to you, you cannot trade away. Your mind is Whole, because God's Mind is Whole. and God's Extension is like God.

7. The correction of your perception of separation from God is not the price of your Wholeness, but it is the price of your *awareness* of your Wholeness. What you chose to 'sell' was kept for you, and now you must invest in It with your Will. What God gives awaits your recognition that you have been saved for It. The Holy Spirit guides you into Eternal Life. but you must relinquish your investment in death, or you will not see that Life is all around you.

5. The Sane Curriculum

1. Only Love is Strong, because It is Undivided. When you are Strong you have no motivation to attack, so before you attack you must have let the idea that you are weak enter your mind. Perceiving yourself as weak is always the first attack you make, and it is an attack on yourself. No longer perceiving Oneness, and regarding yourself as weak, you attack others in the world that you perceive to replace the Strength that you gave away. You use attack because you believe that attack works, since it worked when you attacked yourself to make yourself weak.

2. Your recognition of your inherent Invulnerability as Part of God is essential to restore you to the awareness of your Wholeness. If you accept your Invulnerability, you are recognizing that the attack that you made on yourself by identifying with a personal self has no effect. You seem to have attacked yourself, but nothing real happened, so you have not done anything. Once you recognize this, you will see no value in attack of any kind, because it does not work, and it does not protect you. But your recognition of your Invulnerability has more than a negative value. Your attacks on yourself have failed to weaken you, so you are still Strong.

225

Therefore, you have no need to attack others to establish your Strength.

3. You will only recognize the utter uselessness of attack by recognizing that your attack on yourself by identifying with a personal self has no effects on the Truth in you. If you try to attack others, and you seem to succeed, you will be unable to avoid seeing this as reinforcement of the value of attack. The only place you can cancel out all reinforcement of attack is in yourself. You are always your first point of attack, and if this has never been, then it has no consequences.

4. The Holy Spirit's Love is your Strength while your strength is divided and therefore unreal. You cannot trust your own Love when you attack It. You cannot learn of Perfect Love with a split mind, because when your mind is split you are a poor learner. You have tried to make your separation from God eternal, because you have wanted to retain the characteristics of God's Oneness but with your own content. But God's Oneness is not of you, and as a poor learner you need special teaching.

5. With a split mind, you have learning handicaps in a very literal sense. There are areas in your learning skills so impaired that you can progress only under constant clear-cut direction from a Teacher that transcends your limited resources. The Holy Spirit is your Limitless Resource, because you cannot learn from the limited personal mind. You have placed yourself in an impossible learning situation, and you clearly need a special Teacher and a special lesson plan. As a poor learner, you are a poor teacher for yourself. You cannot turn to yourself in your limited situation to learn how to escape your limitations. If you understood What is beyond the limits that you have made, you would not be handicapped.

6. Your handicap is that, in your identification with a personal self, you do not know What Love is. Don't try to teach yourself from a personal mind What it cannot understand, or try to set up learning goals from a personal mind, which has failed you. Its learning goal for you has actually been for you to *not* learn What Love is, and this does not lead to successful learning for you. You must extend Love to everything for you to understand What Love is, and your

inability to generalize is a crucial learning failure. Generalizing is an essential learning aid for extending Love, but don't ask the personal mind, which has failed to learn, what it is for, because it does not know. If it could interpret generalizing correctly, it would have learned from it.

7. The personal mind's rule is: 'Seek but do not find.' Translated into learning terms this means 'Try to learn, but do not succeed'. The result of this learning plan is obviously that you must misinterpret every legitimate teaching aid, real instruction, and sensible guide to learning What Love is, because they are all for learning What this strange learning plan is *against*. In your identification with a personal mind, you are trying to learn how *not* to learn about Love, and the aim of the personal mind's teaching is to defeat your real learning. Of course you end up confused. The personal mind's lesson plan does not make any sense, and your attempt at learning-by-not-learning has so weakened your mind that you cannot Love, because the lesson plan you have chosen is against Love and amounts to a lesson in how to attack yourself. A supplement to this lesson plan is learning how *not* to overcome your split mind, which makes the primary aim of not-learning believable to you. And you will not overcome your split mind in the personal mind's lesson plan, because all of your learning will be on the personal mind's behalf. The personal mind speaks against your real learning, as your learning from the personal mind speaks against your True Mind, so you fight against all real learning and succeed. But there is Something you want to learn, and that you *can* learn, because it is your choice to do so.

8. In your identification with a personal mind you have tried to learn separation from God, which you do not really want, and this has been depressing for you. But take heart, because the lesson plan that you have made for yourself with the personal mind is merely ridiculous if you look at it. It is not possible that the way for you to attain a goal is for you to not attain it. Resign as your own teacher in your identification with a personal mind, and this resignation will not depress you. It is the result of an honest appraisal of what you have taught yourself from a

personal mind and what has resulted from your teaching. Under the proper learning conditions, which the personal mind cannot provide or understand, you will become an excellent teacher of Love and therefore an excellent learner of Love. It is not so yet, and it will not be so until you have allowed the whole learning situation that you are in to be reversed.

9.   Your learning potential is limitless, because it will lead you to God. You can teach yourself the way to God and learn it if you follow the Teacher within you that knows the way to God and understands God's lesson plan for learning it. This lesson plan is totally consistent, because its Goal is not divided, and its Means and End are One. You only need to offer your undivided attention, and everything else will be given to you. You really *do* want to learn What Love is, and nothing can oppose the decision of you who are One with God. Your ability to learn is as limitless as you are.

6. The Vision of Christ

1.   The personal mind tries to teach you how to gain the whole world and lose your own Spirit. The Holy Spirit teaches you that you cannot lose your Spirit, and there is no gain in the world because it is nothing. For you to invest in nothing steeps you in a sense of lack, and its cost to you seems enormous. You lose your Real Perception by denying your Reality, and the world that you see instead gives you nothing in return. You cannot 'sell' your Spirit, but you can 'sell' your *awareness* of It. You cannot *perceive* your Spirit, but you can *know* It. However, you will not know It as long as you perceive something else as more valuable.

2.   The Holy Spirit is your Strength, because the Holy Spirit knows It is you. It is perfectly aware that you do not know this in your identification with a personal self, and It is perfectly aware of how to teach you What you are. The Holy Spirit loves you and teaches you What you are, because It wills to extend Itself. Remembering What you are for you, the Holy Spirit cannot let you forget your Worth. God never ceases to remind the Holy Spirit of you, and the Holy Spirit never ceases to remind you of God. God is in your memory, because the Holy Spirit is there. You chose to forget God,

but you do not really want to do so, so you can decide again. This is your Christ Mind's decision, so it is your decision.

3.   You do not want the world. The only things of value in the world that you perceive are your extensions of Love there, and they are the only reality it will ever have. The world's value is not in itself, but your Value is in you. You perceive your Value by extending your Loving Thoughts outward to replace the world of separation, and make your perceptions reflect your Reality. Real Perception is the Holy Spirit's Gift, so It belongs to you.

4.   Correction is for you, who cannot see Reality. The Holy Spirit's mission is to open your eyes to Love, because the Holy Spirit knows that you are not blind, but that you merely have your eyes closed. The Holy Spirit wants to undo your denial so that you can remember God. Your Christ Mind's Eyes are open. and Christ will look upon whatever you see with Love if you accept Christ's Perception as yours. The Holy Spirit holds the Real Perception of your Christ Mind for your entire mind. In the Holy Spirit's Perception, your entire mind is perfect, and the Holy Spirit longs to extend Its Perception to be all that your mind perceives. It will show you your Real Perceptions, because God gave you Heaven. Through the Holy Spirit, God calls your entire mind to remember What it is. Your awareness of God begins with your investment in Real Perception, because here you will learn to reinvest in your True Self. Reality is One with God and you, and the Holy Spirit blesses your perceptions with your Oneness.

5.   When you see your Real Perceptions, which you will certainly do, you will remember Oneness. But you must learn What denial costs you and refuse to pay it, because only then will you decide to remember God. Then your Real Perceptions will spring to your sight, because your Christ Mind has never left you. Your Christ Mind waits to be seen by you, because It has never lost sight of you. Your Christ Mind looks quietly on your Real Perceptions, Which It wants to extend to you, as God's Love is extended to your Christ Mind. Your Christ Mind wants to give you What is yours. In perfect Peace, Christ waits for you within, holding out God's Love to you in the Quiet Blessing of the Holy Spirit. The Holy Spirit leads your

entire mind Home to God, where Christ waits for Its Self.

6. Every part of your mind and being is One in Christ, as Christ's Mind and Being are One in God. Christ's Love for you is Christ's Love for God, Which is God's Love for Christ. When the Holy Spirit has at last led you to Christ within, your perception will be so Holy that it will transfer easily to God as its natural extension. Love transfers to Love without interference, because It is One. As you perceive God's Love in more and more situations, the Holy Spirit's Perception will increase in you, and become generalized. When you have learned to apply God's Love universally, your perceptions and your Knowledge of God will become so similar that they share God's Law of Oneness.

7. What is One is not separate, and your denial of separation from God reinstates your Knowledge of God. From your awareness of God within you, your mind's perceptions will become so enlightened that your Spirit will rejoin with the Mind of God and become One. Very Gently, God will smile upon Itself, loving the Extension that is Its Oneness. The world that your mind perceives will have no purpose as your entire mind blends into God's Purpose. Your Real Perception will slip quietly into Heaven, Which is Eternal. There, your Whole Mind will join in the Perfect Love of God and of Itself. Heaven is your Home, and being in God, It is also in you.

7. Looking Within

1. Your learning is invisible, but it is attested to by its results. Your experience of miracles demonstrate that you have learned from the Holy Spirit. As you experience a miracle in more and more situations, you demonstrate that you have learned to generalize God's Love. You will recognize that every miracle is whole and complete when you apply them equally to every situation. Miracles apply in every situation, and by your applying them in every situation, you gain your Real Perception. In this Holy perception, you will be made whole again in your awareness, and from your acceptance of the correction of your perception of separation from God, the Holy Spirit will bless your entire mind. The Holy Spirit's blessing lies in

every part of your mind, and in your blessing every perception that your mind has you are blessed.

2. You must extend correction to all of your mind where you perceive a world to recognize that your perception has been corrected. You cannot see the Invisible, but by Its effects you can know that It is here. By perceiving what It does, you recognize Its Being, and by what It does, you learn What It is. You cannot see your Strength, but you gain confidence in Its existence as It enables you to act, and the results of your action you *can* see.

3. The Holy Spirit is Invisible, but you can see the results of Its Presence and learn through them that It is here. What the Holy Spirit enables you to do is clearly not of the world, because it violates the world's 'laws' of reality. Its every law of time and space and of magnitude and mass is transcended, because the Holy Spirit enables you to extend God's Love to everything equally. When you perceive the Holy Spirit's results, you understand that the Holy Spirit is within you, and you finally know that the Holy Spirit *is* you.

4. You cannot see the Holy Spirit, but you can see Its manifestations. If you do not, you will not realize that the Holy Spirit is here. Your experience of miracles witnesses to the Holy Spirit and speak for Its Presence. What you cannot see becomes compellingly real to you as Its Presence becomes manifest *through* you. Do the Holy Spirit's Work, because Its function is your function. As your Function in Heaven is extending God, your function in the world that you perceive is extending healing to all of your mind through corrected perception. God shares Its Function with you in Heaven, and the Holy Spirit shares Its function with you in your perception that you are in a world. As long as you believe that you have other functions, you will need correction. Your Peace is destroyed when you believe that you have a function other than healing your mind, and destroying Peace is a goal in direct opposition to the Holy Spirit's purpose.

5. You see what you expect, and you expect what you invite. Your perception is the result of your invitation to either the personal mind or to the Holy Spirit. You will believe in what you manifest,

and what you see reflected back at you in your perception will convince you of the truth of what is within you. Two ways of perceiving are in your mind, and what you perceive is the result of the guidance that you have chosen.

6. [If you see Jesus, you are seeing a manifestation of the Holy Spirit, because you have invited the Holy Spirit. The Holy Spirit will send you Its Witnesses if you are willing to see them.] You see what you seek, and what you seek for you will find. The personal mind finds the separation that it seeks and only that. It does not find Love, because Love is not what it is seeking. Seeking and finding are the same, and if you seek for two goals you will find them, but you will not recognize either of them, because you will confuse them with each other. Your mind always seeks to be whole, and if it is split and wants to keep the split, it will believe it has only one goal by making two goals seem like one.

7. What you project or extend is up to you, but you must do one or the other, because that is the Law of Mind. You always look within before you perceive. When you look within you choose your guide, and then you look outward and see witnesses for the guide that you chose. You find what you seek. What you want in yourself you will make manifest to you in your perception, and you will accept it, because you put it there by wanting it. When you look on the personal mind's projections and think that you do not want them, understand that you really *do* want them or you wouldn't see them. This conflicted perception arises from your denial that you have two goals: Wholeness and separation from your Wholeness. Instead of seeing its own split, your mind perceives a world outside and divided off from it, so that it can maintain the illusion that it is still whole and pursuing only one goal. As long as you perceive the world as something separate, your mind is not healed, because the world is in your mind. For you to be healed is for you to pursue only one goal, a whole mind, because you have accepted it and you want it.

8. When you want only Love, you will see nothing else. The contradictory witnesses that you perceive reflect your conflicting invitations. You have looked within and accepted the conflict there,

because you want it. But do not believe that the witnesses to your conflict make the conflict real. They only attest to what you want to be real, returning to you the messages that you gave them to give to you. Love is also recognized by its Messengers. Love will manifest to you when you invite It.

9.   Your only freedom in your perception that you are in a world is the freedom to decide. You can decide to see your Real Perceptions. The world that you have made does not reflect Reality, but it does reflect what you *want* to be reality. You cannot really give anything but Love, so you cannot really receive anything but Love. But if you think that you have received something else, it is because you have looked within, and you think that you have the power to give something else. If you want something other than Love, you will find it, because you will seek for it.

10.   You are afraid of the Holy Spirit, because you looked within and saw something that frightened you. Yet you could not have seen Reality, because the Reality of your Mind is Lovely in Its Oneness with God. Being of God, your Mind's Power and Limitlessness can only bring you Peace *if you really look upon It*. If you look within and are afraid, you have looked on something that is not really there. Yet, in your Mind, the Holy Spirit and your Wholeness are in the Perfect Safety of the Oneness of God's Mind, Which Wills only to extend through you.

11.   When you have accepted your mission to extend Peace, you will find Peace, because by making It manifest you will see It. Peace's Holy Witnesses will surround you when you call on Them. Your Christ Mind has heard and answered your call, but you will not see or hear the Answer that you sought until you want *only* Christ. As Christ becomes more real to you, you will learn that you do want only Christ. You will see your Christ Mind as you look within, and then you will look on your Real Perceptions. Only your Real Perceptions exist and can be seen through your Christ Mind. As you decide so you will see, and all that you see will witness to your decision.

12.   When you decide to look within and see Christ it will be because you have decided to manifest Truth. And as you manifest Truth

you will see It within *and* in all that you perceive. You will see It in your perception, *because* you first saw It within. What you see in your perception is a judgment of what you see within. If it is a judgment of the personal mind, it will be wrong, because judgment through the personal mind is not your function. But the Holy Spirit's function is judgment, and It is always right. You share the Holy Spirit's function only when you judge through the Holy Spirit. With the personal mind, you will always judge against yourself. But the Holy Spirit will always judge *for* you.

13. When you look at the world that you perceive and react unfavorably to what you see, you have judged yourself unworthy and have condemned yourself to death. The personal mind's ultimate goal for you is death because it believes that you are guilty and deserving of death. God knows that you are deserving of Life. The wish for your death never leaves the personal mind, because that is what it reserves for you in the end. It wants to kill you as the final expression of its feeling for you, but it lets you live only to wait for death. It will torment you while you live, but its hatred for you will not be satisfied until you die. Your destruction is the one end toward which the personal mind works and the only end with which it will be satisfied.

14. The personal mind is not a traitor to God, because God cannot be betrayed. But you are a traitor to yourself when you identify with a personal self and believe that you have betrayed God. That is why undoing your guilt is an essential part of the Holy Spirit's teaching. As long as you identify with a personal self you will feel guilty and believe that you deserve death, because you will believe that you have betrayed God. You will think that death comes from God and not from your split mind, because when you identify with a personal self you project its goal onto God. As long as you want to identify with a personal self, God cannot save you.

15. When you are tempted to give into the desire for death, remember that Jesus demonstrated that the Christ Mind does not die. You will realize this is true when you look within and see your Christ Mind. Jesus overcame death through Christ, and Christ is in you. Eternal Life is given to your Christ Mind, so It is given to you. When you

234

learn to make Christ manifest, you will never see death. You will look upon the deathless in yourself, and you will see only the Eternal as you look upon a Perception that cannot die.

8. The Attraction of Love for Love

1. Do you really believe that you can kill What is One with God? You are safe in God's Oneness and truly far from your destructive thoughts, but you do not know God or yourself because of these thoughts. You attack your Real Perceptions every moment, and yet you are surprised that you cannot see Them. If you seek Love only to attack It, you will not find It. Love extends naturally, and you can find It only by extending It. Offer Love and It will come to you, because It is drawn to Itself. But offer attack and Love will be hidden from you, because It lives in Peace.

2. Your Christ Mind is safe in God, and It knows that It is safe in God, so It cannot fear. God's Love holds your Christ Mind in perfect Peace, and, needing nothing, Christ asks for nothing. Yet Christ seems far from you, whose Self It is, because you chose to attack yourself, and your Christ Mind disappeared from your awareness. But your Christ Mind has not changed, though you have. Your split mind and all that it has done are not of God, and it cannot live in an awareness of God.

3. When you chose to see what is not true, What *is* True became invisible to you. But It is not invisible to Itself, because the Holy Spirit sees It clearly. It is only invisible to you, because you are looking at something else. It is not up to you to decide what reality is. What *can* be seen is What the Holy Spirit sees. God defines Reality, not you in your split mind. God *is* Reality. You knew this, but you have forgotten, and because God has given you a way to remember, you are not condemned to oblivion.

4. God loves you, so you can never forget God, because you cannot forget What God has placed in your mind. You can deny God, but you cannot lose God. The Holy Spirit will answer every question you ask, and the Holy Spirit's Perception will correct your perception of everything. What you have made invisible to you is the only Truth, and What you do not hear is the only Answer. God

wills to reunite your mind, and God did not abandon you in your distress. You are only waiting for God, but you do not know this. But God is still in your mind and cannot be obliterated. Your Memory of God is not in the past or in the future; It is here Forever, Always.

5. You only have to ask to remember God and you will. But you cannot remember God if you want to obliterate God. Your Memory of God can only come to you if you want to remember God, and you give up your insane desire to control reality. You cannot even control the personal self, so you should hardly try to control reality. Look at what you have tried to make real, and be glad that it is not real.

6. You who are One with God should not be content with nothing. You cannot really see what is not real and has no value. God does not offer you what has no value, and, being God's Extension, you can not receive what has no value. You were corrected the instant that you thought that you left God. Everything that you have made has never been and is really invisible, because the Holy Spirit does not see it. Yet, What the Holy Spirit *does* see is yours to see, and through the Holy Spirit's Perception, your perception is healed. You have made invisible to you the only Truth that your perception holds by seeing a world of separation instead. You have valued nothing, and you have sought nothing. You have made nothing real to you, so you think that you have seen it, but *nothing is there*. Your Christ Mind is invisible to you because of what you have made visible to yourself.

7. It does not matter how much distance you have tried to put between Truth and your awareness of Truth. You can see your Christ Mind because you can extend It. The Holy Spirit sees only Christ and sees only your Christ Mind in you. What is invisible to the personal mind is Perfect in the Holy Spirit's Perception, and encompasses all that the Holy Spirit sees. The Holy Spirit remembers you, because the Holy Spirit remembers God. You look upon the unreal and you find despair. The unreal world *is* a thing of despair, because it can never be real. And you who are One with God can never be content without Reality. What God did not give

to you has no power over you, and the attraction of Love for Love remains irresistible. It is the Function of Love to extend only Love and to hold all things together in Its Wholeness.

8. God gives you Real Perception in exchange for the world that you made and see. Take your Real Perception from your Christ Mind, and look upon It. Its reflection of Reality will make everything else invisible to you, because your beholding It is your wholly corrected perception. As you use your Real Perception, you will remember that What It reflects was always so. Nothingness will become invisible to you, because you will at last see Truly. Your corrected perception is easily translated into God, because only perception is capable of error, and perception is not real. When your perception is corrected, it will give way to God, because God is the Only Reality. Your acceptance of correction is your way back to What you never lost. God cannot cease to love you.

Chapter 13

The Guiltless World

1. You would not attack another if you did not feel guilty for attacking God. Your condemnation of yourself is the root of all of your attacks. You project away from you your condemnation of yourself by judging *another* as unworthy and deserving of punishment. Here lies the split in your mind: Your mind perceives itself as separate from the mind that it is judging, believing that by punishing another, it escapes punishment. This is only a delusional attempt of your mind to deny itself and escape the penalty of its denial. This does not undo your denial, but preserves it through projection. Your guilt obscures God to you, and it is your guilt that makes you seem to be insane.

2. The beginning of your belief in your separation from God was your acceptance of guilt into your mind; the end of your perceiving separation is your acceptance of correction for this misperception. The world of the personal mind is a delusional system that shows that you have been driven insane by guilt. Look honestly at the world that you perceive, and you will see that this is so. The world that you perceive is the symbol of your punishment of yourself for separating from God, and the laws that govern it are the laws of death. You are born into it through pain and in pain. Your growth is attended by suffering as you learn of sorrow, separation, and death. Your mind seems to be trapped in a brain that declines if your body is hurt. You seem to love, but you desert others, and they desert you. Most insane of all, you seem to lose what you love. In the end, the body that you identify with withers and gasps and is laid in the ground. If you think that this is of God, then you must think that God is cruel.

3. If this was Reality, God *would* be cruel. God would not be Loving if It subjected you to this as the price of salvation. *Love does not kill to save.* If It did, attack would be salvation. This is the personal mind's

interpretation of attack, not God's. Only a world of guilt can command you to die, because only the guilty can conceive of death. Your belief in separation could not touch you if you did not project it onto God and believe that God has driven you out of Heaven. In this belief of yours, God *is* lost to you, because you do not understand God if you believe this.

4.   The personal mind's world *is* the picture of your crucifixion. You will see this world until you realize that you cannot be crucified. And you will not accept that you cannot be crucified until you accept the Eternal Fact that you are not guilty. You deserve Love, because, in Truth, you give only Love. You cannot be condemned, because in Truth you have never condemned. The correction of your perception that you are separate from God is the final lesson that you need to learn, because it teaches you that you have never sinned, and so you do not need salvation.

1. Guiltlessness and Invulnerability

1.   As a Teacher, the Holy Spirit only wants to make Itself unnecessary to you by teaching you all that It knows, because, sharing God's Love for you, the Holy Spirit wants to remove all the guilt from your mind, so that you can remember God in Peace. Peace and guilt are diametrically opposed, and you can only remember God in Peace. Love and guilt cannot exist together, and for you to accept one is for you to deny the other. Guilt hides your Christ Mind from you, because your guilt is the denial of your Innocence.

2.   In the strange world that you have made it seems that you who are Christ have sinned, but you only seem to have done so by making your Christ Mind invisible to you. Your Christ Mind is blocked by a world of retribution that has risen in your mind in the guilt that you have accepted and hold dear. The Innocence of your Christ Mind is the proof that the personal mind never was and can never be. The personal mind cannot exist without guilt, and, as Part of God, you *are* without guilt.

3.   You may be tempted to wonder how you can be Innocent when you look at the personal self and judge what it does. But you are Innocent in Eternity, not in time. Your 'sins' are in the past, but the

past does not exist, because *always* has no direction. Time seems to have a direction, but when you let it go, it will disappear. As long as you believe that you are guilty, you will walk in time believing that it leads to death. And the journey will be long and cruel and senseless.

4.   The journey of the personal self on which you have set yourself *is* useless, but the journey of correction on which God has set you releases you to Joy. God is not cruel, and, in Truth, you cannot hurt yourself. The retaliation you fear and see will never touch you, because, although you believe in it, the Holy Spirit knows it is not true. The Holy Spirit stands outside of time Where you truly are, because the Holy Spirit is with you. The Holy Spirit has already undone everything unworthy of you, because that is Its mission, given to It by God. And What God gives has always been.

5.   You will perceive your Christ Mind as you learn that you are Innocent. You have always sought your Innocence, and now you have found It. You seek to escape the limitations that you have made for yourself, and you are not denied the way to find Freedom, because It is in you, and you have found It. *When* you find Freedom is a matter of time, and time is an illusion. You are Innocent *now*, and your Purity shines untouched Forever in God's Mind. You will always be One with God. Deny the world that you perceive, and do not judge yourself, because your Eternal Innocence is in God's Mind, and It protects you Forever.

6.   When you have accepted correction of your perception of separation from God, you will realize that there is no guilt to perceive. Only if you look on Innocence everywhere can you understand Oneness. Your concept of guilt brings you the concept of condemnation, and results in you projecting separation in place of the Oneness of your mind. But you can only condemn *yourself*, and, when you do so, you forget that you are One with God. You deny your Innocence, Which is the condition of God's Being. But God extends Love to you, and you live with God in Love. Goodness and Mercy always follow you, because in Truth you extend God's Love.

7.   As you perceive your Holiness in place of the personal mind's projections, you will realize that there is no journey, only your

growing awareness of God's Eternal Presence. Your Christ Mind has kept faith with God for you. There is no road for you to travel on, and no time for you to travel through. God does not wait for you, because God is unwilling to be without you, and it has always been that you are with God. Let the holiness of your Christ Mind undo the guilt that darkens your mind, and, as you accept Christ's Purity by extending It everywhere, you will learn that it is *your* Purity.

8. You are safe, because you are Innocent. Guilt and time go hand-in-hand. Your guilt seems to establish that you will be punished in the future for what you have done in the past, so it depends on one-dimensional time that proceeds from past to future. When you believe in time, you cannot understand 'always' so guilt deprives you of an understanding of Eternity. You are Immortal, because you are Eternal; 'always' means endless *now*. By holding the past and the future in your mind, guilt ensures the personal self's continuity through your expectation of punishment. But the guarantee of *your* continuity comes from God, not from the personal mind. Immortality is the opposite of time, because time passes away, while Immortality is constant.

9. Accepting correction for your perception of separation from God teaches you What Immortality is, because by accepting your Innocence, you learn that the past has never been, so a future is unnecessary. In time, the future is always associated with 'atoning[1] for your sins', and only your sense of guilt makes you feel that you need to do that. Teaching you to accept your Innocence by extending It to be all that your mind perceives is God's way of reminding you of What you are in Truth. God has never condemned any part of you, and, being Innocent, you are Eternal.

10. You cannot undo your guilt by making it real and then paying for it. This is the personal mind's plan, which it offers you in place of undoing your guilt. It is committed to the insane idea that attack is salvation, because *its* continuity is your continuing to attack yourself by identifying with it. The personal mind then teaches you that your 'atonement' comes through attacking yourself further by punishing yourself. Attack, this version of 'atonement', and

salvation all become the same in your mind in your identification with a personal self. Only by identifying with a personal self can you cherish guilt, which you do not really want, and value attack.

11.   Attacking yourself because you are guilty, then, only increases your guilt, because attack always results in guilt. So, in the personal mind's teaching, you have no escape from guilt. Attack makes your guilt real to you, and, if guilt is real, there is no way for you to overcome it. The Holy Spirit, however, looks on your Innocence and dispels guilt simply through Its Calm Recognition that you are not separate from God. This being True, you cannot attack yourself, because without guilt there is no need for attack. You are saved because you are Innocent. And, being Wholly Pure, you are safe from attack.

2. The Guiltless Son of God

1.   The ultimate purpose of projection for you is supposed to be to get rid of your guilt. Characteristically, the personal mind wants you to keep guilt while *seeming* to get rid of it. But *you* find guilt intolerable, because God is irresistible to you, and guilt stands in the way of you remembering God. This is where the deepest split in your mind occurs, because to keep guilt as the personal mind insists *you cannot be you*. By persuading you that *it* is you, the personal mind induces you to project guilt, which actually keeps guilt in your mind, while only *seeming* to get rid of it.

2.   This strange solution of the personal mind has you project guilt onto a world that you perceive outside of you to get rid of it, which only results in you concealing that the guilt that you see is in your own mind. So you still experience the guilt, but you do not know why. You explain this to yourself by associating your guilt with your failure to meet certain ideals of the personal mind, but you have no idea that you are failing yourself by seeing yourself as guilty. Because you believe that you are no longer you, you do not realize that you are failing yourself.

3.   In the darkest corner of your identification with a personal self, your belief in your guilt is hidden from your awareness. In that dark place, you realize that you have betrayed your Christ Mind by

condemning It to death. You do not suspect that this murderous and insane idea is hidden there, but the personal mind's destructive urge is so intense that nothing short of your Christ Mind's crucifixion can ultimately satisfy it. It does not understand What your Christ Mind is, because it is blind to Truth. But if it perceives Innocence anywhere, it will try to destroy I,t because it is afraid of It.

4. Much of your strange behavior can be attributed to the personal mind's strange definition of guilt: *The guiltless are guilty.* When you do not attack, you are the personal mind's 'enemy', because it values attack as salvation, and when you do not value attack, you are in an excellent position to let it go. From this position you can look into the deepest, darkest secret of the personal mind, and while it can stand you questioning anything else, it guards with its life the secret that you have 'killed' Christ within you, because its existence depends on this being hidden from you. So you *must* look at this secret, because the personal mind cannot keep the Truth from you, and in Its Presence the personal mind is dispelled for you.

5. In the Calm Light of Truth, recognize that you believe that you have crucified your Christ Mind. You will not admit to this 'terrible' secret, because you still want to crucify your Christ Mind if you can find It. You hide this wish, because you are afraid of it, so you are afraid to find your Christ Mind. You have handled this wish to kill your True Self by not knowing that you are Christ, and by identifying with a personal self instead. You project your guilt blindly and indiscriminately, because you will not look at its source. The personal mind *does* want to kill you, and in your identification with it, you believe its goal is yours.

6. Crucifixion is the symbol of the personal mind. When the world that you made with your split mind was confronted with the real Innocence of Christ as modeled by Jesus, it *did* attempt to kill Christ by killing Jesus, and the reason given was that the perception of Innocence is blasphemous to God. In your mind where you perceive a world, the personal mind is god, and the perception of Innocence is interpreted as the final guilt that fully justifies murder. You do not yet understand that any fear that you

experience in connection with this course ultimately stems from this interpretation, but if you honestly examine your reactions to it, you will see that this is so.

7. This course explicitly states that its goal for you is Happiness and Peace, and yet you are afraid of it. You have been told repeatedly that it will set you free, but sometimes you react as if it is trying to limit you. You often dismiss it more easily than you dismiss the personal mind. You must believe, then, that by *not* learning this course you are protecting yourself. You do not yet realize that only your Innocence can protect you.

8. The plan of the Atonement has always been interpreted in your world as the release from guilt, and this is correct if you understand that Atonement is the correction of your perception of separation from God. Yet you may reject even this interpretation and not accept it for yourself. You may have looked at the personal mind and its offerings and recognized them as futile, but, though you don't want them, you may not yet be willing to accept correction with gladness. In the extreme, you are afraid of correction, and you believe that it will kill you. Do not mistake the depth of your fear. You believe that in the Presence of Truth, you will be destroyed.

9. This is not so. Your 'guilty secret' is nothing, and, if you bring it to the Holy Spirit, the Holy Spirit will dispel it. Then no dark secret will remain between you and your remembrance of God, because you will remember the Innocence of your Christ Mind, Which is Immortal. Your perception of separation is corrected in your Christ Mind, from Which you have never been separated. Your understanding this is your remembering God, because it is your recognition of Love without fear. There will be great Joy in Heaven on your Homecoming, and the Joy will be yours. Your corrected split mind is your Innocent Christ Mind. and to recognize your Christ Mind everywhere *is* your correction.

3. The Fear of Redemption

1. You might wonder why it is important for you to look on the personal mind's hatred and realize its full extent. You might also think that it would be easy for the Holy Spirit to show it to you and

to dispel it without you needing to raise it to your awareness. But there is one more obstacle that you have interposed between yourself and full correction of your perception that you are separate from God. You will not tolerate fear if you recognize it, but, in your disordered state of mind, you are not really afraid of fear. You don't like it, but it is not the personal mind's desire to attack that frightens you, and you are not really disturbed by its hostility. You keep its hatred hidden, because you are more afraid of what it covers. You would even be willing to look on the deepest secret of the personal mind without fear if you did not believe that without the personal mind you would find something within yourself that you fear even more. You are not really afraid of cruci-fixion; *your real terror is of correction.*

2.   Under the dark secret of the personal mind's 'attack' on your Christ Mind is your Memory of God, and it is of God that you are really afraid. Your remembering God will instantly restore you to your Proper Place in God, and it is This Place that you have sought to leave. Your fear of attack is nothing compared to your fear of Love. You might be willing to look on the personal mind's savage wish to kill the Christ in you, except that you believe that not looking at it saves you from Love. Your wish to be separate from Love is what caused your perception of separation from Love, and you protect this wish, because you do not want to heal this perception. You realize that if you remove the dark secret of the personal mind that obscures your Love for God, you will be impelled to answer God's Call and leap into Heaven. You believe the personal mind's attack is your salvation, because it saves you from God. Because, deeper than your secret attack on your True Self by identifying with a personal self, and much stronger than it will ever be, is your intense and burning Love for God and God's Love for you. This is What you really want to hide.

3.   In all honesty, isn't it harder for you to say 'I love' than 'I hate'? You associate Love with weakness and hatred with strength, and your Real Power seems to you to be a real weakness. You could not control your Joyous response to the Call of Love if you allowed yourself to hear It, and the whole world that you made would

vanish at Its sound. The Holy Spirit, then, seems to be attacking what you have made to shut out God, because God does not Will to be excluded.

4. You have built yourself an insane belief system, because you think that you would be helpless in God's Presence, and you want to save yourself from God's Love, because you think that God wants to crush you into nothingness. You are afraid that God's Love would sweep you away from yourself and make you little, because you believe that greatness lies in defiance and attack. You think that you have made a world that God wants to destroy, and that by loving God, *which you do*, you would throw away the world, *which you would*. So you have used a world to cover your Love, and the deeper that you go into the personal mind's thought system, the closer that you come to the Love that is hidden there. *And it is This that frightens you.*

5. You are willing to accept insanity, because you made it, but you will not accept Love because you did not make It. You would rather be a slave to crucifixion than accept your Christ Mind as correction. Your individual death is more valuable to you than your Living Oneness with God, because What is given to you is not so dear to you as what you have made. You are more afraid of God than of the personal mind, and Love cannot enter where It is not welcome. But hatred seems to enter your mind of its own will, and it does not care for your True Will.

6. You must not hide your illusions but look at them, because they do not rest on their own foundation. While they are hidden, they appear to be self-sustained, and this is the fundamental illusion on which all illusions rest. But beneath your illusions, and concealed with them, is your Loving Mind that thought It made them in anger. When It is uncovered, the pain in your mind will be so apparent that you will not deny your need for healing. Not all the tricks and games that the personal mind offers can heal it, because this is the real crucifixion of your Christ Mind.

7. And yet your Christ Mind is not crucified. In your mind is both your pain and your healing, because the Holy Spirit's Perception is Merciful, and Its Remedy is Quick. Do not hide suffering, but bring

it gladly to the Holy Spirit. Lay before the Holy Spirit's Eternal Sanity all of your hurt, and let It heal you. Do not leave any spot of pain hidden from the Holy Spirit, and search your mind carefully for any thoughts that you may fear to uncover. The Holy Spirit will heal every little thought that you have kept to hurt yourself, and It will cleanse your mind of limitedness by restoring it to the Limitlessness of God.

8. Beneath the self-inflation of the personal mind that you hold so dear is your real call for help. You call to God for Love as God calls you to Itself. In the Holy Place Which you have hidden within yourself, you will only to be One with God, in Loving remembrance of God. You will find this Place of Truth as you extend It in place of the limited world that you perceive, because your mind longs for the Limitlessness within you. By perceiving It, you will welcome It, and It will be yours. Limitlessness is your Right as Christ, and no illusions can satisfy you or save you from What you are. Only your Love is Real, and you will be content only with Reality.

9. Save your mind from its illusion of a world of separation so that you can accept the Limitlessness of God in Peace and Joy. But do not exempt any perception from Love or you will be holding back a part of your mind where the Holy Spirit is not welcome, and exempting yourself from the Holy Spirit's healing power. You must offer Love totally to be totally healed. You must let healing completely undo your fear, because Love cannot enter your mind when there is one spot of fear to mar Its welcome.

10. You who prefer separation to Sanity cannot obtain separation in your True Mind. You were at Peace until you asked to be separate, and God could not give this to you because it is an alien request to What is One. So you made God an unloving God in your mind by demanding of God what only an unloving God could give. Your Peace was shattered, because you no longer understood your Oneness with God. You fear what you have made, but you fear God even more, because you attacked your glorious Oneness with God.

11. In Peace you need nothing, and you ask for nothing. In conflict you

demand everything, and you find nothing. How can the Gentleness of Love respond to your demands, except by departing from you in Peace and returning to God? If you do not want to remain in Peace, then Love cannot remain with you at all. When your mind is full of illusions you cannot live in Reality, and you must seek a place of illusions where you can believe you are where you are not. God has not allowed this to happen, but you have demanded that it happen, and so you believe that it is so.

12. To 'single out' is to make alone, and therefore to make lonely. God does not do this to you, because your Peace lies in God's Oneness. God denies only your request for pain, because suffering is not of God. God is One with you, and God will not take this Oneness away from you. But God answers your insane request for pain with a Sane Answer that is with you in your insanity. When you hear the Holy Spirit, you will give up insanity, because the Holy Spirit is the Reference Point beyond illusions from Which you can look back on your illusions, and see that they are insane. Seek this Place within you, and you will find It, because Love is in you and will lead you there.

4. The Function of Time

1. Now the reason that you are afraid of this course should be apparent: This is a course in Love, because it is about you. Your function in the world that you perceive is healing your mind of its perception of separation from God, as your Function in Heaven is to be One with God. But the personal mind teaches you that your function in the world is destruction, and that you have no function in Heaven. So the personal mind wants to destroy you in the world and bury you in the world, leaving you nothing but the dust out of which it thinks that you were made. As long as the personal mind is satisfied with you in its judgment, it offers you oblivion at the end of your 'life' in the world. When it is not satisfied with you, it becomes openly savage and offers you hell.

2. But neither oblivion nor hell is as unacceptable to you as Heaven. To the personal mind, which wants to destroy you, Heaven *is* oblivion and hell, and in your identification with a personal self,

the real Heaven is the greatest threat that you think that you can experience. Oblivion and hell are ideas that you made up, and you are determined to establish their reality to establish the personal identity as your reality. If you question oblivion and hell as your final destination, then you believe that you are questioning your reality, because you believe that separation from God *is* your reality, and your destruction is the final proof that you are right.

3. Putting aside the fact that you *are* wrong, isn't it more desirable to be wrong in this circumstance? While you might argue that death suggests there *was* life, you cannot claim that it proves that there *is* life. Even the life that has passed into death could only have been futile if it ends in death and needs death to prove it ever was. You question Heaven, but you do not question this. But you could heal yourself if you *did* question this. Even though you don't seem to know Heaven, couldn't It be more desirable to you than death? You have been as selective in your questioning as you have been in your perception. An open mind is more honest.

4. In your identification with a personal self you have a strange idea of time, and it is with this idea that your questioning should begin. The personal mind invests heavily in the past, because it believes that the past is the only aspect of time that is meaningful, since the personal mind exists for you only in the past. Remember that the personal mind emphasizes your guilt in your identification with it to ensure that *it* continues by projecting a future for you from the personal self's past, so it avoids the present. If you are to pay for the 'sins' of the personal self's past in the future, then the personal self's past determines your future, which makes the personal self's past continuous, and leaves you without any real present. The personal mind regards the present only as a brief transition to the future, in which it brings the personal self's past to the future by interpreting your present through the personal self's past.

5. 'Now' has no meaning for the personal mind. Unable to tolerate your release from the past, it projects onto the present the past hurts that you perceive in your identification with a personal self, so that you react to the present as if it were the past. It dictates

your reactions to those you meet in the present from a past reference, so that in effect you react to others as though they are someone from the personal self's past, and you do not see that God's Love is What is present. In your identification with a personal self, you receive messages from others out of the personal self's past, making the personal self's past real to you in the present, and thereby making you hold onto the personal self's past. You thus deny yourself the message of release that you could see by extending God's Love *now*.

6.   Your projections from the personal self's past are exactly what you must escape. They are not real, and they have no hold over you unless you bring them with you. They carry spots of pain in your mind, directing you to attack in the present in retaliation for a past that is gone. This is your decision for future pain. Unless you learn that the past is an illusion, you are choosing future illusions and losing the many opportunities that you have for release in the present. The personal mind wants to preserve your illusions, prevent you from becoming aware of God, and prevent you from understanding that your illusions are gone. You cannot perceive your own Holiness when you perceive an individual past. Nothing real happens when you do this, but you miss opportunities to extend salvation, which would make every situation Holy. The Holy Spirit teaches you that every encounter that you have in the world is an encounter with an extension of your own Holiness. The personal mind teaches you that you always encounter the personal self's past, and because the personal self's past was not Holy, *your* future will not be, and the present is without meaning.

7.   The Holy Spirit's perception of time is the exact opposite of the personal mind's perception of time, because their perceptions of the *goal* of time are exactly opposite. To the Holy Spirit, the purpose of time is to render your need for time unnecessary. It perceives the function of time as temporary, because time serves only the Holy Spirit's Teaching Function, Which is temporary by definition. The Holy Spirit's emphasis, then, is on the only aspect of time that can extend to the Infinite: *now*. *Now*, without past or future, is as close as you can get to Eternity in time. Only *now* is here, and only *now*

presents you with opportunities to extend your Holiness and find salvation.

8.   The personal mind regards the function of time as one of extending itself in place of Eternity, because, like the Holy Spirit, it regards the goal of time as the same as its own goal. Continuing the personal self's past in the future is the only purpose that the personal mind has for time, and it closes over the present, so that no gap in its own continuity can occur. So the personal mind wants to keep you in time to ensure *its* continuity, while the Holy Spirit wants to release you from time. If you want to share the Holy Spirit's goal of salvation for you, then you must accept the Holy Spirit's interpretation of time.

9.   You, too, will interpret the function of time as you interpret your own function. If you accept that your function in your perception that you are in a world is healing your mind of its perception of separation, then you will emphasize the present, because it is the only aspect of time in which your healing can occur. Your healing cannot occur in the past, because the past is gone, and you are released from the future only through healing your mind in the present. If you use time this way, your future will become an extension of your present healing, rather than of the personal self's past 'sin'. But if you interpret your function as destruction, you will ignore the present and hold onto the personal self's past to ensure your fear of future destruction for your guilt. Time is nothing in itself, and it will be to you however you interpret its function.

5. The Two Emotions

1.   You have only two emotions: Love and fear. Love is Changeless and continually exchanged, being offered by the Eternal to the Eternal. In this exchange, Love is extended, and It increases as It is extended. But fear has many forms, because the content of individual illusions varies greatly, though they all have one thing in common: they are insane. They are made of sights and sounds that are not here. They make up a private world that you cannot extend. They are meaningful to you only in the personal mind

where you make them, so they have no real meaning at all. In this world of illusion you move alone, because only you perceive your own illusions.

2. You people the world that you perceive with projections from the personal self's individual past, and this is why private worlds differ. But the figures that you see were never real anyway, because they were entirely made up of your own projections. You do not see that you made them, and that they are not whole. These figures have no witnesses, because they are perceived only in your separate mind.

3. Through these strange and shadowy projections you relate in insanity to your insane world. You see and relate to only the projections that you make from the personal mind. You communicate with what is not here, and what is not here seems to answer you with what you gave them to answer you, and only you believe in them. Projection makes perception, and you cannot see beyond your projections. Again and again you attack others for your projections onto them. But you must have attacked yourself first, because you are not really attacking others, but you are attacking yourself by seeing yourself as a personal self. The only reality others have is in your own mind, and, when you attack others, you are attacking what is not there.

4. In your delusions you can be very destructive, because you do not recognize that you are condemning yourself. You may not wish to die, but you will not let go of condemnation. So you separate into your private world where everything is disordered, and where what is within your mind appears to be outside of you. But what is truly within you, you do not see, and the Reality beyond your projections you cannot recognize.

5. You have only two emotions, and in your private world you react to each as though it was the other. You cannot see Love in a world of separation, because you will not recognize It. If you see your own hatred of yourself in another, you are not seeing Love. You are drawn to what you 'love', and you recoil from what you fear, so you react to Real Love with fear, and you draw away from It. Separation attracts you, and, believing it is 'love', you call fear to

you. Your private world is filled with projections of fear that you have invited, and all the Real Love that you could see in their place you do not see.

6. If you look with honesty on the world that you perceive, it must occur to you that you have withdrawn into insanity. You see what is not there, and you hear what makes no sound. You fear Love, and you love fear. You have no real connections, and you are isolated and alone in your private personal mind. In your madness, you overlook Reality completely, and you perceive only your own split mind everywhere. God calls to you and you do not hear, because you are preoccupied with the personal mind's voice. And you do not perceive with your Christ Mind's Perception, because you perceive only the projections of a private personal self.

7. Would you offer this to God? If you offer it to yourself you *are* offering it to God. But God will not return it to you, because it is unworthy of you, since it is unworthy of God. But God wants to release you from it and set you free. The Holy Spirit is God's Sane Answer, and It tells you that what you offer to yourself is not true, and that God's Offer is unchanged. You know not what you do, but you can learn that it is insane and look beyond it. Extension is the means given to you to learn how to deny insanity, and to come out of your private world in Peace. You will learn that, because you have denied Love in yourself, you have denied the Love that lies beyond your mind's projections. You will extend Love in your perception, drawing yourself to Love and Love to you, perceiving Love as a Witness to the Reality that you share with God. Your Christ Mind is your entire mind, and you will be drawn out of your private world as you unite your mind in Christ by perceiving only Christ. God welcomes your Wholeness in Gladness, and gladness is what you should offer to God. Your Whole Mind is given to you to extend God as God extends God to you. You must extend God in place of your projections to recognize God's Gift to you.

8. The Perception of your Christ Mind depends on your willingness to Truly See, and you cannot Truly See when you deny your Christ Mind. You have made what you see in the private illusions of the personal mind. But let go of your denial and all that you have

made you will no longer see, because you can only see it by denying your Christ Mind's Perception. But your denial does not mean that you have lost the ability to perceive through your Christ Mind. What it does mean is that you accept insanity and believe that you can make a private world and rule your own perception, and for this you must exclude your Christ Mind. Your illusions will disappear when you accept your Christ Mind's Perception and Truly See.

9. Do not seek to Truly See through the personal mind, because you made its way of seeing so that you could see illusions to deceive yourself. Beyond your illusions, but still within you, is the Perception of your Christ Mind, Which looks on everything with Love. The personal mind's perception comes from fear, but your Christ Mind sees for you as the Witness to your Real Perception. Your Christ Mind always uses your Real Perception and calls forth Witnesses to Itself. Your Christ Mind loves Its Self, which It sees in you, and It wants to extend It. Your Christ Mind will not return to God until It has extended your Real Perception up to God. In God, perception is gone, because your Christ Mind returns to God with you.

10. You have two emotions: fear, which you made; and Love, which was given to you by God. Each is a way of perceiving, and different perceptions arise from them. See through the Perception that God has given to you, because through your Christ Mind's Perception you will look on Christ, and, seeing Christ, you will know God. Beyond your darkest illusions, your Christ Mind sees God's Innocence within you, Perfect and untouched by your illusions. This is What you will see when you look with your Christ Mind, because your Christ Mind's Perception is Its Gift of Love to you, given to your Christ Mind from God for you.

11. Your Christ Mind is revealed to you through the Holy Spirit. If you want to perceive your Christ you *can* perceive It, because you have asked for Truth. You will not perceive Christ in the isolation of a personal mind, because your Christ Mind is not limited to a personal mind. When you perceive Christ you will rise in It to God, and you will understand this, because you will look within and see

beyond illusions to your Christ Mind and recognize God. In the Sanity of your Christ Mind's Perception you will look upon yourself with Love, and see yourself as the Holy Spirit sees you. And with this Perception of the Truth in you comes all the Beauty of your Real Perceptions.

6. Finding the Present

1. For you to perceive Truly is for you to see your Real Perceptions through the awareness of your own Reality. But you cannot hold onto any illusions to do this, because Reality has no room for error. This means that you must perceive only as you can perceive *now*. The past has no reality in the present, so you cannot see it. The personal self's past reactions are also not here, and if it is to them that you react, then you will see only an image of the past that you have made and that you cherish. As you question illusions, ask yourself if it is really sane for you to perceive the past as though it is happening now. If you remember the personal self's past as you look at the world, you will be unable to perceive your Real Perceptions.

2. You consider it 'natural' to use the personal self's past experience to judge the present. But this is *unnatural*, because it is delusional. When you have learned to perceive with no reference to the past at all, you will be able to learn from your Real Perceptions, Which you can see *now*. The past can hold no illusion over the present *unless you are afraid of Truth*. Only if you are will you choose illusions and, by holding them in your mind, see them as a veil that conceals your Real Perceptions from your sight.

3. *This veil of illusions is in your mind*. The Christ that you can see now has no past, because your Christ Mind is Changeless, and in your Christ Mind's Changelessness lies your release. Your Christ Mind is One with God, and there is no guilt in your Christ Mind. Guilt cannot obscure your Christ Mind, and Christ is revealed to you everywhere, because you can see Christ through the Christ Mind in you. For you to be 'born again' is for you to let go of the personal self's past and to look without guilt and condemnation on the present. The illusions that obscure your Christ Mind to you are

past, and if you want them to be past and gone, you must not see them now. If you see the past in your illusions now, the past has not gone from you, although it is not here.

4. Time can free as well as limit you, depending on whether you use the Holy Spirit's or the personal mind's interpretation of it. Past, present, and future are not continuous unless you force continuity on them and perceive them that way for yourself. Do not be deceived and believe that that is how time is. To believe that reality is what you want it to be according to your use for it *is* delusional. You break time into past, present, and future for the personal mind's purposes. You anticipate and plan for the future based on the personal self's past experiences. This aligns past and future and doesn't allow the experience of the miracle, which intervenes between past and future *now*, to free you to be born again.

5. Your experience of the miracle enables you to see others in the world that you perceive without your projections of the personal self's past on them, so your perceptions are born again. All of your errors are in a personal past, and by perceiving others without your projections of error onto them, you release your mind where you perceive a world. Do not let your illusions of the past block the Truth in the present, and you will find the Truth that is here. You have looked for Truth where It is *not*, so you have not found It. Learn to seek for the Truth in the present, and you will see the Truth. You made the personal self's past in anger, and if you use it to attack the present, you will not see the freedom that the present holds for you.

6. Your self-judgment and condemnation are behind you, and, unless you bring them with you into the present, you will see that you are free of them. Look Lovingly at the present, because it holds the Truth. All of your healing lies in the present, because Truth's continuity is real. Every healing that you accept extends to your entire mind at once, and enables it to be One. God *is*, before time was, and God will be again in your awareness when time is no more for you. *Now* all things are Timeless, and therefore Eternal and One. There is no separation in the present. Only the past can separate, and it is nowhere.

7. The present offers you the Love that unites your mind and frees you from the past. Do not hold the personal self's past against anyone or anything in the world that you perceive. If you do, you are choosing to remain in illusions, and you are refusing the Love that is offered to you. The Love of Perfect Perception is freely given to you, and you must freely receive It; It can only be accepted by you without limits. *Now*, in this one, still dimension of time that does not change, and where you hold no idea of what you *were*, you look at Christ and call to you Witnesses to your Christ Mind. They will not deny the Truth in you, because you looked for the Truth and found It within.

8. *Now* is the time of your salvation, because *now* is your release from time. Extend God's Love everywhere and touch everything with your Christ Mind. In Timeless Union, your Mind is Continuous and Unbroken, because It is wholly extended. God's Innocent Extension is only Love. There are no illusions in It, because It is Whole. Call on all that you perceive to witness to the Wholeness of God's Extension, as your Christ Mind calls to you to be One. Everything that you perceive has a part in your correction, in gladness and thanksgiving for the Love of God. The Holy Love that extends from you is the Witness that your Love is God's Love.

9. Extend God's Love everywhere in remembrance of God, because you remember God as you call forth Witnesses to God's Love. Every extension that you make to heal your perception of separation witnesses to your healing, because, in them, you see your own Wholeness. As your gratitude rises to God, God will return your thanks to you through the Holy Spirit, Which is the Answer to your call. You will always be answered by God. God's Call to you is your call to God. And, in the Holy Spirit, you are answered by God's Peace.

10. You who are One with Love do not know that Love is in you. But you will find It through Its Witnesses, because, by extending Love, you will find It returned to you. Each time that you replace a projection of the personal mind with Love, you bring Love closer to your full awareness. Love always leads to Love. The personal mind's projections of separation are your call for Love, and when

you supply Love in their place, you will be filled with gratitude and Joy. The personal mind's projections are your guides to Joy, because when you replace them with Love, Love remains. You establish these projections as guides to Peace, because you make Peace manifest in their place. And Peace's Beauty calls you Home.

11. There is a Love that the world that you perceive cannot give. But you can give It, because It was given to you by God. As you extend God's Love, It calls you to follow It out of your perception of a world. This Love attracts you as nothing in the world can. You *will* lay aside the world of the personal mind and find your Real Perceptions. Your Real Perceptions are bright with the Love that you have extended to Them. Everything in your Real Perceptions reminds you of God, and your Oneness with God. Love is Limitless, and It spreads across your Real Perceptions in Quiet Joy. All of the personal mind's projections will be replaced by your extensions of Love, and you will Love them in gratitude, because they brought you to Love. The Love in you will join with the Love that you extend in your perception with a Power so compelling that your entire mind will be drawn out of illusions.

12. For you to become aware of your Christ Mind is for you to follow the Law of Love and Free Will, because the Truth is in Them. The attraction of Love must attract you willingly, and your willingness is signified by your extension of Love. Your extensions of Love become your willing Witnesses to the Love within you by reflecting Love back to you. In illusions you are alone and separate from the rest of your mind, and your awareness is narrowed to a personal self. That is why it is a nightmare. You have an illusion of isolation, because you are in denial. You do not see your entire mind, because, in your illusions of a world of separation, you do not see your Love in your mind's perceptions.

13. But the Law of Love is not suspended because you are in denial. You have followed this Law, even in your illusions, and you have been faithful in your extension of Love, because you are not a personal self alone. Even though you deny It, your Christ Mind ensures your Real Perceptions when you are ready to be aware of Them. Your Christ Mind has extended Christ for you and to you. In

Truth, you are still as Loving as God, One with God, and with no past to keep you apart from God. So you have never ceased to be God's Extension. Although you have denied It, your Christ Mind's Perception has not left you. And so you can call Witnesses to you to teach you that your denial is not real.

7. The Attainment of the Real World

1. Sit quietly and look at the world that you perceive and tell yourself: 'My Real Perception is not like this. It has no buildings, and there are no streets where people walk alone and separate. There are no stores where people buy an endless list of things they do not need. It is not lit with artificial light, and night does not come upon It. There is no day that brightens and then grows dim. There is no loss. The Love There extends Forever.'

2. You must deny the world that you perceive, because seeing it costs you your Real Perception. You cannot perceive both the world and your Real Perception, because each of them involves a different type of perceiving, and each depends on what you cherish. You perceive one when you have denied the other. They do not both reflect Truth, but either one will be as real to you as you hold it dear. Their power is not the same, because their real attraction to you is unequal.

3. You do not really want the world that you perceive, because it has always disappointed you. Its homes do not shelter you, and its roads lead nowhere. None of its cities can withstand the crumbling assault of time, and everything in it has the mark of death upon it. Do not hold it dear, because it is old and tired and ready to return to the dust out of which you made it. The aching world does not have the power to touch your Real Perception at all. You cannot give it that power, and, even though you turn from it in sadness, you cannot find in it the way that leads to your Real Perception.

4. Yet, because you love your Real Perception, It can touch you even in your perception that you are in a world. What you call with Love will come to you. Love always answers you, because It is unable to deny your call for help and your cries of pain, which arise to It from your perception of a world of separation that you

259

do not really want. All that you need to give up your perception of a world of separation and to exchange it for your Real Perception, is your willingness to learn that the world that you made shows you a lie.

5. You have been wrong about what is real, because you have misjudged yourself. From a twisted reference point, you see a twisted world. All of your perceiving starts with you, the perceiver, and you judge what is true and what is false for you. What you judge as false you will not see. You have judged Reality, and you cannot see It, because when you judge, Reality slips away. What is out of your mind *is* out of your sight, because what you deny in your mind is there, but is not recognized by you. Christ is still in your mind, although you do not know it. But Christ's Being does not depend on your recognition. Your Christ Mind lives within you in the Quiet Present, and It waits for you to leave the past behind and accept the Real Perception that your Christ Mind holds out to you in Love.

6. Even in the distracted world that you perceive you have had glimpses of your Real Perception. But while you value the personal mind's perception of a world, you will deny your Real Perception, while maintaining that you love a world that you cannot love. And you won't follow the road that Real Love so gladly leads you upon. As you follow your Christ Mind, you will rejoice that you are Whole, and that you have learned of your Christ Mind the Joyful journey Home. You only wait for yourself. It is *your* Will to give over the personal mind's sad world and exchange your errors for the Peace of God. Your Christ Mind will always offer you God's Will in recognition that you share God's Will.

7. It is God's Will that nothing else touch you; only God, and nothing else, *can* approach you. You are as safe from pain as God is, and God watches over you in everything. Your Real Perception surrounds you and shines with God's Love, because, in Truth, you are in God, Where there is no pain, only the Love that surrounds you without end or flaw. Your Peace can never be disturbed. In Perfect Sanity you can look on Love, because It is all around you and within you. You will deny the world of pain that you perceive

the moment that you perceive the Arms of Love around you. From this Point of Safety, you can look quietly around yourself, and recognize that your Real Perception is with you.

8. Only in your perception of a personal self's past can you not understand God's Love. The Peace of God is *here*, and you can understand It *now*. God loves you Forever, and you return God's Love Forever. Your Real Perception is your way to remember that God is the One Thing that is Wholly True and wholly yours. Everything else you have lent yourself in time, and it will all fade. But God is always yours, being God's Gift to you. Your One Reality is given to you in your Oneness with God.

9. You will first perceive Peace, and then you will become fully aware of It. Your first exchange of what you made for What you want is the exchange of the personal mind's projections for your Perceptions of Love. These are your *Real Perceptions*, because the Holy Spirit corrects at the level of perception. God does not need correction, but your corrected Perceptions of Love lead you to God. In your Perceptions of Love there is nothing for you to fear, so they welcome God. Love waits on your welcome, not on time, so your Real Perception is your welcome of What always *is*. The Call of Joy is in your Real Perception, and your Happy Response is your full awareness of What you have not lost.

10. Thank God for your Perfect Sanity. God knows that you do not need anything in Heaven, because Eternity does not lack. But scarcity is all that you can perceive in your mind where you perceive a world of separation, because you lack God there. You can only find yourself with the Holy Spirit in your perception that you are in a world, because the Holy Spirit is the Mediator between your perception of a world of scarcity and your Real Perception. The Holy Spirit knows what you need and what will not hurt you. Ownership is a dangerous concept of the personal mind, because the personal mind tells you to want things for your salvation, and possession is its law. Possession for its own sake is the personal mind's fundamental creed; a part of the foundation of its thought system. It demands that you get what it tells you that you need to be whole, and then it leaves you no joy in it.

11. Everything that the personal mind tells you that you need will hurt you. Although the personal mind tells you over and over again to *get*, it leaves *you* nothing, because what you get it wants to validate *itself*. Once you get what it tells you to seek, whatever it is will fade into emptiness, because where the personal mind sees salvation it always sees separation. So you lose by whatever you get to appease the personal mind. Do not ask the personal mind what you need, because it does not know, and its advice will hurt you. What you think that you need in your identification with a personal self will merely tighten up your mind where you perceive a world against Love. And you will be unwilling to question the value of what the world can hold for you.

12. Only the Holy Spirit knows what you need, and It will give you all things that do not block your way to Love. This is all that you *can* need. In time, the Holy Spirit gives you all the things that you need, and the Holy Spirit will renew them as long as you have need of them. Nothing will be taken from you as long as you have need of it. But the Holy Spirit knows that what you need in your perception that you are in a world is temporary, and that your perception of need will only last for you until you realize that all of your needs are fulfilled in God. So the Holy Spirit has no investment in what It supplies, except to be sure that you will not use it to linger in time. The Holy Spirit knows that you are not at home in a world, and It wills that there be no delay to your Joyous Homecoming in God.

13. Leave your needs to the Holy Spirit, because the Holy Spirit will supply your needs without any emphasis on them. What comes to you from the Holy Spirit comes to you safely, because the Holy Spirit will ensure that it can never become a hidden attachment that keeps you in separation. Under the Holy Spirit's guidance you will journey lightly, because the Holy Spirit's Sight is always on the journey's Goal. No world is your Home, and, no matter how Holy your perception becomes in the world, it cannot hold All that God gives to you. Within you, you have no needs, because Love needs nothing but to be in Peace and to extend Peace into Infinity from Itself.

14. Whenever you are tempted to walk away from Love by following the personal mind, remember What you really want, and say to yourself:

'The Holy Spirit leads me to Christ, Where I want to go. My only need is to be aware of my Christ Mind.'

15. Then follow the Holy Spirit in Joy, with faith that It will lead you safely through all threats to your Peace of mind that your perception that you are in a world may set before you. Do not worship sacrifice, and do not seek what certainly leads to loss for you. Be content with What you will certainly keep, and do not be restless, because you undertake a Quiet journey to God, Where God wants you to be in Quietness.

16. In your Christ Mind, you have already overcome every temptation to be separate from God that could hold you back. Christ is with you as you walk in a Quietness that is the Gift of God. Hold your Christ Mind dear, because you need only Christ. With Christ, you will find the Peace of mind that you must extend in your mind where you perceive a world. The Holy Spirit will teach you to be aware of yourself in your Oneness with Christ. This is the only real need that you have to be fulfilled in time, and your salvation from your perception that you are in a world lies only here. Your Christ Mind gives you Peace, so take It in glad exchange for all that the world offers, but that leaves you empty. Through your Christ Mind, extend Peace in your mind where you perceive a world, and replace all thoughts of separation.

17. You can only accept correction of your perception of separation from God with your entire mind. Your Christ Mind's job is not done until your entire mind is lifted to Christ. Your Whole Mind, Which is your Christ Mind's Gift to you, is God's Gift to your Christ Mind in Oneness. Christ will banish all sorrow from your mind, where sorrow cannot abide. In time you need healing, because Joy cannot establish Its Eternal Reign where sorrow dwells. But you do not dwell in sorrow, but in Eternity. You are safe at Home, but you seem to travel through illusions. Give thanks to every Perception

through which you teach yourself to remember your True Self. Thus you give thanks to God for your Purity.

8. From Perception to Knowledge

1. All of your healing is your release from the personal self's past, so the Holy Spirit is the only Healer. The Holy Spirit teaches you that the past does not exist, which is a fact in God, but which you cannot understand while you perceive yourself in a world. The world would not exist for you if you knew this. The Mind in you that wholly knows this is in Eternity, and It does not use perception at all, so It does not consider 'where' It is, because 'where' does not mean anything to It. This Mind in you knows that It is Everywhere, Everything, and Forever.

2. The very real difference between perception and God is obvious if you consider this: There is nothing incomplete about God. Every Part of God is Whole, therefore no Part of God is separate. Being in God's Mind, you are Part of God. All of God is yours, because you are in God. But even at its highest level, perception is never complete. Even your Perception of the Holy Spirit, Which is as Perfect as perception can be, is without meaning in Heaven. Your Perception of the Holy Spirit will extend to be all that you perceive, because the Perception of your Christ Mind perceives everything in Love. But no perception, no matter how Holy, will last Forever.

3. Perfect Perception has many aspects in common with God, and It makes your mind ready for God. After your perception is wholly corrected, the Last Step, Which *seems* to be in the future, is taken by God, because your Oneness with God has always been. Your perception of separation has not interrupted God's Oneness; it is merely a false reality in your mind that has no real effect at all. Your experience of the miracle, which you don't need in Heaven, you need while you perceive yourself in a world. You can perceive Reflections of Reality in the world through your extension of God's Love to replace unreality. You can see God's Love everywhere and in everything, but only God can gather Its Love all together into Oneness and Eternity.

4. The Holy Spirit has no function apart from God and you. It is not

separate from either, being in your mind and in God's Mind, because It knows that your minds are One. The Holy Spirit is the Thought of God in your mind, and God has given you the Holy Spirit, because God extends Its Thoughts everywhere. The Holy Spirit's message speaks of Timelessness in time, and that is why your Christ Mind's Perception looks on everything with Love. But even your Christ Mind's Perception is not Reality. The Loving Reflections of Reality that you see through your Christ Mind are only partial glimpses of the Heaven that lies beyond perception.

5. The miracle of Creation is that It is One Forever. Every extension of God's Love that you offer is one True Perception of a Reflection of the Whole of God. Even though every Reflection of God *is* Whole, you cannot see this until you perceive that this Reflection is the same Reflection everywhere in everything, and that It is therefore One. Every projection of the past that you replace with God's Love brings you closer to the end of time by bringing healing Perception into your mind. This enables you to use your Real Perception. Love must come into your mind where you perceive a world to bring your Christ Mind's Perception to it. Help your Christ Mind to extend Love to be all that you perceive, and let Christ gather your entire mind into Its Quiet Perception.

6. Everything in your Mind is equally Beautiful and Holy. Your Christ Mind will offer all of your Real Perceptions to God as you have offered Them all to your Christ Mind. There is only one miracle, because there is only One Reality. Every extension of Love that you make contains every other extension of Love that you have made, because every Reflection of Reality that you perceive blends quietly into the Reality of God's Oneness. You are the only miracle that ever was, at One in the Reality that is God. Your Christ Mind's Perception is God's Gift to you. Christ's Being is God's Gift to your Christ Mind.

7. Be content with healing yourself, because you can bestow your Christ Mind's Perception on all that your mind perceives, and you cannot lose Christ's Being. Offer your Christ Mind's Perception to everything, because miracles that you offer through the Holy Spirit through your mind's perception attune your mind to Reality. The

Holy Spirit knows what you need to do in your perception that you are in a world to undo your perception that you are separate from God. Reality is beyond your concern as long as you perceive yourself as a separate self. You who are One with God only need to realize that God is Reality, and that what you have made is not. The part that you seem to play in your perception that you are in a world will lead to correction of your perception that you are separate from God by re-establishing Oneness in your mind.

8. When all that you perceive is Oneness, you will be released to God, having learned through the Holy Spirit to free yourself from your perception of a world. Unite with your Christ Mind through the Holy Spirit's teaching, and as you grow in the Power of your Christ Mind, you will leave nothing untouched and separate. Suddenly, time will be over, and your entire mind will unite in the Eternity of God. The Holy Love that you perceived in a world that seemed outside of you will be returned to you. Knowing that God's Love is in you, your Extension of God's Love will be with you as you are in God.

9. As miracles join your mind by extending Love to be all that you perceive, so does your Extension of God establish you as One with God in Heaven. As God's Extension you Witness to God, as your extension of God Witnesses to your Oneness with God. When you deny yourself an opportunity to exchange a projection of the personal mind with an extension of God's Love, you deny yourself a witness to your Oneness with God in Heaven. The miracle that you are in your Oneness with God is Perfect, as are the miracles that you extend in your perception that you are in a world. You do not need healing when you accept God's Love, because this miracle *is* your healing.

10. But your Perfection has no witnesses in the world of separation that you perceive. God knows your Perfection, but you do not know It in your mind where you perceive a world, so you do not share God's Witnesses. And you do not witness to God, because Reality is witnessed to as One. God awaits your Witness to your Christ Mind and to God. Your extensions of God's Love in the world that you perceive are lifted up to God in Heaven. They witness to What you

266

do not know, and as they reach Heaven. God will open Heaven's Gate for you. God will never leave Part of Itself outside of Heaven and beyond Itself.

9. The Cloud of Guilt

1. Your guilt is the only thing that hides God from you, because your guilt is your attack upon your Oneness with God. When you believe that you are guilty you condemn yourself, and you project your condemnation into the future, linking the future to the past, as is the personal mind's law. Your fidelity to this law lets no Love into your mind, because it is your fidelity to illusions, and it forbids your awareness of God. The personal mind's laws are strict, and it severely punishes any breaches. Do not give obedience to these laws, because they are the laws of punishment. If you follow them, it is because you believe that you are guilty of separating from God, and you condemn yourself for it. Between the past and the future, the Law of God intervenes for you to free yourself. Correction stands between them, with the Love that undoes all of your illusions of separation from God.

2. Release yourself from guilt, and completely undo the personal mind. Do not project guilt and condemnation onto others, or you will make yourself fearful, because by obeying the personal mind's harsh commandments, you bring condemnation *on yourself*, and you will not escape the punishment that the personal mind offers. The personal mind rewards your fidelity to it with pain, because your faith in the personal mind *is* pain. Your faith is always rewarded in the terms of the belief in which you place your faith. Your faith is the power behind your belief, and where you invest your faith determines your reward. You always put faith in what you treasure, because what you treasure is returned to you.

3. The world is nothing but your projection, and it can give you only what you have projected or extended to it. Its meaning is the meaning that you have given to it. Be faithful to illusions, and you will see nothing, because your faith is rewarded as you give it. You *will* accept what you treasure, and if you put your faith in the personal self's past, your future will be like it. Whatever you hold

dear you think is yours, because the power of your valuing will make it so to you.

4.   To correct your perception of separation from God, you must re-evaluate everything that you cherish, because this is the means by which the Holy Spirit within you can separate Truth from illusion. You have accepted both into your mind without distinguishing between them, so you value them both, and guilt has become as true for you as Innocence. You do not believe that you are Innocent, because you see the personal self's past, and you do not see your Oneness with God. When you condemn another you are saying: 'I who was guilty choose to remain so.' When you project guilt onto another, you are denying your own freedom from guilt. You can easily see freedom from the personal self's past instead by extending God's Love in place of your projection, and lift guilt from your entire mind. As you release all that you perceive from guilt, you find your own freedom from guilt.

5.   Do not reinforce guilt in another, because any guilt that you see is a projection of your own mind. Teach yourself that guilt is a delusion. The idea that you who are One with God and Innocent can attack yourself and make yourself guilty, is insane. In any form, anywhere, *do not believe that guilt is real*. Your belief in sin and in guilt is the same, and your belief in one is your faith in the other, calling for punishment instead of Love. Nothing justifies insanity, and calling for punishment on yourself is insane.

6.   Deny guilt everywhere, and you will affirm the Truth of your Innocence. In every condemnation that you offer anywhere in the world that you perceive,lies your conviction of your own guilt. If you want your Christ Mind to free you of guilt, accept your Christ Mind's correction of your perception that you are separate from God throughout your entire mind. This is how you will learn that *you* are Innocent. It is impossible for you to condemn only some perceptions, and not condemn your entire mind. If you see guilt anywhere, it witnesses to guilt in you, and you will feel it is within you, because your belief in your guilt is there until it is undone. Guilt is always in *your* mind, which has condemned itself. Do not project it, or it cannot be undone within you. Your every exchange

of God's Love for a projection of guilt brings great Joy to Heaven, Where the Witnesses to your Oneness with God rejoice.

7. Even one spot of guilt that you see within your mind makes you blind to Love. When you project guilt, you see a world of illusions shrouded in your guilt, and you become unable to look within, because you know that you will find there the guilt you are trying not to see. But guilt is not there, either. *The guilt you fear is gone.* If you truly look within, you will see correction of your perception that you are separate from God shining in the Quiet and the Peace of your Christ Mind.

8. Do not be afraid to look within. The personal mind tells you that all is dark with guilt within you, and tells you to not look. It tells you to look on guilt in others instead. But you cannot do this without remaining blind to Love. When you see guilt in others, it is because you are too afraid to look within, believing that the guilt is really there. But it is not there, though you put your faith in it. Within you is the Holy Spirit, the Holy Sign of Perfect Faith that God has in you. God does not value you as the personal mind does. God knows Itself, and God knows the Truth in you, and God knows there is no difference, because God does not know of anything different from God. You cannot see guilt Where God sees Perfect Innocence. You can deny God's Knowledge, but you cannot change It. Look upon the Love that God placed in you, and learn that the guilt that you feared was there has been replaced.

10. Release from Guilt

1. You are used to the idea that your mind can see the source of your pain where it is *not*. This displacement is to hide that the real source of guilt is within your own mind, and to keep you unaware that the idea of guilt is insane. Displacement is maintained by your belief that guilt is true, so your attention must be diverted from the true source onto something less fearful to you. You are willing to look on all sorts of 'sources' for guilt, as long as they do not bear any relationship to the deeper source: your mind.

2. You cannot relate with insane ideas, and this is why they are insane. No real relationship can rest on guilt or hold one spot of it

to mar its purity. You use all relationships in the world on which you have projected guilt to avoid the person *and* your guilt. You have made strange relationships for this strange purpose. The only Real Relationship is between your Christ Mind and the Christ that It extends in your perception, and this Relationship is Holy, and cannot be used by the personal mind. It is used by the Holy Spirit, and it is this that makes It Pure. If you displace your guilt onto relationships in the world, the Holy Spirit cannot use them, because, by using them for the personal mind's ends, you prevent the Holy Spirit from using them for your release through your extension of God's Love. You will not find release from the world that you perceive in any relationship in which you join with another for your individual 'salvation'. What is for you alone as a personal self cannot be extended, and so it is not real.

3. In any relationship with another where you attempt to make them guilty, or to see guilt in them, or to share guilt with them, *you* will feel guilty. You will not find satisfaction and Peace in that relationship, because your Relationship with Christ will not be real to you. You will see guilt in that relationship, because you have projected it there. It is inevitable that when you feel guilt you will try to displace it elsewhere, because you believe it is real. Even though you suffer, you will not look within and let go of guilt. You will not know that you love, and you will not know what Real loving is. Your primary concern will be to perceive the source of guilt outside of you, and out of your control.

4. When you maintain that you are guilty for something that the personal self did in the past, you are not looking within. The past is not *in* you. Your weird associations to a personal past have no meaning in the present, but you let them stand between you and your Christ Mind, and you do not form any real relationships. You cannot expect to use others to 'solve' a personal past and to still see Christ in place of your projections on them. You will not find salvation by using others to solve problems that are not here. You did not want salvation in the past, so why do you impose your idle wishes on the present and hope to find salvation now?

5. Determine to be not as you were in a personal past. Do not use any

relationship to hold you to the personal self's past, but, with each one, be born again by extending your Christ Mind to it. An instant will be enough to free you from the personal self's past, and to give your mind over to correction of your perception that you are separate from God. When you welcome your Christ Mind as you want to be welcomed by God, you will not see guilt. You will have accepted correction, which was within you always when you thought that you were guilty, and would not look within and see it.

6. As long as you believe that guilt is justified in any way in anyone, you will not look within where you will always find correction for your belief in guilt. Guilt will end for you when you find there is no reason for it. You must learn that guilt is always insane, because it has no justification. The Holy Spirit is not seeking to dispel reality. If guilt were real, there could be no correction. The purpose of correction is to dispel your illusions, like guilt, not to make them real to you, and then to try to forgive them.

7. The Holy Spirit does not keep illusions in your mind to frighten you and then fearfully demonstrate to you what It has saved you from. What the Holy Spirit saves you from is *gone*. Do not give reality to guilt or see any justification for it. The Holy Spirit has always done what God wants It to do. The Holy Spirit sees your belief in your separation from God, but It knows of your Oneness with God. It teaches you healing, because It knows of Oneness. The Holy Spirit wants you to see and teach yourself healing *through* the Holy Spirit. What the Holy Spirit knows, you do not yet remember, though It is yours.

8. *Now* it is given you to heal and to teach; to make What *is, now*. But It does not seem to be *now*, because you believe that you are lost in guilt, alone in a frightening world, where pain is pressing on you from all over. But when you look within and see Love there, you will remember how much God loves you. And it will seem unbelievable to you that you ever thought that God did not love you and looked at you with condemnation. The moment that you realize that guilt is insane and wholly unjustified, you will not fear to look within and accept the correction of your perception that you are separate from God.

9. You have been unmerciful to yourself, so you do not remember God's Love for you. Looking unmercifully upon the world that you perceive, you do not remember how much you love God. But your love for God is Forever True. In Peace within you is the Perfect Purity of your Oneness with God. Do not fear to look at the Lovely Truth within you. Look through the cloud of guilt that dims your True Perception, and look past your illusions to the Holy Place Where you will see God's Love. Your Mind is as Pure as God's Mind. Nothing can keep you from What your Christ Mind wants you to see. Christ's Will is God's Will, and your Christ Mind offers mercy to all that you perceive, as your Christ Mind wants you to do.

10. If you want to be released from guilt, you must release all of your perceptions of guilt. There is no other way for you to look within and see the Love that is there, as certainly as God loves you *and you love God*. There is no fear in Love, because Love is guiltless. You who have always loved God have no reason to fear looking within and seeing your Holiness. Your guilt is unjustified, because it is not in the Mind of God, Where you are. This is the awareness to which the Holy Spirit wants to restore you. The Holy Spirit only removes illusions; All Else the Holy Spirit wants you to see. With your Christ Mind's Perception, the Holy Spirit wants to show you the Perfect Purity that is Forever within you.

11. You cannot enter into a real relationship with anything but Christ, Which you must love as your entire mind. Love is not special, and if you single out individuals to love to the exclusion of your Christ Mind, you are making relationships about guilt and unreality. You can love only as God loves, because there is no Love apart from God's Love. Until you recognize this as Truth, you will have no idea What Love is. When you single out another for special-love, you make the personal self real to you and you feel guilty. You do not see your Innocence, and that you are in the Peace of God. You are delusional and not seeing yourself as you are. Say to yourself:

    Let me look on my Christ Mind's Holiness and be grateful that I cannot be guilty of separating from God.

12. No illusion that you have ever held has touched your Christ Mind's Innocence in any way. Christ's Purity, wholly untouched by guilt and wholly Loving, is within you. Look upon Christ with your entire mind and love Christ. In your love of Christ is your Innocence. Look upon your True Self within with gratitude and happiness, because What you see will banish guilt Forever.

Thank You, God, for the Purity of my Christ Mind, Which is One with You and Innocent Forever.[1]

13. Like you, your Christ Mind's faith and belief are centered on what It treasures. The difference is that your Christ Mind loves only What God loves. Therefore, your Christ Mind treasures you more than you treasure yourself in your identification with a personal self; Christ treasures you as much as God does. Christ loves All that is One with God, and It offers all of Its faith and belief to God's Oneness. Christ's faith in you is as strong as the Love that It gives God. Its faith in you is without limit and without the fear that you will not hear It. Christ thanks God for your Loveliness, and for the many extensions of Love that you let your Christ Mind offer for you to remember God's Oneness.

14. Praise be to you who make God's Wholeness complete! Isolated in a personal mind you are lowly, but with your Christ Mind your Love is so Great that you cannot even conceive of It in the limitation of a personal mind. Before the Oneness of God your guilt melts away and is replaced by Kindness. Every reaction that you experience in your awareness of your Oneness with God will be so purified that it will praise God. See only the Love of God everywhere, because God will never cease to love you. With your mind united in praise to God you stand before Heaven, Where you are sure to enter in your Innocence. God loves you. To love God perfectly, your Christ Mind must have complete faith in you.

11. The Peace of Heaven

1. Denial and illusions and death are the personal mind's best advice to you for dealing with the harsh intrusion of your perceived guilt.

In your split mind, you see yourself ravaged by conflict because you see both Truth and illusion as real. You feel you must escape this conflict somehow, because it destroys your peace and could destroy you. But if you realize that the conflict is between Real and unreal powers, you can look within and see your Freedom. You will no longer see yourself as torn and ravaged when you recognize that the conflict that you perceive is without meaning.

2.   God does not want you in conflict, so your imagined 'enemy' is totally unreal. You are trying to escape from a conflict that you *have* escaped. Your conflict is over, because you have heard the Holy Spirit. Your gratitude and Joy belong to God for your release, because you did not make Freedom, but you also have not made any conflict that can endanger your Freedom. Nothing destructive ever was or will ever be. Your conflict, your guilt, and the personal self's past are all gone as one into the unreality from which they came.

3.   When your mind is united and in Heaven, you will value nothing that you have valued in your perception that you are in a world. You do not value anything in the world wholly, so you do not value it at all. Value is in Heaven, Where God places Value, and you cannot judge the Value of Heaven, because God has established Its Value. Heaven is wholly of Value, and you can appreciate It or not, but for you to partially value It is for you to not value It at all. In Heaven is Everything that God values and nothing else. Heaven is Unified and Clear, and It calls forth only one response: extension. There are no illusions, no conflict, and no variations in Heaven. It is continuous. In Heaven there is a Peace so deep that no illusion in the world that you perceive has ever brought you even a dim imagining of It.

4.   Nothing in the world that you perceive can give you the Peace of Heaven because nothing in the world is wholly extended. Perfect Perception can merely show you that only God's Love is capable of being wholly extended. It can also show you the results of extending God's Love while you still remember the results of *not* extending It. The Holy Spirit quietly points to the contrast, knowing that you will let It judge the difference for you, so It can

demonstrate that only God's Love is True. The Holy Spirit has perfect faith in your final judgment, because the Holy Spirit knows that It will make it for you. For you to doubt this is for you to doubt that the Holy Spirit's mission can be fulfilled, and this is not possible, because the Holy Spirit's mission is from God.

5. Your mind is darkened by doubt and guilt, but remember this: God has given the Holy Spirit to you to remove all doubt and every trace of guilt that you have laid upon yourself. It is impossible that this mission fail, because nothing can prevent from accomplishment what God wants accomplished. Whatever reactions you have to the Holy Spirit's Voice, whatever voice you choose to listen to, whatever strange thoughts may occur to you, God's Will *is* done. You will find the Peace in Which God has established you, because God does not change Its Mind. God is as Unchanging as the Peace in Which you dwell and of Which the Holy Spirit reminds you.

6. In Heaven you will not remember change and shift. You need contrast only in your perception that you are in a world. Contrast and differences are necessary learning aids, because by them you learn what to avoid and what to seek. When you have learned What to seek, you will find the Answer that makes your need for differences disappear. Truth comes to Its Own of Its Own Will. When you have learned that you belong to Truth, It will flow lightly over you without variation of any kind, because you will not need contrast to teach you that Truth, and only Truth, is What you want. Do not fear that the Holy Spirit will fail in what God has given It to do. The Will of God cannot fail.

7. Have faith only in this, and it will be enough: God Wills you be in Heaven and nothing can keep you from It or It from you. Your wildest misperceptions, your weird imaginings, and your darkest illusions all mean nothing. They will not succeed against the Peace that God wills for you. The Holy Spirit will restore your Sanity, because insanity is not the Will of God. That is enough for God, so It is enough for you. You will not keep what God wants removed, because it interferes with your communication with God. You *will* hear God's Voice.

8. The Communication Link that God placed within you to join your mind with Its Own cannot be broken. You may believe that you want It broken, and this belief does interfere with your knowing the deep Peace Which is the Sweet and Constant Communication that God extends to you. But God's Channels of reaching out cannot be wholly closed and separated from God. Peace will be yours again, because God's Peace still flows to you from God's Will. You have Peace now. The Holy Spirit will teach you how to extend It to learn that It is in you. God wills you Heaven and will always will you only This. The Holy Spirit knows only of God's Will. There is no chance that Heaven will not be yours again, because God is sure, and What God wills is as sure as God.

9. You will learn salvation by learning how to extend salvation. You cannot exempt yourself from what the Holy Spirit will teach you. Your salvation is as sure as God, and God's Certainty is enough. Learn that even the darkest illusion that disturbs your mind in your denial of God has no power over you. You *will* learn to be aware of God again. God watches over you, and God's Love surrounds you.

10. You cannot lose yourself in illusions when God has placed within you the Call to undo them and be Happy. You cannot separate yourself from What is within you, and your denial will not withstand the Call of God. Your mission of correction will be fulfilled as surely as your Oneness with God remains unchanged throughout Eternity. You do not have to know that Heaven is so to make it yours. It *is* so. Yet, to know it, you must accept the Will of God as your will.

11. The Holy Spirit will undo for you everything that you have learned that teaches you that what is not true must be made into truth. This is the union that the personal mind wants to substitute for your re-union with Sanity and Peace. The Holy Spirit has a very different kind of Union in Its Mind for you, and One It will accomplish as surely as the personal mind will not accomplish what it attempts. Failure is of the personal mind, not of God. You cannot wander from God, and there is no possibility that you will not perfectly accomplish the plan that the Holy Spirit offers to you for the salvation of your entire mind. You will be released from your

illusions, and you will not remember anything that you made that was not given to you by God in your Oneness with God. You cannot remember what was never true, and you must remember What is always True. Heaven lies only in your Union with Truth.

Chapter 14

Teaching for Truth

1. Yes, you are indeed blessed. But in your perception of a world as reality you do not know it. However, you do have the Means for learning it and seeing it quite clearly. The Holy Spirit uses logic as easily and as well as the personal mind, but the Holy Spirit's conclusions are Sane. They take a direction exactly opposite the personal mind's direction, pointing as clearly to Heaven as the personal mind points to illusions and death. In this course you have followed much of the personal mind's logic, you have seen its logical conclusions, and you have realized that they can only be seen in illusions where alone they can seem clear. Now you will turn away from them and follow the simple logic of the Holy Spirit, Which teaches you the simple conclusions that speak for Truth and only Truth.

1. The Conditions of Learning

1. You are blessed and do not know it, and so you need to learn it must be so. God's Blessing cannot be taught to you, but you must acquire the *conditions* of knowing that you are blessed, because this is what you have thrown away. You can extend only what you already have, and you can extend blessing and learn that you already have it. You must accept blessing for yourself before you can extend it. This is why your experience of miracles offers you the testimony that *you* are blessed. If you offer complete forgiveness, you must have let go of guilt, accepted correction for yourself, and learned of your Innocence. You learn What you have, even if It is unknown to you, by extending It.

2. You need indirect proof of Truth in a world that you made out of denial of Truth and without direction. You will perceive your need for this if you realize that 'to deny' is 'the decision to *not know*'. The logic of the world that you perceive therefore leads to nothing,

because its goal is 'to not know'. If you decide to have and give and be nothing, you must direct your thoughts to oblivion. And if you have and give and are Everything and you have denied this, then your thought system is closed off and wholly separated from the Truth. The world that you perceive *is* insane, and do not underestimate the extent of its insanity. There is no area of your perception that insanity has not touched, and your illusions *are* sacred to you. That is why God placed the Holy Spirit in your mind where you placed your illusions.

3.   Your perceiving is always outward. If your thoughts were only of the personal mind, your thought system would be forever dark. The thoughts that you project or extend have all the power that you give to them. In your identification with a personal self, the Thoughts that you share with God are beyond your belief, but the thoughts that you have made *are* your beliefs. And it is these thoughts that you have chosen to defend and love. They will not be taken from you, but they can be given up *by* you, because the Source of their undoing is within you. There is nothing in the world that you perceive to teach you that the logic of the world is totally insane and leads to nothing. But in you who made this insane logic is One Which knows that the world's logic leads to nothing, because It knows Everything.

4.   Any direction in which the Holy Spirit does not lead you goes nowhere. Anything that you deny that the Holy Spirit knows to be True, you have denied to yourself, and the Holy Spirit must teach you to not deny It. Undoing *is* indirect, just as doing is indirect. You are One with God, in Which there is no perceiving or doing. Perceiving and doing are indirect expressions of your Will to Live, Which you have blocked with your unpredictable and unholy whim of death and murder that God does not share with you. You have set yourself the task of extending what cannot be extended, and while you think that it is possible for you to learn to do this, you will not believe What it *is* possible for you to learn to do.

5.   The Holy Spirit must therefore begin Its teaching by showing you what you have tried to learn but that you can never learn. Its message is not indirect, but the Holy Spirit must introduce the

simple facts into your thought system, which has become so twisted and complex that you cannot see that it means nothing. The Holy Spirit merely looks at the personal mind's foundation and dismisses it. You, however, cannot undo what you have made with the personal mind, nor see through the heavy burden of it on your mind. It deceives you, because you chose to deceive yourself. When you choose to be deceived you attack direct approaches, because they seem to encroach on and attack your deception.

2. The Happy Learner

1. The Holy Spirit needs a happy learner in whom Its mission can be accomplished. You are steadfastly devoted to misery, and you must recognize that you are miserable and not happy. The Holy Spirit cannot teach you without this contrast, because you believe that misery *is* happiness. This has so confused you that you have tried to learn to do what you can never do, believing that unless you learn to be completely separate from God, you will not be happy. You do not realize that the foundation that this peculiar learning goal depends on means absolutely nothing, so it seems to make sense to you. Have faith in nothing and you will find the 'treasure' that you seek. You add another burden to your already burdened mind by valuing nothing. A diamond, a speck of dust, a body, or a war are all the same, because if you value one thing made of nothing you believe that nothing can be precious, and that you *can* learn to make the untrue true.

2. The Holy Spirit sees that you believe that you are in a world but knows that you are Elsewhere, so It begins Its lesson with the simple and fundamental teaching that *only the Truth is True*. This is the hardest lesson that you will ever learn, and, in the end, the only one. Simplicity is very difficult for your twisted mind. Consider all the distortions that you have woven out of nothing: strange forms and feelings and actions and reactions. Nothing is so alien to you as the simple Truth, and there is nothing to which you are less inclined to listen. The contrast between Truth and illusion is obvious, but you do not see it. The simple and the obvious are not apparent to you who want to make illusions of great things out of

nothing and believe that you are great because you make them.

3. The Holy Spirit sees all this and simply teaches that none of it is true. To you who want to teach yourself nothing and delude yourself into believing that it is *not* nothing, the Holy Spirit says with Steadfast Quietness:

    'Only the Truth is true. Nothing else matters, nothing else is real, and nothing else is here. Let Me distinguish Truth from illusion for you, which you cannot do with a personal mind, but which you need to learn. Your faith in nothing is deceiving you. Offer your faith to Me, and I will place it gently in the Truth, Where it belongs. You will not find deception There, and you will love It because you will understand It.'

4. Like you, the Holy Spirit did not make Truth. Like God, the Holy Spirit knows Truth. The Holy Spirit brings Love into your illusions and extends It to you. As you extend Love, you will realize that you did not make Love, and that you are more than what you have made. You will be a happy learner of the lesson Love brings, because It teaches you release from nothing and all the works of nothing. The heavy illusions that you project from a personal mind, and that seem to bind you to despair, you do not see are nothing until you extend Love in their place. And then you see your illusions have disappeared, so they *must* have been nothing. Because you teach Happiness and Freedom, you will see Happiness and Freedom reflected back to you.

5. When you teach that only the Truth is True by extending Truth, you learn Truth. You learn that what seemed hardest is easiest. Learn to be a happy learner, because you will never learn how to make nothing into Everything. But recognize that this has been your goal and recognize how foolish it is. Be glad that it is undone, and, when you look at it in simple honesty, it *is* undone. Do not be content with nothing. You have believed that you could be content with nothing, and *it is not so*.

6. To be a happy learner you must give everything that you have learned from the personal mind to the Holy Spirit to be unlearned

for you. Then you will begin to learn the Joyous lessons that come quickly on the firm foundation that only the Truth is True. What you learn on this foundation is Truth, and is built on Truth. The universe of learning will open up to you in all its gracious simplicity, and, with Truth before you, you will not look back.

7.   As a happy learner you meet the conditions of learning at this foundation, just as you meet the Condition of God in Oneness. This foundation lies in the Holy Spirit's plan to free you from the personal mind's past. Truth *is* True; nothing else could ever be or ever was. This simple lesson undoes the fear that you thought could never be undone. You made fear, and fear is nothing. This lesson is the Love that undoes the shapes and forms and fears of nothing. Accept Freedom from your Christ Mind, Which frees you to join in the Holy task of extending Love. Because you believe in a world of separation from God, you do not realize that Love has come and freed you from that world's dark illusions.

8.   Behold Freedom in place of the world that you perceive, and learn of It how to be Free. The Love in you will extend to be all that you perceive, and you will not be left in illusions. The Perception of your Christ Mind is extended the very moment that you perceive Christ, making everything Clear and Holy to you. The Quietness of Its simplicity is so compelling that you will realize it is impossible for you to deny the simple Truth. There is nothing else. God is Everywhere, and you are in God with Everything. You cannot be sorrowful when this is True.

3. The Decision for Guiltlessness

1.   To be a happy learner, you cannot feel guilty about learning. This is so essential to your learning that you should not forget it. When you are guiltless you learn easily, because your thoughts are free. But this means you recognize that guilt is interference, not salvation, and that it serves no useful function at all.

2.   Perhaps you are used to valuing your Innocence only to offset the pain of your guilt and you do not look at It as having value in Itself. You believe that your guilt and your Innocence are both of value, each representing escape from what the other does not offer to you.

You do not want either alone, because without both you do not see yourself as whole and therefore as happy. But you are Whole only in Innocence, and only in your Innocence can you be Happy. There is no conflict in your Innocence. If you wish for guilt in any way, in any form, you will lose appreciation of the Value of your Innocence, and push It from your sight.

3.   There is no compromise that you can make with guilt and escape the pain that only your Innocence can allay. In your perception that you are in a world, learning is living, just as Oneness is Being in Heaven. Whenever you are attracted to the pain of guilt, remember that if you give into it, you are deciding against your Happiness, and you will not learn how to be Happy. Say gently to yourself, with the conviction of God's Love for you:

'What I experience I will make manifest in my awareness.
I am Innocent, so I have nothing to fear.
I choose to testify to my acceptance of the correction of my
   perception that I am separate from God.
I accept my Innocence by extending It in my awareness.
Let me extend the Peace of God to be all that I perceive.'

4.   Each day, each hour, each minute, and every second you are deciding between crucifixion and resurrection; between the personal mind and the Holy Spirit. The personal mind is your choice for guilt; the Holy Spirit is your choice for Innocence. The power of decision is all that you have. You have only two choices, because there are no alternatives but Truth and illusion. They cannot overlap, because they are complete opposites that cannot join and cannot both be true. Your choices are: guilt or Innocence, limitedness or Limitlessness, unhappiness or Happiness.

5.   Your experience of miracles teaches you that you have chosen Innocence, Limitlessness, and Joy. Your experience of miracles is not a cause, but an effect: the natural result of your choosing right. It attests to your happiness in choosing to be free of guilt. Every extension of healing that you offer returns to you; every attack that you make holds guilt and condemnation in your mind. It is impos-

sible for you to offer what you do not want without this consequence. The cost of your giving *is* your receiving. Your giving is either a penalty from which you suffer, or your happy purchase of a Treasure that you hold dear.

6.   Only you ask for penalty of and for yourself. Every chance that you have to extend healing is another opportunity for you to replace illusions with Truth, and fear with Love in your mind. If you refuse an opportunity to heal, you bind yourself to illusions, because you did not choose to free your mind with a Perception of Love. By giving power to nothing, you lose a Joyous opportunity to learn that nothing has no power. By not dispelling your illusions, you become afraid of Truth and Love. The Joy of learning that illusions have no power over you is the Happy lesson that the Holy Spirit teaches and wants you to teach yourself. It is the Holy Spirit's Joy to teach this, as it will be your Joy.

7.   The way to teach yourself that illusions have no power is to teach yourself that your Innocence cannot be harmed. Make your Invulnerability manifest by teaching yourself that no matter what another may try to do to you, you cannot be harmed, because your Innocence is your Reality and It cannot be touched. No one can hurt you, and by refusing to be hurt, you teach yourself that you have accepted correction of your perception that you are separate from God, and you undo all of your perceptions of guilt. There is nothing to forgive. No one can hurt your Christ Mind. Your guilt has no cause, therefore it does not exist.

8.   God is the only Cause, and God did not make guilt. Do not teach yourself that you can be hurt, or you teach yourself that what is not of God has power over you. *The causeless cannot be.* Do not attest to it or foster belief in it anywhere in your mind. Remember that Mind is One and Cause is One. You will learn of Oneness only when you learn to deny the causeless and to accept God as your Cause. The Power that God gives to you *is* yours, and if you choose anything else to perceive, you penalize yourself with guilt in place of all the Happy teaching that the Holy Spirit offers to you.

9.   Whenever you choose to make a decision with the personal mind you are thinking destructively, and the decision will be wrong. It

will hurt you because of your concept of decision that led to it. It is not true that you can make decisions by and for the personal self alone. The effects of your thoughts are not isolated to the personal mind. Every decision that you make is for your entire mind, directed inward and out in your mind where you perceive a world, and influencing more than you can conceive.

10. When you accept correction of your perception that you are separate from God you *are* invulnerable. But if you believe that you are guilty of separating from God you will respond to guilt, because you will think that separation is salvation, and you will see it and side with it. You will believe that increasing separation, and therefore your guilt, is self-protection. You will fail to understand that you do not really want guilt, and that what you do not want must hurt you. All this happens because you do not believe that What you really want is God, and that God is Good. But your Holy Will brings to you all that you need as naturally as Peace without limit. What your Will does not provide has no value. But because you do not understand your Will, the Holy Spirit quietly understands It for you, and gives you What you *do* want without effort or strain or the burden of deciding in the isolation of a personal mind what you need and want.

11. You never have to make decisions alone with the personal mind. You have Help in the Holy Spirit, Which knows the Answer that you need. Do not be content with little, which is all that the personal mind can offer you, because the Holy Spirit offers you Everything. The Holy Spirit will never ask you what you have done to be worthy of God, so do not ask this of yourself. Instead, accept the Holy Spirit's Answer, because the Holy Spirit knows that you are worthy of everything that God wills for you. Do not try to escape the Gift of God that the Holy Spirit so gladly offers to you. The Holy Spirit offers you What God gave It to give to you. You do not have to decide whether or not you are deserving of God; God knows that you are.

12. Do not deny the Truth of God's Decision by substituting the personal mind's pitiful appraisal of you for God's Calm and Unswerving Value of you. Nothing can shake God's Conviction of

the Perfect Purity of All that is One with God, because It *is* Wholly Pure. Do not decide against It, because being of God It must be True. Peace abides in your mind when you quietly accept the plan that God has set for your correction and you let go of the personal mind's plan. You do not understand salvation in your identification with a personal self. Do not make any decisions with the personal mind about what your salvation is or where it lies, but ask the Holy Spirit everything, and leave all decisions to Its Gentle Counsel.

13. The Holy Spirit knows the plan that God wants you to follow, and It can teach you what the plan is. Only the Holy Spirit's Wisdom is capable of guiding you to follow It. Every decision that you undertake with the personal mind signifies that you want to define alone what your salvation is, and from what you need to be saved. The Holy Spirit knows that your whole salvation is in your escape from guilt. You have no other 'enemy', and against this strange distortion of your Purity, the Holy Spirit is your only Friend. The Holy Spirit protects your Innocence, Which will set you free. And it is the Holy Spirit's decision to undo everything that obscures your Innocence in your awareness.

14. Let the Holy Spirit be the only Guide that you want to follow to your salvation. It knows the way, and It leads you gladly on it. With the Holy Spirit you will not fail to learn that What God wills for you *is* your Will. Without the Holy Spirit's guidance you will think that you know that your salvation is in the isolation of a personal mind, and you will decide against your Peace. But salvation is of the Holy Spirit, given to the Holy Spirit by God for you. The Holy Spirit has not forgotten you, so do not forget the Holy Spirit, and It will make every decision for you, for your salvation, and for the Peace of God within you.

15. In your identification with a personal self do not seek to appraise the worth of you who are One with God, because when you do, you evaluate God and judge against God. You *will* feel guilty for this imagined crime, though it cannot really be committed. The Holy Spirit teaches you only that your 'sin' of replacing God with a personal self is not a source for guilt, because what cannot happen can have no effects for you to fear. Be quiet in your faith in the Holy

Spirit, Which loves you and wants to lead you out of insanity. Madness may be your choice, but it is not your Reality. Never forget God's Love, because God has not forgotten you. It is impossible that God will ever let you drop from the Loving Mind in Which you are One with God and Where your Home is secured in Perfect Peace Forever.

16. Only say to the Holy Spirit, 'Decide for me' and it is done. The Holy Spirit's decisions are reflections of what God knows about you, and, in Light of this Love, no error of any kind is possible. You do not have to struggle frantically to anticipate all that you cannot know when Knowledge of God lies behind every decision that the Holy Spirit makes for you. Learn from the Holy Spirit's Wisdom and Love, and extend them in your perception, because you decide for your entire mind.

17. How gracious it is for you to decide all things through the Holy Spirit, Which loves your entire mind without exception! The Holy Spirit does not leave out one of your perceptions. The Holy Spirit gives you What is yours, because God wants you to extend It with the Holy Spirit. Be led in everything by the Holy Spirit, and do not reconsider. Trust the Holy Spirit to answer quickly, surely, and with Love for every perception of yours that will be touched by a decision in any way. And your entire mind *will* be touched. Do not give the personal mind the sole responsibility of deciding what can bring good to your entire mind, because it does not know this.

18. You have taught yourself the most unnatural habit of *not* communicating with God. But you remain One with God, and Everything in God is in you. Unlearn isolation through God's Loving Guide, and learn of all the Happy Communication that you have rejected but can never lose.

19. Whenever you are in doubt about what to do, think of the Holy Spirit's Presence in you, and tell yourself only this:

    'The Holy Spirit leads me and knows the way to God.
    The Holy Spirit will never keep from me What It wants me to learn,
    So I trust It to communicate to me all that It knows for me.'

Then let the Holy Spirit quietly teach you how to perceive your Innocence, Which is already here.

4. Your Function in the Atonement

1. When you accept your Innocence in place of your perception of a world of separation, you will see the correction of your perception that you are separate from God. By proclaiming your Innocence in your perception, you make It yours, because you see what you seek. But you will not perceive your Innocence while you still believe that It is not here to be perceived. Yet the Innocence that you can perceive in place of your perception of a world of separation is your correction. Grant Innocence in your perception, and you will see the Truth of What you have acknowledged. Truth is offered to you first and foremost to be received by you, as God extends It to you. [The first in time means nothing, but God is the First in Eternity. God is both First and One. There is nothing beyond the First, because there is no order in Oneness.]

2. You who are One with God are more than merely without guilt. Your state of guiltlessness is the condition in which the guilt that is not there has been removed from your disordered mind, which thought it was there. This is the state that you must attain with God beside you. Until you do, you will still think that you are separate from God. You may feel God's Presence next to you, but you will not know that you are One with God. You cannot be taught Oneness. You must learn the *condition* of remembering your Oneness with God, and then Oneness will happen of Itself.

3. When you have let all that obscured the Truth in your Holy Mind be undone for you, and you stand in Grace before God, you will be aware of God extending Itself to you as God has always done. Extending God is all that God knows, so it is all Knowledge. What God does not know cannot be, therefore it cannot be extended. Do not ask to be forgiven, because that is already accomplished. Ask instead to learn how to forgive and to restore to your mind What always is. Correction will become real and visible to you when you use it. In your perception that you are in a world ,correction is your only function, and you must learn that correction is all that you

want to learn. You will feel guilty until you learn to correct your mind, because, in the end, whatever form it takes, your guilt arises from your failure to fulfill with your entire mind your Function of Oneness in God's Mind. You cannot escape this guilt by failing to extend your Function to all that your mind perceives.

4.   You do not need to understand Oneness to do what must be done before Knowledge of Oneness will be meaningful to you. God does not make barriers or break barriers. When you release them, they are gone. God cannot fail you. Decide that you are wrong about yourself in your identification with a personal self, and that God is right about you. You are One with God, and God knows What you are. Remember, there is nothing but God, so there cannot be anything without God's Holiness, or anything unworthy of God's Perfect Love. Do not fail in your function of extending Love in your mind where you perceive a loveless world of deceit and illusions, because this is how deceit and illusions are undone in you. Do not fail yourself, but offer to God and yourself God's Innocent Oneness. For this small gift of appreciation for God's Love, God will give you the Gift of God.

5.   Before you make any decisions, remember that you have decided against your Function in Heaven by identifying with a personal self. Consider carefully whether you want to make decisions with a personal self for the 'life' that you perceive you live in a world. Your function in your perception that you are in a world is only to decide *against* deciding with a personal mind what you want, because with it you do not know what you want, so you cannot decide what you should do. Leave all decisions to the Holy Spirit, Which speaks for God, and for your function. The Holy Spirit will teach you to remove the awful burden that you have laid upon yourself by not loving the Truth in you, and by trying to teach yourself guilt instead of Love. Give up this frantic and insane attempt that cheats you of the Joy of living with God,and of being aware of the Love and Holiness within you that make you One with God.

6.   When you have learned to decide with God, all of your decisions will become as easy and as right as breathing. You will not make

any effort, and you will be led as gently as though you were being carried down a quiet path in summer. Only your perception that you have a separate will seems to make deciding with God difficult for you. The Holy Spirit will not delay in answering your every question about what to do, because the Holy Spirit knows what to do. And the Holy Spirit will tell you and then do it for you. You who are tired will find this more restful than sleep, because you can bring guilt into your sleeping, but not into the Holy Spirit's guidance.

7.   You cannot know God unless you are guiltless, and God's Will is that you know God, so you *must* be guiltless. But if you do not recognize your guiltlessness, you deny God, and you do not recognize God though God is all around you. You cannot know God without yourself, and your recognizing your guiltlessness is the condition for your knowing God. When you accept yourself as guilty you deny God so completely that Knowledge of God is swept away from your mind, where God placed It. Learn how impossible this is! Do not endow God with attributes that you understand with a personal mind. You did not make God, and anything that you understand with a personal mind is not of God.

8.   Your task is not to make Reality, because Reality is here, and you are Part of It. You who have tried to throw yourself away and have valued God so little, hear your Christ Mind speak for God and for yourself: You cannot understand how much God loves you, because there is no parallel in your experience of a world to help you understand this. There is nothing in the world with which God's Love can compare, and nothing that you have ever felt apart from God resembles God's Love even faintly. You cannot yet give a blessing in perfect gentleness, so you do not know of One Which gives Forever and Which knows only giving.

9.   You who are of Heaven live in the Blessing of God, because you are without sin. The Atonement as correction of your perception of separation from God was established as the means of restoring your Innocence to your mind, which has denied It, so has denied itself Heaven. Correction teaches you your True Condition of guilt-lessness. It does not teach you What you are or What God is. The

Holy Spirit remembers This for you, and teaches you how to remove the blocks in your awareness that stand between you and What you know. The Holy Spirit's Memory is yours. If you remember what you have made, you are remembering nothing, but the Memory of Reality is in the Holy Spirit, so It is in you.

10. Your perceptions of yourself as both guiltless and guilty cannot communicate, because they are completely opposed. True Communication is extension, and can only occur between What is the same. God can communicate only to the Holy Spirit in your mind, because only the Holy Spirit shares with God Knowledge of What you are. And only the Holy Spirit can answer God for you, because only the Holy Spirit knows What God is. Everything else that you have placed in your mind does not exist, because what cannot communicate with the Mind of God has never been. Your communication with God is Life. Nothing without God exists at all.

5. The Circle of Atonement

1. The only part of your mind that has any Reality is the Part that still links you with God. Let your entire mind be transformed into a Radiant Reflection of God's Love by extending God's Love in place of those perceptions which seem to deny God. *God makes this possible.* Do not deny God's yearning to be known by you, because you yearn for God as God yearns for you. This is Forever Changeless, so accept the Unchanging. Leave behind the world of death that you perceive, and return quietly to Heaven. There is nothing of value in the world that you perceive, and everything of Value is in Heaven. Listen to God through the Holy Spirit in you. The Holy Spirit speaks *of* you *to* you. There is no guilt in you, because you are One with God.

2. You have a special part to play in the plan of the Atonement, and the message of your part is always: *I am Part of God, and I am guiltless.* You will teach and learn this in a way that is uniquely meaningful to you. But until you teach and learn this, you will suffer the pain of a dim awareness that you are not fulfilling your True Function. Your burden of guilt is heavy, but God does not

want it so. God's Plan for your correction is as Perfect as the personal mind's plan is fallible. You know not what you do in your identification with a personal self, but the Holy Spirit knows what you need to do, and the Holy Spirit is with you. The Holy Spirit's Gentleness is yours, and all the Love that you share with God the Holy Spirit holds in trust for you. The Holy Spirit teaches you only how to be Happy.

3.   Joy is for you who are blessed in your Oneness with God. You cannot condemn whom God has blessed. There is nothing in the Mind of God that does not share God's Innocence, because Perfect Purity naturally extends Itself. Your only calling in your perception that you are in a world is to devote yourself with active willingness to the denial of guilt in all of its forms. To accuse is *to not understand*. When you are a happy learner of the correction of your perception that you are separate from God, you become a teacher of the Innocence of God's Oneness. Deny Innocence anywhere in your mind where you perceive a world, and you deny It to yourself.

4.   Your Oneness with God is your Right. Do not try to make a reality to replace It, or you will be asking for guilt, and you will experience guilt. Protect the Purity of your Innocence from every thought of guilt that keeps your Innocence from your awareness. In answer to the Call of the plan of the Atonement, bring Innocence into your awareness. Do not let your Purity remain hidden, but undo the guilt in which you hide your True Self from your perception.

5.   Only the plan of the Atonement unites your mind into wholeness. The world of separation in your mind will slip away, and Full Communication will be restored between you and God through this correction. Your experience of miracles acknowledges the Innocence in you that you have denied to produce your need for healing. Extend God's Love in your awareness, because your hope of Happiness and release from suffering of every kind lie in Its extension. You wish to be free from pain, but you may not yet have learned how to exchange guilt for Innocence, nor yet realized that only in this exchange can you be freed from pain. But when you fail to learn you need to be taught, not attacked. If you attack yourself when you need teaching, you fail to learn.

6. As you teach yourself your Innocence, you take up your unique part in the plan of the Atonement. This is the only unified and unifying lesson plan there is. There is no conflict in this lesson plan, which has One Aim, no matter how It is taught. Every effort that you make on Its behalf you offer for the One Purpose of releasing yourself from guilt to the Eternal Glory of God's Oneness. Your every teaching that points to this points straight to Heaven and the Peace of God. There is no pain, no trial, no fear that you cannot overcome by teaching yourself your Innocence. The Power of God supports this teaching and guarantees Its Limitless results.

7. Join your efforts to the Power of God, Which cannot fail and must result in Peace. Everything in your mind where you perceive a world must be touched by teaching such as this. You will not see yourself beyond the Power of God if you teach only Innocence. You will not be exempt from the Effects of this Most Holy Lesson, Which seeks to restore What is your Right in your Oneness with God. From every perception of guilt that you release you will inevitably learn of your own Innocence. The Circle of Atonement has no end. You will find ever-increasing confidence in your safe inclusion in this Circle, with every perception that you correct within Its Safe and Perfect Peace.

8. Peace unto you who are becoming a teacher of Peace! Peace is your acknowledgment of Perfect Purity, from Which nothing is excluded. Within the Atonement's Holy Circle is God's Oneness. Joy is Its Unifying Attribute, and guilt is not left in anything that you perceive. The Power of God draws your entire mind to the Atonement's Safe Embrace of Love and Oneness. Stand quietly within the Atonement, and undo all torturous thoughts in the Safety of Its Peace and Holiness. Abide within It in your Christ Mind as a teacher of correction, not of guilt.

9. Blessed are you who teach yourself with your Christ Mind, because your Power is of God. In your guiltlessness you know God, as God knows that you are guiltless. Your Christ Mind stands in the Circle of Atonement and calls you to Peace. Teach yourself Peace with Christ, and stand with Christ on Holy Ground. For your entire mind, remember the Power of God that is given to you. Do not

believe that you cannot teach yourself God's Perfect Peace, but join your Christ Mind within the Circle. Do not fail the only purpose to which Christ's Teaching calls you. Restore God's Oneness by teaching yourself your Innocence.

10. Jesus' crucifixion had no part in the plan of the Atonement; Jesus's part in the Atonement was only the resurrection of Christ in His mind. The resurrection of Christ is the symbol of your release from guilt by Innocence. When you perceive guilt anywhere, you crucify yourself, but you restore Innocence to your mind when you perceive guiltlessness. The personal mind's goal is always your crucifixion. It sees your guilt everywhere, and it wants to kill you with its condemnation. The Holy Spirit sees only your guilt-lessness, and in Its Gentleness It wants to release you from fear and re-establish the reign of Love in your mind. The Power of Love is in the Holy Spirit's Gentleness, Which is of God and therefore cannot crucify or be crucified. Restoring your mind to Innocence is your gift to God, and everything that you extend to God is yours. In Heaven, God extends God, and this is Creation. In the 'life' that you perceive yourself living in a world, you restore your mind to God by extending your Innocence in your awareness.

11. Every perception that you have is either within the Holy Circle of Atonement or outside of It, depending on whether it is your judgment of crucifixion or your choice for correction. If you correct your perception, you will rest in Purity with your perception. But if your perception is the personal mind's judgment of condemnation, you condemn yourself. Judge only in the Quietness of the Holy Spirit. Refuse any perception that is not a blessing of correction. You must extend Holiness, because Holiness *is* extension. Come gladly to the Holy Circle of Atonement within you, and look out in Peace at all that only *seems* outside of you. Do not deny Peace to anything that you perceive, because Peace is what *you* seek. Join your entire mind in the Holy Place of Peace.

6. The Light of Communication

1. The journey that you undertake with your Christ Mind is the exchange of your denial of God for your acceptance of God, and

your ignorance of God for your understanding of God. What you understand, you do not fear. It is only in your denial and ignorance of God that you perceive a justification for your fear of God, and you shrink from God into further denial. But What is hidden terrifies you, not for What it is, but *because* It is hidden. The Obscure scares you, because you do not understand Its meaning. If you did, It would be clear, and you would no longer be in ignorance. ['Hidden value' means nothing, because you cannot extend what is hidden, so you cannot know its value. What is hidden is kept apart, but Value always lies in What is universally extended.] You cannot love What you have concealed, so you must fear It.

2. The Quiet Love in Which the Holy Spirit dwells within you is Perfectly Open and hides nothing, so It is not frightening to you. The thoughts that you have that seem to separate you from God will always give in to Love if you bring them to Love and don't hide them from Love. You have no belief in separation from God that Love will not dispel. unless you conceal it from Love's Beneficence. What you keep apart from Love cannot share Love's healing power, because you keep it separated off from Love and denied. The personal mind carefully hides all the forms that your belief in separation from God take, and you who made the illusion of the personal mind out of nothing are now afraid of it.

3. Do not continue to give the personal mind the power to protect you. It is not safe or unsafe; it cannot protect or attack. Being nothing, it does nothing. The personal mind is the guardian of your perception of separation from God. and you can only look to it for fear, because, by seeming to hide something, it *is* frightening to you. Let go of the personal mind and fear will be gone from you. Only Love remains with you when your illusions are gone, because only Love is Real and can live in openness. Everything else must disappear.

4. Death gives in to Life, because destruction is not true. Innocence undoes guilt when they are brought together, because the Truth of Innocence makes the falsity of guilt perfectly clear. It is meaningless for you to try to keep both guilt and Innocence in your

mind, and if you do, they will both be meaningless to you, because you will confuse them with each other. Only Innocence means anything; guilt makes no sense at all.

5. You have looked at separation as a means of breaking Communication, or Oneness, with God. But the Holy Spirit reinterprets your means of separation as the means of re-establishing your Communication with God, Which has not been broken, only obscured to you. All that you have made has use for the Holy Spirit for Its Most Holy Purpose. The Holy Spirit knows that you are not separate from God, but perceives much in your mind that makes you think that you are. The Holy Spirit only wants to separate this perception from you. You made the power of decision to replace the Power of Oneness, but the Holy Spirit will teach you how to decide on your own behalf. You made the concept of 'deciding' to crucify yourself, and you must learn from the Holy Spirit how to apply it to the Holy Cause of restoring you to God.

6. In your identification with a personal self you use dark and devious illusions to communicate with yourself, but you cannot really understand them. They have no meaning, because their purpose is not really communication but the disruption of True Communication, Which is your Oneness with God. Your illusions cannot communicate anything to you, because their purpose is to not communicate. Yet, even the strange and twisted world of illusions in your mind holds enough Love in it to make it meaningful if it is interpreted by the Holy Spirit and not your split mind, which made it. The world that you perceive is meant to communicate conflict back to you, and the Holy Spirit wants to release you from conflict. Leave communication to the Holy Spirit, because the Holy Spirit will interpret to you with perfect clarity, since It knows that you are in Perfect Communication with God.

7. You do not know what you are communicating to yourself with the world that you perceive, so you do not know what it communicates to you. But the Holy Spirit interprets meaning in your mind where you perceive a world, and will use it to communicate the Meaningful to you. The Holy Spirit will separate out all that reflects Meaning and will let go of the meaningless, offering you True

Communication to extend so that True Communication will be returned to you. You try to communicate to yourself with both the personal mind and the Holy Spirit, and this must lead to confused communication. But the personal mind communicates nothing, and the Holy Spirit communicates Everything, so only the Holy Spirit is possible for True Communication. The personal mind only interferes with True Communication.

8.   The Holy Spirit's entire Function is True Communication, so It must remove whatever interferes with True Communication in order to restore It to you. The personal mind is the source of interference, so do not keep it from the Holy Spirit, because the Holy Spirit will not attack it but will teach you in Gentleness and Love that the personal mind is not frightening, and that it hides nothing. You must open your mind and let Love in, because there is nothing hidden in God's Mind. God's Mind is open wide to greet you, and you cannot fail to know that you are in God, unless you choose to not be aware of this.

7. Sharing Perception With the Holy Spirit

1.   Do you want awareness or denial, Knowledge or ignorance? Opposites conflict, and you cannot have both. Your mind seems to be split by opposites, and they must be brought together, because your mind is healed by uniting. In your united mind, what is not True in your mind disappears, because Truth *is* union. As your denial of God is undone by your acceptance of God, so your ignorance of God is undone when you accept Knowledge of God. Perception is the means by which your ignorance of God is brought to Knowledge of God. Yet your perception must be cleansed of deceit, because otherwise it becomes the messenger of ignorance rather than a means for your remembering Truth.

2.   To find Truth you must honestly search out everything in your mind that interferes with your awareness of Truth. Truth *is*. It cannot be lost or sought or found. It is here within you. But Truth can be recognized or not recognized, which makes It real or false to you. If you hide Truth by denying It, It becomes unreal to you, because you hid It and made It frightening to you. Truth lies

hidden under the fear on which your split mind's insane belief system rests. You do not know this, because, by hiding Truth in fear, you see no reason to believe that the more you look at fear the less you see it and the clearer Truth becomes.

3.   It is not possible to convince you that you know God when you believe that you don't know God. From the point of view of not-knowing-God it is not true that you know God. But it *is* true, because God knows it. These are clearly opposite points of view of what 'not knowing God' is. To God, it is impossible for you to not know God. It is therefore not a point of view at all, but a belief in something untrue. If you think that you do not know God it is only a *belief*, and you are wrong about yourself. Your Oneness with God is not a point of view but a Certainty. An untrue belief brought to Truth is undone.

4.   The emphasis of this course has been on bringing what you do not want, separation from God, to What you do want, God. You will realize that your salvation must come to you this way if you consider what your perception of separation from God is. It is your maintenance by denial of two thought systems in your mind which cannot coexist: God and the personal mind. If they are brought together in your mind, it will be impossible for you to accept both. So to maintain the personal mind as your identity, you deny God either completely or you project God outside of you. From this point of view, either the personal mind alone is real, or the personal mind and a separate God are real, but never only God is Real. So you are afraid to look at both God and the personal mind together in your mind, because you know that you will withdraw your acceptance of one of them, because they cancel out each other. When you see them apart through denial, you cannot see that they cancel out each other, because you see each in a separate place – the personal mind within you and God outside of you – so you can believe in both equally if you want to. But bring them together in your mind, and you instantly see that they are incompatible. The personal mind will go, because it is only an illusion, and God is already in your mind.

5.   Awareness of God cannot enter your mind when you believe in

illusions and will not let them go. Truth does not struggle against illusion, and Love does not attack fear. Truth *is*, and It does not need to defend Itself against what *is not*. You make defenses; God does not. The Holy Spirit uses your defenses on behalf of Truth, only because you made defenses *against* Truth. The Holy Spirit's perception of your defenses is used for Its Purpose, and It changes your defenses into your call for God, Which your defenses were made to attack. Like everything else that you made, defenses must be gently turned to your Real Good, transformed by the Holy Spirit from a means for your self-destruction to a means for your preservation and release. The Holy Spirit's Task is great, but the Power of God is in the Holy Spirit. To the Holy Spirit, Its Task was accomplished the instant that It was given to the Holy Spirit for you. Do not delay your return to Peace by wondering how the Holy Spirit can fulfill What God has given It to do. Leave that to the Holy Spirit. You are not asked to do great tasks in your identification with a limited personal self; you are merely asked to do the little that the Holy Spirit suggests. Trust the Holy Spirit to the little extent that what It asks you to do you *can* do. You will see how easily you accomplish all that the Holy Spirit asks.

6. The Holy Spirit asks only this of you: Bring to It every secret that you have locked away from It in your identification with a personal self. Open your entire mind to the Holy Spirit, and ask It to undo your illusions with Its Love. At your request, the Holy Spirit will gladly enter your mind, and undo your illusions when you reveal them to It. But what you hide the Holy Spirit cannot undo. The Holy Spirit is *your* Sight, and unless you look with the Holy Spirit, the Holy Spirit cannot see. The Perception of your Christ Mind is for you with the Holy Spirit, so bring all of your dark and secret thoughts to the Holy Spirit, and look on them with the Holy Spirit. The Holy Spirit is the Love in your split mind, and Love and fear cannot coexist in your mind when you look on fear with Love. The Holy Spirit's judgment will prevail,l and it is yours when you join your perception with the Holy Spirit.

7. Seeing with the Holy Spirit is the way in which you learn to extend the interpretation of perception that leads to God. You cannot

really see in the isolation of a personal mind. Perceiving with the Holy Spirit teaches you that what you see in the isolation of a personal mind means nothing. Seeing with the Holy Spirit will show you that all Meaning, even your own, comes not from your seeing with two minds, but from your gentle fusing of everything into *One* meaning, *One* emotion, and *One* purpose. God has One Purpose, Which It shares with you. The single Perception Which the Holy Spirit offers to you will bring this Oneness to your mind so clearly that you will not wish, for all that you perceive in a world, to reject What God gives to you. Perceive that your Will is God's Will, and all of God's Love is yours.

8. The Holy Meeting Place

1. In your illusions, you obscure the Glory God gives to you and the Power that God bestows on you as an Innocent Part of God. All of This lies hidden in your every illusion of separation, shrouded in guilt and in your denial of your Innocence. Behind your denial is nothing real, because nothing can obscure God's Gift. It is the act of denial that interferes with your recognition of the Power of God within you. Do not banish Power from your mind, but let all the illusions that you use to hide your Glory be brought to the judgment of the Holy Spirit to be undone. You whom the Holy Spirit wants to save for Glory *are* saved for It. The Holy Spirit is God's Promise that you will be released from limitedness to Limitlessness. The Holy Spirit is faithful to this Promise, because the Holy Spirit shares with God the Promise that was given to It from God to share with you.

2. And the Holy Spirit still shares It with God for you. Everything else that seems to promise you otherwise, great or small, however much you value it, the Holy Spirit will replace with the One Promise given to It for your Mind in Its Oneness with God. God's Mind is your Mind. Anything in your mind that is not equally worthy of both God and you will be replaced by Gifts wholly acceptable to Both. You cannot offer guilt to God, so you cannot offer it to yourself. You are not separate from God, and the gifts that you offer to One, you offer to the Other. You don't seem to know God,

because you don't seem to know this. But you *do* know God, and you *do* know this. All of this is safe within you in the Holy Spirit. The Holy Spirit is not in your perception of separation from God, but in the Meeting Place within you Where God, united to your Christ Mind, speaks to you through the Holy Spirit. You cannot be separate from God, so Communication between you and God cannot cease. The Holy Meeting Place of the united God and Christ lies in the Holy Spirit within you. Any interruption in Communication between you and God is impossible Here, because it is not God's Will. Unbroken and Uninterrupted Communication flows constantly between you and God, as you Both want it to be. And so it is.

3.   Don't let your mind wander through illusions, away from Love's Center. You may choose to lead yourself astray with the personal mind's projections, but your mind can be joined in wholeness by the Guide appointed for you by God. The Holy Spirit will surely lead you to Where God and your Christ Mind await your recognition. You are joined in Oneness with God through your Christ Mind, and through this Gift all separation disappears from your mind. Unite with What you are; you can only join with Reality. God's Glory belongs to you in Truth. It has no opposite, and you cannot bestow anything else upon yourself.

4.   There is no substitute for Truth, and Truth will make this plain to you as you are brought into a Place within you Where you can meet with Truth. And There you must be led through Gentle Understanding, Which can lead you nowhere else. Where God is, There you are; such is the Truth. Nothing can change this Knowledge, given to you by God, into untruth. Everything that is One with God knows God, because Knowing God is what Oneness is. God and you and your Extension of God are joined in the Holy Meeting Place within you. God is the One Link that holds Oneness together.

5.   The Link between you and God can never be dissolved. Heaven Itself is Oneness, and Heaven remains God's Will for you. Accept no other Gift in your mind, because nothing else can exist with It. Your little illusions will be brought together with God's Gift of

Heaven, and only What is worthy of God will be accepted by you for whom It was intended. To whom God gives Itself, God *is* given. Your little 'gifts' of separation will vanish in your mind where God has placed Its Own Gift of Oneness.

9. The Reflection of Holiness

1. The plan of the Atonement, which corrects your perception of separation from God, does not make you Holy. You are always Holy in your Oneness with God. Correction merely brings your perception of your unholiness to your Holiness, or what you made to What you are. Bringing illusions to Truth, or the personal mind to God, is the Holy Spirit's only Function. Do not hide what you have made from God, because hiding it has cost you Knowledge of God and of yourself. This Knowledge is Safe, but you do not feel safe apart from It. You made time to replace Timelessness in your decision to be not as you are, so Truth was made to seem past to you, and you dedicated the present to illusion. And then you changed the past, too, and interposed it between What has always been and now. The personal past that you remember never was, and it represents your denial of What always *is*.

2. For you to bring the personal mind to God is for you to bring your error to Truth Where it is corrected, because it is the opposite of Truth. Your error is undone, because the impossible nature of the contradiction between your error and Truth can no longer stand. What disappears in Truth is not attacked; it merely vanishes, because it is not True. It is meaningless for you to think that different realities can exist, because Reality must be One. It cannot change with time or mood or chance. Its Changelessness is what makes It Real. You cannot undo this, because undoing is for unreality. And undoing unreality is what Reality will do for you.

3. Merely by being What It *is*, Truth releases you from everything that It *is not*. Correction is so gentle that you only need to whisper to the Holy Spirit, and all of the Holy Spirit's Power will rush to your assistance and support. You are not frail with God within you, but without God you *would* be nothing. Correction offers you God, and this Gift is Held by God within you through the Holy Spirit. God

has not left your mind, though you worship the personal self. Your mind is still Holy, because the Presence Which dwells within it *is* Holiness.

4.   In your mind Holiness waits Quietly for you to return to It in Love. The Presence within you knows that you will return to Purity and Grace. The Graciousness of God will gently take you in and cover all of your sense of pain and loss with the Immortal Assurance of God's Love. There your fear of death will be replaced with Joy of Life, because God is Life, and you live in God. Life is as Holy as God, with Which It is One. The Presence of Holiness lives in every-thing that lives, because Holiness is One with Life, and It does not leave What is One with Itself.

5.   Your mind can become a spotless mirror in which the Holiness of God shines forth through your perceptions. Through this process you can see a Reflection of Heaven in your mind, but no images of the personal mind must dim the mirror that you want to hold God's Reflection. God will shine of Itself on the mirror of your mind, and you will perceive only the clear Reflection of God through it.

6.   Reflections of your mind are seen clearly only in the Light of Truth. In the darkness of illusions, your mind's reflections are obscure, and their meaning lies only in your shifting interpretations rather than in themselves. The Reflection of God needs no interpretation, because It is clear. Clean the mirror of your mind, and the Message that shines forth from your mind will cover everything that you perceive, and you will not fail to understand It. It is the same Message that the Holy Spirit is holding in the mirror of your perceptions. You will recognize the Message, because you have been taught your need for It, but you did not know where to look for It. See It in you, then, and extend It to replace the world that you perceive.

7.   If you realized for a single instant the Power of Healing that the Reflection of God shining in your perception can bring to all of your mind, you would not wait to make the mirror of your perception ready to receive the Image of the Holiness that can heal your entire mind. The Image of Holiness that shines in your mind

is not obscure, and It will not change. Its meaning to you is not obscure when you look upon Its Reflection everywhere in your mind where you perceive a world. All of your problems find healing in It.

8.   The Response of Holiness to any form of separation is always the same, and there is no contradiction in what It calls forth. Its One Response is Healing, without regard to what is brought to It. When you have learned to offer only healing, you will be ready at last for Heaven, because of the Reflection of Holiness within you. In your perception, Holiness can only be *reflected*. In Heaven, Holiness is not a reflection, but the actual Condition of God. God is not an image, and What is One with God holds God within Itself in Truth. What is One with God does not merely reflect Truth; It *is* Truth.

10. The Equality of Miracles

1.   When no perception stands between God and you, or between you and your Extension of God, your Knowledge of God's Oneness will extend Forever. The reflections that you accept into the mirror of your mind in time bring Eternity nearer to, or push It further from, your awareness. But Eternity Itself is beyond time. Reach out of time and touch Eternity with the help of Eternity's Reflection within you. You will turn away from time toward Holiness, as surely as Holiness calls to you to let go of guilt in your entire mind. Reflect the Peace of Heaven in your mind where you perceive a world, and bring your entire mind to Heaven. The Reflection of Truth draws your entire mind to Truth, and, as you enter Truth, you will leave all reflections behind.

2.   In Heaven, Reality is extended, not reflected. But by extending Reality's Reflection in your mind where you perceive a world, Reality's Truth becomes the only Perception that your Christ Mind accepts. This is how your Memory of God dawns on you, and you will find that you can no longer be satisfied with anything but your Reality. In the world that you seem to live in, you have no conception of Limitlessness, because it is a world of limits. In the world, every action is classified and ranked according to how easy or difficult it is to perform in different circumstances, so your

experience of the miracle, being the same in every circumstance, has a unique function. It is motivated by the Holy Spirit, Which brings the Law of Oneness to all that you perceive. Extending God's Love is the one thing that you can do in the world that transcends categorization, because it undoes differences by being exactly the same in every situation.

3.   Miracles do not compete with each other or with your non-mirac-ulous thoughts, and you can extend them without limit. They can be simultaneous with each other and with your non-miraculous thoughts, and they can occur in great numbers. This will not be difficult for you to understand once you can conceive of miracles as possible at all. What you may find more difficult to grasp is that the sameness of miracles stamps them as something that must come from Somewhere other than the world that you perceive. From the perspective of the world, it is impossible for any two situations to be exactly the same, or for you to respond to them in exactly the same way.

4.   Perhaps you are aware that your thoughts do not compete, though they may conflict, and they can occur together in great numbers. You may be so used to this that you give it no thought at all. But you are also used to classifying some of your thoughts as more important, larger, better, more productive, or more valuable than other thoughts. This is how your split mind thinks, because some of your thoughts reflect Heaven, while others are motivated by the personal mind, which only *seems* to think.

5.   The result of your thinking with a split mind is that your mind never rests and is never still, because it is full of weaving, changing patterns. It is a mirror that is swept constantly with alternating reflections of Truth and illusion, and the little sanity that you maintain is held together by a sense of order that you establish and that attests to the fact that you are not a personal mind. The personal mind is chaos, and if you were only the personal mind, ordering your thoughts would not be possible. But ordering your mind does not limit only the personal mind; it limits *you*. To order your mind is to arrange your thoughts through judgment, so it is really the Holy Spirit's function, not yours in your split state.

6. You must learn that in your identification with a personal self you have no basis at all for ordering your thoughts. The Holy Spirit teaches you this by giving you the experience of miracles to show you that there is a better way to order your thoughts. The miracle offers exactly the same response to every call for help without judging some calls as louder, greater, or more important. You may wonder how you can accept this when you are still so bound to judgment, and the answer is very simple: The Power of God, not of the personal mind, engenders your experience of miracles. Your extension of God's Love witnesses to the Power of God within you. The Power of God's Love is Limitless, and that is why every miracle extends to be all that you perceive, and blesses your entire mind. God does not classify your calls for help; all calls for help are given help.

7. The Holy Spirit's judgment divides every perception that you have in the world into two categories: Your extension of Love and your call for Love. You are too confused in your identification with a personal self to recognize Love, or to believe that everything else is nothing but your own call for Love. The personal mind is bound to form, and what it considers 'content' is really another version of form. From the personal mind you do not respond to the opportunities to extend Love that the world that you perceive really offers to you; you respond to the particulars of the personal mind's judgments and projections.

8. The personal mind is incapable of understanding content, and is totally unconcerned with it. It assumes that if a form is acceptable to it the content must be, otherwise it will attack the form. If you believe that you understand the personal mind's 'dynamics', you do not understand it *from* a personal mind, because it cannot be understood *by* a personal mind. The personal mind enjoys studying itself, and thoroughly approves of analyzing itself, because doing so validates its reality. But the study of the personal mind, or 'ego', is not the study of the mind; it is the study of a form with meaningless content. A personal mind studying the personal mind is senseless, though this is carefully concealed behind impressive-sounding words, and its conclusions lack any consistent sense.

9. It is characteristic of the personal mind's judgments that separately they seem to stand, but put them together, and the personal mind's thought system is revealed as incoherent and chaotic. Form is not enough for meaning, and the lack of underlying content in the personal mind makes a cohesive system impossible. Separation remains the personal mind's chosen condition, because, in the isolation of it, you cannot find Truth. But extend your True Mind to encompass your mind where you perceive a world, with a personal mind, and the personal mind can no longer defend its lack of content. The fact that what seems to be 'your mind' and what seems to be a separate 'world' can join means that the isolation of the personal mind is not your Truth.

10. It is impossible for you to remember God in the secret solitude of a personal mind, because your remembering God means that you are not isolated to a personal mind, and that you are willing to remember this. Do not think with a personal mind, because its thoughts are not for *you*. If you want to remember God, let the Holy Spirit order your thoughts, and accept only the answer that the Holy Spirit gives to any question or problem. Your entire mind seeks for Love, and if you join in Love with your mind where you perceive a world,, then everything that you perceive will be given meaning for you. The isolated journey of a personal mind fails you, because it excludes the Wholeness that it is supposed to find.

11. As God communicates to the Holy Spirit in you, so does the Holy Spirit translate Its Communications through you to your perceptions so that you can understand Them. God has no secret communications, because Everything of God is Perfectly Open and Freely Accessible to your entire mind, because It is *for* your Whole Mind. Nothing lives in secret, and what you hide from the Holy Spirit *is* nothing. Every interpretation of the personal mind's perceptions of others that you make is senseless. Let the Holy Spirit show you how your perceptions are either Love, or your call for Love. Your split mind holds only these two orders of thought.

12. In your experience of miracles, you will recognize that this is true. Where you perceive Love you must know that you have It, because for you to perceive It, It must've been extended from you. And

where you call for Love you must extend It, because Love is What you are. This course will teach you how to remember What you are, restoring you to your True Identity. This Identity extends everywhere, and your experience of the miracle is your means for extending It in your awareness. By supplying your True Identity wherever you do not recognize It, you *will* recognize It. God wills to be One with you Forever, and every time that you recognize your Christ Mind, God will bless you with all of the Love that God has for your Christ Mind. The Power of God's Love is with every miracle that you extend, so every miracle is the same.

11. The Test of Truth

1. The essential thing for you to learn is that in your identification with a personal self you do not know anything. Knowledge is power, and all Power is of God. You have God's Power, but, in your attempt to keep power to a little self, you have interposed so much between God's Power and your awareness of It that you cannot use It. Everything that you have taught yourself through a personal mind has made your Power more and more obscure to you. You don't know What or Where It is. You have made something that looks like power but is a show of strength so pitiful that it must fail you, because Power is not a *seeming* strength, and Truth is beyond appearances of any kind. All that stands between you and the Power of God in you is your learning of the false and your attempts to undo the Truth.

2. Be willing to have it all undone, and be glad that you are not bound to your illusions forever. You have taught yourself how to limit your Christ Mind, a lesson so unthinkable that only in insanity could you think of it. God cannot learn how to be not-God, and you who are One with God, and who have been given all Power by God, cannot learn to be powerless. Do you prefer to keep what you have taught yourself in place of What you have, and What you are?

3. Correction teaches you how to escape forever from everything that you have taught yourself in the past in your identification with a personal self by showing you only What you are *now*. You must learn something before the effects of what you have learned are

308

made manifest to you, so your learning is in the past, but its influence determines your present by giving it whatever meaning it holds for you. Your learning with the personal mind gives the present no meaning at all. Nothing that you have ever learned with it can help you understand the present or teach you how to undo the past. A personal past is what you have taught yourself through a personal mind. *Let it all go.* Do not attempt to understand anything in the 'light' of a personal past, because the illusions through which you try to see can only obscure. Do not put your confidence in illusions to bring you understanding, because you will contradict Truth and believe in separation. But you cannot really *see* illusions, because they are nothing more than a condition in which your seeing Truth becomes impossible.

4.   You have not yet brought all of the illusions that you have taught yourself to the Truth within you, so you can hardly judge the truth and value of this course. But God has not abandoned you, so you have another lesson already learned for you by the Holy Spirit, Which was given this lesson for you. This lesson shines with God's Glory, and in it lies God's Power, Which God shares so gladly with you. Learn of the Happiness of God, Which is yours. But, to accomplish this lesson, you must willingly bring all of your thoughts of separation's reality to Truth and joyously lay them down with a mind that is open to receive. Every thought of separation that you bring to the Holy Spirit It will gladly accept from you, because you do not want separation. And the Holy Spirit will gladly exchange each one for the Happy lesson It has learned for you. Never believe that any lesson that you have learned apart from the Holy Spirit means anything.

5.   You have one test by which to recognize if what you have learned is true: If you are wholly free of fear of any kind, and if everything that you see shares in your Perfect Peace, then you can be sure that you have learned God's lesson and not the personal mind's lesson. Unless this is true, you still have thoughts of separation that hinder you and that you project onto your perception of a world. The absence of Perfect Peace means one thing: You think you do not will for yourself What God wills for you. Whatever form it takes,

every lesson of separation teaches this. And every lesson of correction with which the Holy Spirit replaces your thoughts of separation teaches you that you will with God in your Christ Mind.

6.   Do not be concerned with how you can learn a lesson so completely different from everything that you have taught yourself. Your part is very simple: You only need to recognize that you do not want anything that you have learned through a personal mind. Ask the Holy Spirit to teach you, and do not use the personal self's experiences to confirm what you learn. When your Peace is threatened or disturbed in any way, say to yourself:

'I do not know what anything, even this, means, so I do not know how to respond to it. I will not use the personal mind's past learning to guide me now.'

By refusing to teach yourself through a personal mind that does not know, you open yourself to the Holy Spirit's guidance. The Holy Spirit will take up Its rightful place in your awareness the instant that you open your awareness to the Holy Spirit.

7.   In the isolation of a personal mind you cannot be your own guide to miracles, because it is your identification with a personal mind that makes them necessary. But the Means on Which you can depend for the experience of miracles has been provided for you in the Holy Spirit. You can make no need that God cannot meet, if you turn to God ever so little. But God cannot compel you to turn to God and still remain God, because God does not compel. God cannot be unlike God, because it is impossible for God to lose Its Identity, because It is *your* Identity. And your Identity is Changeless. In your experience of the miracle, you acknowledge God's Changelessness by seeing yourself as you always are and not as you want to make yourself. Your experience of the miracle brings you the effects that only your Innocence can bring, so it establishes in your awareness the Fact that your Innocence must be True.

8.   It is impossible for you to establish your Innocence in your awareness when you are firmly bound to perceiving separation from God, and you are committed to perceiving yourself as guilty.

Be sure that you are willing to acknowledge that this *is* impossible, because the guidance of the Holy Spirit is limited when you think that you can run or deal with some aspects of your 'life' in the world that you perceive without the Holy Spirit. By holding back parts of your life for the personal mind, you make it appear as though it is the Holy Spirit that is undependable, and you use this as further justification for holding back more. By limiting what guidance you will accept from the Holy Spirit, you put yourself in a position where you cannot depend on the experience of miracles to answer all of your problems for you.

9. The Holy Spirit does not withhold from you What It wants you to give. You have no problems that the Holy Spirit cannot solve with an extension of God's Love. Miracles are for you, and every fear or pain or trial that you have has already been undone. The Holy Spirit has already brought them all to Love for you and has recognized that they never happened. There are no lessons of separation that the Holy Spirit has not already corrected for you, and they do not exist in the Holy Spirit's Mind at all. The personal self's past does not limit the Holy Spirit, therefore it does not limit you. The Holy Spirit does not see time as you do, and each miracle that It offers to you corrects your use of time, and gives time to the Holy Spirit to use on your behalf.

10. Being your True Mind, the Holy Spirit has freed you from the personal self's past, and It wants to teach you that you *are* free of the past. The Holy Spirit wants you to accept Its accomplishments as yours, because the Holy Spirit *is* you. The Holy Spirit has already freed you from what you made. You can deny the Holy Spirit, but you cannot call on It in vain, because the Holy Spirit always gives Its Gifts in place of what you offer to It. The Holy Spirit wants to establish its Teachings of Love firmly in your mind, so that no lessons of guilt will abide in What is made Holy by the Holy Spirit's Presence. Thank God that the Holy Spirit is here, and that It works through you, and that all that It does is yours. The Holy Spirit offers you the experience of the miracle with everything you let It do through you.

11. Your Christ Mind will always be indivisible. As you are One with

God, so do you learn with one, entire mind. The Holy Spirit is as like God as your Christ Mind is like God, and through the Holy Spirit, God proclaims God's Oneness and yours. Listen in silence to the Holy Spirit ,and do not raise a voice against It, because the Holy Spirit teaches you the miracle of Oneness, and before this lesson all division disappears. Teach like the Holy Spirit in your perception that you are in a world, and you will remember that you have always extended God as God extends God. The miracle of your Extension of God has never ceased, because in its Holiness it is Immortal. Immortality is the Will of God and of God's Oneness.

12. When you remember that you don't know anything without the Holy Spirit, and you become willing to learn Everything, you *will* learn Everything. But when you trust that in the personal mind you already know everything, then you will not learn anything, because you will have destroyed your motivation for learning. Do not think that you know anything until you pass the test of Perfect Peace, because Peace and Knowledge go together and cannot be found alone. It is the Law of God that Peace and Knowledge go together, because they are cause and effect, each to the other, so that if one is absent so is the other.

13. You will really learn when you recognize that Peace is the evidence that you have Knowledge, because for True Knowledge you must want Peace and nothing else. Whenever you think that you have Knowledge but really do not, you will not have Peace, because you will have abandoned the Holy Spirit. Whenever you fully realize that you *do not* have Knowledge, Peace will return, because you will have invited the Holy Spirit by abandoning the personal mind on the Holy Spirit's behalf. The only thing that you need to do is to *not call* on the personal mind for anything. The Holy Spirit will fill your every perception if you make room for It.

14. If you want Peace, you must abandon the teacher of attack. The Teacher of Peace will never abandon you. You can desert the Holy Spirit, but It will never desert you, because the Holy Spirit's faith in you is Its Knowledge. It is as firm as Its faith in God, because the Holy Spirit knows that faith in God must encompass faith in you who are One with God. In this constancy lies the Holy Spirit's

Holiness, Which It cannot abandon, because it is not Its Will to do so. With your Perfection always in the Holy Spirit's Sight, the Holy Spirit extends Peace to your every perception that needs it. Make way for Peace and It will come to you, because Knowledge is in you, and from It Peace must come to you.

15. The Power of God, from Which both Knowledge and Peace arise, is yours as surely as It is God's. You think that you don't know God, because in the isolation of a personal mind, it is impossible for you to know God. But see the Mighty Works that God does through you, and you will be convinced that you did them through God. You will not deny that God is the Source of effects so powerful, because they could not be of the personal mind. Leave room for God in your mind, and you will find yourself so filled with Power that nothing will touch your Peace. This will be the test by which you recognize that you *know*.

Chapter 15

The Holy Instant

1. The Two Uses of Time

1. Imagine what it means to have no cares, no worries, and no anxieties but to be Perfectly Calm and Quiet all the time. For you to learn just this, and nothing more, is what time is for. The Holy Spirit will not be satisfied with Its teaching until Its teaching is all that you learn. The Holy Spirit's teaching function is not fulfilled until you have become such a consistent learner that you learn only of the Holy Spirit. When this has happened, you will no longer need a teacher or time in which to learn.

2. You may be discouraged by believing that learning of the Holy Spirit takes time, and that the results of Its teaching are far in the future, but this is not so. The Holy Spirit uses time in Its own way and is not bound by it. Time is the Holy Spirit's friend in teaching. Time is not wasted by the Holy Spirit, as it is wasted by the personal mind, which uses it to support its belief in destruction. The personal mind, like the Holy Spirit, uses time to teach you the inevitability of the goal and end of its teaching. But, for the personal mind, the goal is your death, which *is* its end; for the Holy Spirit, the goal is Life, Which *has* no end.

3. The personal mind is an ally of time but not its friend. It is as mistrustful of death as it is of Life, and the death that it wants for you it cannot tolerate for itself. The outcome of this strange religion is the personal mind's conviction that it can pursue you beyond the grave. Out of its unwillingness that you find peace even in death, it offers you immortality in hell. It speaks to you of Heaven, but assures you that Heaven is not for you. If you are guilty of separation from God, you cannot hope for Heaven.

4. In your identification with a personal self you cannot escape the belief in hell. Your nightmares and fears are all associated with it. The personal mind teaches that hell is in the future, because hell is

its teaching goal. Although the personal mind aims at death as an end for you, it does not believe in it, because the goal of death it craves for you leaves it unsatisfied. If you learn of the personal mind you cannot escape the fear of death, but if you thought of death merely as the end of pain there would be nothing for you to fear. You can clearly see the strange paradox of the personal mind here: It must keep fear *from* you to hold your allegiance to it, but it must engender fear *in* you to maintain itself. The personal mind frequently succeeds in doing both by using denial to hold together contradictory goals so that they can seem to work. It teaches you that your death is the end as far as your hope of Heaven goes, but because it cannot conceive of its own death or be without you, then it must go with you in death, and your separation from God must be eternal. This is the personal mind's version of Immortality, and this is the version of time it supports.

5. The personal mind teaches that you must find Heaven here and now in your perception that you are in a world, because hell is in your future. But it also tells you that hell is here and now, even sometimes to the point of attacking you so savagely that it tells you to take your own life. The only part of time that the personal mind allows you to look on calmly is the past, and even the past's only value to you is that it is no more.

6. How bleak and despairing and terrifying is the personal mind's use of time! But, underneath its fanatical insistence that your future be like the personal self's past, it hides a far more insidious threat to your Peace: the belief that you are guilty. The personal mind does not advertise this, because it wants you to still believe that it can offer you escape from hell. But your belief in guilt will always lead to your belief in hell. For you to experience fear of hell, the personal mind brings hell to you now in your perception that you are in a world as a foretaste of the future. If you believe that you deserve hell, you cannot believe that your punishment will end in Peace.

7. The Holy Spirit teaches that there is no hell, except for the hell that the personal mind makes of the present. Your belief in hell is what prevents you from understanding the present, because it makes you afraid of the present by holding the personal self's past against it.

The Holy Spirit leads you as steadily to Heaven as the personal mind drives you to hell. The Holy Spirit knows only the present and uses it to undo the fear by which the personal mind wants to make the present useless to you. There is no escape from fear for you in the personal mind's use of time, because time, according to its teaching, is a teaching device for compounding your guilt until it becomes all-encompassing and demands vengeance on you forever.

8. The Holy Spirit wants to undo all guilt and fear and thoughts of vengeance in you *now*. Fear is not of the present but of the past and future, which do not exist. You experience no fear in the present when each instant stands clear and separate from the past and without the past's shadow creeping over it into the future. This Instant is a clear, untarnished birth in which you emerge from the personal self's past into a present that extends Forever. It is so beautiful, and so clean and free of guilt, that nothing but Happiness is here. No guilt and fear are remembered this Instant, and Immortality and Joy are *now*.

9. This lesson takes no time for you to learn, because what is time without a past or future? It has taken you time to misguide yourself so completely, but it takes no time at all for you to be What you are. Practice the Holy Spirit's use of time as a teaching aid to Happiness and Peace. Take this instant, *now*, and think of it as all there is of time. Nothing can reach you here out of the personal self's past, and it is here that you are completely absolved, completely free, and wholly without guilt. From *this* Holy Instant, Where Holiness is born again in your awareness, you will go forth in time without fear and with no sense of change with time.

10. Time and change go together, but Holiness does not change. Learn more in this Instant than that hell does not exist; learn in this Instant of correction that Heaven is here. Heaven will not change, and your birth into the Holy Present is your salvation from change. Change is an illusion taught to you by the personal mind, which cannot conceive of your Innocence. There is no change in Heaven, because there is no change in God. In this Holy Instant, in Which you see yourself Free, you remember God. Remembering God *is* remembering your Freedom.

11. If you are tempted to be dispirited by thinking how long it could take to change your mind so completely, ask yourself, 'How long is an Instant?' Give this Instant to the Holy Spirit for your salvation. The Holy Spirit asks for nothing more, because It needs nothing more. It takes far longer for the Holy Spirit to teach you to be willing to give this tiny Instant to the Holy Spirit than for the Holy Spirit to use It to offer you the Whole of Heaven. In exchange for this Instant, the Holy Spirit stands ready to give you the Memory of Eternity.

12. You will never give the Holy Instant to the Holy Spirit for your release while you are unwilling to extend It in place of the personal mind's projections onto others. The Holy Instant is one of extending Oneness to your mind where you perceive a world, and it is not for the isolation of a personal mind. Remember, when you are tempted to attack another for your projections onto them, that the Holy Instant is your release from separation. Your experiences of miracles are the Holy Instants of release that you extend and receive. They attest to your willingness to *be* released and to offer time to the Holy Spirit for Its use.

13. How long is an Instant? It is as short for your mind where you perceive a world as it is for you. Practice extending this Blessed Instant of Freedom in place of the personal mind's projections, and make time a friend of your entire mind. The Holy Spirit extends this Blessed Instant to you through your willingness to extend It. As you extend It, It is extended to you. Be willing to extend What you want to receive of the Holy Spirit, because you join with the Holy Spirit in extending It. Your own instantaneous escape from guilt is in the Purity of the release that you extend. You must be Holy if you offer Holiness.

14. How long is an Instant? As long as it takes for you to re-establish Perfect Sanity, Perfect Peace, and Perfect Love for your entire mind and for God. As long as it takes for you to remember Immortality and your Immortal Extension of God, Which shares Immortality with you. As long as it takes for you to exchange hell for Heaven. Long enough for you to transcend all that the personal mind has made and to ascend to God in your awareness.

15. Time is your friend if you leave it to the Holy Spirit to use. The Holy Spirit needs very little to restore God's Whole Power to you. The Holy Spirit transcends time for you and understands what time is for. Your Holiness does not lie in time, but in Eternity. There never was in instant in which you could lose your Purity. Your Changeless State is beyond time, and your Purity remains Forever beyond attack and without variation. Time stands still in your Holiness and does not change, so it is not time at all. Caught in this single Instant of the Eternal Sanctity of God's Oneness, the present is transformed into Forever. Extend this Eternal Instant for the Holy Spirit to remember Eternity for you. Offer the miracle of the Holy Instant through the Holy Spirit, and leave the Holy Spirit's giving It to you up to the Holy Spirit.

2. The End of Doubt

1. The plan of the Atonement, or the correction of your perception that you are separate from God, is *in* time but is not *for* time. Being in you, It is Eternal, because What holds the Memory of God cannot be bound by time. *You* are not bound by time. You can be bound only if God is bound. An Instant that you offer to the Holy Spirit is offered to God, and in that Instant you gently remember God. In that Blessed Instant you let go of all your past learning through a personal mind, and the Holy Spirit quickly offers you the whole lesson of Peace. This does not take time, because all of your obstacles to learning It have been removed. Truth is so far beyond time that all of It happens at once. Truth is One, and Oneness does not depend on time at all.

2. Do not be concerned with time, and do not fear the Holy Instant that will remove all of your fear. The Instant of Peace is Eternal, *because* It is without fear. It will come to you, because It is the lesson that God gives to you through the Holy Spirit, Which is appointed by God to translate time into Eternity for you. Blessed is God's Teacher, the Holy Spirit, Which is Joyous as It teaches you of your Holiness. The Holy Spirit's Joy is not contained in time, and Its teaching is for you, because Its Joy is yours. Through the Holy Spirit, you stand before God's Mind Where God gently translates

318

hell into Heaven. God wants you to be only in Heaven.

3. It takes you no time to be Where God wants you to be. You *are* in Heaven, Where you have Forever been and will Forever be. All that you have There you have Forever. This Blessed Instant reaches out to encompass time, as God extends Itself to encompass you. You, who have spent time in limiting your mind to perception of a world to support and strengthen the personal mind, do not perceive the True Source of Strength. In this Holy Instant you release your entire mind and refuse to support weakness anywhere in your mind.

4. You do not realize how you have misused your relationships with others by seeing in your projections onto them sources of support for the personal mind. As a result, in your perception, you see them as witnesses to the personal mind, and they seem to provide you with reasons for not letting it go. Yet you could use your relationships with others as stronger and much more compelling Witnesses for the Holy Spirit, and as a support for the Holy Spirit's Strength, by extending God's Love to others instead of the personal mind's projections. It is therefore your choice whether your relationships with others support the personal mind or the Holy Spirit in you. And you will recognize which one you have chosen by how you see them. When your Christ Mind has been released through the Holy Spirit in you, you will always recognize It. You cannot deny your Christ Mind, and if you remain uncertain of what you perceive, it is only because you have not given complete release to your Christ Mind. If you do not clearly see Christ it is because you have not given a single instant completely to the Holy Spirit. When you have you will be sure that you have, because the Witness to the Holy Spirit will be so clear that you will know. You will doubt all this until you have seen one Witness which you have wholly released through the Holy Spirit, and then you will doubt no more.

5. You have not experienced the Holy Instant yet, but you will, and you will recognize It with Perfect Certainty. You recognize All Gifts of God in this way. You can practice the mechanics of the Holy Instant, and you will learn much from doing so. But your Perception of It will blind you to the world, and This you cannot

supply. Here It is in this Instant, complete, accomplished, and wholly given.

6.   Start now to practice your little part in separating out the Holy Instant. You will receive very specific instructions as you go along. For you to learn to separate out this single Instant and to experience It as Timeless, is for you to begin to experience yourself as *not separate* from God. Do not fear that you will not be given help in this. The Holy Spirit and Its lessons will support your Strength. It is only the weakness of the personal self that will depart from you in this practice, because it is the practice of the Power of God within you. Use It for just one Instant, and you will never deny It again. You cannot deny the Presence of What God's Wholeness bows to in appreciation and gladness. Before your recognition of the Wholeness that Witnesses to It, your doubts must disappear.

3. Littleness versus Magnitude

1.   Do not be content with limitedness, and be sure that you understand what it is and why you can never be content with it. Limitedness is the offering that you make to yourself in your identification with a personal self. You offer this to yourself in place of Limitlessness, and you accept it. Everything in the world that you perceive is limited, and is made out of the limited, in your strange belief that limiting yourself can content you. When you strive for anything in the world that you perceive in the belief that it will bring you Peace, you are limiting yourself and blinding yourself to Limitlessness. Limitedness and Limitlessness are the choices open to your striving and to your attention. You will always choose one at the expense of the other.

2.   But what you do not realize is that, each time that you choose, you are evaluating yourself, and that your choice is your evaluation. Choose limitedness and you will not have Peace, because you will have judged yourself unworthy of It. Whatever you offer yourself as a substitute for Peace is much too inadequate a gift to satisfy you. It is essential that you gladly accept the fact that there is no form of limitedness that will ever content you. You are free to try as many forms of limitedness as you wish, but all that you will be doing is

delaying your Homecoming in God. You can only be content with Limitlessness, Which *is* your Home.

3.   There is a deep responsibility that you owe to yourself and one that you must learn to remember all the time. It may seem hard at first, but you will learn to love it when you realize that it is true and is a tribute to your Power. You have sought and found limitedness but remember this: Every decision that you make stems from what you think you are and represents the value that you put upon yourself. Believe that the limited can content you, and you limit yourself, and you will not be satisfied. Your function is not limited, and It is only by finding your function and fulfilling it that you can escape from limitedness.

4.   There is no doubt about what your function is and the Holy Spirit knows what it is. There is no doubt about its Limitlessness because it reaches through the Holy Spirit *from* Limitlessness. You do not have to strive for your function, because you have it. All of your striving must be directed *against* limitedness, because it *does* require effortful attention on your part for you to maintain your awareness of your Limitlessness in the limited world that you perceive. This is not a task that you can undertake with a limited personal mind, and you are not asked to do this with a personal mind. Seek for the limited and you deny yourself God's Power. But the Power of God will support every effort that you make on behalf of your Limitlessness in Christ. God does not will that you be content with less than Everything, because God is not content without you, and you cannot be content with less than God has given to you.

5.   You can be limited by the personal mind or Limitless in God. Let the Holy Spirit ask you which you want every time that you make a decision, because with every decision that you make, you do choose one of these, and you invite sorrow or Joy accordingly. In your Oneness with God, you hold God within you Forever. God does not leave you and you do not leave God. All of your attempts to deny God's Limitlessness and make yourself limited to a personal self cannot limit you or God. Every decision that you make is for Heaven or for hell and brings you the awareness of

what you decided for.

6.   The Holy Spirit holds your Limitlessness Clearly and Perfectly Safe within your mind, untouched by every little 'gift' that the world of limitedness that you perceive seems to offer to you. But, for you to know this, you cannot side against What the Holy Spirit wills for you. Decide for God through the Holy Spirit, because limitedness, and your belief that you can be content with limitedness, are decisions *you* make about yourself. The Power and the Glory of God within you are for your entire mind. They can be extended in your mind to replace all of the limitedness that you perceive in a world. Do not extend limitedness or accept it. The personal mind's limitedness deceives you, but God's Limitlessness is within you and encompasses you. For your Christ Mind's sake, then, do not extend limitedness, because your Christ Mind holds God within It Eternally.

7.   In this season (Christmas), which celebrates the birth of the awareness of your Holiness in your split mind, join with your Christ Mind, Which decides for Holiness for you. Your task, through your Christ Mind, is to restore the awareness of your Limitlessness to your entire mind, which is appointed by God to hold only God. It is beyond the limitedness of a personal mind to give the Gift of God, but it is not beyond you. While never leaving you, God wants to give God *through* you by reaching from you to your mind where you perceive a world and beyond that to your Extension of God. Far beyond your perception of a limited world, but still within you, God extends Forever. God brings Its Whole Extension to you, because God is within you.

8.   It is not a sacrifice for you to leave limitedness behind and to no longer wander in vain. It is not a sacrifice for you to wake to Glory. But it *is* a sacrifice for you to accept anything less than Glory. Learn that you *must* be worthy of Christ, Which is born in your awareness in honor of God within you. You don't know what Love means, because you have sought to purchase It with the limited gifts of a personal mind, so you have valued Love too little to understand Its Limitlessness. Love is not limited, and It dwells in you, because you hold God within you. Before the Greatness that is within you, your

poor appreciation of yourself as a personal self, and all the limited offerings that you give yourself through it, slip into nothingness.

9. You who are a Holy Part of God will learn that only Holiness can content you and give you Peace. Remember that you do not learn for the personal mind, as Jesus also did not. It is because Jesus learned of His Christ Mind that you can learn of your Christ Mind. Your Christ Mind teaches you What is yours so that you can replace the shabby limitedness that binds you to guilt and weakness with the glad awareness of the Glory within you. The birth of Christ in your awareness is your awareness of your Limitlessness. Do not welcome Christ into a manger but into your mind, where Holiness abides in Perfect Peace. Your Christ Mind's Oneness with God is not of the world that you perceive, because It is in you and you are of God. Join with your Christ Mind in honoring you, because you remain Forever beyond limitedness.

10. Decide with your Christ Mind. Your Christ Mind wills as God wills, knowing God's Will is Constant and at Peace with Itself Forever. You can be content only with God's Will. Accept no less, remembering that Everything Jesus learned is yours. What God loves, your Christ Mind loves as God loves. Your Christ Mind can accept only God's Love as God can accept only God's Love, and you can accept only God's Love. When you have learned to accept What you are, you will not make anymore 'gifts' for yourself from the personal mind, because you will know that you are Complete, without needs, and unable to be limited. And you will gladly extend God, because God is within you. You have God within you, and you do not need to seek for anything.

11. You will be given salvation if you are wholly willing to leave your salvation to the plan of God, and you are unwilling to try to grasp for Peace with a personal mind. Do not think that you can substitute the personal mind's plan for God's plan. Join your Christ Mind in God's plan by releasing all of your perceptions to your Christ Mind, so that your entire mind can hold God within it. If you do not let any thought in your mind contain the denial of God, you will remember God.

12. In your relationships with others, see only your Extension of God

and of Heaven. You will think that you are in Heaven or in hell depending on what you extend or project in your perception. In your projections of hell and limitedness, see only your call for Heaven and Limitlessness, and answer the call with your Christ Mind. God's Power is Forever on your side, because It protects only the Peace in Which God dwells. Do not limit your mind, because God's Limitlessness is in it.

4. Practicing the Holy Instant

1. You can learn this course immediately, unless you believe that what God wills takes time. This only means that you would rather delay your recognition that God's Will *is*. This instant, and every instant, is the Holy Instant. The instant that you want to be Holy *is* Holy; the instant that you don't want to be Holy is lost to you. You decide when the Holy Instant is. Do not delay It, because beyond the past and future, in each of which you will *not* find the Holy Instant, It stands ready for your acceptance. But you cannot bring the Holy Instant into your glad awareness while you do not want It, because It holds your whole release from limitedness.

2. Your practice of the Holy Instant must therefore rest upon your willingness to let all limitations go. The Instant in which Limitlessness dawns on you is only as far away as your desire for It. Cherish limitedness instead, and Limitlessness will seem far away from you. But when you want It, you will bring It nearer. Do not think that you can find salvation in a personal mind. Give over every plan that it has made for your salvation to be exchanged for God's plan. God's plan for your salvation will content you, and nothing else will bring you Peace, because Peace is of God and nothing else.

3. Be great *in* God by deferring *to* God. Do not value any plan of the personal mind in place of the plan of God. You leave your place in God's plan empty when you decide for any plan not of God. You are called by your Christ Mind to fulfill your Holy part in the plan that God has given you to release your mind from the limitation of its perception of a world. God wants you, who hold God within you, to abide in Perfect Peace. Every allegiance that you have to a

plan of salvation that does not come from God diminishes the value of God's Will in your own mind. And yet it is your mind that holds God within it.

4. You will recognize how Holy and Immaculate is the Holy Mind that you share with God in the Holy Instant in Which you willingly and gladly give up every plan but God's Plan. Peace lies here, Perfectly Clear, because you have been willing to meet Its conditions. You can claim the Holy Instant any time and anywhere you want It. In your practice of the Holy Instant, give up every plan that you have made for finding Perfect Freedom in limitedness. *It is not there.* Use the Holy Instant to recognize that you cannot know where Freedom is in the isolation of a personal mind, and that there you can only deceive yourself about It.

5. Your Christ Mind stands within this Holy Instant, as clear as you want your Christ Mind to be. The extent to which you learn to accept Christ is the measure of the time in which the Holy Instant will be yours. Christ calls to you to make the Holy Instant yours at once, because, for you whose Mind holds God, release from limitations depends on your willingness, not on time.

6. The reason this course is simple is that the Truth is simple. Complexity is of the personal mind, because the personal mind seeks to obscure the obvious. You could live Forever in the Holy Instant beginning now and reaching to Eternity, but for a very simple reason. Do not obscure the simplicity of this reason; if you do, it is because you prefer not to recognize it and to let go of your resistance to it. The simple reason is this: In the Holy Instant, you are in Perfect Communication with God. Your mind is wholly open to receive God and to extend God. In the Holy Instant, you recognize that Mind is One, therefore you do not seek to change anything, but to accept Everything that *is*.

7. You cannot do this when you prefer to have and keep private thoughts, because to do this you must deny the Perfect Communication that makes the Holy Instant What It is. You believe that you can harbor thoughts that cannot be extended, and that your salvation lies in your keeping these thoughts in the isolation of a personal mind. Because in private thoughts known

only to you in a personal mind, you think that you find a way to keep what you want for yourself alone, and to extend what *you* choose to extend. Then you wonder why you feel alone and isolated from the world that you perceive and from God, Which encompasses you and all of your mind where you perceive a world.

8.   Every thought that you want to keep hidden shuts off your Communication with God, because you want it to be so. It is impossible for you to recognize Perfect Communication while breaking Communication has value for you. Ask yourself honestly, 'Do I want Perfect Communication with God, and am I wholly willing to let go of everything that interferes with It?' If your answer is 'no', then the Holy Spirit's readiness to give It to you is not enough, because you are not ready for It. Perfect Communication cannot come into your mind when you have decided to oppose It. The Holy Instant is given by the Holy Spirit and received by you with equal willingness, because It is your acceptance of the One Will that governs all thought.

9.   The Holy Instant does not require that you have only Pure Thoughts; Its only condition is that you be willing to let go of thoughts that are not of God. You do not make Innocence, and It is given to your awareness the moment that you want It. The plan of the Atonement would not exist if your correction wasn't necessary. You will not accept Perfect Communication as long as you hide It from yourself, because what you hide *does* seem gone from you. In your practice of the Holy Instant, then, make an effort against deception, and do not seek to hold onto thoughts of the personal mind. Let the Holy Spirit's Purity brush them away and bring all of your awareness to readiness for the Purity that the Holy Spirit offers to you. And so the Holy Spirit will make you ready to remember that God is in your mind, and that you are Limitless.

5. The Holy Instant and Special Relationships

1.   The Holy Instant is the Holy Spirit's most useful means for teaching you Love's Meaning, because Its purpose is for you to entirely suspend judgment. The personal self's past is the personal mind's basis for judgment, so you need the past to make judgments. You

think that without the past you cannot understand anything, and this frightens you, because you believe that without the personal mind everything will be chaos. But be assured: Without the personal mind all will be Love.

2. In your identification with a personal self the past is your chief means of learning, because it was in the personal self's past that you learned to define your needs, and you acquired methods for getting them met on your own terms. By limiting your 'love' to some others in the world that you perceive, you put yourself in a relationship with guilt and you make Real Love unreal to you. It is your attempt to have parts of the separation meet your needs as you define them in a personal self to turn separation into your salvation. Guilt must enter your mind then, because your perception of separation from God is the source of your guilt, and for you to look to separation for your salvation is for you to believe that you *are* separate. And for you to believe that you are separate from God *is* for you to believe that you are guilty, because to experience yourself as separate from God you must deny your Oneness with God and seem to attack Reality.

3. Your mind in its Wholeness *is* Reality, so you cannot pick out only certain of your mind's perceptions to 'love' and still understand that Love means Oneness and that Oneness is Reality. With *special*-love you make yourself unlike God, because God does not know special-love. For you to believe that *special* relationships and *special*-love can offer you salvation is for you to believe that separation from God is your salvation. But it is in the Wholeness of your mind that your correction and your salvation lie. You cannot decide that certain of your mind's perceptions are special and can give you more than the rest of your mind. The personal self's past has taught you this, but the Holy Instant teaches you that it is not so.

4. All special relationships have elements of fear, because they foster guilt. They shift and change frequently, because they are not based on God's Changeless Love alone. Love where fear has entered is not Perfect, so you cannot depend on It. But in the Holy Spirit's function as Interpreter of what you have made, the Holy Spirit will

use your special relationships. You have chosen to use them to support the personal self; the Holy Spirit uses them as learning experiences for you that point to Truth. Under the Holy Spirit's teaching, every relationship in your perception that you are in a world becomes for you a lesson in the Oneness of Love.

5. The Holy Spirit knows that your mind is One and that no part of it is 'special'. But It also perceives that you have made special relationships with others in your perception that you are in a world, and It will purify them and not let you destroy them. However unholy your reasons for forming these relationships, the Holy Spirit can translate them into Holiness by removing as much separation and fear from them as you will let It. You can place any relationship under the Holy Spirit's care and be sure that it will not result in pain if you offer your willingness to let the relationship serve only the Holy Spirit's Goal. All of the guilt in your relationships comes from the personal mind's use of them; all of the Love in your relationships comes from the Holy Spirit's use of them. Do not be afraid to let go of your imagined needs, which will destroy your relationships. Your only need is the Holy Spirit.

6. Love has no substitute. When a relationship in the world that you perceive does not meet your needs as defined by the personal mind, and you find another relationship to substitute for it, you teach yourself that some of the personal mind's projections are more valuable than others, you make them real to you, and you make separation real to you. You have not offered your relationships to the Holy Spirit for Its use. But before judging these relationships you first judged against yourself, or you would not have imagined that you have needs and looked to others to meet them. And because you saw yourself without Love, you also perceived others as lacking Love and unable to fill your needs.

7. In your identification with a personal self your relationship to your mind where you perceive a world is so fragmented that you take fragmentation even further by separating out certain parts of some people for your purposes while you prefer different parts of others. This is how you assemble a 'reality' for the personal mind's unpredictable desires, offering yourself a picture of 'perfection' that does

not exist to seek for in others. There is nothing in the world that you perceive or in Heaven that resembles this picture, so no matter how much you seek for it you will not find it, because it is not real.

8.   You have formed special relationships in your perception that you are in a world, and even though they are not real in Heaven, Where all is One, the Holy Spirit knows how to bring a touch of Heaven to them. In your extension of the Holy Instant to your relationships with others, you will not see specialness, because the personal self's needs will not intrude. Without values from the personal self's past, you will see only Oneness and that there is no separation. In the Holy Instant, you see in each relationship the Oneness that you can perceive only in the present.

9.   God knows you *now*. God remembers nothing, because God has always known you exactly as God knows you now. The Holy Instant reflects God's Knowing you by undoing all of the personal mind's past perceptions in your mind, thereby removing the frame of reference that the personal mind has built, and by which you judge and make the world real to you. Once the past is gone from your mind, the Holy Spirit substitutes Its Frame of Reference, Which is simply God. The Holy Spirit's Timelessness is only in the Holy Instant. In the Holy Instant, free of a personal past, you see that Love is in you, and you have no need to look out at your perception of others to snatch love guiltily from them.

10. All of your relationships are blessed in the Holy Instant, because Its Blessing is not limited like special-love. In the Holy Instant, your mind is One, and it becomes One in your awareness. The Meaning of Love is Oneness, and this is the Meaning God gave to It. Give Love any other meaning and you do not understand It. God loves your entire mind, not one perception more, and another perception less. God needs all of your mind, as you do. You have been told, in time, to extend miracles as the Holy Spirit directs to replace the personal mind's projections. But in the Holy Instant, you unite directly with God, and your mind joins as One in Christ. There is no separation in your Christ Mind, because your Christ Mind is your Self in Wholeness, as God extends Its Whole Self to your Christ Mind.

11. Do not think that you can judge the Self of God. God created It beyond judgment out of God's need to extend God's Love. With Love in you, your only need is to extend Love. In the Holy Instant you have no conflict of needs, because you have only this one need. The Holy Instant reaches to Eternity, and to the Mind of God. Only There does Love have Meaning, and only There can you understand Love.

6. The Holy Instant and the Laws of God

1. In your perception that you are in a world, to satisfy the needs that you think you have in your identification with a personal self, you use every relationship at the expense of other relationships, and then you suffer from guilt. You also condemn parts of each of your relationships, and fail to find Peace within them. You feel guilt and lack Peace, because these relationships are for and about splitting your mind and separating you from God. But under the Holy Spirit's teaching, there is only One Relationship, Which is Total, and completely without conflict, and that is your Relationship with the Holy Spirit. Your Perfect Faith in Its ability to satisfy you completely comes from your Perfect Faith in yourself as you are in Truth. You cannot have this Perfect Faith while guilt remains in your mind, and you will feel guilt while you accept and cherish the personal mind's projections onto others over your extensions of the Holy Spirit.

2. You have little faith in yourself because you are unwilling to accept that Perfect Love is in you. So you seek outside of yourself in your perceptions of 'others' for what you can never find outside of yourself. Your Christ Mind offers you Its Perfect Faith in you in place of all of your doubts. But do not forget that your Christ Mind's Perfect Faith is extended to your entire mind, or It will be a limited Gift to you. In the Holy Instant, you and your Christ Mind are One in faith in you, because you recognize through your Christ Mind that you are Wholly Worthy of your faith, and, in your appreciation of your Worth, you cannot doubt your Holiness. And so you love yourself.

3. All separation vanishes for you as you extend Holiness. Holiness is

Power, and by your extending It, It strengthens in your awareness. If you seek for satisfaction for the needs that you think that you have in your identification with a personal self, you must believe that your strength comes from others, and that what you gain they lose. If you perceive yourself as weak, someone must always lose. But there is another interpretation of relationships that completely transcends the concept of loss of power.

4. You do not find it difficult to believe that when another calls on God for Love, your call remains just as strong. And when another is answered by God, your hope of answer is not diminished but strengthened. That is because you recognize, however dimly, that God is an Idea, so your faith in God is strengthened by extension. But what you find difficult to accept is that, like God, *you* are an idea. And, like God, you can extend yourself completely, wholly without loss, and only with an awareness of gain. Your Peace is in this, because in this there is no conflict.

5. In the world of scarcity in which you perceive yourself, Love has no meaning, and Peace is impossible, because you accept both gain and loss as real, so you are not aware that Perfect Love is within you. In the Holy Instant, you recognize the Idea of Love in yourself, and you unite with this Idea in God's Mind, Which thinks It and cannot relinquish It. By holding Love within Itself and extending It from There, there is no loss in God's Mind. The Holy Instant, then, is a Lesson in how to hold Love in your entire mind by extending It everywhere to experience Completion. And this *is* Love, because extending Love is only natural under God's Law. In the Holy Instant, only God's Law prevails and has meaning for you, and the laws of the world that you perceive cease to have any meaning to you at all. When you accept God's Law as what *you* will, it will be impossible for you to be limited in any way. In the Holy Instant you are free, as God wants you to be, because the Instant that you want to be Limitless, you *are* Limitless.

6. What happens in the Holy Instant has always been, but the veil that you have drawn across your *awareness* of Reality is lifted. Nothing Real changes, but your *awareness* of Changelessness comes swiftly to you as you push aside the veil of time. Only when you

have experienced the lifting of this veil, and felt yourself irresistibly drawn to the Love that it seems to hide, will you have faith in Love without fear. The Holy Spirit gives you this Faith, because it is your Christ Mind's Faith. Do not fear that the Holy Instant will be denied to you, because your Christ Mind does not deny It. Do not let any need that you perceive obscure your need for the Holy Instant. In the Holy Instant you will recognize that the Holy Instant is your only need, and, in this recognition, you will join with your Christ Mind to extend It.

7.   Peace will come to you through your identification with your Christ Mind. Join with your Christ Mind in the Idea of Peace, because ideas can be extended. If you extend yourself as God extends Itself, you will understand What you are. Extension is Love's Meaning. Remember that Understanding and Knowledge of God are of the mind, and Their conditions are in your mind as well. If you were not an idea, and *only* an idea, you would not be in full Oneness with God. As long as you prefer to be something other than an idea, or to be an idea and something else at the same time, you will not remember your Oneness with God, Which you *do* Know Perfectly.

8.   In the Holy Instant, you remember your Oneness with God, and your entire mind is in Perfect Communication with God. Your mind where you perceive a world is included in the Holy Instant, because the personal self's past is gone, and with it goes the whole basis for excluding any part of your mind. This permits God, the Source of your Whole Mind, to replace in your awareness all ideas of exclusion. In the Holy Instant, God and the Power of God take Their rightful place in your mind, and you fully experience yourself as an Idea in Perfect Communication with the Idea of God. Through your ability to do this, you learn What you must be, because you begin to understand What God is, and that you are One with God.

7. The Needless Sacrifice

1.   Beyond your poor attraction to the special-love relationship, and always obscured by it, is your powerful attraction to God. Only God's Love can satisfy you, because there is no other Love. Being

One, God's Love is the only Love that is fully given to you and fully received by you. Being Complete, God's Love asks for nothing. Being Wholly Pure, when your entire mind is joined in God's Love, you have Everything. None of this is the basis for any relationship in which the personal self enters. Every relationship that you make with a personal self *is* special, because it is based on your perception of your separation from God, and it proceeds from your fragmented mind.

2. In your identification with a personal self you establish relationships with others to get something for yourself, and you hold the perceived giver to yourself through guilt. With the personal self you can only enter relationships in anger[1], and you believe that anger and guilt are the way to make friends. The personal mind does not state this to you outright, but its purpose *is* to keep attack and guilt in your mind. In your identification with it you really believe that you can get and keep what you want by *making guilty*. Guilt, being the result of your perceived separation from God, is the one thing that the personal mind is attracted to, but this attraction is so weak that it would have no hold on *you* except that you do not recognize it. The personal mind always seems to attract you to it through love, and it would not attract you at all if you perceived that it attracts you to it through guilt.

3. You must recognize your sick attraction to guilt for what it is. Having made guilt real to yourself by believing that you have really separated yourself from God, it is essential that you look at it clearly, and, by withdrawing your investment in it, learn to let it go. You will not let go of guilt as long as you think that your separation from God, and the personal self that you have made for it, have value. Guilt has value to you only because you have judged that separation from God is valuable without looking at it clearly. But as you look at guilt, your only question will be why you ever wanted it. You have nothing to lose by looking at your attraction to guilt, because it does not belong in your Holy Mind. You who are One with God can have no real investment in separation from God.

4. The personal mind maintains and increases guilt in *your* mind by projecting it onto others, so that you do not recognize what your

guilt is doing to you. Its fundamental doctrine is: *What you do to others you have escaped*. The personal mind does not wish you well, but its survival depends on your belief that you are exempt from its evil intentions. It tells you that, if you identify with it, you will be able to direct its anger outward and protect yourself from it. So with it you embark on an endless, unrewarding chain of special relationships, made in anger, and dedicated to this one insane belief: The more anger that you invest outside of yourself, the safer you are.

5. It is this chain of special relationships that binds you to the personal self and guilt, and it is this chain that the Holy Spirit wants to remove from your Holy Mind. These savage relationships do not belong to you who are One with God and who cannot make the personal self real. For the sake of your release and for God, Which wants to release you, look more closely at the relationships that the personal mind contrives, and let the Holy Spirit judge them truly. It is certain that, if you look at them clearly, you will offer them to the Holy Spirit. You do not yet know what the Holy Spirit can make of them, but you will become willing to find out if you are first willing to perceive them honestly.

6. The personal mind values sacrifice, because it believes that you sacrificed God to be with *it*. And it values guilt, because it is through your guilt over separating from God and your fear that God will punish you that the personal mind holds you to itself. So in one way or another, every relationship that you make with the personal self is based on the idea that by sacrificing yourself to another you can get what you want from them. This 'sacrifice', which the personal mind regards as a form of 'purification', is actually the root of its bitter resentment. It would really rather attack you directly and not delay getting whatever it wants from you, but it recognizes that *you* would not confuse direct attack with love. But to make someone else guilty *is* to attack yourself directly, because it still makes guilt real in your mind. It only does not seem like a direct attack because you feel that you are guilty, you expect attack, and, having asked for it, you are attracted to it and you want it.

7. In these insane relationships, your attraction to the guilt that you do not really want seems much stronger to you than your attraction to the Love that you do really want. In your identification with a personal self, you think that you have sacrificed something to another, and you hate them for it. And this is what you think you want. You are not really in love with another; you are in love with sacrifice. And, for this sacrifice that you demand of yourself, you demand that the other feel guilty, and you demand that they sacrifice as well. You cannot forgive your projection of guilt on the other, because, in the personal mind, you believe that to do so is to lose. It is only by attacking that you can ensure the guilt that holds the personal self's relationships together.

8. But you can only *seem* to be together with another, because relationships that you make through the personal self mean only that bodies are together. This is what the personal mind demands, and it doesn't care where your mind goes or what you think, because mind and thought are unimportant to the personal mind. As long as a body is there to accept your sacrifice, the personal mind is content. To the personal mind, your mind is private, and only a body can be shared with another body. Ideas are of no concern to it except as they bring the body of another closer or push them further off. It is in these terms that the personal mind evaluates ideas as 'good' or 'bad': What makes another seem guilty and holds them to you through guilt is 'good'; what releases them from your projection of guilt is 'bad', because you will no longer believe that bodies unite, so you would 'lose' the other.

9. Suffering and sacrifice are the 'gifts' with which the personal mind blesses all unions in the world that you perceive. United with another at the personal mind's altar, you accept suffering and sacrifice as the price of union. In this angry alliance, born of fear and loneliness, and dedicated to the continuance of their source – your perception of separation from God – you seek relief from your guilt by increasing it in your projection onto the other, because you believe that this decreases it in you. You perceive the other as always attacking and wounding you, maybe in little ways, maybe 'unconsciously', but never without demand that you

sacrifice. The fury that you experience when you join with another at the personal mind's altar far exceeds your awareness of it. You do not realize that the personal mind wants your total sacrifice to *it*.

10. Whenever you are angry, you can be sure that you have made a special relationship which the personal mind 'blesses', because anger *is* its 'blessing'. Anger takes many forms, but it will not long deceive you when you learn that there is no guilt in Love, and that what brings guilt cannot be Love and must be anger. All anger is nothing more than your attempt to make someone else feel guilty, and this is the only basis that the personal mind accepts for a special relationship. Your guilt is the only need that the personal mind has, and as long as you identify with it, guilt will be attractive to you. Remember this: To be with a body is not union, and if you think that it is, you will feel guilty about union, and you will be afraid to hear the Holy Spirit, recognizing in Its Voice your own need to be united with God.

11. The Holy Spirit cannot teach you through fear. The Holy Spirit cannot unite with you while you believe that to unite is to make yourself more isolated and alone. It is clearly insane for you to believe that by uniting you will be abandoned. But you do believe it, and you think that you must keep your mind isolated and private, or you will lose it. You think that if bodies are united your mind is your own. Uniting bodies, then, is the way to keep your mind apart, because the body cannot forgive your perception of separation; it can only do as the mind directs.

12. The illusion of the independence of the body, and the illusion of its ability to overcome loneliness, is the personal mind's plan to establish its own independence from the Truth in you. As long as you believe that to be with a body is companionship, you will be compelled to project personal selves onto bodies and to hold them there with guilt. You will see safety in guilt and danger in Oneness with God. The personal mind will always teach that loneliness is solved by guilt and that union is the cause of loneliness. Despite the evident insanity of this lesson, you have learned it.

13. Forgiveness for yourself lies in your awareness of your Oneness

with God, as surely as your belief in your damnation lies in your belief that you are guilty for separating from God. It is the Holy Spirit's teaching function to instruct you, who believe that union is damnation, that your Union with God is your salvation. The Power of God in the Holy Spirit and in you is united in a Real Relationship that is Holy and Strong and can overcome this belief without fear.

14. It is through the Holy Instant that you accomplish What seems impossible, making it evident to you that It is not impossible. In the Holy Instant, guilt holds no attraction for you, because Oneness has been restored to your awareness. Guilt, which is supposed to disrupt True Union, has no function in the Holy Instant. In the Holy Instant, you hide nothing, and you have no private thoughts. Your willingness to be One with God attracts Oneness to you and completely overcomes your sense of loneliness and isolation. You experience complete forgiveness in the Holy Instant, because you have no desire to exclude the part of your mind where you perceive a world in recognition of the value of your mind's wholeness. Your Completion is God's Completion, Which only needs you to be Complete. Your Completion makes you God's Completion in your awareness. In the Holy Instant, you experience yourself as you are in Oneness with God.

8. The Only Real Relationship

1. The Holy Instant does not replace your need for learning, because the Holy Spirit must not leave you as your Teacher until the Holy Instant has undone time for you. For Its Teaching Assignment, the Holy Spirit must use for your release everything in the world that you perceive. It must side with every sign of your willingness to learn of It What the Truth is. The Holy Spirit is swift to use whatever you offer to It on behalf of this. Its concern and care for you are Limitless. Faced with your fear of forgiving, which the Holy Spirit perceives clearly, the Holy Spirit will teach you to remember that forgiving is not loss but your release and salvation. In complete forgiving, in which you recognize that there is nothing to forgive, you are absolved completely.

2. Hear the Holy Spirit gladly, and learn of It that you have no need of special relationships at all. You only seek in them What you have thrown away. You will never learn through them the value of What you have cast aside but still desire with all your Being. Join your Christ Mind in making the Holy Instant all that there is by desiring that it *be* all that there is. You have such great need of your willingness to strive for this, that you cannot conceive of a need so great. This is the only need that you and God share and will meet together. You are not alone in this. The Will of your Extension of God calls to you to be One again. Turn in Peace to God and to your Extension of God.

3. Relate only with What will never leave you and with What you can never leave. If you could really separate from God, then God *would* be lonely. Do not refuse to be aware of your Completion, and do not seek to restore It to yourself through a personal mind. Do not fear to give your need of correction over to the Holy Spirit's Love. The Holy Spirit will never fail you, because It comes from God, and God cannot fail. Your sense of failure is nothing more than your mistaken belief about who you are. You who are One with God are beyond failure, and nothing that you Will can be denied. You are Forever in a Relationship so Holy that It calls to your entire mind to escape from its perception of isolation, and to join in your Love. You will seek with your entire mind Where you are in Truth, and you will find yourself There.

4. Think about this for an instant: God extends Oneness to you to ensure your Perfection. This is God's Gift to you, because as God does not withhold Itself from you, God does not withhold Its Own extension. All that is in God is yours. Your Relationship is with God's Wholeness, and this Wholeness is far beyond the petty sum of all of the separate bodies that you perceive through a personal mind. Every Part of God's Wholeness joins in God through your extension of your Christ Mind, so that your mind becomes like God. Your Christ Mind does not know separation from God, and God is your Christ Mind's One Relationship, in Which It extends God as God extends God to It.

5. The Holy Spirit is God's Means of freeing you from what God

cannot understand. Because God is the Source of the Means, It will succeed. The Holy Spirit asks you to respond to everything with Love as God does, because the Holy Spirit will teach you What you do not think you understand in your identification with a personal self. God responds to your every need, whatever form it takes, so God keeps the Holy Spirit in you open as a channel for you to receive God's Communication to you and for you to send yours to God. God does not understand your problem in Communication, because God does not share it. You only think this problem is understandable in your identification with a personal self. The Holy Spirit knows that it is not understandable in Truth, but It understands it, because you made it.

6.   In the Holy Spirit alone lies the awareness of both your perception of separation that God cannot know and the Oneness that you do not understand in your identification with a personal self. It is the Holy Function of the Holy Spirit to accept them both and remove every element of disagreement to join them into one. Leave to the Holy Spirit what seems to you to be impossible. The Holy Spirit knows that it is possible, because it is the Will of God. Let the Holy Spirit, Which teaches you only of God, teach you the meaning of relationships. God created the only Relationship that has Meaning, and that is God's Relationship with you.

9. The Holy Instant and the Attraction of God

1.   The personal mind wants to limit your perceptions of others to bodies; the Holy Spirit wants to release your Real Perception through others by seeing in their place the Limitless Love that reaches to God. It is this shift to Spiritual Perception that you accomplish in the Holy Instant. You need to know what this shift entails, so that you will become willing to make it permanent. Spiritual Perception *is* Permanent, and you only need to be willing to know this. Once you have accepted It as the only Perception that you want, It is translated into God in the only part that God plays directly in the correction of your perception of separation from God. There is no delay in this when you are ready for it. God is ready now, but you are not.

2. With the Holy Spirit, your task is to continue, as fast as possible, the necessary process of looking straight at all that interferes with your awareness of God, and to see it exactly as it is. It is impossible for you to recognize that your perception of separation from God is wholly without gratification for you while you think that you want it. The body is the symbol of the personal self, as the personal self is the symbol of your separation from God. Both are nothing more than your attempts to limit your Communication with God to make Oneness impossible. Communication must be Limitless to have Meaning, and deprived of Meaning, It will not satisfy you completely. Limitless Communication is the only Means by Which you can establish your Relationship with God, Which has no limits, having been established by God.

3. In the Holy Instant, Where Limitless Love replaces the body in your awareness, you recognize your Limitless Relationship with God. In order to see this, it is necessary for you to give up every use that the personal mind has for the body, and to accept the fact that you do not want to share the personal mind's purpose. The personal mind wants to limit your awareness of relationships to bodies for its purpose of keeping you separate from God, and, while you share its purpose, you will use the means it does to accomplish this purpose. Though the purpose of separation will never be accomplished, you surely recognize that the personal mind, whose goal is unattainable, will strive for it with all its might, and will do so with the strength that you have given to it.

4. It is impossible for you to divide your strength between God and the personal mind, and to release your Power to extend God's Oneness, Which is the only Purpose for Which It was given to you. Love *always* extends Itself. Limits are demanded by the personal mind and represent its desire to make you little and ineffectual. Limit relationships to bodies, which you do when you do not extend your Relationship with God in their place, and you have denied the Gift of Wholeness that your Relationship with God can give to you. A body cannot give you this Gift, and do not seek for It through a body. Your mind and God's Mind are Continuous; you only need to accept your Oneness with God, and

Heaven is Whole again.

5. Let the Holy Spirit tell you of God's Love for you and of the need your Extension of God has to be with you Forever, and you will experience Eternity's attraction. You cannot hear the Holy Spirit speak of this and wish to linger in your perception of a world for long. It is your Will to be in Heaven, Where you are Complete and Quiet in such a Sure and Loving Relationship that limits are not possible. Exchange your limited perception of relationships for your Relationship with God. The body *is* little and limited, and only the Relationship that you can see without the limits that the personal mind puts on It can offer you the Gift of Freedom.

6. You have no idea of the limits that you have placed on your perception and no idea of all the Loveliness that you could see. You must remember this: Your attraction to separation from God opposes your attraction to God. God's attraction for you remains Limitless, but, because your Power is God's Power and is just as Great, you can choose to turn away from Love. When you invest in separation you invest in guilt, and you withdraw from God, and your perception becomes limited, because you have attempted to separate yourself from God and to limit your Communication with God. Do not seek for correction of your perception of separation from God in further separation. Do not limit your Perception of Christ to what interferes with your release to your Christ Mind, or even to what the Holy Spirit must do to set you free. Your belief in limits is what limits you.

7. When the body ceases to attract you, and when you no longer value it as a means for getting anything, then there will be no interference in your Communication with God, and your Thoughts will be Free. As you let the Holy Spirit teach you how to use the body only as a means for communication, and as you renounce the personal mind's use of the body as a means for separation and attack, you will learn that you have no need of a body at all. In the Holy Instant, there are no bodies, and you experience only your attraction to God. Your attraction to God is Limitless, and you join with God wholly in an Instant, because you place no limits on your Oneness with God. The Reality of this Relationship becomes the

only Truth that you could ever want. All Truth is in God.

10. The Time of Rebirth

1. It is within your power in time to delay your Perfect Union with God, because, in your perception that you are in a world, your attraction to the guilt of separation *does* stand between you and God. Neither time nor season mean anything in Eternity, but in your perception that you are in a world, the Holy Spirit can use them both, but not the way that the personal mind uses them. This is the season (Christmas) when you celebrate the birth of the awareness of Christ in your split mind, but you do not know how to do it. Let the Holy Spirit teach you, and let Christ celebrate *your* birth through the Holy Spirit. The only Gift your Christ Mind can accept of you is the Gift that your Christ Mind gives to you. Release Christ as Christ releases you. You celebrate the Time of Christ with your Christ Mind, or it has no meaning.

2. The Holy Instant is the true Time of Christ. In this liberating Instant, you do not lay guilt upon yourself, and your Limitless Power is restored to you. This is the only Gift that your Christ Mind offers to you, so this is the only Gift that you can offer to your Christ Mind. To see your Christ Mind you extend Christ in place of the personal mind's projections, so you offer your Christ Mind the Gift of Wholeness. Your Christ Mind is as incapable of receiving sacrifice as God is, and every sacrifice that you ask of yourself you ask of your Christ Mind. Learn that sacrifice of any kind is only a limitation that you impose on your extension of God. By this limitation you limit your acceptance of the Gift that your Christ Mind offers to you.

3. You are One with Christ, and you cannot extend apart from your Christ Mind. When you are willing to accept that your Relationship with your Christ Mind is real, the guilt of separation will no longer attract you. In your Oneness with Christ you will accept your entire mind as Christ. The Gift of Oneness is the only Gift that your Christ Mind was created by God to extend. Extend Oneness back to your Christ Mind so that *you* may have It. The Time of Christ is the time appointed for the Gift of Freedom, offered everywhere without

limit. By accepting this Gift, you extend It everywhere.

4. It is in your power to make this season Holy, because it is in your power to make the Time of Christ be *now*. It is possible for you to do this all at once, because there is only one shift in perception that is necessary for you to make, because you made only one mistake. It seems like you have made many mistakes, because the personal self takes many forms, but it is all the same. What is not Love is always fear and nothing else.

5. It is not necessary for you to follow fear through all the circuitous routes by which it burrows into your unconscious and hides in denial to emerge in forms that seem quite different from what it is. But it *is* necessary for you to examine each one as long as you want to retain the principle of separation that governs all of them. When you are willing to regard them all as manifestations of the same idea, and one that you do not want, they will all go away. The idea that they all represent is this: Identify with the personal self and be free, or identify with God and be bound. This is the choice that you think you have and the decision that you think you must make. You see no other alternatives, because you cannot accept that the sacrifice of your Oneness with God that you made for the personal self does not get you anything. Sacrifice is so essential to the personal mind's thought system that, while you identify with it, salvation without sacrifice means nothing to you.

6. In your identification with a personal self you believe that you can give all your guilt away by projecting it onto others and thereby purchase peace. It does not seem as though you pay, because though the personal self always demands payment, it never seems to be demanding it of *you*. You are unwilling to recognize that the personal self with which you choose to identify is treacherous only to you. It will never let you see this, because then you will let it go. But when the recognition of its treachery to you dawns on you clearly, you will not be deceived by any form that the personal self takes to protect itself from your awareness of this. Each projection of the personal self that you make you will recognize as only a cover for one idea that hides behind them all: Love demands sacrifice and is therefore inseparable from attack and fear. And guilt is the 'price'

of 'love', which must be paid by fear.

7.   How fearful, then, God has become to you, and how great a sacrifice you believe that God's Love demands of you! Total Love seems to demand your total sacrifice, so the personal self seems to demand less of you than God. The personal self seems the lesser of two evils, maybe to be feared a little, but God has to be destroyed. You see Love as destructive, and your only question is: *Is it me or another who is to be destroyed?* You try to answer this question in the special relationship, in which you seem to be part-destroyer and part-destroyed but able to be neither completely. And you think that this saves you from God's Total Love, Which you think will destroy you completely.

8.   You think that everyone outside of you demands your sacrifice, but you do not see that only you demand sacrifice and always of yourself. You sacrifice yourself by identifying with a personal self. Your demand for your sacrifice is so savage and frightening that you cannot accept that it is within you. Rather than look at this, you have given away God, because if God demands your total sacrifice, it seems safer for you to project God away than to accept your Oneness with God. You ascribe to God the personal mind's treachery, and you replace God within you by identifying with a personal self to protect you from God. You don't recognize that it is the personal mind that wants to destroy you, and that it demands total sacrifice from you. No partial sacrifice will appease the savage personal mind, which seems to offer you kindness only to make your sacrifice complete.

9.   You will not succeed in being only partially bound by the personal mind, because it does not keep bargains, and it wants to leave you nothing. You cannot only partially identify with a personal self, because freedom and bondage are both total, and you must choose one or the other. You have tried many compromises to avoid recognizing this one decision that you must make. But if you recognize the decision *just as it is* it is easy. Salvation is of God, therefore simple and easy to understand. Do not project it away from you, and see it outside of you. Within you are your only choices: the demand for sacrifice and the Peace of God.

11. Christmas as the End of Sacrifice

1. Do not be afraid of recognizing that the idea of sacrifice is solely of your own making. Do not try to protect yourself from sacrifice by projecting it outside of you. God and others have become frightening to you because you have projected your demand for sacrifice onto them, and you want to bargain with them for a few special relationships in which you think that you see some safety from guilt. Do not try any longer to keep the personal mind's thoughts apart from the Holy Spirit. When they are brought together in your mind, the choice between them is nothing more than your gentle awareness that illusions mean nothing beside Truth.

2. The sign of Christmas is a star; a light in darkness. Do not see it outside of you but shining in Heaven within you, and accept it as a symbol that the Time of Christ has come. Christ does not demand anything; no sacrifice is asked of you. In Christ's Presence, the idea of sacrifice loses all meaning for you, because your Christ Mind is One with God. You only need to call on your Christ Mind and recognize that nothing alien to God can abide in God's Oneness. Your Love must be Total to welcome Christ, because your Christ Mind and Love are Whole and One. No fear can touch you who cradle God in the Time of Christ, because you are as Holy as the Perfect Innocence you protect, and God's Power protects you.

3. This Christmas, give to the Holy Spirit every thought that hurts you. Let yourself be completely healed of your perception of separation by joining the Holy Spirit, and celebrate your Freedom in Christ by extending healing to be all that you perceive. Leave no perception behind, because Freedom is total, and when you have accepted your Freedom *in* Christ, you will extend your Freedom *with* Christ. All of your pain and sacrifice and littleness will disappear in your Relationship with Christ, Which is as Innocent and Powerful as your Relationship with God. Your pain will be brought to your Relationship with Christ, and it will disappear. Without pain there is no sacrifice, and without sacrifice there is Love.

4. In your identification with a personal self you believe that sacrifice is 'love', so you must learn that sacrifice is separation from Love.

Your sacrifice brings guilt to you as certainly as your Love brings you Peace. Guilt is the condition of sacrifice, as Peace is the Condition of your awareness of your Relationship with God. Through guilt you exclude God and the part of your mind where you perceive a world from yourself. Through Peace you invite them back, realizing that they are both within you where you want them to be. You cannot perceive part of yourself as loathsome and live with yourself in Peace, so you must project the loathsome perception away from you. But when you exclude something from yourself it seems frightening, because you endow it with fear when you project it away from you. You cannot resolve the 'conflict' between Heaven and hell within yourself by projecting Heaven away from you and giving it the attributes of hell, without experiencing yourself as incomplete and lonely.

5. As long as you perceive the body as your reality, you will perceive yourself as lonely and deprived; a victim of sacrifice that is justified in demanding that others sacrifice for you. You will thrust God aside, so you will experience sacrifice and loss and seek to restore yourself to wholeness through others. But you cannot restore yourself to wholeness in your identification with a personal self, because then the basis for your attempts at wholeness is your belief that deprivation is real. Deprivation breeds attack, because it is a form of attack, so it is also your belief that attack is justified. As long as you retain deprivation through your identification with a personal self, attack will mean salvation for you and sacrifice will mean 'love'.

6. In all of your seeking for 'love' through a personal self, you are really seeking for sacrifice, and you find it, but you don't find Love. You cannot deny What Love is and find It. The Meaning of Love lies in God, Which you have cast outside yourself. Love has no meaning apart from *you*. It is the personal self that you prefer to keep that has no meaning, while God, Which you want to keep away from yourself, holds all the Meaning of Reality and holds Reality together in Its Meaning. Because Reality is within you, It is within God. For you to be without God *is* for you to be without Meaning.

7. In the Holy Instant, the Condition of Love is met, because, without the body's interference, you are aware that your mind is One. And, where there is True Communication, there is Peace. Your Christ Mind *is* Peace, and It has been represented in the world that you perceive as Jesus to re-establish Peace in your mind by teaching you that True Communication remains intact even when the body is destroyed, as long as you do not see the body as necessary to communication. If you understand this lesson, then you will realize that you cannot sacrifice the body, because it is nothing, and you cannot sacrifice True Communication, Which is of the mind. *There is no sacrifice*. Jesus' lesson is that sacrifice is nowhere, and Love is Everywhere. True Communication embraces Everything, and, in the Peace that It re-establishes in you, Love comes naturally to you.

8. Do not let the despair of the personal mind darken the Joy of Christmas for you, because the Time of Christ is meaningless without Joy. Join your Christ Mind in celebrating Peace by not demanding sacrifice anywhere as a means of offering to your Christ Mind the Love that It offers to you. Nothing is more Joyous than for you to perceive that you are not deprived of anything. This is God's message for the Time of Christ, which your Christ Mind extends to you, so that you may extend it back to your Christ Mind, and to God in your Oneness with Them. In the Time of Christ, True Communication is restored to you, and God joins in celebrating Its extension.

9. God offers thanks to you who, in your awareness of your Holiness, have let God come and stay where God wants to be. You are welcome in God, because God is in you. You celebrate God's Wholeness when you welcome God into your awareness. You are One with God, and, by allowing God to enter your awareness, you remember the Only Relationship that you have ever had, and that you ever want to have.

10. This is the time in which a new year will soon be born from the Time of Christ. Your Christ Mind has Perfect Faith in you to do all that you need to accomplish. You will lack nothing, and you will make yourself Complete in your awareness, as you will not

destroy anything. Say to the part of your mind where you perceive a world:

'As part of myself, I extend the Holy Spirit to you.
You are released from my illusion of separation, unless I want to use you to limit myself.
I choose your freedom from my illusions, because I recognize that I am set free with you.

And so your new year will begin with Joy and Freedom. There is much for you to do, and you have been long delayed. Accept the Holy Instant as the year is born, and take your place in your Great Awakening. Make this year different from the past by making it all One in God's Love. Look only on your Holy Relationship with God. This is your Will in Christ. Amen.

Chapter 16

The Forgiveness of Illusions

1. True Empathy

1. From the Holy Spirit's perspective, to *empathize* does not mean to
    join in suffering, because suffering is what you must *refuse* to
    understand. Empathizing to share pain is the personal mind's
    interpretation of empathy, and it always uses it to form a special
    relationship. But the capacity to empathize is very useful for the
    Holy Spirit when used in the Holy Spirit's way. The Holy Spirit
    does not understand suffering, and It wants you to teach yourself
    that suffering is not understandable. When the Holy Spirit relates
    to another through you, It does not relate from personal mind to
    personal mind. The Holy Spirit does not join in pain, because
    healing pain is not accomplished by entering into a delusion and
    attempting to lighten it by sharing it.

2. The clearest proof that, when you are identified with a personal
    self, you use empathy destructively, is in the fact that you apply it
    only to some problems and to some people that you select out to
    join with. From the personal mind you only join to strengthen the
    personal mind, and, having identified with what you think that
    you understand in another, you want to increase the personal mind
    in you by joining only with that. So the personal mind always
    empathizes to weaken *you* by increasing itself in your awareness,
    and to weaken *is* to attack. In your identification with a personal
    self you do not know what empathizing means. But you can be
    sure of this: If you will merely sit quietly by and let the Holy Spirit
    relate through you, you will empathize with your True Strength,
    and you will gain in your awareness of your True Strength.

3. Your part is only to remember that you do not want anything that
    the personal mind values to come of any relationship. Do not
    choose to hurt any relationship, and do not choose to heal any
    relationship, because, in your identification with a personal self,

you do not know what healing is. All that you know of empathy is from the personal self's past, and there is nothing from the past that you really want to keep. Do not use empathy to make the past real to you and so to perpetuate it. Put the personal mind aside, and let healing be done for you by the Holy Spirit. Keep one thought in your mind, and do not lose sight of it, however much you may be tempted to respond to any situation with the personal mind's judgment. Focus your mind only on this:

'The Holy Spirit is with me, and I will not intrude the past on It. I only need to not interfere.'

4.   True Empathy is of the Holy Spirit. You will learn the Holy Spirit's interpretation of empathy if you let It use your capacity for empathy for your Strength and not to weaken yourself. The Holy Spirit will not desert you; be sure that you do not desert the Holy Spirit. Humility is strength in this sense only: For you to recognize and accept that in your identification with a personal self you do not know how to use anything, is for you to recognize and accept that the Holy Spirit *does* know how to use everything. You are not sure that the Holy Spirit will do Its part, because you have not yet done your part completely. You cannot know how to respond to what you do not understand. Do not be tempted to try, and do not yield to the personal mind's use of empathy for its own glory.

5.   Weakness is not what you should wish to extend, and yet, in your identification with a personal self, this is what you recognize as worth extending. This does not come from God, and the form of empathy which reinforces weakness in your mind is so distorted that it limits you, whom it should set free. In your mistaken identification with a personal self you cannot correct your perception of weakness as strength, but you have the Holy Spirit with you for correction. Do not attempt to teach the Holy Spirit, because you are the learner, and the Holy Spirit is the Teacher. Do not confuse the personal mind's role with the Holy Spirit's Role, because this will not bring you Peace. Offer your empathy to the Holy Spirit, because it is *Its* Perception and *Its* Strength that you want to extend. So let

the Holy Spirit offer you Its Perception and Its Strength to extend through you.

6. The Meaning of Love is lost to you in any relationship where you look to the personal self and hope to find Love there. The Power of Love, Which is every relationship's Meaning, lies in the Strength of God that replaces the personal mind's projections and blesses every relationship silently by enveloping it in healing. Let this *be*, and do not substitute the personal mind's 'miracle' for this. [If, in your perception that you are in a world, another asks you to do a foolish thing, you should do it, because opposing it will only make it real to you. But this does not mean that you should do a foolish thing that seems to hurt either of you. All requests in the world that you perceive are foolish because they conflict with Reality, therefore they contain some element of specialness. Only the Holy Spirit recognizes the needs that you think you have in the world as well as your one real need for God. And the Holy Spirit will teach you how to meet your real need for God as well as your needs in the world, without loss to you.

7. If you listen to the personal mind, you will think that by meeting one of these needs you jeopardize the other, because the personal mind wants to keep them separate and secret from each other. This does not lead to Life and Truth. All of your real and perceived needs will soon be met if you leave them to the Holy Spirit, Which has the function of meeting your needs. Meeting your needs is not the personal mind's function. The Holy Spirit will not meet your needs in secret, because the Holy Spirit extends to you Everything that you extend through It. What you extend through the Holy Spirit is for all of your mind where you perceive a world, not just for some of it.] Leave the Holy Spirit Its function, and It will fulfill it if you ask It to bless every relationship that you perceive by extending to it your awareness of your One Relationship with God.

2. The Power of Holiness

1. You may still think that it is impossible for you to understand Holiness, because you cannot see how It can be extended to be

every perception that you have. And you have been told that it *must* be extended to include your entire mind to *be* Holy. In your identification with a personal self do not concern yourself with how miracles extend Holiness, because from the personal mind you do not understand the nature of miracles, and you do not do them. It is their extension far beyond the limits that the personal mind perceives that demonstrate that you do not do them through the personal mind. You do not have to worry about how the miracle extends to fill your entire mind when you do not understand the miracle itself. One attribute of the miracle is no more difficult to understand than the whole miracle, because every attribute of the miracle is miraculous.

2.   The personal mind fragments, so it is only concerned with making 'true' just a little part of any whole thing. It avoids looking at the whole by looking at a part that it thinks it can better understand, so as to keep understanding to itself. A more helpful way for you to look at miracles is this: In your identification with a personal self you do not understand miracles in whole or in part. But they *have* been done *through* you, so there is Something in you that *does* understand them.

3.   In your identification with a personal self your experience of the miracle does not seem natural to you, because this identification is so hurtful and unnatural for your mind that you do not remember what *is* natural for you. So when you are told what is natural you cannot understand it. Recognizing that the Part is Whole and the Whole is in every Part is Perfectly Natural, because it is the way that God thinks, and what is Natural to God is Natural to you. Wholly Natural Perception shows you instantly that every extension of God's Love takes the same effort from you in every situation, or the miracle would contradict itself. If you can understand that the meaning of miracles is Oneness, their attributes will not confuse you.

4.   You *have* experienced miracles, and it is quite apparent that they did not come from a limited personal mind. You have succeeded whenever you have extended God's Love in place of a projection of the personal mind. When you extend God's Love to your

perception of another in the world that you perceive, and you see God's Love reflected back to you from your extension, the first link in your awareness of your mind as One has been made. When you make this extension as the Holy Spirit guides you, the Holy Spirit's Natural Perception of it enables the Holy Spirit to extend Its Own understanding of the miracle to you. It is impossible for you to be convinced of the reality of what has clearly been accomplished through your willingness, while you still believe that the personal mind must understand it for it to be real.

5.   You cannot have faith in Reality while you are determined to make Reality unreal. You are not safer maintaining the reality of illusions than you would be Joyously accepting Truth for What It is and being thankful for It. Honor the Truth, and be glad that the personal mind does not understand It. Miracles are natural to the Holy Spirit, because Its task is to translate your experience of miracles into the Knowledge of God, Which they represent, and Which you have hidden. Let the Holy Spirit's understanding of miracles be enough for you, and do not turn away from all of the Witnesses to Its Own Reality that the Holy Spirit has given to you.

6.   No evidence will convince you of the Truth of What you do not want. But your Relationship with the Holy Spirit *is* Real. Do not fear this, but rejoice that the One that you called upon is with you. Welcome the Holy Spirit, and honor the Witnesses that show you that the Holy Spirit is here. It is true, just as you fear, that for you to acknowledge the Holy Spirit is for you to deny all that you think is true in your identification with a personal self. But what you think is true was never true, and there is no gain to you in clinging to it and denying the Evidence for Truth. You have come too near to Truth to renounce It now, and you *will* yield to Its compelling attraction. You can only delay this now, but not for long. Your Christ Mind has called to you and you have heard, and never again will you be wholly unwilling to listen.

7.   This is a year of Joy in which you will listen to the Holy Spirit more and more, and your Peace will grow as you do. The Power of your Holiness and the weakness of your attack on yourself through your identification with a personal self are both being brought into your

awareness. And this has been accomplished in your mind, which was firmly convinced that Holiness is weakness and attack is Power. This should be a sufficient miracle to teach you that your Teacher is *in* you, but not *of* you. Remember also that when you have listened to the Holy Spirit's interpretations, the results have brought you Joy. Consider honestly the results of the personal mind's interpretations, and ask yourself if you prefer them. God wills you better than they offer, and you can look with greater charity on yourself, whom God loves with Perfect Love.

8.   Do not interpret against God's Love, because you have many Witnesses that speak of It so clearly. This year, determine to accept What has been given to you by God. Be aware of God's Love, and extend God's Love, because this is why God has called to you. The Holy Spirit has spoken, but you have little faith in What you have heard, because you have preferred to place greater faith in the disaster of separation that you seem to have made. Resolve today to accept with Joy the fact that disaster is not real, and that Reality is not disaster. Reality is Safe and Sure and Wholly Kind Everywhere. There is no greater Love than for you to accept this and be Happy. Love asks only that you be Happy, and It will give you Everything that makes for Happiness.

9.   Every problem that you have given to the Holy Spirit, the Holy Spirit has solved for you, and It will always do so. Any problem that you have tried to solve with the personal mind has not been solved. It is time you brought these two facts together and made sense of them. This is the year for you to apply the ideas that have been given to you in this course. These ideas are mighty forces to be used and not set aside. They have already proven their power sufficiently for you to place your faith in them. This year, invest in Truth and let It work in Peace. Have faith in the Holy Spirit, Which has faith in you. Think about What you have really seen and heard, and recognize that you cannot be limited to a personal mind with Witnesses like these.

3. The Reward of Teaching

1.   You have already learned that you teach yourself all the time. You

may have taught yourself the Truth but without accepting the Comfort of your teaching. If you consider What you have taught, and have therefore learned, and how alien It is to what you thought you knew before, you will be compelled to realize that your Teacher came from beyond the personal mind's thought system. The Holy Spirit can look fairly on the personal mind's thought system from a very different thought system that has nothing in common with it, and the Holy Spirit can perceive that it is untrue. Certainly, What you learn from the Holy Spirit as you teach yourself *through* the Holy Spirit has nothing in common with what you taught yourself through a personal mind. And your results have been Peace where there was pain and Joy where there was suffering.

2. You have taught yourself freedom without learning how to be Free. At the end of Chapter 9, Part 5 this course says: 'Extend God's Love, and you will know yourself by your results' because it is certain that you judge yourself according to what you teach yourself. What you teach yourself through the personal mind produces immediate results, because you immediately accept what you decide through the personal mind. This acceptance means that you are willing to judge yourself by the results of your teaching. Cause and effect are very clear in the personal mind's thought system, because all of its teaching has been directed toward establishing them. You have faith in what you diligently teach yourself to believe. But notice how much care you have exerted in choosing the personal mind's witnesses, and in avoiding Witnesses that speak for the Cause of Truth and Its Effects.

3. The fact that you have not learned the Truth that you have taught yourself shows that you do not perceive your mind as One. It is impossible for you to teach yourself wholly without conviction, and your conviction cannot be outside of you. You *have* taught yourself Freedom, because you *did* believe in It, and it must be that What you taught came from within yourself. Yet this Self that teaches you Freedom you clearly do not know or recognize, even though It functions. But What functions must be there, and it is only if you deny What It has done that you can possibly deny Its Presence.

4. This is a course in how to know yourself. With the personal mind you have tried to teach yourself what you are, but you have not let What you are in Truth teach you. You have been very careful to avoid the obvious, and to not see the Real Cause and Effect Relationship that is perfectly apparent. Within you is Everything True that you have taught, so what has not learned it must be a part of you that is outside of you, not by projection, but in fact. It is this part that is not-you that you have taken in. But what you accept into your mind does not really change it, because illusions are only beliefs in what is not there. You can only resolve the seeming conflict between Truth and illusion within you by separating yourself from illusion and not from Truth.

5. Your teaching has already done this, because the Holy Spirit is part of you. Being One with God, the Holy Spirit has not left God or you. The Holy Spirit is both God and you, as you are God and the Holy Spirit together. God's Answer to your perception of separation adds more to you than you tried to take away by trying to separate from God. God keeps you together with your Extension of God, though you want to exclude your Extension of God from your awareness. Your Extension of God *will* replace the world that you made to replace It. It is quite Real; a Part of the True Self that you deny. Your Extension of God communicates to you through the Holy Spirit, and It Gladly offers Its Power and Its Gratitude to you for Its Oneness with you and for your teaching of yourself. You who are One with God are also One with your Extension of God. Nothing Real has ever left the Mind of Its Creator. What is not Real has never existed.

6. You are not two selves in conflict; there is nothing beyond God. You hold God and God holds you, and together you are One, and there is nothing outside of Oneness. You *have* taught yourself this, and Witnesses to your teaching extend from Oneness within you to replace the personal mind's projected witnesses to separation. Their gratitude joins with yours and God's to strengthen your faith in What you teach, because you teach Truth. In the isolation of a personal mind you stand outside your True teaching. But with the Witnesses to Oneness you learn that you only teach yourself, and

you learn from the conviction with which you teach.

7.   This year you will begin to learn What you teach. You have chosen this by your own willingness *to* teach. Though through the personal mind you seemed to suffer for teaching, the Joy of teaching will yet be yours, because Joy is in you as both Teacher and learner. As you learn, your gratitude to your True Self, Which teaches you what It is, will grow and help you honor It. You will learn your True Self's Power and Strength and Purity, and you will love your True Self as God does. God's Oneness is Limitless and Eternal and Perfect. All of this is *you*, and nothing outside of this is you.

8.   All praise is due to your most Holy Self for What you are and for What God, your Creator, is. Sooner or later you must bridge the gap that you imagine exists between the illusory personal self and your True Self. The Bridge is your Relationship with the Holy Spirit. You will build this Bridge to carry you over to Truth as soon as you are willing to expend a little effort on Its behalf. Your little efforts are powerfully supplemented by the Strength of Heaven and by the One Will that makes Heaven What It is. When you choose to cross over to Heaven, you will be literally carried over There.

9.   Your Bridge is stronger than you think, and your feet are planted firmly on It. Do not fear that your attraction to the Love that stands on Heaven's side of the Bridge will not draw you safely across. You *will* arrive Where you want to be, and Where your Self awaits you.

4. The Illusion and the Reality of Love

1.   Do not be afraid to look at the special hate relationship, because your freedom lies in your looking at it. You would know the Meaning of Love if not for the special hate relationship. In the special-love relationship, the Meaning of Love is hidden from you. In your identification with a personal self you undertake the special relationship to offset the personal mind's hatred of you but not to let it go. Your salvation will clearly rise before you as you look on this, because you cannot limit hate. The special-love

relationship will not offset the personal mind's hatred of you, but it will merely drive it underground and out of your sight. It is essential for you to look at this and to not keep it hidden, because Love is meaningless to you in your attempt to balance hate with special-love. You do not realize the extent of the split in your mind that lies in this, and until you do, you will not be able to heal it.

2.   The special relationship is only a symbol. The symbols of hate against the symbols of love play out a conflict that does not exist, because Love has no symbol, since It is Everything. [You will go through this last undoing unharmed and will emerge at last your True Self. This is the last step in your readiness for God. Do not be unwilling, because you are too near and you will cross the Bridge of your relationship with the Holy Spirit in perfect safety, translated quietly from war to Peace.] The illusion of love will never satisfy you, but Love's Reality, Which awaits you on the other side of the Bridge that is your relationship with the Holy Spirit, will give you Everything.

3.   The personal self does not love you. It is a symbol of your 'attack' on God. The personal mind teaches you that you are guilty of separating from God, and that you must fear that God will punish you for this. It must keep attack, guilt, and fear in your mind to keep you away from God. The personal mind attempts to limit the destructive effects of its hatred of you with the special relationship, which is meant to be a haven in its storm of attack, guilt, and fear, which it projects outside the relationship. The special relationship does not undo attack, guilt, and fear in your mind; instead it emphasizes them by teaching you to build defenses against their onslaught *from outside*. So, in your identification with the personal self, you do not really perceive the special-love relationship as valuable in itself, but as a place where hatred is split off and kept outside of you. The special-love partner is acceptable to you only as long as they serve this purpose. Hatred can enter the special relationship, and you actually welcome it in some aspects of the relationship, but an illusion of love must still hold it together. If this illusion of love goes, then you break up the relationship on the

grounds of 'disillusionment'.

4.   Love is not an illusion; It is a Fact. If disillusionment is possible, then you are experiencing hate, not Love. Hate *is* an illusion, and what can change was never Love. God's Love is Everywhere in your mind, and to know this you must extend It everywhere in your mind where you perceive a world. But if instead you select out certain people for some form of special-love, then you are trying to live *with* separation from God, and mitigate the guilt and fear that it produces. In your belief in the reality of your separation from God, you think your only choice for relief from guilt and fear is between the special relationship and returning to God and being killed for your 'sin'. Special-love, then, is only your temporary reprieve from God's punishment and your death. You *do* desperately seek for Love, but not in the Peace that Gladly comes Quietly to you. And when you find that your fear of God and death are still with you, the special-love relationship loses its illusion that it can save you. When your defenses against guilt and fear are broken, they rush in, and hatred triumphs.

5.   [Love does not 'triumph'; only hate is concerned with the 'triumph of love'. An illusion of love can triumph over an illusion of hate, but only in illusions can love seem to 'triumph'.] As long as the illusion of hatred is real to you, love will be an illusion to you, and the only question that you have then is: *Which illusion do I prefer?* There is no conflict for you in the choice between Truth and illusion, because Truth undoes illusion. Conflict enters only when your choice is between two illusions, but then your choice is meaningless *because* they are both illusions. When one choice is as dangerous to your Peace of mind as the other, your decision can only be one of despair.

6.   Your task is not to seek for Love, but to seek for and find within yourself all the barriers that you have built against your awareness of Love. It is not necessary for you to seek for What is True, but it is necessary for you to seek for what is false. Whatever form it takes, every illusion is fear, and escaping from one illusion into another will not bring you relief from fear. If you seek for Love outside of yourself, you can be certain it is because you perceive

hatred within yourself, and you are afraid of it. Peace will never come to you from the illusion of love but only from Love's Reality.

7. Recognize this fact to help you sort out Truth from illusion: The special-love relationship is your attempt to bring Love into separation and fear, and to make illusions real to you. In violation of Love's Oneness, the special relationship is meant to accomplish the impossible, and this can only be done in an illusion. It is essential that you look very closely at exactly what it is that you think you can do to solve the dilemma of self-hatred, which is very real to you in your identification with a personal self, but which does not exist. You have come *this close* to Truth, and only your perception of this dilemma stands between you and your Relationship with the Holy Spirit, Which is the Bridge that leads you into Truth.

8. Heaven waits Silently, and your own Extension of God reaches to you to help you cross the Bridge and welcome It. It is your Extension of God that you really seek, because It is your Completion. The special-love relationship is only a shabby substitute for What makes you Whole in Truth. Your Relationship with your Extension of God is without guil,t and this enables you to gratefully extend God's Love in your perception while you perceive yourself in a world. Your acceptance of your Extension of God is your acceptance of the Oneness of God, Which is your Completion. No specialness can offer you the Oneness that God extends to you and Which you extend.

9. Across the Bridge of your Relationship with the Holy Spirit is your Completion in God, Where you wish for nothing special, and you only want to be wholly like God and to complete God as God completes you. Do not be afraid to cross into your Home of Peace and Perfect Holiness. Only There is God's Completion and your Completion established Forever. Do not seek for completion in your illusion of a bleak world, where nothing is certain, and every-thing fails to satisfy you. In the Name of God, be wholly willing to abandon all illusions. In any relationship in which you are wholly willing to extend God's Completion, and only This, God is completed, and you are completed with God.

10. The Bridge that leads to the union of your mind must lead to God. because It was built with God beside you, and It will lead you straight to God, Where your Completion rests with God's Completion. Every illusion that you accept into your mind by judging it to be attainable removes your own sense of Completion and is your denial of God's Wholeness. Your every fantasy of love or hate deprives you of God, because fantasies are the veil behind which Truth is hidden. To lift this seemingly dark and heavy veil, you only need to value Truth beyond all fantasies, and to be unwilling to settle for illusions in place of Truth.

11. Your journey seems to be through fear to Love. Love calls to you, but in the personal mind's hatred for you it wants you to stay away from Love. Do not hear the call of hate, and do not look on fantasies. Your Completion lies in Truth and only There. In every call of hate, and in every fantasy that tempts you, hear the call of Love that rises ceaselessly from you to God. God will answer you whose Completion is God's Completion. God loves you wholly without illusion, as you must love, because Love is wholly without illusion and therefore wholly without fear. What is One with God is Whole, and God has never forgotten that you make God Whole. In your Completion lies your Memory of God's Wholeness, and God's Gratitude to you for God's Completion. In God's Link with you lie both God's inability to forget you and your ability to remember God. In the Holy Spirit, your willingness to love, and all of God's Love, are joined.

12. God can no more forget the Truth in you than you can fail to remember It. The Holy Spirit is your Bridge to God, made from your willingness to unite with God and by God's Joy in Union with you. Your journey, which seems endless, is almost complete, because What *is* Endless is very near. You have almost recognized It. With your Christ Mind, turn firmly away from all illusions now, and let nothing stand in the way of Truth. With your Christ Mind you will take the last useless journey away from Truth, and then go straight to God in Joyous answer to God's Call for Completion.

13. Special relationships of any kind hinder God's Completion, so they can have no value for you. What interferes with God must interfere

with you. Only in time does interference in God's Completion seem possible. The Bridge that God wants to carry you across lifts you from time into Eternity. Leave time behind, and fearlessly answer the Call of God. God gives you Eternity in Oneness. On the time side of the Bridge to Timelessness you do not understand anything. But as you step lightly across It, upheld *by* Timelessness, you are directed straight to God. In God, and only There, you are Safe Forever, because you are Complete Forever. The Love of God in you can lift any veil in your mind. The Way to Truth is open; follow It with your Christ Mind.

5. The Choice for Completion

1. As you look at the special relationship, it is first necessary for you to realize that it involves a great amount of pain. Anxiety, despair, guilt, and attack all enter into it, broken up by periods in which they seem to be gone. All of these you must understand for what they are. Whatever form they take, they are an attack on yourself that you project onto another and for which you make them feel guilty. This has been discussed earlier in this course[1],but there are some aspects of what you are really attempting in the special relationship that have not yet been touched on.

2. Your attempts to make someone else guilty are really always directed at God. In your identification with a personal self you want to see God and God alone as guilty, with you and the world that you perceive open to attack from God and unprotected from God. So the special-love relationship is your substitute for Heaven and your chief weapon for keeping you *from* Heaven. It does not appear to be a weapon, but if you consider how you value it and why, you will realize why it must be a weapon.

3. The special-love relationship is the personal mind's most boasted 'gift' to you, and the one which has the most appeal to you when you are unwilling to relinquish your belief in your separation from God. The personal mind's goal of independence from God is clear here, and it is counting on the attraction of this gift to you. Your fantasies that center on the special relationship are often quite overt, and the personal mind judges them as acceptable and

natural, along with the anxiety, despair, guilt, and attack that are part of them. In your identification with a personal self, you do not consider it bizarre that you love and hate together, and, even if you believe that hate is a 'sin', you merely feel guilty for it and do not correct it. This is the 'natural' condition of the separation, and when you learn that it is not at all natural *to you*, you will seem unnatural in the world of separation. The world that you perceive *is* the opposite of Heaven, being made to be Its opposite, and everything in the world takes a direction exactly opposite of What is True. In Heaven, Where you know the Meaning of Love, Love is the same as Oneness. In the world that you perceive, where you accept the *illusion* of love in Love's place, 'love' fosters further separation and exclusion.

4.   It is in the special-love relationship, born of your hidden wish for special-love from God, that the personal mind's hatred of you seems to triumph. The special relationship is your rejection of God's Love and an attempt to get the special-love that God denies you. It is essential for the preservation of the personal self that you believe that specialness is Heaven, not hell. The personal mind will never let you see that separation can only be loss for you, because even it recognizes that Heaven could not be loss.

5.   Heaven is Completion, and the personal mind and the Holy Spirit do agree on this. But they disagree on what *completion* is and on how it is accomplished. The Holy Spirit knows that Completion lies first in Oneness and then in the extension of Oneness. To the personal mind completion lies in triumph and in extension of its 'victory' to its final triumph over God. This is where it sees the ultimate freedom for itself, because then nothing will interfere with it. This is the personal mind's idea of Heaven, so Oneness, Which is a Condition in which the personal mind cannot interfere, is hell to it.

6.   The special relationship is a strange and unnatural device of the personal mind to try to join Heaven and hell, or Oneness and separation, thereby making them indistinguishable to you. This attempt to find the imagined 'best of both worlds' has merely led you to fantasies of both and to your inability to perceive either as

they are. The special relationship is the triumph of this confusion, because it is a kind of union from which Oneness is excluded, and the basis for your attempt at union is preservation of separation. There is no better example of the personal mind's maxim: 'Seek but do not find.'

7. Most curious of all is the concept of the 'self' which the personal mind fosters in a special relationship. In your identification with a personal self you seek to make yourself complete in the special relationship, but, when you find one in which you think that you can find completion, you give yourself away and you try to 'trade' yourself for the other's self. This is not Oneness, because there is no extension or increase. Each of you tries to sacrifice the self that you do not want for the other's self, which you think that you would prefer, and each of you feels guilty for the 'sin' of taking and giving nothing of value in return. You cannot put much value on a self that you want to give away for a 'better' one.

8. The 'better' self that you seek in your identification with a personal self is always one that is more special, and that you love for what you can take from him or her. When each of you sees this special self in the other you see a union 'made in Heaven.' Neither one of you will recognize that you have asked for hell, and you will not interfere with the personal mind's illusion of Heaven. This illusion is what the personal mind offers to you to interfere with the Real Heaven. But all of your illusions are of fear, because they seem to make separation from God real to you, and the illusion of Heaven is nothing more than an 'attractive' form of fear, in which the guilt that you feel for separating from God arises as the illusion of 'love'.

9. The appeal of hell for you lies only in your terrible attraction to guilt, which the personal mind holds out to you when you put your faith in it. Your certainty that you are limited to a personal self lies in every special relationship that you make, because only if you are limited will you value specialness. Your demand for specialness, and your perception that giving specialness is an act of Love, makes Love hateful to you, because It seems to limit you. In strict accordance with the personal mind's goal, your real purpose for the special relationship is to destroy Reality and to substitute illusions

in Its place. The personal mind itself is an illusion, and it needs illusions like the special relationship to witness to its 'reality'.

10. Would you want the special relationship if you perceived it as a 'triumph' over God? Put aside the fearful nature of this idea, the guilt it must entail, and the sadness and loneliness that are its result. These are only attributes of your whole religion of separation from God and of the total context in which you think separation occurs. The central theme of your perceived separation's litany to sacrifice is that God must die so that you can live. So what you think you have done to God is acted out in the special relationship with another: Through the death of your 'self', you think that you can attack another and snatch away their self to replace the self that you despise. You despise it because you do not think it offers you the specialness that you demand. And, hating it, you have made it limited and unworthy, because you are afraid of it.

11. You cannot accept that What you have 'attacked' has Limitless Power. Truth has become so fearful to you that you will not dare to look at It, unless you perceive It as weak and little and unworthy of value. You think it is safer to endow the little self that you made with power that you supposedly wrested from Truth, triumphing over Truth, and leaving Truth helpless. Notice how exactly this ritual is enacted on the altar of the special relationship: Two separate people each seek to kill their self and to raise on a body another self to take power from the death of Truth in themselves. Over and over and over this ritual is enacted and is never completed; nor will it ever be completed. This ritual for completion cannot complete, because Life does not arise from death, and Heaven does not arise from hell.

12. Whenever any form of special relationship tempts you to seek for Love in this ritual, remember that Love is Content and not form of any kind. The special relationship is a ritual of form aimed at raising form to take the place of God at the expense of Love's Content of Oneness. There is no Meaning in form and there never will be. You must recognize the special relationship for what it is: a senseless ritual in which strength is extracted from the seeming

death of God and given to you, God's killer, as the sign that form has triumphed over Content, and Love has lost Its Meaning of Oneness. Apart from the fact that this is impossible, do you want it? If it *were* possible you'd be making yourself helpless. God is not angry, because God cannot let this happen. You cannot change God's Mind. No rituals that you have set up to delight in death can bring death to the Eternal. Nor can your chosen substitute for the Wholeness of God have any influence upon God's Wholeness.

13. See in the special relationship your meaningless attempt to raise other gods before God, and, by worshiping them, obscure both their puniness and God's Greatness. In the Name of your Completion, you do not want this. Every idol that you raise to replace God stands before *you* and will replace What *you* are.

14. Your salvation lies in the simple fact that illusions are not frightening, because they are not True. They seem to be frightening to the extent that you do not recognize that they *are* illusions, and you will fail to recognize them *as* illusions to the extent that you want them to be true. To this same extent you are denying Truth, so you are failing to make the simple choice between Truth and illusion; God and fantasy. Remember this, and you will have no difficulty in perceiving the decision as just what it is.

15. The core of your illusion of separation from God lies in your fantasy of the destruction of Love's Meaning, Which is Oneness. Unless Love's Meaning is restored to you, you will not know that you share It. Your perception of separation from God is only your decision to not know yourself. The separation's whole thought system is a carefully contrived learning experience that is designed to lead you away from Truth and into fantasy. Yet for everything you learn that could hurt you, God offers you correction and complete escape from all of the consequences of your perceiving separation.

16. Your decision whether or not to listen to this course and follow it is only your choice for Truth or illusions. Here Truth is separated from illusion and not confused with it at all. The choice is simple when you perceive it as it is. Only fantasies make your choice confusing, and fantasies are unreal.

17. This year is the time to make the easiest decision that has ever confronted you. It is also the *only* decision that has ever confronted you. You will cross the Bridge into Reality simply because you will recognize that God is on the other side, and that the world where you perceive yourself is nothing. You will make the natural decision for Truth when you realize this.

6. The Bridge to the Real World

1. Your search for the special relationship is the sign that you equate yourself with a personal self and not with God, because the special relationship has value only to the personal mind. For the personal mind, a relationship only has meaning if it has special value, because it perceives all love as special. But this is not natural, because it is unlike God's Relationship with you, and all relationships that are unlike this One must be unnatural. God's Love is One, and God extends Love in Oneness with Everything. Love's Meaning is only as God defines It by God's Will. It is impossible for you to define Love any other way and understand It.

2. Love is Limitless. For you to look for Love by limiting yourself to a personal self is for you to separate yourself from Love. For the Love of God, do not seek for Union in separation or for Freedom in the limited! As you release the world that you perceive from your mind, you will be released. Do not forget this, or Love will not be able to find you or comfort you.

3. If you want the Holy Spirit's Help there is a way for you to extend Help so as to learn that you have It. The Holy Instant is the Holy Spirit's most helpful Aid in protecting you from the attraction of guilt that draws you to the special relationship. You do not recognize that guilt is the real appeal in the special relationship, because the personal mind has taught you that freedom lies in separation. But the closer you look at the special relationship, the more apparent it will be that it fosters guilt and therefore limits you to a personal self.

4. The special relationship is totally meaningless to you without a body, so if you value it, you must also value the body. What you value you will keep, so the special relationship is about limiting

your identity to a body and for limiting your perception to a world full of other bodies. If you look upon God's Limitless Love instead, It will be clear to you that the special relationship has no value. When you look on God's Love you do not see bodies, because they have no value, so you have no reason to see them.

5. You perceive what you value. On the side of the Bridge to God where you perceive that you are in a world, you seek a separate body to join with in a separate union and become 'one' by losing your Self. When you try to become 'one' with another, you are really trying to limit yourself to a personal self. You are denying your Power, because a separate union excludes the Oneness of your entire mind. Far more is excluded from the union than is taken in, because God is excluded, and you take in nothing. If in a perception of another you truly saw your Oneness in place of a projection of the personal self, Reality would enter into your awareness. But the special relationship that the personal mind seeks does not even include one whole individual, much less the awareness that your mind is everywhere. The personal mind wants a part of another and sees only a projection of this, and nothing else.

6. Across the Bridge to God it is so different! For a time you will still perceive a body but not exclusively, because God's Limitless Love within you cannot long be limited to it. Once you have crossed the Bridge through your Relationship with the Holy Spirit, the value of the body will be so diminished for you that you will see no need to magnify it. You will realize that the only value that the body has is to enable you to extend God's Love to replace your perception of a world, so to release your entire mind as one.

7. The Bridge that is your Relationship with the Holy Spirit is nothing more than a transition in your perspective of what is real. On the side where you perceive a world, everything is grossly distorted and completely out of perspective. What is insignificant you see as important and What is Strong and Powerful you see as insignificant. In your transition there will be a period of confusion and disorientation but do not fear this because it only means that you have been willing to let go of your hold on the distorted frame of reference which seemed to hold your 'reality' together. This frame

of reference is built around the special relationship. Without this illusion you would not still seek for meaning in a world of separation.

8. Do not fear that you will be abruptly lifted up and hurled into Reality. Time is kind if you use it on behalf of Reality, and it will keep gentle pace with you in your transition. The urgency is only in dislodging your mind from its fixed position in the illusion. You will not be left homeless or without a frame of reference. The period of disorientation, which precedes your actual transition, is far shorter than the time your mind has been fixed firmly on illusions. Delay will seem to hurt you now, only because you realize that it *is* delay, and that it is really possible for you to escape from pain. Find hope and comfort rather than despair in this: You will not find even the illusion of love in any special relationship for long, because you are no longer wholly insane, and you want to recognize the guilt of Self-betrayal for what it is.

9. Anything that you seek to strengthen in the special relationship is not really a part of you. You cannot keep part of the personal mind's thought system, which teaches you that the special relationship is real, and understand the Holy Spirit, Which knows What you are. You have invited the Holy Spirit to enter your mind, and It abides with you. Your Love for the Holy Spirit will not allow you to betray yourself, and you cannot enter into any relationship where It will not go with you, because you do not really want to be apart from It.

10. Be glad that you have escaped the mockery of salvation that the personal mind has offered to you in the special relationship, and do not look back with longing on the travesty it has made of your relationships. You do not need to suffer, because you have come too far to yield to the illusion of the 'beauty' and 'holiness' of guilt. Only if you are wholly insane can you look on death and suffering and sickness and despair and see them this way. What guilt has made is ugly, frightening, and very dangerous; do not see any illusion of truth and beauty in it. Be thankful that there *is* a Place Where Truth and Beauty wait for your awareness. Go to meet Them gladly, and learn how much awaits you for your simple

willingness to give up nothing, because you recognize that it *is* nothing.

11. The new perspective that you will gain while crossing over the Bridge to God through your Relationship with the Holy Spirit will be your understanding that Heaven is within you. From the side where you perceive a world, Heaven seems outside of you and across the Bridge. But as you cross the Bridge to join with Heaven, Heaven will join with you and become One with you. And you will think in glad astonishment: *For all this I gave up nothing!* The Joy of Heaven, Which has no limit, is increased with each extension of Love that you return to It. Do not wait any longer for the Love of God and *you*. The Holy Instant will speed you on the way if you will let It come to you.

12. The Holy Spirit asks only this little help from you: Whenever your thoughts wander to a special relationship which still attracts you, enter a Holy Instant with the Holy Spirit, and let It release you from illusions. The Holy Spirit needs only your willingness to share Its Perspective to give It to you completely. Your willingness does not have to be perfect, because the Holy Spirit's is Perfect. It is the Holy Spirit's Task to correct your unwillingness with Its Perfect Faith, and It is the Holy Spirit's Faith that you share with the Holy Spirit. The Holy Spirit's Perfect Willingness is given to you out of recognition that you are still unwilling to be free of illusions. Call upon the Holy Spirit, because Heaven is at Its Call, and let the Holy Spirit call on Heaven for you.

7. The End of Illusions

1. To let go of the personal self's past you must let go of the special relationship, because the special relationship is your attempt to re-enact the personal self's past and change it. Through the special relationship, the personal mind seeks to restore its wounded self-esteem for the imagined slights, pain, disappointments, injustices, and deprivations of its past story. There is no other basis for choosing a special partner. The choice that you make in your identification with a personal self is because of some perceived 'evil' in the past to which you cling, and for which someone else must pay.

2. In the special relationship, you take vengeance on the present by seeking to remove suffering in the personal self's past. You overlook the present in your preoccupation with and total commitment to the personal self's past. You never experience the special relationship in the present, and shades of the past envelop it and make it what it is. Since it has no meaning *now*, it cannot have any real meaning at all. You can change the past only in fantasy, because who can give you what you think you were deprived of in the past? The past is nothing, so do not seek to lay blame on it for your sense of deprivation. The past is gone, and you cannot really *not* let go of what is already gone, so you must be maintaining an illusion that it has not gone, because you think it serves some purpose that you want fulfilled. You must also believe that this purpose could not be fulfilled in the present, but only in a past that is not here, so what the personal mind seeks to do in the special relationship cannot be done.

3. Do not underestimate the intensity of the personal mind's drive for vengeance on you in the present for the past. It is completely savage and completely insane, because it remembers everything that you have done that has offended it, either through your identification with it or through the Holy Spirit, and it seeks retribution on you. The fantasies that the personal mind brings to the special relationship are fantasies of your destruction. The personal mind holds the personal self's past against you, and in your escape from the past, it sees itself deprived of the vengeance it believes you merit. But without your allegiance to it, the personal mind cannot hold you to the past. In the special relationship you are allowing your destruction through your identification with a personal self, and it is obvious that this is insane. But what is less obvious to you is that the present is useless to you while you pursue the personal mind's goal.

4. The past is gone. Do not seek to preserve it in a special relationship that tries to teach you that salvation is in the past, and that you must return to the past to find it. The personal mind has no fantasy that does not contain the dream of retribution on you for the past. It is your choice whether you act out the dream, or you let it go.

5. In the special relationship, it does not seem like you are seeking to act out vengeance on yourself through the personal mind. Even when the hatred and savagery of the personal mind briefly break though the illusion of 'love', the relationship is not profoundly shaken. But the one thing that the personal mind will never allow to reach your awareness is that the special relationship is the acting out of vengeance on *yourself*. Yet it could not be anything else, because, in seeking the special relationship, you do not look for God in yourself. You deny that God is within you, and the special relationship becomes the substitute for God. Vengeance becomes your substitute for correcting your perception of separation from God, and escaping from vengeance by letting go of the special relationship seems like loss to you.

6. In place of the personal mind's insane idea of salvation, the Holy Spirit offers you the Holy Instant. The Holy Spirit must teach you through comparisons, and It uses opposites to point to Truth. The Holy Instant is the opposite of the personal mind's fixed belief in salvation through vengeance for the past. In the Holy Instant, the past is gone for you, and, with it, the personal mind's drive for vengeance disappears. The Stillness and Peace of *now* enfolds you in Perfect Gentleness, and everything is gone except the Truth.

7. For a while you may try to bring illusions into the Holy Instant to hinder your full awareness of the complete difference between your experiences of Truth and illusion. But you will not attempt this for long, because, in the Holy Instant, the Power of the Holy Spirit will prevail, since you have chosen to join the Holy Spirit. The illusions that you bring with you will weaken your experience of the Holy Spirit for a while and will keep you from holding the experience in your mind. But the Holy Instant is Eternal, and your illusion of time will not prevent the Timeless from being What It is, nor you from experiencing It as It is.

8. What God extends to you, you receive, because the Reality of God's Gift is in your Oneness with God. God extends the Holy Instant to you, and you must receive It, because God extends It to you. God Wills your Freedom, so you *are* Free. The Holy Instant is God's Reminder to you of your Oneness with God. Everything that the

Holy Spirit teaches you is to remind you that you have What God extends to you.

9. You cannot hold anything against Reality. Reality has no past, and you can forgive only illusions. All that you must forgive are the illusions that you project to perceive a world. God holds nothing against anything, because God is incapable of illusions. Release your mind by forgiving it your illusion of a world, and you will learn that you are forgiven. In time this is done for you in the Holy Instant, to bring you the True Condition of Heaven.

10. Remember that you always seek between Truth and illusion; between real correction and the personal mind's 'atonement',[1],which wants to destroy you. The Power of God and God's Limitless Love will support you as you seek only for your place in the plan of the Atonement, Which arises from God's Love. Be an ally of God, and not of the personal mind, in seeking how correction can come to you. God's Help is enough, because the Holy Spirit understands how to restore the awareness of Oneness to you, and how to place all your investment in your salvation in your Relationship with God.

11. Seek and find the Holy Spirit in the Holy Instant, Where you forgive all illusions. From the Holy Instant that you extend, the miracle blesses all that you see and resolves all problems, whether you perceive them as great or small, possible or impossible. There is nothing that will not be replaced by the Holy Spirit's Love. For you to join in close Relationship with the Holy Spirit is for you to extend Reality to your relationships in your perception that you are in a world, and, through the Reality that you perceive there, to give up all illusions for the Reality of your Relationship with God. Praise be to your Relationship with God and to no other relationship! The Truth lies Here, and nowhere else. You choose your Relationship with God, or you choose nothing.

12. *God, You forgive me my illusions, so help me to accept my Oneness with You, in Which there are no illusions and Where none can ever enter. Your Holiness is my Holiness. There is nothing in me that needs to be forgiven. because Your Forgiveness is Perfect. My forgetting You is only my unwillingness to remember Your Forgiveness and Your Love. I will not be*

tempted to forget You, because it is not Your Will. I will receive only What You extend to me and accept into my mind only Your Oneness and Your Love. Amen.[2]

Chapter 17

Forgiveness and The Holy Relationship

1. Bringing Fantasy to Truth

1. Your betrayal of yourself is only an illusion, and all your 'sins' are only in your imagination. Your Reality is Forever sinless, so you do not need to be forgiven; you only need to undo your illusion of separation from God. In your illusions, you seem to have betrayed yourself, everyone that you perceive, and God. But what is done in illusions has not really happened. Yet in your identification with a personal self it is impossible to convince you of this, because you believe your illusion of separation is your reality. Only by your becoming fully aware of God again will you be fully released from your illusion, because then it will be perfectly apparent to you that it has had no effect on Reality at all. Illusions seem to have the purpose of changing reality, but they cannot do so *in Reality*; they only seem to do so in your mind, when you want reality to be different.

2. It is only your wish to change what is real that makes Reality frightening to you, because by your wish you think that you have made it happen. In a sense, this acknowledges your Power, but by distorting It and devoting It to 'evil', it also makes your Power unreal to you. You cannot be faithful to two Teachers who ask conflicting things of you. What you use to make an illusion of separation, you deny to Truth; what you give to Truth to use for you is safe from your illusions.

3. When you maintain that it is too difficult for you to extend God's Love to be everything that you perceive, all that you mean is that there are some illusions that you want to withhold from God. You believe that God cannot deal with them, only because you want to keep them from God. Very simply, your lack of faith in the Power that heals all pain comes from your wish to retain some part of your mind for illusions. If you only realized how this destroys your

appreciation of your Whole Mind! What you reserve for illusions you take away from the Holy Spirit, Which wants to release you from illusions. Unless you give your illusions to the Holy Spirit, it is inevitable that you will believe in a warped reality, and your mind will be uncorrected.

4. As long as you want it, you will keep the illusion that there are some things that you perceive to which you cannot extend God's Love. You have established this idea by giving some of your illusions to the personal mind and others to the Holy Spirit, so that you have learned to deal with parts of the world that you perceive with one and with other parts with the Other. You confuse illusion with Truth, and this is your 'reality'. But to fragment Truth is to make It meaningless to you. There are no orders of Reality, because Reality is One.

5. You cannot bring Truth to illusions and learn What Truth is from the perspective of illusions. Truth has no meaning in illusions, and Truth's Frame of Reference is Itself. When you try to bring Truth to illusions, you are trying to make illusions real and to keep them by justifying your belief in them. But if you truly give illusions to Truth, Truth will teach you that illusions are not real, and this will enable you to undo them. Do not hold back any idea from Truth, or you will establish different realities for yourself that will limit you. There is only One Reality, and only What is There is True.

6. Be willing to give all that you have held apart from Truth to the Holy Spirit, Which knows Truth and in Which all is brought to Truth. For your salvation to be at all, you must be completely saved from your perception of separation. Be concerned only with your willingness to have this accomplished, and the Holy Spirit will accomplish it for you. Do not forget this: When you become disturbed and lose your Peace of mind because you perceive others in their own illusions, you are not forgiving *yourself* for perceiving illusions. You are holding part of your mind away from Truth and salvation. As you forgive the personal mind's perceptions of others, you restore Truth to your entire mind. You will see forgiveness where you have extended it.

2. The Forgiven World

1.   You cannot imagine how Beautiful your perception of others will be to you when you have forgiven the personal mind's projections onto them. You have never seen anything so Beautiful in your illusions, and you will value nothing above this. Nothing that you remember in the personal self's past has made your heart sing with the Joy this Perception will bring to you. You will see Christ. You will see the Beauty the Holy Spirit sees, and for Which the Holy Spirit thanks God. The Holy Spirit is given to you to see this for you, until you learn to see It for yourself. All of the Holy Spirit's teaching leads you to seeing Christ and to your giving thanks to God for your Christ Mind.

2.   This Loveliness is not an illusion. It is your Real Perception, bright and clean and new. There is nothing hidden in your Real Perception, because, with It, you have forgiven everything, and you have no illusions to hide the Truth. The bridge between your Real Perception and the world of separation that you perceive is so little and so easy to cross, that you will not believe that it is the meeting place of perceptions so different. This little bridge is the strongest thing that touches on the world that you perceive. The little step it takes you to stride across this bridge takes you from time into Eternity; beyond all ugliness into enchanting Beauty that will never cease to cause you wonderment at Its Perfection.

3.   Over the bridge to Real Perception the next step you take is the smallest of steps, and, yet, the greatest accomplishment in God's plan of Atonement. You learn everything else, but this final step is given to you wholly Complete and Perfect. Only God can complete it. Crossing the bridge you learn to reach your Real Perception's Loveliness, Where all illusions are undone, and, by your own forgiving, you are freed to see Truth. But what you see is only the perception that you made with the blessing of your forgiveness on it. With this final blessing of your Christ Mind on Itself, the Perception that reflects Reality has served Its purpose.

4.   In the final step taken by God, the world will disappear from your mind. Perception will be meaningless to you, because it will have been perfected and everything that you used for learning will no

longer have a function. Now nothing will ever change for you; no shifts or shadings or differences or variations will happen for perception to occur. When you have reached for Real Perception, and you have been made ready for God, your Real Perception will be so short that you will barely have time to thank God for It before God will take the last step swiftly and lift you into Heaven.

5.   You attain Real Perception simply by your complete forgiving of the world of separation in your mind. The Holy Spirit will undertake with you the careful searching of your mind, which made the world, and uncover with you the seeming reason you had for making it. The Holy Spirit's Reason for the world that you perceive is to reflect Reality, and in Light of this Reason, you will see that the world has no reason at all. Every spot that the Holy Spirit touches with Its Reason will become Beautiful to you, and what seemed ugly in the empty reason of the personal mind, you will release to Loveliness. Even what you have made in insanity has a hidden spark of Beauty that is released in Gentleness.

6.   All this Beauty will rise to bless your sight as you look on all that you perceive with forgiving eyes. Your forgiving literally transforms your perception and lets you see your Real Perception, Which reaches quietly and gently across chaos and removes all the illusions that had twisted your perception and fixed it on the personal self's past. The smallest leaf will become a thing of wonder to you, and a blade of grass will become a sign of God's Perfection to you.

7.   From your forgiving perception you will easily be lifted Home to God, and you will know that you have always rested There in Peace. Salvation will become an illusion and then vanish from your mind, because salvation is the end of illusions, and it has no meaning without them. You will have no need of an illusion of salvation when you are aware of Heaven.

8.   How much do you want salvation? It will give you your Real Perception, Which is trembling with readiness to be given to you. The eagerness of the Holy Spirit to give you your Real Perception is so intense that the Holy Spirit does not want to wait, although It waits in Patience. Meet the Holy Spirit's Patience with your

impatience to meet It. Go in gladness to meet the One Which corrects your perception of separation from God, and walk in trust out of your perception of a world of separation and into your Real Perception of Beauty and forgiveness.

3. Shadows of the Past

1. When you forgive the personal self's past, you remember only your Loving Thoughts of the past, and you forget everything else. Your forgiving is your selective remembering, but it is not based on the personal mind's selection. The 'shadow figures' from the personal self's past that the personal mind projects onto others and wants to make immortal are your 'enemies' of Reality. Be willing to forgive your Christ Mind for what your Christ Mind did not do, because the shadow figures are the witnesses the personal mind brings to make it seem as though you have separated from God, which you have not done. You bring them to your relationships, but you do not understand how they come into your mind or what their purpose is. The shadow figures represent the 'evil' that the personal mind tells you was done to you in the past, and you bring them with you only so that you can return evil for evil by projecting guilt onto another in the present and seem to not harm yourself. They seem to witness clearly to the reality of your separation from God, and you see them only because you are obsessed with keeping the separation real to you. They offer you the 'reasons' why you should enter into unholy relationships to support the personal mind's goals and use these relationships to witness to the personal mind's power.

2. It is these shadow figures that seem to make the personal self holy in your sight and to teach you that what you do to keep the personal self safe is 'love'. The shadow figures always speak for you getting vengeance on the personal self's past in the present, and all relationships in which you see them are totally insane. Without exception these relationships have as their purpose the exclusion of the Truth from your mind, both in you and in your mind where you perceive a world. This is why you see in both yourself and others what is not there, and you enslave both to

379

vengeance; why whatever reminds you of the personal self's past grievances attracts you and seems to go by the name of 'love', no matter how distorted are the associations by which you arrive at the connection; why all special relationships attempt union through bodies, since only bodies can be seen as a means for vengeance. It is obvious that bodies are central to all unholy relationships, and your own experience has taught you this. But what you may not realize are all the reasons that make the relationship unholy. Unholiness seeks to reinforce itself, just as Holiness does, by gathering to itself what it perceives as like itself.

3. In the unholy relationship, it is not the body of the other with which you attempt union but the bodies of those from the personal self's past, whose shadow you bring with you. The body of the other, which already severely limits your perception of what is real, is not really your central focus. You separate off as valuable only the parts of the body of the other that you can use for your fantasies of vengeance and that you can most readily associate with those from the personal self's past on whom you seek vengeance. Every step that you take in the making, the maintaining, and the breaking off of an unholy relationship is a move you make toward further separation and unreality. The shadow figures enter your relationship more and more, and the one on whom they are projected decreases in importance to you.

4. Time is kind when you use it for Gentleness, but time is cruel when you use it for the personal self, and it is indeed unkind to the unholy relationship. In your identification with a personal self, almost at once the attraction of the unholy relationship begins to fade for you and you question it. Once the special relationship is formed, you must begin to doubt it, because its purpose of true union is impossible. The 'ideal' special relationship, from the personal mind's point of view, is one in which the actual personal self of the other does not enter to 'spoil' your fantasy of them, so that the less the other really brings to the relationship the 'better' it becomes for you. This attempt at union really becomes your means of excluding even the personal self with whom you sought union. You formed the special relationship to get the other out of the

Forgiveness and the Holy Relationship

relationship so that you could join with your fantasies of the personal self's past in 'bliss'.

5.   So how can the Holy Spirit bring into relationships, whose only purpose is supposed to be your separation from Reality, *Its* interpretation of the body as a means for uniting your mind? *Forgiving* enables the Holy Spirit to do so. When your forget everything but your Loving Thoughts from the past, What remains is Eternal, and your transformed past is made like the present. Then the past will no longer conflict with *now*. This continuity extends the present by increasing its Reality and its value in your perception of it. Your Loving Thoughts from the past provide the Spark of Beauty in the ugliness of the unholy relationship, where hatred is supposed to be remembered. This Spark comes alive as you give the relationship to the Holy Spirit, Which gives it Life and Beauty. This is why the plan of the Atonement centers on your perception of the personal self's past, which is the source of your perception of separation from God, and where it must be undone. Your perception of separation must be corrected where it is made.

6.   The personal mind seeks to 'resolve' your problems where they are *not* to guarantee that they will have no solution. The Holy Spirit only wants to make Its solutions complete and perfect, so It seeks for and finds the source of your problems where they are, and It undoes them. With each step in the Holy Spirit's plan of undoing, your perception of separation is undone more and more, and True Union is brought closer to your mind. The Holy Spirit is not at all confused by any 'reason' for your perception of separation, and It only perceives that your perception of separation must be undone. Let the Holy Spirit uncover the Loving Thoughts in your relationships and show them to you. Love will so attract you that you will be unwilling to ever lose sight of Love again, and you will let Love transform your relationships so that you can see Love more and more. You will want Love more and more, and you will seek for and establish the conditions in which you can see Love.

7.   All this you will gladly do if you let the Holy Spirit hold Love before you to make the Goal clear. Your mind is One, and What God has joined as One, the personal mind cannot put asunder. No

matter how hidden, Holiness is safe in every relationship that you perceive, because your One Relationship with God has not left your mind. The Holy Spirit sees only the Holiness that you extend to any relationship, because It knows that only Holiness is True. You have made unholy and un-real relationships by not seeing your One Relationship with God. Give the personal self's past to the Holy Spirit to change your mind about it for you. But first, be sure that you fully realize what you have made the past to represent to you and why.

8. The personal self's past is your justification for entering into a continuing, unholy alliance with the personal mind against the present. The present *is* forgiveness, so you do not perceive or feel *now* the relationships that your unholy alliance with the personal mind dictates. The personal mind uses the personal self's past as a frame of reference for the present. But this is an *illusion* of a past in which you keep those elements that fit the purpose of the unholy alliance, and you let go of everything else. What you let go of, then, are all the Loving Thoughts that the past could ever offer to the present as Witnesses to Reality. What you keep, then, seems to witness to the reality of illusions.

9. It is always up to you to choose to join with Truth or with illusion. But remember, to choose one is to let go of the other. Which one you choose you will endow with beauty and reality for yourself, because your choice depends on which one you value more. Your awareness of Love or the veil of separation; your Real Perception or the world of guilt and fear; Truth or illusion; Limitlessness or limitedness – it is all the same. Your only choice is between God and the personal mind. Thought systems are either True or false, and their attributes come from what they are. Only the Thoughts of God are True, and All that follows from Them are as True as the Holy Source from Which they come.

10. Christ will enter all relationships in your mind where you perceive a world, and It will step between you and your fantasies. Let your Relationship with Christ be Real to you by extending your Christ Mind in your relationships in your perception that you are in a world. God does not extend Its Mind to you so that you can hurt

yourself with a world of separation. Your mind is meant to be Whole and to extend God. This is the Truth that your awareness of Christ will interpose between you and your goal of separation from God. Do not be separate from your Christ Mind, and do not let the Holy Purpose of correction of the plan of the Atonement be lost to you in the personal mind's fantasies of vengeance. Relationships in which you cherish fantasies exclude Christ. In the Name of God, let Christ enter your relationships and bring you Peace so that you may extend Peace to your entire mind.

4. The Two Pictures

1. God's Relationship with you is for Joy, and nothing you do that does not share this Purpose can be Real. The Purpose God ascribes to anything is its only Function, so, because of your Relationship with God, the Function of relationships is forever 'to make happy' *and nothing else*. To fulfill this Function, you must relate to your Extension of God as God relates to you, because Everything that is One with God is Joyful and extends Joy as God does. Whatever does not fulfill this Function cannot be Real.

2. Oneness is impossible in the world that you perceive, but the Happiness in your mind can be reflected in your perceptions. You have been told earlier in this course that the Holy Spirit will not deprive you of your special relationships, but that It will transform them. This means that the Holy Spirit will restore to them the Function of Happiness given to relationships by God. The function that the personal mind has given to relationships is clearly not 'to make happy', but the Holy relationship shares God's Purpose and does not seek to make a substitute for It. Every special relationship that you have made in your identification with a personal self is meant to be a substitute for God's Will and glorifies the personal self instead of God, because you believe the illusion that your will is different from God's Will.

3. Even in your belief that you are in a world you have a very Real Relationship with the Holy Spirit, but you do not recognize this Relationship because, as a substitute for It, when Truth calls to you – which It does constantly – you answer with the special

relationship. Every special relationship that you have made has, as its fundamental purpose, the aim of occupying your mind so completely that you will not hear the Truth.

4.   The Holy Spirit is God's Answer to your perception of separation from God and, in a sense, the special relationship is the personal mind's answer to the Holy Spirit. Although the personal mind does not understand the Holy Spirit, it *is* aware of a 'threat' to it in your mind. The personal mind's whole defense system evolved to protect from the Holy Spirit your belief in separation from God, because the Holy Spirit is the Gift God has given to you to heal your perception. The Truth is that the Holy Spirit is in Close Relationship with you, and through the Holy Spirit, your Relationship with God is restored to you. Your Relationship with God has never been broken, because the Holy Spirit has not been separate from you since your perception of separation began. Your Holy Relationship with God is carefully preserved by the Holy Spirit to serve God's Purpose for you.

5.   The personal mind is always alert to threat, and the part of your mind into which you have accepted the personal mind is very anxious to preserve its 'sanity' as it sees it. You do not realize that the personal mind is totally insane, but you must realize this if you want to be restored to Sanity. In insanity you project your thought system and you do so insanely. All of your defenses are as insane as what they are supposed to protect. Every part of your perception of separation is insane, and its 'protection' is part of it and as insane as the whole of it. The special relationship, which is your chief defense for your perception of separation from God, is therefore insane.

6.   You have little difficulty realizing now that the personal mind's thought system is delusional, and, at least in general terms, that the personal mind is insane. But the special relationship still seems somehow *different* to you. You have looked more closely at the special relationship than at many other aspects of the personal mind's thought system that you have been willing to let go. But while the special relationship remains, you have not let the others go, because it is *not* different from them. Hold onto this one aspect

of your perception of separation, and you hold onto all of it.

7. All of your defenses do what they defend. You defend your perception of separation from God by offering yourself further perceptions of separation. Your defense of your perception of separation takes elaborate forms, but they all frame a miniature picture of separation. Your defense is meant to be of value in itself, to divert your attention away from the fact that it is framing a perception of separation from God. But you cannot have the defense without the perception of separation it is defending, although the defense is meant to make you think that you can.

8. The special relationship is the most imposing and deceptive of defenses that the personal mind uses. Separation from God is the picture that it offers to you, but the special relationship frames it with the illusion of love, fantasies of sacrifice, personal self-promotion, and Self-destruction. It is an offering of blood and tears in an elaborate disguise.

9. But look at the *picture* of separation from God inside the frame of the special relationship, and do not let the special relationship distract you. It is a gift of damnation given to you by the personal mind, and if you take this gift, you will believe that you *are* damned. The frame has no meaning without the picture; the special relationship has no meaning without separation from God. You value the special relationship because you do not see the conflict in it, but it is only the frame for a gift of conflict. Do not be deceived by the superficial aspects of the personal mind's thought system, because they enclose your whole belief in separation from God. Death is its real gift to you, so do not be hypnotized by the special relationship, but look at what it is framing.

10. This is why the Holy Instant is so important in defending your awareness of Truth. You need to defend yourself against the gift of death, because when you who are Truth accept an idea that would undo Truth, you threaten to destroy your awareness of Truth. The Power of Heaven, the Love of God, the Joy of Christ and Its Holy Spirit are All marshaled to defend you from your own attack. You attack Them when you attack yourself, because you are One with Them, and they must save you because They Love Themselves.

11. The Holy Instant is a miniature Picture of Heaven sent to you *from* Heaven. It is a Picture of Timelessness set in the frame of time. If you accept this Gift you will not see the frame of time at all, because you can accept this Picture of Timelessness only through your willingness to focus all of your attention on *It*. If you focus on the Picture, the frame will fade away, and you will see only Eternity. Just as the whole thought system of the personal mind lies in its gifts, so does the Whole of Heaven lie in this Holy Instant, borrowed from Eternity and set in time for you.

12. You are offered two gifts; each is complete and cannot be partially accepted. Each is a picture of all that it offers to you, but around the picture of your separation from God you look only on the frame of the special relationship that seems to defend it. You cannot compare a picture to a frame, or the Holy Instant to the special relationship. You must compare picture to picture, the Holy Instant to your perception of separation from God, for the comparison to have any meaning, because the picture is the gift. Only if you look clearly at both pictures are you free to make a choice. The picture of separation is a tiny miniature obscured by the enormous frame of the special relationship; the Holy Instant is so lightly framed by time that Its Lovely Image is all that you see.

13. You have tried hard to fit the better picture into the wrong frame – to make a god of the special relationship. They cannot be combined, so accept this, and be glad: Each picture is framed perfectly for what it represents. Your perception of your separation from God is framed by the special relationship to be out of focus and not seen. The Holy Instant is framed for perfect clarity, because you have nothing to hide in It. The picture of denial and death that is your perception of separation from God will grow less appealing as you seek it within its heavy frame. As you examine each senseless aspect of the special relationship, it will cease to attract and distract you. And, as you finally look on the picture of separation from God it is meant to hide, you will see that the picture has no meaning.

14. The Picture of the Holy Instant is lightly framed by time, because time cannot contain Eternity. The frame does not distract you from the Picture. The Picture of Heaven and Eternity grows more

convincing as you look at It. Through real comparison now, a transformation of both pictures can happen. When you see both in relation to the other, the picture of your perception of separation from God will not frighten you, but you will recognize it is only a picture; something you mistakenly thought was real and nothing more. There is nothing beyond this picture.

15. The Picture of the Holy Instant, in clear-cut contrast, is transformed into the Eternity that lies beyond the Picture. The Holy Instant is not a Picture; It is Reality. It does not merely represent a thought system; It *is* the Thought of God, and what It represents is here. The frame of time will fade gently as you remember God, Which offers you Oneness in exchange for your little valueless and meaningless picture of separation.

16. As God ascends to Its Rightful Place in your mind, and you ascend to yours with God, you will again experience the Joyful Meaning of *Relationship*, and know It to be True. With your Christ Mind, ascend in Peace to God by giving God ascendance in your mind. You will gain Everything by seeing Power and Glory in God, and by letting go of your illusory belief that They can be found in the personal mind. They are in you through God's Ascendance in your mind. What God has given to you is God's in every Part of God and in the Whole of God. The Whole Reality of your Relationship to God lies in your relationship to your entire mind. The Holy Instant shines equally on all that your mind perceives, because your mind is One. In the Holy Instant, your mind is completely and perfectly healed, because God is here. And only the Perfect and Complete can be where God is.

5. The Healed Relationship

1. Your Holy relationship with another in your perception that you are in a world can be an expression of the Holy Instant. It can represent the healing of your mind by uniting your mind with the part of it that you perceive as a world outside of it. Like everything else that the Holy Spirit uses for your salvation, it is practical, and its results witness to it. The Holy Instant never fails you, and you can always experience It, but without Its expression you will not

remember It. Your Holy relationship is your constant reminder of the experience of the Holy Instant, in Which your Relationship with the Holy Spirit *is*. As the unholy special relationship represents hatred of you through its praise of the personal self, so your Holy relationship is Happy praise for the Holy Spirit, Which corrects all of your relationships.

2. You learn a Holy relationship, and it is a major step toward your Real Perception. It is an unholy relationship with another in the world that you allow to be transformed, and that you see with Real Perception. It is a phenomenal teaching accomplishment, because as it begins, develops, and becomes accomplished it represents for you the reversal of the unholy relationship. Be comforted that the only difficult phase is the beginning, because this is when your unholy goal for the relationship is abruptly shifted to the exact opposite of what it was. This is the first result of your offering a relationship to the Holy Spirit to use for Its purposes.

3. Your invitation to the Holy Spirit to enter your relationship is accepted immediately by the Holy Spirit, Which wastes no time in introducing you to the practical results of your invitation. At once, the Holy Spirit's Goal of Oneness replaces the personal mind's goal of separation, and, since this is accomplished very rapidly, it makes the relationship seem disturbed, disconnected, and distressing for you. This is because the relationship as it *is*, is out of line with its new Goal and it is clearly unsuited for this new Purpose that you have accepted for it. In its unholy condition, the personal mind's goal of specialness was all that seemed to give the relationship meaning for you, so its new Purpose seems to make the relationship make no sense to you. You may be tempted to break off your relationship at this point to pursue the old goal of specialness in another relationship, because, once you have accepted the Goal of Holiness for an unholy relationship, it can never again be what it was.

4. With this shift in goals, the temptation to follow the personal mind will become extremely intense for you, because the relationship will not yet have changed enough to make its former goal of specialness completely unattractive to you. The structure of the

relationship will seem 'threatened' by your recognition of its inappropriateness for meeting its new Purpose of Holiness. The conflict between your new Goal and the structure of the relationship will be so obvious that they cannot coexist. But now the Goal cannot be changed back, so the only course for you is to change the relationship to fit the new Goal. Until you accept that this happy solution is the only way out of conflict, the relationship may seem to you to be severely strained.

5. It would not be kinder to shift the goal of the relationship more slowly, because the contrast would be obscured for you, and the personal mind would have time to reinterpret each slow step according to its goal. Only a radical shift in purpose will induce you to completely change your mind about what the relationship is for. As this change develops and is finally accomplished, the relationship will grow increasingly beneficial and Joyous for you. But at the beginning, you will experience the relationship as very precarious. You have entered the relationship for your unholy purposes, and you now have Holiness for your goal. As you contemplate your relationship from the point of view of this new Purpose, you will inevitably be appalled. Your perception of the relationship might even become quite disorganized, but the former organization of your perception will no longer serve the Purpose that you have agreed to meet.

6. This is the time for *faith*. You let the Goal be set for you, and that was an act of faith, so do not abandon faith now that the rewards of faith are being introduced to you. You believed that the Holy Spirit was there to accept the relationship, and you can believe that the Holy Spirit is here to purify what It has taken under Its guidance. Have faith in your new perception of your relationship in what seems to be a trying time. The Goal *is* set, and your relationship now has Sanity as its purpose. In Light of your new Goal, you can see that your relationship *was* insane.

7. Now the personal mind will counsel you to substitute for your Holy relationship another relationship that serves your former goal of specialness. It will tell you that you can only escape from your discomfort by getting rid of the other. You won't have to get

rid of the other completely, but you must exclude the other from major areas of your life in the world to protect your sanity. *Do not listen to this!* Have faith in the Holy Spirit, Which has answered you very clearly. You are not wholly insane. The Holy Spirit asks for your faith in the midst of your bewilderment, because this confusion will go away, and you will see your faith justified. Do not abandon the Holy Spirit by abandoning the other, because your relationship has been reborn as Holy.

8.   Accept with gladness a relationship that you do not understand, and let it be explained to you as the Holy Spirit's Purpose works in it to make it Holy. It will seem at times to have no purpose, and the personal mind will find many opportunities to blame the other for the 'failure' of your relationship. A sense of aimlessness may come to haunt you and to remind you of all the ways in which you used to seek for satisfaction for the personal self and in which you thought that you had found it. But do not forget the misery that you really found, and do not breathe life into the failing personal mind. Your relationship has not been disrupted; it has been saved.

9.   You are very new to the ways of salvation, and you may think that you have lost your way. The personal mind's way *was* loss for you, so do not think that giving it up is loss. In your newness, remember that, by recognizing your Holiness in your perception of another in the world in your mind, you walk along a road to God that is far more familiar to you than you now believe. It is certain that you will remember the Oneness that is unchanged throughout Eternity. You have chosen the Goal of God, from Which your True intentions have never left.

10. Your Christ Mind sings the song of Freedom in Joyous echo of your choice. You have joined your entire mind in the Holy Instant. Your choice will not leave you comfortless, because God blesses your Holy relationship. Join in God's blessing by blessing the relationship yourself, because this is all that it needs for you to see that in it rests your salvation. Salvation has come to you, so welcome it, because in this relationship your entire mind is blessed.

11. You have invited the Holy Spirit into a relationship in your perception that you are in a world; the Holy Spirit could not have

entered it otherwise. Although you may have made mistakes by projecting the personal mind onto the other since then, you have also made enormous efforts to help the Holy Spirit. The Holy Spirit appreciates all that you have done for It, and It does not see your mistakes at all. Have you done the same in your relationship with the other? Have you gratefully extended Holiness to your perception of the other in place of the personal mind's projections? Or have you looked on the personal mind's projections as real? Maybe you are now embarking on a campaign to blame the other for your discomfort in this relationship. By your lack of gratitude to the other for the opportunities your relationship with them gives to you to extend Holiness in your awareness, you make yourself unable to express the Holy Instant, so you lose sight of It.

12. No matter how compelling you find the experience of the Holy Instant to be, you will easily forget it if you allow time to close over It. It must be kept graciously in your awareness of time, but not buried in it. The Holy Instant is always here, but where are you? For you to be grateful for your Holy relationship is for you to appreciate the Holy Instant and to enable yourself to experience and extend its results. For you to attack the other in your relationship is not for you to lose the Holy Instant but for you to make It powerless for you.

13. You *have* received the Holy Instant, but you may have established a condition in which you cannot use It, so you do not realize that It is still with you. By cutting yourself off from the Holy Instant's expression through the Holy relationship, you deny yourself Its benefits. You reinforce this every time that you attack the other with the personal mind's projections, because the attack blinds you to yourself by blocking the reflection of your Holiness in your perception. When you deny yourself, you cannot recognize the Holiness that God has given to you and that you have.

14. In your relationship with the other, you stand in the Holy Presence of God. Here is the Goal, and the Goal Itself will gladly arrange the means for you to accomplish It. The discrepancy between the Purpose that you have accepted for your relationship and the relationship as it is now makes Heaven glad, although in your

identification with a personal self this discrepancy seems to make you suffer. Because Heaven is within you, you can share Its Gladness. Through your relationship with another who once seemed outside of you, your mind is united in Purpose, but you still remain conflicted on the means to attain It. But the Goal is Fixed, Firm, and Unalterable, and the means will fall into place because the Goal is sure. You will share your Christ Mind's gladness that this is so.

15. As you begin to recognize and accept the Gifts of God that you freely extend in your relationship, you will also accept the effects of the Holy Instant and use them to correct all of your mistaken projections and to free yourself from their results. Learning this, you will learn how to free all of your relationships in your mind where you perceive a world by offering them to the Holy Spirit in gladness and thanksgiving. The Holy Spirit has freed you and will extend your Freedom through you.

6. Setting the Goal

1. The practical application of the Holy Spirit's Purpose of extending God's Truth in your awareness is extremely simple and clear. In fact, to be simple it must be clear. The Holy Spirit's Goal of Truth, being Everywhere, is general, but, for now, the Holy Spirit will work with you to apply It in specific situations. There are certain very specific guidelines that the Holy Spirit provides for you in any situation, but you do not yet realize their potential for application everywhere. So, for now, it is essential for you to use them in each situation separately until you can more safely look beyond each situation in an understanding far broader than you now possess.

2. In every situation, the first thing for you to consider is: *What experience do I want to have?* Your goal will determine your experience of any situation, so clarifying your goal belongs at the beginning of every situation. The personal mind reverses this procedure and teaches you that the situation determines your experience, which can be anything. It does this because it does not know what it wants you to experience. It is aware that it does *not* want you to experience God, but it has no positive goal at all.

3. When you don't have a clear-cut positive goal set at the beginning of a situation it just seems to happen to you, and it makes no sense to you until it has already happened and you try to piece it together and give it meaning. Then your judgment will be wrong, because the situation is in the past, and you have no idea what it should have meant. You did not set a goal to make the situation a means for meeting it. Now the only judgment left to you is whether or not the personal mind finds the situation acceptable or thinks it calls for vengeance on you. The absence of a goal that you set in advance of a situation leaves you doubting its meaning and makes your evaluating it impossible.

4. The value of your deciding on a goal in advance is simply that you will perceive the situation as a means for achieving that goal. You will therefore make every effort to overlook what interferes with the goal's accomplishment, and you will concentrate your efforts on what helps you to meet the goal. Notice that this approach has brought you closer to the Holy Spirit's sorting out of Truth from illusion. The True is What you extend to meet the Goal of God, and everything else you perceive as useless. The situation has meaning for you, only because your Goal has made it meaningful for you.

5. The personal mind teaches you that a situation's meaning can be anything and that the situation itself causes your experience of it. The Holy Spirit teaches you that your goal determines a situation's meaning for you, as well as the experience that you will have. Besides giving a situation meaning for you, another practical advantage of your setting the Goal of God at the beginning of any situation is that what you use for Truth and Sanity results in Peace for you. This is quite apart from the outcome of the situation that shows up in the world that you perceive. God is always here, and if you experience Peace, it is because you have accepted and extended this Truth in your awareness. You will recognize that you see a situation Truly when the result for you is Peace.

6. The Goal of God requires your faith that God is Real. Faith is implied in your acceptance of the Holy Spirit's Purpose, and this faith includes everything in a given situation. Where you set the Goal of God, you must have faith in It. The Holy Spirit sees a

situation as a whole, and you must extend God's Truth to everyone and everything involved in it for you to see it as whole. This is inevitable and will not fail. This seems to ask for faith beyond you and beyond what you can give, but this is only so from the personal mind's viewpoint. The personal mind believes in 'solving' conflict through fragmentation, and it does not perceive any situation as whole. It seeks to split off segments of a situation and to deal with them separately, because its faith is in separation and not in wholeness.

7. When you are confronted with a problem situation and it seems too difficult for you to extend your awareness of God to all of it, the personal mind will try to keep some parts away from Truth and resolve them itself. This can seem to be successful, except that this obscures the Goal of God for you by conflicting with Oneness. If you experience peace doing this, it is only a temporary illusion of peace. You have lost sight of God, because you have lost faith that only God is Real. The situation will lose the Meaning for you that the Goal of God would have given to it. Illusory solutions bring you illusory experiences, and an illusion of peace is not the condition of Truth.[1]

7. The Call for Faith

1. When you accept the personal mind's substitute 'solutions' for parts of a problem situation in place of the Holy Spirit's extension of your awareness of God, they witness to your lack of faith that only God is Real. They demonstrate that you do not believe that the problem situation is only your perception of separation from God. Any problem that you perceive is *always* your lack of faith that only God is Real, because if you extended your awareness of God to the situation, the problem would be gone. And then the situation would be meaningful to you, because there would be no interference in your extension of Truth. When you see a problem as outside of your mind you keep it, because this makes it seem unsolvable to you.

2. Your faith that only God is Real can solve any problem in any situation. But if you shift parts of a problem to the personal mind

to solve, you make real solution impossible, because your perception of separation *is* the problem. Your problems have all been solved, but you have removed yourself from the Solution. Your faith must be in the Holy Spirit, Which *is* the Solution to your perception of separation from God, and Which you can see by extending It.

3. Every situation in your perception that you are in a world is your relationship with yourself, because it is made up of thoughts in your mind that you project onto the world. If you perceive problems, it is because your thoughts are conflicting. But if your Goal is God, conflict is impossible. So, if you are conflicted, some thought making bodies real to you must have entered your mind, because you cannot allow yourself to see your mind as attacking itself, and you need to project the source of attack onto *something*. Bodies cannot solve anything, and your thinking that bodies are real indicates that you lack faith that only God is Real. In your relationship with yourself, bodies seem to intrude and justify your lack of faith that God is True, but your seeing bodies as real is just an error in your thoughts. You will make this error, but do not be concerned with it, because errors do not matter. If you bring your errors to Truth, then they cannot interfere with Truth. But use your errors *against* Truth and your faith in Truth will be destroyed. When you believe in error, ask that your faith that only God is Real be restored in your mind where it was lost, and do not seek to have your lack of faith corrected elsewhere as though you have been unjustly deprived of your faith by something outside of you.

4. Only what *you* have not extended to any situation can be lacking. Remember this: The Goal of Holiness was set for your relationship with another, and it was not set by the personal mind. The personal mind did not set it, because you can see Holiness only through your faith in Holiness' Reality, and your relationship was not Holy before, because you limited your perception of the other to the personal mind's projections. Your faith will grow to meet the Goal that has been set for you by the Holy Spirit within you. The Goal's Reality will call forth your faith, and you will learn that your faith and Peace come together. You cannot be faithful to yourself in any

situation where you lack faith that only God is Real.

5.   Every situation in which you find yourself in your perception that you are in a world is a means for you to perceive the Holiness that is the Goal for your relationship with the other and is therefore your Goal for your relationship with yourself. See a situation as for something else, and you lack faith that only God is Real. Let the personal mind's goals enter your mind, look on them calmly, and then let them go. Your lack of faith that only God is Real serves the personal mind and its illusions. Use the personal mind and you will go straight to illusions. Do not be tempted by what it offers you, because it interferes, not with your Goal of God, but with the value that you place on God. Do not accept the illusion of peace it offers to you, but look on it, and recognize that it *is* an illusion.

6.   Your lack of faith that only God is Real results in your having illusions as your goal; your faith that only God is Real results in God as your Goal. If you commit a situation to God in advance and then lack faith by not extending your awareness of God to the whole situation, then your commitment is divided. You will have lacked faith that God is in your mind and can be extended in your perception, and you will have used this lack of faith against yourself. Holiness goes everywhere with a Holy relationship. Since Holiness and faith go hand-in-hand, faith must go everywhere with Holiness. The Reality of your Goal of God will call forth and accomplish every miracle that you need for Its fulfillment. Everything – small, enormous, weak, compelling – in the world that you perceive will be gently turned to the Holy Spirit's use and Purpose. Reality will serve your mind where you perceive a world as the world serves your awareness of Reality, as long as you do not allow the personal mind to interfere.

7.   The Power set in you, in whom the Holy Spirit's Goal of Holiness has been established, is so far beyond the personal mind's little conception of the Infinite, that you have no idea how Great is the Strength that goes with you. You can use this Power in perfect safety. Yet, for all of Its Strength, so great that It reaches past all that you can perceive, your little lack of faith can make It useless if you want to use your faithlessness instead.

8. Think about this: You think that you hold against the other in your Holy relationship what they have done to you, but what you really blame them for is what *you* have projected onto *them*. You do not hold their past against them but *your* past against them, and you do not extend your awareness of God's Oneness to your perception of them because of *your* guilt for *your* past. But your past is the personal mind's illusion, and you are Innocent. What never was has no cause and is not here to interfere with God. There is no cause for you to lack faith that only God is Real, but there is Cause for your faith that only God is Real. The Cause for your faith that only God is Real is the Holy Spirit, and the Holy Spirit enters any situation that you have given to the Holy Spirit's Purpose of extending Holiness. Truth extends from the center of any situation that you have devoted to Truth and calls to It the whole of your mind where you perceive a world. There is no situation that you enter that does not involve your whole Holy relationship with the other in every aspect and in every part, because your mind is whole. You cannot leave any of your perceptions outside of the relationship and keep the situation Holy. Every situation in your perception that you are in a world *is* your Holy relationship with the other, because everything is your relationship with yourself, and from this everything derives its meaning for you.

9. Enter every situation in your perception that you are in a world with the awareness of God that you extend to your Holy relationship, or you will lack faith in your Holy relationship. Your faith in the Holiness of this one relationship will call all that you perceive to share the Purpose of God. You will see the means that you once employed to make your illusions real to you transformed into means for your remembering God. God calls for your faith, and your faith makes room for God. When the Holy Spirit changed the purpose of your one relationship with another to Holiness, Holiness became the Goal for every situation you will ever enter in your perception that you are in a world. Every situation is thereby made free of the personal self's past, which would make it purposeless.

10. You call for faith because of the Holy Spirit, Which walks with you

in every situation. You are no longer wholly insane or limited to a personal mind. Limitation in God must be an illusion. You, whose relationship shares the Holy Spirit's Goal, are freed from limitation, because the Truth has come into your awareness. Its call for your faith is strong. Do not lack faith in Truth, because It calls you to your salvation and to your Peace.

8. The Conditions of Peace

1. The Holy Instant is an extreme example of what every situation is meant to be in the Holy Spirit's perception of the world. The Meaning that the Holy Spirit's Holiness gives to the Holy Instant It also gives to every situation that you perceive. The Holy Instant calls for a suspension of your faith in the personal mind, so that your faith can answer the Call of God. The Holy Instant is the shining example, the clear and explicit demonstration, of the Meaning that you can extend to every relationship and every situation that you perceive. You can extend your faith that only God is Real to every aspect of every situation and not allow the personal mind to force any aspect to be excluded from God. Then a situation will become one of Perfect Peace for you by you allowing What *is* to simply *be* in your awareness.

2. The Holy Spirit asks you for just this simple courtesy: Let God be What God is. Do not intrude the personal mind upon God, do not interrupt God's coming to you, and let your awareness of God's Reality encompass every situation and bring you Peace in your perception that you are in a world. God does not ask for anything, not even for faith. Let God's Reality enter your mind, and It will call forth and secure from you the faith in It that you need to be at Peace. Do not let the personal mind rise against Truth, because Truth cannot come when you oppose It.

3. Don't you want to make every situation that you perceive a Holy Instant? This is the gift of faith that you freely give whenever you put aside faith in the personal mind. This frees you to use the Power of the Holy Spirit's Purpose, Which instantly transforms all situations into one sure and continuous means for establishing your Holiness in your mind and for demonstrating the Reality of

your Holiness to you. What is demonstrated calls your faith to It ,and It becomes a Fact from Which you can no longer withhold your faith. The strain for you in your refusing faith in the Truth in you is enormous and far greater than you realize. But there is no strain for you in answering Truth with faith.

4. You have acknowledged the Call of the Holy Spirit, and now the strain of not responding to It seems greater than before, but this is not so. Before, the intolerable strain of your refusing to have faith that only God is Real took the form of sorrow and depression, sickness and pain, dark and terrifying imaginings, fearful fantasies, and dreams of hell.

5. Such was the crucifixion of the Christ in your. You did this to yourself through your lack of faith that only God is Real. Think carefully before you put your faith in the personal mind, because Christ is within you, and you have accepted Christ's Cause as your own. You have accepted your part in correcting your perception of separation from God, and you are now responsible to your Christ Mind. Do not fail to give your faith to your Christ Mind, because you now know What your lack of faith will cost you. Your salvation is now your only purpose, so see only this purpose in every situation, and every situation will be a means for bringing you salvation.

6. When you accepted Truth as the Goal for your relationship with another, you became an extender of Peace as surely as God extends Peace to you. You can accept the Goal of Peace only when you have faith in It, and you only put your faith in what you believe is real. Your purpose has not changed, and it will not change, because you have accepted What can never change. You can no longer withhold yourself from God's Changelessness. Your Freedom is certain, so extend It as you have received It, and demonstrate to yourself that you have risen far beyond any situation in the world that you perceive that once would've held you back and kept you separate from God.

Chapter 18

The Passing of the Dream

1. The Substitute Reality

1.   To substitute is 'to accept instead'. If you consider what this entails, you will perceive how much substituting one illusion for another conflicts with the Goal of Oneness that the Holy Spirit has given to you, and that the Holy Spirit wants to accomplish for you. In your relationships with others in your perception that you are in a world, your substituting one person for another is your choosing one of the personal mind's projections as more valuable and 'special' than another of its projections, making all of its projections real to you. Your relationship with yourself is then fragmented, and you see its purpose as split between an isolated 'you' and a world that seems outside of you. Substituting one illusion for another is the strongest defense that the personal mind has for your perception of separation from God.

2.   The Holy Spirit never uses substitutes. Where, in your identification with a personal self, you perceive one person as a replacement for another, the Holy Spirit sees them as the same. Your relationships with others are either opportunities for you to project separation or for you to extend Love in your awareness, but either way they are all the same, and substitution is clearly a process in which you think that they are different. The Holy Spirit wants you to extend Love everywhere and unite with Truth; the personal mind wants you to project differences everywhere and to be separate from everyone and everything that your mind perceives. Nothing can split your mind, which God joins, and which the Holy Spirit sees as One. But in the fragmented relationships that the personal mind sponsors to destroy Truth, illusions seem to come between your mind and what it perceives.

3.   Love, being One, is the one emotion in which it is impossible for you to substitute. But fear involves substitution by definition,

because it is meant to be Love's replacement. Fear is both a fragmented and fragmenting emotion that seems to take many forms. Each form of fear seems to require a different form of acting out for your satisfaction. While this makes your behavior unstable, a far more serious effect of fear lies in the fragmented perception that is the source of your behavior. In fear, you cannot extend your awareness of Wholeness to your perception of anyone, because the personal mind emphasizes the body, especially certain parts that are used as a standard of comparison for acceptance or rejection for acting out fear as special love.

4.   You have tried to make only one substitution for Love: You've tried to substitute fear for God. This substitution has taken many forms, because it was the substitution of illusion for Truth; of fragmentation for Wholeness. Your substitution for God has become so splintered and subdivided and divided again, over and over, that it is now almost impossible for you to perceive that your mind once was One, and that it still is. That one error, which seemed to bring Truth to illusion, Infinity to time, and Life to death, was all that you ever made. The whole world that you perceive rests upon it, everything that you perceive in the world reflects it, and every special relationship that you have ever made is part of it.

5.   You may be surprised to learn how very different Reality is from what you think of as reality. The magnitude of your one error is so vast and incredible that a world of total unreality *had* to emerge from it. Nothing else *could* come of it. Its fragmented aspects are frightening enough to you as you begin to look at them, but nothing you see in them begins to show you the enormity of your original error. It seems to have cast you out of Heaven, to have shattered your mind into meaningless bits of disunited perceptions, and to have forced you to make more substitutions.

6.   You projected your error outward, and the physical world arose to hide it and to be the screen between you and the Truth on which you could project your error. But Truth extends inward, where the idea of loss is impossible, and only increase is conceivable. It is not strange that a world where everything is backward and upside down arose from your projection of error; in fact it was inevitable.

Truth brought to illusion can only remain within you in Quiet, and It takes no part in all of the mad projections by which you make the world that you perceive. Do not call your perception of separation from God 'sin', but call it madness, because that is what it is. Do not invest it with guilt, because guilt implies that it has really happened. Above all, *do not be afraid of it.*

7. When you seem to see some twisted form of the original substitution of fear for Love arise to frighten you, say to yourself: 'God is Love, not fear' and let it disappear. The Truth will save you, because It has not left you so that you can go out into a mad world. Within you is Sanity; outside of you is insanity. You believe that it is the other way around, and that Truth is outside of you, and that error and guilt are within you. Your little, senseless substitutions for God have no substance. They fuse and merge and separate in shifting and totally meaningless patterns that you do not need to judge at all. To judge individual projections is pointless, because their tiny differences in form are not real differences at all. None of them matters, and *that* they have in common and nothing else. They are all the same.

8. Let go of all of your illusions, and let them disappear from your sight. Turn to the Stately Calm within where the Living God, Which has never left you, dwells in Holy Stillness. The Holy Spirit will gently guide you as you retrace with It the mad journey that you took outside yourself, and It will lead you back to the Truth and Safety within you. The Holy Spirit brings to Truth all of the insane projections and wild substitutions for God that you have placed outside of yourself, reversing the course of your insanity and restoring you to Sanity.

9. In your Holy relationship with another, where the Holy Spirit has taken charge of everything as you have requested, the Holy Spirit has set your course inward to the Truth that you extend to your relationship. In the personal mind's perception of the mad world that seems outside of you, nothing can be extended, only substituted. Extension and substitution have nothing in common. From within yourself, you extend Perfect Love to your relationship with the other, and your relationship is Holy ground on which no substi-

tution can enter, and where only the Truth can abide. Here you join your mind with God to replace your perception of a world. The original error of substitution has not entered here, and it never will. Here is the Radiant Truth to Which the Holy Spirit has committed your relationship. Let the Holy Spirit bring your relationship here, where you want it to be. Give the Holy Spirit a little faith in your extension of Love to your relationship with the other to help the Holy Spirit show you that no substitute that you have made for Heaven can keep you from It.

10. In you there is no separation, and no substitute can keep you from extending Oneness to your relationship with the other. Your Reality is God's Reality, and It has no substitute. Your mind is so firmly united in Truth, that only God is There. God loves your mind as One, and as God loves you, so you are. You do not unite your mind through illusions of a world, but in the Thought so Holy and so Perfect that illusions cannot remain. God is with you. In Peace and Gratitude, join with your Christ Mind in God, and accept God as your most Holy and Perfect Reality.

11. Heaven is restored to your mind through your Holy relationship, because in it lies your Christ Mind, Whole and Beautiful and Safe in your Love. Heaven has quietly entered your relationship, because all illusions have been gently brought to the Truth in you, and Love shines upon you, blessing your relationship with Truth. God's Oneness has entered your relationship, and how Lovely and Holy your relationship is with the Truth shining on it! Heaven beholds it, and rejoices that you have let It come to you, and God is glad that your relationship extends God's Oneness. Reality within you stands with you and with your extension of Love to the other. Heaven looks with Love on what joins in It and with God.

12. God has called to you, and you should hear no substitutes for God. Their call is only an echo of your original error, which seemed to shatter Heaven and destroy your Peace. Return with your Christ Mind to Heaven, walking with your Holy relationship out of the world of separation that you perceive and through your Real Perception to the Loveliness and Joy that is only *reflected* in your Real Perception. Do not further weaken and break apart your

mind, which already seems broken and hopeless. Heal it instead, and join in making whole what has been ravaged by separation.

13. You have been called to the most Holy Function that you have in your perception that you are in a world. It is the only one that has no limits and that extends to every seeming broken fragment of your mind with healing and uniting comfort. This is offered to you through your Holy relationship. Accept It here, and you will extend It as you have accepted It. The Peace of God is given to you with the purpose in which you extend Love to your relationship with another. As you accept the Holiness that you extend to your perception of one other, It must be extended to all that your mind perceives.

2. The Basis of the Dream

1. When you dream while you sleep at night, the world that arises in your dream seems very real to your mind. But think about what it is: It is not the world that you see before you go to sleep, but a distortion of the world that you perceive awake, planned solely around what you prefer. In the dream, you are free to make over whatever seemed to attack you while you were awake, and to change it into a tribute to the personal self, which was outraged by the perceived 'attack'. This is *your* wish, because you see yourself as one with the personal mind, which always looks on itself as under attack and highly vulnerable.

2. The dreams that you have while you are asleep are chaotic, because they are governed by your conflicting wishes, and they have no concern with what is real to you when you are awake. They are the best example you can have of how you can use perception to substitute illusion for truth. You do not take dreams seriously when you awaken, because, in them, what you think is real when you are awake is so outrageously violated. But they are a way of looking at the world and changing it to suit the personal self better. They provide striking examples of both the personal mind's inability to tolerate any 'reality', even the one that it makes, and your willingness to join with the personal mind to change whatever reality you perceive on its behalf.

3. You do not find disturbing the differences between what you see
    while you sleep and what you see while you are awake. You
    recognize that what you see when you are awake is blotted out in
    dreams, and you are not surprised that the world that you left to
    sleep and dream is still there when you wake up. In dreams *you*
    arrange everything: people become what you want them to be, and
    you order what they do. There are no limits on the substitutions
    you make, because for a time it seems as though the world is given
    to you to make of it what you wish. What you do not realize is that
    you are attacking the world and trying to triumph over it and make
    it serve you.

4. Dreams are perceptual temper tantrums in which you literally
    scream, 'I want it like this!' and so it seems to be. But the dream
    cannot escape the mind that is its origin. Anger and fear pervade it,
    and in an instant your illusion of satisfaction is invaded by the
    illusion of terror. It *is* terrifying to dream that you can control
    reality by substituting a world that you prefer. Your attempts to
    blot out what you think is real are frightening, but you are not
    willing to accept this. So you substitute the fantasy that what you
    think is real is frightening, instead of seeing that it is what you
    want to do to reality that is frightening. And so you make guilt
    real.

5. Sleeping dreams show you that you have the power to make a
    world as you want it to be, and that because you want it, you see
    it. And while you see it, you do not doubt that it is real. A dream is
    a world that is clearly in your mind but that seems outside of your
    mind while you are dreaming it. You do not respond in the dream
    as though you made it, nor do you realize that the emotions that
    the dream produces come from you. You think that the figures in
    the dream and what they do make your dream. You do not realize
    that you are making them act out for you, because if you did realize
    this, your guilt would be yours, not theirs, and your illusion of
    satisfaction would be gone. When you are dreaming the dream
    seems clear; then you wake up and the dream is gone. What you do
    not recognize is that the thoughts that caused the dream have not
    gone away with the dream. Your wish to make a world that is not

real remains with you, and what you seem to awaken to is but another form of the same illusory world you see in sleeping dreams. *All* of your time is spent in dreaming. The dreams that you have when you are asleep and when you are awake take different forms, and that is all. Their content is the same, because they are your protest against Reality, and your fixed and insane belief that you can change Reality. In the dreams you see when you are awake, the special relationship has a special place. It is the means by which you try to make your sleeping dreams come true, and you do not awaken from this. The special relationship is your determination to keep your hold on unreality and to prevent yourself from waking to God's Reality. While you see more value in dreaming that you are separate from God than in awakening to God, you will not let go of the special relationship.

6. The personal mind uses your dream of separation from God to maintain your dream of separation from God. But the Holy Spirit is very practical in Its Wisdom, and It accepts your dreams of separation and uses them as a means to awaken you to God. The first change before the dream of separation disappears completely from your mind is that it is changed into a happy dream that reflects God's Love. This is what the Holy Spirit does with the special relationship. The Holy Spirit does not destroy the special relationship or snatch it away from you. But the Holy Spirit does use it in a way that is different from the personal mind's use of it. The Holy Spirit uses the special relationship to make the Holy Spirit's purpose real to you. The special relationship will remain with you, not as a source of pain and guilt, but as a source of Joy and Freedom. It is not for you in your identification with a personal self, because that is the source of the relationship's misery. Its unholiness keeps it a thing of separation, but its Holiness becomes an offering that you extend your mind where you perceive a world.

7. Through your extension of the Holy relationship, your special relationship becomes your means for undoing guilt in everything that you perceive. It is a happy dream and one which you will extend to all of your perceptions. The Holy Spirit has not forgotten

you or any part of your mind in the purpose that the Holy Spirit has given to you. The Holy Spirit uses every call for Love that you perceive as an opportunity to extend salvation to your entire mind. And your entire mind will be awakened to God through your Holy relationship. If you only recognized the Holy Spirit's Gratitude to you! And your Christ Mind's Gratitude through the Holy Spirit! Your Christ Mind is joined with you in the Holy Spirit's purpose, because you are of One Mind with the Holy Spirit.

8.   Do not let your dream of separation from God take hold and make you unaware of God. It is not strange that dreams can make an unreal world. What is incredible is your *wish* to make an unreal world. Your relationship with the other is now one in which this wish has been removed, because its purpose has been changed from a dream of separation to Truth. You are not yet sure of this, and you think that *this* may be the dream. That's because you are so used to choosing among dreams that you do not see that you have finally made the choice between Truth and *all* illusions.

9.   Yet Heaven is sure, and It is no dream. Heaven's coming into your awareness means that you have chosen Truth, and Heaven has come into your awareness because you have been willing to let your special relationship meet Its Conditions. The Holy Spirit has gently laid your Real Perception in your relationship. It is the perception of Happiness from which you will awaken to God, naturally and easily. Just as your sleeping and waking dreams in the world that you perceive represent the same wishes in your mind, so do your Real Perceptions and the Truth of Heaven join in the Will of God. Your dream of awakening to God is easily transferred to God. This dream reflects your Will, Which is One with God's Will. What this Will is has always been.

3. Light in the Dream

1.   You who have spent your life denying Truth and Reality for illusions and fantasy have walked the way of dreams. You were once awake in God, and then you chose to be asleep to God, and you have gone deeper and deeper into sleep. All of your dreams lead to more dreams, and all of your fantasies, which seem to make

truth out of illusion, only make your illusion deeper. Your goal was a denial of God in which no awareness of God could enter. You sought a denial so complete that you could hide from Truth Forever in complete insanity. What you forgot was that God cannot destroy God. *God is within you.* In denial you can hide God from you, but your denial cannot destroy God.

2. As you become more aware of God you will rush to denial, shrinking from the Truth. Sometimes you will retreat into lesser forms of fear; sometimes you will retreat into stark terror. But you will advance to Truth, because It is your Goal. The Goal that you have accepted is Knowledge of God, and you have signified your willingness for It. When you are afraid, you have stepped back into denial. When this happens, quickly join with your Christ Mind in a Holy Instant, and this will be enough to remind you that your Goal is God.

3. Truth has rushed to meet you since you called upon It. If you knew that Christ is with you on the way that you have chosen, it would be impossible for you to be afraid. You do not know this, because your journey into denial has been long and cruel, and you have gone deep into it. A little flicker of your eyelids, which have been closed in denial so long, has not yet been sufficient to give you confidence in your True Self, which you have despised for so long. You go toward Love still hating It and terribly afraid of Its judgment on you. You do not realize that you are not afraid of Love, but you are afraid of *what you have made of Love.* You are advancing toward Love's Meaning and away from all the illusions in which you have surrounded Love. When you retreat from Love to illusions, your fear increases, because, from illusions, what you think Love means *is* fearful. But that is nothing to you who travel swiftly away from fear with your Christ Mind.

4. You who extend Holiness to your perception of another extend your Christ Mind, because when you extended your True Self you chose to no longer be isolated to a personal mind. Christ will not leave you in denial, because you have made the choice to leave denial to remember Christ. The Love that replaces your perception of a world.is in your Holy relationship with another, and fear must

disappear before you now. Do not be tempted to snatch away the gift of faith in God that you have extended to the other, because you will only frighten yourself. Your gift of faith extends Forever, because God receives it, and you cannot take it back; you have accepted God. The Holiness of your relationship is established in Heaven. You do not understand What you have accepted, but remember that your understanding is not necessary. All that is necessary is your *desire* to understand, because that is your desire to be Holy. God's Will is granted to you, because you desire the Only Thing that you ever had or that you ever were.

5.   Each instant that you spend with Christ will teach you that your Goal of Holiness is possible and will strengthen your desire to reach It. In your desire for Holiness, Holiness is accomplished because your desire is in complete accord with all of the Power of the Holy Spirit's Will. No little, faltering footsteps that you may take can separate your desire from the Holy Spirit's Will or from the Holy Spirit's Strength. Christ is with you, as surely as you chose to extend your True Self to your perception of another. You will not separate, because your Christ Mind is with you in your advance to Truth. Where you go with Christ, you carry God with you.

6.   In your relationship with the other, you have extended your Christ Mind to bring Heaven to your perception, where Heaven was hidden by your denial. You have become willing to undo your denial, and this willingness has strengthened the awareness of God in your perception. If you are willing to be aware of God, you *will* be aware of God. The denial that remains in your mind you will bring to your Christ Mind, and it will be removed Forever. Christ's Need for you is your need for salvation. Your Christ Mind will extend to you what you extend to your Christ Mind. When you extended yourself to encompass your perception of another, you answered Christ.

7.   You bring salvation with you now as you bring Love to replace your perception of a world. Denial in you has been undone. From the Holy Instant, carry your awareness of God with you throughout the world that you perceive. You are made whole in

your desire to make yourself whole. Do not let time worry you, because all of the fear that you experience is really past. Time will be readjusted to help you do with Christ what the personal self's separate past tries to hinder. You have gone past fear, because you have united your mind in Love.

8.   All of the Love of Heaven goes with you; God's Eternal Love shines on you. Heaven joins with you in your advance to Heaven. When such Power is with you to give your little desire Strength, you cannot remain in denial. You are uniting your mind after a long and meaningless journey of separation that led nowhere. You have extended your Love to your perception of another, who seemed outside of your mind, and your Love will light your way. From this Love, God's Love will extend back through your denial and forward to God to undo the personal self's past and make room in your awareness for God's Eternal Presence, in Which Everything is radiant with Love.

4. The Little Willingness

1.   The Holy Instant comes to you as a result of your determination to be Holy. It is the *Answer*. Your desire for It, and your willingness to let It come, precede Its coming. You prepare your mind for It only by recognizing that you want It above everything else. It is not necessary that you do more than this; in fact, it is necessary that you realize that you cannot do more. Do not attempt to give to the Holy Spirit what It does not ask for, or you will confuse the personal mind with the Holy Spirit. The Holy Spirit asks little, and It is the Holy Spirit that adds Greatness and Might. The Holy Spirit joins with you to make the Holy Instant far greater than you can understand with a personal mind. It is your realization that you need do so little that enables the Holy Spirit to give so much.

2.   Do not trust your good intentions; they are not enough. But trust completely your *willingness* to experience the Holy Instant, whatever else may enter. Concentrate only on this and do not be disturbed by the thoughts of the personal mind which surround it. They are why you need the Holy Instant, and if they were not here, you would not need the Holy Instant. Don't come to the Holy

Instant arrogantly assuming that you must achieve what It brings. The miracle of the Holy Instant lies in your willingness to let It be What It is. And in your willingness for this lies your acceptance of yourself as God means you to be.

3. You are not being humble when you are content with littleness. True humility requires that you not be content with less than the Greatness that comes from God. Your difficulty with the Holy Instant comes from your fixed conviction that you are unworthy of It. This is only the personal mind's determination that you be what *it* wants to make of you. God dwells within you, and God's Dwelling Place is not unworthy of God. If you believe that you can block God from being within you, then you are trying to interfere with God's Will. You do not need the Strength of willingness to come from you, but from God's Will.

4. The Holy Instant comes to you from your little willingness combined with the Limitless Power of God's Will. You have been mistaken in thinking that you need to prepare yourself for God. If you make arrogant preparations for Holiness it is because you believe that it is up to you to establish the conditions for Peace. God has already established them, and they do not wait upon your willingness to be what they are. You only need to be willing to be taught the conditions for Peace. If you hold onto the belief that you are unworthy of learning this, you are interfering with the lesson by believing that you have to make the learner different. You did not make yourself, and you cannot make yourself different. Would you first make a miracle and then expect one to be made *for* you?

5. In the Holy Instant, you ask the question of God, 'What are You?' and the Answer is given to you by God. Do not seek to answer yourself in your identification with a personal self, but receive the Answer as It is given to you by God. Do not attempt to make yourself Holy to be ready to receive the Answer, because that is for you to confuse your role with God's Role. Real Correction cannot come to you when you think that you must make correction before Real Correction can come. Real Correction comes when you offer It nothing more than the simple willingness to let It come. God's

coming into your awareness *is* your Correction. Instead of preparing yourself for God, think instead:

'I, in whom God dwells, am worthy of God.
God created Its Dwelling Place as God wants It to be.
I do not have to make myself ready for God, but I only need to not interfere with God's plan to restore me to the awareness that I am Eternally Ready.
I do not need to add anything to God's plan.
But to receive God's plan, I must not substitute my own in place of It.'

6. And that is all. Add more and you take away the little that is asked of you. Remember that in your split mind you made guilt, and that your plan for escaping your guilt for separating from God has been to increase your guilt and to make salvation fearful. You will only add fear if you try to prepare yourself for Love. Your preparation for the Holy Instant belongs to the Holy Spirit, Which gives the Holy Instant to you. Release yourself to the Holy Spirit, Which has the function of releasing you. Do not assume the Holy Spirit's function, but give the Holy Spirit what It asks so that you will learn how little is your part, and how Great is the Holy Spirit's part.

7. It is the little that is asked of you that makes the Holy Instant so easy and so natural for you. You make It difficult, because you insist that there must be more that you need to do. You find it difficult to accept that you need to do so little to receive so much. You find it personally insulting that your contribution and the Holy Spirit's contribution are so extremely disproportionate. You are still convinced that your understanding is a powerful contribution to the Truth, and that it makes Truth What It is. But you do not need to understand anything. Your salvation is easy, because it asks of you only what you can give right now.

8. Do not forget that it was your decision to make everything that is easy and natural for you seem impossible. If you believe that the Holy Instant is difficult for you, it is because you have made yourself the judge of what is possible, and you are unwilling to give

this position to the Holy Spirit, Which *knows* What is possible. Your whole belief that some miracles are harder than others is centered in this. Everything that God Wills is not only possible but has already been done. The past is gone, because it never happened in Reality. Only in your mind, which believes it has a past, is its undoing needed.

5. The Happy Dream

1. Prepare *now* for undoing what never was. If you already understood the difference between Truth and illusion you would not need correction. The Holy Instant, the Holy relationship, the Holy Spirit's Teaching, and all the other means by which your salvation is accomplished would have no purpose. These are all aspects of the plan to change your illusions of fear into happy illusions, from which you will easily become aware of God again. Don't put the personal mind in charge of this, because through it you cannot distinguish between advance and retreat. The personal mind has judged as failure some of your greatest advances toward Truth, and it has evaluated as success some of your deepest retreats into fear.

2. Do not approach the Holy Instant after you have tried to remove all fear and hatred from your mind; that is the Holy Instant's function. Do not attempt to overlook guilt before you ask the Holy Spirit for help; that is the Holy Spirit's function. Your part is only to offer to the Holy Spirit your little willingness to forgive yourself by letting the Holy Spirit remove all fear and hatred and guilt from your mind. To build your part in the plan of the Atonement, the Holy Spirit will join Its understanding of Truth to your little faith, and It will make sure that you fulfill it easily. With the Holy Spirit, you will build a ladder that is planted firmly in the solid rock of your faith and that will rise to Heaven. You will ascend to Heaven with a mind that has been made whole again.

3. Through your Holy relationship, which is reborn and blessed in every Holy Instant that you extend to it from the Holy Spirit, you lift your entire mind to Heaven. You cannot plan for this or prepare yourself for this with a personal mind. It is possible, because God

Wills it, and God will not change Its Mind about it. Your purpose, and the Means for accomplishing it, both belong to God. You have accepted your purpose, and the Means will be provided for you to meet it. A purpose without the means is inconceivable, and God will provide the Means because you share God's Purpose.

4. Happy illusions translate easily into Truth, not because they are illusions, but because they are Happy, so they must be Loving. The message of a Happy illusion is, 'God's Will be done', not 'I want it this way'. It is impossible for you to understand from the personal mind how the Means and the purpose align. You do not even realize that you have accepted the Holy Spirit's purpose as your own, and the personal mind only wants to bring unholy means to the Holy Spirit's accomplishment. Your little faith is all that is needed to change your purpose to the Holy Spirit's purpose, and for you to receive the Means and to use Them.

5. It is not an illusion for you to extend your True Self in place of the personal mind's projections, so your Holy relationship is not an illusion. All that remains of illusions within your relationship with the other is that it is still special. But it is very useful to the Holy Spirit, Which *has* a special function in your perception that you are in a world. Your Holy relationship will become the Happy illusion from which the Holy Spirit will extend Joy in your mind where you perceive a world through corrected perception and teach you that Love is Happiness, not fear. Let the Holy Spirit fulfill the function It gives to your relationship by letting the Holy Spirit accept the relationship's function for you. Your relationship will have everything that the Holy Spirit needs to make it Holy, as the Holy Spirit wants it to be.

6. When you feel that your awareness of the Holiness of your relationship is threatened by anything, stop instantly and offer your willingness to the Holy Spirit, despite fear, to make this instant a Holy Instant. The Holy Spirit will never fail in answering. Do not forget that in your relationship your mind is made One in your awareness again, so whether the threat to your Peace seems to come from you or from the other it is the same. The Power of your extending blessing lies in the fact that it is now impossible for you

to experience fear without including the other, or for you to deal with fear without including the other. This is not necessary or possible. Just as this is impossible, it is impossible for the Holy Instant to come to your mind and not extend to the other in your Holy relationship. When you perceive fear in yourself or in the other, the Holy Instant will come to your mind when you request It.

7. When your awareness of the Holiness of your relationship is threatened, you should remember how deeply you are indebted to the other, and how much gratitude you owe them for the opportunity to extend Holiness in your awareness that your relationship with them gives to you. Pay your debt by extending Happiness. Say to yourself:

    'I desire that this instant be Holy for me so that I may extend it to the other, whom I love.
    It is not possible for me to be aware that I have Love without extending it, or for me to perceive Love without being aware that It is in me.
    It is wholly possible for me to extend Love now.
    So I choose this instant as the one to offer to the Holy Spirit, so that Its Blessing may extend to my relationship and keep Peace in my awareness.'

6. Beyond the Body

1. There is nothing outside of you. This is what you ultimately must learn, because it is in this realization that your Oneness with God is restored to your awareness. God extends only God, and God does not depart from God's Extension or make It separate from God. God's Oneness is your Home, and you have never left God or your Home. Heaven is neither a place nor a condition; It is merely your awareness of Perfect Oneness, and your Knowledge that there is nothing else outside or within this Oneness.

2. God can extend only Knowledge of God. There is nothing else to give. Your belief that you can give something outside of yourself, and get something outside of yourself, has cost you your

awareness of Heaven and of your Identity. But you have done a stranger thing than you yet realize. You have projected guilt from your mind onto the body. But a body cannot be guilty, because it cannot do anything of itself. You deceive yourself if you think that you hate the body. You hate your mind, because guilt has entered into it, and you want guilt to be separate from you, so you project it onto others. But this does not remove guilt from your mind.

3.   Mind is One, bodies are not. Only by assigning the body's properties to your mind does a split mind seem possible to you. So it is your mind that seems fragmented and private and isolated. The guilt in your mind keeps your mind split as your guilt is projected onto the body. The body then suffers and dies, because you attack it to keep your mind split, so you won't remember your Identity. Though your mind cannot attack, you can make fantasies of attack and direct the body to act them out. But it is not what the body is really capable of doing that satisfies you. Unless you believe that the body is actually acting out your fantasies, you will attack the body by increasing your projection of guilt onto it.

4.   Your mind is clearly delusional in this. It cannot attack, but you maintain that it can, and you hurt the body to prove that it can. Your mind cannot attack, but you can deceive yourself, and this is all that you do when you believe that you have attacked the body. You can project guilt, but your mind does not lose guilt by projecting it. Though you can clearly misperceive the function of the body, you cannot change the body's function from what the Holy Spirit wants to use it for. The body was not made by Love, but Love does not condemn it. It can use the body Lovingly, respecting what you have made and using it to save you from your illusions.

5.   Let your instruments of separation be reinterpreted as means for your salvation, and let them be used for Love. Welcome and support your shift from illusions of vengeance to release from them. Your perception of the body can clearly be sick, but do not project this onto the body. Your wish to make destructive what cannot destroy has no real effect at all. What is One with God is only as God wants It to be, this being God's Will. You cannot make

God's Will destructive. You can only make illusions in which your will conflicts with God's Will.

6. It is insane for you to use the body as the scapegoat for your guilt, directing its attack, and blaming it for what you wished it to do. It is impossible for you to act out illusions, because it is still the illusions that you want, and they have nothing to do with what the body can do.[1] The body does not make illusions, and illusions make the body a liability where it could be an asset to you. Your illusions make the body your enemy: weak, vulnerable, treacherous, and worthy of the hate that you invest in it. How has this served you? In your identification with a personal self, you identify with this thing that you hate: an instrument of vengeance and the perceived source of your guilt. You have done this to a thing that has no meaning, proclaiming it to be your Christ Mind's home but turning it against your Christ Mind.

7. The body is the host that your split mind has made for God, but neither God nor your Christ Mind can enter a home that harbors hate and where the personal mind has sown the seeds of vengeance, violence, and death. This thing that you made to serve your guilt stands between you and the unity of your mind. Your mind *is* joined, but you do not identify with the part that you have projected away onto a world that seems outside of you. Identifying with a body, you see yourself locked in a separate prison, removed from what you perceive, and as incapable of reaching out as being reached. You hate the body as a prison that you have made, and you want to destroy it. But you refuse to escape from it and leave it unharmed and without your guilt upon it.

8. Yet only by releasing the body from your guilt can you escape from it. The home of vengeance is not your Home; the place that you made to house your guilt is not a prison. The body is an illusion of yourself. The body is a limit imposed on the Oneness that is an Eternal Property of Mind. Oneness is internal, and It reaches to Itself. It is *not* made up of different parts which reach to each other. Oneness does not go outside Itself. Within Itself It is Limitless, and there is nothing outside of It. Oneness encompasses everything. It encompasses you entirely; you within It and It within you. There is

nothing else, anywhere or ever.

9. The body is outside of your Reality, and it only *seems* to surround you, shutting you off from the rest of your mind, and keeping you apart from it and it from you. It is not there. There is no barrier between God and you who are One with God, and you can only be separated from your Oneness with God in illusions. The body is not your Reality, though you believe that it is, and it could only be so if God were wrong. God would have had to separate Itself from What is One with It to make this possible. God would have had to make different things and to establish different orders of reality, only some of which were Love. But Love must be Forever like Itself: Forever Changeless and Forever without alternative. And so It is. You cannot put a barrier around yourself, because God has not placed a barrier between you and God.

10. You can stretch out your mind and reach to Heaven. You, who have extended your Identity to encompass another who seemed outside of you, have begun to reach beyond the body, but not outside yourself, to recognize your Limitless Identity. This cannot be outside of you, where God is not. God is not a body, and God did not make you what God is *not* and where God cannot be. You are surrounded only by God. There are no limits on you who are encompassed by God.

11. Even in your identification with a personal self you have sometimes had the experience of what you would call being 'transported beyond yourself'. This feeling of liberation far exceeds the illusion of oneness and freedom that you sometimes hope for in a special relationship. It is a sense of actual escape from limitations. If you consider what this 'transportation' really is, you will realize that you are suddenly unaware of the body, and that you join with something else that your mind enlarges to encompass. It becomes part of you as you unite with it, and both you and it become whole as you perceive neither as separate. What really happens is that you give up your illusion of limitation and you lose your fear of union. The Love that instantly replaces fear you extend to what has freed you, and you unite with it. And, while this lasts, you are not uncertain of your Identity, and you do not want to limit It. You have

escaped from fear to Peace, and you don't ask what is real; you *accept* What is Real. You have accepted Reality in place of the body, and you have let yourself be one with something beyond the body simply by not letting your mind be limited to a body.

12. This occurs regardless of the physical distance, the respective positions in space, and the differences in size and quality that seem to be between you and what you join. Time is not relevant, because you can join with something past, present, or anticipated. The 'something' can be anything and anywhere: a sight, a sound, a thought, a memory, or even a general idea without specific reference. Yet, in every case, you join it without reservation, because you love it and want to be with it. You rush to meet it, letting your sense of limitation melt away, suspending and gently setting aside the seeming 'laws' that the body obeys.

13. There is no violence in this escape from the body. You don't attack the body; you only perceive it properly. It does not limit you, because you don't want it to. You are not really 'lifted out' of it, because it cannot contain you. You go where you want to be, and you don't lose but you gain a sense of Self. In these instants of release from physical restrictions, you experience much of what happens in the Holy Instant: the lifting of the barriers of time and space, the sudden experience of Peace and Joy, and, above all, you lack awareness of the body. When it happens, you do not question whether or not all this is possible.

14. This is all possible, because you want it. The sudden expansion of your awareness of yourself that takes place with your desire for the Holy Instant is the irresistible appeal that the Holy Instant has for you. The Holy Instant calls to you to be your Self within Its Safe Embrace. The laws of limits lift from your mind to welcome you to an Open Mind that is Free. Come to this Refuge, Where you can be yourself in Peace. This does not happen through your destroying or breaking out of barriers, but through your quiet melting inward. Peace will join you in the Holy Instant simply because you have been willing to let go of the limits that you have placed on Love. You will join Love Where Love is, and Where Love has led you, in answer to Love's Gentle Call to you to be at Peace.

7. I Need Do Nothing

1. You still have too much faith in the body as a source of strength. All of your plans involve the body's comfort, protection, or enjoyment in some way. This means that you interpret the body as an end in itself and not as a means for correction, and that you still find separation from God attractive. You have not accepted correction if you still have separation as your goal, therefore you have not met your *one* responsibility – accepting correction of your perception that you are separate from God. You will not welcome correction while you prefer pain and Self-destruction.

2. There is one thing you that have never done: completely forgotten the body. Perhaps it has sometimes faded from your awareness, but it has never completely disappeared from your awareness. You are asked to do this for only an Instant, but in that Instant the miracle of correction happens. After that Instant, you will be aware of the body again, but never in quite the same way. Every Instant that you spend without an awareness of the body will give you a different view of it when you return to an awareness of it.

3. There is no instant in which the body exists at all. You always remember it or anticipate it, but you never experience it *now*. Only the personal self's seeming past and projected future make the body seem real to you. Time controls your perception of the body entirely, because your perception of separation from God is never wholly in the present. In any single Instant, you would experience the attraction of separation from God as pain and nothing else, and if you recognized this, you would avoid it. Guilt has no attraction to you *now*. Its whole attraction to you is imaginary, therefore you must think of in the past or in the future.

4. Until you are willing to see no past and no future for just an Instant, you will have reservations about the Holy Instant. You cannot *prepare* for the Holy Instant without placing It in the future. The instant that you desire the Holy Instant you will be released in It. In your perception that you are in a world, one way to God is to spend your time preparing for the Holy Instant, and this does have its moments of success. This course does not attempt to teach you more than that path teaches in time, but it does aim at saving you

time. You may be trying to follow a very long road to the Goal of God that you have accepted. It is extremely difficult for you to reach total correction of your perception that you are separate from God by fighting against perceived 'sin'. You will have to expend enormous effort trying to make Holy the body that the personal mind despises. It is also not necessary for you to spend a lifetime in contemplation and long periods of meditation aimed at detachment from the body. All of these attempts would ultimately succeed because of their Purpose, but these means are tedious and very time consuming, and they all look to the future for release from a present state of unworthiness and inadequacy.

5. Your way is different from these paths, not in Purpose, but in means. A Holy relationship is your means for saving time. One Instant of Holiness that you extend to your relationship with another restores Reality to your mind. You *are* prepared for the Holy Instant, and all that you now need to remember is that you *need do nothing*. It is far more useful now for you to concentrate on this than to consider what you *should* do. When Peace comes at last after wrestling with temptation and fighting against 'sin', when enlightenment comes after a lifetime of contemplation, or when the Goal is achieved in any way, it will come with the happy realization: *I need do nothing*.

6. Here is the ultimate release that you will eventually find. You do not need time for this, because time has been saved for you since you extended your True Self to your perception of another. This is the special means that this course uses to save you time. You are not making use of this course if you insist on neglecting the means that was made for you in favor of other means. Save time for your Christ Mind with this one preparation, and practice doing nothing else: 'I need do nothing.' This is a statement of undivided allegiance to Christ. Believe it for just one Instant, and you will accomplish more than you would accomplish in a century of contemplation or of struggle against temptation.

7. To 'do' involves the body. When you recognize that you need do nothing, you will withdraw the body's value from your mind. This is the door through which you will quickly slip past centuries of

effort to escape from time. This is the way that the separation loses all of its attraction for you *now*, because you deny time, and the past and the future are gone for you. When you need do nothing you have no need for time. For you to do nothing is for you to rest and to make a place within your mind where the activity of the body ceases to demand your attention. The Holy Spirit then comes into, and abides in, this place of rest within you. And the Holy Spirit will remain with you when you forget again, and the body's activities return to occupy your conscious mind.

8.   There is always this place of rest within you. Within it, you are more aware of the Quiet Center than of the storming personal mind raging around it. This Quiet Center in Which you do nothing remains with you and gives you rest in the midst of all of the busy doing to which the Holy Spirit sends you. From this Center, you will be directed in how to use the body for correction of your perception of separation from God. It is this Center, from Which the body is absent, that will keep you aware that the body cannot separate you from God.

8. The Little Garden

1.   It is only your awareness of the body that makes Love seem limited to you, because the body *is* a limit on Love. Your belief in limited Love was the body's origin, and it was made by you to limit the Limitless. This is not merely a metaphor; the body was made to limit *you*. You cannot know yourself as an idea when you see yourself in a body. Through the personal mind, everything that you recognize is some external *form*. You cannot even think of God without a body or some form that you think you recognize.

2.   The body cannot *know*, and while you limit your awareness to its tiny senses, you will not see the Limitlessness that surrounds you. God cannot come into a body, and you cannot join God in a body. Your limits on Love will always seem to shut out God from your mind and seem to keep you apart from God. A body is like a tiny fence around a little part of a Glorious Completion. It's like an infinitely small circle around a very tiny segment of Heaven that is splintered from the Whole and that proclaims that God cannot

enter its tiny kingdom.

3.   The personal mind rules cruelly within this kingdom. To defend this speck of dust, it wants you to fight against Reality. This fragment of God's mind that has been limited to a body and a personal self is such a tiny part of your Whole Mind, that, if you could see your Whole Mind, you would see instantly that it is like the tiniest sunbeam to the sun, or the faintest ripple on the surface of the ocean. In their amazing arrogance, the tiny sunbeam has decided that it is the sun, and the almost imperceptible ripple has decided that it is the ocean. Think how alone and frightened are these little thoughts, these infinitesimal illusions that hold themselves apart from their limitless selves. To the sunbeam the sun is its devouring 'enemy', and the ripple is terrified of the ocean that wants to swallow it.

4.   But neither the sun nor the ocean is even aware of all this strange and meaningless activity. They merely continue, unaware that they are feared and hated by a tiny segment of themselves. But that segment is not lost to them, because the sun would not be the sun without its beams of light, and the ocean would not be the ocean without ripples on its surface. And what the sunbeam and the ripple think in no way changes their total dependence on the sun and the ocean for what they are. Their whole existence remains in the sun and the ocean. Without the sun the sunbeam would be gone, and the ripple is inconceivable without the ocean.

5.   And so it is with you who seem to be in a world inhabited by bodies. Each body seems to house a separate, disconnected thought that lives isolated and apart from your mind, which perceives it. And you seem separate from the Mind of God, with Which you are One. Your tiny fragment of mind seems self-contained, needing others for some things but by no means wholly dependent on God's Mind, with Which it is One, for everything. But it needs the Mind with Which it is One to give it meaning, because by itself it means nothing. It does not have a life apart and by itself.

6.   Like the sun and the ocean in the metaphor above, your Wholeness continues, completely unaware that you regard yourself as an

isolated personal self. This tiny part of your Wholeness, which you have given over to identify with a personal self, is not missing from the Whole, because it could not exist if it were separate from the Whole, and the Whole would not be Whole without it. It is not a separate kingdom ruled by the idea of separation from the Whole, nor does a fence surround it and prevent it from joining with God, Which *is* your Wholeness. This little part of you is no different from the Whole of you, being continuous with It and One with It. It does not lead a separate life, because its Life is the Oneness of your Being in God.

7. Do not accept the little, fenced-off personal self as you. The sun and the ocean are nothing beside What you are. Neither the sun nor the ocean has the Power that resides in you. Do you want to remain within your tiny kingdom, a sorry and bitter ruler who looks on nothing, yet would die to defend it? The little personal self is not your home. Surrounding it is the Glorious Wholeness of God's Love, Which offers all of Its Happiness and Deep Content to every part of Itself. The little part that you think you have separated off is no exception.

8. Love does not know bodies, and Love reaches to everything that is One with It. Love's Limitlessness *is* Its Meaning. It is extended completely impartially, and It encompasses Everything to preserve and keep Itself Complete. In your tiny kingdom of the personal mind, you have so little! This is where you need to call on Love to enter. Look at the dry, unproductive, scorched, and joyless desert that makes up your little kingdom, and realize the Life and Joy that Love will bring to it from God. You will return to God with Love.

9. The Thought of God surrounds your little kingdom, and It waits at the barrier you have built to It to come inside and rain life-giving water upon the barren ground. See how life springs up everywhere! The desert of your mind becomes a green, deep, and quiet garden from which you can extend Love in your awareness in place of the personal mind's barren projections. Everything to which you extend Love will return Love from Heaven to you. You extend Holiness one by one, but the Love that you extend in your perceptions of others will stay with you. Under Love's Beneficence, your

little garden will expand and reach out to your perceptions, which thirst for living water but cannot find it in the isolation of a personal mind.

10. Extend your True Self in place of the world of separation that you perceive, and turn your mind into a quiet garden where you receive Its blessing. This blessing will grow and extend across the desert of your mind, leaving nothing that you perceive locked away from Love. As you extend your True Self, you will recognize your True Self and see the Loving garden of your mind gently transformed into Heaven, with all of God's Love shining upon it.

11. The Holy Instant is your invitation to Love to enter into your bleak and joyless kingdom to transform it into a garden of Peace and welcome. Love's Answer is inevitable. It will come into the Holy Instant, because you came without a body, and you didn't put up any barriers to interfere with Love's glad arrival. In the Holy Instant you ask of Love only What It offers without Limit. You ask for Everything, and you receive Everything. Your Wholeness will lift straight to Heaven the tiny part of your mind that you tried to hide from Heaven. No part of Love calls on the Whole of Love in vain. No Part of God remains outside of God.

12. You can be sure that Love has entered your special relationship, and It entered fully at your weak request. You do not recognize that Love has come, because you have not yet let go of all of the barriers that you project onto the other. You will not be able to welcome Love without extending It to your perception of the other to replace the personal mind's projections. You cannot know God in the isolation of a personal mind, and God cannot know you without the part of your mind where you perceive a world. In the Wholeness of your mind, you are aware of Love, and Love does not fail to recognize you.

13. You have reached the end of your ancient journey of separation, but you have not yet realized that it is over. You are worn and tired, and the desert's dust still seems to cloud your eyes and keep you blind. But you have welcomed the Holy Spiri,t and the Holy Spirit has come and welcomes you. The Holy Spirit has waited long to give you welcome, so receive it now, because the Holy Spirit wants

you to know the Holy Spirit. Only a little wall of dust is projected between you and your perception of the other in your Holy relationship, so blow on it lightly and with happy laughter, and it will fall away, so that you can walk into the garden Love has prepared for your entire mind.

9. The Two Worlds

1.   You have been told to bring illusion to Truth and guilt to Holiness, and that error must be corrected at its source. And so it is the tiny part of your Mind that seems split off and separate from the rest of your Mind that the Holy Spirit needs. The rest of your Mind is fully in God's Keeping, and It doesn't need a guide. But this small part, which is wild and delusional, needs help, because in its delusions it thinks it is its own god, whole and omnipotent, sole ruler of a kingdom it set apart to tyrannize and limit with madness. This is the little part that you think you stole from Heaven. Give it back to Heaven, because Heaven has not lost sight of it, but *you* have lost sight of Heaven. Let the Holy Spirit remove from this tiny part of your mind the withered kingdom in which you have set it off from the rest of your mind. Your split mind has surrounded it with illusions, guarded it with attack, and reinforced it with hate. But within its barricades a tiny Part of God *does* reside, Complete and Holy and Serene, unaware of what you think surrounds It.

2.   Do not be separate from God, because God surrounds this tiny part of your mind. God has brought Oneness to it, exchanging Truth for your little offering of illusion. This is done simply because of what the little kingdom you offer really is. You see illusions and lifelessness only through the body's eyes and the personal mind's perceptions. The body's sight is so distorted, and the messages that it transmits to you who made it to limit your awareness are little and limited and so fragmented that they are meaningless.

3.   Insane messages seem to be returned to your mind from the world of bodies that you made with insanity. These messages bear witness that the world is true, because you projected these messages onto it to make it seem true. Everything that these messages relay to you is external, and there are no messages that speak to you of What lies

within your mind, below this level of perception, because the body cannot communicate Truth. Its eyes cannot perceive Truth, its senses are unaware of Truth, and its tongue cannot relay Truth's Messages. But God can bring you to Truth, if you are willing to follow the Holy Spirit through the seeming terror of the level of your mind that lies between the level of the world that you perceive and God, and if you trust the Holy Spirit to not leave you there. It is not the Holy Spirit's purpose to frighten you, but it seems to be your purpose in your identification with a personal self. You are severely tempted to abandon the Holy Spirit at the outside ring of fear, but the Holy Spirit will lead you safely through fear and far beyond it.

4.   The circle of fear lies just below the level of your mind that the body sees, and it seems to be the whole foundation on which the world-level of your mind is based. Here are all of your split mind's illusions: its twisted thoughts and insane attacks; its fury and vengeance and betrayal, which were made to keep your guilt in place so that the world could arise from it and keep it hidden. But the shadow of guilt rises to the surface to darkly color the external manifestations on the world-level of your mind and to bring despair, loneliness, and joylessness there. The intensity of your guilt is veiled by the heavy form of a world that seems to be separate from your mind to keep guilt hidden. The body cannot see this level of guilt and fear, because the body was made to protect that level from your awareness. The body's eyes will never look at the guilt in your mind, but they will see what guilt dictates.

5.   As long as you believe that your guilt is real, you will project it onto the body and see it there, and the body will act as guilt directs it. The seeming reality of your guilt is the illusion that makes guilt seem heavy, opaque, impenetrable, and a real foundation for the personal mind's thought system. Your guilt's thinness and trans-parency are not apparent until you see the Love beyond it, and then you see it is a fragile veil before the Truth.

6.   Guilt is like a bank of low clouds that looks solid as it blocks the sun. But its impenetrable appearance is wholly an illusion. The clouds give way to the mountain tops that rise above them, and

they have no power at all to hold you back if you are willing to climb above them and into the sun. Try to touch guilt, and like a cloud it disappears; attempt to grasp it, and your hands hold nothing.

7.   In clouds you can imagine you see a whole world rising: A solid mountain range, a lake, a city – all this rises in your imagination, and what you project onto them you see there to assure you that it *is* there. Figures move about, actions seem real, and forms shift from loveliness to grotesque. They go back and forth as long as you want to play the game of make-believe. But, however long you play at it, and regardless of how much imagination you bring to it, you do not confuse what you imagine in clouds with the world you stand on, and you do not seek to make it real.

8.   This is how it should be with the dark clouds of your guilt, which are no more impenetrable and substantial than the clouds in the sky. You will not bruise yourself against them as you travel through them. Let the Holy Spirit teach you that your guilt is insubstantial as It guides you past it, because beyond your guilt is your Real Perception, which reflects Love. Guilt's shadow falls on the world that you perceive that is far from Love, but guilt cannot cast a shadow on Love.

9.   Love is your Real Perception, Where guilt meets with forgiveness. Here, the world that seems outside of your mind you see without the shadow of guilt upon it. Here is your new Perception, Where everything is bright and shiny with Innocence, washed in the waters of forgiveness, and cleansed of every evil thought that you laid upon it. Here, you do not attack your Christ Mind, so *you* are welcome. Here is your Innocence, waiting to protect you and to make you ready for your final step inward to God. Here, you lay guilt aside, and it is gently replaced by Purity and Love.

10. But your forgiving is not the end. Your forgiving makes you aware of Love, but it does not make you One with Love. Your forgiving is the source of your *healing*, because it reminds you of Love, but it is not the source of *Love*. Your forgiving leads you up to the Source of Love, Where Love can *be* without interference, so that God can take the final step unhindered. You cannot take the step yourself beyond

this Holy Place before God, because God will transport you to Someplace completely different from the world in your mind. In God is the Source of Love, and in God nothing is perceived, forgiven, or transformed. In God, Everything is Known.

11. This course will lead you to God, but God is still beyond the scope of its lesson plan. There is no need to speak of What must Forever lie beyond words. Your learning cannot go beyond your Real Perception, and, when you attain your Real Perception, you will go beyond It, but in a way that is different from *learning*. Where your learning ends, God begins. You do not learn in God, because God is Complete. Do not dwell on What you cannot yet attain, because there is too much for you to learn. You still must attain your readiness for God.

12. You do not learn Love, because Its Meaning lies within Itself. Your learning ends when you have recognized all that Love is *not*. What Love is *not* is what interferes with Love in your awareness, and this is what you need to undo. You don't learn Love, because there never was a time when you did not know Love. Learning is useless in the Presence of God, because God's Knowledge of you and your Knowledge of God transcends all learning. In God's Presence, everything that you have learned is meaningless and is replaced Forever by the Knowledge of Love and Its One Meaning.

13. The once unholy purpose of your relationship with the other has been uprooted from the world of fear that you perceive, safely brought through your barrier of guilt, washed with forgiveness, and firmly rooted in your Perception of Love. From Love it calls to you to follow the course it took, rising high above illusions and landing gently before the gates of Heaven. The Holy Instant, Which you extend to your Holy relationship, is the Love that comes to you from beyond your forgiving and that reminds you of All that lies beyond your forgiving. It is through forgiving that you remember Love.

14. When your Memory of God comes to you in the Holy Place of forgiving within you, you will remember nothing else, because memory will be as useless to you as learning. Your only Purpose will be extending God. You cannot know this until your every

perception has been cleansed, purified, and finally removed Forever. Your forgiving only removes the untrue from your mind by lifting your projections of guilt and fear where you perceive a world and gently replacing them with a Perception of Innocence and Safety. This is your purpose *now*, and it is here that Peace awaits you.

Chapter 19

The Attainment of Peace

1. Healing and Faith

1. As was stated earlier in this course, when you have wholly dedicated a situation to Truth, your attainment of Peace is inevitable. Your attainment of Peace is the proof of the wholeness of your dedication. You cannot attain Peace without your faith that only God is Real, because what you have dedicated to Truth as its only Goal is brought to Truth *by* your faith that only God is Real. Your faith that only God is Real must encompass all of your mind where you perceive a world for you to perceive it as meaningful and whole. If your entire mind is not included in your faith that only God is Real, then your faith is limited, and your dedication is incomplete, because you have faith in another reality beside God.

2. Properly perceived, every situation is an opportunity for you to heal your entire mind of your perception of separation from God. You are healed when you offer faith that your Christ Mind is your Reality and you release yourself from the personal mind's demands. You share the Holy Spirit's Perception when you see yourself freed of the personal mind, and you let the Holy Spirit heal your perceptions through you. You joining your mind with the Holy Spirit in this purpose is what gives this purpose any Reality, because you make It Whole, and Wholeness *is* healing. When you join the Mind in Which all healing rests, the body is healed, because you came without it.

3. The body cannot heal, because it cannot make itself sick. The body does not need healing, because its health or sickness depends entirely on how your mind perceives it, and the purpose for which your mind wants to use it. It is obvious that a segment of your mind can see itself as separated from Oneness. When this happens, the body becomes a weapon of the personal mind to use against Oneness and to demonstrate the 'fact' that your separation from

431

God has occurred. The body is then the instrument of illusion, and it acts accordingly: It sees what is not there, it hears what Truth has never said, and it behaves insanely, because it is imprisoned by insanity.

4. Do not overlook the earlier statement that your lack of faith that only God is Real will lead you straight to illusions. When you lack faith that only God is Real, you look on bodies as real, and bodies cannot be One as mind can. If you look on bodies as real, then, you have established a condition in which it becomes impossible for you to unite your mind, because then the world outside of you seems real to you and not just made up of your own thoughts. Your lack of faith that only God is Real results in your mind being split, and it keeps you from being healed. Your lack of faith that only God is Real opposes the Holy Spirit's purpose of healing, and it brings illusions, centered on bodies, to your mind to stand between you and the Holy Spirit. The body then seems to be sick, because you have made it to be an 'enemy' of healing and the opposite of Truth.

5. Obviously, your faith that only God is Real must be the opposite of your lack of faith that only God is Real. But the difference in how your faith and your lack of faith operate may be less apparent to you, even though how they operate follows directly from their fundamental differences. Your lack of faith that only God is Real always limits you and attacks you, because you are really One with God; your faith that only God is Real removes all of your limitations and makes you Whole again in your awareness. Your lack of faith that only God is Real interposes illusions between you and God; your faith that only God is Real removes all obstacles that seem to rise between you and God. Your lack of faith that only God is Real always results in your dedication to illusions; your faith that only God is Real always leads to your dedication to Truth. It is impossible for you to be partially dedicated to each, because in Truth there are no illusions, and in illusions there is no Truth. Truth and illusions cannot be perceived in the same place. For you to dedicate yourself to both illusions and to Truth is for you to set up a goal for yourself that is forever unattainable. The illusion part of the goal sets up the body as reality and is therefore a means of

attacking Truth; the Truth part of the goal wants to heal and therefore calls on your mind, not on the body.

6. The compromise that you try to make to keep both Truth and illusion as your goal is the belief that the body, not the mind, must be healed. This divided goal gives both the body and the mind equal reality to you. This results in your perception that your mind is divided into little parts that seem whole but are limited to bodies and so are unconnected. This illusion does not harm bodies, but it does maintain the delusional thought system of your split mind. Healing is needed in your mind, and it is in your mind that healing *is*. God brings healing where it is needed. Sickness and healing are together in your mind, and when you see them together, you will recognize that all of your attempts to keep both Truth and illusion in your mind resulted in your dedication to illusions. And you will give up illusions when they are brought to Truth, and you see that they are totally irreconcilable with Truth in every way.

7. Truth and illusion can have no connection, and this is forever true, no matter how much you seek to connect them. But illusions are always connected to illusions as Truth is always connected to Truth. Each is a united, complete thought system that is completely disconnected from the other. When you perceive this, you will recognize that your separation from God is only in your mind, and that it is there that it must be healed. The result of an idea is never separate from its source. Your idea of separation resulted in the body and remains connected to it. The body is sick because of your mind's misidentification with it. You think that you are protecting the body by hiding this connection from your awareness, because this concealment seems to keep your identification with the body safe from the 'attack' of Truth.

8. Understand how much this strange concealment has seemed to hurt your mind, and how confused you are about your own identity because of it. You do not see how great is the devastation wrought by your lack of faith that only God is Real. Your lack of faith that only God is Real is an attack on yourself that seems justified by its results. By withholding faith that only God is Real, you see only what is unworthy of your faith, and you cannot see

beyond this barrier of seeming unworthiness to your Oneness with God.

9. For you to have faith that only God is Real is for you to heal yourself. It is the sign that you have accepted correction of your perception of separation from God, and therefore that you want to extend it. Through your faith that only God is Real, you receive the Gift of Freedom from the personal self's past, and you extend Freedom to replace the world in your mind. In your Holy relationship, you do not use the personal mind's perceptions of the past to condemn the other; you freely choose to overlook all errors of separation and to look on Oneness instead. Your faith in Oneness is fully justified. There is no justification for your lack of faith, but your faith that only God is Real is always justified.

10. Your faith that only God is Real is the opposite of fear, and it is as much a part of Love as fear is a part of attack. Your faith that only God is Real is your acknowledgment of Oneness. It is your gracious acknowledgment that your Whole Mind is loved by God and you as yourself. It is God's Love that joins your mind in Oneness, and, for you to be aware of God's Love, you must not project any part of your mind away from yourself by perceiving a world of separation. In your faith in God, your mind is joined in the Holy Instant to release you from guilt. Look on your Christ Mind in place of the world of separation, and your mind will be healed, because you will see What makes your faith Forever justified everywhere.

11. Faith is God's Gift to you through the Holy Spirit. In your lack of faith that only God is Real, you look on the personal mind and its projections onto a world, and you judge them as unworthy of forgiveness. But through your faith, which sees that only God is Real, you are already forgiven the personal mind, and you are freed of all of the guilt that you have laid upon yourself through it. Through your faith that only God is Real, you see your mind only as it is *now*, because you do not judge it by the personal self's past, but you see only your Christ Mind. Through your faith that only God is Real, you do not look through the body's eyes or look to bodies for its justification. Your faith calls forth your Real Perception.

12. Your faith that only God is Real, and the Real Perception that you see through your faith, are easily translated to God, because this faith arises from the Holy Spirit's Perception, and is the sign that you share Perception with the Holy Spirit. Your faith that only God is Real is extended to your Christ Mind through the Holy Spirit, and it is as wholly acceptable to God as it is to your Christ Mind. It is therefore offered to you. Your Holy relationship with the other, with its new purpose, offers you the faith that only God is Real to extend in your mind where you perceive a world. Your lack of faith has driven your mind apart so that you do not recognize salvation in your mind because of your perception of a world of separation. Yet your faith unites your mind in the Holiness that you perceive, not with the body's eyes, but with the Holy Spirit in Which your mind is One.

13. Grace is given to your mind, not to a body. When your mind receives Grace, it looks instantly beyond the body, and it sees the Holy Place in your mind where your mind is healed of its perception of separation from God. Your mind is where Grace is given to you and where It remains. Extend Grace and blessing to the other in your Holy relationship, because you and the other and Grace are together in your mind. Your entire mind is healed by Grace so that you can heal through your faith that only God is Real.

14. In the Holy Instant, you stand before the Mind that you share with God. Put aside your lack of faith that only God is Real, and bring your mind and all that it perceives to God. There you will see that by your faith your relationship was made Holy, and that by your faith you forgive yourself everything. Before God's Mind, no error interferes with your Calm Perception, Which easily brings the miracle of healing to all of your errors equally. What your extensions of Love are meant to do they do, returning Love to your entire mind from the Mind of God.

15. As your lack of faith will keep your mind divided and barren, so will your faith that only God is Real help the Holy Spirit prepare your mind to be aware again of Wholeness and Life. Your faith that only God is Real brings you Peace, so it calls on Truth to fill your prepared mind with Love. Truth follows faith and Peace and

completes the process that they began by bringing Love to your awareness. Your faith that only God is Real is still a learning goal for you, and you will no longer need it when you have learned that only God is Real. But Truth stays with you Forever.

16. Let your dedication be to the Eternal and learn how to not interfere with It or to limit It with time. What you think you do to the Eternal, you do to *you*. You are One with God and Limitless, with Power over Everything. You can limit a body, but an idea is free, and it can only be limited by the mind which thinks it. An idea remains joined to the mind which thinks it, and the mind limits it or sets it free, depending on the purpose that the mind chooses for itself.

2. Sin versus Error

1. It is essential that you do not confuse error with *sin*, because it is the distinction between them that makes your salvation possible. Error can be corrected, but sin, were it possible, would be irreversible. Your belief in sin is based on your firm conviction that minds, not bodies, can attack, and that your mind is forever guilty unless, or until, a mind that is not part of it gives it absolution. Error calls for correction, but sin calls for punishment. Your belief that punishment is correction is clearly insane.

2. Sin is not error, because the idea of sin entails an arrogance which the idea of error lacks. Sin is the idea that you have successfully violated Reality. Your belief in sin proclaims that your attack on God is real, and that your guilt is justified. It assumes that you have succeeded in losing your Innocence and in making yourself into something that is not of God. So you do not see that God's Oneness is Eternal, and you see God's Will as open to opposition and defeat. The idea of sin is the grand illusion underlying all of the personal mind's self-inflation, because the personal mind believes that it has changed God and has rendered God incomplete.

3. You can be mistaken, you can deceive yourself, and you can turn your mind against yourself, *but you cannot sin*. There is nothing real that you can do that will change your Reality or make you guilty. But sin would do this, because this is its purpose. Yet, for all the

436

wild insanity inherent in the idea of sin, it is impossible, because the wages of sin *is* death, and you are Immortal and cannot die.

4. A major tenet in the personal mind's insane religion is that it is not an error for you to believe in sin because sin is 'truth', but that for you to believe in your Innocence is to deceive yourself. The personal mind believes it is arrogant for you to believe in your Purity, and your acceptance of yourself as 'sinful' it perceives as 'holiness'. It is this doctrine that replaces the Reality that your Oneness with God is Willed by God Forever. This doctrine is not humility but an attempt to wrest you away from Truth and to keep you separate from It.

5. The personal mind finds it indefensible for you to attempt to reinterpret your belief in separation from God as an error. The idea of sin is wholly sacred to its thought system, and if you must approach this idea, you must do so with reverence and with awe. Sin is the personal mind's most 'holy' concept; wholly true to it, and, as such, necessarily protected with every defense at the personal mind's disposal. Your perception of your 'sinfulness' is the personal mind's best defense of itself, and the one which all of its other defenses serve. Your perception of your sinfulness is its armor, its protection, and the fundamental purpose it has for the special relationship.

6. You can indeed say that the personal mind makes its world on the idea of sin, because only in such a world could everything be upside down. The idea that separation from God is real is the strange illusion that makes guilt seem heavy and impenetrable to you, and that makes the foundation of the world that you perceive seem solid. Sin is the idea that *seems* to have changed Creation from God's Oneness to an ideal that the personal mind wants: a mindless, corruptible, and decaying world of bodies that it rules. But this is only your *mistake*, which can easily be undone by Truth, because Truth corrects mistakes when Truth is left to judge them. Yet, if you give your mistake the status of 'truth', then to what can you bring it to be judged? The 'holiness' of sin is kept in place for you by you giving it the status of 'truth'. If sin is 'truth', then you must bring everything to *it* to be judged. But your perception that

separation from God is real is only a mistake which must be brought to Truth. It is impossible for you to have faith in sin, because your belief in sin means that you *lack faith*. But it *is* possible for you to have faith that a mistake can be corrected.

7.   There is no thought more defended by the personal mind than the idea that your separation from God is real. To the personal mind, the idea of sin is not a mistake; sin is the natural expression of what you have made yourself to be. To the personal mind, sin is your 'reality'; the 'truth' that it is impossible for you to escape. Sin is your past, present, and future. You have corrupted part of God and changed God's Mind completely. Mourn the death of God, Which sin has killed! This is the personal mind's wish, which, in its madness, it believes you have accomplished.

8.   Don't you want to know that your idea of separation from God, and all that it has made, is nothing more than a mistake that you can so easily correct that it is like walking through a mist into the sun? That *is* all that it is. Maybe you are tempted to agree with the personal mind, that it is far better to be sinful than mistaken. But think carefully before you allow yourself to make this choice, because it is your choice between hell and Heaven.

3. The Unreality of Sin

1.   You can see your attraction to separation from God in the idea that it is a sin, but not in the idea that it is an error in perception. When you perceive separation from God as sin, and therefore as real, you repeat it over and over again in many forms, because you are attracted to it. You might become so afraid of punishment that you do not act out certain forms of separation, but, while you are attracted to separation from God, you will suffer from guilt and not let go of the idea that it is a sin. Separation from God will still call to you, and your mind will hear it and yearn for it, making you a willing captive to guilt's sick appeal. Sin is the idea that your separation from God is an evil that you cannot correct but that you will always desire. It is an essential part of the personal mind, and as long as you want the personal mind, you will want your separation from God to be a sin – to be real. From this perspective,

you fear an avenging separate God as the only thing that can stamp out your sin.

2. The personal mind thinks that your separation from God calls for punishment, and it does not think it possible that your belief that it is real calls for Love to correct it. And that *Love always answers*. The personal mind brings sin to fear in its demand for punishment. But punishment is another form of protecting your idea that separation and guilt are real, because only what has really happened can deserve punishment. Punishment is the great preserver of the idea that your perception of separation from God is real; that sin has occurred. You want what you think is real, and you will not let go of what you think is real.

3. While you still want to be separate from God, the idea that separation from God is only an error in your perception is not attractive to you. What you see clearly as a mistake you will want to correct. Sometimes, you can repeat a form of separation over and over again with obviously distressing results but without its losing its appeal to you, because it's a sin, and is therefore uncorrectable. But if you change its status from a 'sin' to a 'mistake' you will not repeat it; you will merely stop it and let it go. However, if guilt remains, you will simply change to another form of separation, granting that the other form was a mistake and correctable, but this one is a sin and therefore is not. This is not really a change in your perception, because you will still believe that some forms of separation are a sin, and that they are in need of punishment, not correction.[1]

4. The Holy Spirit cannot punish sin, because the Holy Spirit cannot perceive sin, only mistakes. Correcting mistakes is what God has entrusted the Holy Spirit to do. The Holy Spirit does not know sin, and the idea that some of your mistakes cannot be corrected is meaningless to the Holy Spirit. Every mistake calls for correction. Your call for punishment is meaningless, and your every mistake must be a call for Love. The idea of sin is the idea that separation from God is real, and your belief in sin is only a mistake that you want to keep hidden. It is a call for Love that you want to keep unheard and unanswered by the Holy Spirit.

439

5.   Like you, the Holy Spirit can clearly see that you make mistakes in time. But you do not share the Holy Spirit's recognition of the difference between time and Eternity. When correction is completed, the only time is *now*, which *is* Eternity. The Holy Spirit can teach you to look on time differently, and to see beyond it to Eternity, but not while you believe in sin; you must believe that your perception of separation from God is an error that can be corrected in your mind. Your belief in sin is your belief that your perception is unchangeable and that your mind must accept as true what it is told through your perception of separation. And if you do not accept what your belief in sin seems to show you, then the personal mind judges you as insane. But if you believe in the personal mind as the only power that can change your perception, you keep your mind impotent, and your hold it to the body by your fear of the changed perception that the Holy Spirit in your mind can bring you.

6.   When you are tempted to believe that separation from God is real, remember this: If the separation is real, you and God are not Real. Creation is extension, and God extends only God, so it is impossible that What is Part of God is totally unlike the rest of God. If separation is sin and not a mistake, then God must be at war with God. God must be split between good and evil; partial sanity and partial insanity. God would've created what wills to destroy God and has the power to do so. Isn't it easier to accept that you have been mistaken than to believe this?

7.   While you believe that bodies are real, you will believe that separation from God is real and that it is therefore not a mistaken perception, but a sin. While you believe that bodies can unite, you will find separation from God attractive and believe that it is precious. Your belief that bodies limit your mind leads to your perception of a world that seems to 'prove' your separation from God everywhere. God's Oneness seems split apart and overthrown. If separation is sin, it 'proves' that God's Wholeness cannot remain Itself or prevail against your desire for separation. If separation is sin and not error, then you perceive the personal mind as mightier than God. Is this humility or madness?

8. If your separation from God is sin and not just a mistaken perception, then it is forever beyond the hope of healing. The idea of sin implies a power beyond God's Power that is capable of making another will that can attack and overcome God's Will. So you seem to have a will apart from God that is stronger than God's Will, and God's Oneness seems to be fragmented into different wills that are eternally opposed to God's Will and to each other's wills. But your Holy relationship now has as its Purpose the goal of proving that this is impossible. Heaven smiles on your relationship, and your belief in sin has been uprooted by Heaven's Love. You still see the separation, because you do not yet realize that its foundation is gone. The source of your perception of separation from God has been removed, so you can cherish it only a little while before it vanishes. It is only your habit of looking for it that remains in you.

9. Yet now you can look at your perception of separation with Heaven's Smile on your lips and Heaven's Blessing on your sight. You will not see separation for long, because, in your new Perception, your mind corrects separation when you seem to see it, and it becomes invisible. You will recognize errors quickly and give them over for correction to be healed, not hidden. You will be healed of your belief in sin, and of all of its ravages, the instant that you stop giving it power over your perceptions. You will overcome your mistaken projections Joyously when you release your mind from the belief that separation from God is possible.

10. In the Holy Instant, you see Heaven shining in your entire mind, and you shine upon all that you perceive in happy acknowledgment of the Grace that has been given to your entire mind. Your perception of separation from God will not prevail against the Oneness of your mind when Heaven shines upon it. Forget what you have seen in the personal self's past, and raise your eyes in faith to What you can see now. Your barriers to Heaven will disappear before your Holy Perception, now that you can see Truth. Don't look back at what has been removed from your mind, but look for the Glory that has been restored to your mind.

11. In your Holy relationship, look on your Christ Mind instead of on

the personal mind's projections on the other, and do not let the belief in sin rise to blind you. Your belief in sin will keep your mind split, but your Christ Mind wants you to look on your True Self to replace the world in your mind. Your Holy relationship is now a healing place where you can bring all of the personal mind's weary projections to be exchanged. Here is your rest after a long journey. Your Holy relationship brings rest closer to your entire mind.

4. The Obstacles to Peace

1. As Peace extends from deep within you to embrace your entire mind and give it rest, It will encounter many obstacles. Some of them you will recognize that you impose; other obstacles will seem to come from the world that you perceive outside of you. Yet Peace will gently undo these obstacles and extend past them completely unencumbered. The extension of the Holy Spirit's purpose from your Holy relationship to your entire mind will quietly extend to every aspect of your life, surrounding you with the glowing Happiness and calm awareness of Complete Protection. You will carry your relationship's message of Love and Safety and Freedom to exchange for the personal mind's projections and to heal your mind. You will not wait to extend this message, because you will recognize in the personal mind's projections your call for God. You will extend rest to your entire mind as rest was extended to you from your Holy relationship.

2. You will do all this when the Peace that already lies deep within you first extends in your mind and then flows across the obstacles that you have placed before It. You will do this, because you undertake it with the Holy Spirit, Which leaves nothing unfinished. There is nothing outside of you to be sure of, but you can be sure of this: The Holy Spirit within you asks that you offer to the Holy Spirit a resting place where you can rest in the Holy Spirit. The Holy Spirit answered your invitation and entered your relationship to make it Holy. Now return the Holy Spirit's Graciousness, and enter into a Relationship with the Holy Spirit. The Holiness of your relationship comes from the Holy Spirit or you would not be able to see Christ in place of the personal mind's projections onto the other.

3.   The gratitude that you owe to the Holy Spirit, the Holy Spirit asks you to accept, because you are One. When you look with Gentle Graciousness on your perception of the other, you are beholding the Holy Spirit, because you are looking with What the Holy Spirit *is*. You cannot see the Holy Spirit, but you can look out from your mind and choose to perceive Truth, and, seeing Truth, you will see All that you need to know. When the Peace in you has been extended to be all that you perceive, the Holy Spirit's function will be complete. You will have no need for perceiving then. When God takes the last step, the Holy Spirit will gather all of the thanks and gratitude that you have offered to the Holy Spirit and will lay them Gently before God in the name of Christ. And God will accept them in Christ's Name. You have no need of perception in the Presence of your Christ Mind's Gratitude.

a. *The First Obstacle: The Desire to Get Rid of It*

1.   The first obstacle within you that Peace must flow across is your desire to get rid of It. Peace cannot extend unless you keep It, because you are the center from which It radiates outward in your awareness. You are Peace's Home, Its Tranquil Dwelling Place from Which It gently reaches out, never leaving you. If you make Peace homeless, then Peace cannot abide in What is One with God. For Peace to spread across your entire mind and bring it rest, It must begin within you and be extended by you to replace all of the personal mind's projections.

2.   Why don't you want Peace? What do you think that Peace must replace to dwell within you? What seems to be the cost that you are unwilling to pay for Peace? A little barrier of separation still seems to stand between you and your Holy relationship. Do not reinforce it, because you are not asked to let it go for the isolation of a little personal mind but for the Limitlessness of your Christ Mind. Your Christ Mind wants to extend Peace across your entire mind, and this must begin within you. Do not let a tiny barrier stand between you and salvation for your entire mind. The little remnant of separation that you still cherish is the first obstacle that the Peace within you encounters as It tries to extend to be all that you

perceive. This little wall of Self-hatred still opposes the Will of God and keeps It limited in your awareness.

3.   The Holy Spirit's purpose rests in Peace within you, but you are unwilling to wholly join with It. You still oppose the Will of God by just a little, and that little is a limit that you impose upon the Whole. God's Will is One, not many. It has no opposition, because there is no other will. The little personal self that you still contain behind your little barrier, keeping it separate from the rest of your mind, where you perceive a world, seems mightier than God, because it holds God away from your awareness. Your little wall of separateness hides the Purpose of Heaven and keeps you from Heaven.

4.   Your salvation has become your purpose, so do not thrust it away from yourself. Peace can no more leave you than It can leave God. Do not fear the little obstacle that is your desire for separation, because it cannot hold back the Will of God. Peace *will* flow across it and join you in Wholeness. Salvation cannot be withheld from you, because it is your purpose, and there is no other purpose for you to choose. You asked the Holy Spirit to share Its purpose with you, and that purpose is for your entire mind. Your little wall of separation will fall away so quietly beneath Peace, and Peace will extend to replace the world in your mind, as all the barriers that you have made fall away.

5.   It is no more difficult for you to overcome the world that you perceive than it is for you to surmount your little wall of separation in your Holy relationship. Without this barrier, every miracle is contained in the miracle of your Holy relationship. No miracle is harder than another, because they are all the same. In each miracle, for you the Appeal of Love wins over the appeal of separation. This is accomplished for you wherever you undertake to experience a miracle. Your guilt for your perception that you have separated yourself from God can raise no real barriers to Love, and all that seems to stand between you and what your mind perceives will fall away because of the Appeal you answer. The Holy Spirit calls to you *from* you. The Holy Spirit's Home is in your Holy relationship. Do not attempt to stand between the Holy Spirit and Its Holy

purpose, because It is yours. Let the Holy Spirit quietly extend the miracle of your relationship to be all that you perceive, because your entire mind is contained in your relationship.

6. In acknowledgment of the end of your fruitless journey, there is a hush in Heaven, a Happy expectancy, and a little pause of Gladness. Heaven knows you well, as you know Heaven well. No illusion stands between you and the Wholeness of your mind now. Do not look at illusions, because Truth has returned to your awareness, and illusions cannot keep you from God. Your every experience of a miracle is the end of an illusion. Your journey was through illusions, and miracles are your journey's ending. All illusions must end in the Goal of Truth that you have accepted.

7. You invited the Holy Spirit into your mind, so your little insane wish to get rid of the Holy Spirit *must* produce conflict in you. As you look at the world that you perceive, your little wish can settle briefly on anything, because it has no fixed purpose now. Before you welcomed the Holy Spirit, your wish to keep the Holy Spirit from your awareness seemed to have a mighty purpose: your fixed and unchangeable dedication to your separation from God and the illusions that it made. Now your wish for separation from God is aimless and pointless and causes no more than tiny interruptions in Love's Appeal for you.

8. A world that seems outside of you is all that remains of this microscopic remnant of your belief that separation is real, but it is no longer an unrelenting barrier to your Peace. Your pointless, wandering perceptions of what is left of your belief in separation make its results *appear* to be more erratic and unpredictable than before, but nothing is more unstable than a tightly organized delusional system. Its *seeming* stability is its inherent weakness throughout. The varying perceptions that the remnant of your wish for separation induces in your mind merely show you the limits of the personal mind's thought system.

9. Your microscopic wish for separation from God cannot stand before the Reality of your Oneness with God. This little wish is easily undone forever, so part with it in gladness, not regret. It is nothing, and it has always been nothing. Greet the Love of God,

and do not look upon your fading illusions.

1. The Attraction of Guilt

1.   Your attraction to separation from God makes you fear Love, because Love does not see separation at all. It is the Nature of Love to look only on Truth, because Love sees Itself in Truth and unites with It in Holy Union and Completion. Love looks past fear as fear looks past Love, because Love contains the end of your guilt for a separation that never happened, and fear depends on your guilt for proof that your separation from God did happen. Love overlooks separation and guilt completely and is wholly without attack Itself, so It cannot be afraid. Fear is attracted to the guilt that Love cannot see, and fear and Love each believe that what the other looks upon does not exist. Fear looks on guilt with the same devotion that Love looks on Itself. Fear projects and Love extends, and each perceives what it understands and what it wants to increase in its awareness.

2.   Love's extensions are gentle and increase in your mind your awareness of Love and Gentleness. Fear's projections increase guilt in your awareness, and it cherishes every scrap of proof of your separation from God that it can find. Your perception cannot obey two masters that ask for different things that are alien to each other. Love overlooks the separation that fear feeds upon. The guilt that fear demands, Love cannot even see. Fear's fierce attraction to guilt for your separation from God is wholly absent from Love's Gentle Perception of your Oneness with God. And the Oneness that Love looks upon is meaningless and invisible to fear.

3.   Your relationships to others in your perception that you are in a world are the result of what you see the world is for. Your seeing depends on which emotion – fear or Love – that you choose to experience and that you therefore project or extend. Fear projects guilt and increases guilt in your awareness. Fear is merciless, and no one escapes its projection of sin and guilt.

4.   Do not project fear's savage desire for guilt onto a world that you made to replace Reality, because it will teach you that you are limited to a body that is prey to corruption and decay. To guilt and fear this is beautiful. Guilt is frantic with the pain of fear, and it

offers itself to fear to allay punishment.

5. The Holy Spirit extends Love instead of fear, and Love is eager to return Itself to your awareness, just as fear is eager to increase your fear. When you extend Love, you look only on the Innocence of your Christ Mind. In the world that you perceive, every little act of charity or forgiveness or Love is what stands out. Do not be afraid of this, because it offers you salvation. The world that you perceive is a place of safety and kindness when safety and kindness are what you extend in your perception.

6. If you extend only the Love that the Holy Spirit extends to you, and you want only This, you will no longer see fear. The perceptions in your mind will be purified of guilt and softly brushed with Beauty. All of the fear that you see in the world that you perceive is fear that you have laid upon it. You can extend Love instead to remove the fear. The Holy Spirit has extended Love to you to extend to your Holy relationship to return Love to your awareness. Love was extended to you to replace the fear that you projected, and Love signifies the end of your fear.

7. Love sets a Pure, Quiet Joy before you that honors your Holy relationship and invites all that you perceive to join with It. In a Holy Instant of Grace, your mind is One in Christ, as Christ has promised to be with you. In your newly Holy relationship, you welcome Christ in your awareness, and where Christ is made welcome, there Christ is.

8. Your awareness of your Christ Mind is made welcome by you in the State of Grace in Which you at last forgive yourself your perception that you have separated from God. To the personal mind, sin calls for death and 'atonement' is achieved through murder. Your split mind projected sin onto Jesus so that He could die instead of you. To the personal mind, salvation is 'God's Son' being murdered so that you can live and continue to identify with *it*. But no one can die for anyone, and death does not 'atone' for sin. You can live to show yourself that death is not real. While you believe that a body can get you what you want, the body will appear to you to be a symbol that separation from God is real. While you believe that the body can give you pleasure, you will

also believe that it can bring you pain. To think that you can be satisfied and happy with so little is to hurt yourself, and when you limit your happiness, you call upon pain to make your life complete. This *is* completion as the personal mind sees it, because guilt creeps in to substitute for Happiness. But your Oneness with God is a Completion that goes beyond guilt, because it goes beyond the body.

b. *The Second Obstacle: The Belief the Body is Valuable for What It Offers*

1. Peace must first surmount the obstacle of your desire to get rid of It, and where you are attracted to separation from God, you do not want Peace. The second obstacle that Peace must flow across is closely related to the first: your belief that the body is valuable for the separation from God that it seems to offer you. Here is your attraction to separation made manifest in the body.

2. Your identification with a body is the thing that you value and that you think Peace will take from you. You think that Peace will replace the body and leave you homeless, so you deny Peace a home within you. Giving up the body is the 'sacrifice' that you think is too great for you to make and that you think is too much for the Holy Spirit to ask of you. But is it a sacrifice or a release for you to give up the body? What has the body given to you that justifies your strange belief that in it lies your salvation? With the body comes your belief in death and the focus of your belief that you must 'atone' for separating from God by letting God kill you. Your attachment to the body is the source of your fear of Love.

3. The Holy Spirit's extensions of God's Love reach beyond your mind's perceptions of bodies to join your mind in Oneness and Peace. This is what your Christ Mind gives to you. Only fear perceives bodies, because it looks for what can suffer. It is not a sacrifice for you to no longer identify with what can suffer. The Holy Spirit does not demand that you sacrifice all hope of the body's pleasure, because the body has no hope of pleasure. But the body cannot bring you pain, either, because the body does not choose your experience for you. The Holy Spirit *does* ask you to give up the pain of limiting yourself to a body, and the Holy Spirit wants

to remove this source of pain from your mind.

4. Peace extends from the Eternal to the Eternal in your mind, and It flows across everything else. Your second obstacle to Peace is no more solid than the first, because you do not really want to get rid of Peace or to limit It. The obstacles that you interpose between Peace and its extension are barriers that you place between your Will and Its accomplishment. You want Oneness with God, not fear; you want salvation, not the pain of guilt; you want God, not a body, to be your Home. Christ is in your Holy Relationship, and Christ is always One with you and with God. When you agreed to join your mind by extending your Christ Mind to another who seemed to be outside of your mind, you acknowledged this. This does not cost you anything, but it releases you from the cost of separation.

5. You have paid dearly for your illusions, and they have not brought you Peace. Be glad that you cannot sacrifice Heaven, and that you cannot be asked to sacrifice. There is no obstacle that you can place before the union of your mind, because, in your Holy relationship your Christ Mind is already here. With Christ, you will surmount all seeming obstacles, because you are no longer outside the gates of Heaven but within them. And, from within Heaven, it is easy for you to let Peace bless your tired mind where you perceive a world. You have joined the Limitless, so it is easy for you to pass any seeming barriers. It is now up to you to end guilt, so do not stop now to look for guilt in the other in your Holy relationship.

6. Let Jesus be a symbol to you of the end of guilt, and extend your Christ Mind in your Holy relationship as you extend your Christ Mind to Jesus. Forgive Jesus for all of the sins that the personal mind projects onto everyone, and in your forgiving you will remember your Christ Mind and forget your illusions. Jesus asks for your forgiveness, because if you are guilty, Jesus must be guilty. Jesus surmounted guilt and overcame His perception of a world as reality, and, in your Christ Mind, you are with Jesus in this. You see Jesus as a symbol of guilt or of the end of guilt, depending on what you see within yourself.

7. From your Holy relationship, Truth proclaims the Truth, and Love

looks on Love. Salvation flows from deep within the home that you have offered to your Christ Mind and to God, and you are all One in Quiet Communion. Come faithfully to the Holy Union of God and Christ within you, and do not keep yourself apart from Their gratitude for giving Peace Its Home in Heaven. Extend in your perception the Joyous message of the end of guilt, and this message will be increased in you. Think of your Happiness as everyone becomes for you a Witness to the end of sin and shows you that the power of sin is gone forever. You have no guilt when your belief in guilt is gone, and there is no death when guilt no longer calls for it.

8.   Forgive your mind your illusions, and release your Christ Mind from punishment for what It did not do. So you will learn the Freedom that Christ teaches by extending Freedom to others and releasing your Christ Mind. Christ is within your Holy relationship, but you block your awareness of Christ behind the obstacles that you raise to Freedom. It is not possible for you to keep away What is already in your relationship. From your Christ Mind, your new Perception will extend to replace the world in your mind.

1. The Attraction of Pain

1.   Your little part is to give to the Holy Spirit the whole idea of sacrifice and to accept the Peace that the Holy Spirit extends to you in its place without limiting your awareness of Its extension. What the Holy Spirit extends *to* you must be extended *by* you if you want Its Limitless Power to release your Christ Mind. You do not really want to be rid of Peace, and, having It within you, you cannot really limit It. If Peace is homeless, so are you. so is Christ, and so is God, Which *is* your Home. Do you want to search for Peace forever and invest your hope for Peace and Happiness in what must fail?

2.   Your faith in the Eternal is always justified, because the Eternal is Forever Kind, Infinite in Its Patience, and Wholly Loving. It will wholly accept you and give you Peace, but It can only unite with What is already at Peace in you and is as Immortal as Itself. The body can bring you neither Peace nor chaos, neither Joy nor pain, because it is a means and not an end. The body has no purpose of

its own but only the purpose that you give to it. Whatever goal that you assign to the body, the body will seem to you to be a means of attaining that goal. Peace and guilt are both conditions of your mind; they are goals to be attained. These conditions are home of the emotions – Love or fear – that call on them and are therefore compatible with them.

3. Which emotion is compatible with you? In this your choice *is* free, but what lies in your choice will come with it, and what you think you are can never be apart from your choice. The body seems to have betrayed your faith in it, because it has disappointed you, but only because you ask of it what it can never give. But your mistaken faith in it is not grounds for depression, disillusionment, and retaliation on the body. Do not use your error of expecting something from the body that it cannot give to justify your lack of faith in it. You have not sinned, but you have been mistaken in where you have put your faith. The correction of your mistake will justify your faith in What deserves your faith.

4. It is impossible for you to seek for pleasure through the body and to not find pain. It is essential that you understand why this is, because the personal mind uses the pain of guilt that comes with the body's pleasure as proof of 'sin'. The relationship between pleasure and pain is not punitive at all, but it is the inevitable result of your mind identifying with a body. This limitation on yourself invites pain, because it invites guilt for separating from God and fear of God's punishment. Guilt and fear are your purpose when you identify with a body. Your attraction to separation from God is the source of your identification with a body, and whatever the personal mind directs the body to do is therefore painful for you. The body will share the pain of all illusions, and the illusion of pleasure will be the same as the illusion of pain for you.

5. Under the personal mind's orders, the body pursues separation through the illusion of pleasure and thereby serves the personal mind's attraction to the guilt and fear that maintain the illusion of its existence. This is your attraction to pain. Ruled by the perception that the pain of separation from God is really pleasure, the body serves pain and seeks it out dutifully. This false idea

underlies all of the personal mind's heavy investment in the body. And the insane relationship between pleasure and pain keeps this investment hidden from you while the personal mind feeds upon it. To you the personal mind whispers: 'The body's pleasure is happiness' but to itself it whispers: 'The body is death.'

6. Why should the body be anything to you? It is certainly not made of anything precious, and, just as certainly, it has no feeling of its own. The body transmits to you the feelings that you want. Like any communication medium, it receives and sends the messages that it receives, and it has no feeling for the messages. All of the feelings that the body has are given to it by you – the sender and the receiver of the messages that you want it to give to you. Both the personal mind and the Holy Spirit recognize this, but the Holy Spirit tells you this with Joy, and the personal mind hides this from you. You would not send messages of hatred and attack if you understood that you send them to yourself. You would not accuse, make guilty, and condemn yourself if you understood that this is what you are doing.

7. The personal mind always projects its messages away from you to cause someone else to suffer for your attack on yourself and for the guilt this causes you. You might suffer, yes, but someone else will suffer more. The personal mind recognizes that this is not really so, because your thoughts do not leave your mind, but as the 'enemy' of Peace, it urges you to send out all of your messages of hate to free yourself from them. To convince you that this is possible, it calls on the body to find pain by attacking another, calls it pleasure, and offers you this as freedom *from* attack.

8. Do not hear the personal mind's madness, and do not believe that the impossible is true. The personal mind has dedicated the body to the goal of making separation from God real to you, and it places all of its faith in its accomplishing this. In your identification with a personal self, you see praise of the body everywhere in celebration of the personal mind's rule over God. But you cannot really believe that yielding to your attraction to separation from God, which brings you guilt and fear, is the way to escape from pain. You think that you would die without the body, but in your

identification with the body your death is inevitable.

9. You do not see that in your identification with a personal self that you have dedicated yourself to death. Freedom from death is offered to you, but you do not yet accept it. What is offered to you, you must accept for it to be truly given, because you give only to yourself. The Holy Spirit is also a Communication Medium, receiving God's Message of Love and extending It to you. Like the personal mind, the Holy Spirit is both the sender and receiver, because What is sent *through* the Holy Spirit is received *by* the Holy Spirit. What the Holy Spirit sends seeks and finds Itself. So does the personal mind seek the death it wants for you, and this is what you receive when you identify with it.

c. *The Third Obstacle: The Attraction of Death*

1. In your Holy relationship, the means are given to you to be released from your dedication to death. They were offered to you and you accepted them, but you must learn more about this strange dedication of yours, because it contains the third obstacle that Peace must flow across. You cannot die unless you choose death, and what seems to be your fear of death is really your attraction to it. Guilt, too, is frightening to you, but it has no hold over you unless you are attracted to it and you seek it out. The concept of death was made by your split mind, and death's shadow falls across everything in the world that you perceive, because the personal self is the 'enemy' of Life.

2. But a shadow cannot kill, and what is a shadow to the Living? Walk past death, and it is gone. Those in the world that you perceive who seem to be dedicated to the idea of sin and death need only to be forgiven for your projection of death onto them and you are freed from death. You can forgive the death sentence that your belief in separation from God lays on the world that you perceive and therefore on yourself. This is not arrogance but the Will of God. Nothing is impossible for you who choose God's Will as your own. Death is nothing to you, and your real dedication is not to death nor to its master, the personal mind. When you accepted the Holy Spirit's purpose in place of the personal mind's

purpose, you rejected death and exchanged it for Life. An idea does not leave the mind that thinks it, and death is the result of your belief that the personal self is you, as surely as Life is the result of you knowing that you are a Thought in God's Mind.

1. The Incorruptible Body

1. The ideas of sin and guilt and death come from your split mind, in opposition to Life and Innocence and the Will of God. This opposition can only lie in a sick mind that is dedicated to madness and that is set against the Peace of Heaven. One thing is sure: God made neither sin nor death, and God does not will that you be bound by them. God does not know of separation from God or of its seeming results. If you honor death, you do not honor God, Which wills that you live. If you honor death, you are not following God's Will; you are opposing It.

2. What is the body that you will bury? It is a symbol of your dedication to death and corruption and of your sacrifice to separation from God. It is your offering of 'sin' to the personal mind to keep it alive. It is a thing condemned and damned by the personal mind, which made it, and it is lamented by other bodies that look on it as themselves. If you believe that you have condemned Part of God to this, you *are* arrogant, but if you release your mind from its projections of separation, you are honoring God's Will. The arrogance of your belief that your separation from God is real, the pride that you take in your guilt for this, and your denial that only God is Real are all part of your unrecognized dedication to death. The guilt that the personal mind lays on the body *will* kill it, because what the personal mind loves it kills for obeying it. But what does not obey the personal mind cannot be killed by it.

3. But through your acceptance of the Holy relationship, you now have a dedication to Life that will keep the body incorruptible and perfect as long as it is useful for your Holy purpose. The body can no more die than it can feel. Of itself it is neither corruptible nor incorruptible. It does nothing, and it *is* nothing. The body is just the result of your tiny, mad idea of corruption, which you can correct.

God has answered your insane idea with the Holy Spirit within you. The Holy Spirit has not left God, therefore It brings God to your awareness.

4. Through your acceptance of the Incorruptible, you have the Power to release yourself from your belief in the corruptible. There is no better way to teach yourself the fundamental principle of miracles that all miracles are equal than to show that what seems to be the hardest can be accomplished first. The body will serve your chosen purpose, and what you see in the body it will seem to be to you. If death were true, it would be the final and complete destruction of your Oneness with God, which *is* the personal mind's goal.

5. You seem to fear death, but you do not see how often and how loudly you call to death to come to save you from Oneness with God. In your identification with a personal self, you see death as your safety, the great savior from Truth, the answer to, and silencer of, the Holy Spirit. But your retreating to death does not end the conflict of your split mind. Only the Holy Spirit is the Answer to your conflict. Your seeming 'love' for death seems to be a great obstacle for Peace to flow across, because in this obstacle lies hidden all of the personal mind's strange devices for deceiving you into believing that separation from God is your salvation. Death seems to be the end of Oneness, the triumph of the personal mind's limitations over God's Limitless Extension, the victory of lifelessness over Life Itself.

6. The personal mind wants to slay a body that is supposed to be you and that is buried by its orders under the dusty mantle of its insane world. A decaying body is 'proof' that God is powerless before the personal mind and is unable to protect the Life Which is One with God from the personal mind's savage wish to kill. You who are One with God should know that death is only an *illusion*. The body does not lead you to death, so do not ask it for release from death. Free it from the merciless and unrelenting orders that you have laid upon it, and forgive it what you ordered it to do. In your identification with a personal self, you exalt the body, and you command it to die, because only death can conquer Life. Only in insanity can you look upon the defeat of God as something real.

7.   Your fear of death will go from you as your attraction to it yields to the real attraction of Love. The end of your perception that separation from God is real is very near. It is nestled quietly in the safety of your Holy relationship, and it is protected by the Oneness that you extend to your relationship as it grows into a mighty force for your remembering God. The beginning of your salvation is carefully guarded by Love, is preserved from every thought that wants to attack it, and is quietly made ready to fulfill the mighty task for which it was given to you. Your newborn purpose is nursed by Thoughts of God, cherished by the Holy Spirit, and protected by God Itself. It does not need your protection, because It *is* your Protection. It cannot die, and within it lies the end of death.

8.   When you are aware that you are wholly Innocent, you will not be able to conceive of attack or danger of any kind. Fear will not enter to disturb your Peace when your belief in separation from God is gone. Your Holy relationship, even at the beginning, is One with God and with you. Within it in perfect safety is every miracle that you will ever extend. The miracle is ageless, born in time but nourished in Eternity. Behold the miracle, which you have given a resting place in your forgiveness of the personal mind's projections on the other, and see in it the Will of God. Here is your Christ Mind, reborn in your awareness, and you will follow Christ, not to the cross but to the resurrection and the Life.

9.   When any thing or situation seems to be the source of your fear, remember that it is always for one reason: the personal mind perceives it as a symbol of fear; a sign that your separation from God and death are real. Remember, then, that as a symbol what you are looking on you can see to stand for Something Else. Its meaning is not in itself, but in your mind, so it can represent Love or fear depending on what you choose it to reflect to you. When you are uncertain how to look on something, do not judge it with the personal mind. Remember the Holy Presence of the Holy Spirit, Which is given to you to judge for you. Give the situation to the Holy Spirit, and say:

'Take this from me, and judge it for me.

I will not use it as a sign of separation from God or of death.

Nor will I use it as an obstacle to Peace.

Teach me how to use it to bring Peace back into my awareness.'

d. *The Fourth Obstacle: The Fear of God*

1. What will you see and think and feel without the fear of death or your attraction to separation from God? Very simply, you will remember that only God is Reality, extending Infinitely. As you begin to remember God, Peace must still surmount a final obstacle within you. After this, your salvation is complete, and you will be entirely restored to Sanity. Here the world in your mind *does* end.

2. This fourth obstacle hangs like a heavy veil before your perception of Christ. But, as you begin to extend your Christ Mind, and to perceive Christ's Joy in God's Love beyond the veil, the Peace within you will lightly brush aside this veil and rush at last to join in Christ your mind where you perceive a world. This dark veil, which seems to make your Christ Mind frightening to you, will fade from your mind when your attraction to separation and to death is gone.

3. This is the darkest veil, upheld by your belief in death and your attraction to separation from God. Your dedication to death and to death's authority is the solemn vow that you have made to the personal mind to never lift this veil or even to suspect that it is there. This veil is the secret bargain that you have made with the personal mind to keep What lies beyond the veil forever blotted out of your memory. It is your promise to never allow Oneness to call you out of separation. And it is the great amnesia in which you seem to have forgotten God, and you seem split from your Self. *Your fear of God* is the final step in your denial of God.

4. See how your belief in death seems to 'save' you? If death is gone, what is there left for you to fear but Life? It is your attraction to separation from God that makes God seem ugly, cruel, and tyrannical. You are really no more afraid of death than you are of the personal mind, because they are your chosen friends. In your secret alliance with them, you have agreed to never let your fear of God be lifted so that you can perceive your Christ Mind and unite with God.

5. You surmount every obstacle that Peace must flow across in the same way: your fear, which raised the obstacle, gives way to Love and is gone. Your desire to get rid of Peace and to drive away the Holy Spirit from your mind fades in your quiet recognition that you love the Holy Spirit. Your adoration of the body gives way to the Holy Spirit, Which you love as you could never love the body. And the appeal of separation and death is lost to you forever as Love attracts and calls you to Oneness. From beyond each of your obstacles to Love, Love Itself calls to you, and you surmount each by the Power of your attraction to Love. Your desire for separation, and the fear that defends it, seem to hold your obstacles in place. But when you hear the Voice of Love beyond them, they disappear in your answer.

6. Now you stand in terror before the veil that you swore to never look upon. You remember your promise to your 'friends' – your desire for separation from God, guilt, fear, and death. They scream at you to not look at your fear of God, and you fear the personal mind will get revenge on you because you are deserting it. You realize that, if you look on your fear of God and let the veil be lifted, your 'friends' will be gone forever and your 'protection' and 'home' will vanish. You know that you will not remember anything that you remember now.

7. It seems to you that the world that you perceive will utterly abandon you if you look on your fear of God. But all that will happen is that you will let go of the world. This re-establishes *your* Will. Look on your fear of God with open eyes, and you will never again believe that you are at the mercy of things outside of you, forces out of your control, or thoughts that come to you against your will. It *is* your Will to look on this. No mad desire for separation from God, no trivial impulse to forget God again, no stab of fear or terror at seeming death can stand against your True Will. The Love that attracts you from beyond the veil of your fear of God is also deep within you, and you *are* One with It.

1. The Lifting of the Veil[1]

1. Do not forget that it is not the personal mind that has led you this

far in your Holy relationship. You cannot use the personal mind's help to surmount your obstacles to Peace, because it does not open its secrets to you and ask you to look on them and then go beyond them. The personal mind does not want you to see its weaknesses and learn that it has no power to keep you from Truth. The Holy Spirit is the Guide that has brought you to your Holy relationship and that remains with you. When you are ready, you will look on terror with no fear at all. But first, look in Innocence on the other in your relationship with faith born of your complete forgiveness of the personal mind's projections.

2.   You cannot look on your fear of God without terror unless you have accepted correction of your perception that you are separate from God and learned that illusions are not real. You cannot stand before the obstacle of your fear of God without first extending your Holiness to your perception of another in the world that seems outside of you, because you will not dare to look at your fear without first forgiving yourself your perception of separation from God. Stand before this obstacle and do not tremble; you are ready. Join with your Christ Mind in a Holy Instant in this place where the Holy Instant has led you. Join in faith that God, the Source of your Christ Mind, offers you the Innocence that you need and in faith that, for your Love of Christ and of God, you will accept Innocence.

3.   It is not possible for you to look on your fear of God too soon. It is inevitable that you will reach this place when you are ready, and, once you have seen your Holiness in your perception of another in the world that you thought was outside of you, you *are* ready. But merely to reach this place is not enough. A journey without a purpose is meaningless, and you won't know that it is over until you realize that its purpose is accomplished. Here, with the journey's end before you, you see its purpose – to look upon your fear of God. And, here, you choose whether to look upon it or to wander off, only to return later and make the choice again.

4.   You do need some preparation to look on your fear of God. Only the Sane can look on insanity with pity and compassion instead of fear. Only if you share in insanity is it frightening to you, and you

do share in insanity until, in faith, you extend Love in your perception of another in your mind where you perceive a world. You have not forgiven yourself, though you stand before forgiveness in your Holy relationship. You are afraid of God, *because* you are afraid to extend Love to another. You fear those to whom you do not extend forgiveness, and you cannot reach Love while fear is still real to you.

5. You still see the personal mind's projections of separation on the other, and your interpretation of the other *is* frightening. You still attack the other to keep what seems to be yourself unharmed. Yet, in your relationship with the other is your salvation. You see in the other the personal mind that you project onto them, and you hate it because it is in *your* mind. All the forgiveness that you could extend to heal your mind gives way to fear. But you need to forgive the other *your* projections, because you see your own mind reflected in your relationship with the other, and this can be madness or Heaven. You must extend your faith that only God is Real to all of your mind where you perceive a world, or you do not have faith at all.

6. Beside you is one who offers you correction when you choose to extend the Holy Spirit in your perception of them. Your choice is to hold the personal mind's projections against the other or to accept the Gift of Love's Extension by seeing Love instead. You will receive from your perception of the other what you extend to them. In your perception of the other you have the power to forgive your perception of separation from God. You cannot accept forgiveness for yourself in the limited, isolated personal mind. Your salvation is in taking back your mind where you perceive a world and in letting your mind be What it is as Part of God. Do not seek to make part of your mind a separate enemy when it is Love, and you are One with it.

7. Your Christ Mind, Holy and Beautiful, is with you as you perceive yourself walking through a world. You thought that sin was real, because you chose to throw the veil of separation that is the world across your mind to hide your Christ Mind. But Christ is still here holding out forgiveness to you so that you can share in Christ's

Holiness. The seemingly separate world still offers you salvation when you use it to perceive a reflection of your Christ Mind. When you worship separation from God, you do not see that you attack yourself.

8. Your mind seems crucified by your perception that separation from God is real, and it waits to be released from pain. Forgive your perception of illusions, because only then can your perception offer *you* forgiveness. Correct your perception that the world is real, and your mind will be corrected as surely as you are One with God and God loves you. You *will* find correction in the world that you perceive, because you both extend it there and receive it there. You can extend the Grace of Heaven to the world to receive Grace from your Christ Mind. Do not let the world that you perceive withhold Grace from you by not extending Grace in place of the world yourself. Correction is yours to extend, and so to increase in your awareness. What you forgive in your perception is freed, and you are freed with your perceptions. Forgive the world all the 'evidence' of your separation from God and all the guilt that you think you see there.

9. With your Christ Mind, you will return again and again to correction until you accept complete correction. Before you condemn the other in your Holy relationship, remember that your perception of them is your perception of yourself. Thank God for your Holiness, Which you can see in your perception of the other. Unite your mind in gladness, and remove all traces of the guilt that you have projected onto the other to disturb and torture your mind. Do not project separation onto the other and believe that it is uncorrectable and hopeless, but lift all belief in sin from your mind and toss it away.

10. Extend your faith in Christ to your Holy relationship, because faith and hope and mercy are yours to give and so to increase in your awareness. Look on the other and see the Gift of God that is for you. It is almost Easter, the time of resurrection. Extend correction that you may rise with Christ in resurrection, not separate from Christ in death. Through the Holy Spirit, your Christ Mind extends Freedom to you for you to extend to your relationship and to

return to the Holy Spirit. Through extension of your Oneness everywhere, you learn that you are One and Free. The Holy Spirit unites you with your Christ Mind so that you can again make the decision for correction.

11. Extend your Christ Mind to your relationship to free yourself, because you can only be Free in your awareness that you are One with God. See Innocence, not guilt, in place of the personal mind's projections on the other, because this is what your Christ Mind sees. This is how you are prepared for the resurrection of Christ in your mind. Let God rise in your memory. God does not know of separation or death, only Eternal Life.

12. With Christ you will disappear into the Presence beyond the veil. Here you will find your Home, and you will go beyond perception to God. God's plan for your salvation will be done. God is your journey's Purpose and Meaning. Beyond the veil, you are in God's Eternal Peace; in the Rest and the Quiet that you seek. This is the whole reason for the journey that you have undertaken. Heaven is the Gift that you owe to your entire mind. It is the dept of gratitude that you owe to your Christ Mind for What you are in Oneness with God.

13. Think carefully about how you want to look upon the other in your Holy relationship, because, as you look on them, you look upon the gift that you want to receive from them. The other *seems* to offer you either guilt or salvation, but *you* extend to them what you want to receive. If you want pain, then you will project the source of your pain onto them. But, if you want correction, then you will extend Joy to them, because you want to be healed of pain. You will recognize your choice by what you extend and what is increased in your awareness. The choice is yours, and nothing can interfere with it.

14. You have come this far in your Holy relationship, because the journey to God was your choice. You would not have undertaken this journey if you thought it was meaningless. What you had faith in still has faith in you. The Holy Spirit's Strong, Gentle faith in you will lift you far beyond the veil and will place you in the Sure Protection of God. Going beyond the veil is the only purpose for the

world that you perceive and your journey through it. Beyond the veil, you have no need for a world or a journey. You still lack conviction that the world has a purpose or that there is a journey for you to take, but it is given to you to see your Purpose in your Holy relationship, where you extend your Christ Mind, and you recognize your True Self.

Chapter 20

The Vision of Holiness

1. Holy Week

1. This is Palm Sunday, a day to celebrate your overcoming the personal mind through your acceptance of Truth. Do not spend this Holy week brooding on your crucifixion in your identification with a personal self, but happily celebrate your Christ Mind's release. Easter is the sign of Peace, not of pain. A slain Christ is meaningless, but a risen Christ is the symbol of your forgiveness of yourself. It is the sign that you look upon yourself as healed and whole.

2. This week begins with palms that symbolize the success of your journey of overcoming the personal mind, and ends with white lilies that represent your Christ Mind's Innocence. Do not let any dark symbol of crucifixion intervene between your journey and its purpose: your acceptance of Truth and Its expression. This week, celebrate Life, not death. Honor the Perfect Purity of your Christ Mind, and not the personal mind's perceptions of 'sin'. Extend to the other in your Holy relationship the gift of lilies (Love), not the 'gift' of thorns (fear). You stand beside the other with Love and fear in your mind, uncertain which to extend or project. Join with Christ and throw away the thorns and extend lilies in their place. This Easter you will forgive Christ the illusions that you project onto It, and you will have your forgiving returned to you. You cannot unite with Christ in crucifixion and death. The resurrection of your Christ Mind is not complete until, as Jesus did, you wholly forgive the illusions that you have projected onto your Christ Mind.

3. A week is short, but this Holy week is the symbol of the whole journey that you have undertaken with your Christ Mind. It starts with the promise of your resurrection, so do not wander into the temptation of crucifixion and delay yourself. Go in Peace beyond the crucifixion with the Innocence of your Christ Mind offering you

correction and release from your perception of separation from God. Do not hold yourself back with thorns and nails when full correction is so near, but let your Innocence speed you on your way to resurrection.

4.   If you catch glimpses of Christ beyond the veil of your denial as you forgive the illusions that the personal mind projects onto the other in your relationship, you will recognize Truth. Christ seemed to be a stranger to you, and yet you have become willing to extend God's Love to remember your Christ Mind. In your forgiveness of your illusions lies your Christ Mind's release and your correction. The time of Easter is a time of Joy, not of mourning. Look on Christ, Which has risen in your awareness, and celebrate your Christ Mind's Holiness. Easter is the time of your salvation as well as Jesus'.

2. The Gift of Lilies

1.   Look upon all of the trinkets that are made to hang on the body, to cover it, or for it to use. See all the useless things you made for the body's eyes to see, and think of the many offerings that you make for the body's pleasure. And then remember that all of these were made to make a body that you hate seem lovely. In your identification with a personal self, you use the body to attract others to you, not recognizing that you are offering yourself fear by trying to justify the body's value to you through another's acceptance of it. Your 'gift' of the body also makes the other worthless to you, because their acceptance and delight in the body acknowledges the lack of value that they place on their self.

2.   What you can truly give and receive cannot be given through the body. Bodies can neither offer, nor accept; neither hold back, nor take away. Only your mind can value, and only your mind decides what it will project or extend and therefore receive. What you offer with your mind depends on what you want to increase in your awareness. Your split mind will adorn your chosen home carefully, making it ready to receive what you want. If the body is your chosen home, you will adorn it to attract others to increase separation, guilt, and fear in your awareness. But if you recognize

that your mind is your home, you will adorn it with Love and extend Love to increase Love in your awareness. With your mind you will project or extend what you judge yourself worthy of receiving.

3. What you extend in your perception is an evaluation of your own mind. Your chosen home (mind or body) is an altar to yourself, and you will see in your perception witnesses to your choice that will reinforce your devotion to it. From your mind, you project or extend what you want increased in your awareness. Here is the value that you place on your entire mind; your judgment of what you are. Do not forget that in your perception you see your condemnation or your salvation. Project fear and *you* are crucified; extend Love and *you* are Free.

4. Your Christ Mind has a great need for you to extend Love, because you have not yet forgiven yourself your illusions. Your Christ Mind cannot offer you forgiveness when you still project guilt and fear and think that they are real. You are against Christ, then, and you cannot be whole without your Christ Mind. Forgive the illusions that you perceive in others so that you can see Christ and know that you are Whole. Look in your mind and see whether Love or fear is your chosen home. If you see fear, then the body is your chosen home and you offer Christ separation. And yet your mind is not what it was, and, if you look closer, fear is gone.

5. You still see with the body's eyes, and all that they can report is separation. But you have asked for and received another Perception. You share the Holy Spirit's purpose now, so you also share the Holy Spirit's Perception. The Holy Spirit's ability to extend Love everywhere is yours now, too. The Holy Spirit does not see separate selves; only One Holy Self everywhere. The Holy Spirit does not see fear; only Innocence shining Peacefully on Everything that the Holy Spirit loves.

6. This Easter, look with a different Perception on your Holy relationship. You *have* forgiven Christ your illusions, and yet your Christ Mind cannot use your Love while you do not see It. You cannot use What your Christ Mind gives to you unless you choose to use It *with* your Christ Mind. The Holy Spirit's Perception is not

an idle gift to be played with for a while and then tossed aside. Listen carefully: Don't think that the Holy Spirit's Perception is an illusion, a careless thought to play with, or a toy to pick up from time to time. If you do, this is what It will be to you.

7. You have the Perception now to look past illusions. It has been given to you to no longer see fear, separation, or obstacles to Peace. Your fear of God is nothing to you who can now see Christ in place of the personal mind's projections on the other. With your Christ Mind in your awareness, your Real Perception has become the greatest Power for the undoing of illusions that God can give. What God gives to the Holy Spirit *you* receive. Your Christ Mind looks to you for release, because you have asked for the strength to look on the final obstacle of your fear of God and to no longer see fear or death.

8. The Home that you have chosen is beyond the veil of your fear of God. It is ready to receive you. You will not see It with the body's eyes, yet all that you need to see It you already have. Your Home has called to you since time began, and you have never failed to hear It. You just did not know how or where to look for It; now you know. In you, God lies ready to be unveiled, and your awareness of God is ready to be freed from the terror that has kept God hidden from you. There is no fear in Love. Easter is a symbol that Christ was never crucified. Lift your eyes with Christ, not in fear, but in faith that only God is Real. There is no fear in your Christ Mind, because your Christ Mind's Perception does not see illusions, only a path to Heaven, your Quiet, Gentle, Peaceful Home.

9. The Holiness that you extend in your perception of the other in your Holy relationship will lead you Home. The Innocence that you extend will light your way, guiding you and protecting you, shining from the Holiness that you extend in your forgiving your illusions. Let your Perception of the other in your Holy relationship be your Savior from illusions, as you look on them with the new Perception that looks on Love and that brings you Joy. With your Christ Mind, you go beyond the veil of fear. The Holiness that leads you is within you, just as your Home is within

you. You will find What God means for you to find.

10.   This is the way to Heaven and the Peace of Easter: Join Christ in the glad awareness that you have risen from a personal past to awaken to the present. Now, you are Free and Limitless in your Oneness with All that is within you. Now, your Innocence is untouched by guilt and perfectly protected from fear and the belief that separation from God is real. Your extension of Love to your relationship saves you from pain and fear, and Christ, Which you see in it, is the Strength that guides you through and beyond fear. Walk in your Holy relationship rejoicing, because Christ has come into your awareness to save you from your illusions and to lead you Home.

11.   The Christ that you see in your Holy relationship is your Savior, and your mind is released from crucifixion through your Perception of Christ in everything. In your pain, your Christ Mind will not leave you, who are One with Christ. With Christ, you will gladly walk the way of Innocence as you behold the open door of Heaven, and recognize the Home that has called to you. Joyously extend your Freedom and your Strength to lead you Home and to replace the world in your mind. Extend your Holiness, Where Strength and Freedom are, to receive the awareness that leads you Home. Christ is in you and in your mind where you perceive a world, and your Christ Mind will lead you past fear to Love.

3. Sin as an Adjustment

1.   Your belief that separation from God is real is an adjustment in your mind. An adjustment is a change or a shift in perception. In this case, it is your belief that God was True before the adjustment and has been made different by your adjustment. Every adjustment that you make is therefore a distortion of Truth and needs defenses to hold it up against Reality. Your Knowledge of God does not require any adjustment and is in fact *not* Knowledge of God if any shift or change occurs. Change of any kind reduces your Knowledge of God to perception, because your certainty is lost when doubt has entered. It *is* necessary for you to make adjustments in this impaired condition of perception, because it is not

True. You don't need to adjust to Truth, because Truth is What you are and you inherently understand It.

2. Only the personal mind makes adjustments. It is the personal mind's fixed belief that all relationships depend on adjustments to make them what it wants them to be. To the personal mind, Oneness, Which is a Relationship in Which there is nothing to interfere with Eternal Extension, is dangerous. It appoints itself mediator of all of your relationships in your perception that you are in a world to make whatever adjustments it deems necessary to interpose obstacles to your awareness of Oneness and to keep your mind separated. It is this studied interference that makes it difficult for you to extend Oneness in your perception of the other in your Holy relationship.

3. In your Holiness, you do not interfere with Truth or fear It, because it is within Truth that you recognize your Holiness and rejoice. In your Holiness, you look directly at Truth and do not attempt to adjust to It or to adjust It to you. So you learn that Holiness is in you, and you do not decide to see It someplace else. Looking out from your Holiness is a way of asking, 'Who am I?', and the Holiness that you extend in your looking is What answers you. But in your identification with a personal self, you make a world on which to look, and then you adjust to the world that you perceive and make the world adjust to you. And you see no difference between you and the world because you made both.

4. A simple question remains, and it needs an answer: Do you like this world of murder and attack, through which you thread your timid way through constant dangers, isolated and frightened, hoping that death will wait a little longer before it overtakes you and you disappear? *You have made this up.* It is a picture of what you think you are. You believe that you are a murderer of God, and you are frightened because those who kill fear death. What you perceive are your fearful thoughts, as you adjust yourself to a world made fearful by your adjustments. You look out in sorrow from sadness within and see the sadness outside of you.

5. Do you wonder what your perception will be through Happy eyes? The world that you perceive is a judgment on yourself. It is not

really there at all, but judgment lays a sentence on it, which justifies it and makes it real to you. Such is the world that you see: a judgment on you *by* you. This sickly picture of yourself is carefully preserved outside of you by the personal mind, because it is *its* image and it loves it. This is the world to which you must adjust as long as you believe that it is outside of you, and that it has you at its mercy. This world *is* merciless, and if it were outside of you your fear of it would be justified. But you are the one who made mercilessness and you can correct this.

6. Your awareness of unholiness cannot long remain now that you have a Holy relationship. When you perceive through your Holiness, your mind is One, just as the personal mind sees a world that is like itself. The Holiness that you perceive is Beautiful, because you see your Innocence in It. In your awareness of your Holiness, you do not make a world and then make it adjust to fit your orders. You gently ask 'What are you?' of the part of your mind where you perceive a world, and the Holy Spirit answers with a Perception of Holiness. Do not take the judgment of the personal mind's world as an answer to your question 'What am I?' The personal mind's world is the belief that separation from God is real, and this belief is not outside of *your* mind.

7. You are One with God, so do not seek to adjust to your insanity. There is a stranger in your mind that you invited to wander into Truth, but the stranger *will* wander off. This stranger came without a purpose, and it will be gone, because you accepted the Love that the Holy Spirit offered. In Love, the stranger is made homeless, but *you* are welcome. Do not ask this transient stranger, 'Who am I?', because this stranger is the one thing that cannot know. Yet it is the stranger that you ask, and it is the stranger's answer to which you try to adjust. This one wild thought, fierce in its arrogance, but so tiny and meaningless that it slips by unnoticed in Reality, has become your guide. To it you turn to ask the meaning of all that you see. Of this one thing that is blind to God you ask, 'How should I, who am One with God, look on myself?'

8. Do not ask for the judgment of what is totally without judgment. If you have asked it, why would you believe its answer and adjust to

it as if it were the truth? The world of separation that you perceive is the answer that it gave to you, and you have given it the power to adjust the world to make its answer seem true. You have asked this puff of madness for the meaning of your unholy relationship, and you adjusted the relationship according to its insane answer. Did it make you happy? Did you bless yourself with Joy by extending Christ in your perception of the other, to give thanks for all the Happiness that your Christ Mind extends to you? Did you see in your relationship with the other the Eternal Gift of God to you? Did you see your Holiness reflected in your perception of the other? That is the purpose of your Holy relationship. Do not ask how to attain this of the one thing that still wants your relationship to be unholy. Do not give it any power to adjust the means and the end.

9. Prisoners who are bound with heavy chains for years, starved and emaciated, weak and exhausted, with eyes so used to darkness that they don't remember the light do not leap with joy the moment that they are freed. It takes them a while to understand what freedom is. You groped in the dust and found Christ's Hand ,and now you are uncertain whether to let It go or to hold on and remember a Life you have forgotten. Strengthen your hold and raise your eyes to your Strong Companion, in Which the Meaning of your Freedom lies. Your Holy relationship *seemed* to reflect your crucifixion, and yet your Holiness remains untouched and Perfect, and you can see This instead. You will this day enter Heaven with Christ, and know the Peace of God.

10. This is your Christ Mind's Will for you and your Will for yourself. Heaven is Holiness and Oneness without limit. Heaven is Oneness without the veil of fear upon It. In Heaven, your mind is One, and you look with Perfect Gentleness on everything and yourself. In Heaven, all thoughts of separation are impossible. You were a prisoner to separation, and now you are free in Heaven, Where Christ is One with you and your entire mind, which is Christ's Self.

11. Your extension of Holiness to your relationship gives your Christ Mind the certainty that you will soon be aware of your Oneness again. Share Christ's faith in this and know that it is justified. There

is no fear in Perfect Love, because it has no separation in It. Love looks only on Itself. Looking with charity within, It cannot fear that anything is outside of it. In Innocence, you see your Safety, and in your Purity, you see God in your mind and you trust your Christ Mind to lead you to God. Where else would you go but Where you will to be? As certainly as God is One with you, all that you perceive will now lead you to God, as you lead your mind to God by extending God to replace the world in your mind. In your Holy relationship, you can see God's Eternal Promise of Immortality. There is no fear in you if you do not see separation.

4. Entering the Ark

1. Nothing can hurt you unless you give it the power to hurt you. But, in your identification with a personal self, you give power as the world that you perceive interprets *giving*: What you give you lose. Yet it is not up to you to give power at all. Real Power is of God, given by God, and reawakened in you by the Holy Spirit. The Holy Spirit knows that as you give, you gain. The Holy Spirit gives no power to your belief in separation from God, so it has none. The Holy Spirit also does not give power to the results of your belief in separation: sickness, death, misery, and pain. These things have not occurred, because the Holy Spirit cannot see them and does not give any power to their seeming source. This is how the Holy Spirit keeps you free of them. Having no illusions about you, the Holy Spirit gives everything to God, Which has already given and received All that is True. God has neither given nor received the untrue.

2. Your idea of separation from God has no place in Heaven. Its results are alien There, as is your split mind, which thinks it. Here is your need to see your Holiness in place of the personal mind's projections of separation on another. Heaven *is* in your entire mind, though you perceive a world. When you see separation, Heaven is lost to you. But see Truth and What is yours returns to your awareness. When you extend only Love in your relationship with another, you receive only Love, so what you receive from a relationship is up to you. You must overlook all projections of the

472

personal mind, whether they seem to be from you or from others, and this is your salvation. This is the reawakening in you of the Law of God that Mind is One. You have established other laws and given them the power to enforce what is not of God.

3. You made your insane laws to guarantee that you will continue to make the mistake of believing in your separation from God. You give this idea power over you by accepting the results of this belief as your just due. This is madness. Is this what you want to see in your Holy relationship, which can save you from insanity? Free your mind from your perception of separation by extending Oneness in place of it. You share in what you extend. What God gives follows God's Law alone. If you follow God's Law, you cannot suffer from the results of any other laws.

4. When you choose Oneness, you will experience only Its results. Your Power will be of God, and you will extend only What God extends to you to share in It. Nothing but Oneness will touch you, because Oneness will be All that you see, extending your Power according to the Will of God. And so your Limitlessness is established and maintained. It is upheld through all of your temptation to see limitations and therefore to limit yourself. Ask only of Limitlessness What Limitlessness is. Do not ask the limited personal mind about Limitlessness, because the limited does not have the Power to know Limitlessness.

5. In your Innocence, you give What you receive. Extend the Power of Innocence in your Holy relationship and be released from your belief in separation from God. A relationship is given to you, who seem to walk isolated in a world of separation, for you to release another from the personal mind's projections, so that you can be released. In the world of separation that you perceive, it appears as though others are separate from you, but, being in your mind, they are really part of you. If you already knew this, you would not need salvation. You found a Holy relationship when you were ready to look on your Christ Mind and to see your Innocence.

6. This plan is not of you, and you do not need to be concerned with anything except the part that you must learn. The Holy Spirit will see to the rest without your help. But don't think that the Holy

Spirit does not need your part. In your part lies the whole of the plan, because without your part the plan would be incomplete. You enter Peace by extending your True Self to encompass your perception of another who seems to be in a world outside of you, and the beginning of a new Perception goes with you. Your Holy relationship must enter Peace for you to learn your special function in the Holy Spirit's plan. Now you will share the Holy Spirit's purpose. As you fulfill this purpose, a new Perception will rise in your mind, in which there will be no separation, therefore no fear. You will be able to rest your entire mind here a while to forget limitations and to remember your Limitlessness. Your entire mind is what you think of as you as well as all that your mind perceives, or it is not complete. And It is Completion that you have come to the Holy relationship to remember.

7.   This is the purpose that you have been given. Do not think that your forgiving the personal mind's projections will leave you limited to a personal self. A whole new Perception will extend in your mind, and you will know that it is your mind that you see. Christ will shine in your mind as you remember God's Law of Oneness. You will forget any other laws as you yearn to have God's Law perfectly fulfilled in your entire mind. Do not think that you can rest while any part of your mind where you perceive a world is left outside of Oneness. You can no more leave part of your mind out than your Christ Mind can leave you and forget part of Itself.

8.   You may wonder how you can be at Peace while you still perceive yourself in time, and while it seems that there is so much that must be done before Peace will be available to you. If Peace seems impossible to you, ask yourself if it is possible that God has a plan that does not work. Once you accept God's plan as the one function that you want to fulfill in your perception that you are in a world, there will be nothing else that the Holy Spirit will not arrange for you without your effort. The Holy Spirit will go before you, making your path straight and undoing all obstacles. Nothing that you need will be denied to you. Every difficulty will melt away before you reach it. You will not need to think or to care about anything, except the only purpose that you want to fulfill. As the purpose was given to

you, so will its fulfillment be given to you. God's Guarantee holds against all seeming obstacles, because It rests on Certainty. It rests on *you*. What can be more certain than What is One with God?

5. Heralds of Eternity

1. In your perception that you are in a world, you come closest to your True Self in a Holy relationship. In this relationship, you begin to find in yourself the Certainty that God has in you. This is where you find your function of restoring God's Law of Oneness to your mind, which seems to have lost part of itself by projecting it away onto a world that seems outside of it. Only in time can you lose anything, but never Forever. Your mind gradually unites in time as you extend Love in your perception more and more, and with each joining of your mind with what seems outside of it, the end of time will be brought closer for you. Each miracle that you extend is a mighty herald of Eternity. You cannot be afraid when you have Oneness as your purpose. And everything to which you extend your purpose shares your purpose with you.

2. Each herald of Eternity sings of the end of your perception that you are separate from God and so of the end of fear for you. Each speaks in time of What is far beyond time. Your uniting your mind with what once seemed outside of it calls to your entire mind to be One. And, in that Oneness, you proclaim and welcome Love. Peace to your Holy relationship, which has the power to hold the Oneness of God in your awareness! You extend your True Self in your perception of another to unite your entire mind, and this makes your entire mind glad. Do not forget that the Holy Spirit extends Oneness to you, and that God extends Oneness to the Holy Spirit to extend Oneness to you.

3. It is impossible for you to overestimate the value of the other in your Holy relationship by your choosing to see your Christ Mind in your perception of them instead of the personal mind's projections. When the personal mind overestimates the other's value, it is because it wants the other for itself. But this means it actually values the other too little, because it wants to use the other for the purpose of limiting you to a personal self. Your Christ Mind is

invaluable and cannot be evaluated. You don't see the fear that arises in you from your meaningless attempt to judge What lies far beyond the judgment of the personal mind. Do not judge with the personal mind What is invisible to the personal mind, or you will never see It. Wait patiently for your Christ Mind to come into your awareness. You will see the other's value when all you want is to extend Peace in your relationship with them. And you will receive the Peace that you extend.

4.   You cannot estimate the worth of another who offers you the opportunity to extend Peace to increase Peace in your awareness. What could you want but this opportunity? The Worth of your mind has been established by God, and you will recognize this as you receive God's Gifts by extending them in your Holy relationship in your perception that you are in a world. The Oneness of your Christ Mind, Which is reflected back to you in your grateful Perception of the other, will make you Love the other and be glad. You will not think to judge them, because when you look on the Oneness of your Christ Mind, you have no need to return to the personal mind's judgments to make separation real to you. Insisting on the personal mind's judgments will only blind you to Christ. Your choices are your Christ Mind's Perception or the personal mind's judgment; you cannot have both.

5.   The other's body has little use for you, and, when you use it as the Holy Spirit teaches, it has no function. Your mind does not need bodies to unite itself. The sight that sees the body has no use in the Holy relationship. While you value the other's body, your awareness of the Holiness of your relationship has not been accomplished. Why does it take so many Holy Instants to let this be accomplished when one would do? There *is* only one Holy Instant. The little breath of Eternity that runs through time like a golden thread is always the same. There is nothing before It and nothing after It.

6.   You look on each Holy Instant as a different point in time, but It never changes. All that It will ever hold is here right now. The past takes nothing from It, and the future will add nothing to It. Here in this Instant is Everything. Here is the Loveliness of your Holy

relationship already accomplished. Here, the perfect faith that only God is Real is extended to you, as you will one day extend it to be all that you perceive. Here, Limitless forgiveness is extended to you to extend to your perception of the other. Here is your Christ Mind.

7. You cannot evaluate the other who offers you the opportunity to extend, and so to receive, this Gift. Do you want to exchange this Gift for another? The Gift of the Holy Instant returns God's Law of Oneness to your mind. Merely by your remembering God's Law you forget the laws that held you to pain and death. This is not a Gift that the other's body gives to you. The veil of your fear of God, which the body represents, hides the Gift of the Holy Instant, so it hides your Christ Mind from you. Christ is the Gift that you can see in your Holy relationship, though the other may not be aware of this. And you may not be aware of this, either. Have faith that the Holy Spirit sees this Gift in all parts of your mind, and extends It and receives It for you. Through the Holy Spirit's Perception, you will see It, and through the Holy Spirit's understanding, you will recognize It and love It as your own.

8. Be comforted and feel the Holy Spirit's Love and Perfect Confidence in you. The Holy Spirit knows that you are Christ, and the Holy Spirit shares God's Certainty that Reality rests in you in Safety and in Peace. Consider now what you must learn to share God's Confidence in you. What are you that God offers you all of Reality and knows that It is Safe? You don't look on yourself as God looks on you. But God's Confidence is not misplaced.

6. The Temple of the Holy Spirit

1. Your Meaning lies solely in your Relationship with God. If your meaning was elsewhere, it would rest on chance, but there *is* nothing else. Your Relationship with God is wholly Loving and Eternal. But you have invented an unholy relationship with yourself that attempts to replace the Relationship between you and God. Your Real Relationship with God is of Perfect Oneness and Infinite Continuity. The relationship that you have made with the part of God that you seem to have broken away, fragments your

mind, is centered on a limited self, and is full of fear. The Relationship that God extends to you encompasses and extends God's Oneness. The relationship that you made attempts to destroy God's Oneness, so as to limit you.

2.   The contrast between What God extends to you and what you have made is clear in the very different experiences of the Holy and the unholy relationships. The Holy relationship is based on the Oneness of Love, and it rests on It serene and undisturbed. The body does not intrude upon it. Any relationship in which the body enters is based on idolatry, not Love. Love wants to be known and extended. It has no secrets, nothing to keep apart, or to hide. It is Open and Calm and Welcoming and so Simple that It cannot be misunderstood.

3.   You make idols to hide God, Which you do not want in your mind. You make these idols seem outside of your mind so that they can accept your mind's projections. They are nothing in themselves. You can 'love' them because you made them, but you will not see your Real Love reflected in them, because they are made to hide Real Love. They cannot be used for your Real Relationship with God, because they are separate from you, and they are meant to uphold your perception of your separation from God.

4.   Love does not use idols to hide anything. Love does not seek for power but for your Real Relationship with God. The body is the personal mind's chosen weapon for seeking for power *through* relationships. The personal mind's relationships are unholy, because it cannot even see your Real Relationship with God. It wants relationships solely for projecting onto idols. The personal mind throws away everything else, because it does not value the Oneness that your Real Relationship with God offers. Having no real home, the personal mind seeks for as many bodies as it can collect to make idols for its projections and to establish them as temples to itself.

5.   The Holy Spirit's Temple is a Holy relationship, not a body. The body is an isolated, secret, tiny spot of mystery in your mind that is meaningless and that really hides nothing. It is where the personal mind projects its unholy relationship to escape Reality and to keep

itself alive. It is with the body that the personal mind holds the world of idolatry in your mind. The personal mind is safe in the body, because Love cannot enter it. But the Holy Spirit does not build Its Temple where Love can never be. The Holy Spirit, Which looks on your Christ Mind, does not choose the only place in your mind where Christ cannot be seen.

6.   You cannot make the body the Holy Spirit's Temple, and it will never be the seat of Love. It is the home of the personal mind, the idolater; it is the home of Love's condemnation. Believing that you are a body makes Love seem fearful and hopeless to you. Even the body-idols that you worship seem mysterious and separate from you. The body is a temple that is dedicated by the personal mind to undoing your Real Relationship with God. When you worship the body, you perceive the 'mystery' of the separation in awe, and you hold it in reverence. What God will never make is kept 'safe' from God. But what you do not realize is that what you fear in another, but that you deny that you see there, is what makes God seem frightening and unknowable to you.

7.   If you worship idols, you will fear Love, because Love will seem to threaten your idols. If, as an idolater, you *do* let Love draw near, then Love will overlook the body and you will retreat from Love in fear, feeling the firm foundation of your temple shake and loosen. But What you will fear is the Sign of your escape from limitations. The body is not your home; your Temple is not threatened. And you are no longer an idolater, because the Holy Spirit's purpose lies safe in your Holy relationship, not in a body. You have escaped the body through your Holy relationship, which is the Holy Spirit's Temple. The body cannot enter this Temple.

8.   The only Relationship is your Oneness with God. The Oneness that you experience in the Holy relationship reflects your Relationship with God. An unholy relationship is not really a relationship at all. It is a state of isolation that only *seems* to be a joining. The instant that your mad idea of undoing your Relationship with God seemed possible, the Oneness of your mind was made meaningless to you. In that unholy instant, time was born, and bodies were made to house your mad idea of separation from God and to give it the

illusion of reality. So it seems that in time this mad idea has a home to hold it together, but it has really vanished. Only for an instant could your mad idea stand against Reality.

9. Your idols *must* disappear and leave no trace behind in your mind. The unholy instant of their seeming power is frail. Do you want this frail instant to substitute for the Eternal Blessing of the Holy Instant and Its Unlimited Beneficence? Do you prefer the malevolent unholy relationship, which seems powerful, but which you misunderstand and invest with a false attraction, to the Holy Instant, Which offers you Peace and Knowledge? If not, then lay aside the body and transcend it, quietly rising to welcome What you really want. From the Holy Spirit's Holy Temple, do not look back at your illusion of separation from God, which you have undone. No illusions can attract your mind when you have transcended them and left them far behind.

10. Your Holy relationship reflects your Oneness with God in Reality. The Holy Spirit rests within it, certain that it will endure Forever. Its firm foundation is Eternally upheld by Truth, and Love shines on it with the Gentleness and Tender Blessing that It offers to Its Own. Here, you gladly exchange the unholy instant for the Holy Instant of your safe return to God. Here, the way to your True Relationship with God is held open and you walk it with your entire mind, thankfully leaving behind the body to rest in God. Love is open to receive you and to give you Peace Forever.

11. The body is the personal mind's idol. It is your belief in separation from God made into form and then projected outside your mind. This makes it seem like there is a wall of flesh around your mind, limiting it to a tiny spot of space and time, obligated to die, and given an instant to sigh and grieve and die in honor of separation. This unholy instant of despair that is set uncertainly upon oblivion seems to be 'life' to you. Here, you who are One with God stop briefly to offer your devotion to death's idols, and then to die yourself. Here, you are more dead than Living. But it is also here that you can choose between idolatry and Love; you can choose to spend an instant paying tribute to the body, or you can free yourself from the body; you can accept the Holy Instant to replace the

unholy instant that you chose before; and you can learn to look on relationships as your salvation and not as your doom.

12. You are learning this, and you might still be afraid, but you are not immobilized. The Holy Instant is of greater value to you now than the unholy instant, and you have learned that you really want the Holy Instant. This is not a time for sadness; perhaps confusion, but not discouragement. You have a real relationship in the Holy relationship, and it has real meaning. In your Holy relationship is your Real Relationship with God. Idolatry is past and meaningless. Perhaps you still project fear onto your relationship; maybe you still fear God a little. But that is nothing when you have one true relationship beyond the body. You cannot hold yourself back from looking on your Christ Mind for long; you cannot hold back remembering your Oneness with God or your awareness of God's Love for long.

7. The Consistency of Means and End

1. The *means* for making you aware of your Holiness and the *end result* of this awareness must be brought into line before your Holy relationship will bring you only Joy. The means to meet the Holy Spirit's Goal comes from God, the same Source as the Holy Spirit's purpose. Being simple and direct, this course has nothing in it that is not consistent. The parts that seem inconsistent or more difficult to you are areas where you still keep means and end apart in your mind. This produces great discomfort for you, but it does not need to be this way. This course requires almost nothing from you. It is impossible to imagine one that asks so little or that offers you more.

2. The period of discomfort that follows your changing your relationship's purpose from separation to Holiness may now be almost over. To the extent that you still experience it, you are refusing to leave the means for attaining this new purpose to the Holy Spirit, Which changed the purpose for you. You recognize that you want the Goal, but are you also willing to accept the means to reach It? If you are not, admit that it is *you* who are inconsistent. Every purpose is attained by some means, and if you want

the purpose you must be willing to accept the means. You cannot sincerely say, 'I want this above all else, but I don't want to learn how to get it.'

3. The Holy Spirit indeed asks little of you for you to obtain your Goal, but the Holy Spirit also does not ask any more of you to give you the means. The means are second to your Goal, and when you hesitate to use them, it is because the Purpose frightens you, not the means. Remember this, or you will make the mistake of believing that the means are difficult. They cannot be difficult *for* you, because they are given *to* you. The means guarantee your Goal, and they are perfectly in line with It. Before you look at them a little closer, remember that if you think that they are impossible, it is because you are not sure that you want the Purpose. If your Goal is possible to reach, the means must be possible, too.

4. It is impossible for you to see Innocence while you believe that bodies are real. This is perfectly consistent with the Goal of Holiness. When you let the effects of your belief in separation be lifted, your recognition of your Holiness is the result, because your Holiness is always True. It is impossible for you to see an Innocent body, because Holiness is positive, and the body is merely neutral. The body is not guilty or innocent. Since it is nothing, the body cannot be invested with attributes of your Christ Mind or of the personal mind. Either view of the body is an error, because both give attributes of the mind where they cannot be. For you to remember Truth, you must undo both views of the body.

5. The body is the means by which the personal mind seeks to make you unholy by making separation from God real to you. The time of bodies *is* the unholy instant. Its purpose *is* to make separation real to you. You can only attain this in an illusion, so the illusion of bodies is quite in keeping with the purpose of unholiness. Because of this consistency, you don't question the means for unholiness while you cherish the goal of unholiness. Perception adapts to your wishes, because you always see what you desire. If you see the body, you have chosen the personal mind over the Perception of your Christ Mind. The Perception of your Christ Mind, like your Real Relationship with God, is One. You either see Christ, or you do

not really see at all.

6.   For you to see another's body as real is for you to judge your separation from God as real and to not see your mind Truly. In the darkness of separation, the Reality in your perception is invisible to you. You can only fill in this blank with illusions. Here, illusions and Reality are kept apart. Here, illusions are never brought to Truth but hidden from It. In the darkness of separation, you imagine a reality in which bodies enter unholy relationships with other bodies to serve the cause of separation before they die.

7.   There is indeed a difference between these vain imaginings and the Perception of your Christ Mind. Their difference does not lie in them but in their purposes. Both are the appropriate means to the end for which you employ them. Neither can serve the other's purpose, because each one is your *choice* of purpose and is employed on behalf of your chosen purpose. Either is meaningless without the purpose for which you intend it, and you value both as part of their purpose. The means seem real when you value the Goal. And judging your separation from God as real has no value for you, unless your goal *is* separation.

8.   You can only see the body through your judgment that separation from God is real. For you to see the body as real is for you to deny the Perception of your Christ Mind, Which is the Means the Holy Spirit uses to serve *Its* purpose. The Holy relationship cannot achieve its purpose through the means for separation. You taught yourself to judge the separation as real, but the Perception, of your Christ Mind is taught to you by the Holy Spirit, Which will undo your teaching. The Holy Spirit's Perception cannot look on the body, because It cannot see separation from God, so It leads you to Reality. The Perception of your Christ Mind, which you see to replace the personal mind's projections in your Holy relationship, is not an illusion. Do not look on your relationship from the personal mind, because from there your imaginings will seem real to you. With the personal mind, your purpose is to deny the Truth, and, while this purpose has meaning for you, you will evaluate the means for its attainment as worth seeing. You will not be able to see Truly.

9.   Don't ask, 'How can I not see bodies?'; ask instead, 'Do I really want to see Innocence?' As you ask, remember that the Innocence that you see is *your* escape from fear. Your salvation is the Holy Spirit's Goal, and Its Means is the Perception of your Christ Mind. What you see with your Christ Mind's Perception *is* Innocence. You cannot love and then judge the separation as real and see guilt. When you love, you do not see what you made, but you see Christ, Which is given to you to see with the Perception that makes seeing Christ possible.

8. The Vision of Sinlessness

1.   As you choose to overlook the personal mind's projections on the other in your Holy relationship, the Holy Spirit's Perception will come to you at first in glimpses, and these will be enough to show you your Innocence. Truth is restored to you through your desire for Truth, just as Truth was lost to you because of your desire for something else. Open the Holy Place in your mind that you have closed off by valuing the 'something else', and What you have never lost will quietly return to your awareness. Your Real Perception would not be necessary for you if you had not judged the world as real. When you want judgment to be undone for you, it will be undone.

2.   Do you want to know your own Identity? Do you want to happily exchange your doubts for Certainty? Do you want to be free of misery and to learn of Joy again? Your Holy relationship can do all of this; these are the *effects* of your Holy relationship. But just as its Holy purpose was not made by the personal self, its happy results are not of it, either. Rejoice in what is yours for the asking, and do not think that you need to make either the means or the end. These effects are given to you when you decide to see Innocence instead of the personal mind's projections on the other in your relationship. All this is waiting on your desire to receive it. The Holy Spirit's Perception is freely given to you when you ask to see Truth.

3.   With the Holy Spirit's Perception, Innocence is yours to see in place of the personal mind's projections. Rejoice with the Holy Spirit! Peace will come to you when you ask for It with real desire, and

you sincerely agree with the Holy Spirit about what is salvation. Be willing to see Innocence so that Christ may rise in your perception and give you Joy. Place no value on bodies, which hold you to illusions. Your entire mind desires Innocence, though you perceive a world of separation. Bless your mind where you perceive a world with your Holy relationship, and do not see what the personal mind has made in the world that it projects outside of you.

4. The Presence of the Holy Spirit in your mind guarantees that What God wills and extends to you is yours. Remembering this is your Purpose now, and the Perception that will make you aware of It is ready to be given to you. You *have* the Real Perception that enables you to overlook the body. As you look on your Holy relationship, you can see an altar to God, as Holy as Heaven, glowing with Purity, and shining with your forgiveness. Can you value anything more than this? The body is not a better home or a safer shelter. Why look on the body instead of on Truth? How can you prefer the engine of destruction to the Holy Home that the Holy Spirit offers to share with you?

5. The body is a symbol of weakness, vulnerability, and loss of power. Can this save you? Do not turn to the helpless in your distress and in your need for help. The pitifully little is not the perfect choice for you to call upon for strength. Judging bodies as real will seem to make your mind weak when you need to see the Strength that is in your mind. There is no problem, no event, no situation, and no perplexity that the Holy Spirit's Perception will not solve for you. Your mind is healed when you look upon everything with the Holy Spirit's Perception, because this is not the personal mind's sight, and It brings with It God's Beloved Law of Oneness.

6. Everything that you look upon with your Real Perception falls gently into place according to the Law of Oneness, Which is brought to It by the Holy Spirit's Calm and Certain Perception. The end for everything that the Holy Spirit looks upon is always sure, because, in unadjusted form, it is suited perfectly to meet the Holy Spirit's purpose. Under the Holy Spirit's Gaze, destructiveness becomes benign and separation is turned to blessing. But the body's eyes cannot correct. Its eyes adjust to separation and cannot

overlook it in any form. It sees separation everywhere and in every-thing. Look through its eyes and everything is condemned by guilt. All that could save you, you will not see. Your Holy relationship, the source of your salvation, will be deprived of meaning by the body, and its most Holy purpose will lack the means to be accom-plished.

7. The personal mind's judgment is a toy, a whim, the senseless means to make separation and death real to you. But the Holy Spirit's Perception sets all things right by bringing them within Heaven's kindly Law of Oneness. What if you recognized that the world is a hallucination? What if you really understood that you made it up? What if you realized that those who seem to walk about in it separate from God, attacking, murdering, self-destructing, and ultimately dying are wholly unreal? If you accept that all of this is unreal, you will not have faith in it; you will not even see it.

8. Hallucinations disappear when you recognize that they *are* halluci-nations. This is their healing and their remedy: do not believe in them and they are gone. Once you accept this simple fact and take back the power that you have given to your illusions, you will be released from them. One thing is sure: Hallucinations serve a purpose, and when you no longer consider their purpose valuable, they disappear. So your question is never 'Do I want the illusions?' but 'Do I want the purpose that illusions serve?' The world that you perceive seems to hold out many different purposes with different values. But they are all the same purpose - separation from God - and their values only *seem* to have a hierarchy.

9. Only two purposes are possible for you: separation from God or Oneness with God. They cannot be joined. Which you choose deter-mines what you see, because what you see is your means to meet your chosen purpose. Hallucinations are the means to meet the goal of madness. They are the means by which the world that you have projected outside of your mind from within it adjusts to the separation and seems to witness to its reality. Nothing is outside of your mind, and your projections are made upon nothing. It is the projections that give 'nothing' all the meaning that it holds for you.

10. You cannot perceive what has no meaning. Meaning always comes

from within you and is then projected or extended outward in your awareness. All of the meaning that you give to the world that seems outside of your mind reflects whether you looked within and saw Truth or whether you looked within and judged against God. The Holy Spirit's Perception is your means for translating the personal mind's nightmares into Happy illusions; the personal mind's wild hallucinations of fearful outcomes for your guilt into the Calm and reassuring Perception of your Oneness with God. You will look on the Holy Spirit's Gentle Perceptions with Joy. They are the Holy Spirit's Substitutes for all of the terrifying sights of the personal mind, which fill you with horror. They step away from separation and remind you that what frightens you is not reality but errors that you can correct.

11. You will not have to be persuaded to accept the Gift of the Holy Spirit's Perception when you look on what should seem terrifying and you see Peace instead. And you will not refuse God, Which comes after your Real Perception is as complete as the Holy Spirit's. Think for an instant on this: You can behold the Holiness that God gives to your Christ Mind, and you never need to think that there is anything else for you to see.

Chapter 21

Reason and Perception

1. Projection makes perception. The world that you see is what you have put there to see; nothing more and nothing less, so it is important to you. The world that you perceive is the witness to your state of mind; the outward picture of your inward condition. As you think so do you perceive. So do not seek to change the world, but choose to change your mind about the world's reality. What you perceive is a result, not a cause. That is why no miracle is harder than another. What you look upon with your Christ Mind's Perception is healed and Holy. and nothing you perceive without It means anything. Where there is no meaning, there is chaos.

2. Through your identification with a personal mind, you have damned yourself, and this is the judgment that you project onto the world that you perceive. See the world as damned, and what you see is what you have done to hurt What is One with God. If you behold disaster and catastrophe, then you have tried to crucify yourself, but if you perceive Holiness and hope, then you have joined God's Will to set yourself free. There is no choice that lies between these two decisions. What you see witnesses to the choice you make.

1. The Forgotten Song

1. What the blind 'see' they imagine, because they do not know what anything really looks like. They infer what things look like indirectly, and they construct their inferences as they stumble or fall against them or walk around or through them unhurt. This is how it is with you without your Christ Mind's Perception. The cues that you use to infer your situation are wrong, so you get hurt. You fail to realize that the way to Heaven is open before you, and that you will be welcomed There.

2. It is foolish for you to use the personal mind's judgment, which always makes separation real to you, when you can use the Perception of your Christ Mind instead. It is not necessary for you to imagine what Reality must look like, because you must see It before you recognize It for What It is. And you can be shown which way to go and where you will feel safe in your mind; which way leads to despair and which way to Love. The personal mind's judgment will always mislead you, but your Real Perception shows you Reality. Why should you guess?

3. There is no need for you to learn through pain. You acquire Gentle lessons Joyously, and you remember them gladly. You *want* to learn What brings you Happiness, and you want to remember It. You don't deny this. But you question whether the means that this course uses will bring you the Joy that it promises. If you believed it would, you would have no problem learning it. You are not yet a Happy learner, because you still remain uncertain that your Christ Mind's Perception gives you more than the personal mind's judgment. You have not yet learned that you cannot have both.

4. In your blindness to God, you have become accustomed to the world that you made by adjusting to it. You think that you know your way about in it, and you learned this through the stern necessity of limits that you believed were real. Believing in them still, you hold your lessons dear, because you feel like you cannot know anything real without them. You do not understand or believe that your lessons *keep* you from knowing Reality, so you keep the world that you see in your imagination, believing that this and nothing else is real. You hate this world, because you learned it through pain, and everything in it reminds you that you are incomplete and bitterly deprived.

5. You adjust to the world of bodies where you think you are because you are afraid that this is all that you have, and you don't want to lose it. You try to reach for real union with others in the world that you perceive, and you fail again and again. You adjust to loneliness, because you believe that keeping the body is the way to save the little that you have. But listen, and try to remember this:

6. Perhaps you catch a hint of a former State of Being that you have

not entirely forgotten. It may be dim, but It is not altogether unfamiliar. It is like a song that you once heard, but you don't remember where or what it is called.[1] Just a wisp of the melody has stayed with you, but you remember from this little part how lovely the whole song was, how wonderful was the setting where you heard it, and how you loved those who were there with you.

7. The notes are nothing, but you have kept them with you as a soft reminder of what would make you weep if you remembered how dear it was. You are afraid to remember, because you believe that you would lose the world that you have learned since then. And yet, you know that nothing that you have learned in this world is half so dear. Listen, and see if you remember an ancient song that you knew long ago and once held more dear than any melody that you have taught yourself to cherish since then.

8. Beyond the body, beyond the sun and the stars, past everything that the body's eyes can see, and yet more familiar to you, is an arc of golden light that stretches as you look into a great and shining circle. The circle fills with light, and then the edges disappear and the light is no longer contained. The light extends into Infinity without break or limit. Everything within it is joined in perfect continuity. There is nothing outside of it, because this light is every-where.

9. Such is the Perception of your Christ Mind, Which you know well. It is the Perception of that Which knows God. It is the Memory of What you are: a Part of God with All of God within you, and joined to All of God as surely as All of God is joined with you. Accept your Real Perception, Which can show you this instead of the body. You know this ancient song well, and nothing will ever be as dear to you as the hymn that your Christ Mind sings to God.

10. Now you who were once blind with the personal mind's judgments can see, because your former State of Being, Which you dimly remember, is yours. The denial that you have made cannot withstand your Memory of God. You will look upon your Christ Mind's Perception and remember God. Your remembering God is what your experience of the miracle is. No part of your mind where you perceive a world can be left out of your remembering. Any

perception of Love that you extend, extends to your entire mind. When you see Love, you *are* remembering It for your entire mind.

2. The Responsibility for Sight

1. It has often been repeated in these pages how little is asked of you for you to learn this course. Your little willingness can transform to Joy your relationship to your mind where you perceive a world. Your little willingness is all that you need to offer to the Holy Spirit in return for Everything. This is all that your salvation rests on. This is the tiny change of mind by which your crucifixion is changed to resurrection. This little willingness is so simple that you cannot fail to understand what is asked of you. You can refuse to offer it, but you cannot be confused about what is being asked of you. If you choose to not offer your little willingness, it is not because what is asked of you is obscure to you, but because you think it is too high a price to pay for Peace.

2. The only thing that you need to do to have your Christ Mind's Perception, Happiness, release from pain, and to escape from separation from God, is to say this and mean it without reservations:

    'I *am* responsible for what I perceive.
    I choose the feelings that I experience by choosing the goal that I want to achieve.
    And separation from God or Oneness with God comes to me as I ask for it.'

    Do not deceive yourself any longer that you are helpless in the face of what is done to you. Acknowledge that you have been mistaken, and the effects of your mistake will disappear.

3. It is impossible for you who are One with God to be driven by events outside of yourself. It is impossible that what happens to you is not your choice. Your power of decision determines your experience in every situation in which you find yourself 'by accident' or 'by chance'. There is no accident or chance in What is One with God, and there is nothing outside of God. If you suffer, it

is because you have chosen separation from God as your goal. If you are Happy, it is because you gave the power of decision to the Holy Spirit, Which decides for God for you. This is the little gift that you give to the Holy Spirit, and even this the Holy Spirit gives to you to give to yourself. The power of decision is given to you to release your mind from the world that you perceive so that you may see your salvation.

4. Do not begrudge the Holy Spirit your little offering. Withhold the power of decision from the Holy Spirit, and you hold onto the world as you perceive it now. But give the power of decision to the Holy Spirit, and what you now perceive goes away. Never was so much given for so little. This exchange occurs and is maintained in the Holy Instant. Here is the world that you *do not* want brought to the Real Perception that you *do* want, and you are given your Real Perception. But for this to happen, you must recognize the power of your wanting. You must perceive that your mind, which is strong enough to make a world, can let it go. If you are willing to see that you were mistaken, you can accept correction.

5. The world that you perceive is an idle witness that you are right in thinking that you are separate from God. It is insane for you to listen to this witness. In your identification with a personal self, you project the message that you are separate from God onto the world, you listen to this message, and then you are convinced by it. Recognize only this, and you see how circular is the 'reasoning' of the personal mind. This was not given to you by God. This is your 'gift' to yourself, and this is what you project onto your Holy relationship. Be willing to extend Truth in its place. As you look on Truth instead of the personal mind's projections, you will see your True Self.

6. Perhaps you do not see the need that you have for you to give a little willingness to the Holy Spirit. Look closer, then, at what it is you are afraid of losing, and see in it the whole exchange of separation for salvation. All that the personal self is, is your idea that it is possible for things to happen against the Will of you who are One with God and therefore against the Will of God. It is your replacement for your True Will; your mad revolt against What must

Forever *be*. The personal self is your statement that you have the power to make God powerless, to take this power for yourself, and so to leave yourself without What God wills for you. This is the mad idea that you enshrine upon the many personal selves that you see and worship. Everything that threatens this seems to attack that which you have faith in. Do not think that you lack faith when you identify with a personal self; your belief and trust in the personal mind are strong indeed.

7.   The Holy Spirit can give you faith in Holiness and the Perception to see It easily, but you have not left your mind open and unoccupied. Where Holiness and your Real Perception should be, you have set up idols to the personal self. You give reality to this other 'will', which seems to tell you what must happen, so What can show you Reality seems unreal to you. All that you are asked to do is to make room for Truth. You are not asked to make or do what lies beyond your understanding. Just *let Truth in* and stop your interference with What will happen of Itself. Recognize the Presence of What you thought you gave away.

8.   Be willing, for an Instant, to leave your mind open, and you won't fail to see What is really here. The Holy Instant does not make you One with God; in It you recognize that you are *already* One with God. You recognize this when you suspend the personal mind's judgments, and you use the Holy Spirit's Perception. Only then do you look within and see What must be here. Undoing your perception of separation from God is not your task, but it is up to you to *welcome* its undoing. Your faith and your desire go together, because you believe in what you want.

9.   Wishful thinking is how the personal mind makes what it wants. There is no better demonstration of the power of your wanting and your faith to make goals real to you and to make them seem possible. Your faith in the unreal leads to you making mental adjustments to make a reality to fit your goal of madness. Your goal of separation from God induces your perception of a fearful world to justify its purpose. What you desire you will see, and if it is unreal, you will make it seem real to you by denying the adjustments that you make to make it seem real.

10. When you deny your Christ Mind's Perception, it is inevitable that you confuse the cause and effect relationship of your perceptions. Then your purpose becomes obscuring the cause and effect relationship of your perceptions to make it seem that your perceptions, which are the effects of your thoughts, stand on their own. Your mind's effects then seem independent of your mind and they seem to be the cause of events and your feelings about them. Earlier in this course it was mentioned that you desire to make your own god and to not be One with God. Your confusion of cause and effect is the same desire. You who are God's Effect deny that God is your Cause. Now you seem to be your own god, a cause that produces real effects, though you hide this by giving your effects power over you and you make them seem to be your cause. Every effect has a cause, and if you confuse cause and effect, you fail to understand both.

11. Believing that you *did not* make the world that you see and believing that God *did not* create you *are the same mistake*. What is *not* One with God has no influence over you who *are* One with God. If you think that what you made can tell you what you think and feel, then you deny that God created you, and you believe that the effects of your mind made you. If you think that the world that you made has the power to make you what it wills, then you are confusing the effect of your mind with God.

12. In your Oneness with God, your extension of God is like God's extension of God to you. And in your extending God, you do not delude yourself that you are independent of God. Your Oneness with God is the Source of your extension of God. Apart from God you have no power to create, and what you make is meaningless. What you make changes nothing in God's Creation; it depends entirely on your madness, and it cannot serve to justify your madness. Others in the world that you made seem to validate the reality of the world. Thus they seem to deny your Oneness with God. They seem to believe, with you, that the world made you and them. Thus they validate your denial that you made the world and them.

13. But the Truth is that your entire mind is One with a Loving God.

See what 'proves' otherwise and you deny your whole Reality. But acknowledge that it is only what you have made in secret that seems to keep your mind divided into an isolated mind and a world outside of it, and that this keeps you in a perception of separation from God, and the instant of release has come to you. All of your perception of separation's effects are gone when its source has been uncovered in your mind. It is your perception of separation's seeming independence from your mind that keeps you bound to it. This is the same mistake as thinking that you are independent of your Source, with Which you are One, and Which you have never left.

3. Faith, Belief and Vision

1. Your goal for all special relationships is to make separation from God real to you. Special relationships are a compromise that you make with Reality, Which is One, by attempting a *form* of union. But compromises are limits, and you hate anyone with whom you have a limited relationship. In the name of 'fairness', you sometimes demand more of yourself and sometimes more of the other to maintain the seeming union. You attempt this 'fairness' to ease your guilt for your accepted purpose of separation from God for the relationship. So the Holy Spirit *must* change the purpose of your relationship to make it useful to the Holy Spirit and harmless to you.

2. If you accept this change of purpose, you will accept the idea of making room for Truth. Then the source of your guilt will be gone from your mind. You may imagine that you still experience its effects, but it will not be your purpose, and you will no longer want it. But you will not allow your purpose to be changed while you still desire separation from God, because you cherish and protect the goal that you accept for your mind. Your mind will follow your goal, grimly or happily, with faith and persistence. You never recognize the power of your faith when it is placed in separation from God, but you will always recognize it when it is placed in Love.

3. Why is it strange to you that your faith can move mountains? This

is a little feat for such a power. Your faith can keep you limited as long as you believe you are limited. You will be released from limitations when you no longer believe in limitations and you place your faith in Limitlessness instead. You cannot place equal faith in opposite things. What faith you give to your perception of separation from God, you take away from your Holiness; what faith you give to your Holiness, you take away from your perception of separation from God.

4.   Your faith and belief and Real Perception are the means by which you reach the goal of being aware of your Holiness. Through them, the Holy Spirit leads you to Truth and away from illusions. Holiness is the Holy Spirit's direction; the only one that the Holy Spirit sees. When you wander, the Holy Spirit reminds you that there is only one direction. The Holy Spirit's faith and belief and Perception are all for you, and when you have accepted them completely in place of the personal mind, you will no longer need them. Your faith and belief and Real Perception are only meaningful before you reach the state of Certainty that only God is Real. Though they are *how* you reach Heaven, you do not need them in Heaven.

5.   It is impossible for you to lack faith, but you can choose where to put your faith. For you to lack faith that only God is Real is for you to put your faith in nothing. The faith that you give to illusions does not lack power, because, by this faith, you who are One with Power believe that you are powerless. You may lack faith in your Truth, but your faith in your illusions about yourself is strong. You made faith, perception, and belief as the means to lose your certainty that only God is Real and to make separation from God real to you. This mad direction was your choice, and, by your faith in it, you made what you desired.

6.   The Holy Spirit can use everything that your split mind made to make separation from God real to you. But as the Holy Spirit uses these things, they will lead you *away* from separation from God, because the Holy Spirit's Purpose lies in the opposite direction. The Holy Spirit sees the means that your split mind made, but not the goal of separation it made them for. The Holy Spirit will not take

what you made away from you, because the Holy Spirit sees value in them as a means for what the Holy Spirit wills for you. You made perception so that you could choose among personal selves to make relationships that make separation from God real to you. The Holy Spirit sees perception as a means to teach you that the Real Perception of the Holy relationship is all that you want to see. When you learn this, you will give your faith and belief to Holiness, because you want It.

7. Your faith and your belief will become attached to the Perception of your Christ Mind as they are redirected toward Holiness. What you think of as separation from God limits you, and when you limit your mind to looking on bodies as real, you hate others because they remind you of your fear. In your refusal to forgive your own projections of bodies you project your guilt onto others, because then the means for separation from God are dear to you, so the body has your belief and faith. But your extending Holiness will set you free, removing hatred from your mind by removing fear, not as a symptom, but at its source.

8. You will have no fear if you free yourself from seeing your projections of bodies as real. If you do so, you will be renouncing your means for making separation real to you by letting all limitations be removed from your mind. As you desire to look on Holiness instead, the power of your faith and belief will go far beyond the body. They will support your Christ Mind's Perception, not obstruct It. But first you must choose to recognize how much your faith in the body has limited your understanding of what is real. And you must *want* to place the power of your faith and belief in What the Holy Spirit gives to you. Your experience of miracles, which follows this decision, is born of your faith. When you choose to look away from separation from God, you are given your Christ Mind's Perception, and you are led to Holiness.

9. When you are attached to separation from God, you must think that the Holy Spirit is asking you to sacrifice the body by asking you to let go of the body. This is because sacrifice is how the personal mind's purpose is accomplished. But the Holy Spirit knows that sacrifice brings nothing, and the Holy Spirit does not

make compromises. If you limit the Holy Spirit, you will hate the Holy Spirit, because you will be afraid. The Gift of Itself that the Holy Spirit gives to you is worth more than anything in the world that you perceive. It is time for you to recognize this. Join your awareness to What has already been joined. The faith that you have extended in your Holy relationship can accomplish this. The Holy Spirit sees your entire mind through Love for you, without one spot of separation upon it, and in the Innocence that makes it as Beautiful as Heaven.

10. Your faith in sacrifice has made sacrifice powerful to you, and you do not recognize that you cannot use the Perception of your Christ Mind because of your belief in sacrifice. For sacrifice to occur, it would have to be a body that demands sacrifice from another body, because your mind cannot ask for or receive sacrifice of itself. But a body cannot ask for sacrifice. The intention is in your the mind, which uses bodies to carry out the separation from God that you believe in. Confusing your mind with the body is inescapable when you value separation from God. Sacrifice is your means for limitation and therefore for Self-hate.

11. The Holy Spirit is not concerned with sacrifice, because the Holy Spirit does not ask of you what it is Its Purpose to lead you *from*. You think that the Holy Spirit wants to deprive you 'for your own good', but 'good' and 'deprivation' are opposites that cannot be meaningfully joined. If you see one then the other has disappeared. Neither demands the sacrifice of the other, but the absence of one does lead to your awareness of the other.

12. Identifying with a body is the sacrifice that you make to be separate from God, and even in your perception that you are in a world, you are aware that the body limits you. Yet, in your Christ Mind's Perception you look upon the body very differently. You can have faith in the body to serve the Holy Spirit's Goal, and you can give it the power to serve as a means to help you see with your Christ Mind's Perception. But with your Christ Mind's Perception you look past the body. The faith and belief that you have given to the body belong beyond it. From your mind, you gave perception and faith and belief to the body. Give them back to your mind so that

they can be used to save you from what you made.

4. The Fear to Look Within

1. The Holy Spirit will never teach you that you are sinful. The Holy Spirit *will* correct your errors, but this is not frightening for you. You are indeed afraid to look within and see the sin that you think is there, and you are not afraid to admit this. The personal mind deems it appropriate for you to feel fear in association with sin. It smiles approvingly at this, and it has no fear in letting you feel ashamed. The personal mind does not doubt your belief and faith in sin, so it is not threatened. Your faith that sin is within you witnesses to your desire that it *be* there. But your belief that you are sinful is not the real source of your fear.

2. Remember that the personal mind is not all that is in your mind. Its rule is limited by its 'enemy', the Holy Spirit, Which it cannot see, but Which it fears. The personal mind screams loudly at you to not look within, because you will see your sin and God will strike you blind. You believe this and you do not look. But this is not the personal mind's real fear, nor yours. There is another fear hidden beneath this one. Underneath its constant and frantic demand that you not look within is the personal mind's uncertainty that sin is there to see. Beneath your fear to look within because of sin is this other fear that makes the personal mind tremble:

3. What if you looked within and did *not* see sin? This is the 'fearful' question that the personal mind never asks. And now that you are asking it you are threatening the personal mind's whole defense system too seriously for it to pretend to be your friend. When you extended the Holiness in your mind to encompass your perception of another, you detached yourself from the belief that your identity lies in a personal self. A Holy relationship is one in which you join with What is part of you in Truth. Your belief in separation from God has already been shaken, and you are no longer wholly unwilling to look within and *not* see sin.

4. Your liberation is still only partial, limited, and incomplete, but it is born within you. No longer wholly mad, you are willing to look on much of your insanity and recognize it *is* madness. Your faith is

499

moving inward, past insanity, and on to Sanity. The personal mind cannot hear what your Sanity tells you now. The Holy Spirit's Purpose has been accepted by the Part of your mind that the personal mind does not know and that you did not know. But this Part, with Which you now identify, is not afraid to look on Itself. It does not know sin, and this is how It is willing to see the Holy Spirit's Purpose as Its own.

5. This Part has seen Christ in place of the personal mind's projections in your Holy relationship, and It has recognized Its Self. It desires nothing more than to join with Its Self and be Free again. It has been waiting for you to accept release. Now you recognize that it was not the personal mind that joined the Holy Spirit's Purpose, so there must be Something Else in your mind. Do not think that *this* is madness. It is your Sanity that tells you that there *is* Something Else, and this follows perfectly from what you have already learned.

6. The Holy Spirit's teaching is wholly consistent. This is the reasoning of the Sane. You have perceived the personal mind's madness without fear, because you did not choose to share in it. Sometimes the personal mind still deceives you, but in your saner moments its ranting does not scare you. You have realized that you do not want all the 'gifts' that the personal mind will withdraw from you in rage at your 'presumptuous' wish to look within. A few might draw your attention still, but you will not trade Heaven for them.

7. Now the personal mind *is* afraid. But what it perceives with terror the other Part of your mind perceives with gladness. It has longed for your mind's Oneness since the personal self came into your mind. The personal mind's weakness is the Holy Spirit's Strength. Another Perception is rising in your sight, and It brings you hope for Peace. You are remembering Heaven, Which the personal mind's rule has kept from your mind for so long. Heaven has come into your awareness, because It finds a home in your Holy relationship, and the world that you perceive can no longer contain what belongs to Heaven.

8. Look gently on your Holy relationship, and you will see the

personal mind's weakness. Your mind, which the personal mind wants to keep split, *has* joined, and it looks on the personal mind without fear. You who are Innocent should gladly follow the way to Certainty. Do not be held back by fear's insistence that sureness lies in doubt. This is meaningless, and what does it matter to you how loudly the personal mind proclaims it? The senseless is not made meaningful by repetition and clamor. The Quiet Way is open. Follow It happily and do not question What must be so.

5. The Function of Reason

1. Your perception makes the world that you see. It literally picks things out in it as your mind directs it. Laws that govern size and shape and brightness would hold if you had no preferences, but you do. You are far more likely to find what you are looking for than you are to find what you want to overlook. If you want to hear It, the still, small Voice of the Holy Spirit is not drowned out by the personal mind's raucous screams and senseless ravings. Your perception sees your choices, not facts, and far more than you may realize depends on your choices. Your whole belief in what you are depends entirely on the voice that you choose to hear and on the sights that you choose to see. Your perception is a witness to this but never to Reality. But it can show you those conditions in which you can become aware of Reality or those conditions in which you can never be aware of Reality.

2. Reality does not need your cooperation to be Itself, but your *awareness* of Reality is your choice. Listen to the personal mind, and see what it tells you to see, and you will certainly see yourself as tiny, vulnerable, and afraid. You will experience depression, a sense of worthlessness, and feelings of impermanence and unreality. You will believe that you are the helpless prey of forces beyond your control that are much more powerful than you. And you will think that a world outside of your mind directs your destiny. This will be what you have faith in, if you believe in the personal mind. But don't believe in it, because it is your faith that makes it reality to you.

3. There is another Perception and another Voice in Which your

Freedom lies, and they are awaiting your choice. If you place your faith in Them, you will perceive another Self in you. This other Self experiences miracles as natural. Miracles are as natural to It as breathing is to the body. Miracles are Its obvious response to your calls for help; the only response this Self makes. Miracles seem unnatural to the personal mind, because it cannot understand how your mind can influence your perception of others who seem separate. And if they *were* separate from your mind, then your mind could *not* influence your perceptions of them. But your mind is not split, and this other Self is perfectly aware of this, so It recognizes that miracles do not affect something outside but only what is in Its Own Mind. There *is* nothing else.

4.   You do not realize the extent to which the idea of your separation from God has interfered with your ability to think clearly. Your True Reasoning lies in the other Self that you have cut off from your awareness. Nothing that you have allowed to stay in your awareness is capable of True Reasoning. How can the segment of your mind devoid of True Reasoning understand what True Reasoning is or grasp the information that True Reasoning will give you? All sorts of questions may arise in the personal mind, but when the basic question 'What if I looked within and saw no sin?' arises from your True Reasoning Mind, the personal mind will not ask it. Like all that stems from your True Reasoning Mind, the basic question is obvious, simple, and remains unasked by the personal mind. But your True Reasoning Mind can answer the question.

5.   God's plan for your salvation could not have been established without your will and consent. It must have been accepted by your Christ Mind because, being One with God, What God wills for your Christ Mind, your Christ Mind receives. God does not will apart from your Christ Mind, and the Will of God does not wait upon time to be accomplished. Being Eternal, What is joined with the Will of God is in you now. You have within you a Place Where the Holy Spirit has been since your need for the Holy Spirit arose and was fulfilled in the same instant. Your True Reasoning Mind will tell you this if you listen. But this is not the personal mind's thinking. The alien nature of your True Reasoning Mind to the

personal mind is proof that you will not find in the personal mind the answer to 'What if I looked within and saw no sin?' But the answer exists for you, and it has as its given purpose your freedom from belief in sin, so you must be free to find it.

6.   God's plan is simple; never circular or self-defeating. God's Thoughts are all Self-extending, and your Will is included in this. So there must be a Part of you that knows God's Will and shares It. It is not meaningful for you to ask if What must be is so, but it is meaningful for you to ask why you are unaware of What is so. The question 'What if I looked within and saw no sin?' must have an answer if the plan of God for your salvation is complete. And It *is* complete, because God does not know incompletion.

7.   The answer must be in God, the Source of the plan for your salvation. And where are you but in God with the answer? Your Identity is as much an Effect of God as is the Innocence Which is the answer, so they must be the same. Oh yes, you know this and much more. But any part of this Knowledge threatens your perception of separation from God as much as all of It does, because all of It comes with any part. This you can accept, because What your Clear Mind points to you can see, because Its Witnesses are Clear. Only in total insanity can you disregard them, and you have gone past this. Your True Reasoning is a Means which serves the Holy Spirit's purpose. Unlike other means, It cannot be reinterpreted or redirected by the goal of separation from God. Your True Reasoning is beyond the personal mind's range of means.

8.   Your faith, perception, and belief can be misplaced to serve the personal mind's needs. But your True Reasoning has no place at all in madness, and It cannot be adjusted to fit its goal. Your faith and belief in madness can be strong, guiding your perception toward what your mind values. But your True Reasoning does not enter into this at all. If your True Reasoning is applied, the personal mind's perceptions fall away. There is no True Reasoning in insanity, because insanity depends entirely on the absence of True Reasoning. The personal mind does not use True Reasoning, because it doesn't realize that True Reasoning exists. In your partial insanity, you have access to True Reasoning, Which you need. But

God does not depend on It, and madness keeps It out.

9.	The Part of your mind where your True Reasoning lies was dedicated, by your joint Will with God, to the undoing of your insanity. Here you accepted the Holy Spirit's purpose, and it was accomplished at once. Your True Reasoning is alien to insanity, and when you use It, you gain a Means Which cannot be applied to separation from God. Knowledge of God is far beyond what you can attain, but your True Reasoning opens your mind, which you have closed against God.

10.	You have come very close to this open mind. Your faith and belief have shifted, and you have asked the question that the personal mind will never ask. Your True Reasoning must tell you that the question came from Something that you do not know, but Which must be in you. Your faith and belief, upheld by True Reason, cannot fail to lead to changed perception in you. In this change, you make room for the Perception of your Christ Mind. Your Real Perception extends beyond Itself, as does the purpose that it serves.

6. Reason versus Madness

1.	Your True Reasoning Mind cannot see sin, but It can see errors, and It leads to their correction. Your True Reasoning Mind does not value the errors but their *correction*. Your True Reasoning Mind will also tell you that when you think that you sin, you call for Help. If you do not accept the Help that you call for, you will not believe that It is yours to extend, you will not extend It, and you will maintain your belief that Help is not for you. Any error in your mind that you leave uncorrected deceives you about the Power that is in you to make correction. This Power can correct, but, if you do not allow It to do so, you deny correction to yourself through your perception of the other in your Holy relationship. You will share with your perception of the other your belief that you are damned. You can spare yourself and your perception of the other this, because your True Reasoning can correct your perception of both.

2.	You can only accept or refuse correction of your mind by including your perception of the other. Your belief in sin maintains that this isn't necessary. But True Reasoning tells you that you cannot see yourself or the other as having the purpose of separation from God and still perceive one of you as Innocent. You cannot feel guilty and perceive Innocence any more than you can perceive a guilty world and see yourself as Innocent. Sin maintains that you must be separate from the world that you perceive; True Reasoning tells you that this is a mistake. Your Mind is One, so how can your thoughts have no effect at all in your mind where you perceive a world? This is impossible.

3. God cannot think without you who are One with God; no more can you think without including all that your mind perceives. Only if bodies are real is it possible for there to be more than one mind. But bodies can only be separate, and they are therefore unreal. The home of madness cannot be the home of True Reason, but it is easy for you to leave the home of madness if you Reason Truly. You do not leave insanity by going somewhere else; you leave it by accepting True Reason in its place. Madness and True Reason see the same things, but it is certain that they look on them differently.

4. Madness is an attack on True Reason; it drives True Reasoning out of your mind and takes Its place. Your True Reasoning Mind does not attack, but, if it is your choice to listen to It, It quietly takes the place of madness. In insanity, you do not know your Will, because you see the body, and you let your madness tell you that it is real. True Reasoning is incapable of this, and if you defend the body against your True Reasoning Mind you will not understand the body or yourself.

5. The body does not separate you from the world that you perceive, and if you think that it does, you are insane. Madness has a purpose, and it believes it has the means to make its purpose real. It is insane to see the body as a barrier to a Mind that True Reasoning tells you must be One. You will not see the body if you hear the Voice for True Reason. Nothing can stand between What is One and so must be Continuous. Since there *is* nothing between, what enters part of One cannot be kept from the other parts. True Reasoning will tell you this. But think about what you must recognize:

6. If you choose sin over healing, you condemn your Whole Mind to

what can never be corrected. You tell It that, by your choice, It is damned, split within Itself, and separated from God Forever, without hope of safe return. You teach your Whole Mind this, and you will learn exactly what you teach. You can teach your Whole Mind only what you want It to be, and what you choose for your Whole Mind, you of course choose for yourself. But don't be frightened by this. That your Mind is One is a Fact, not an interpretation. A fact is only frightening when it disagrees with what you hold more dear than truth. True Reasoning tells you that this Fact is your release.

7. You cannot attack yourself or another without it affecting your perception of both. But you also cannot accept the experience of a miracle for either without its blessing and healing encompassing both. True Reasoning, like Love, seeks to reassure you, not to frighten you. The power to heal your mind is yours *because* your mind is One. You *are* responsible for what you perceive. True Reasoning tells you that it is given to you to change your entire mind, which is One, in just an instant. Any Instant will serve to bring complete correction of all of your errors and make you Whole in your awareness again. In the Instant in which you choose to let yourself be healed, your entire mind's salvation is complete. True Reasoning is given to you to understand that this is so. True Reasoning, Which is as Kind as Its Purpose, leads you steadily away from madness and toward the Goal of Truth. Here, you will lay down the burden of denying Truth. Truth is not a burden, but your *denying* Truth is a terrible burden.

8. That your Mind is One is your salvation. This is the Gift of Heaven, not the gift of fear. Heaven seems to burden you only in your madness, but what you see in madness is dispelled by True Reasoning. True Reasoning assures you that Heaven is What you want, and that It is all that you want. Listen to the Holy Spirit, Which speaks with True Reasoning and brings your thinking into line with It. Be willing to let True Reasoning be the means by which the Holy Spirit directs you to leave insanity behind. Do not hide behind insanity to escape from True Reasoning. What madness wants to conceal from you, the Holy Spirit still holds out to you to

look upon with gladness.

9. Christ in you and Christ in your perception of the other in your Holy relationship is your Savior, because your mind is One. True Reasoning speaks happily of this to you. This Gracious Plan was given to Love by Love. What Love plans is like Itself in this: Being One, It wants you to learn that you must be One, too. And, since you are One with Love, Love extends Love to you to extend. Spend only an Instant in the glad acceptance of What is extended to you to extend in your Holy relationship, and learn What has been given to your entire mind. To give is no more blessed than to receive, but neither is it less.

10. Your entire mind is always blessed as One. You cannot stand apart from the blessing or the gratitude that you extend to your mind where you perceive a world. The gratitude that you experience is God's Gratitude for God's Completion through you. Here alone does True Reasoning tell you that you can understand What you must be. God is as close to you as is all that you perceive. What can be closer to you than your Self?

11. The power that you have over your entire mind is not a threat to its Reality; it attests to It. If you want to be Free, where does the whole of your mind's Freedom lie but within you? If you want to deny your Freedom, who can limit you but yourself? God is not thwarted, and you can be limited only by your own desire. It is also by your own desire that you are freed. This is your strength, not your weakness. You are at your own mercy, and where you choose to be Merciful, you are Free. And where you choose guilt instead, you are limited, waiting for your own pardon to be Free.

7. The Last Unanswered Question

1. Can you see that all of your misery comes from your strange belief that you are powerless? Being helpless is the cost of your belief that separation from God is a sin. Helplessness is sin's condition, the one requirement that it demands for you to believe in it. Only if you are helpless *can* you believe in sin, because being 'bad' appeals to you as a defense for the smallness and vulnerability of the personal self. Treachery to your Christ Mind is your defense

against your Christ Mind when you do not want to identify with It. Either you are for Christ, or you are against It; either you Love Christ, or you attack It; either you protect your awareness of your Christ Mind's Oneness, or you perceive your Christ Mind as shattered and slain by your attack.

2. You cannot believe that What is One with God is powerless, so if you see yourself as helpless you must not believe that you are One with God. This splits your mind and makes your Christ Mind your 'enemy'. Then you envy your Christ Mind's Power and your envy makes you afraid of It. You project outside of your mind a world where you live with others with whom you each walk alone and isolated in personal selves, secretly afraid of a Power that will strike you all dead and that you are all helpless against. You and these seeming others wage a war of vengeance, bitterness, and spite on each other to make yourselves one with the vengeful, bitter, spiteful 'Christ' that you have made in your own image. But, because you do not know that you *are* One with Christ, you do not know What Christ really is. You are as likely to attack others, or even yourself, as you are to remember that you are supposed to have a common cause against this 'alien' Power.

3. The world that you have projected outside of your mind seems frantic and loud and strong, but though you all hate your 'enemy', you do not really know What It is. You have joined with these seeming others in hatred, but you are not One with them. If you saw that they are in your mind, and that you *are* One with them, hatred would be impossible for you. In the Presence of True Strength, your world of powerlessness would be undone. In Strength, you are never treacherous, because you have no need to act out an illusion of power. But you can act any way in an illusion. You can attack anyone or anything. Illusions are not True Reasoning. Love is turned to hate easily in illusions. There is no real joining in powerlessness, only insanity, and what seems to be a planned attack against an 'alien' Power is really chaos.

4. You are indeed weak when you are powerless, but you have no real weapons and no real enemy. You can overrun the world and seek an enemy, but you will never find one. You can have an illusion that

you have found an enemy, but this will shift even as you attack, and you will have to run and find another, never resting. You will turn against yourself or anyone in whom you see a glimpse of your elusive 'enemy'.

5. Your hate must have a target. You cannot have faith in your separation from God without an enemy, because for you to believe in your separation from God you cannot admit that you made it up and made yourself powerless. True Reasoning tells you to stop seeking for what is not here. But first, you must be willing to perceive that you have no enemy to take your power. It is not necessary for you to understand how you can see this, and you shouldn't try. If you focus on what you cannot understand, you will emphasize your helplessness, and your belief in sin will tell you that your enemy must be yourself. Ask yourself only these questions:

    'Do I desire a perception that I rule instead of one that rules me?'
    'Do I desire to perceive that I am powerful instead of powerless?'
    'Do I desire to perceive that I do not have enemies, and that I cannot sin?'
    'Do I want to see that I *do* rule my perception, that I *am* powerful, that I do *not* have enemies, and that I *cannot* sin, *because these are the Truth*?'

6. You may already have answered the first three questions but not yet the last one. This last one may still seem fearful to you and unlike the others. But True Reasoning shows you that they are all the same. Earlier, you were told that this year your lessons will emphasize the sameness of things that are the same. This last question, which is the last that you need to decide, still seems to hold a threat to you that the others do not. This imagined difference attests to your belief that Truth may yet be the enemy that you have to find. This seems to be your last remaining hope of finding sin and of not accepting Power.

7. Do not forget that, as you choose between sin and Truth, and helplessness and Power, you are choosing whether to attack or to

heal your mind through your perceptions. Your healing comes from your Power, and you attack when you feel helpless. When you attack your perceptions, you cannot want to heal, and when you want to heal, you will not attack your perceptions. The decision that you make is your choice: to look through the body's eyes and the personal mind's projections, or to let your Christ Mind be revealed to you through your Real Perception. How this decision leads to its effects is not your concern; this is a course in cause, not in effect.

8. Carefully consider your answer to the last question. Let your True Reasoning Mind tell you that it must be answered, and that it is answered in the other three. Then it will be clear to you that as you look on the effects of your belief in sin in any form, all that you need to do is ask yourself:

'Is this what I want to see?'

9. This is your one decision; the condition for what you see. How it happens is irrelevant, but not why. You *have* control over what you see, and if you choose to perceive that you have no enemy, and that you are not helpless, the means to see this will be given to you.

10. True Reasoning will tell you why the last question is so important. It is the same as the other three questions, except in time. The others are decisions that you can make, unmake, and then make again. But Truth is constant and does not vacillate. You can desire a perception that you rule, and then change your mind. You can desire to exchange helplessness for Power, and then lose this desire as a glint of separation attracts you. And you can see Innocence, and then let a projection of the personal mind tempt you to believe what the body's eyes show you.

11. In content, all of the questions are the same, because each asks if you are willing to exchange your world of separation for the Real Perception of the Holy Spirit. Your Real Perception is what your world of separation denies so that when you look on separation you are seeing your denial of your Real Perception. But the last question asks for consistency in your desire for your Real Perception so that this desire becomes the only one that you have.

By answering the final question with 'yes', you add sincerity to your affirmative answer to the other questions. Only then will you have renounced the option to change your mind again. When you no longer want this option, all of the questions are wholly answered.

12. You are unsure that the other questions have been answered, and this is why they are asked so often. Until you decide to answer the last question 'yes' your answer is both 'yes' and 'no' to the other questions. You have answered 'yes' without perceiving that 'yes' means 'not no'. You do not *mean* to decide against your Happiness; you do not recognize that this is what you are doing. You decide against your Happiness when you see its source as ever changing: coming from this, then that; an ever-elusive shadow attached to nothing.

13. Happiness that shifts with time and place is an illusion that has no meaning. Your Happiness must be constant, because It is attained by your giving up your wish for the *in*constant. You can only perceive Joy through the Constant Perception of your Christ Mind. And you can only have Constant Perception when you wish for Constancy. The Power of your Mind is the proof that you are wrong to perceive yourself as helpless. What you desire you see and think is real. All of your thoughts have the power to either release you or seem to kill you. Your thoughts cannot leave your mind or leave you unaffected.

8. The Inner Shift

1. Your thoughts are dangerous only to the body. The thoughts that seem to kill you are those that tell you that you *can* be killed, so, when you identify with a body, you 'die' because of what you taught yourself. Going from life to death is meant to be the final 'proof' that you value the inconstant more than Constancy. You think that you want Happiness, but you do not yet want it *because* it is the Truth and therefore must be Constant.

2. The Constancy of Joy is alien to the personal mind's understanding. If you could even imagine What It must be you would desire It, even though you cannot understand It. The Constancy of

Happiness has no exceptions and no variations of any kind. It is as Unshakable as God's Love for you who are One with God. As sure in Its Perception as God is in What God knows, Happiness looks on everything and sees it is like Itself. It does not see the temporary, because It wants everything to be Eternal like Itself. Nothing can frustrate Its Constancy, because Its Own desire cannot be shaken. Happiness will come to you when you want Power and Innocence because they are the Truth, just as Peace will come to you when you choose to heal instead of to judge your perception of separation from God as real.

3. Your True Reasoning Mind will tell you that you cannot ask for Happiness inconstantly. Happiness is Constant, and, since you always receive what you desire, then you only need to ask for Happiness once to have It always. So, if you do not always have Happiness, you did not ask for It from What can really give It. You ask for Happiness only from something that you believe holds some promise of giving It to you. You may be wrong in how you ask for It, or wrong about what can give It to you, but you will ask for Happiness, because you desire It and your desire is a request. God will never fail to answer you. God has already extended God to you, Which is What you really want. But if you are uncertain that God is Happiness, you will not be aware that you have It. You do not desire God while you remain uncertain of God, and God's extension of God to you is incomplete unless you accept It.

4. You who complete God's Will and who are God's Happiness, whose will is as Powerful as God's Will and whose Power is not lost in illusions, think carefully why you have not yet decided that you want Happiness and Power *because* they are your Truth. You are already partly Sane because you do not want to be powerless or sinful. But accepting Happiness and Power because they are your *Truth* means that you are willing to be wholly Sane.

5. The Holy Instant is God's Appeal to you to recognize What God has given to you. Here is the Great Appeal of True Reasoning, the awareness of What is always here for you to see, and the Happiness that can always be yours. Here is the Constant Peace that you can experience Forever. Here is What your denial has denied revealed

to you. Here, Truth is given to you *because* It is the Truth, and What you have asked for is given to you. Here, What seems to be in the future is *now*, because time is powerless in your desire for What will never change. You have asked that nothing stand between the Holiness of your entire mind and your *awareness* of its Holiness.

Chapter 22

Salvation and the Holy Relationship

1. Take pity on yourself, as you have been limited by a personal mind for so long. Rejoice that God joins your mind in Oneness, and that you can no longer look on separation from God as real. You never see 'sin' in the same way at different times and in different places. You see sin in others, but you really believe it is in yourself. Everyone seems to represent a different sin to you, but every manifestation of separation from God is really the same, projected by your mind and forgiven by you. But your awareness of the Holiness of your relationship forgives you your perception of separation, and undoes its effects. With the undoing of the effects of separation, your need to see sin is undone.

2. Only in your desire for the separateness of a personal self do you need the idea of sin to justify your perception that others are separate from your mind. The differences that you perceive between you and others are necessary to maintain this belief. But separate selves, differences, and 'sin' can only be real if your mind is not One and separation from God is real. An unholy relationship upholds your belief in separation. It is based on lack and differences, and its result is that you believe that others have what you are missing. You join with them only to rob them so that you can complete yourself. You stay with them until there is nothing left to steal, and then you move on. You wander through a world of strangers, and perhaps you live with some of them under a common roof that does not really shelter you, and you share space with them without ever really joining with them in Oneness.

3. A Holy relationship starts from a different premise: You have looked within, and you see that you are not lacking. Accepting your Completion, you naturally extend It to replace your perception of separation. You see no difference in your mind between you and your perception of another because differences are only of the

body/personal self, and you are overlooking bodies/personal selves. Therefore, you do not look on anything that you want to take. *Because* this Oneness is the Truth, you are no longer denying your own Reality. You stand just under Heaven, but close enough to It to not return to perceiving separation. Your relationship has Heaven's Holiness, so how far from Home can it be?

4.   Think what a Holy relationship can teach you! Here, your belief in your separation from God is undone, and your faith shifts to Oneness. Your True Reasoning Mind leads you to the logical conclusion that your mind's perceptions are part of your mind. Just as your awareness of your Oneness extended *to* your perception of the other in your Holy relationship, It must now extend *from* your perception of them. Your Holy relationship must extend beyond you and this one other, just as you extended your True Self beyond the body when you extended your Holiness to your perception of them. Now, your Oneness will extend and remove all of your sense of separation between you and what your mind perceives. Here is where you recognize your Christ Mind. Your awareness of Oneness, which was born in your Holy relationship, can never end.

1. The Message of the Holy Relationship

1.   Let your True Reasoning take another step: If you attack what God wants to heal, and you hate what God loves, then you and God must have different wills. But, if you *are* God's Will, then if you believe this past sentence, you must believe that you are not yourself. And in your identification with a personal self you *do* believe you are not your True Self. You have faith in this, and you see much evidence on its behalf. And you wonder where your strange uneasiness, your sense of disconnection, and your haunting fear of lack of meaning in yourself come from! It is as though you have wandered into separation from God with no plan *but* to be separated from God, because only this is certain about it.

2.   Earlier in this course there is a similar description, but it is not of you. But this strange idea which it does describe you think of as you. Your True Reasoning will tell you that a world that you see through eyes that are not yours must not make sense to you. To

whom would this seeing return its messages? Certainly not to you, because your True Perception, is wholly independent of the eyes that look on the world. This is not your True Perception, so what can it show you? The brain cannot interpret What your True Perception sees, and you understand this. The brain interprets to the body, of which it is a part. You cannot understand what it says, yet you have listened to it. And you have tried to understand its messages for a long, hard time.

3. You have not yet realized that it is impossible for you to understand messages that completely fail to reach you. You have received no messages that you understand, because you have listened to what can never communicate with you. Think what happens then: denying What you are, and firm in your conviction that you are something else, this 'something else' that you have made becomes your guide. It must be the 'something else' that sees and interprets what it is seeing to you. Of course, your True Perception makes all of this unnecessary. But your mind is closed to your True Perception, and you have called on this other thing to lead you and to explain to you the world that it sees. You have no reason to not listen to this thing or to suspect that what it is telling you is not true. But True Reasoning will tell you that it cannot be true *because* you do not understand it. There are no secrets in Truth. God does not lead you through a world of misery only to tell you in the end why It did this to you.

4. Nothing is secret from God's Will, but you believe that you have a secret. Your secret is another 'will' that is your own, separate from God's Will. True Reasoning will tell you that this is not a secret to be hidden as a 'sin', but it *is* a mistake. Do not let your fear that it is a sin protect this mistake from correction, because fear is what attracts you to separation from God. Whatever form it takes, fear is the only emotion that you have made. It is the emotion of secrecy, of private thoughts, and of the body. It is the emotion that opposes Love, so it always leads you to perceiving differences instead of Oneness. Fear keeps you blind to Truth and dependent on the personal self that you think you made to lead you through a world that it made for you.

5. Your True Perception was given to you, along with Everything that you can understand. You have no difficulty understanding Everything your True Perception sees, because you only see What you are. What your True Perception shows you, you understand *because* It is the Truth. Only your True Perception can show you What you are really capable of seeing. It reaches you directly, without needing to be interpreted to you. What needs to be interpreted to you must be alien to you, and it will not be made understandable to you through an interpreter that you cannot understand.

6. Of all of the messages that you have received in your perception that you are in a world, this course alone is open to your understanding. This course is in *your* language. You may not fully understand it yet, because your ability to communicate is like a baby's. What a baby babbles, and what it hears is highly unreliable, meaning different things to it at different times. Sights and sounds are not stable to a baby. But what a baby hears will one day be the baby's language. And the strange, shifting images about the baby will one day be the baby's comforters and the baby's home.

7. So, in your Holy relationship, True Communication is reborn and replaces separation in your mind. But a Holy relationship so recently reborn from an unholy relationship, though it is older than time, is like a baby. Still, early in this relationship, True Perception is returned to you, and you will understand What you see. Your Holy relationship is not nurtured by the 'something else' that you thought was you. It does not come from a personal mind, but it is received by *you*. Your mind and its perception can only unite in Christ, Which sees only Oneness.

8. Think what is given to you! This Holy relationship will teach you What you do not understand and make It plain, because It is not alien to you. You will not need an interpreter, because What this relationship teaches you, you already know. The Holy relationship can only come to *you*, not to the 'something else' that you made. Christ cannot be isolated to a personal mind, because Christ is not at home in separation. But Christ must be reborn into your awareness, which seems new, but is as Timeless as Christ Christ is dependent on your awareness of the Holiness of your relationship

517

to live in your awareness.

9. You can be certain that God does not entrust your Christ Mind to the unworthy. Only what is Part of God is worthy of being joined, and what is not part of God cannot join at all. True Communication must have been restored to your mind, because you cannot unite with a body. So what has joined? Your True Reasoning will tell you that you see the other in your Holy relationship through a Perception that is not of the body, and that you communicate with your Perception of them in a language that the body does not speak. It cannot be fear that joins your mind into One. What you see instead is a Perfect Shelter where your True Self can be reborn in your awareness, in Safety and Peace. This is what your True Reasoning tells you, and this is what you must believe *because* it is the Truth.

10. Here is the first, direct Real Perception that you can make, and you make it through an awareness that is older than perception, but is reborn in just an Instant. What is time to What is always so? Think what the Holy Instant brings to you: the recognition that the 'something else' that you thought was you is an illusion. Then Truth comes instantly to show you your True Self. When you deny illusions, you call on Truth, because for you to deny illusions is for you to recognize that fear is meaningless. Love thankfully enters the Holy home Where fear is powerless, and Love is grateful that It is One with you, who joined with It to let It enter.

11. Christ is drawn only to what is like Itself, and Christ can come into only what is like Itself. Your Holy relationship is like Christ, and the Christ that you extend in your Holy relationship draws Christ into your awareness. In your Holy relationship, your Christ Mind's gentle Innocence is protected from attack, and Christ returns to your awareness, because your faith in your Holy relationship is your faith in Christ. You are indeed correct in extending Christ's Home to your relationship, because in this you Will with your Christ Mind and with God. This is God's Will for you and your Will with God's. Your attraction to Christ is your attraction to God, and your Christ Mind and God are attracted to your Holy relationship, which is Their home as the world gives way to Heaven for you.

2. Your Brother's Sinlessness

1. The opposite of illusions is not disillusionment, but Truth. Only to the personal mind, to which Truth is meaningless, do illusions and disillusionment seem to be different from each other and your only alternatives. They are actually both the same. Both bring you misery, though they seem to bring relief from the misery that the other brings. Every illusion carries pain and suffering in the dense, heavy appearances in which it hides its nothingness. You are buried in these appearances and hidden from the Joy of Truth.

2. Truth is the opposite of illusions, because It offers Joy, and Joy is the opposite of misery. For you to leave one kind of misery for another is not for you to escape from misery. For you to exchange illusions is for you to make no change at all. Your search for Joy in misery is senseless. All that is possible for you in the dark world of misery that you made is for you to select out some aspects, see them as different from the rest, and then define them as joy. But for you to perceive differences where there are none will make no real difference to you.

3. Illusions carry only guilt, suffering, sickness, and death to you when you believe in them, so the form in which you accept illusions is irrelevant. Your True Reasoning Mind knows that no form of misery can be confused with Joy. Joy is Eternal, and any seeming happiness that does not last is really fear. Joy cannot turn to sorrow, because the Eternal cannot change, but sorrow can turn to Joy, because time gives way to the Eternal. Only the Timeless remains unchanged, but everything *in* time changes *with* time. Real change is illusions giving way to Truth, not to other illusions that are equally unreal. There is no difference between illusions.

4. Your True Reasoning will tell you that the only way for you to escape from misery is to recognize it and *go the other way*. Truth is all the same and misery is all the same, but they are different from each other in every way, without exception. If you believe that one exception can exist, then you confuse what is the same with what is different. One illusion that you cherish and defend against the Truth makes all Truth meaningless to you and all illusions real to you. Such is the power of your belief, which cannot compromise.

Your faith in Innocence is changed to faith in separation from God if you hold one illusion apart from your forgiving.

5.   Both your True Reasoning Mind and the personal mind will tell you this, but they do not arrive at the same conclusion. The personal mind will assure you that it is impossible for you to *not* see separation from God, so your guilt must be Eternal. But your True Reasoning Mind sees the *source* of an idea as what makes it either True or false, because all ideas are like their source. Since the Holy Spirit was given the purpose of undoing your sense of separation from God *by* God, Which wills only the Possible, then the means for your attaining it must be more than possible. They must be here now, and you must have them.

6.   This is a crucial period for you in this course, because here the separation of you from the personal mind must be made complete. You have the means to let the Holy Spirit's purpose be accomplished, and you can use them. Through your use of them you will gain faith in them. To the personal mind, undoing your separation from God is impossible, and it will not undertake what it has no hope can be done. But *you* know that what God wills is possible, even though what you made does not know this. Now you must choose between your True Self and an illusion of yourself. You can choose only one. There is no point in your trying to avoid this one decision; you must make it. Your faith and belief can fall to either, but your True Reasoning will tell you that one leads you to misery, and the Other leads you to Joy.

7.   Do not forsake your Holy relationship now. Because your mind is One, what you decide will be the same for you and for your perception of the other in your Holy relationship. You extend to the other either Life or death; you see in them either your salvation or the personal mind's judgments. Your Holy relationship is your Sanctuary or your condemnation. You will believe this course either entirely or not at all. It is wholly true or wholly false for you, and you cannot partially believe in it. You will either escape misery entirely or not at all. Your True Reasoning will tell you that there is no middle ground where you can pause uncertainly to wait to choose between the Joy of Heaven and the misery of hell. Until you

choose Heaven, you *are* in misery and hell.

8. There is no part of Heaven that you can weave into illusions, and you cannot bring illusions into Heaven. You cannot judge as separate from you the one in whom you want to perceive your salvation, and there is no mercy in condemnation. Your Christ Mind's Perception cannot damn; It can only bless. The Holy Spirit *will* fulfill Its function, which is your salvation. How the Holy Spirit will do this is beyond your understanding, but *when* is your choice. You made time, and you command time. You are no more a slave to time than you are a slave to the world in your mind.

9. Look closer at the illusory idea that what you have made can enslave you. This is the same as the belief which caused the separation: Thoughts can leave the mind of their thinker, be different from it, and in opposition to it. If this is true, your thoughts are not your mind's extensions, but its enemies. Here we see again another form of the same fundamental illusion we have seen many times before: Part of God can leave God, make itself different from God, and oppose God's Will. Only if this is possible can the self that you made, and all that *it* made, be master over you.

10. Behold your great projection! But look on it without fear and with the decision that it must be healed. What you have made has power over you only if you want to be apart from God and with a will opposed to God. Only if you believe that Part of God can be God's enemy is it possible that what you made is really your enemy. You want to condemn God's Joy to misery and to make Part of God different from God. But all the misery that you have made is your own. Aren't you glad to learn that it is not true? Is it not welcome news to you to learn that not one of the illusions that you have made actually replaces the Truth?

11. Only the personal mind's thoughts have been impossible. Your salvation *cannot* be impossible. It *is* impossible for you to look upon the other as your enemy and see salvation in your relationship. But it *is* possible for you to recognize your True Self in place of the personal mind's projections, because God wants it so. What God has extended to your Holy relationship is there, because What God gave to the Holy Spirit to extend to you *the Holy Spirit extended*.

Look upon the salvation that has been given to you in your Holy relationship. Exchange, in gratitude, the function of executioner that you have projected onto the other in your relationship, for the function that your relationship with them has in Truth. Receive of the other in your Holy relationship What God has extended to them through your Perception of them, and not what you tried to give yourself through the personal mind's projections.

12. Beyond your mind's perception of a world of bodies, and shining with God's Eternal Love, is your Holy relationship, Beloved of God. How still your Holy relationship rests, in time, but from beyond time; Immortal, but in the world that you perceive. How great is the Power that lies in it! Time waits upon the will of your Holy relationship, and all of your perceptions are corrected to Holiness as your relationship wants it to be. In your relationship, you do not have a will that is separate from God, nor the desire that anything be separate. Its will is whole, and What it wills is True. Every illusion that you bring to your Holy relationship's forgiveness you will gently overlook, and it will disappear. At the center of your Holy relationship, your Christ Mind is reborn in your awareness with the Perception that overlooks the world that you made. Don't you want this Perception for your own? There is no misery in your Holy relationship; only Joy.

13. All that you need to do to dwell in Quiet with Christ is to extend your Christ Mind's Perception. Christ's Perception will come to you quickly when you are willing to see Innocence in place of sin. If you want to be released entirely from all of the effects of your belief in your separation from God, not one perception can remain beyond your willingness to let it go. You cannot want only partial forgiveness for yourself, and you cannot reach Heaven while a single bit of separation from God tempts you to remain in misery. Heaven is the Home of Perfect Purity, and God extends It to you. Look on Holiness in your relationship with the other, and see *your* Innocence, and let It lead you to Heaven.

3. Reason and the Forms of Error

1. The introduction of True Reasoning into your thought system is the

beginning of the personal mind's undoing, because your True Reasoning Mind and the personal mind contradict each other. It is not possible for them to coexist in your awareness. Your True Reasoning Mind's goal is to make Truth plain and simple to you. You can *see* True Reasoning; It is the beginning of your True Perception, Which has Meaning. Your True Perception is quite literally *sense*. What is not the body's sight you *must* understand, because it is plain, obvious, and unambiguous. Here your True Reasoning Mind and the personal mind go their separate ways.

2. The personal mind's continuance depends on its belief that you cannot learn this course. If you share this belief, your True Reasoning Mind will be unable to see your errors and correct them. Your True Reasoning Mind sees *through* errors, telling you that what you thought was real is not real. Your True Reasoning Mind can see the difference between 'sin' and mistakes, because It wants correction. It tells you that the separation from God that you thought was uncorrectable can be corrected, so it must've been an error. The personal mind's opposition to your correction leads to its fixed belief in sin and its disregard of errors. The personal mind does not look on anything as something to be corrected. The personal mind damns you; your True Reasoning Mind saves you.

3. Your True Reasoning is not your salvation in itself, but It makes way for Peace, and It prepares you to accept salvation. Your belief that your separation from God is real, and therefore sin, is like a heavy locked gate across your road to Peace. You cannot try to pass it without the help of your True Reasoning Mind. The personal mind sees your separation from God as a solid fact, and it teaches you that it is madness for you to attempt to pass it. But your True Reasoning Mind sees through your perception of separation from God easily, because it is only an error. The form that 'sin' takes cannot conceal its emptiness from your True Reasoning Mind.

4. Only the form of your error attracts the personal mind, because the personal mind does not recognize meaning, and it doesn't even know if meaning is there or not. Everything that the body's eyes see and that the personal mind perceives is a mistake, an error in your perception; a distorted fragment of wholeness without the

meaning that the whole gives to it. But your mistakes, no matter the form that they take, can be corrected. 'Sin' is an error in a special form that the personal mind honors. The personal mind wants to preserve all of your errors and make them uncorrectable 'sins'. The concept that 'sin' is real is the personal mind's stability, its heavy anchor in the shifting world that it made; the rock on which its churches are built and where worshippers bound to bodies/personal selves believe that the body's freedom is their own.

5.   Your True Reasoning Mind, however, will tell you that the *form* of your error is not what makes it a mistake, but what the form *conceals* is your mistake, so the form cannot prevent your correction. The body's eyes see only form, and they cannot see beyond what they were made to see. They were made to look on error and to not see past it. The body's eyes have a strange perception indeed, because they see only illusion, and they are unable to look past the personal mind's heavy block of perceived separation from God. But they stop at the outside form of nothing. To this distorted form of perception, the external sights that are the block between you and your awareness of Truth *are* truth. But sight that stops at nothingness as if it were a solid block cannot see Truly. This sight is held back by form, having been made to guarantee that you will perceive nothing but form.

6.   The body's eyes, made to *not* see Truth, will never see Truth. The idea of separation from God that they represent has never left its maker, the personal mind, and it is its maker that sees through them. The body's maker's goal is for you to not see Truth, and for this the body's eyes are perfect, because they do not go beyond external sights. They stop at nothingness, unable to go beyond form to meaning. Your seeing form means your understanding has been obscured.

7.   Only mistakes take different forms, so that they can deceive. You can change form, because form is not true. Form is not Reality, *because* it can be changed. Your True Reasoning will tell you that if form is not reality it must be illusion, so it is not there for you to Truly See. If you see form, you must be mistaken, because you are seeing what is not real as though it were real. What cannot see

524

beyond what is not there is distorted perception, and it must perceive illusions as truth. It cannot recognize the Truth.

8.   Do not let the form of your mistaken perception of the other in your Holy relationship keep you from perceiving your Holiness. Do not let your Perception of Holiness, Which shows you forgiveness, be kept from you by what the body's eyes can see. Do not block your awareness of Truth with your perception of 'sin' in the other. What you attack in the other is what you associate with a body, which you believe can make your separation from God real. Beyond this error in your perception is your Holiness and your salvation. You tried to see your sins in the other to save yourself, but the Holiness that you can extend in your Perception of the other is *your* forgiveness. You cannot be saved by making sinful the other to whom you must extend Holiness for your own salvation.

9.   In your Holy relationship, however newly born into your awareness, you must value Holiness above all else. Valuing unholiness will produce confusion in your awareness. In an unholy relationship, you value the other because they justify your own separation from God. You see in the other what compels you to 'sin' against your will. Having laid your sins on the other, you are attracted to them to perpetuate your sense of separation from God. It therefore becomes impossible for you to see that you are causing your sense of sin by your own desire that your separation from God be real. Yet your Clear Mind sees a Holy relationship as a unified state of mind, where you gladly give your sense of separation from God over to correction, so that your mind will be healed in Oneness.

4. The Branching of the Road

1.   You will come to a place in your journey to God where the road branches. If you go straight ahead, continuing on the way that you came, you will go nowhere. The whole purpose of your coming this far is for you to decide to take the branch. The way that you came no longer matters, because it can no longer serve you. When you reach this branch, you cannot make the wrong decision, but you can delay. If you refuse to take the branch, there is no part of

your journey that will seem more hopeless and futile to you.

2.   It is only the first few steps along the branching road that will seem hard to you. But you have chosen, and though you may think that you can still go back and make the other choice, you cannot. A choice that you make with the Power of Heaven to uphold it cannot be undone. Your way is decided. If you acknowledge this, there is nothing that you will not be told.

3.   Here, in this Holy place, you stand in your Holy relationship with the veil of your belief in separation from God between you and your perception of the other obscuring your Christ Mind. Let it be lifted! Lift from your mind what looks like a solid world, but is only a veil. In the isolation of a personal mind, it seems like a solid block to you, and you cannot see that it is only thin drapery that separates your mind. This veil is almost undone in your awareness, and Peace has reached you even here before the veil. Think what will happen after: The Love of Christ will fill your awareness and will extend in your mind where you perceive a world, which calls for Love. From this Holy Place, Christ will extend to replace the world in your mind, not leaving It or you. You will be Christ's Messenger, returning Christ to Christ.

4.   Think of the Loveliness that you will perceive when you are aware of your Christ Mind! Think how beautiful your Holy relationship will be to you! How happy you will be in your Limitless Christ Mind after a long journey where you walked isolated in a limited personal mind. Heaven is open now for you, and you will extend It to the rest of your sad mind. Your entire mind will rejoice as you extend Christ to it. How Beautiful is the Perception beyond the veil, Which you bring with you now to rest your weary mind where you perceive a world. How thankful your entire mind will be as you extend Christ's forgiveness to dispel your faith in sin.

5.   Every mistake that you make will be gently corrected in your corrected perception of your Holy relationship. Your salvation is in the Loveliness that you extend in your perception, and you will want to protect It from harm. Every obstacle that seems to rise between you and your awareness of the Holiness of your relationship will be undone. So shall you walk with Christ, in your

perception that you are in a world,, with a Message that you must extend to be all that you perceive. You have reached this point, so let It be received by your entire mind. God's Offer of Love is here to be received by you, but you must accept It first. From your acceptance of Love, Love is extended in your awareness. Love is safely given to your mind, which is united in the Holy relationship, because, by extending Love, you have become Love's guardian and protector.

6. Grace is given to you who extend God's Love, so that you learn that It is yours Forever. All barriers to Love's extension will disappear before you now, just as you finally surmounted every obstacle to God that seemed to block you before. The veil that you lifted from your perception of one other in your perception that you are in a world opens the way to Truth for your entire mind. When you let illusions be lifted from your mind, you joined with your Christ Mind, and you will extend Christ's Message of Hope and Freedom to be all that you perceive.

7. How easy it is for you to extend God's Love to all that you perceive! Having received It for yourself, you cannot find this difficult. By your receiving God's Love you have learned that it was not given to a personal self. This is the function of a Holy relationship: for you to receive God's Love in one relationship in your mind where you perceive a world, so as to extend God's Love to your entire mind. Standing before the veil of sin, this may seem difficult to you. But join your mind in wholeness, and the heavy-seeming block is revealed to you as nothingness. Only an illusion stands between you and the Holy Self that is your Whole Mind.

5. Weakness and Defensiveness

1. You do not overcome illusions by force or by anger or by opposing them in any way. You overcome them by letting your True Reasoning Mind tell you that they contradict Reality; that they go against What must be True. Opposition comes from illusions, not from Reality, because Reality does not oppose anything. What merely *is* does not need defense and offers none. Illusions need defense because they are weak. It is not difficult for you to walk the

way of Truth when only weakness interferes. *You* are the strong one in this seeming conflict, and you don't need defense. You do not really want what needs defense, because your accepting what needs defense will only weaken you.

2.   Consider what the personal mind wants defenses for: to justify what goes against Truth, flies in the face of True Reasoning, and makes no sense. This cannot *be* justified, and your defending the personal mind is only your invitation to insanity to save you from Truth, Which you fear. Your belief in separation from God needs great defense at an enormous cost to you. You must defend the personal mind *against* the Holy Spirit, and you must sacrifice all that the Holy Spirit offers. Your belief in separation from God is a block between you and the return of Peace to you.

3.   But your Peace cannot be blocked; It is still Whole, and nothing stands before It. See how the means and the material of bad illusions are nothing? In Truth, your Mind is Whole, and It is not separated into what seems like 'you' and a world outside of you. God is your Wholeness, and nothing can separate What is joined in Oneness with God. It is impossible for you to keep Love out of your mind. God rests within you in Quiet, wholly without defense, because in this Quiet State alone is Strength and Power. There is no weakness in God, because there is no attack and no illusions in God. Love rests on Certainty. Only uncertainty is defensive, and all uncertainty is doubt about yourself.

4.   How weak is fear! How little, meaningless, and insignificant it is before the Quiet Strength of you whose mind has been joined by Love. This is your enemy: a tiny, frightening idea that wants to attack Reality. How likely is it that it will succeed? It cannot be difficult for you to disregard its feeble squeaks, which tell you of its own omnipotence, and that want to drown out the Praise that your Whole Mind expresses Forever to God. Is this tiny idea stronger than God's Oneness? Your mind is not One in limitedness, but in the Limitless Will of God. A limited idea of yourself cannot betray your Oneness with God.

5.   If you only recognized how little stands between you and your awareness of your Mind's Oneness! Do not be deceived by the

illusion of size, thickness, weight, and solidness of the body of the other in your Holy relationship. To the body's eyes, a solid body seems as immovable as a mountain. But within you is a Force that no illusion can resist. The body only *seems* immovable, and this Force is Irresistible in Truth, so what must happen when they come together? An illusion of immovability cannot long be defended from your True Perception, Which quietly passes through it and goes beyond it.

6. Do not forget that when you feel the need arise to defend yourself over anything it means that you have identified yourself with an illusion, and that you feel that you are weak, because you are limited to a personal self. This is the cost of your illusions. All of them rest on your belief that you are separate from God, and that your mind is split. They seem to stand heavy and solid and immovable outside of you. And yet, the Truth in your mind can pass over all of them so lightly and easily that you must be convinced, in spite of what you thought that they were, that they are nothing. This must happen when you forgive the personal mind's projections on the other in your Holy relationship. It is your unwillingness to overlook what seems to be a world outside of your mind that makes it look impenetrable and that defends the illusion of its immovability.

6. The Light of the Holy Relationship

1. Do you want freedom for your mind or for the body? You cannot have both, so which do you value? Which is your goal? One will be your means to the goal of the other. One will serve the other and lead to its predominance in your awareness, increasing the importance of the goal for you and diminishing its own importance. Means serve an end, and as the end is reached, the value of the means decreases as its function is no longer needed. You yearn for freedom, and you try to find it, and you will seek for it where you believe that it can be found. You will believe that freedom is of the mind *or* of the body, and you will make the other serve your choice as the means to find it.

2. When you choose freedom for the body, you value the mind only

as a means to contrive ways to achieve the body's freedom. Yet freedom for the body has no meaning, so your mind is then dedicated to serve an illusion. This is such a contradictory and impossible situation that when you choose this you can have no idea of What is Truly Valuable. Yet, even in your profound and indescribable confusion, the Holy Spirit waits within you in Gentle Patience, as certain of the outcome as It is certain of God's Love for you. The Holy Spirit knows that you who have made this decision are as dear to God as Love is to Itself.

3. Do not concern yourself with how the Holy Spirit can change the roles of means and end so easily in your mind, which God loves and wants to be Free Forever. Be grateful instead that the body that you made can be the means to serve the Holy Spirit's Goal. This is the only service for the body that leads to your Freedom. Your Goal is Innocence, so you must perceive the body without sin and guilt. This lack of contradiction between means and end will make for a soft transition that is as easy as your shift from hate to gratitude before your forgiving mind. You will sanctify bodies, using them only to serve your extension of Innocence. It will be impossible for you to hate what serves healing.

4. Your Holy relationship, lovely in its Innocence, mighty in its Strength, and blazing with God's Love, is chosen by God for God's Own plan. Be grateful it does not serve the personal self at all. You cannot misuse anything that you have entrusted to your Holy relationship, and everything that you give to it *will* be used. Your Holy relationship has the power to heal all of your pain, regardless of its form. Your split mind cannot do this. Only joining your mind with the part that you once perceived outside of you can do this. Your Holy relationship heals your mind, and it is here that you accept correction of your perception that you are separate from God.

5. There is no separation from God in a Holy relationship. You no longer see the many forms that the error of separation takes, and your True Reasoning Mind, joined with Love, looks quietly on all confusion and merely observes, 'This is a mistake.' The correction that you have accepted in your relationship corrects all of your

perceptions of error and lays an Extension of Heaven in their places. How blessed are you who let this Gift be extended *through* you, because this is how It is given *to* you. Heaven shines on you now. You are the Means of Innocence, and you can be unafraid, because you carry only Love with you.

6. You are One with Peace, and Love *has* come into your awareness. The Love that you bring with you, you do not yet recognize, but you will remember It. You will not deny that within you is the Perception of Love that you extend to replace the world in your mind. You will not fail to recognize the Gift that you have extended to Heaven through yourself. The gentle service that you give to the Holy Spirit is service to yourself. You are now the Holy Spirit's means, and you must love all that the Holy Spirit loves. What you bring is your Memory of Everything that is Eternal. No trace of time can long remain in your mind when it serves the Eternal. And no illusion can disturb the Peace of your relationship, which has become the means for your Peace.

7. When you have completely forgiven the other in your Holy relationship for all of the personal mind's perceptions that you have projected onto them, without exception, there will be no mistake anywhere that you will not overlook. No form of suffering will block your Real Perception and prevent you from seeing past it. You will recognize all illusions as mistakes; shadows through which you walk completely unaffected. God will not let anything interfere with you, whose Will willingly serves God's Will, because you recognize that they are the same. Your remembering God's Will and your own cannot be long delayed.

8. You will see your Value in your Holy relationship as you extend your Value to it, and you will be released as you see salvation in place of the personal mind's attacks, which you thought were there. Through this releasing, your mind will release the whole world that it perceives. This is your part in bringing Peace to yourself. You have asked what your function is, and this is the answer. Do not seek to change it or to substitute another goal for it. Accept your function, and serve it willingly. What the Holy Spirit does with the Gifts that you extend to your Holy relationship, and

where and when they are offered to you, is up to the Holy Spirit. You will receive these Gifts when you welcome them, and the Holy Spirit will use every one of them for your Peace. Not one little smile, or willingness to overlook the tiniest error, will be lost to you.

9. It can only bless *you* when you look on What God loves with charity. Extending forgiveness is the Holy Spirit's function, so leave this to the Holy Spirit. Your concern is only that you give to the Holy Spirit What can be extended. Do not hold onto anything that the Holy Spirit cannot use, but offer the Holy Spirit your tiny gifts of Love, Which the Holy Spirit can extend Forever. The Holy Spirit will take your tiny gifts and make of them a potent Force for Peace. The Holy Spirit will bless them and will not limit them in any way. The Holy Spirit will join your tiny gifts to all of the Power that God has given to the Holy Spirit to make them a source of healing for your entire mind. Each little gift of Love that you extend in your Perception of the other in your Holy relationship is extended to your entire mind. Do not be concerned with illusions. Look away from them and toward the Oneness that you extend in your perception of the other. Let illusions be dispelled by the Holy Spirit, Which knows Truth and lays Truth gently in each quiet smile of faith and confidence with which you bless your Holy relationship.

10. The welfare of your entire mind depends on what you learn. It is only in arrogance that you deny the power of your Will. The Will of God is not powerless, and it is not humility for you to think that God's Will is not your own. You do not see what this denial has done to you. You see yourself as vulnerable, frail, easily destroyed, and at the mercy of countless attackers more powerful than you. Look straight at how this error came about, because here lies buried the heavy anchor that seems to keep the fear of God unmoving in your mind. While this error remains in your mind, it will seem to be as solid as a rock.

11. You cannot attack yourself and not attack God. What is One with God can be weak, frail, and easily destroyed only if God is these things. You do not see that the separation and guilt that you perceive and justify *are* an attack on God. That is why they cannot

happen and are not real. You do not see that *you* do all of this, because you think that you and God are separate. In fear, you *must* think that you are separate from God. It seems safer to think that you attack yourself or a perceived 'other' than to see that you attack God, Which has a Power that you know.

12. If you recognized your Oneness with God, you would know that God's Power is your own. But you will not remember this while attack of any kind has value to you. Attack is unjustified in any form, because it has no meaning. You could justify it only if you and the world that you perceive were truly separate and both were truly separate from God. Only then would it be possible for you to attack the world without attacking God, to attack another without hurting yourself, or to attack yourself without perceiving your pain in your perceptions of the world. You want to believe that you can do this, but only because you want to attack in safety. But attack is neither safe nor dangerous; it is impossible. This is so, because your Mind *is* One. You choose to attack your Mind's Oneness, because it is essential in your concept of attack that you think that the source of attack is separate from you. So it seems to you as though *Love* can attack and be frightening.

13. You only attack what is different from you. So you conclude that, because you attack, differences must be real. Yet the Holy Spirit sees this differently: Because differences are not real you cannot attack. Each position comes to a logical conclusion, and each can be maintained, but never both. Your only question is: *Are differences real?* From the point of view of what you think that you are in your identification with a personal self, the answer is 'yes', so you think you *can* attack. This seems natural to, and in line with, your experience as a personal self. So it is necessary that you have other experiences that are in line with Truth to teach you What is True and Natural for you.

14. This is the function of your Holy relationship: What you extend in your perception of the other you will experience. What does this mean, but that your mind is One? Do not fear this happy fact, and do not think it lays a heavy burden on you. When you have accepted it with gladness, you will realize that your relationship

reflects your Oneness with God. In a Loving Mind there is no separation. Every Loving Thought that you have extends Gladness to your entire mind. Joy is Limitless, because each Thought of Love extends Its Being and increases It. There is no difference of any kind in One Mind, because every Thought is like Itself.

15. The Love that joins your mind extends throughout Reality, and, because It joins you, It makes you One with God. In God, All of Reality is joined. Do not regret that you cannot get rid of fear by projecting it onto another when your Holy relationship can also teach you that the Power of Love is within you, and that It makes all fear impossible. Do not attempt to keep a little of the personal mind with this Gift of the Holy relationship. The Holy relationship is meant to be used, not obscured. What teaches you that your mind cannot be split denies the personal mind. Let Truth teach you if differences or Oneness is real.

Chapter 23

The War Against Yourself

1. You must recognize that the opposite of frailty and weakness is Innocence. Innocence is Strength, and nothing else is strong. In your Innocence, you do not experience fear, but in your belief that you are a 'sinner', you believe that you are weak. The show of 'strength' that attack is supposed to be is meant to conceal your frailty, but it does not work, because the unreal cannot be hidden. You are not strong if you have an 'enemy', and you will not attack unless you think that you have one. If you believe in 'enemies', then you believe that you are weak, but weakness is not the Will of God. Weakness is opposed to God's Will, and, if it were real, it would be God's 'enemy'. If you believe that you are weak you fear God as an opposing Will.

2. How strange is this war against yourself! You believe that everything that you made for separation from God can hurt you and is your 'enemy'. You fight against everything to weaken it, and you think that you succeed, so you continue to attack, believing that attack has value. But it is certain that you fear what you attack, and that you love What you perceive as Innocent. When you travel in Innocence, you walk in Peace on the way that Love shows you. Love walks with you, protecting you from fear, and you see only Innocence, Which cannot attack.

3. Walk in Glory, and do not fear evil. You are safe in your Innocence, because you extend your Innocence. Do not see the harmful, because your awareness of the Truth can release your mind where you perceive a world from the illusion of harmfulness. What seemed harmful can stand in your Innocence, released from your belief in sin and fear and happily returned to Love. You share the Strength of Love when you look on Innocence. Every error disappears when you do not see it. Look for Glory and find It, Where It is in Innocence.

4. Do not let the personal mind's little interferences draw you into limiting yourself. Guilt is not attractive to you when you know that you are Innocent. Think what Happy Perceptions you see with Truth in your awareness! Do not give up perception of your Freedom for a little sigh of seeming guilt, or for the tiny stirrings of your attraction to separation from God. Do not lay Heaven aside for these meaningless distractions. Your Destiny and purpose lie far beyond them in the Pure Place in your mind Where limitations do not exist. Your purpose conflicts with limitations of any kind, so it conflicts with your perception of separation from God.

5. Do not let yourself be tempted by limitations. The Glory of your Christ Mind is beyond limitation, measureless, and Eternal. Do not let Time intrude upon your awareness of Christ. Do not leave yourself frightened and alone in your temptation, but rise above it, and perceive the Love of Which you are a Part. Extend your Innocence to protect It in your awareness. You cannot know your Glory and perceive limitations and weakness around you. You cannot walk trembling in a frightening world and realize that Heaven's Glory is in you.

6. Everything around you is part of you. Look on it all Lovingly, and see the Love of Heaven in it all. This is how you will come to realize All that is given to you. In your Kind forgiving, the world that you perceive will sparkle and shine, and everything that you once thought sinful will now be reinterpreted for you as part of Heaven. How Beautiful it is for you to walk through the world with corrected and Happy perceptions that were in bitter need of the correction that your Innocence bestows on them. You cannot value anything more than this, because here is your salvation and your Freedom. It must be complete for you to recognize that it is so.

1. The Irreconcilable Beliefs

1. Your Memory of God comes to your Quiet Mind. It cannot come where there is conflict in your mind, because when your mind is at war with itself, it does not remember Eternal Gentleness. The means of conflict are not the Means of Peace, and what you remember in conflict is not Love. You have no conflict, unless you

believe that it is possible for you to win. Your conflict implies that you believe it is possible for the personal mind to overcome God. Why else would you identify with it? Surely you recognize that the personal mind thinks that it is at war with God. Just as surely the personal mind has no real enemy, though it is its fixed belief that God is the enemy it must overcome, and it believes that it will succeed.

2. Realize that your war against yourself is a war on God. Victory is not conceivable, but if it were, is this a victory that you want? If God dies, you die. Is this victory for you? The personal mind always marches to defeat, because it thinks it is possible to triumph over you. God thinks otherwise. There is no war, only your mad belief that you can attack and overthrow the Will of God. You may identify with this belief, but it will never be more than madness. Fear will reign in your madness and seem to replace Love. This is conflict's purpose, and when you think it is possible, the means to make it so seem real to you.

3. Be certain that it is impossible that God and the personal mind, and you and the personal mind, will ever meet. You *seem* to meet with the personal mind and make your strange alliance with it on grounds which have no meaning, because your beliefs converge on the body, the personal mind's chosen home, which you believe is yours, too. You meet at an error in your self-evaluation, and the personal mind joins with you in an illusion of you that you share with it. But illusions cannot join. They are all the same, and they are all nothing. Two illusions are as meaningless as one or a thousand. The personal mind, being nothing, joins with nothing. The victory over God that it seeks is as meaningless as itself.

4. Your war against yourself is almost over. Your journey ends at Peace. Accept the Peace offered to you here. You will recognize the 'enemy' that you fought as an intruder on your 'peace' as the Giver of your Peace. Your 'enemy' was God, to Which all conflict, attack, and victory of any kind are unknown. God loves you Perfectly, Completely, and Eternally. For you who have God within you, your being at war with God is as ridiculous as the wind saying that nature is no longer part of it. Could the wind make this true? It is

also not up to you to determine What is within you or what can never be part of you.

5. You undertook this war against yourself to teach yourself that you are *not* One with God. For this you must forget God, and you *do* forget God in the body's 'life'. If you believe that you are a body, you will believe that you have forgotten God. But Truth can never be forgotten by Itself, and you have not forgotten What you are. Only a strange illusion of yourself, a tiny wish to triumph over What you are, seems to have forgotten.

6. Your war against yourself is only a battle of two illusions in your mind – the personal mind and what it has made of God – that you struggle to make different from each other in the belief that the one that wins will be true. There is no conflict between these illusions and Truth. They are not different from each other, because both are not true. It does not matter what form they take. Your wish, which made them, is insane, and they remain part of the insanity that made them. Madness does not threaten Reality, and it has no influence on Reality. Illusions cannot triumph over Truth or threaten It in any way. The Reality that illusions deny is not a part of illusions.

7. The Truth that you remember *is* a part of you, because you must be One with God. Truth does not fight against illusions, and illusions only have an illusion of fighting against Truth. Illusions only battle themselves. Being fragmented, they fragment, but Truth is indivisible and far beyond their little reach. You will remember What you know when you learn that you cannot be in conflict. One illusion about yourself can battle another illusion about yourself, but this war of illusions is a state where nothing real happens. There is no victor or victory. And Truth stands apart, untouched and Quiet in the Peace of God.

8. Conflict must be between two opposing forces. It cannot be between Power and nothingness. Anything you attack is part of your mind. By attacking, you make two illusions of yourself in conflict with each other: the attacker and the attacked. Your mind is One with God, and attack occurs whenever you look on anything that your mind perceives with anything but Love. Conflict is fright-

ening, and it is the birth of your fear. But what is born of nothing cannot make itself real through battle. Why would you fill your mind with perceptions of conflicts with yourself? Let all this madness be undone for you, and turn in Peace to your Memory of God, Which is still in your Quiet Mind.

9. See how the conflict of illusions disappears when it is brought to Truth? The conflict seems real only as long as it seems to be between two truths, the winner being the more real and the defeated becoming the illusion. But conflict is always a choice between illusions, one to be crowned as real and the other to be despised in defeat as an illusion. You will never remember God here. But no illusion can drive God out of your mind, which God loves Forever. What God loves must Forever *be* Quiet and at Peace, because It is God's Home.

10. You who are Beloved of God are not an illusion, being as True and as Holy as God. The Stillness of your Certainty of God and of your True Self is Home to Both, Which are One. Open your mind, God's Holy Home, and let forgiveness sweep away all trace of your belief in separation from God, which keeps God and you homeless. There are no strangers in God's Home. Welcome all that you perceive to God's Home, Where God has set Serenity and Peace for your entire mind, and Where God dwells. Illusions have no place Where Love abides, and Where Love protects you from everything that is not true. You dwell in Peace that is as Limitless as God, and Everything is given to you when you want to remember God. The Holy Spirit watches over your mind, God's Home, sure that Its Peace can never be disturbed.

11. You are God's Resting Place, and you cannot turn on yourself and seek to overcome God. Think what happens when you, the House of God, perceive yourself divided: Love disappears, you perceive separation from God as real, and guilt and fear follow. You remember nothing but illusions. Illusions conflict because their forms are different, and they battle each other only to establish which form must be 'true'.

12. Illusion meets illusion; Truth meets Truth. The meeting of illusions leads to conflict. Peace, looking on Itself, extends Itself. Conflict is

the condition in which fear is born, grows, and seeks to dominate. Peace is the State Where Love abides and seeks to extend Itself. Conflict and Peace are opposites: where one is, the other cannot be. Your Memory of God is obscured when your mind becomes conflict's battleground. But far beyond this senseless conflict your Memory of God waits, ready to be remembered when you side with Peace.

2. The Laws of Chaos

1. The 'laws' of the chaos that seem to uphold in your mind your perception of separation from God must be brought to your conscious awareness, though you will never understand them. Chaotic laws cannot be meaningful, so they are out of the sphere of your True Reasoning. But they appear to be an obstacle to your True Reasoning and to Truth. Look on them calmly so that you can look beyond them, understanding what they are but not what they are supposed to maintain. It is essential that you understand what they are for, because it is their purpose to attack the Truth and to make It meaningless to you. These are the 'laws' that rule the world that you made in your mind to be separate from God. But they govern nothing, and you don't need to break them. You only need to look at them and then go beyond them.

2. The *first* chaotic law that upholds in your mind your separation from God is your belief that *the truth is different for everyone* that you perceive in the world in your mind. You perceive each person as separate and with a different set of thoughts from everyone else. This principle evolves from your belief that there is a hierarchy in illusions, where some illusions are more valuable to you, and these you consider to be 'true'. You, and everyone that you perceive, establish what is valuable for yourselves, and then you make it true for yourselves by attacking what others value. You see this as justified, because values *do* differ in the world that you perceive, and everyone *is* different from each other, therefore everyone is everyone else's enemy.

3. Think of how this seems to interfere with your understanding the principle of miracles that one miracle is not harder than another. By

establishing degrees of truth among illusions, some seem harder for you to overcome than others. But if you realize that all illusions are the same, and all are equally untrue, it will be easy for you to understand that a miracle applies to all of them equally. You can accept correction of errors of any kind *because* they are untrue. When errors are brought to Truth instead of to other errors, they merely disappear. No part of nothing can be more resistant to the Truth than can another part of nothing.

4. The *second* law of chaos that upholds in your mind your perception of separation from God, which is dear to you when you want separation to be real, is that *everyone must sin* in the world that you perceive, so everyone deserves attack and death. This principle, closely related to the first one, which makes separation real to you, insists that your perception of separation calls for punishment instead of for correction. Destroying the one who makes an error then puts them beyond correction and forgiveness. You interpret their error as an irrevocable sentence on them, which even God is powerless to overcome. 'Sin' cannot be canceled out, because 'sin' is the belief that you can make mistakes for which your destruction by God becomes inevitable.

5. Think what this seems to do to your Relationship with God: It appears that you can never be One with God again. You and God must always seem to condemn each other, because you are different; you are enemies. Your relationship is one of opposition, just as you meet the others that people the world in your mind only to conflict, never to join. Whether it's God or another in the world that you perceive, you always perceive one of you as weak and the other as made strong by the defeat of the weak one. Your fear of God and of others now appears sensible, having been made real to you by what you have made of yourself and of God.

6. The arrogance of the laws of chaos cannot be more apparent than they are here. Here is the principle that defines what God and Reality must be, what God must think and believe, and how God must respond. You do not see it as necessary to ask God what the Truth is. *You* tell God what the truth is, and God has the choice to either accept it or to be mistaken. This leads directly to the *third*

541

preposterous belief that seems to make your perception of separation from God and chaos eternal to you: *If God cannot be mistaken, then God must accept what you believe you are and hate you for it.*

7. Do you see how your fear of God is reinforced in this third principle? Now it is impossible for you to turn to God for help in your misery. God has become the 'enemy' that causes your misery, and to Which it is useless for you to appeal. And your salvation cannot lie in the world, either, which you perceive as justifiably at war with God, too. Conflict seems inevitable to you and beyond the help of God. You think that your salvation is impossible, because your Savior is your enemy.

8. Under this principle you have no release or escape, because you view correction of your perception that you are separate from God as a myth, and vengeance, not forgiveness, has become for you the 'Will of God'. There is no help for you that can succeed. Only your destruction can be the outcome, and God seems to side with this to overcome you. Do not think that the personal mind will enable you to find escape from the destruction that it wants for you. Escape is the function of this course, which does not value what the personal mind cherishes.

9. The personal mind values only what it takes from someone or something else. This leads to the *fourth* law of chaos, which upholds in your mind your separation from God, and which must be true if you accept the others. This seeming law is the belief that *you only have what you have taken from God or from others*. You therefore see another's loss as your gain. This law fails to recognize that your mind is One, and that it can only ever take from itself. But all the other laws *must* lead to this, because they say that separation is real, so enemies are real. You must take from God and others what you want, because enemies do not give willingly to one another or share what they value. And you believe that what your 'enemies' keep from you *must* be worth having, because they keep it hidden from you.

10. All of the mechanisms of the madness of your belief in separation emerge here: others as the 'enemy' who are made strong by hiding

what should be yours, your justified attack on them for what they are withholding from you, and the inevitable loss that they must suffer for you to save yourself. This is how, in your guilt, you protest your 'innocence': If you were not forced into this foul attack by the unscrupulous behavior of the enemy, you would be kind instead. But, in a savage world, the kind cannot survive, so you must take or be taken from.

11. Now there is a vague, unanswered question that has not yet been 'explained': What is this precious hidden treasure that you must wrest from your cunning 'enemies' in righteous wrath? It must be what you have been seeking for and have never found. Now you understand why you have never found it. It was taken from you by your enemies and hidden where you would not think to look. They hide it in their bodies, the cover for their guilt, and the hiding place for what belongs to you. Now they must be destroyed and sacrificed so that you can have what belongs to you. Their treachery demands their death, so that you can live. You attack only in self-defense.

12. But what is it that you want and that you need others to die for? Can you be sure that your murderous attack is justified? Here, the *final* principle of chaos that upholds in your mind your perception of separation from God comes to the 'rescue': *There is a substitute for Love.*[1] This is the magic that you think will cure all of your pain; the missing factor in all of your madness that makes it 'sane'. This is the reason why you must attack and what makes your vengeance justified. Behold unveiled the personal mind's secret gift, torn from the body of another where it was hidden in hatred from you to whom it belongs! The other wants to deprive you of the secret ingredient that would give your life meaning. This substitute for Love, born of the hostility between you and others, must be your salvation. *It* has no substitute, and it is the only substitute for Love. All of your relationships in the world that you perceive have the purpose of seizing it from others and making it your own.

13. Never is your possession of the substitute for Love complete, and never will others cease their attack on you for what you stole from them. And God will never end Its vengeance on you and others,

because, in God's madness, God must have this substitute for Love and kill all of you. You believe that you walk in sanity on solid ground through a world where meaning can be found. But consider this: These *are* the principles which make the world that you perceive seem solid, and it *is* here that you look for meaning. These are the laws that you made for your salvation. They hold in place in your mind the world that you substitute for Heaven, and which you prefer to Heaven. This is their purpose; what they were made for. It is apparent that there is no point in asking what they mean, because the means of madness must be insane. But are you as certain that you realize that the goal *is* madness?

14. You don't want madness, and you would not cling to madness if you saw that it *is* madness. What protects your madness is your belief that it is the truth. It is the function of insanity to take the place of Truth, and you must see it as truth to believe it. If madness is the truth, then its opposite, *Truth*, must be madness. This reversal, where madness is 'sanity', illusions are 'truth', attack is 'kindness', hatred is 'love', and murder is 'benediction', is the goal that the laws of chaos serve. These are the means that seem to reverse the Law of God that Mind is One. Here, the laws of separation from God appear to hold Love captive and to let 'sin' go free from correction.

15. These do not seem to be the laws of chaos. In this reversal, they seem to be the laws of order. Chaos is lawlessness, so for you to believe its 'laws', you must perceive them as real, and you must see the goal of madness as sanity. You must confuse fear with Love, Which fear conquered, substitutes for, and 'saves' you from. The laws of fear make separation seem lovely to you. Give thanks to fear, which has saved you for death!

16. How can it be that you believe laws like these? There is a strange device that makes it possible. It is not unfamiliar; you have looked on it in this course before. In Truth, this device does not function, but in illusions, where only shadows play major roles, it seems powerful. The laws of chaos compel your belief because of their emphasis on *form* and their disregard of content. When you think that these laws are true it is because you do not see what they really

say. Some *forms* that these laws take have meaning for you, but that is all.

17. Actually, every form of separation from God attests that death is real, attack in any form cannot mean Love, guilt is not a blessing, and you cannot make your Christ Mind powerless and find salvation. Do not let the *form* of attack that you make on your Christ Mind deceive you. You cannot seek to harm your Christ Mind and be saved, because you cannot find safety from attack by turning it on yourself. It does not matter what form madness takes. It is a judgment that defeats itself, condemning you, whom it is supposed to save. Do not be deceived when madness takes a form that you think is lovely. What is intent on your destruction is not your friend.

18. You want to maintain, and think it true, that you do not believe these senseless laws, and that you do not act on them. And when you look at them directly, you *cannot* believe them. But you *do* believe them. With content such as this, how else can you perceive the form that they take, except that you believe the content? Can any form of these laws be supported? Yet you believe them *for* the form that they take, and you deny their content. But their form never changes their content. You cannot paint rosy lips on a skeleton, dress it, pet it, and pamper it to make it live. You cannot be content living an illusion.

19. There is no Life outside of Heaven; Life is only Where God wants It to be. In any state apart from Heaven, life is an illusion. At best, it *seems* a type of 'life'; at worst like death. But both are your judgments on what is *not life*, equally inaccurate and lacking in meaning. Life outside of Heaven is impossible, and what is not in Heaven is not anywhere. Outside of Heaven is only the conflict of illusions: senseless, impossible, and beyond all reason, yet perceived by you as an eternal barrier to Heaven. Illusions are only forms; their content is never true.

20. The laws of chaos govern all illusions. The forms that illusions take conflict so that it seems possible for you to value some illusions above others. But they all rest on your belief that the laws of chaos are the laws of order. Each form of illusion upholds these laws

545

completely, offering a witness that these laws are true. The seemingly gentler forms of separation from God are no less certain in their witnessing or in their results. Illusions bring you fear because of the beliefs that they imply, not because of their form. Your lack of faith that only Love is Real, in whatever form, attests to chaos as reality.

21. Your faith in chaos must follow from your belief that separation from God is real. It is because it follows that it seems to be a logical conclusion; a valid step in ordered thought. Your steps to chaos do follow neatly from their starting point of your belief in 'sin'. Each is a different form in the progression of Truth's reversal, leading you deeper into terror, and away from Truth. No step is smaller than another, and your return from each is the same. Your whole descent from Heaven to hell lies in each one. Where your thinking starts, there must the descent end.

22. Do not take one step in the descent to hell, because, having taken one, you will not recognize the rest for what they are. And they will follow. Your belief in separation from God in any form places your foot on the twisted stairway that descends from Heaven. But you can have it all undone in an Instant. How do you know if you have chosen the way to Heaven or the way to hell? Easily: How do you feel? Is Peace in your awareness, and are you certain that you can reach the Goal of Heaven? If not, you are listening to the personal mind. Ask the Holy Spirit to join you and to make you certain about the way that you go.

3. Salvation Without Compromise

1. It is true that you do not recognize some of the forms that your attack on God, and therefore on yourself, can take. Your desire for separation from God in any form will hurt you, whether you recognize that this is what you want or not, and that is why you do not always recognize the source of your pain. Your mind is One, and all thoughts in it that make separation real to you are attack thoughts, and they are all equally destructive. Their purpose never changes. Their sole intent is to make God unreal to you by making death real to you, and what form of murder can cover the massive

guilt and frantic fear of punishment that you must feel? You may deny that you are a murderer and justify your savagery with smiles while you attack, but you will suffer and look on your true intent in nightmares where the smiles are gone and where your purpose rises to your horrified awareness. You cannot think of murder and escape the guilt that this thought entails. What does it matter what form your intent of death takes?

2. Any form that your belief in separation from God takes is a form of death, no matter how lovely and charitable it may seem to you to be. It cannot be a blessing, nor a sign that you are extending the Holy Spirit to in your mind where you perceive a world. The wrapping does not make the gift. An empty box, however beautifully wrapped and gently given, still contains nothing. Withhold forgiving the personal mind's projections on the world that you perceive, and you are attacking your mind. You extend nothing, so nothing is what you receive.

3. Your salvation can contain no compromise of any kind. To compromise is to accept only part of what you want and to give up the rest. Your salvation can give up nothing; it must extend completely to your entire mind. Let the idea of compromise enter your mind and salvation's purpose of restoring Oneness to your mind is lost to you, because you won't recognize it. Your salvation is denied to you when you try to compromise by holding onto some forms of separation, because this compromise is your idea that Oneness is impossible. Your compromise maintains that you can separate a little, and be One a little, and know the difference. It teaches you that a little of What is One can be different, and yet Oneness can remain intact. This does not make sense, and you cannot understand it.

4. This course is easy precisely because it does not compromise, but it seems difficult to you as long as you believe that compromise is possible. If compromise is possible, then salvation is a form of separation and attack. Certainly your belief that salvation is impossible does not uphold your quiet, calm assurance that salvation has come. You cannot withhold forgiveness a little. You cannot be separate here, and One there, and understand that forgiveness

overlooks all separation and sees only Oneness. The only way to *not* lose sight of your Peace is to recognize your assault on It in all of its forms. You can keep Peace forever clear in your perception if you do not defend It.

5.   If you believe that you can defend Peace, and that your attack on Its behalf is justified, then you do not perceive that Peace already lies within you. You will not overlook all separation while you still believe that some forms of separation are necessary for your Peace. You do not see that your savage purpose of separation is directed toward yourself. You cannot look at the world that you perceive as your enemy and be one with it in purpose. If you compromise and try to keep some separation with Oneness, you will still hate the world that you perceive, because it will seem to be keeping Peace from your mind.

6.   Do not mistake a temporary truce with the personal mind for Peace, or the personal mind's offering of compromise for an escape from conflict. For you to be released from conflict means that the conflict is over because you have left the personal mind behind. It does not mean that you linger with the personal mind in cowering hope that the conflict will not return because the personal mind is quiet an instant and your fear is not apparent. There is no safety in the conflict of the personal mind, but you can look on it safely from the Holy Spirit. No illusion of protection that the personal mind offers to you can stand against your faith in murder. Here is the body, torn between your True Mind's natural desire for Oneness and the personal mind's unnatural intent to murder and to die. Don't think that any form of separation can offer you safety from murder. Guilt cannot be absent from your wish for death.

4. Above the Battleground

1.   Your fear of God is your fear of Life, not of death. But God is the only Place of Safety, because in God there is no attack, and no illusion in any form stalks Heaven. Heaven is wholly True. There are no differences in Heaven, and what is all the same cannot contain conflict. You are not asked to fight against your wish to kill God, but you are asked to realize the forms that conceal this intent.

It is this intent that you fear, not the forms it takes. What is not Love is murder; what is not Loving is attack. Every illusion that you hold onto is an assault on Truth, and your attachment to it does violence to the idea of Love, because then separation seems to be as true as Love.

2. But what is equal to the Truth cannot be different. Murder and Love are different, so both cannot be Truth. If they were both True, they would be indistinguishable from each other. And this is what you believe when you believe that bodies are real. It is not the body that is like God. What is lifeless cannot be One with Life. A body cannot be extended to hold all of Reality, it cannot extend itself and be what it extends, and it cannot offer its extensions all that it is and never suffer loss.

3. God does not share Its Function with a body. God gave the Function to extend to your Mind, because your Mind is God's Extension. It is not sinful for you to believe that your function is murder, but it is insane. What is the same cannot have a different function. Your Whole Mind is the Means for God's extension, and what is God's must be yours as well. Either both God and you are murderers or neither is. Life does not make death, as Life only extends Itself.

4. The Loveliness of your Holy relationship is like the Love of God. It cannot yet assume the Holy function God gave to your Christ Mind, because your forgiving the personal mind's projections on the other is not yet complete, so it cannot yet be extended to your entire mind. Each form of separation that still attracts you, and that you therefore do not recognize as attack and murder, limits the healing and the miracles that you have the Power to extend to your entire mind. But the Holy Spirit knows how to increase your little gifts and make them mighty. The Holy Spirit also understands how your Holy relationship is raised above the personal mind's projections of separation, where it is no longer. This is your part: to realize that separation from God in any form is murder and not your will. Overlooking the personal mind's projections of separation is now your purpose.

5. Look on the personal mind's projections of separation from the

Holy Spirit within you, and your perspective will be quite different from what it has been. From the perspective of the personal mind, its projections seem quite real. You have chosen to be part of them; murder is your choice. But from the Holy Spirit, your choice is miracles instead. And this perspective shows you that the separation is not real, and it is easily escaped. Bodies may battle, but the clash of forms is meaningless. It is over when you realize it was never begun. You cannot perceive that the personal mind's projections are nothing when you engage in them. You will not recognize the Truth of miracles if you want murder to be your choice.

6.   When the temptation to attack and make the separation real to you occurs, remember that you *can* detach yourself from it. Even if you do not recognize all of the forms that attack takes, you do know the signs: a stab of pain, a twinge of guilt, and above all, the loss of your Peace. When this occurs, do not leave the Holy Spirit, but quickly choose to experience a miracle in place of separation. God and all of the Love of Heaven will gently lean toward you and hold you up, because you will have chosen to remain in Heaven, Where God wants you to be. No illusion can attack the Peace of God's Oneness.

7.   Look on anything from the perspective of the personal mind, and you will see nothing. The personal mind does not have a reference point that can give meaning to what you see. Only a body can be separate, and if attack and murder are your purpose, then you will want to be a body. Only a purpose unifies, and what you extend your purpose to is one with you. The body has no purpose, and it must be separate and isolated. From the personal mind, you cannot surmount it. But from the Holy Spirit, the limits it exerts on you are gone. The body stands between God and the Oneness that God extends to you *because* it has no purpose.

8.   Think what will be given to you when you become fully aware that God's Purpose is *your* Purpose: you will want nothing, and sorrow of any kind will be inconceivable to you. Only Love will be in your awareness, and only Love will shine on you Forever. Love will be your past, present, and future; always the same, Eternally

Complete, and wholly extended. You will know that your Happiness cannot change. But perhaps you still think that the personal mind offers you something of value? Can it offer you Perfect Calmness and an Eternal Love so Deep and Quiet that no touch of doubt can ever mar your Certainty of It?

9.   With the Strength of God in your awareness you will never think of the personal mind's conflict. What can it give to you but loss of your Perfection? Everything that the personal mind fights for is of the body – something that the body seems to offer or to own. When you know that you have everything, you will not seek for the limitations of the body, and you will not value anything that the body offers. The senselessness of conflict is quite apparent to you from the Quiet of the Holy Spirit. What can conflict with Everything? What, that offers less than Everything, could you want more than Everything? With the Love of God upholding you, you cannot find the choice of miracles or murder hard to make.

Chapter 24

The Goal of Specialness

1. Your motivation for doing this course is attaining and keeping the State of Peace. In this State, your mind is Quiet, and this is the Condition in Which you remember God. It is not necessary to tell God what to do, because where God wills to be, God already *is*. A shadow cannot hold back the Will that holds Reality secure. God does not wait on illusions to be God, and you do not wait on illusions to be One with God. You and God *are*. No illusion that seems to drift between you and God has the power to defeat your joint Will.

2. To learn this course, you must be willing to question every value that you hold in your identification with a personal self. Any value that you keep hidden and obscure will jeopardize your learning. No belief is neutral, and every belief that you have has the power to dictate each decision that you make. A decision is a conclusion based on everything that you believe. A decision is the outcome of your belief, and it follows as surely as suffering follows guilt and Freedom follows Innocence. There is no substitute for Peace; there is no alternative to What is One with God. Truth arises from God's Knowledge. Your decisions come from your beliefs as certainly as all of Creation rose in God's Mind *because* of What God knows.

1. Specialness as a Substitute for Love

1. Love is extension, so for you to withhold Love anywhere is for you to not know Love's Purpose. Love offers Itself to everything Forever. If you hold onto one belief in Love's place, then Love is gone from your mind, because you asked a substitute to take Its place. Now must conflict, the substitute for Peace, come to you with the separation that you asked to substitute for Love's Oneness. Your choosing separation has given separation all the reality that it seems to have for you.

2. Conflicting outcomes are impossible, so your beliefs will never openly attack each other. But your not recognizing your beliefs is your decision to secretly attack yourself, and to deny the results of your conflict, which you never bring to your True Reasoning Mind to be judged as sensible or not. In your identification with a personal self, you have reached many senseless outcomes, and you have made many meaningless decisions that you have kept hidden to become beliefs themselves that direct your subsequent decisions. Do not mistake the power of these hidden decisions to disrupt your Peace, because your Peace is at their mercy while you decide to leave them hidden. Any decision where you choose separation instead of Love, no matter how small, is a secret enemy of your Peace and is quick to lead you into a conflict that encompasses all that your mind perceives. These decisions are there by your choosing, so do not deny their presence or their terrible results. You can only deny their reality, not their outcome.

3. Your hidden beliefs always defend your faith in your specialness, though you don't recognize this. This takes many forms, but it always clashes with the Reality of your Oneness with God and with your Limitlessness in God. Only defending your specialness can justify your attack, because you would not hate if you recognized that your Self is in your mind where you perceive a world . Only in separation do you perceive enemies, because you perceive differences, not Oneness. Differences of any kind impose orders of reality, and a need to judge that you cannot escape.

4. What is One with God cannot be attacked, because there is nothing in Reality unlike Reality. But when you want differences to be real, you call for judgment, and your judgment must be that you are 'better than', 'above', and 'sinless' compared to whom you condemn. Specialness is your means and end at once, because you are not only separate from whom you judge, but you see your attack on who is 'beneath' you as natural and just. In specialness, you are weak because of your separateness, and the personal self that makes you special *is* your enemy. Yet you protect the personal mind's hatred of you, and you call it 'friend'. You fight against Reality on its behalf, because you value nothing more than the

separate personal self.

5. Specialness is the great dictator of your wrong decisions. It is the grand illusion of what you are and of what you project onto others, and it makes the body dear to you and worth preserving in your judgment. You must defend specialness. Illusions can attack it, and they do, because the attack that you must perceive as coming from others to keep your specialness intact *is* an illusion. You must attack the other who is 'worse' than you, so that your specialness can live on their defeat. Your specialness is triumph, and its victory is another's defeat and shame. With your separation projected onto them, they do not deserve to live, and you must be their conqueror.

6. You would not hate others and attack them if you realized that they were perceptions in your mind, and that as such they journey to the Goal of God with you. If you perceived this, you would do every-thing that you could to perceive God in their place *now* to attain your Goal of God. In specialness, you are an enemy to the others that you perceive, but you are their friend in the shared Purpose of remembering God. In specialness, you do not share, because your goal is for you alone in the isolation of a personal mind. In specialness, you feel your goals are jeopardized when another shares them. Love has no meaning for you when your goal is triumph. Any decision that you make for triumph over another will hurt you.

7. The others that you perceive are your friends, because your mind is One. There is no difference between you and what you perceive in the world in your mind. Your relationships with others are for you to extend Love to, not for you to use to cut yourself off in separation. What you keep for yourself alone in the personal mind is lost to you. God extends God to your entire mind, and to remember this now is the only purpose that you share with your mind where you perceive a world, so it is the only purpose that you have. You are not attacking another if you choose to overlook all specialness. In your Holy relationship, look fairly at whatever makes you only sometimes extend Love to the other, or that makes you think that you would be better off apart from the other. It is always your belief that your specialness is limited by the Holy

relationship. Your desire for specialness is what makes the other an 'enemy' to you.

8.	Your fear of God and of the other in your Holy relationship comes from your unrecognized belief in your specialness, because your specialness demands that others bow to it against their will. Even God must honor your specialness or suffer vengeance. Your every twinge of malice, stab of hate, or wish to separate arises from your desire for specialness. Here, the Purpose of Oneness that you share with your perception of the other in your Holy relationship becomes obscured. You oppose this course, because it teaches you that your mind is One. But you share your purpose with the part of your mind where you perceive a world, and it comes from God. Your relationship has been made clean of special goals, so do not defeat the Goal of Holiness that Heaven has given to it. In specialness, your perspective changes with every seeming blow, each imagined slight, and every fancied judgment on it.

9.	In your specialness, you must defend illusions against the Truth, because you perceive your specialness as an attack on the Will of God, and you expect God to attack you back. And you do not extend Love to your perception of the other in your relationship, because you are defending your perceived attack on God. It seems to you that the other attacks your specialness, too, and that you must defend it against them as well. Your specialness is the grounds for conflict between you, so you must see the other as your enemy and not as your friend. There cannot be Peace among the different, but the other is your friend *because* your mind is One.

2. The Treachery of Specialness

1.	Comparisons must come from the personal mind, because Love, being One, doesn't make comparisons. Your specialness always makes comparisons, because your specialness is established by the differences that you project onto another, and it is maintained by your searching for and keeping clear in sight all of the differences that you can perceive. Separation is all that your specialness looks upon. But you can extend Christ instead to those whom you diminish for the sake of your specialness. Compared to the littleness that the personal mind projects onto others, you see your specialness as tall and stately, clean and honest, pure and unsullied. But you do not see that it is yourself that you diminish by this comparison because of your identification with a personal self.

2. Your pursuit of specialness always costs you Peace. Attacking another to whom you could extend Christ leaves you without the Strong Support extending Christ to them would give to you. You cannot detract from your Christ Mind's Omnipotence and share Its Power. You cannot use part of your mind as a judge of limitedness and be released from all limits. You have a function in your salvation, and Its pursuit will bring you Joy. But your pursuit of specialness brings you pain, because it is a goal that defeats your salvation, so runs counter to God's Will. For you to value your specialness is for you to esteem an alien will in which an illusion of yourself is dearer to you than Truth.

3. Your specialness turns your perception of separation from God into a *sin* in your mind, because it seems to make separation real. It is impossible for you to imagine sin without your specialness as its base, because your idea that separation from God is real comes out of your desire for specialness. But specialness is nothingness, and the idea of sin is like an evil flower with no real roots. Your specialness is your self-made 'savior', the 'creator' that creates unlike God, which made Part of God like itself and unlike God. Now, Part of God's Mind perceives many special 'selves', never One Self. Each of these selves seems separate from you and from God. You choose your own specialness instead of Heaven and Peace, and you wrap it in the idea of sin, which cannot be undone, to keep it 'safe' from Truth.

4. You are not special. You cannot know the Truth when you think that you are special, and you defend it against the Truth that you are really One with God. You cannot hear the answers that the Holy Spirit gives to you when you listen to your specialness, which both asks the questions and then answers them. And yet, your specialness' tiny answer, which is soundless in the Eternal Communication Which flows from God to you in Loving Praise of What you are, is all that you listen to. God's Honor and Love for

What you are seem silent and unheard by you before the 'mightiness' of your specialness. As you strain to hear its soundless voice, you are deaf to the Call of God.

5.   You can defend your specialness, but you will never hear the Holy Spirit beside it. Your specialness and the Holy Spirit speak to you of different things, and they seem to be heard in different parts of your mind. It seems that every special person in the world that you perceive has a different special message that is the truth for them. But the Truth cannot be different for parts of a mind that is One. The special message that you hear in your specialness convinces you that you are different and separate in your special form of separation, and that you are 'safe' from the Oneness of Love, Which does not see specialness at all. Your Christ Mind's Perception is your 'enemy' in your specialness, because It does not look on the specialness that you want to see, and It shows you that the specialness that you want is an illusion.

6.   What does your Christ Mind's Perception show you? The Love of God, Which is so like God that It brings God instantly to your mind. With Christ, you remember your own Extension of God, Which is as like to you as you are to God. And the entire world that you made, all of your specialness, and all of the forms of separation that you held onto to defend your specialness, vanish as you accept the Truth about yourself, and you let It take their place. This is the only 'cost' of Truth: You no longer see what never was, nor hear what makes no sound. Is it a sacrifice for you to give up nothing and to receive the Love of God in your awareness Forever?

7.   You have chained your Holy relationship to your specialness by projecting specialness onto the other instead of extending Christ in your perception of them, but remember this: By extending Christ in your perception of the other, you extend the Power to forgive *you* all of the sins that you think that you perceive between the other and the function of salvation that has been given to your relationship with them. You cannot change the function of your Holy relationship any more than you can change your Oneness with the Truth beyond the personal mind's projections onto the other. The Truth is the same for both you and your perception of

the other in your Holy relationship, Its Message is the same for both, and Its Message has One meaning. It is a Message that you can understand and that releases you and your perception of the other to your Christ Mind. Here, your Holy relationship stands, holding out the key to Heaven to you. Do not let the illusion of specialness remain between you and your perception of the other, because a Mind that is One is joined in Truth.

8. Think of the Loveliness that you will see within yourself when you have looked on the other in your Holy relationship as your friend. In your perception of Holiness, the other *is* the enemy of your specialness, but a friend to the Christ that is Real in you. None of your attacks on the other has taken away the Gift of Love that God has given to you to extend to them. You mind where you perceive a world needs this Gift as much as you. Let your relationship forgive your specialness by extending to it the Wholeness of your Mind to make you One. Your relationship waits for your extension of forgiveness so that you may be forgiven. God has not condemned you, but you have condemned God's Oneness to save your specialness and to kill your Self.

9. You have come far along the way to Truth; too far to falter now. Just one more step, and every vestige of your fear of God will melt away in Love. The other's specialness and your specialness *are* enemies, bound in hate to kill each other and to deny that they are the same. But it is not an illusion of yourself that has reached this final obstacle that seems to make God and Heaven so remote to you that you cannot reach Them. Here, in this Holy Place, Oneness stands waiting to receive your entire mind in silent blessing, and in Peace so Real and so Encompassing that nothing stands outside of It. Leave all illusions outside of this Place to Which you come in hope and honesty.

10. In Holiness, your perception of the other is your Savior *from* specialness. You need to accept that you and your perception of the other are Part of One Mind. Together, you are as alike to God as God is to God. God is not special, because God does not keep any Part of God cut off from the rest of God. And you fear this, because, if God is not special, then God's Will is that you are not special. So

your relationship *is* in your One Mind, not special, but possessed of Everything, including you. Extend to your perception of the other the Oneness that is already here, remembering that God extends God to your entire mind with equal Love, so that you can share Reality with God. In God, Love is never divided and kept from the Oneness that It is and must be Forever.

11. Your Holy relationship with the other in your perception is Oneness, because Love is not denied to any part of your mind. You do not lose because you perceive Completion in your relationship. The Truth beyond the personal mind's projections onto the other makes you Complete, as It makes your perception of your relationship Complete. God's Love gives your Holy relationship to you, because God gives God, and What is the same as God is One with God. Only your specialness makes the Truth of your Oneness with God seem like something other than Heaven to you, and makes it seem that you can find the hope of Peace in specialness.

12. Your specialness is the seal of treachery on your gift of 'love'. Whatever serves specialness' purpose you give to kill the Truth in you. What your specialness offers brings treachery to you as giver and receiver. What you look on through specialness is death. Believe in its potency, and you will seek out bargains and compromises with Truth where you want to make separation from God the substitute for Love, which will serve it faithfully. Any relationship in which you hold your specialness dear clings to murder as a weapon for safety and to the personal self as a defense against the 'threat' of Love's Oneness.

13. Your hope that specialness is real makes it seem possible to you that God made the body, which keeps you 'safe' from God. Your specialness demands a special place where God cannot enter; a hiding place where only a tiny personal self is welcome. What is sacred in the body is for you alone, separate from others, safe from all intrusions of Sanity on illusions, safe from God, and safe *for* everlasting conflict. The body is the gate of hell that you have closed on yourself so that you can rule your special kingdom in madness and isolation, apart from God, away from Truth, and away from salvation.

14. You can find the key to the gate of hell that you threw away in your extension of Oneness in your Holy relationship. Your Holiness, which you see in your perception of the other, offers this key to you when you are ready to accept God's plan for your salvation in place of the one that you made with the personal mind. You reach this readiness by perceiving your misery, and through your awareness that the personal mind's plan has failed, and always will fail, to bring you Peace and Joy of any kind. You travel through this despair now, but it is only an illusion of despair. The death of your specialness is not *your* death but your awakening into Eternal Life. You will emerge from an illusion of what you are to your acceptance of your Oneness with God.

3. The Forgiveness of Specialness

1. Your forgiving your perception of separation from God is the end of your specialness. You can only forgive illusions, and when you do, they disappear. Real forgiving releases *all* illusions, and that is why it is impossible for you to partly forgive. You cannot see your Innocence if you cling to even one illusion, because then you are cherishing an error that is 'unforgivable' and is therefore a sin. And, you cannot wholly extend forgiveness if you are not ready to wholly accept forgiveness for yourself. You will receive forgiveness wholly the instant that you wholly extend it. Your secret guilt will disappear, forgiven by yourself.

2. Whatever form of specialness that you cherish, you make a sin to you. It stands unchanged and strongly defended by the personal mind's puny might against the Will of God. This sin stands against *you*; it is your enemy, not God's enemy. It seems to split you off from God, because your defense of it means that you are protecting what is *not* One with God. But this idol of specialness that is supposed to give you power takes True Power away from you. You give to it the power that belongs to the Truth in your Holy relationship, leaving you perceiving you and the other in separation and misery before an idol of specialness that cannot save you.

3. It is not the Truth in you that is so vulnerable and open to attack that just a little whisper that you do not like, a circumstance that

doesn't suit you, or an event that you did not anticipate upsets your world and hurls it into chaos. Truth is not frail; illusions leave It perfectly unmoved. Specialness is not the Truth in you. *It* can be thrown off balance by anything, because it rests on nothing, and it can never be stable. However large and overblown specialness seems to be, it still rocks and turns and twirls about with every breeze.

4.   Nothing is secure without a foundation, and God has not left you in a state where safety has no meaning. You *are* safe, resting on God. It is your specialness that is attacked by everything that walks and breathes, creeps or crawls, or even lives at all. Your specialness attacks everything, and your specialness is never safe. It is Forever unforgiving, because it is your secret vow that What God wants for you will never be, and that you will oppose God's Will Forever. It is not possible that your specialness and God's Will will ever be the same, because your specialness makes an enemy of God.

5.   God asks you for your forgiveness for the specialness that God cannot give to you. God does not want separation, like an alien will, to rise between What God Wills for you and What you Will for yourself. The Will of your Christ Mind and God's Will *are* the same, because neither one wills your specialness. How could They will the death of Love Itself? But Christ's Will and God's Will are powerless to attack your illusions. They are not bodies; as One Mind, they wait for you to bring illusions to Them and to leave illusions behind. Your salvation doesn't even challenge death. Even God, Which knows that death is not your Will, must say, 'Thy will be done' when you think that death *is* your will.

6.   Forgive the Creator of All; the Source of Life, Love, and Holiness; the Perfect Whole of Which you are a Perfect Part your illusions of your specialness. Your specialness is the hell that you chose to be your home. God did not choose this for you; do not ask God to enter into it. In this hell, your way to Love and salvation is barred. But, if you release the personal mind's projections of hell on the other in your Holy relationship, you forgive God, Which wills that you live Forever in the arms of Peace, in Perfect Safety, and without the malice of one thought of specialness to mar your rest. Forgive

God the specialness that God cannot give and that you made instead.

7.   In specialness, it is as though you are asleep, surrounded by a Loveliness that you do not perceive. Freedom, Peace, and Joy are beside the bier on which you sleep, and they call you to waken from your dream of death. But you do not hear them when you are lost in dreams of specialness. You hate the Call that will awaken you, and you curse God, because God did not make your dream into Reality. Curse God and die, but not by God. God did not make death, and you die only in your dream of separation from God. But you open your eyes a little by seeing the salvation that God offers to you in your Holy relationship. What you extend to your relationship *is* yours.

8.   Though you are a slave to specialness, you will yet be free from all limitations. This is the Will of God, and your Will. God does not condemn Itself to hell and damnation. Do you will to see this in your perception of the other in your Holy relationship? God calls to you from your Holy relationship to join God's Will to save your entire mind from hell. Look at the crucifixion that the personal mind perceives in the other and holds out for your forgiveness. God asks that you have mercy on your Christ Mind and on God. Do not deny Them. They ask only that you let your Will be done. They seek your Love so that you will love yourself. Do not love your specialness instead of Them. The crucifixion that you perceive in the other is yours. Forgive God for not making your crucifixion God's Will.

4. Specialness versus Sinlessness

1.   Your specialness results in you lacking trust in anyone but the personal self with which you identify. You invest your faith in this personal self alone, and everything else becomes your enemy: feared and attacked, deadly and dangerous, hated and worthy only of destruction. Whatever offers you gentleness you see as deception, but if it offers you hate you believe it is real. Everything is out to kill you, because it is in danger of destruction from you, so you are drawn to kill it first. This is your attraction to your

separation from God: death is enthroned as your savior, crucifixion is your redemption, and your salvation means the destruction of the world, except for you.

2.	In your identification with a personal self, your purpose for the body is only your specialness. It is this that makes it frail and helpless in defense of itself. You conceived of the body to make *you* frail and helpless in your identification with it. Your goal of separation is the body's curse. But the body does not have goals; purpose is of the mind, and your mind can change as you desire. You cannot change What your mind is or any of its attributes, but you can change what you hold as your mind's purpose, and the body's condition will shift with this change. The body can do nothing of itself. See the body as a means to hurt you, and it is hurt; see it as a means to heal your mind, and it is healed.

3.	You can only hurt yourself. This has often been repeated in this course, but it is impossible for you to grasp when your mind is intent on specialness. But when you choose to heal instead of to attack, it is quite obvious. The purpose of attack is in your mind, and you feel its effects there. Your mind is not limited, so your harmful purpose shows up in your perception. Nothing makes less sense to your specialness or more sense to miracles. Your experience of miracles merely shifts the purpose of your mind from hurt to healing. This shift does 'endanger' your specialness, but only because all illusions are 'threatened' by the Truth. Illusions will not stand before the Truth. But you have never found comfort in illusions, so why keep from God the miracles that God asks you to extend in their place? Extend Love to God, and All is yours. But the 'love' that you give to illusions is never returned to you. What you give to an illusion leaves you bankrupt, and leaves your treasure house barren and empty. And then you invite in everything that will disturb your Peace.

4.	Earlier in this course, it tells you to not consider the means by which you attain salvation, but to consider well whether or not you wish to see Innocence in place of the personal mind's projections on the other in your Holy relationship. To your specialness the answer must be 'no', because Innocence is an 'enemy' to your specialness, while sin, if it were possible, would be its friend. If your separation from God were real, then the sin that you project onto the other would justify your specialness and give it the meaning that Truth denies to it. But All that is Real proclaims the Innocence of all that your mind perceives; all that is false proclaims that the separation that you perceive in the other is real. If the other is not sinful, then the 'reality' that you have made for yourself is not real; only an illusion of your specialness that lasts an instant before crumbling into dust.

5.   Do not defend this senseless illusion in which God is bereft of What It loves and you remain beyond salvation. Only this is certain in your perception that you are in a shifting world that has no meaning in Reality: When you are not entirely Peaceful, or when you suffer pain of any kind, you have beheld some form of separation as real, and you have rejoiced at it, because your specialness seemed safe because of it. And so you have saved the specialness that the personal mind has appointed as your savior, and you have crucified your Christ Mind, Which you could have extended in its place. You are bound to your perception of the other in your Holy relationship because your mind is One, so specialness is the 'enemy' of your True Mind.

5. The Christ in You

1.   Your Christ Mind is very Still. It looks on What It loves and knows It as Itself, and It rejoices because It knows that What It sees is One with It and with God. Your specialness also takes joy in what it sees, although what it sees is not true. What you seek for is a source of joy for you *as you conceive of joy*. What you wish for is true for you. It is not possible for you to wish for something and to lack faith that it is real. Your wishing makes something real to you, as surely as Will extends Itself. The power of your wish upholds illusions as strongly as Love extends Itself. But wishes delude, and Love heals.

2.   You have no illusion of specialness in which you do not suffer your own guilt, no matter how hidden, how disguising the form, how lovely it may seem to be, or how much it delicately offers you hope

of peace and escape from pain. In your illusions, cause and effect are interchanged, because you, the maker of the illusion, believe that what you made is happening to you. You do not realize that you picked a thread from here, a scrap from there, and wove a picture out of nothing. The parts do not belong together, and the whole does not give any meaning to the parts.

3. Your Peace can *only* arise from your forgiving your illusion that you separated from God. Your Christ Mind looks only on the Truth, and It does not see any guilt that needs forgiving. Your Christ Mind is at Peace *because* It sees no separation. Identify with Christ and you will have Everything that Christ has. Christ will be your eyes, your ears, your hands, your feet. How Gentle will be the sights and sounds that you hear through your Christ Mind! How Beautiful will be your hand, which, in your perception of your Christ's Mind's Oneness, holds the hand of another who once seemed separate from you in a world that you thought was outside of your mind. Through your Christ Mind you will see and hear What you *can* see and hear, and you will overlook the nothingness where there are no real sights or sounds.

4. But see specialness in the other in your Holy relationship, and you will believe that you are special. You will see the other as dangerous to you, and you will want to destroy them, because specialness delights in killing. It seeks death, and it leads to destruction. But do not think that what it sees and hates in the other it sees in them first. The 'sin' that specialness loves to see in the other it saw in you first, and it still looks on it with joy. But is it joy for you to look on decay and madness and to believe this crumbling thing is like yourself?

5. Rejoice that you do not really have eyes to see, or ears to listen, or hands to hold, or feet to guide. Be glad that your Christ Mind can lend you these while you still perceive yourself in a world. They are illusions, too, but they serve a different purpose and are given this purpose's Strength. What they see and hear and hold and lead to is Love so that you may extend Love as It was given to you.

6. Your Christ Mind is very Still. Christ knows Where you are going, and It leads you There in Gentleness and Blessing all the way.

Christ's Love for God replaces all of the fear that you thought that you saw within yourself. Christ's Holiness shows you Christ in your Holy relationship. Through your Christ Mind, What you see is like yourself, because, in your Christ Mind, there is only Christ to see and hear and love and follow Home. Your Christ Mind looked within you and saw that you were unaware that you are Complete, so Christ seeks for your Completion in everything that It beholds and loves so that everything might offer you the Love of God.

7.   Your Christ Mind is Quiet, because It knows that Love is in your awareness now, and that It is safely held by the same hand that holds a perception of Oneness in your Holy relationship. Christ holds all that you perceive in Itself. Christ gives you your Real Perception, where you were once blind to Christ, and Christ speaks to you of Heaven, so that you do not hear of conflict and death anymore. Christ reaches through all that you perceive so that everything may be blessed with Holiness. Christ rejoices that you share these Perceptions, so that you can share Christ's Joy. Christ offers you Its perfect lack of specialness, so that you may see Life instead of death, receiving from everything the Gift of Life that your forgiving offers to your True Self. The Sight of Christ is all that there is for you to see, the Sound of Christ is all that there is for you to hear, and the Hand of Christ is all that there is for you to hold. The only journey for you in your perception that you are in a world is for you to walk with your Christ Mind in your awareness.

8.   You who want to be content with specialness and seek for salvation in a war with Love, consider this: Your Christ Mind has come into your awareness to offer you your own Completion. What belongs to your Christ Mind is your own, because in your Completion is your Christ Mind's Completion. God wills to be One and can never leave you incomplete. Christ is in your perception of the other in your Holy relationship, as Perfect as yourself, and as like to God in Holiness as you must be.

9.   You must have doubt before you can be in conflict, and all of your doubt must be about yourself. Your Christ Mind has no doubts, and your Christ Mind's Quiet comes from Its Certainty. You will have Christ's Certainty to replace your doubts, if you agree that you are

One with Christ, and that this Oneness is Endless, Timeless, and within your grasp, because Christ's Hands are yours. Christ is within you, and yet Christ is beside you and before you, leading the way that your Christ Mind must go to find Completion. Your Christ Mind's Quietness is your Certainty. You have no doubt when Certainty has come.

6. Salvation from Fear

1.   The world is still before the Holiness that you perceive in your relationship, and Peace descends in Gentleness and blessing so complete that not one trace of conflict still remains to haunt you. Christ, Which is in your perception of the other in your Holy relationship, is your Savior from your illusions of fear. Christ heals your sense of sacrifice, and your fear that what you have will scatter with the wind and turn to dust. In your perception of Christ in place of the body of the other is your assurance that God is here with you now. While you look on Christ, you can be sure that you can know God. God can never leave Its Own Extension. The sign that this is so is in your perception of Christ in your Holy relationship, which is offered to you so that all your doubts about yourself may disappear in your perception of Holiness. See God's Extension in your relationship, because, in this, God awaits your acknowledgment that *you* are God's Extension.

2.   Without you, God would lack, Heaven would be incomplete, and God's extension of God would cease. There would be no Oneness and no Reality, because What God wills is Whole and is Part of God, because God's Will is One. All that *is* is alive in God. The Holiness that you see in your perception of the other shows you that God is One with you, despite your perception of a world of separation; that What God has is yours, because your mind is not split, nor are you separate from God.

3.   Nothing is ever lost to you. God lays Lovingly before you All that God extends as yours Forever. Every Thought in God's Mind is in your mind. It is God's Will that you share God's Love for you, and that you look on yourself as Lovingly as God looked on you before the world entered your mind, and as God looks on you still. God

does not change Its Mind about you with passing circumstances that have no meaning in Eternity, Where God abides, and Where you abide with God. It is this that saves you from a world that God did not create.

4.   Do not forget that healing your mind is all that the world that you perceive is for. That is the only purpose that the Holy Spirit sees in it, therefore that is the only one that it has. Until you accept your mind's total healing as all that you wish to be accomplished in time and perception, you will not know God or yourself. If you use the world that you perceive for another purpose, you will not escape its laws of violence and death. But it is given to you to be beyond the perceived world's laws in every respect, in every way, in every circumstance, in all temptation to perceive what is not there, and in all belief that What is One with God can suffer pain, because It sees Itself as something other than What It is.

5.   Look on Holiness in your relationship in the world that you perceive, and behold in it the whole reversal of the laws that seem to rule the world. See your Freedom from limitation as you extend Freedom to your relationship. Do not let your desire for specialness obscure the Truth in your relationship, because any law of death that you project onto the other will bind *you*. Any sin that you see in the other keeps *your* mind in hell. Yet, your Perfect Innocence will release your mind, because Holiness is impartial, judging everything in your mind the same. That judgment is made by the Holy Spirit, Which speaks for God in Everything that shares God's Being.

6.   Perceiving Truly, your mind can look on God's Innocence. It is God's Loveliness that it can perceive in everything. It is God that your mind can look for everywhere, and there is no sight, no place, and no time that it will not find God. The Holiness that you see in your relationship is the perfect frame for the salvation of your entire mind. Your Memory of God is set in this Holiness, in Which your entire mind lives. Do not let your mind live in denial because of the veil of specialness that hides your Christ Mind from you. No longer let your fear of God hold from you the Perception that you are meant to see. The other's body cannot show you Christ; Christ

is in the Holiness that you extend in your perception of the other.

7.   You choose what you want to perceive - either bodies or Holiness - and which you look upon is what you believe is true for you. You will choose in countless situations until you decide only for Truth. You do not regain Eternity by seeing one more denial of Christ in the body of another. Where is your salvation if even one body is the truth? Where is your Peace, but in the Holiness that you extend to replace the personal mind's projections? God is Forever in that Part of God that God has set Forever in the Holiness that you extend in your perception of the other, so that you can see the Truth about yourself in terms that you recognize and understand.

8.   The Holiness that you extend in your perception of the other is sacrament and benediction to you. The errors of separation that you perceive in the other cannot withhold God's blessing from your perception when you decide to perceive the other Truly. The mistakes that you project onto the other can cause you delay, but the means are given to you to correct these mistakes, and to end a journey that has never really begun, so needs no end. What never was is not part of you, but you will still think that it is until you realize it is not true for your mind where you perceive a world. In your perception of the other is the mirror of your mind, where you see the judgment that you have laid on yourself and on your mind where you perceive a world. Your Christ Mind beholds only Holiness; your specialness looks on the other's body and doesn't see anything real.

9.   See Truth in place of the personal mind's projections on the other so that you may be delivered soon. The other choice offers you only senseless wandering without purpose or accomplishment of any kind. You will be haunted by a sense of futility while your Christ Mind lies dormant in your perception of the other and until you lift your projections of the personal self's past from them, and, as you have been assigned, you extend Christ in your perception of them. The other is given to you to save yourself from condemnation by lifting condemnation from your perception of them. You looked on Part of God's Mind and saw flesh, and you thought it was real, and you bound Part of God's Mind to laws that can have no power over

It, but you shall see God's Glory in your Christ Mind everywhere.

10. Gladly realize that the laws of flesh are not for you by not seeing your perception of the other as bound by these laws. What governs any Part of God's Mind must hold for all the rest. You place yourself under the laws that you see ruling your perception of the other. Think, then, how great the Love of God for you must be that God has given Part of God to you to save you from pain and to give you happiness. Never doubt that your specialness will disappear before the Will of God, Which loves every Part of God with equal Love. Your Christ Mind can perceive Truth in the other. Do you want to decide against the Holiness that your Christ Mind perceives?

11. Your specialness is the function that you have given to yourself in your identification with a personal self. Your specialness stands for you alone: self-created, self-maintained, in need of nothing, and not joined with anything beyond the body. In the eyes of specialness, you are a separate universe with all of the power to hold itself complete within itself, with every entry shut against the intrusion of Truth, and with every window barred against the Light of Love. Always attacked and furious, with anger fully justified, you have pursued the goal of specialness with a vigilance that you never thought to yield and an effort that you never thought to cease. All this grim determination was because you wanted specialness to be the truth.

12. You are asked now to pursue another Goal with far less vigilance, little effort, little time, and with the Power of God maintaining It and promising success. Yet, of the two, this is the goal that you find more difficult. You understand the 'sacrifice' of your True Self to specialness, and you do not deem this cost too heavy. And a tiny willingness to nod to God, or to greet Christ you find a burden too wearisome, tedious, and heavy to be tolerated. But dedication to the Truth as God established It does not ask you for sacrifice or strain, and all the Power of Heaven and the Might of Truth provide the means and guarantee the Goal's accomplishment.

13. You believe that it is easier to perceive bodies than to perceive Holiness, but be sure that you understand what has made this judgment. Here you clearly hear the voice of your specialness

judging against your Christ Mind and telling you which purpose you can attain and which Purpose you cannot attain. Do not forget that this judgment applies to you only as an ally to specialness, because what you do through your Christ Mind your specialness does not know. To your Christ Mind, your specialness' judgment does not make sense at all, because only What God Wills is possible, and there is no alternative for your Christ Mind to see. Your Peace comes out of your Christ Mind's lack of conflict, and the means for effortless accomplishment and rest comes from your Christ Mind's Purpose.

7. The Meeting Place

1. In your attachment to the world that you perceive, you bitterly defend your specialness, which you want to be the truth. Your wish is your law, and you obey it. In your love for it, you do not withhold anything that your specialness demands, and you do not deny it anything that it needs. While your specialness calls to you, you do not hear the Holy Spirit. You judge that no effort is too great, no cost is too much, and no price is too high for you to save your specialness from the least slight, the tiniest attack, a whispered doubt, or a hint of threat. You reserve only the deepest reverence for your specialness. It is a part of you, as beloved of you as you are beloved of God. But it stands in place of your Extension of God, Which *is* part of you, so that you can be One with God. What is this thing that you have made to be your strength? What is this self, in a world that you made, on whom you lavish so much love? What is this parody of God's Creation that takes the place of your Extension of God? Where is your Extension of God now that your mind has made something else that it prefers?

2. Your Memory of God does not shine in the isolation of a personal mind. The Holiness that you perceive in the other in your Holy relationship contains all of God's Extension: What seems to have gone by, What you are aware of now, and What is yet to dawn on your awareness. The Holiness that you perceive in the other is Changeless, and you recognize *your* Changelessness by acknowledging It. Your Holiness belongs in your mind's perception, and,

571

by your seeing It in the other, It returns to your awareness. All of your love and care, your strong protection, your thoughts night and day, your deep concern, and your powerful conviction that this is you belong to the Holiness that you perceive in your relationship. What you have given to specialness is due to Holiness, and what is due to Holiness is due to you.

3.   You cannot know your Worth while specialness claims you instead. You cannot fail to know your Holiness when you see It in your perception of the other. Do not seek to make your specialness the truth, because if it were the truth you would indeed be lost. Be thankful that it is given to you to see your Holiness in your relationship instead *because* It is the Truth. What is True in your perception of your relationship must be True in you.

4.   In your identification with a personal self, can *you* protect your mind? The body you can protect, not from time, but temporarily. But what you think that you save you hurt, because what would you save the body *for*? In your answer lies the body's health and its harm. Save the body for show, as bait to catch another body, to house your specialness in better style, or to weave a frame of loveliness around your hate, and you condemn yourself to decay and death. If this is the purpose that you see in *any* body, you condemn yourself to it. But choose to see Holiness in place of bodies so that you may see the Truth, and you are saved from decay.

5.   God keeps safe What God extends. You cannot touch God's Extension with the false ideas that you made, because God's Extension was not made by you. Do not let your foolish fancies frighten you. You cannot attack the Immortal, and what is temporal has no real effects. Only the purpose that you see in anything gives it meaning for you, and if you see its purpose is Truth, then its safety is secure. But if you see its purpose is not Truth, then it is means for nothing. Whatever you perceive as means for Holiness shares in Holiness' Purpose and rests in safety. When it is gone, the Holiness remains, Immortal, a gift to your Extension of God as a sign that you have not forgotten It.

6.   The question to ask of everything in the world that you perceive is:

What is it for? Your answer makes it what it is for you. Nothing in the world that you perceive has any meaning in itself, but you give reality to it according to the purpose that *you* serve. So in your perception that you are in a world, *you* are a means as well. In Heaven, God is Means and End. This is the State of Extension, Which is found in Eternity, but not in time. It is not describable in the world, and there is no way for you to learn what this Condition means. You will not understand It until you go past learning to What is Given to you by God, and you make a Holy Home in your Mind for your Extension of God.

7. In Oneness with God, you must extend God, and your Extension of God must be like God: a Perfect Being, All-encompassing, Whole, needing nothing; no size, no place, no time, no limits, nor uncertainties of any kind. In God, Means and End are One, and this Oneness has no end at all. All of this is True. But It has no meaning when you still retain one thought that you haven't forgiven, a divided purpose, or one wish to be something else.

8. This course attempts to teach you only what you can easily learn. It does not exceed your own capacity, but What is yours will come to you when you are ready for It. In your perception of a world, means and end are made separate, so this course deals with them as though they are. It is essential for you to keep in mind that all of your perception is upside down until you understand its purpose. What you perceive seems to be reality, not a means, and this is what makes it hard for you to grasp the extent to which what you perceive depends on what you think that perception is for. What you perceive seems to teach you what is real, but it actually witnesses to what you teach yourself. It is an outward picture of a wish; an image that you want to be true.

9. Look at what you think that you are, and you will see a body. This body will look different in a different light, and if you turn the light off, it will seem to be gone. But you are reassured that it is there because you can feel it with its own hands and hear it move with its own ears. This is an image that you want to be you; the means to make your wish come true. It gives the eyes with which you look on it, the hands that feel it, and the ears with which you

listen to the sounds that it makes. The body proves its own reality to you.

10. So the body is made a theory of you, with no evidence for anything beyond itself and no escape from itself. Its course is sure when seen through its own eyes: it grows and withers, flourishes and dies. You cannot conceive of yourself apart from it. You brand it sinful, and you hate it, judging it evil. But your specialness whispers, 'Here is my beloved son, in whom I am well pleased.' So does the body become the means to serve specialness' purpose. Means and end here are not identical or even alike, because the body is physical material and specialness is an idea, yet you still offer the body to specialness for it to get what it wants. This is a travesty of God's Creation. Just as God's extension of God to you gives God Joy and witnesses to God's Love and Oneness, so does the body testify to the idea of specialness with which you made it and which speaks for its reality and truth.

11. So you seem to have two selves in your perception that you are in a world – one extended to you by God, another you made – and both appear to walk the world that you perceive without a meeting place. The one that you made you perceive as a body outside of your mind, in a world outside of your mind; the Part of God rests within your mind, and you can perceive It through extension from your mind. The difference between these two selves does not lie in how they look, where they go, or what they do. They have a different purpose, and it is this that joins them to what is like them and separates each from the other. The Part of God retains God's Will; the self of the world perceives it has a will alien to God and wishes it were so. This self's perception serves its wish by giving it the appearance of truth. But perception can serve another Goal. It is only bound to specialness by your choice. You can make a different choice and use perception for a different purpose. What you perceive will serve that purpose well, and prove Its Own Reality to you.

Chapter 25

The Justice of God

1. Christ is in *you*, but not in a body, so it must be that you are not in a body. What is within you cannot be outside of you, and it is certain that you cannot be apart from What is at the very center of your Life. What gives you Life cannot be housed in death, so neither can you. But instead of a body, you can perceive a Frame of Holiness for your extension of your Christ Mind. This Frame is for Christ to be made manifest to you where you once thought a body was real. Your perception of bodies will melt away from you, and you will be aware only of the Holiness of your mind.

2. You carry your Christ Mind with you, so you cannot fail to perceive Christ everywhere – *except* when bodies are real to you. As long as you believe that you are a body, you will think that you are where Christ cannot be. You carry Christ within you unknowingly, so you do not make Christ manifest, and you do not recognize that Christ is within you. A person is not the risen Christ, yet Christ does abide in your mind exactly where you perceive a person. Your Christ Mind perceives Holiness as plainly as your specialness perceives a body.

3. The body does not need healing, but, if your mind thinks that it is a body, it is sick indeed! It is in your mind that Christ sets forth the remedy. Christ's Purpose perceives bodies through Love and fills them with the Holiness that shines from your Christ Mind. Nothing that a body says or does can prevent Christ from manifesting in your awareness. A body will carry you to other bodies where you think that you do not know Christ, and you will extend your Christ Mind to them in Gentleness and Love to heal your mind. The mission that the other in your Holy relationship has is to be here for you to fulfill your mission of extending your Christ Mind in your perception of them.

1. The Link to Truth

1. It cannot be hard for you to do the task that your Christ Mind appoints you to do, since it is Christ that does it. In doing it, you will learn that the body only *seems* to be the means of doing it. Your mind is Christ's, so It must be yours. Christ's Holiness directs the body through your mind, which is One with Christ. The Holiness of your mind is made manifest to you in the Holiness that you extend to your perception of another. Here is the Holy Meeting Place of Christ and Christ. You will perceive no differences standing between these Aspects of your Christ Mind's Holiness, Which meet and join and raise your Christ Mind to God, Whole and Pure and Worthy of God's Everlasting Love.

2. How can you manifest the Christ in your mind except to look on Holiness and perceive Christ There? You use perception to manifest what you believe about yourself. Look on bodies and you will believe that you are a body. Every body will remind you of your sinfulness and your death. You will despise the bodies that you see, because they remind you of this, and you will seek their death instead. The message and the messenger are one. You must perceive others as you perceive yourself. Your sinfulness and condemnation are framed in your perception of another's body. But see a frame of Holiness instead of a body, and Christ will proclaim Itself as you.

3. What you perceive is a choice of what you want yourself to be, the reality that you want to live in, and the state in which you think that your mind will be content and satisfied. What you perceive is your decision about where you think that your safety lies. Your perceptions reveal yourself to you as you want you to be. They are always faithful to your purpose, from which they never separate, and for which they are always the only witnesses. What you perceive is a part of your purpose, because means and end are never separate. So you learn that what you perceive that seems apart from you is not separate from you at all.

4. *You* are the means for God, not separate from God, nor with a life apart from God. God's Life is manifest in you, who are One with God. Every aspect of your mind is an aspect of God and is framed

in Holiness, Perfect Purity, and Heavenly Love so Complete that It wishes only to release all that It looks upon. Your Mind's Radiance can shine through each body that you look upon, brushing them away by looking past them to God's Love. The veil of illusion in your mind is lifted through Love's Gentleness and nothing hides Christ when you want to look on It. Now, in your Holy relationship, you stand with Christ to let It draw aside the veil that seems to keep your mind separated.

5. Since you believe that you are separate, Heaven presents Itself as separate, too. It is not in Truth, but the Holy Spirit that has been given to you to link you with Truth must reach you through what you can understand. God and your Christ Mind and the Holy Spirit are One, as you and what your mind perceives are One in Truth. Your Christ Mind and God are never separate, and your Christ Mind abides within your understanding in the Part of you that shares God's Will. The Holy Spirit links the part of your mind that is home to your tiny, mad desire to be separate, different, and special to your Christ Mind to make Oneness clear to you, who are really One already. You cannot understand this from the perspective of the world that you made, but you can learn it.

6. The Holy Spirit serves your Christ Mind's Purpose, so that the error of your goal of specialness can be corrected in your mind, where it is. The Holy Spirit knows What you really will, because the Holy Spirit's Purpose is still One with God through your Christ Mind. You understand this in your Christ Mind, Which perceives Itself as One and experiences Itself as One. It is the Holy Spirit's function to teach you how to experience this Oneness, what you must do to experience It, and where you should go within yourself to experience It.

7. All of this takes note of time and space as if they were separate from your mind, because while you think that part of your mind is separate, the concept of Oneness is meaningless to you. It is obvious that your split mind cannot be a teacher of a Oneness Which unites all things within Itself. So the Holy Spirit within your split mind, Which *does* unite all things together, must be a Teacher

to your split mind. It must use a language that your split mind can understand in the condition in which your split mind thinks that it is. It must use all of your learning to transfer your illusions to the Truth, taking away all of your false ideas of what you are to lead you beyond them to the Truth that *is* beyond them. All of this can be simply reduced to:

What is the Same cannot contain differences.
And What is One cannot have separate parts.

2. The Savior from the Dark

1. Isn't it evident that what the body's eyes perceive fills you with fear? Maybe you still think there is some hope of satisfaction in the world that you perceive, or that you can attain some Peace in it. But it must be evident to you that the outcome of pursuing goals in the world never changes. Your hopes and dreams always result in despair. There is no exception to this and there never will be. The only value that the personal self's past can hold for you is that you learn that it gave you no rewards that you want to keep. Only then will you be willing to relinquish the world in your mind and have it gone forever.

2. It is strange that you should still cherish some hope of satisfaction in the world that you perceive. In no respect, at any time or place, has anything but guilt and fear been your reward. How long do you need to realize that the chance that this might change is hardly worth your delaying change that must result in a Better Outcome? One thing is sure: The world that you perceive gives no support to your hopes for the future and no suggestion that success is possible at all. To place your hope where there is no hope must make you hopeless. But this hopelessness is your choice while you seek for hope where none can ever be found.

3. It is also true that you have found some hope apart from all of this. Though inconstant, wavering, and dim, you *have* seen glimpses of Something not of the world that you have made that gives you justification for hopefulness. And yet your hope that the world that you perceive will yet satisfy you still prevents you from giving up

the hopeless and unrewarding task that you have set for yourself. It makes no sense for you to continue to pursue what has always failed you in the belief that it will suddenly succeed and bring you what it has never brought before.

4.   The personal self's past *has* failed you. Be glad that it is gone from your mind and can no longer darken What is there. And do not mistake form for content, because the world that you perceive is the form that is the means for the content of separation. The purpose of the world is to make separation real to you.

5.   When you see bodies, you see nothing, and you obscure your Christ Mind. Christ is All that there really is for you to perceive, and bodies cannot conceal Christ. Do you want to see bodies instead of Christ?

6.   The Holy Spirit is the Frame that God has set around the part of God's Mind that you perceive as separate from God. The Holy Spirit is One with you, who fills the Frame, and with God, Which encompasses the Frame. Joining you and God is the Holy Spirit's Purpose. You do not change this by choosing to see bodies instead, but you do block your *awareness* of this when you choose to cherish bodies. The body is the frame that the personal mind has put around separation. God's Frame will endure Forever, while the personal mind's frame will crumble to dust. But don't think that this will affect you. What is One with God is safe from all corruption, unchanged, and Perfect in Eternity.

7.   Accept God's Frame around all that you perceive, and you will see Christ within It. Look on Christ's Loveliness and understand the Mind that thought It. Your Christ Mind's Frame is the Holy Spirit, not flesh and bones. The Holy Spirit lights up your Christ Mind's Innocence to reflect It back to God, but the body seems to hide your Innocence in the darkness of illusions. Do not think that Christ was ever gone from your mind because you saw death there instead. God has kept your Holiness safe, so you can look on It.

8.   Instead of looking on the dark frame of the illusion of the other's body, extend Christ, your Savior *from* illusions, to your perception of them, and understand your mind as God's Mind shows it to you. Your Christ Mind will emerge from your illusions as you

choose to look on Christ and your illusions are gone. Your illusions have not touched your Christ Mind or you. Christ's Innocence is yours. Your Christ Mind's Gentleness will become your Strength, and you will gladly look within and see the Holiness that must be there because of the Christ that you perceive in place of the other's body. Your perception of the other will become the Frame in Which your Holiness is set, and What God extends to It will also extend to you. However much the other may seem to not see Christ and only see the dark frame of the body, it is still *your* only function to behold Christ. In this perception is your Real Perception, Which looks on Christ instead of death, and extends to be all that you perceive.

9. God is Glad when you appreciate your Christ Mind. God offers you thanks for loving What is One with God as God loves It. God makes known to you God's Love when you share God's Praise of What God loves. In Perfect Wholeness, God cherishes What is One with God, so God's Joy is made complete when you join in God's Praise to share God's Joy. See God's Perfect Oneness in place of the body of the other, and God's Thanks and Gladness will shine on you, who want to complete God's Joy and yours. You will not see illusions when you make God's Happiness complete, and yours along with God's. God's Gratitude is freely offered to you when you share God's Purpose. It is not God's Will to be incomplete, and it is not your Will, either.

10. Forgive the personal mind's perception of the other, and you will not separate your mind from What you perceive or from God. You don't need forgiveness, because the Wholly Pure has never sinned. But extend the Love that God extends to you, so that you may see that your Mind is One and thank God as God thanks you. Believe that all God's Praise is given to you. What you extend is God's, and by extending It, you learn to understand God's Gift to you. Give to the Holy Spirit the Love that the Holy Spirit gives to God and to you. Only God's Will and your Will, Which extends God's Will, have power over you. God extends God to you, so that you can extend God in Oneness with all that you perceive.

11. You and your mind where you perceive a world are the same, just

as God is One and not divided. You have One Purpose, Which God gave to your entire mind. God's Will is brought together as you join your Will with what your mind perceives, so that you are made Complete in your awareness by extending Completion to your perception of the other. Do not see sin in the other, even if that's what the other seems to see, but honor Christ instead and esteem your entire mind through your Real Perception. The power of salvation is given to your entire mind, so that you may escape from dark illusions and see that your One Mind has never been split or apart from God's Love.

3. Perception and Choice

1. You will perceive a world where attack is justified to the extent that you value guilt because you want separation from God to be real. To the extent that you recognize that guilt is meaningless because you *cannot* be separate from God, you will perceive that attack cannot be justified. This is in accord with perception's only law: You see what you want to believe is there. Everything that you perceive supports this law. Perception's law is an adaptation of God's Law that Love extends only Itself.

2. God's Law does not apply directly to the world that you perceive because perception has no meaning in God. But God's Law is still *reflected* everywhere in your mind. This does not make the world real at all, but *you* believe that the world is real, and you cannot be completely separate from God. God cannot enter your insanity, but God's Sanity is still with you, and you cannot be lost forever in your mad wish to be separate from God.

3. Perception rests on choice; God's Knowledge does not. Knowledge has One Law, because God is One. But you have the choice of two makers of your perception - the personal mind and the Holy Spirit - and they do not see your world in the same way. To each maker of your perception the world has a different purpose, and to each the world is perceived as the perfect means to serve its goal. For the personal mind, the world that you perceive is the perfect frame to set off your specialness, the perfect battleground to play out your conflict, and the perfect shelter for illusions that it wants to make

real to you. This is the world that the personal mind's perception upholds and justifies.

4. Simultaneously, the other Maker of your perception, the Holy Spirit, corrects your mad belief that you have established and maintained a world without a Link that still keeps it within the Law of God. In your perception of a world, God's Law is not used as God uses It to uphold Oneness, but It is adapted to a form to fit the need that you seem to have in your perception of separation from God. Corrected error undoes error, and this is how God protects your Christ Mind, even as you seem to live in error.

5. There is another purpose for the world that your error made, because your perception has another Maker Which reconciles the world that you perceive with God's Purpose. In the Holy Spirit's perception of the world, everything justifies your forgiving and your Perception of Perfect Innocence. You can meet everything that arises with instant and complete forgiving, and then nothing will remain to obscure the Innocence Which shines unchanged in your mind. Your Innocence is beyond the pitiful attempts of your specialness to put It out of your mind and to make the body real to you instead. It is not up to you to decide what is real. If you elect to see as real something that can never be real, then the Holy Spirit must correct your error so that you do not remain in illusions.

6. You have entered illusions, but not without Heaven's Help within you ready to lead you out and into Reality at any time. The time you choose can be any time, because your Help is here waiting on your choice. When you choose to avail yourself of the Holy Spirit's Help, then you will see every situation that you thought justified your anger turned into an event that justifies your Love. You will plainly hear that the calls to conflict that you used to hear are really your Calls to Peace. You will perceive that where you used to attack, you can, with equal ease, and far more happiness, bestow forgiveness. And you will reinterpret all temptation to forget that only God is Real as just another chance to remember and bring yourself Joy.

7. Misperception is not a sin. Let the personal mind's perceptions of

error be a chance for you to see with the Real Perception of the Holy Spirit. Which perception is justified? Which do you want? These two questions are the same to you, and when you see that they are the same, your choice is made. Seeing these questions as the same releases you from the belief that there are two ways to see. The world that you perceive presents you with many opportunities to extend your Peace and your own forgiveness. This is its purpose when you want Peace and forgiveness to descend on you.

8. The Holy Spirit, Maker of your Perception of Gentleness, has the Perfect Power to offset the world of violence and hate that seems to stand between you and Gentleness. The Holy Spirit's forgiving mind does not see the world, so *you* do not need to see it. 'Sin' is your idea that your separation from God is a fact, and that therefore you cannot change your perception. What is damned is damned forever and is unforgivable. But if you *do* forgive your perception of separation from God, then what you think of as 'sin' must have been a mistake and change is possible for you. The Holy Spirit, too, sees What It sees as far beyond the chance of change. But your perception of separation from God cannot encroach on the Holy Spirit's Perception, because your perception of separation from God is *corrected* by the Holy Spirit's Perception. So your separation from God must be an error and not real, because what you claimed was sin and could never be undone *is* undone. To punish your separation from God as a sin is to preserve it in your mind as reality. But to forgive your perception of a world of separation is to use it for Truth.

9. You are One with God and cannot sin, but you can wish for what hurts you, and you have the power to think that you can be hurt. This can only be a misperception of yourself. Is this a sin or a mistake? Is it forgivable or not? Do you need help or condemnation? Is it your purpose to save yourself or to damn yourself? Do not forget that the choice that you make for your mind where you perceive a world you make for yourself. You make this choice *now*, the instant when all time becomes a means to reach the goal that you choose. Make your choice, but recognize that in this choice you

choose for yourself the purpose of the world that you perceive, and it will be justified.

4. The Light You Bring

1   Your mind is One, and when you recognize that this is so you will not feel guilt, because there will be nothing to attack. You will rejoice and see your Safety in this Happy Fact. Your Joy will be in the Innocence that you see, and you will seek for Innocence, because it is your purpose to behold It and rejoice. You always seek for what will bring you Joy. It is not your aim of Joy that varies, but what you believe will bring you Joy makes inevitable your choice of the means to get It, unless you change your mind. Then you will change the means to fit your goal of Joy.

2.   Perception's basic law can be stated: 'You will rejoice at what you see, because you see it to rejoice.' While you think that suffering and separation from God will bring you Joy, then this is what you will see. What you wish determines what you believe is harmful or beneficial to you, because your wish makes it what it is in its effects on you. You choose the means to get the effect that you want, because you believe that what you want will bring you Joy. This law also holds in Heaven, because you extend God to bring you Joy, just as God extends God to you for God's Own Joy.

3.   You have made a world that is not real, but you can take rest and comfort in another Perception Where Peace abides. You can bring this Perception with you to all the weary sights of separation to undo them and to rest. From you can arise a Perception that you will rejoice to see, and in Which you will be glad. In you, there is a Perception that extends to all of separation, and covers it in Gentleness and Love. In this widening Perception of Love, the dark illusions that you thought were in your mind will be pushed away until they are far away, not long to be remembered by you. All your 'evil' thoughts and 'sinful' hopes, your illusions of guilt and merciless revenge, and every wish to hurt and kill and die will disappear before the Love that you extend.

4.   Do this for the Love of God and of yourself. Think what this will do for you: the 'evil' thoughts that haunt you now will seem increas-

ingly remote and far away from you. They will go further and further away because the Love in you will replace them. They will linger for a while in twisted forms too far away for you to recognize, and then they will be gone forever. In Love, you will stand in Quiet and in Innocence, wholly unafraid. The rest that you will find will extend from you, so that your Peace will never fall away or leave you homeless. When you offer Peace to all that you perceive, you will find a Home in Heaven that the personal mind's world cannot destroy, because Heaven is large enough to encompass all that your mind perceives in Its Peace.

5.   In you is All of Heaven. Every leaf that falls is given life in you, every bird that ever sang will sing again in you, and every flower that ever bloomed has saved its perfume and its loveliness for you.[1] You can have no goal before God's Will and your Will that Heaven be restored to you to whom God extends Heaven as your only Home. Nothing can come before Heaven or after It. There is no other place, no other state, no other time, nothing beyond, nothing closer – nothing else in any form. You can extend your Perception of Heaven everywhere to correct the mistaken thoughts that have entered your mind. In no better way can your own mistakes be corrected by Truth than by your willingness to bring the Love of Heaven with you as you walk through the world of illusions and beyond it to Truth.

5. The State of Sinlessness

1.   The State of Innocence is merely this: You have no desire to be separate from God, so there is no reason for you to attack your Mind and perceive It as other than It is. Guilt has no purpose and is meaningless without your goal of separation. Your desire for separation from God, attack, and your belief in sin are bound together in one illusion, each the cause and aim and justifier of the other. Each depends on the others for whatever sense it seems to have, and if you believe in one, you believe that the others are true, because each attests that the others are true.

2.   Your desire for separation from God is your 'attack' on God, and it seems to make your Christ Mind and God your 'enemies'. You *must*

585

be afraid with 'enemies' like this. And you are afraid of yourself, because you have hurt yourself by making your True Self your enemy. You must believe that you are not you, that you are an alien; 'something else' to be feared instead of loved. You would not attack yourself if you perceived your Total Innocence, and because you wish to attack, though you want Innocence, you must perceive yourself as guilty for this wish. So you project your own guilt onto the 'something else', your Christ Mind, so you can justify wanting It dead. Yet, each time that you look on your Holy relationship, your Christ Mind is there. Your Christ Mind is not gone because you deny It. There is nothing to see when you perceive the other through your denial of your True Perception.

3. It is not your Christ Mind that you see when you deny your True Perception. It is the 'enemy' that you have made of Christ and believe is real, and that you hate because there is really no 'sin' in Christ. Nor do you hear in the personal mind's perception of the other in your Holy relationship, in whatever form it takes, your own plaintive call to unite your mind in Innocence and Peace. Yet beneath the senseless shrieks of the personal mind is your own call, which God wants you to hear so that you will hear God's Call to you and answer by returning to God your mind, which belongs to God.

4. Your Christ Mind asks only this of you: that you extend Christ in your perception of the other in your Holy relationship, so that you may be aware of the Christ in you. In the isolation of the personal mind, you cannot be aware of your Christ Mind, so It is useless to you there. But extend Christ in your perception of the other and you will have the Strength to save your entire mind. Forgive the other your projections of the personal mind onto them, and in them you will perceive your Savior. But condemn them through the personal mind's projections, and they will seem to offer you death. In everyone you see the reflection of what you choose to have them be to you. If you decide against their proper function of being there for you to forgive the personal mind's projections, which is the only function that they have in truth, you deprive yourself of the awareness of Joy that you can have in their place. But don't think

that Heaven is lost to you. You can regain Heaven by extending Heaven to your relationship so that you may find It.

5.   It is not a sacrifice for you to see your salvation in your perception of the other, because in the Freedom that you extend to them you gain your own. To let the other's function be fulfilled is to fulfill your function. This is how you walk toward Heaven or toward hell through your perception that you are in a world. How beautiful Innocence will be to you when you perceive It in place of the personal mind's perceptions of separation! How great will be your Joy when you free your perception of the other from the personal mind's projections and you extend your Perception of Christ instead, as God wants it to be! Your relationship has no need but that you allow it to complete the function that God has for it. Remember this: that as you perceive the other you perceive yourself. And you define the function that your perception of the other will have for you: to make separation from God real to you, or to forgive your perception of separation from God.

6.   In the hatred that you may still cherish toward yourself, you believe God to be without the power to save you, who are One with God, from the pain of hell. But in the Love that you show yourself, God's Will is set free through you. In your perception of the other, you see the picture of your own belief in what the Will of God must be for you. In your forgiving the personal mind's projections, you will understand God's Love for you. Through your attack on the other you believe that God must hate you and that Heaven must be hell. Look on your perception of the other with the understanding that your perception of them is the way to Heaven or to hell for you. Don't forget that the role that you perceive in the other is given to you, and that you will walk the way that you project or that you extend to your perception of them, because it is your judgment on yourself.

6. The Special Function

1.   God's Grace rests gently on your forgiving mind, and everything that it perceives brings God to your awareness. From forgiveness, you do not see evil, anything in your perception to fear, or

anything that is different from you. As you love what you see, you look on yourself with Love and Gentleness. You do not condemn yourself for your mistakes, any more than you can damn another in your perception of a world. You are not an arbiter of vengeance, nor a punisher of sin. The Kindness of your Real Perception rests on yourself with the Tenderness that It extends to all that you perceive, because you only heal and bless. Being in accord with What God wills, in your forgiving you have the Power to heal and bless all that you look on with the Grace of God in your perception.

2.   You have become used to illusions, and the Clarity of Truth seems painful to you, because you are used to arbitrarily supplying your own meaning. You turn away from Truth, because Its stark Clarity makes you aware that your illusions are illusions. Illusions seem better to you, because their meaning is ambiguous and supplied by you. But this is not what your mind is for, and you cannot say that you prefer illusions and maintain that you want the Truth.

3.   Your wish to be aware of Truth calls on God's Grace and brings you the Gift of Love that makes your True Perception possible. Do you want to see your Christ Mind? God is Glad to have you look on Christ in place of the personal mind's projections on the other in your Holy relationship. God does not will that Christ be unrecognized by you, nor does God will that the other be without the function that God has given to them to be here for you to forgive the personal mind's projections. Do not let the other remain separate from you or without a function, or you leave part of your mind outside of you.

4.   This is the Holy Spirit's Kind Perception of specialness, the healing use that the Holy Spirit makes of what you made to harm: You have a special function, which is forgiving, that you alone can fulfill. The Holy Spirit's plan is not complete until you find your special function and fulfill it, bringing your Completion to your awareness in your perception that you are in a world where incompletion rules.

5.   In the world that you perceive, where God's Law of Oneness does not prevail in perfect form, you can do *one* perfect thing and make *one* perfect choice. By this special act of extending Christ to your perception of another who seemed separate from you, you increase

your awareness of your Christ Mind, and you learn that your mind must be One. Forgiving your illusion of separation is the only meaningful function for you in time. It is the means that the Holy Spirit uses to translate your specialness from 'sin' into salvation. Your forgiving is for everything that you perceive in your mind as a world. When your forgiving of separation rests on all that you perceive it is complete, and the only real function that the world has for you is completed with it. Then time is gone for you. But while you perceive yourself in time, there is much forgiving for you to do, and you must do what is allotted to you to do, because the whole plan depends on your part. You *have* a special part in time, because you chose to have one. Your wish is not denied, but changed in form to serve your Whole Mind, and become a means to save you instead of for you to lose.

6. Salvation is nothing more for you than a reminder that the world that you perceive is not your home. Its laws are not imposed on you, and its values are not yours. You will see this and understand it as you take your place in undoing the world that you made. As always, you have the means for making separation or for undoing it. From the very instant that you made specialness to hurt yourself, God appointed it to be the means for your salvation. Your special 'sin' became your opportunity for your special Grace; your special hate became your means for extending God's Love.

7. The Holy Spirit needs your special function so that Its Function can be fulfilled. Do not think that you lack a special value in your perception that you are in a world. You wanted it, and it is given to you. All that you have made can serve your salvation easily and well. You cannot make a choice that the Holy Spirit cannot use on behalf of the Truth in you. Only in illusions does your specialness appear to be an attack on the Truth in you. In the Light of Truth, you can see your special function in the plan to save your Mind from all attack, and you can understand that you are safe, as you have always been, in time and in Eternity. Forgiving is the function given to you to extend to all that you perceive. Extend it gently to be all that you perceive, and let salvation be perfectly fulfilled in your mind. Do this *one* thing that Everything be given to you.

7. The Rock of Salvation

1. Since the Holy Spirit can translate everything that you made to make separation real to you into a blessing, then what you made cannot be sin. Sin is the idea that your perception of separation from God cannot be changed, and that the world is real. The 'magic' of the world that you perceive can seem to hide the pain of sin and deceive you with glitter and with guile, but you know that the cost of separation from God is death. Your belief that separation from God is real is your request for death, a wish to make a world as sure as Love, as dependable as Heaven, and as strong as God. The world that you perceive is safe from Love when you think that separation from God is sin and unchangeable. But it is not possible that what cannot be One with God, and that opposes God in every way, is like God.

2. It cannot be that your 'sinner's' wish for death is just as strong as God's Will for Life. Nor can a world that God did not make be as Firm and Sure as Heaven. Heaven and hell cannot be the same. It must be possible that what God did not will can be changed. Only God's Will is Unchanging, and only God's Will can share attributes with God's Will. No wish can rise against God's Will and be unchanging. When you realize that only God's Will is Unchanging, this course will not be difficult for you. You do not believe this yet, but there is nothing else that you could believe if you looked at God's Will as It really is.

3. Look more carefully at what was said earlier in this course: Either God is insane or the world that you perceive is insane. No Thought of God makes any sense in the world that you perceive, and nothing that the world believes is true has any meaning in God's Mind at all. What makes no sense and has no meaning is insanity, and insanity cannot be Truth. If one belief that the world that you perceive values is true, then every Thought of God is an illusion. But, if One Thought of God is True, then all beliefs in the world that you perceive are illusion. The choice of which is insane, and is therefore unreal to you, is the choice that you make for yourself. Do not attempt to see this differently or to twist it into something else. This is the only choice that you can make; the rest is up to God.

4. For you to justify one value that the world that you perceive upholds is for you to deny God's Sanity and yours. God's Mind and your Christ Mind do not think differently. This is what makes your Christ Mind capable of extending God's Mind, Which extends Itself to your Christ Mind. But if you choose to believe one thought that is opposed to Truth, then you are deciding that you are not Christ, and that your Christ Mind and God must be insane. Do not think that this belief depends on the form that it takes. When you think that the world is sane in any way, is justified in any of its beliefs, or is maintained by any form of reason, then you believe that God is insane. But sin is not real *because* God and your Christ Mind are not insane. And the world that you perceive is meaningless *because* it rests on the idea that your perception of separation from God is real, and therefore a sin. Only the Changeless can rest on Truth.

5. The Holy Spirit has the Power to change the whole foundation of what you perceive to one that is not insane. Your True Perception has nothing in It to contradict Sanity and Joy. Nothing in It attests to death or cruelty or separation or differences. In your True Perception, you perceive everything as One, and there is no loss for you to perceive, only increase in your Peace.

6. Test everything that you see by whether you perceive loss or increase in your Peace, and understand that only the Perception that meets the one demand that it increase your Peace is worthy of your faith. What is not Love is your belief that separation from God is real, is sin, and Love and sin perceive each other as insane and meaningless. If you are a 'sinner' then you believe that your perception of Love is wholly mad, because sin is the way to sanity. But sin is equally insane to Love, and Love looks gently beyond insanity to rest Peacefully on Truth. Both Love and sin see their perception as unchangeable as each one's perception defines for them the changeless and eternal truth of what you are. To make their viewpoint meaningful and sane, each reflects the view of what God and you must be.

7. Your special function of forgiving takes a special form in which the fact that God is not insane appears most sensible and meaningful to you. The content is unchanged by the form, which is suited to

your special needs, to the special time and place in which you think you are, and can free you of time and place and all that you believe must limit you. Your Christ Mind is not bound by time or place or anything that God did not will. But if you see God's Will as insanity, then the form of Sanity Which makes It most acceptable to you requires special choice. This choice cannot be made by you in your insanity, because then your choice is not free and made with your True Reasoning Mind.

8. It would be insane for God to entrust your salvation to you in your insanity. *Because* God is not insane, God has appointed the Holy Spirit to raise True Perception in you, who chose insanity as salvation. The Holy Spirit chooses the form of True Perception most suitable to you, one which will not attack the world that you made, but enter into your mind in Quietness to show you that you are not insane. The Holy Spirit points to another way of looking at the world, where you think that you live and that you think that you recognize and understand.

9. Now you will question what you thought you recognized and understood before, because this new Perception is one which you cannot deny, or overlook, or fail completely to accept. Your special function of forgiving is designed to be perceived as possible by you, and more and more desired by you as it proves to you to be what you really want. From this position, your 'sinfulness' and every form of separation from God that you perceive, offers you less and less until you understand that it has cost you your Sanity. No part of your perception will be left in insanity, because your special part in the plan releases your entire mind. You can no more leave out any perception in your mind from your special function, than God can overlook your Christ Mind in careless thoughtlessness.

10. Only God's Love is Dependable, and your Sanity abides only in God. The Holy Spirit can show you this in the new Perception chosen especially for you. It is God's Will that you remember this and emerge from deepest mourning to Perfect Joy. Accept the function that has been assigned to you in God's Own plan to show you that hell and Heaven are different. In Heaven, you and God are the Same, without the differences that would make Heaven into

hell, and which seem in an impossible insanity to make a hell of Heaven.

11. Your whole belief that loss is possible reflects the underlying tenet of the personal mind: God is insane. In the world that you perceive, it does seem that one must gain *because* another losses. But if this were Truth, then God would indeed be insane! This belief is a form of the personal mind's basic tenet that separation from God is real and sin rules the world. In the world that you perceive, you believe that for every little gain that you make, someone else must lose and pay the exact amount in blood and suffering, because otherwise evil will triumph, and your destruction will be the total cost of any gain. You who believe that God is insane, look at this carefully, and understand that either God or this is insane, but not both.

12. Your salvation is the rebirth of the idea in your mind that there is no loss of any kind in Truth, because Mind is One. For you to gain, you must perceive the Truth that you want to gain everywhere. This is how your Sanity is restored. Your faith in God's Eternal Sanity rests in Perfect Confidence and Perfect Peace on the Truth of One Mind. Your True Reasoning Mind is satisfied, because all of your insane beliefs are corrected in One Mind, and sin is impossible because One Mind is Truth. One Mind is the Truth on which your salvation rests, and the Vantage Point from Which the Holy Spirit gives meaning and direction to the plan in which your special function has a part. Here, your special function is made whole, because it shares the function of Wholeness.

13. Remember that all temptation to believe that your separation from God is real is this: your mad belief that God needs to be insane for you to be sane and have what you want; that either God or you must lose to insanity, because your aims cannot be reconciled. Death demands Life, but Life is not maintained at any cost. Suffering of any kind is against the Will of God, and salvation is God's Will, because it is yours. Salvation is not for you in your identification with a personal self, but for the Self that is in you and that is in all that you perceive. Your True Self cannot lose, because, if It could, the loss would be God's, and no loss is possible in God. This is Sane, because It is the Truth.

8. Justice Returned to Love

1. The Holy Spirit can use for your salvation all that you give to the Holy Spirit. But the Holy Spirit cannot use what you hold back, because the Holy Spirit can only take what you give *willingly*. Otherwise you will believe that the Holy Spirit is wresting things from you against your will, and you will not learn that it *is* your True Will to be without them. You do not need to give everything to the Holy Spirit *wholly* willingly, because, if you could do this, you would not need the Holy Spirit. But the Holy Spirit needs you to prefer that the Holy Spirit take it than that you keep it for the personal mind to use, and that you recognize that you do not want what results in you perceiving separation anywhere. This much and nothing more is necessary to reinforce in you the idea that your perceiving separation anywhere will never result in gain for you.

2. This is the only principle that you need for salvation. It is not necessary that your faith in it be strong, unswerving, and without attack from all beliefs opposed to it, because if this was the case, you wouldn't need salvation. You are not expected to have a fixed allegiance yet. While you are still divided against yourself, you are not asked to do what you still find impossible. Wisdom cannot be found in such a state of mind. Be thankful that only a little faith is asked of you, because only a little faith is left to you who believe that your separation from God is real, and who do not yet remember Heaven and the Justice of Oneness of the saved.

3. There is a Justice in salvation about which the world that you perceive knows nothing. In the world, justice and vengeance are the same, because when you perceive yourself as a 'sinner' you equate justice with punishment, maybe to be endured by someone else, but never escaped. The personal mind's 'laws' of sin demand a victim, and it makes little difference to the personal mind who it is. Death is the cost of sin, and it must be paid. But this is not justice; this is insanity. But of course you define justice insanely where Love means hate, and you see death as triumph over Eternity and Life.

4. You who do not yet know of the Justice of Oneness can still ask about It and learn the Answer. The Justice of Oneness sees the

Wholeness of your True Mind everywhere, instead of some separation and some Wholeness. Your perception of separation, in whatever form it takes, is a form of vengeance on yourself. The Justice of Oneness, unlike justice in the world that you perceive, does not demand sacrifice of any kind, because sacrifice preserves the idea that separation from God is real. Sacrifice from you is a payment that the personal mind demands that you make for the cost of making separation from God real to you, but it is not the total payment. The rest of the payment is taken from another who seems separate from your mind in the world that you perceive to make up for the part of the payment that you want to hold back and not give up. So you see yourself as partly a victim, with someone else more of a victim. In the total cost, yours is less, because the other's is greater. The world's justice, being blind, is satisfied being paid; it doesn't matter by whom.

5. This cannot be the Justice of Oneness, because God does not know of separation or sacrifice. But God knows the Justice of Oneness well. God is Wholly Fair to all that you perceive and vengeance is alien to God's Mind, because God knows the Justice of Oneness. To be Truly Just is to be Fair, not vengeful. Vengeance can never be Fair, because vengeance and Fairness contradict each other and each denies that the other is real. It is impossible for you to extend the Holy Spirit's Justice of Oneness with a mind that can conceive of specialness. But the Holy Spirit would not be Just if It condemned you for crimes that you think you did but that you did not really do. And it would not be Justice for the Holy Spirit to demand that you lay aside your obsession with punishment without helping you to perceive that punishment is never called for.

6. While you still believe that your separation from God is real, it is extremely hard for you to understand the Holy Spirit's Justice of Oneness. You believe that the Holy Spirit shares your own confusion about what justice is, so you cannot avoid the vengeance that your own belief in justice entails. You fear the Holy Spirit because of the 'wrath' of God that you believe is in the Holy Spirit. You can't trust that the Holy Spirit will not strike you dead. You *do* believe that Heaven is hell, and you *are* afraid of Love. Deep

suspicion and the chill of fear come over you when you are told that you have never sinned. Your world depends on separation from God being real, and you perceive God's Justice of Oneness as a 'threat' that is more destructive to you and your world than vengeance, which you understand and love.

7.   The loss of sin is a curse to you when you believe that separation from God is real. You flee from the Holy Spirit, Which you see as a messenger from hell disguised as a Deliverer and Friend, but sent from Heaven in treachery and guile to work vengeance on you. The Holy Spirit seems like a devil in angel's cloak to you. The Holy Spirit's Escape for you is a door to hell that only looks like Heaven's Gate.

8.   But the Justice of Oneness cannot punish you who ask for punishment, but whom the Holy Spirit as True Judge knows is Wholly Innocent in Truth. In the Justice of Oneness, the Holy Spirit is bound to set you free and to give you all the honor that you deserve but have denied in yourself, because, in your identification with a personal self, you are not fair, and you do not understand that you are Innocent. In your perception of yourself as a 'sinner' you do not understand Love, because you think that justice is split off from Love and stands for something else. You perceive Love as weak and vengeance as strong, because you see Love as lost without justice and too weak to save you from punishment. From this perspective, vengeance is strong for being separate from Love, so only vengeance can help and save you, while Love stands helplessly by, without justice and vitality, and powerless to save you.

9.   What can Love ask of you who think that all of this is true? In Love and Justice, the Holy Spirit cannot believe that in your confusion you have much to give. You are not asked to trust the Holy Spirit far. The Holy Spirit offers only what you are willing to see, and what you recognize that you cannot give to yourself. In God's Own Justice, the Holy Spirit recognizes All that you deserve, but the Holy Spirit understands that you cannot accept it All for yourself yet. It is the Holy Spirit's function to hold out to you the Gifts that the Innocent deserve. And every Gift that you accept brings Joy to the Holy Spirit as well as to you. The Holy Spirit knows that Heaven is made richer by every Gift that you accept, and that God

rejoices that you receive What Loving Justice knows is your due. Love and the Justice of Oneness are not different. God is Merciful because They are the same, and God gives you the Power to forgive yourself your perception of separation from God.

10. Nothing can be kept from you, who merit Everything True. If it could, *that* would be injustice and unfair indeed to the Holiness in you, even though you do not recognize It. God does not know the injustice of separation and will not allow your Christ Mind to be judged by the personal mind, which seeks Christ's death and does not see Christ's Worth at all. What honest witnesses can the personal mind call on to speak for Christ that would plead for Christ and not against It? No justice can be given the Christ in you by the personal mind. But God ensures that the Justice of Oneness will be done to you, whom God loves, and God will protect you from all the unfairness that you seek in your belief that vengeance is your proper due.

11. Just as specialness does not care where you perceive that the cost of sin is paid as long as it is paid somewhere in the world that you perceive, the Holy Spirit does not care where you see Innocence, as long as you see It and recognize It. Your witnessing to Innocence in your perception of one other is enough; the Justice of Oneness does not ask for more. As you look on your perceptions of others in the world that you perceive, the Holy Spirit will ask you if each will be the one that you replace with an extension of Innocence, so that the Justice of Oneness will be returned to Love and be satisfied. The special function that the Holy Spirit allots to you is that you learn that Love and the Justice of Oneness are not separate, and Both are strengthened by the Other. Without Love, justice is weak and prejudiced toward separation, and Love without the Justice of Oneness is impossible. Love is Fair and cannot chasten without cause, and what cause can warrant an attack anywhere in the Innocence of your Perception? In the Justice of Oneness, not in vengeance, Love corrects your mistaken perception of separation from God. Vengeance *would be* unjust to your Innocence.

12. You can be a perfect witness to the Power of Love and the Justice of Oneness if you understand that it is impossible that anything

that you perceive merits vengeance. You do not need to perceive that this is true in every circumstance, nor do you need to look to your experiences within the world that you perceive, which are only shadows of all that is really happening within your mind. The understanding that you need comes from your True Self, Which is so Great and Holy that It does not doubt Its Innocence. Your special function is to call to your True Self, so that It may smile on you, who share Its Innocence. Your True Self's understanding will be yours, and the Holy Spirit's function will be fulfilled. You have found in your True Self a Witness to your Innocence instead of to sin. You need give little to the Holy Spirit so that the Justice of Oneness can be given to you.

13. The Justice of Oneness is Impartial, and It extends Oneness to all that you perceive. Your specialness cannot be just. You cannot judge the world that you perceive with a personal mind, not because in your identification with a personal self you are a miserable sinner, but because a personal mind doesn't know the Truth. In specialness, you cannot know that the Justice of Oneness sees your entire mind as One. For you to judge others is for you to make the personal mind and separation real to you, which is an injustice to your entire mind, since the Holy Spirit sees your entire mind as One. God extends Oneness to your entire mind. For you to see yourself as having more or less than anyone in the world that you perceive is for you to identify with a limited personal self and to not know that you have Everything. You will think that you are deprived and not know that your entire mind deserves Love. In its sense of deprivation, the personal mind is envious of others, and it tries to bolster itself by judging others. The personal mind is not impartial, and in your identification with it, you cannot fairly perceive Love, because you have made your Right to Love obscure to you.

14. You have a Right to Oneness, to Perfect Peace, to complete deliverance from all of the effects of your belief that your perception of separation from God is sin, and to the Eternal, Joyous, and Complete Life that God extends to you. This is the Justice of Heaven and all that the Holy Spirit brings to your perception. Your special function of forgiving shows you only that Perfect Justice can

prevail for you. You are safe from vengeance in all its forms. You may seem to deceive yourself with a world, but you cannot replace God's Justice of Oneness with a version of your own. Only Love is Just and can perceive the Love that the Justice of Oneness extends to you. Let Love decide what is Just for you, and never fear that in your unfairness to yourself through your identification with a personal self, you will deprive yourself of the Love that God's Justice of Oneness has allotted to you.

9. The Justice of Heaven

1. It can only be the arrogance of the personal mind to think that your little errors of separation cannot be undone by Heaven's Justice of Oneness. If this were true, it would mean that your errors are sins, not mistakes, and forever uncorrectable and due vengeance, not Justice. Are you willing to be released from all of the effects of your belief that separation from God is real? You cannot answer this until you see all that your answer must entail. If you answer 'yes' it means that you will give up all of the values of the world that you perceive in favor of the Peace of Heaven. You will not be able to retain even one form of separation from God, or to keep one doubt that this is possible, to hold your belief in sin in place. Truth will have greater value to you than illusions. And you will recognize that Truth must be revealed to you, because you do not know What It is.

2. What you extend you receive, so when you reluctantly extend Love you do not gain from it, because you are reluctant to receive Love. Your Gifts of Love are saved for you until your reluctance to receive them disappears, and you are willing to accept them. God's Justice of Oneness warrants your gratitude, not your fear. Nothing that you truly extend is lost to you, but It is cherished and preserved in Heaven Where your Treasure of Love is preserved for you and offered to you whenever you are willing to receive It. Your Treasure is not lessened as you extend Gifts from It, but each Gift that you extend adds to your awareness that you have It. God is Fair and does not fight against your reluctance to perceive your salvation as a Gift from God. But God's Justice of Oneness will only

be satisfied when It has been extended to be all that you perceive.

3. Be certain that any answer that the Holy Spirit gives to you for any problem will always be one in which you do not perceive separation of any kind. This must be true, because the Holy Spirit does not ask for sacrifice. Since all of your problems are perceptions of separation, an answer that demands any perception of separation anywhere has not resolved your problem but has added to it, made it greater, harder to solve, and made it more unfair to you. It is impossible for the Holy Spirit to see separation as a solution. To the Holy Spirit, what is unfair to you must be corrected *because* it is unfair. And your every error is a perception of unfairness where you do not offer the Justice of Oneness to be all that you perceive. When you perceive separation anywhere, you see your condemnation as real, and punishment, not the Justice of Oneness, becomes what you think is your due.

4. Your Perception of Innocence makes your punishment impossible and the Justice of Oneness sure. The Holy Spirit's Perception leaves no ground for attack. Only separation justifies attack, and the Holy Spirit cannot see separation. In your perception that you are in a world you solve problems by deciding who shall win and who shall lose; how much one should take and how much the other must still defend. Your problem of separation remains unresolved, because only the Justice of Oneness can see a State Where there is no loser, no unfairness, and no deprivation to justify vengeance. Vengeance cannot solve problems, because at best it adds another problem of separation to the first one in which your intended murder of God was not so obvious.

5. The Holy Spirit's problem solving is the way in which any of your problems of separation end. All is solved by meeting with the Justice of Oneness. Until it does, your problem of separation will recur, because it has not been solved. The principle that the Justice of Oneness means you can have no perception of separation is crucial to this course, because your experience of miracles depends on the Justice of Oneness. True Justice is not as justice is in the world of separation that you perceive but as God knows Oneness, and this Knowledge is reflected in the Real Perception that the Holy

Spirit extends to you.

6.   No part of your mind deserves separation, and any perception of separation that you have is unjust to your mind's Wholeness, and this cannot occur. Healing is for your entire mind, because your mind does not merit attack of any kind. One miracle is not harder than another, because it is not the Justice of Innocence that only some parts of your mind where you perceive a world deserve Love. A miracle *is* the Justice of Oneness, not a special gift to be extended to some of your perceptions and withheld from others because the personal mind's judgment is that they are less 'worthy' of healing. The purpose of salvation is the end of specialness, so how can some of your mind be separate from salvation? Salvation is not the Justice of Oneness if some of your errors are unforgivable and warrant vengeance in place of healing and the return of Peace.

7.   Your salvation is not salvation if it helps you to be more unfair to yourself than you have sought to be. If the Holy Spirit's Gift of miracles was extended only to your perception of a select group of special others in the world that you perceive, and was kept apart from your perception of others that the personal mind judges 'less deserving', then the Holy Spirit would be making separation and specialness real to you. But the separation that the Holy Spirit cannot perceive the Holy Spirit cannot witness to. Every perception that your mind has is equally entitled to the Holy Spirit's Gift of healing, deliverance, and Peace. All of your problems are problems of perceiving yourself separate from your perceptions and from God. When you give any problem to the Holy Spirit to be resolved, it means that you *want* your perception of separation to be resolved. For you to keep a problem to the personal mind is for you to decide that you want your perception of separation to remain unsettled and unresolved, and that you want its injustice and attack on you to last. But you cannot perceive the injustice of separation unless you first decide to be unjust to *yourself* by identifying with a personal self. Then, problems will arise to block your way, and your Peace will be scattered by the winds of Self-hate.

8.   Until you realize that the whole of your mind where you perceive

a world has a right to miracles, you will not claim your right to experience miracles, because you will have been unjust to yourself. What you deny in your perception you deny to yourself. You will not receive the experience of the miracle when you deny it to any part of your mind. Only your forgiving your perception of separation offers you the experience of miracles and, in the Justice of Oneness, your pardon of separation must be extended to be all that you perceive.

9.   The little problems that you keep to the personal mind and do not let the Holy Spirit remove from you are your secret beliefs that separation from God is real. They grow and cover everything that you perceive, leaving you unfair to yourself, because you do not believe that you have a Right to Peace and Love. In your bitterness for your perceived lack, your vengeance seems to be justified, mercy seems to be lost to you, and you feel condemned as unworthy of forgiveness. Believing that you are not forgiven, you are unable to extend forgiveness to be all that you perceive. That is why your sole responsibility is to accept for yourself forgiveness of your perception that you are separate from God.

10.   The miracle that you receive you extend. Each miracle that you experience is an illustration of the Law on Which salvation rests: The Justice of Oneness must be extended to be all that you perceive for your mind to be wholly healed. No part of your mind can be excluded, and your entire mind must benefit. Each miracle that you experience is an example of what the Justice of Oneness can accomplish when It is extended to be your perception without exception. You receive and extend the miracle equally in the awareness that what you extend you receive. Because in the miracle you do not make What is the Same unlike Itself, you do not see differences where none exists. A miracle is the same everywhere in your Perception, because you see no separation. Your experience of the miracle offers you Oneness, and it teaches you one message:

God's Love belongs to your entire mind, which *does* deserve God's Love.

Chapter 26

The Transition

1. The 'Sacrifice' of Oneness

1. You are One with God and with the part of your mind that you have projected outward and see as a world, and your perception of separation from them is an attack on yourself. In the 'dynamics' of attack, *sacrifice* is a key idea. It is the pivot on which all of your compromises that try to make some illusions into Reality, all of your desperate attempts to strike a bargain to make some separation into Oneness, and all of your conflicts achieve some balance. Sacrifice is the symbol of your split mind's central theme that *something must lose* for it to be maintained. In your perception that you are in a world, it is apparent that you focus your separation on a body, which is always your attempt to limit loss. The body is itself your sacrifice; your giving up of True Power to keep a little power for yourself in the isolation of a personal self. And your perception of other bodies is the expression of your wish to make separation real and to sacrifice Oneness. Look at the world that you made and you see nothing attached to anything beyond itself. All seemingly separate entities can move nearer or further from other entities, but they cannot be One.

2. The world that you perceive is based on your 'sacrifice' of the Oneness of your Mind. It is a picture of separation and disunity. Each individual person and thing in the world seems to be a solid, defined form where what is inside cannot reach out, and what is outside cannot join with what is within. Each individual person and thing must 'sacrifice' everything else outside of itself to keep itself complete, because if it joined with something else, each would lose its own 'identity'. In the world that you perceive, identities are maintained by separation.

3. The little part of your mind that the body fences off is your 'self', and it is preserved through your giving up all of the rest of your

mind that you perceive as a world outside of you. And the rest of your mind must lose the little part of it that you have given to a body and remain incomplete to retain your perception of *its* identity. In this perception, you think that losing the body would be a total sacrifice, because the body is meant to limit your sacrifice by holding back some of your mind for a personal self. For this little to belong to you, you must place limits on your perception of every-thing outside of the body, just as you limited yourself to a body. This is because you cannot escape the Law of Mind that what you project or extend is always your perception of yourself. For you to accept the limits of the body for yourself is for you to impose limits on everything that you see, since you must see everything as you see yourself.

4. The body *is* a loss, and it *can* be made to sacrifice. While you see any body as real, you are demanding sacrifice of your entire mind. There is no greater sacrifice that you can demand than that What is One with God be without God, and that God be without Part of Itself. Your every sacrifice demands that God and Part of God be without the other. You deny God and you ask for sacrifice when you see any body as real. No matter how much your Christ Mind Witnesses to the Truth of God's Oneness, there is no Witness to the Wholeness of your Christ Mind in your world of separate bodies. Your Christ Mind is invisible in the world that you perceive, and you cannot perceive the Oneness and Love of Christ there at all. But it is given to your Christ Mind to make the world recede before It, so that the Perception of your Christ Mind can replace what the body's eyes see.

5. In your choice to perceive the Witnesses to Truth instead of the witnesses to illusions, you ask to see a purpose in the world of separation that makes it meaningful for you. The world has no meaning for you outside of your special function of forgiving. With your function, your perception becomes a Treasure House as rich and Limitless as Heaven. Every instant you can choose to see Holiness in your perception of another in the world to add a Limitless supply of Happiness to every meager scrap of Happiness that you allot yourself.

6. You can lose sight of Oneness, but you cannot make a sacrifice of Its Reality. You cannot lose Oneness, nor can you keep the Holy Spirit from showing you that you have not lost It. Let the world recede and take rest by seeing a Witness to Peace in your Holy relationship. If you judge the other as the personal mind does, you will not free yourself or see the Witness to Christ and rejoice. Do not sacrifice your Perception of Holiness to your belief that separation from God is real and a sin. You sacrifice your Innocence by refusing to see It in place of the personal mind's perceptions, and you die each time that you make separation from God real to you by seeing sin.

7. Every instant, you can be reborn to an awareness of Life again. Your awareness of the Holiness of your relationship with the other brings Life to your awareness, and with it you will realize that you cannot die, because you see the Innocence that is known to God. You can no more sacrifice your Innocence than the Love in you can be blotted out because others in the world that you perceive cannot see it. You want to sacrifice Life and make eyes and ears to witness to the death of God and your Christ Mind, but do not think that you have the power to make of God and your Christ Mind what God has not willed. In Heaven, you are not imprisoned in a body or sacrificed in a separate identity to sin. And as you are in Heaven, you are Eternally and Everywhere; you are the same Forever. You are born again each Holy Instant, untouched by time, and far beyond the reach of any sacrifice. You have not made Life, nor have you made death real, and only Life has been given to you by God, Which knows Its Gifts can never suffer sacrifice or loss.

8. God's Justice of Oneness rests in Gentleness upon your Christ Mind and keeps It Safe from all of the injustice of separation that the world that you perceive wants to lay upon you. It cannot be that you can make separation from God reality and sacrifice God's Will for you. Do not condemn yourself by seeing a world of bodies as real. In your special function of forgiving, you extend Christ to replace the personal mind's projections, so that your Christ Mind can give you the Gift of Freedom by receiving It from you. The Holy Spirit's function is to release your Christ Mind

from the prison you've made to keep yourself apart from the Justice of Oneness. Your function is not separate from the Holy Spirit's.

2. Many Forms; One Correction

1. It is difficult to understand why you do not ask the Holy Spirit to solve all problems for you. The Holy Spirit does not have greater difficulty solving some problems over others, because all of your problems are a form of your perceiving separation from God as real, and each problem is solved by correcting your perception that separation is real. That your perception of separation from God is what needs to be solved does not change, no matter what form is takes. Separation will appear to you in many forms while the problem of your perception of separation lasts. It serves no purpose for you to try to solve it in a special form. Your perception of separation will recur again and again until it has been corrected for all time; then it will not occur again in any form. Only then will you be released from it.

2. The Holy Spirit offers you release from every problem that you think that you have. They are all the same to the Holy Spirit, because, no matter what form they take, they are projections of suffering and sacrifice from your mind onto the world that you perceive. The personal mind seems to gain by these problems, because they reinforce the separation in your mind. But when the Holy Spirit works out the situation by showing you that separation from God has not occurred and loss of any kind is not real, then your perception is corrected. One mistake is not more difficult than another for the Holy Spirit to bring to Truth, because there is only one mistake: your whole idea that loss is possible and can result in gain for anything. If this was true, God would be unfair, separation from God would be an uncorrectable sin, attack would be justified, and vengeance would be fair.

3. This one mistake, in any form, has one correction: your recognition that you are not separate from God, so there is no loss. For you to think loss is possible is only a mistake. You don't have any problems, though you think that you do. But you will not think

so as you watch them vanish one by one without regard to size, complexity, place, time, or any attribute that makes you think one problem is different from the others. The limits that you impose on what you are willing to perceive cannot limit God in any way.

4. The miracle of the Justice of Oneness can correct all of your errors, because every problem that you perceive is the error of perceiving yourself separate from God. Every problem represents the injustice of your seeming separation from your Christ Mind and is therefore not true. The Holy Spirit does not judge forms of separation as great or small, or more or less. They have no properties to the Holy Spirit. They are mistaken beliefs in separation from which you who are One with God are needlessly suffering, so the Holy Spirit takes them away. The Holy Spirit does not pause to judge whether your pain is large or little, but It makes the only judgment that what hurts you must be unfair, therefore it cannot be real.

5. You believe it is safe to give only some of your mistakes to the Holy Spirit to be corrected and to keep some for the personal mind, but remember this: The Justice of Oneness is Total, because there is no such thing as partial justice. If you perceive guilt anywhere, then condemnation is real to you, and you think God's mercy is not deserved anywhere. But do not ask God to send punishment because *you* see guilt and want punishment to be real. God offers you the Means to see Innocence. It is not fair to make punishment real to yourself, because you choose to not perceive Innocence. Each time you keep a problem to solve with the personal mind, or you judge that a problem has no resolution, you make it past your hope of healing, and you deny that the miracle of the Justice of Oneness *can* be fairly applied to everything that you perceive.

6. Since God is Just, there are no problems that the Justice of Oneness cannot solve. But you believe that some forms of separation are fair and good and necessary to preserve the personal self. It is these problems that you think are great and cannot be resolved, because you want loss and sacrifice to be real. But consider again your special function of seeing Perfect Innocence in your perception of

one other to replace the world in your mind. In seeing Innocence, you do not look on loss. The miracle of the Justice of Oneness you call on rests on you as surely as it does on your perception of the other. The Holy Spirit will only be content when you perceive Oneness everywhere. The Oneness that you give to the Holy Spirit belongs to your entire mind, and by your extending It, the Holy Spirit can ensure that your entire mind receives It.

7.   Think how great your own release will be when you are willing to accept correction of all of your seeming problems. You will not keep one, because you will not want pain in any form. You will see each little hurt resolved before the Holy Spirit's Perception. All of your problems are little to the Holy Spirit and are worth no more than just a tiny sigh before they are forever undone and forgotten by you. What once seemed to you to be a special problem, a mistake without remedy, or an affliction without a cure becomes an opportunity for you to offer a blessing of Oneness. Sacrifice will be gone, and in its place you will remember God's Law of Oneness, Which shines away all of your thoughts of sacrifice and loss.

8.   You will not remember God until you love the Justice of Oneness instead of fear It. God cannot be unjust to anything, because God knows everything Real is One with God and will Forever be so. What God loves must be Innocent and beyond attack. Your special function opens in your mind your Memory of God's Love, Perfectly Intact and undefiled. All that you need to do is wish that Heaven be given to you instead of hell, and every barrier that seems to block your Memory of God will fall away. It is not God's Will that you extend or receive less than God extends to you in the Perfect Love of your Oneness with God.

3. The Borderland

1.   Complexity is not of God, because all that God knows is One. God knows One Extension, One Reality, and One Truth. Nothing conflicts with Oneness, so there can be no complexity in God. You have nothing to decide in God, because it is conflict that makes you need *choice*. Being One, the Truth is Simple and without opposite. Strife cannot enter Truth's Simple Presence and bring

complexity to Oneness. You have no decision to make in Truth, because there is nothing for you to decide *between* There. Your choosing is necessary only as you step *toward* Oneness, because What is Everything has no room for anything else. But the Magnitude of Oneness is beyond the scope of this lesson plan, and it is not necessary for you to dwell on What you cannot immediately grasp.

2. There is a borderland of thought in your mind between the world that you perceive and the Oneness of Heaven. It is not a place, and it is apart from time. It is where your thoughts are brought together, where your conflicting values meet, and where you lay down all illusions beside Truth to be judged as untrue. This borderland in your mind is just before Heaven, and it is where your thoughts are made Pure and Simple. Here, you deny your separation from God, and you receive Everything that *is* instead.

3. This is the end of your journey to God. It has been referred to in this course as *Real Perception*. Yet there is a contradiction in these words that imply a limited, partial awareness of Truth. This is because God does not attack perception, which is not Knowledge of God, but God corrects it, so that it can easily be translated to Knowledge of God. Your salvation is a borderland where place and time and choice still have meaning, and yet you can see that they are temporary and out of place, and that you have already made every choice.

4. Nothing that you believe can be destroyed, but what you think is truth you must bring to the last comparison that you will ever make, the last evaluation that is possible, the final judgment on the world in your mind. This is the judgment of Truth on illusion and of Knowledge on perception: *It has no meaning and does not exist.* This is not a choice that you make, but a simple statement of simple fact. In the world in your mind there are no simple facts, because what is Truth and what is illusion is confused. Yet the distinction between Truth and illusion is the one essential thing that you must choose to make. In this lies the difference between your perception of a world of separation and your Real Perception. In your perception that you are in a world, choosing Truth seems impos-

sible, but in True Perception choosing Truth is simple.

5. Your salvation stops just short of Heaven, because only your perception needs salvation. Heaven was never lost to you, so It does not need to be saved. But you cannot make the choice between Heaven and hell when they are confused in your mind. Teaching you the difference between Heaven and hell is the goal of this course. It will not go beyond this aim. Its only purpose is to teach you to sort out Truth and illusion so that you can choose Truth, the only real choice for you to make.

6. There is no basis for choice in the complex and overly complicated world that you have made. You do not perceive that illusions are all the same, and you choose between them where there is no real choice. Real Perception offers you a True Alternative, so that you can make a real choice. Choice itself is actually an illusion, because only God is Real, but in choosing Real Perception you undo every illusion of choice, even this one.

7. Isn't this like your special function, where your perception of separation from God is undone by your changing the purpose of a relationship in the world that you perceive from specialness to Oneness? All illusions are the same illusion of separation from God. In your recognizing this, you will find that you are able to give up all attempts to choose between illusions and make them seem different. You experience no conflict or sacrifice in your relinquishment of an illusion that you recognize *is* an illusion. It is not hard for you to give up what is no longer real to you and to choose What must be True.

4. Where Sin Has Left

1. Your forgiving in your perception that you are in a world is the equivalent of Heaven's Justice of Oneness. It replaces the world of separation in your mind with Real Perception, Where the Justice of Oneness is reflected from the Limitlessness beyond forgiving. Nothing in Boundless Love needs forgiving, and the charity that is forgiving in your perception that you are in a world gives way to the Simple Justice of Heaven. You only need to forgive because you have believed that your perception of separation from God is real,

and you still believe that you have much that needs to be forgiven. Your forgiving, then, is the means by which you learn that you have done nothing to forgive. Your forgiving always rests on you, who are doing the forgiving, until you no longer see yourself needing to be forgiven. Your forgiving is the means by which you are returned to your Real Function of extending God.

2. Your forgiving replaces your perception of a world of separation from God with a Perception of your Glory. In this Perception, everything that you see and hear reflects the Joy of Heaven. There is no sadness, no parting, and everything is totally forgiven. Your forgiven perceptions must join, because nothing stands between them to keep them apart. In Innocence, you must perceive that your Mind is One, because there is nothing to push away part of your Mind from the rest of It. All things join as One in the space that your belief in separation from God leaves vacant in your mind through your forgiving, gladly recognizing that What is part of your Mind has never been separate from It.

3. The space that your belief in separation from God leaves behind is the Holiest place in your mind. Here, you see Christ rising in place of your belief in separation, and where you see Christ, you recall God as God really is. You cannot fear Love and remain where your belief in separation has left a place in your mind for Heaven to rise in your awareness, and where you reach beyond the world that you perceive to touch God. Heaven is a song of gratitude and Love and praise by God's Extension to God. The Holiest place in your mind is where you once believed that separation from God was real. Here, all the Love of Heaven comes to be revived and increased in Joy. Here, you who were lost to Love are restored to It and made Whole again.

4. They are not little miracles that your forgiving brings before Heaven. Here, your Christ Mind comes to receive each gift of your forgiving that brings you closer to Home. Not one gift of forgiving is lost or cherished more than another. Each reminds you of God's Love as surely as the others, and each teaches you that What you feared is What you love the most. Only your experience of a miracle can change your mind so that you understand that Love

cannot be feared. This is really the only miracle. What else do you need to make all separation disappear from your mind?

5. In place of your perception of separation from God, a Perception of Truth will rise, and you will join the Love of Heaven there in gratitude and praise. As Love comes to you to be Complete, so will you go to Love. You cannot hear Heaven's Call without joining with It. You join Heaven at the tiny spot in your mind that once belonged to your belief in separation from God, and this tiny spot will disappear into the Magnitude of Oneness.

6. The tiny spot of separation in your mind that stands between you and Heaven holds you back from happily crossing to Heaven. How little is this hindrance that withholds the Abundance of Heaven from you! And how great will be the Joy in Heaven when you join It in the Love of God!

5. The Little Hindrance

1. A little hindrance can seem large to you when you do not understand that miracles are all the same. But teaching this is the only purpose for this course, because this is all that there is for you to learn. You can learn this in many different ways. All of your learning helps or hinders you in opening your mind to the Presence of Heaven. Nothing in between is possible, because you have only two teachers - the personal mind and the Holy Spirit - and each points in different directions. You will go along the way your chosen teacher leads you, and you have only two directions while time and choice remain meaningful to you. The only road through the world that you perceive is the road to Heaven, and you choose to go either toward Heaven or away from It to nowhere. There is nothing else for you to choose between.

2. You can only lose time, and in the end this is meaningless. Time is but a little hindrance to Eternity and quite meaningless to the Holy Spirit, your Real Teacher in your perception that you are in a world. Yet, since you do believe in time, why waste it going nowhere when it can be used to reach God, as high a Goal as your learning can achieve? Do not think that your way to Heaven is difficult at all. Nothing that you undertake with certain purpose, high resolve,

and happy confidence to join your entire mind in Heaven's Oneness is difficult for you to do. But it is hard indeed for you to wander in separation and misery down a road that leads to nothing and has no purpose.

3. God gave the Holy Spirit to you to replace the teacher that you made, not to conflict with it. What God wants replaced *is* replaced. Time was only an instant in your mind that had no effect on Eternity. So all time has really passed, and Eternity is exactly as It was before you made the way to nothingness. The tiny tick of time in which you made your first mistake of perceiving yourself separate from God, and all of your seeming mistakes of separation within that one mistake, also held the Holy Spirit as Correction for all of it. In that instant of simultaneous correction, time was gone, because an instant was all that it was. What God gave Answer to is answered and is gone.

4. You still believe that you live in time, and you do not know that it is gone. The Holy Spirit guides you through an infinitely small and senseless maze that you perceive in time, though it has long since gone. You really live in the past, because each thing that you look on you saw for only an instant, long ago in time, before its unreality became your reality. Not one illusion in your mind remains unanswered. Your uncertainty was brought to Certainty so long ago that it is hard for you to hold onto it as though it is still before you.

5. The tiny instant of separation that you want to keep and make eternal passed away in Heaven too quickly for Heaven to have noticed that it had come. What disappeared too quickly to affect your Knowledge of God can hardly still be here for you to choose to be your teacher. Only in the past – an ancient past too short to make a world to replace God's Extension – did a world seem to rise in your mind. This was so long ago, for such a tiny interval, that not one Part of Heaven was changed.

6. Yet, in each of your unforgiving thoughts, in every judgment of the personal mind that you accept, and in all of your belief that separation from God is real, that instant is called back to you as though it can be made into time again. You keep an ancient

memory in your mind, and living in memories you do not know that you are really in God. These memories are not a hindrance to your living in God. An echo from the past is not a fact that describes Where you are now. Your own illusions about time and place cannot change the Fact that you are really in God.

7. What you do not forgive in your perception of separation from God represents a past that is gone forever. Everything that points to separation as real for you is your wish that what is gone be made here and now in place of God, Which is really here and now. This is not a hindrance to the truth that the past is gone and cannot be returned to you. Do you want to keep that frightening instant, when Heaven seemed to disappear from you and you feared God as a symbol of your hate?

8. Forget the time of terror that was corrected and undone so long ago. Your belief that separation is real cannot withstand the Will of God. It is not up to you to make the past into the present. You *cannot* go back. Everything that points in the direction of the past sets you on a mission that cannot be accomplished. This is the Justice of Oneness that God in Its Love has ensured must come to you. God has protected you from your own unfairness to yourself. You cannot lose your way, because the only Way is God's Way, and you cannot go anywhere but to God.

9. God will not allow you to lose your way along a road that has long since past. A dreadful instant, now Perfectly Corrected, has no value. Let the dead and gone be Peacefully forgotten. Resurrection has come to take their place, and you are part of the Resurrection, not of death. No illusions from the past have the power to keep you in a place of death; a place you entered for an instant to be immediately restored to God's Perfect Love. You cannot be kept in limitations that have long been removed from your mind forever.

10. Your Christ Mind is Free in God. Your Christ Mind was reborn into your awareness the moment that you chose to die instead of live. Forgive yourself now, because you made an error in a past that God does not remember and that is not here. Now you are shifting back and forth between a past that never was and a Present in God. Sometimes the past seems real, as though it *is* present. You are like

one who still hallucinates, but is no longer convinced of what they perceive. This is the borderland between perceptions; the bridge between past and Present. The shadow of the past remains here, but you recognize your Present in God. Once you see this Present you will never forget It. It will draw you from the past into the Present, Where you really are.

11. The shadows from the past do not change the laws of time or of Eternity. They come from what is past and gone, and they do not hinder the Truth that is here and now. Real Perception is the correction for your hallucination that time and death are real. These terrible illusions were denied the instant that God gave Its simultaneous Answer to all illusions for all time. Then they were gone.

12. Every instant you seem to relive the instant when the time of terror took the place of Love in your mind. So you die each instant until you cross the gap between past and Present, which is not a gap at all. Such is each seeming 'life' in the seeming world: an interval between birth and death, repeating an instant gone by long ago that cannot really be relived. All of time is your mad belief that what is over is still here and now.

13. Forgive the past and let it go, because it *is* gone. You no longer stand between two perceptions. You have gone on and reached the Real Perception that is just outside of Heaven. There is no hindrance to the Will of God, nor any need that you repeat again a journey that was over long ago. Look gently on your mind's perception of a world, and behold your perception of hate transformed into a Perception of Love.

6. The Appointed Friend

1. Anything in the world that you perceive that you believe is good and valuable and worth striving for will hurt you, not because it has the power to hurt you, but because, by denying that it is only an illusion, you make it real to you. In your perception that it is real, it is not nothing to you, and the whole world of sick illusions enters your mind. All of your belief in separation and the power of attack, in hurt and harm, and in sacrifice and death comes with

it. You cannot make one illusion real to you and escape the rest. You cannot choose to keep some illusions that you prefer and find the Safety that only the Truth can give to you. You cannot perceive that all illusions are the same while maintaining that even one is best.

2. Do not live your little 'life' in your perception that you are in a world with even one illusion as your friend. This is not a friendship that is worthy of Part of God, and it is not one with which you can be content. God has given you a better Friend in the Holy Spirit, in Which all the Power of Heaven rests. Any one illusion that you think is your friend obscures the Holy Spirit's Grace and Majesty from you and keeps you from welcoming the Holy Spirit's Friendship and forgiveness. Without the Holy Spirit, you *are* friendless. Do not seek another friend to take the Holy Spirit's place; there is no other friend. What God appointed has no substitute, because no illusion can replace the Truth.

3. You are indeed friendless when you live with illusions, and your loneliness is not the Will of God. You would not allow one illusion to usurp the place of the Holy Spirit in your mind if you realized that this leaves you empty. Do not make any illusion your friend, because, if you do, it will take the place of the Holy Spirit, Which God has made your only Friend in Truth. The Holy Spirit brings you Gifts of Love that are not of the world that you perceive, and you can receive them only through the Holy Spirit in you. The Holy Spirit will bring Them to your mind when you make room for the Holy Spirit.

7. The Laws of Healing

1. This is a course in miracles, so you must understand the laws of healing before you can fully accomplish the purpose of this course. It is time to review the principles that have already been covered, and to arrange them in a way that summarizes all that must occur for your healing to be possible. When it is possible, healing will occur for you.

2. All discord that you experience comes from your belief that separation from God is real. When you deny the separation,

discord goes, because it is gone as soon as the idea that brought it is healed and replaced by Sanity. Discord and your belief that separation from God is a sin are consequence and cause in a relationship that you keep hidden from your awareness so that it can not be undone through the Holy Spirit's True Reasoning.

3.   Your guilt asks for punishment, and its request is granted, not in Truth, but in your mind where you perceive a world of separation and illusions that is built on your belief that separation from God is real. You perceive a world of separation because your perception is your wish fulfilled. Perception changes, and it was made to take the place of your Changeless Knowledge of God. Truth cannot be changed, and you cannot perceive It, but you can *know* It. What you perceive can take many forms, but none of these forms has any meaning. Brought to Truth, the senselessness of what you perceive is quite apparent. But, kept apart from Truth, it seems to be real and to have meaning.

4.   Perception's law that you see what *you want* to be real is the opposite of Truth, and What is True of God's Knowledge is not true of anything apart from It. But God has given an Answer to your perception of a world of separation in the form of the Holy Spirit, and this Answer applies to all of the forms separation takes. God's Answer is Eternal, though It works in time where It is needed. But, because the Holy Spirit is of God, the laws of time do not affect Its workings. The Holy Spirit is *in* your mind where you perceive a world, because both your perception of separation from God and God's Answer to it are in your mind. But the Holy Spirit is not *of* the part of your mind where you perceive a world, because the Holy Spirit is Real and dwells in the part of your mind Where all Reality is. Your ideas do not leave their source – your mind – and their effects only *seem* to be apart from you. What seems to be external to your mind are ideas projected out from it. They are only an effect of your mind, and they have not left their source.

5.   God's Answer lies in your mind, along with your belief that separation from God is real, because only in your mind can this belief's effects be utterly undone and can you see them as without cause. The law of perception must be undone, because it is the

total reversal of the Law of Truth. The Law of Truth cannot be reversed, because It is Forever True, but you can see It upside down. This must be corrected in your mind, where the illusion of reversal lies.

6.　It is impossible for one illusion to be less open to correction by Truth than any other illusion. But it is possible that you value some illusions more than others, and that you are less willing to offer these to Truth for healing. No illusion has any Truth in it, but it appears to you that some are truer than others, even though this does not make any sense. All that a hierarchy of illusions can show you is your own preference, not Reality. Preference has no relevance to Truth, Which is One. All illusions are illusions and are false. Your preference cannot make any of them real. Not one illusion is true in any way, and all of them must yield with equal ease to God's Answer to them all. God's Will is One, and any wish that you have that seems to go against God's Will has no foundation in Truth.

7.　Your idea is that your perception of separation from God is not an error to be corrected, but it is a *sin*; it is reality and beyond correction. This has made some forms of separation seem to you to be forever past the hope of healing, and the grounds for hell seem eternal to you. If this were so, Heaven would be opposed by its own real opposite; God's Will would be split in two; and God's Mind would be subjected to the laws of two opposing powers, until God became impatient, split perception into two, and attacked Itself. God would have lost Its Mind and proclaimed that sin has taken God's Reality from God and brought God's Love to vengeance. For this insane idea you can expect to have an insane defense, but you cannot establish that the idea must be true.

8.　Nothing can give meaning to the meaningless, and Truth does not need defense to make It True. Illusions have no witnesses and no effects, and if you see them, you are deceived. Forgiving is your only function in your perception that you are in a world, and it brings the Perception of Joy to your entire mind to replace your perception that separation from God is real. Perhaps you do not see the role that your forgiving plays in ending death and all of your beliefs that arise from guilt. Sins are beliefs that you impose to split your mind between 'you' and a world that you see outside of yourself. They limit you to time and place, and give a little space to you and a little space to each of your separate perceptions. This separating off is symbolized in your perception by a body, which is clearly a separate thing. But what this symbol represents is your *wish* to be separate.

9.   Your forgiving takes away the seeming sins that stand between you and the part of your mind that you have projected outside of you. It is your wish that your mind be One, not split. Your forgiving is called a 'wish' here because it is a choice, and it has not yet reached entirely beyond the level of choice. But this wish is in line with the State of Heaven, and it is not in opposition to God's Will. Although it falls short of giving you All that God extends to you, it does remove the obstacles that you have placed between Heaven and your awareness that you are One with God in Heaven. Facts do not change, but you can deny them and seem to not know them.

10. Your complete and perfect salvation asks that you wish that the Truth be True for you, for a little willingness to overlook what is not there, and that you prefer that your mind be filled with Heaven instead of a perception of a world of death and desolation. When this is so, your Oneness with God will rise within your mind in Joyous Answer to replace with Heaven the world that you now perceive. Your forgiving is only your willingness that the Truth be true in your awareness. Nothing can remain unhealed and broken within a Oneness Which holds all things within Itself. You are not separate from God; it is not a sin to perceive this. Every miracle is possible the instant that your wishes are One with the Will of God.

11. What is God's Will? God's Will is that you have Everything that God has, and this is guaranteed in God's extension of God to you. It is impossible that you lose God, because What you *have* in God, you *are* in God. This is the miracle that establishes extending God as your Function, Which you share with God. You cannot under-stand this apart from God, so it has no meaning in the world that you made. In your perception that you are in a world, you do not

ask for too much, but for too little. You sacrifice your own Identity in God for a little identity of your own apart from God. So of course you have a sense of isolation, loss, and loneliness. This is what you sought to find, but you can only be afraid of it. Is fear valuable? Is uncertainty what you really want? Or are you mistaken about what you really are and what you really will?

12. Look at what your error is so that you can correct it instead of protect it. Your belief that sin is real is your belief that your separation from God can be projected outside of your mind, where the belief arose. Your conviction that ideas can leave their source is made real and meaningful to you in this and gives rise to your perception of a world of separation and sacrifice outside of you. This is your attempt to see yourself as 'innocent', while cherishing the separation that was your 'attack' on God. Its failure lies in that you still feel guilty, though you do not understand why. You see the effects of your guilt separate from their source, your mind, and they seem to be beyond you to control or to prevent. You then keep the world apart from you, and you can never join with it.

13. Cause and effect are one and can never be separate. God's Will is that you learn what has always been True: God extends God to you and this must still be True, because ideas do not leave their source. It is Creation's Law that each Idea that Mind conceives adds to Its Abundance, never takes away from It. This is as true of what you idly wish as of what you Truly Will, because you can wish to deceive yourself, but you cannot make your mind what it is not. For you to believe that ideas can leave their source is for you to invite illusions to be true, but without success. You will never wholly deceive yourself.

14. Your experience of the miracle is possible when your mind and its effects are brought together, not when they are kept apart. Healing the effect of your belief in separation from God without healing the cause in your mind will merely shift the effect to a different form. This is not release. In your Oneness with God, you will never be content with less than full salvation from your perception of separation from God and the guilt that it entails. If you still retain some bit of separation, it is because you are still demanding some

sacrifice of your Oneness with God and denying that Everything that is God's is yours, without limits. A 'tiny' sacrifice has the same effect on you as the whole idea of sacrifice. If loss of any kind is real to you, then you cannot believe that you are Complete and One with God. You renounce God and your Self, and you make Them 'enemies' to you.

15. Illusions serve the purpose that you want them to serve. From their purpose, they derive any meaning that they seem to have for you. Though they were made to serve separation from God, God has given your illusions, no matter what form they take, a purpose that will justify a miracle. All of your healing lies in every miracle that you experience, because God gave One Answer, the Holy Spirit, to all of your calls for healing. What is One to God must be the same, and if you believe that what is the same is different, then you deceive yourself. What God calls One is Forever One, never separate. God's Mind is One, as It is extended and will Forever be.

16. Your experience of the miracle calls to the Christ in you, Which you will recognize, because the Truth is in your Memory. The part of your mind where you perceive a world calls to Christ to be released with you. Heaven is shining in that part of your mind; do not deny this, so that you can be released. Every instant you are reborn, until you choose to not die again. In your every wish to hurt, you choose death instead of the Life that God wills for you. But every instant offers you Life, because God wills that you should live.

17. Correction is laid where you see crucifixion, because healing is needed where you perceive pain and suffering are real. Your forgiving it is the answer to any of your perceptions of separation, so that your seeming attack on God is deprived of its effects in your mind and your Self-hate is answered with Love. All Glory be to you, who have the function of saving your entire mind from cruci-fixion, hell, and death! You have the Power to save yourself, because God has willed this be so. Salvation lies in you to be extended and received by you.

18. It is natural for you to use the Power that God gives to you, as God

wants you to use It. It is not arrogant for you to recognize that you are One with God, nor for you to use the Answer that God has given to your mistakes to set you free. But it *is* arrogant for you to lay aside the Power that God gives to you and to choose a little senseless wish instead of God's Will. God's Answer is a Limitless Gift to you. There is no circumstance It cannot answer and no problem that is not resolved in Its Gracious Love.

19. Abide in Peace, Where God wants you to be. Be the means by which you perceive the Peace in Which your wish is fulfilled. Unite with your Christ Mind to extend blessing to replace all of your perceptions of sin and death. What can save you can save your entire mind, because there is no difference between your mind and the part of your mind where you perceive a world. The Oneness that your specialness denies will wholly save you, because What is One is not divided up by specialness. Everything belongs to your mind, and no wishes can stand between your mind and what is part of it. For you to try to get something from someone in the world that you perceive is for you to limit yourself to a personal mind, but for you to extend blessing to your perception of even one other in the world that you perceive is for you to extend blessing to your entire mind.

20. Your Christ Mind is not split, and It is yours as It belongs to your entire mind. Call on Christ, and God will answer, because you are calling on God. God cannot refuse to Answer when God has already answered. Your experience of a miracle does not change anything, but it can make you, who think you don't know Truth, recognize Truth. By letting your experience of the miracle be what it is, you allow you to be your Self, and your mind to be free as One to call upon Christ.

8. The Immediacy of Salvation

1. The one remaining problem that you have is that you see an interval of time between your forgiving your perception of separation from God and your receiving the benefits of trusting in the Oneness of your Christ Mind. This reflects the little space of separation that you want to keep in your mind. Time and space are

one illusion, which takes different forms. If you project the illusion of separation beyond your mind, you think of it as time. The closer you are to the awareness that the illusion of separation is in your mind, the more you think of it in terms of space.

2.   There is a little space of separation that you want to keep in your mind, and you see this as time. You still believe that your mind is split between 'you' and a world outside of you, and this makes it impossible for you to trust in the Oneness of your Christ Mind. You do not believe that extending Christ will settle all of your problems *now*. You think it is safer to remain wary and watchful of a world that you perceive as separate from you. From this perception, you cannot conceive of gaining the Limitlessness that forgiving separation offers you *now*. The interval that you think lies between your extending forgiveness and receiving it for yourself seems to be one in which you will suffer sacrifice and loss. You see eventual salvation, but not immediate results.

3.   Your salvation *is* immediate, and unless you perceive this, you will be afraid of salvation, because you will believe that the risk of loss is great between the time that you accept salvation as your purpose and you receive its effects. But this obscures the real source of your fear, which is that salvation *will* wipe out all separation in your mind, and your mind will instantly become One again. This is really where you fear loss. Do not project this fear onto time, because time is not the enemy that you perceive. Like the body, time is neutral, and its meaning comes from the purpose that you give to it. If you want to keep in your mind a little space of separation, you will want a little time in which you withhold forgiveness from yourself. This makes the interval between the time that you extend forgiveness and receive it seem dangerous to you, and your fears will seem justified.

4.   Yet the space between 'you' and the world that seems outside of you is apparent to you now, and you cannot perceive it as happening only at a future time. You also can only overlook it right now. Your fear is not future loss, but present Oneness. You feel desolation *now*; its cause is not in the future. Therefore, what you fear must have a present cause, and the present is where you need correction.

5.   The plans that you make for safety are all in the future, where you cannot plan. No purpose has been given to the future yet, and what *will* happen does not yet have a cause. You cannot predict effects without a cause, and you will not fear effects unless you believe that they have already been caused, and you have judged them as disastrous *now*. Your belief that your separation from God is real arouses fear in you and, like the personal mind that causes it, it looks forward and back, but never at what is here and now. But its cause must be here and now if you already judge its effects as fearful. Your refusing to look at the separation in the present protects it and keeps it from healing, because the miracle is *now*. The miracle is already here in Present Grace, within the only interval of time that in separation and fear you have overlooked, but which is all that is real in time.

6.   It takes no time at all for total correction to occur, but your *accepting* correction for all can seem to take forever. The change of purpose that the Holy Spirit brought to you through your Holy relationship has in it all the effects of correction that you can look on *now*. Why wait for them to unfold in time, fearing that they may not come, though they are here now? Everything that comes from God is Good, but it seems to you that this is not so when you put It off into the future. Good then appears like disaster to you, and It is difficult for you to credit It in advance. There is no sense in this idea.

7.   You are deceiving yourself if 'good' seems to appear in the evil form of delay. But if Good appears at all, its Cause must be here. So where are Its Effects? Why do you put Them off into the future? You seek to be content with sighing and with 'reasoning' that you do not understand it now but will 'one day'. This is not reason, because it is the injustice of separation, and it clearly hints at your punishment until the time of liberation is at hand. Your purpose has been changed for the Good, and there is no reason for you to suffer an interval of pain. This is your sacrifice of *now*, which the Holy Spirit does not ask for as the 'cost' for the Good that It extends to you.

8.   This illusion that there must be delay between extending your Good and your receiving It has a cause in your mind. This illusion

is only one effect that the cause of your desire for separation engenders, and one form in which you perceive its outcome. This interval of time where you perceive retribution in the form of delay to be the form in which 'good' appears for you is just one aspect of the little space of separation that you still want and haven't forgiven.

9. Do not be content with future happiness. This has no meaning, and it is not your due. You have Cause for Freedom *now*. There is no freedom in a release that you put off. Why should your deliverance be disguised as death? Delay is senseless, and your 'reasoning', which maintains that Effects with a Present Cause must be delayed, is merely your denial of the Fact that Cause and Effect are One. Do not look to be delivered from time but from the little space of separation that you want to keep in your mind. Do not let this little space be disguised as time and preserved because its form is changed so you will not recognize it. The Holy Spirit's Purpose is yours *now*. Don't you want the Holy Spirit's Happiness as well?

9. For They Have Come

1. Think how Holy you must be that the Holy Spirit extends Lovingly through your perception, so that you may awaken in your entire mind the awareness of the Holy Spirit. Think how Holy your perception is because in it your salvation and Freedom are joined to your entire mind. However much you may wish to perceive condemnation, God is in your entire mind. You will never know that God is in you while you perceive any form of separation, because your entire mind is God's chosen home. Regard all that you see Gently, and look with the Loving Perception of your Christ Mind, so that you may behold Christ's Glory, and rejoice that Heaven is not separate from you.

2. It is not too much to ask of you that you trust in the Christ that you see in your perception of another so that you may forgive your perception of separation from God. Do not forget that an illusion held between yourself and another obscures your Christ Mind and your Memory of God for you. Do not trade God for an ancient Self-hate. Your mind is Holy, because God is with you, blessing your

mind with Its Innocence and Peace.

3.   Your mind is renewed as hate fades from it. Your mind, which once honored death, now honors Life and extends Life to all that you perceive, because you remember God. It is God's Presence Which lifts Holiness to take Its rightful place in your mind. Because of God, miracles replace hatred and desolation in your mind, undoing them. Now your mind is so Holy that Heaven leans to join it and make it One like Itself. Where God has come, the dark shadows cast by illusions are gone forever from your mind.

4.   A hundred, a thousand, tens of thousands of years are nothing to God. When God comes into your mind, time's purpose is fulfilled. What never was passes to nothingness, when God has come. What hatred claimed is given up to Love, and, in Loving Limitlessness, your entire mind is lifted to Heaven, Where Love is increased with every Loving Thought that you extend. What seemed incomplete is made Complete in your awareness again, and Heaven's Joy is increased, because you who belong to It have been restored. So that you can join with God in your awareness again, your mind is purified of the conflicted world that you perceived, along with all of the insanity in it.

5.   Heaven is grateful to you for this gift that you give to It, because God has come again to your mind, which belongs to God. Your mind, which was closed to God, has been opened, and what you held apart from Love is given to God, so that Love may undo any space between you and your mind where you perceive a world.

6.   The Holiest of all spots in your mind is where you have given Self-hatred over to Love. God comes quickly to your mind when it has been prepared for God. There is no place in Heaven Holier. God comes to dwell in your mind, which is made a home to God, to be God's resting place as well as yours. Where you have released hatred to Love is the Strongest Spot of Love in Heaven. All the Love of Heaven grows Stronger in Gratitude for what you have restored to It.

7.   God's Loving Thoughts hover around you to keep away all dark thoughts that separation from God is real and to keep Love in your awareness. Where you walk in the world that you perceive, you

walk with forgiveness, and your entire mind offers thanks to you for restoring its home. God cannot thank you more.

8. Now your mind is restored to be home again to the Living God, Which created your mind by extending Itself to it. Where God dwells, your Christ Mind dwells with God. God gives thanks that you welcome God at last. Where you once perceived a cross of crucifixion, you now see Christ risen in your awareness and your scars of separation are healed by Christ's Perception. A miracle has come to bless and replace a hatred that came to kill. In Gentle Gratitude, God returns to your mind, which is God's now and forever. Now the Holy Spirit's Purpose is done, because God has come!

10. The End of Injustice

1. What, then, remains to be undone for you to realize the Presence of God? You believe that some forms of separation in the world that you perceive are justified, and that others are unfair and should not be allowed. When you perceive unfairness, you think it is justified for you to respond with anger. You therefore see as different, illusions that are the same. Your confusion about what is real and what is illusion is not limited. If it occurs at all it is total. And its presence, in whatever form, will hide the Presence of God in your mind.

2. If you perceive some forms of separation as unfair, then you must perceive some forms of separation as fair. You give some illusions meaning, then, and you perceive them as sensible and others you see as meaningless. This denies that all of separation is senseless, is equally without cause, and cannot have real effects. God's Presence in your mind is obscured by any illusion that stands between God's Innocence and your awareness that It is your own, and that It belongs to your entire mind. God does not limit, and what is limited cannot be Heaven, so it must be hell.

3. Your perception of separation is unfair to *you*, who are One. You cannot be unfairly treated, and your belief that you can is another form of your idea that someone or something outside of you can deprive you. Your projection of the cause of your sacrifice is the root of everything that you perceive to be unfair to you. *You* ask

sacrifice of yourself in deep injustice to your Oneness with God. You have no enemy, except yourself, and you are enemy to your own mind when you do not recognize that your perceptions *are* in your own mind. Nothing could be more unjust than that your mind be deprived of its Wholeness, denied the right to its Wholeness, and asked to sacrifice God's Love and yours as not its due.

4.   Beware of the temptation to perceive yourself as unfairly treated. In this view, you seek to find an innocence in the personal mind that does not come from your Oneness with God, but comes at the cost of separating your mind so that guilt seems to be outside of it. You cannot purchase Innocence by splitting your mind so that you can project guilt away from you. It is not really Innocence that this attack on yourself seeks to get; it seeks to project away responsibility for your own attack on God. You think it is safer to believe that you are an innocent victim of an external world, than that you are responsible for splitting your mind off from God. But whatever way you play the game of guilt, you will lose. Some part of your mind must lose its Innocence so that some other part can seem to be innocent, but the guilt is still in your mind.

5.   You think that the other in your Holy relationship is unfair to you, because you think that someone must be unfair to make you innocent. In this game, the personal mind sees a purpose for your relationship, and you seek to add it to the purpose that was given to it by the Holy Spirit. But the Holy Spirit's purpose for your Holy relationship is to make you aware of the Presence of God in your mind. Nothing can be added to this, because the world that you perceive has only this as its real purpose. For you to add or to take away from this purpose is for you to take away all purpose from the world that you perceive and from yourself in it. Every bit of unfairness that the world seems to lay on you, you have laid on *it* by rendering it without the function that the Holy Spirit gives to it. The Justice of Oneness is then denied to your entire mind.

6.   You cannot calculate what this injustice of separation does to you, who judge unfairly, and who then perceive unfairness. You perceive a dark and threatening world without the Happy Sparkle of salvation. You see yourself deprived of Love, abandoned to fear,

628

and unfairly left without a purpose in a futile world. But you *can* perceive Fairness, because, in your mind, the Holy Spirit has replaced the injustice of separation with the Justice of Oneness, Which has resolved all unfairness. If you perceive the injustice of separation anywhere, say to yourself:

'With this, I deny the Presence of God.
I would rather know God than perceive separation, which God's Presence undoes.'

Chapter 27

Healing the Dream[1,2]

1. The Picture of Crucifixion

1. Your wish to be unfairly treated is your attempt to hold onto attack as something real, while seeing yourself as innocent. But you cannot combine the wholly incompatible in your mind and make them one. Walk the Gentle Way, and you will not fear, but put frightening symbols of attack in your path, and you will crucify yourself and project your crucifixion onto all that you perceive. You cannot limit the idea of crucifixion to the personal mind. If you feel that you are unfairly treated, you will perceive unfairness in the world in your mind. You cannot sacrifice just your little self, because the idea of sacrifice will affect your entire mind. Mind is One, so if sacrifice could occur at all, it would have to involve your entire mind, and entail God sacrificing Part of Itself.

2. As you release yourself from sacrifice, you release yourself from the idea that something outside yourself is making you suffer. But every time that you suffer pain, you see proof that someone or something else is guilty for attacking you. You make yourself the sign that another has lost their innocence, and that they only need to look at you to see that they are condemned. And what has happened to you will now happen to another in righteous retribution, and you believe that when they receive it you will be made free. But do not wish to make yourself the living symbol of another's guilt, because you will not escape the death that you make for them. But choose to perceive your Innocence instead, and you will find your own.

3. Whenever you consent to suffer pain, to be deprived, unfairly treated, or in need of anything, you project responsibility for *your* attack on yourself onto another in the world that you perceive. You hold a picture of your crucifixion before their eyes so that they may see *their* sins are written in Heaven in *your* blood, damning *them* to

hell. But this is written in hell, not in Heaven, Where you are beyond attack and you prove Innocence. The picture of yourself that you offer to others, you show to yourself, and you give it all of your faith. The Holy Spirit offers you a picture of yourself in which there is no pain and no reproach at all. What you martyred to another's guilt becomes the perfect witness to the universal Innocence of your mind.

4.   The power of witness brings conviction, because the witness points beyond themselves to what they represent. If you are sick and suffering, you are witnessing to someone else's guilt, so that they will not forget the injuries that they gave to you and which they cannot escape. You accept this sick and sorry picture of yourself if only it can serve to punish another. In sickness, you are merciless to all that you perceive, and you seek to kill. Your death seems to be an easy price for you to pay if you can blame another for it. Your sickness is the witness to *their* guilt, and your death would prove that *they* are sinful. Your sickness is a little death, a form of vengeance that is not yet total, but it speaks certainly for the death it represents. But this bleak picture of yourself that you show to others *you* look upon with grief, and everything that it shows to you, you have believed, because it witnesses to the guilt that you have projected away from you and onto them.

5.   Now into your mind, which the Holy Spirit has made Gentle, the Holy Spirit lays a different picture of the body that you identify with in your perception that you are in a world. It is still a *picture of a body*, because What you really are, you cannot see or picture. But this picture you do not use for attack, so it does not suffer pain at all. It witnesses to the Eternal Truth that you cannot be hurt, and it points beyond itself to the Innocence that fills your entire mind.

6.   It is not your Will for Life, but your wish for death, that is your motivation for making a world separate from God. Its only purpose is to prove to you that your separation from God is real, and that therefore you are guilty. Every thought that you have about the world, and every act or feeling that you have in it, has this sole motivation. These are the witnesses that you call forth to believe in and to lend conviction to the separation that they speak

for and represent. These witnesses have many voices, but their message is always the same. Your adorning the body only seeks to show you how lovely is your witness to guilt. Your concerns about the body demonstrate how frail and vulnerable your 'life' is in the world, and how easily what you love is destroyed. Your depression represents death, and your vanity is not concerned with anything Real at all.

7. Your sickness, in whatever form it takes, is your strongest witness to the futility of the personal self's 'life' in the world that you perceive, the one that bolsters all of your other witnesses to help them paint a picture in which you see pursuing further separation as justified. In sickness, you have a reason for each of your unnatural desires and strange needs, because, in a life so soon cut short, how could you not esteem the worth of passing joys? No pleasure in the world that you perceive can endure, so, in your frailty, you feel entitled to every stolen scrap of pleasure as your righteous payment for your little 'life'. Whether or not you enjoy their benefits, your death will pay the price for all of them. However you spend your 'life' in the world, it must end, so grab whatever passing pleasure you can.

8. These are not 'sins', but witnesses to your strange belief that separation from God and death are real, and your innocence and sin will end together in the grave. If this was true, you would have reason to remain content to seek for passing joys and little pleasures. But in this you do not perceive that the body is neutral, and that it has no inherent goal within itself. Instead, the body is your symbol of reproach; a sign of your guilt, which still shows the consequences of your sin, which you cannot deny.

9. Your function is to demonstrate to yourself that separation from God is not real, and your guilt does not have a cause. It must seem futile to see yourself as a picture that is proof of what can never be! The Holy Spirit's picture of the body does not change it into something it is not. The Holy Spirit only takes away from it all signs of your guilt and accusation. Without a purpose, you see the body as neither sick, nor well; neither bad, nor good. There are no grounds to judge the body at all. It has no life, but it is also not

dead. It cannot experience Love or fear. It witnesses to nothing, and with its purpose being open, your mind is now free to choose again what it is for. Now it is not condemned, but it waits for a purpose to fulfill.

10. When the goal of separation has been removed from your mind, you are free to remember Heaven in the empty space that the body represents. Here, Peace can come, and perfect healing can take the place of death. The body can become a symbol of Life, a promise of correction, and a hint of Immortality. Let it have healing as its purpose, and it will represent the message that it has received, and, by its health and loveliness, proclaim the value of the Truth it represents. Let it receive the power to represent an Endless Life, forever free from attack by separation and guilt.

11. The simple way for you to let this be achieved is for you to let the body be free from the personal mind's past purposes. In the past, you were sure its purpose was to foster guilt in others, and your crippled picture of it was a lasting sign of this. Your past view of the body leaves no space for a different purpose to be given to it. You do *not* know its purpose. You have given an illusion of purpose to a thing that you made to hide your Function of Oneness from yourself. This thing without a purpose cannot hide the function of forgiving that the Holy Spirit gives to you. Let the body's purpose and your function be reconciled and see them as one.

2. The Fear of Healing

1. You may find physical healing frightening. Accusation is a bar to Love, and a damaged body accuses. It stands firmly in the way of trust and Peace, proclaiming that in its frailty it cannot trust, and that it has no grounds for Peace. If you have been injured by someone or something outside of you, how can you love and trust? You have been attacked, and you will be attacked again. A damaged body shows you that you must be protected from a world outside of you. Your forgiving, then, becomes an act of charity, not something justified. You may pity the separate world for its guilt, but you do not exonerate it. Your forgiving then becomes a way of

adding to all the guilt that the world has earned.

2.   You are not forgiving when you are presenting an unhealed body, because it is a witness that you believe that your forgiving is not justified. The body retains the consequences of the guilty world that you are supposed to overlook. You cannot forgive an attack that you believe is real, and if you see its consequences manifest in the body, it must be real to you, because what it has done is there for you to see. Forgiving is not pity, which only pardons what is supposed to be true. Good *cannot be* returned for evil, because real forgiving does not first make sin real and then forgive it. You cannot say, 'You have injured me, but, because I am better than you, I forgive you' and really mean to forgive. Your forgiving cannot exist with hurt that is supposed to be real. Each denies that the other is real.

3.   For you to witness to someone separate from you harming you, and then for you to forgive them, is a contradiction that the Holy Spirit's True Reasoning cannot see. Your manifesting harm indicates that you believe something real has happened, so it cannot be undone. 'Forgiving' this way means that you grant mercy, while retaining proof that True Innocence is not real. When you are sick, you remain an accuser, unable to forgive the world that you perceive or yourself. But, when you truly forgive, you will not manifest suffering, because you will not hold onto 'proof' of harm, which you will have overlooked as an illusion. To heal your mind, your forgiving must be for yourself as well as all the illusions that your mind perceives. In the body's healing is your proof that you have truly forgiven, and that you retain no trace of guilt to hold against yourself or to project onto anything that your mind perceives.

4.   Your forgiving is not real unless it brings healing to you, and to your perception of your mind where you perceive a world. To demonstrate that the sins of the world that you perceive are not real, you must attest that they have no effects. How else can you see your Innocence, or see It justified, unless you see that your perception of separation from God has no effects? If your separation from God was real, it would be beyond forgiveness, because it would entail effects that you could not undo and

overlook entirely. But in separation's undoing lies your proof that it is merely an error. Forgive yourself by accepting healing and extend salvation to be all that your mind perceives.

5.   A broken body shows that your mind has not been healed. A healed mind extends a miracle to the body to heal it and to manifest that separation from God is not real. When you want to manifest this, you will believe it. The power of witness comes from your belief, and everything that you say or do or think testifies to what you want to teach yourself. The body can be a means to teach you that you have never suffered pain from illusions. In its healing, you offer mute testimony of the total Innocence of your Mind. This testimony can speak with great power, because it is here that your forgiveness is proved.

6.   The healing of the body shows that your mind is healed and has forgiven what has never really happened. So a miracle undoes all the things that the personal mind attests can never be undone. Hopelessness and death disappear before the Clear Call of Life, Which has a Power far beyond the weak and miserable cry of death and guilt. The Call of God to you, and of you to your Extension of God, will be the last sound that you will ever hear. There is no death, and you learn this when you no longer wish to project away from yourself the cause of the pain that you experience by your choice to be separate from God and your mind where you perceive a world.

7.   Miracles are Just, because they bestow on you the gift of full deliverance from guilt to be all that your mind perceives. Healing encompasses your entire mind, and you are healed when you wish that your entire mind is healed. In your experience of the miracle, you see no specialness at all, because the miracle comes from Love, Which is Oneness, not from pity, which is for the separate. The Oneness of Love proves that all suffering is but a vain illusion and a foolish wish for separation that has no effects. The body's health is the result of you no longer wishing to project the source of your pain and guilt onto the world that you perceive. What you wish is what you see.

8.   Your Serenity will 'cost' you the separation, because Oneness must

become all that you perceive. This is the 'price' that the Holy Spirit and the personal mind interpret differently. The personal mind sees this as a statement of the 'fact' that your salvation comes selfishly at the expense of a real world that is separate from you. The Holy Spirit knows that the world is only a perception in your mind, and that your mind's healing cannot be apart from its perception. As long as you perceive a suffering world as real, you will be unhealed. Yet, you can teach yourself that suffering is without a purpose and has no real cause. Heal, and you will no longer consent to suffer, because Innocence will be re-established in your awareness. Laughter will replace your sighs, because you will remember that you are One with God.

9. You fear physical healing when you believe that your sickness makes the world guilty, that the world must be guilty for you to be happy, and that your healing would then represent the world's release from guilt, and your own loss of happiness. The constant sting of guilt that you perceive that the world suffers for your sickness seems to prove to you that it is limited, and that you are free. The constant pain that you suffer seems to demonstrate to you that you are free of guilt *because* you hold the world to guilt. You want sickness to prevent a shift in the balance of guilt. The Holy Spirit will not be deterred an instant to reason with this argument for sickness, and your need of healing does not need to be delayed because you stop to listen to this insanity.

10. Consider how this self-perception must extend, and do not deny the fact that mind always extends itself, because that is its purpose. If your mind is split between 'you' and a world outside of you, then the function of these two parts must be split as well. And then, what you want to correct is only half of the error which you think is all of it. Your target for correction is the world that seems outside of you, so that you don't see that your errors and the errors of the world are happening in the same mind. *You* make *mistakes,* and the world's *sins* are not your own. The world merits punishment, while your mistakes should be overlooked.

11. In this interpretation of correction, you don't even see your own mistakes. The focus of correction is outside of you, on a world that

you do not want to see as part of you while you perceive it as sinful. You hate the world as a symbol of your fear. This 'unworthy' world *must* be outside of you; it *must* be denied as part of you. Only the part of your mind that is not the world – the isolated personal self – can you perceive as 'you'. To you in this identification, the Holy Spirit must represent the rest of your mind until you recognize that what you perceive *is* the rest of your mind. The Holy Spirit does this by giving you and what you perceive a function that is one, not different.

12. Your function is to extend correction through your perception. When it is fulfilled, your corrected perception corrects your mind. You cannot heal your perception without healing your mind, since what you perceive is in your mind. If one was healed and the other wasn't, your mind would remain divided, which is not the Holy Spirit's Purpose of Oneness. Oneness is the only Purpose that the Holy Spirit fulfills, and, in doing so, the Holy Spirit preserves *your* Purpose, despite you seeing your purpose as something else. If the Holy Spirit upheld a divided purpose, you would indeed be lost. But the Holy Spirit's inability to see a goal that separates your mind from its perceptions saves you from a purpose that is not yours, and this is how healing is given to you.

13. Your correction must be left to the Holy Spirit, Which knows that your correction and your forgiveness are the same. You cannot understand this with only part of your mind. Leave correction to a Mind that is One, because it is not split in purpose, and It sees only one function for Itself. Its function of correction comes from God. In the Holy Spirit's acceptance of this function lies the means by which your mind is made One in your awareness again. As you forgive your perception of a world that is separate from your mind, you accept that what you perceive is part of your mind.

3. Beyond All Symbols

1. Everything is its purpose, so True Power cannot oppose anything, because opposition intends to weaken and limit. Power that opposes, then, is actually weakness and limitation. A 'weakened power' is a meaningless contradiction. To be Itself, True Power in

unopposed and opposes nothing. If it is weak, it is not Power. To weaken is to limit and to impose an opposite that contradicts the concept that it attacks. Double concepts like 'weakened power' and 'love/hate' are unintelligible.

2. For you, the world that you made is a symbol of contradictory concepts that cancel out each other: Love and hate, weakness and power, life and death. It is meaningless, and it stands for nothing but an empty space in your mind. Emptiness cannot interfere with your awareness of Reality, except when you believe that something is there.

3. The picture of a world that you see in your mind means nothing. There is nothing to attack, or to deny; to love, or to hate; to endow with power, or to see as weak. This picture cancels out itself with its contradictory ideas, and it has no cause at all. There is no effect without a cause; what isn't caused is nothing. The picture of a world that you see is really an empty space in your mind, so recognize that it is vacant, and that the time that you devote to it is occupied with nothing.

4. An empty space and unoccupied time in your mind, when you recognize them as such, can become your silent invitation to the Truth to enter and make Itself at home. You don't need to make any other preparation, because what you leave empty, God will fill, and where God is, the Truth is. Power without opposite is What God's Oneness is. There are no symbols for this, because no symbol can stand for Everything. But true undoing must be kind, and the first replacement for your picture of a world of separation is another kind of perception.

5. Just as you cannot picture nothingness, there is no symbol for Totality. You ultimately know Reality without form; you cannot picture It or perceive It. You do not yet know that your forgiving is a power that is wholly free of limits, and that it does not set any of the limits that you want to impose. Your forgiving is the means by which Truth is temporarily represented to you in your perception that you are in a world. It lets the Holy Spirit exchange your perceptions, until such aids are meaningless and your learning is done. When a learning aid's function has been accomplished, its use

is over. Yet, while you are learning to forgive, it has a use that you now fear but will love one day.

6.   The Perception that the Holy Spirit will give to you to occupy the space in your mind that you leave unoccupied by a world of separation does not need defense of any kind, because you will give It overwhelming preference. Nor will you delay in deciding It is the only perception that you want. It does not stand for double concepts, and even though It is incomplete, It is all the same within Itself. It does not cancel out God, Which wants to complete It, so God is free to take the final step of completing It. What will ultimately take the place of every learning aid simply *is*.

7.   Forgiveness will vanish and symbols will fade, and nothing that the body's eyes have ever seen or its ears have ever heard will remain for you to perceive. God's Limitless Power will come to you, not to destroy, but to receive Its Own. There is no choice of function in God, and the choice that you fear to lose you have never really had. Only your perception of choice seems to interfere with the Unlimited Power of One Thought, Complete and Happy, and without opposite. You do not know the Power of Peace that never opposes, but there can be no other power. Welcome the Power that is beyond your forgiving and beyond the world of symbols and limitations. God *is*.

4. The Quiet Answer

1.   In Quietness, all things are answered, and every seeming problem is quietly resolved. In conflict, there is no resolution or answer, because its purpose is to make resolution impossible and to make sure that no answer is plain to you. A problem set in conflict cannot have an answer, because you see it in different ways, and what is an answer from one point of view is not an answer from another point of view. In your identification with a personal self, you *are* in conflict, so it must be clear that you cannot answer anything there. But God has given you the Holy Spirit as the Answer to conflict, so there must be a way in which your problems are resolved. What God wills has already been done.

2.   So time must not be involved in the Answer to your problems, and

It must be able to answer your every problem *now*. In your separated state of mind, solution is impossible, so God has given you a way of reaching another State of Mind in Which the Answer *is*. This is the Holy Instant, Where all of your problems should be brought and left. They belong Here, because their Answer is Here. It is pointless for you to try and solve problems where their Answer cannot be.

3.   Attempt to solve problems only in the Certainty of the Holy Instant, because Here the problem *will* be resolved. There are no real answers outside of the Holy Instant, because outside of It you never really ask a simple question. The world that you perceive can only present double questions, and a question with many answers has no answer. The personal mind does not ask a question to be answered, but only to restate its point of view.[1]

4.   All questions asked by the personal mind are not really questions, but they are a means of reinforcing separation in your mind. A question asked in Self-hate cannot be answered, because it is an answer in itself. A double question asks and answers, each attesting the same thing in different form. The personal mind asks only one question, though in different forms: 'Of these illusions, which of them is true? Which illusions can bring me Peace and Joy? Which illusions can bring me escape from all of the pain from which this world is made?' Whatever form they take, the purpose of the personal mind's questions is to make separation from God real to you. Its answer is always for you to choose a form of separation that you prefer, and the other possible answers will become not 'true' for you. So what does the personal self want most? The body is your servant and your friend, so tell it what you want, and it will serve you lovingly and well. The personal mind's questions state that you want separation, and its answers tell you where to go to find it. The personal mind does not question its beliefs, because its questions are really only statements that separation from God is real.

5.   A pseudo-question has no answer; it dictates the answer even as it is asked. The personal mind's questions are actually propaganda for itself. Just as the body's witnesses are its own senses, the

answers to the personal mind's questions are always within the question itself. You learn nothing new from them. But an honest question is a learning tool that asks for something that you do not know. It does not set conditions for response, but asks what the response should be. In the conflict of a personal mind, you are not free to ask honest questions, because you don't really want an honest answer that will end your conflict.

6. Only within the Holy Instant can you honestly ask an honest question. A Meaningful Answer comes to you then, because by going to the only Real Answer, you are asking for It, no matter the form of your question. The personal mind's wishes are separated from the Answer, so you can receive It. The Answer is provided everywhere, but it is only in the Holy Instant that you can hear It. An Honest Answer cannot offer you further separation, because It only answers a questioner that is asking for Truth. The personal mind's questions, however, ask how to perpetuate separation from God, not if separation from God is real. When you identify with a personal self, unless an answer comes in terms of the world that you perceive, then you will not recognize or hear it, and the separation will be preserved in your mind, because the personal mind asked the question of itself. But the Holy Instant is the interval in Which your mind is still enough to hear an Answer that is not included in the question. It offers Something new and different from the question. An answer that repeats the content of the question is not a real answer.

7. Don't attempt to solve problems in a world from which the only Real Answer has been barred. Bring your problems to the Holy Instant, Which lovingly holds the Answer for you. Here, the Answer that solves your problems stands apart from your problems, because It sees what your question *really* is. The personal mind's answers only raise further questions in your mind. In the Holy Instant, you bring the question to the Answer, and you receive the Answer that was made for you.

5. The Healing Example

1. The only way for you to extend healing in your perception is for

you to first accept healing for yourself. The miracle extends God's Love in your awareness without your help, but you are needed for it to begin. Accept the miracle of healing and it will extend, because it is natural for it to do so the instant that it is begun. And a miracle is begun the instant that you receive it. You cannot ask for healing from someone or something outside of you, but you can accept healing for yourself, and then extend it in your awareness. You can extend only what you have. The Holy Spirit speaks to *you*, and, through your listening, the Holy Spirit extends in your awareness, because you have accepted what the Holy Spirit says.

2.   The body's health is your witness to a healed mind. As long as healing is not manifested in the body, your belief in healing will not have conviction. Healing is proved by demonstration that compels your belief. You cannot be healed by teaching yourself conflicting messages. If you wish only to be healed, you will heal. A single purpose makes this possible, but if you are afraid, you will not accept healing. The only thing required for your healing is a lack of fear, because you cannot heal when you are afraid of healing. This does not mean that conflict must be gone from your mind entirely, because then you would have no need for healing. But it does mean that, for an instant, you perceive that Oneness, not separation, is Real. An instant is enough, because miracles are not bound by time.

3.   The miracle abides in the Holy Instant. From the Holy Instant, each miracle is brought forth in your perception as a witness to a State of Mind that has transcended conflict and reached Peace. The miracle carries comfort into your mind, which perceives a conflicted world, and demonstrates that the conflict has no effects.

4.   You are not sad where a miracle has come to heal. The only thing you need for a miracle to occur is just one Instant where you accept Oneness in place of separation. In that one Instant, you are healed, and all healing is done. There is no separation in your mind when you accept the blessing that the Holy Instant brings. Do not be afraid of blessing, because the Holy Spirit, Which blesses you, loves your entire mind, and leaves nothing to fear in your perception. But, if you shrink from blessing, you will perceive a frightening world of death as real, because you will have withheld Peace and

Comfort from your mind.

5.   Your perception of a bereft world must seem like condemnation to you, who can choose to see salvation instead, but who have stepped back from doing so, because you are afraid of healing your mind. Your perception of a world of death and suffering presents you with the question: 'What is there to fear in healing?' This question is asked on your behalf. Your mind asks only that you rest an instant from attacking yourself with the perception of a world of separation, so that it can be healed.

6.   Come to the Holy Instant and be healed, because you leave nothing behind Here when you return to perceiving yourself in a world. Being blessed, you will bring blessing with you. Life is given to you to extend to replace your perception of a world of death. Having given up suffering, you will no longer look on a world that accuses you of separating from God, but Gratitude will shine in your mind as you extend blessing in your perception. The Holy Instant's Radiance will give you your Real Perception to look beyond all suffering, and see your Christ Mind instead. Healing replaces suffering, because you cannot perceive both in the same place. What you perceive witnesses to your mind, as your mind witnesses to what you perceive.

7.   For you to perceive only healing, all that is required is that you accept only healing for your mind. Your mind needs to learn only the one perfect lesson of forgiveness, and when you forget it, your Real Perception will gently remind you of the lesson of forgiveness that you have taught yourself. Your gratitude will reinforce this, because you will let yourself be healed, so that you can perceive only Love. You will look on Witnesses to Christ, because you will extend Christ to Witness to It. The world that seemed to accuse you of separating from God will be replaced by a perception of Oneness, which will release your mind from limitation.

8.   Your problem of separation is not specific, but it takes specific forms. and these make up the world that you perceive. You do not really understand that the nature of all of your problems is your perception that your separation from God is real, because if you did, they would no longer be there for you to see. Since you cannot

be separate from God, the very nature of any problem in the world that you perceive is that it does not exist. But while you perceive it, you do not perceive it as the nothing that it is. So your healing first shows up in the world in specific instances, and then you will generalize it to include all seeming problems. This is because all seeming problems are the same, despite their different forms. All of your real learning aims to be transferred to everything, and it will become complete when you see two situations are the same, despite their differences in form. This will only be attained by the Holy Spirit in your mind, because It does not see the differences that the personal mind sees. The total transfer of your learning to encompass everything that you perceive is not made by you in your identification with a personal self. You will be convinced that the differences could not be real when the transfer has been made in spite of all of the differences that you perceived.

9. Your healing will extend, and it will be brought to problems that you do not even perceive as your own. As you escape any one problem, it will be apparent that your many different problems will be solved. You will realize that the problems are the same, despite their seemingly different forms, because learning does not jump to opposite situations and bring the same results. All healing proceeds in an orderly manner in accord with the Law of Oneness when It is properly perceived, but not when It is violated. Do not fear the laws that the personal mind perceives, because they do not work, but the Holy Spirit within you knows the Law that *does* work.

10. Leave the transfer of your learning to the Holy Spirit, Which understands the Law of Oneness. The Holy Spirit will guarantee that this Law remains inviolate and unlimited within you. Your part is only to apply to yourself what the Holy Spirit teaches you, and the Holy Spirit will do the rest. All of the different witnesses to your learning that you perceive will prove your learning to you. Your Holy relationship is the first you see correctly, but beyond this relationship are thousands more in the world that you perceive. Each relationship may seem to be a different form of separation than the rest, but they will all be solved together. Their common Answer shows you that the question that they represent was the same.

11. Peace be to you to whom healing is extended! You will learn that Peace is given to you when you accept It for yourself. You do not need to appraise Its Total Value to understand that you have benefited from It. What occurs the Instant that Oneness enters your mind and undoes separation will stay with you Forever. Your healing will be one of Its effects. All of the witnesses that you behold will be far lfewer than all that there really are. You cannot understand Infinity by counting up Its separate Parts. God thanks you for your healing, because God knows it is a gift of Love to your Self, therefore it is given to God.

6. The Witnesses to Sin

1. Physical pain demonstrates that the body must be real. It is a loud, obscuring voice whose shrieks are meant to keep the Holy Spirit's Voice from reaching your awareness. Physical pain compels your attention, drawing it away from the Holy Spirit to be focused on the body. The purpose of physical pain is the same as physical pleasure, because both are meant to make the body real to you. What shares a common purpose is the same. It is the law of purpose that what shares in a purpose unites within that purpose. Physical pleasure and pain are equally unreal, because their purpose is to make the body real, which cannot be achieved. They are the means for nothing, because their goal is without meaning. They share the lack of meaning of their purpose.

2. Your perception that you are separate from God is a state where you are constantly shifting between pain and seeming pleasure. Both witness to the same thing: You are a personal self within a body that can be hurt and that can also feel pleasure, but only at the painful cost of Reality. Pain and pleasure come in many forms, and you call them by many names, but all have the same purpose. Call pleasure pain, and it will hurt you; call pain pleasure, and the pain will seem to fade from you. Your witnesses to separation from God shift from name to name as one steps forward and the other steps back, but they all hear the call of death.

3. The body, without a purpose in itself, is the repository of the personal mind's memories and hopes. From the personal mind,

you use the body's eyes to see, its ears to hear, and you let it tell you what it feels. *But it does not know.* The personal mind tells you what to call the pain and pleasure that witness to the body's reality, but you cannot choose which are real, because they are all equally unreal. All that you do is give pain different names and sometimes call it pleasure. But you do not make a witness true just because you have called it 'Truth'. What isn't true is a lie, even if you call it 'God'.

4. God's Witnesses do not witness against the body, nor do they recognize the witnesses to the body's reality. God knows that the body is not real, because nothing can contain you who are One with God, nor can the body tell you what it feels or what its function is. But God must love what you hold dear, and for each of your witnesses to the body's death, the Holy Spirit sends a Witness to your Eternal Life in God. Every miracle that you experience is a witness that the body is not real. God heals the body's pains and pleasures alike, because God's Witnesses replace all of your witnesses to separation from God.

5. When you experience the miracle, you do not distinguish between the forms that separation's witnesses take, because the miracle merely proves that the separation that they represent has no effects. The miracle's own effects take the place of the forms of suffering, no matter what you called them. The Holy Spirit, Which perceives all of your suffering as the same, calls all of suffering's forms *fear of God.* As your fear witnesses to death, your extension of God's Love that is the miracle witnesses to Life. It is a witness that you cannot deny, because it brings the Effects of Life: the dying live, the dead rise up, and pain vanishes. The miracle does not speak for itself, but for God, Which it represents.

6. Love also has Its symbols in your mind where you perceive a world of separation. The miracle forgives, because it stands for the Truth that is beyond forgiving. It is foolish and insane for you to think that miracles are bound by laws they came to undo. Your laws of separation from God have different witnesses with different strengths, and they attest to different sufferings. Yet, to the Holy Spirit, Which sends forth miracles to replace your perception of a

miserable world with a perception of blessing, a tiny stab of pain, a little worldly pleasure, and the throes of death are a single call for healing and help from your split mind. Your experience of the miracle proves the sameness of these illusions, because they are all undone together. The laws that call them different are dissolved and shown to be powerless by the miracle. Accomplishing this is the miracle's purpose, and God has guaranteed the strength of miracles, because they witness to God.

7. Be a witness to the miracle, and not to the laws of separation. There is no need for you to suffer anymore, but you do need to be healed, because the suffering and sorrow of the world that you perceive have made you deaf to salvation and deliverance.

8. Your Real Perception waits to be resurrected in your awareness, so that you may demonstrate your healed and Happy Mind. The Holy Instant will replace all of your perceptions of separation, if you carry Its effects with you. You will no longer elect to perceive suffering, and what better function can you have than this? Be healed, so that you may extend healing to be all that you perceive, and do not suffer from the laws of separation. Truth will be revealed to you, who chose to let Love's symbols take the place of your perception of separation.

7. The Dreamer of the Dream

1. Your suffering emphasizes to you that the world that you perceive has injured you. Here, you can clearly see the personal mind's demented version of salvation. Just like in a dream of punishment that you have at night when you sleep, you are unaware that it is you who brings an attack against you, and you see yourself unjustly attacked by something or someone who is not you. You are the victim of something or someone outside of you, and you have no reason to be held responsible for the attack. You must be innocent, because you don't know that it is you who does it, but you only know that it is done to you. But ideas do not leave the mind of the thinker, so it is obvious that the attack on you comes from you, because you are the one suffering. You cannot escape attack by perceiving the source of the attack as outside of you.

2. Now you are being shown that you *can* escape. All that you have to do is look on the problem as it is, not as you have set it up. This is the only way for you to solve a problem that is very simple but that has been obscured by complications that you made to keep the problem unresolved. Without obscuring complexity, the problem will emerge in its simplicity. Your choice to have it resolved will not be difficult for you, because the problem is absurd when you see it clearly. You won't have a difficult time letting a simple problem be resolved when you see that it is hurting you, and that it is easily removed.

3. The purpose for the world that you made, on which it rests, and by which it is maintained, is to be the source of your pain. In your perception that you are in a world, you exist and think apart from everyone and everything. The world is the cause of what you do. Its injustice justifies your wrath. The world attacks, so you are the innocent one, and what you suffer from is the world's attack. And from the perspective that you are a little self in a world, it does look as if the world is hurting you, so from this perspective you don't think that there is any need to go beyond the obvious to find the source of your pain.

4. There is indeed a need to look. Guilt is in your mind, no matter that you project it away from you so that you can perceive it in a world outside of you. Your mind needs to escape the idea of guilt completely. But you are afraid that if you do your part, all the guilt that you see in the world will rest on you, and you believe that accepting this guilt as your own is actually your part in God's plan for your deliverance. So, for you vengeance must have an external focus, otherwise you will see that it is coming from you, and that it is directed toward you. You must see it coming to you from outside, so that you can be a victim of an attack that you did not choose. You must suffer from an attack that has not come from you.

5. You made the world to hide your own responsibility for your pain, and, in the guilty world that you perceive, it is as though the world fulfills this purpose. But the guilty world is in *your* perception, and it *attests* to your pain; it is not the *cause* of your pain. And you will not change the fact that you are the cause of your pain by seeing the

cause as something else. The guilty world in your perception and your pain both witness that your mind is their cause, not that one causes the other. Look beyond the world in your mind, because it is not the cause of your separation from God or of your suffering. And do not dwell on the separation and suffering of the world that you perceive, because they only reflect the error in your mind.

6.   The part that you play to relieve yourself from a perception of a guilty world is your own escape from guilt. Do not forget that you see an evil world because you have a need to see it. This is where you first saw your guilt. The split of your mind into 'you' and a world outside of you was the first attack upon yourself, and this attack is what you perceive in the world. Do not look for another cause for your pain, or look among the many legions of witnesses to your guilt for its undoing. Your witnesses to guilt support your allegiance to guilt. What conceals the Truth is not where you should look to find the Truth.

7.   Your witnesses to separation from God are all in one little space in your mind. It is here that you find your perspective on the world. Once, you were unaware of the cause of everything that the world thrusts upon you, uninvited, and unasked. But you were sure that of all the causes of your pain and suffering, your guilt was not among them, nor did you in any way request pain and suffering. All illusions come about and are maintained by your not seeing that you make them, and by your denying that their seeming reality depends on you. You must see them as separate from your mind, and whatever cause they have must be something separate from you. You do not doubt the reality of your illusions when you do not see the part that you play in making them and in making them real to you.

8.   You cannot undo illusions that you deny are your own. In your denial, you must be part of a world that has a cause other than you. You are a helpless victim of a reality conceived and cherished by a separate mind. This mind doesn't care about you, and it is as thoughtless of your peace and happiness as it is of the weather and the time of day. It doesn't love you, but it casts you in a role that satisfies itself. Your worth to it is so little that you are a dancing

shadow leaping up and down according to the senseless plot conceived within this mind that idly makes the world that you are in.

9. If you are not the one who makes your illusions, this is the only picture that you can see, the one alternative that you can choose, the only other possibility of the cause of the world that you perceive. This is what you are choosing when you deny that the cause of your suffering is in your own mind. Be glad that it *is* in your mind, because then you are the one to decide your destiny in time. The choice for you to make is between a sleeping death and dreams of evil, and a happy awakening and Joy in Life.

10. Your only choices are between Life and death, awareness and denial, Peace and conflict, Reality and illusions. You may confuse death with Peace, because the personal mind equates the body with the Self that is One with God. But a thing can never be its opposite, and death is the opposite of Peace, because it is the opposite of Life, Which *is* Peace. Awaken and forget all thoughts of death, and you will find that you have the Peace of God. But to see your choices, you must see their causes exactly as they are and where they are.

11. You cannot make a choice between two states when you recognize only one clearly. You are not free to choose between the effects of two states when you see yourself as the cause of only one of them. You can never perceive an honest choice as one in which their causes are split between a tiny you and an enormous world outside of you, each with their different ideas about the truth in you. The gap between Reality and illusions is not between the world and what goes on in your private mind. They are one. The world that you perceive is the part of your own mind that you have projected away and see as though it is its own source. But the world was started by your own secret wish to be separate from God, which you do not perceive, although you see it in the world, and you do not doubt that it is real. How can you doubt that the world is real while you are in such denial, and you believe that the separation that caused it is real?

12. Your illusion of a separate world outside of yourself is one where you are stalked by an attacking world and your inevitable death.

But underneath this illusion is another belief, in which you are the guilty one, the murderer of God, and the destroyer of the world. *This* is the little space in your mind between your illusions and your Reality. This little gap that you do not even see is the birthplace of your illusions and of your fear; of time with all of its terrors, hate, and disasters. This is the cause of your unreality, and it is here that it can all be undone.

13. You are the maker of the illusion of the world. It has no other cause and never will. Nothing more fearful than an idle illusion terrifies you and makes you think that you have lost your Innocence, denied God, and attacked yourself. So fearful is this illusion, and so seemingly real, that you cannot accept Reality without terror and mortal fear, unless a gentler perception precedes It in your awareness and allows your calmer mind to welcome, not fear, the Holy Spirit, Which calls you to Reality. God wills that you remember Reality gently and with Joy, and God has given you the Means to do so without fear.

14. Accept the Holy Spirit's Perception in place of the world of separation that have you made. It is not difficult to change what you perceive when you recognize that you made it. Rest in the Holy Spirit, and allow the Holy Spirit's Gentle Perception to take the place of your illusions of terror and fear of death. The Holy Spirit brings a forgiving Perception in which your choice is not between who is the murderer and who is the victim. There is no murder or death in the Holy Spirit's Perception. Your perception of guilt will fade from your sight, although you will not be wholly aware of God yet. Peace will come to you first in your perception of Happiness.

15. Gently perceive your mind's Holy Innocence in your relationship with one other in the world. From this perception, God will remind you of your Oneness with God. Overlook the personal mind's perceptions of mistakes, and be grateful to the other for the opportunity to forgive yourself your illusion of separation. Do not brush aside the gift that the other offers to you, because they are not perfect in the sight of the personal mind. Your perception of them can represent God to you, and you will see in them Life or death,

according to what you think God offers to you.

16. God extends only Life to you. But what you see as the purpose for your relationship with another in the world that you perceive represents what you believe God extends to you. In charity and kindness to yourself, see your relationship with another as offering you only an opportunity to perceive the Life that God extends to you, and let no pain disturb your appreciation for what it gives to you.

8. The 'Hero' of the Dream

1. The body/personal self is the central figure in your illusion of the world. There is no illusion without a body/personal self, and it only exists within the illusion in which it acts as though it was a real self to be believed in. A body/personal self takes the central place in every seemingly separate story in the illusion, which tells of how it was made by other bodies, was born into a world outside of itself, lives there a little while, and then dies, uniting in the dust with other bodies. In the brief time allotted for it to 'live', it seeks for other bodies/personal selves to be its friends and enemies. Its safety is its main concern, and its comfort is its guiding rule. It looks for pleasure and avoids pain. Above all, it tries to teach itself that its pains and joys are different and can be told apart.

2. Stories of bodies/personal selves in your illusion of the world take many forms, because your split mind seeks in many ways to prove it is independent of God and real. Each personal self puts things on its body that it has bought with little metal discs or paper strips, that it has declared are valuable and real. It works to get these doing senseless things, then spends them for senseless things it does not need and does not really want. It hires other bodies/personal selves to protect it and to collect more senseless things that it can call its own. It looks for special bodies/personal selves that can share its 'life'. Sometimes, it has the illusion of conquering other bodies/personal selves that are weaker than itself. Sometimes it is the slave of bodies/personal selves that want to torture it.

3. The serial adventures of a body/personal self, from birth to dying,

are the theme of every story in the world that you perceive. The 'hero' in these illusions, and his or her purpose, will never change. Though the illusion takes many forms and has a great variety of places and events where the 'hero' finds him- or herself, the illusion has only one purpose taught in many ways again and again: The world is the cause of you, and you, as one of these 'heroes' in one of its stories, are its effect.

4.   So you are not the maker of the illusion; you are *in* the illusion, which seems like your reality. It *is* true that the body/personal self only wanders in and out of places that the world contrives, because it is only part of the illusion of the world. But you wouldn't react to figures in an illusion unless you thought that they were real. The instant that you see them as they are, they will have no effect on you, because you will understand that you give them their effects by causing them and making them seem real to you.

5.   Are you willing to escape from the effects of all of your illusions of the world? Are you willing to stop letting your illusions appear to be the cause of you? Look at the beginning of your illusion, because the part that you see as the world is only its effect. In your denial and identification with a personal self, you do not remember your attack on yourself. You don't believe that there was a time when there was no body and you could never have conceived of a world. You would have seen these ideas as one illusion and too ridiculous for anything but to be laughed away. How serious they appear to be now! You don't remember when you would've laughed at them in disbelief. But you can remember this if you look directly at the cause of your illusions. Then you will see cause for laughter, not for fear.

6.   Return to your mind the illusion that you made but have projected away, so that it seems separate from you and done to you. Into Eternity, Where All is One, there crept a tiny, mad idea of separation at which you who are One with God forgot to laugh. In your forgetting, the thought became serious to you, its accomplishment seemed possible, and its effects seemed real. With the Holy Spirit, you can laugh these effects away and understand that time cannot intrude on Eternity. It is a joke to think that time can

avoid Eternity, Which means there is no time.

7. A Timelessness in Which time is real, a Part of God that attacks Itself, a part of your mind that seems separate and outside that attacks you, and a mind within a body are all forms of circular thinking that end where they began in your mind. The world that you perceive depicts exactly what you thought that you did. But now you think that what you did is being done to you. You project your guilt for your perceived attack on God outside yourself and onto a guilty world that depicts your thoughts and illusions. You do not see that the world's vengeance on you is your own. The world keeps you confined to a limited body, which it punishes because of all of the 'sinful' things that you do in your identification with it. You have no power to stop the body/personal self from doing its evil deeds, because you did not make it, and you cannot control its actions, purpose, or fate.

8. Your illusion of the world does to you exactly what you uncon- sciously believe that you do to it. Once you are deluded into blaming the world, you will not see that you are the cause of what the world seems to do, because you *want* the guilt to rest on it. This is the childish and petulant device that you use to keep your innocence by pushing your guilt onto a world outside of you. But this does not release the guilt in your mind. It is not easy for you to perceive that your guilt is not necessary when your eyes behold its heavy consequences all around you, but never look on its cause as impossible. When you won't see that the cause is merely your own erroneous perception that you are separate from God, these effects seem serious and sad indeed. But they only follow from a cause that is nothing and can only be a joke.

9. The Holy Spirit perceives the cause of your guilt with gentle laughter and does not look at its effects. This is how the Holy Spirit corrects your error, the cause of which you have entirely overlooked. The Holy Spirit asks you to look with It on each terrible effect of your guilt that is made manifest in the world that you perceive, so that you may laugh together at your foolish belief in separation from God, which is their cause. You look at the world and judge the effects of guilt, but the Holy Spirit judges their cause.

By the Holy Spirit's Gentle Judgment, the effects are removed from your mind. Maybe you come in tears, but enter the Holy Instant and hear the Holy Spirit say to you, 'You are One with God, and it is only an idle illusion that separation from God can occur' and you will leave the Holy Instant with your entire mind joining in laughter with the Holy Spirit.

10. The secret of your salvation from a world of separation and attack is this: You are doing this to yourself. No matter what form the attack takes, this is true. Whoever takes the role of attacker, this is true. Whatever seems to be the cause of any pain and suffering you feel, this is true. You would not respond at all to figures in an illusion if you knew that it was an illusion. No matter how vicious and hateful they may be, they could not have an effect on you unless you failed to recognize that they were in *your* illusion.

11. Learn this single lesson, and you will be free from suffering in all of its forms. The Holy Spirit will repeat this one lesson of deliverance, regardless of the form of suffering that brings you pain, until you have learned it. Whatever hurt you bring to the Holy Spirit, It will answer with this very simple truth, because this answer takes away the cause of your every form of sorrow and pain. The form does not affect the Holy Spirit's answer at all, because the Holy Spirit teaches you that the single cause of them all is your own erroneous belief that you are guilty for separating from God. And you will understand that all miracles that you experience reflect this simple statement: 'I have done this thing, and it is this that I want to undo.'

12. Bring all forms of suffering to the Holy Spirit, Which knows that they are all the same. The Holy Spirit does not see differences where none exist, and the Holy Spirit will teach you how each form of suffering is caused. Your perception that you are guilty for separating from God is the cause of them all, and all of them are undone by you learning a single lesson truly. Salvation is a secret that you have kept from yourself; Reality proclaims that this is so. But you do not heed Reality's Witnesses, because they attest to the Oneness that you do not want to know. They seem to keep Reality secret from you, but you need to learn that you choose not to see Reality.

13. How differently you will perceive the world when you recognize this! When you forgive your perception of guilt, you will be free of the world. You do not have to perceive your guilt elsewhere to be Innocent; your Innocence does not depend on a sinful world outside of you. This is obvious, a secret that you keep from yourself. And it is your belief that *something* has to be guilty for you to be Innocent that has kept the world that your mind perceives separate from you. Now you need to learn that you and what your mind perceives are either both Innocent or both guilty. It is impossible that what your mind perceives be unlike your mind, or that your guilt and your Innocence be true together. This is the only secret that you need to learn, and when you do, it will be no secret that you are healed.

Chapter 28

The Undoing of Fear

1. The Present Memory

1. Your experience of the miracle doesn't do anything; it undoes. It cancels out all of your interference to God, Which *is*. It does not add to your mind; it takes away what *is not* from your mind. What it takes away is long since gone, but, being in your memory, it seems to have effects *now*. The world that you perceive was over long ago. The thoughts that made it are no longer in your mind, which thought of it and loved it for a little while. Your experience of miracles shows you that the past is gone, and what has truly gone has no effects. Your remembering a cause can only produce an illusion of its presence, not real effects.

2. All of the effects of your belief that your separation from God is real are not here, because that belief is gone from you. Its consequences went with it. You only cling to its memory, because you want its effects. Remembering is as selective as perception, because it is perception's past tense. It is perception of the past as if it is occurring now and is still here to see. Like perception, memory is a skill that you made up to take the place of your Oneness with God. Like all that you have made, memory can be used to serve the Holy Spirit's Purpose. If you wish, it can be used to heal and not to hurt.

3. What you use for healing does not require effort, because healing is your recognition that you don't have any needs that require that something be done. It is an unselective memory that is not used to interfere with Truth. The Holy Spirit can use everything that you give to the Holy Spirit for your healing, but without the content and the purpose for which you made them. They are neutral skills that wait for an application and use. They have no dedication and aim of their own.

4. The Holy Spirit can use your memory, because God is in your memory. But this is not a memory of Something past, but of a

present State. You are used to thinking that memory holds what is in the past, but it is a skill that can remember *now*.[1] The limitations that the personal mind imposes on your memory are as vast as the limitations that you let it impose on you. There is no link between your memory and the personal self's past, unless you want to put it there. Only your desire for it made this link, and only you have held memory to a part of time where guilt appears to linger.

5.   The Holy Spirit uses memory apart from time. The Holy Spirit does not use it to hold onto a personal self's past, but as a means to let go of the past. Memory holds the message it is given; it does not write the message or appoint what it is for. Like the body, it has no purpose in itself. If it seems to serve your cherishing of an old hate, and if it gives you pictures of injustices and hurts that you are holding onto, it is because this is what you have given it to do. The personal self's 'story' is committed to your memory's vault. All of the strange associations that you make to keep the personal self's past alive and the present dead to you are stored within it, waiting for you to call on them so that you can live them again. This is how time seems to increase the past's effects on you and to hide their cause.

6.   Time is just another part of illusions. It works hand-in-hand with all the other ideas that you use to conceal the Truth about yourself. Time cannot take away or restore anything. But in your identification with a personal self, you make a strange use of time: What happened in the personals self's past caused what is in the present, so the present is only a consequence of the past, and it cannot be changed, because the past is gone. But when change happens, it *must* have a cause that is present, or it will not last. Something cannot be changed in the present if its cause is in the past. The way that the personal mind uses memory is to hold onto the personals self's past, so it is a way of holding that past against *now*.

7.   Do not remember anything that the personal mind has taught you, because you were taught badly. You do not want to keep a senseless lesson in your mind when you can learn and preserve a better one. When old memories of hate appear, remember that their cause is gone so you cannot understand what they are for. Do not let a cause

that you give them now be what makes them what they seemed to be in the past. Be glad that they are gone, because they are what you want to forgive yourself. Instead, perceive the new Effects of accepting *now* that God is your Cause, Which has consequences *here*. They will surprise you with their Loveliness. The 'new' ideas that they bring will be the Happy Consequences of a Cause so ancient that It far exceeds the span of memory that you see in your perception.

8. God is the Cause that the Holy Spirit remembers for you when you want to forget It. God is not past, because the Holy Spirit cannot forget God. Your Memory of God has never changed, because the Holy Spirit has always kept God safely in your memory. The Consequences of remembering God will indeed seem new to you, because you thought that you forgot their Cause. But God is never absent from your mind, because it is not God's Will that Part of God forget God.

9. What you remember through the personal mind never was. It came from nothing, which you confused with a real cause. It can only deserve laughter when you learn that you have remembered consequences that have no cause. In your experience of the miracle, you remember that God is your Cause, Forever Present, perfectly untouched by time and interference, and never changed from What It is. You are God's Effect, as Changeless and as Perfect as God. Your Memory of God does not lie in the past, or wait for the future. It is not revealed to you in the experience of the miracle, which only reminds you that you can no longer deny God.

10. You have sought to lay a judgment on God, so you cannot understand that it is not God Which has laid a judgment on you. You want to deny God Its Effect, but God's Effect has never been denied by God. Never at any time can you be condemned for what has no real cause and is against God's Will. What you remember through the personal mind only witnesses to your fear of God. God has not done the thing that you fear; no more have you done the thing that you fear. Your Innocence has not been lost. You do not need healing to be Whole. Quietly see in your experience of miracles lessons in allowing Cause to have Its Own Effect, without interference.

11. The miracle comes quietly into your mind when you stop an Instant and are still. It reaches gently from that Quiet Instant, and from your mind, which is healed in that Instant, to extend to be all that you perceive. And What you perceive will do nothing to prevent your mind's extension back into the Mind Which caused it to be. Born from you extending your mind, the miracle is not delayed by any pause in time to bring an Instant's Stillness to be all that you perceive, and to return the Memory of God to you. Your remembering is Quiet now, and you will not wholly forget What has come to take the place of the personal mind's memories when you return to time.

12. The Holy Spirit thanks you for every Quiet Instant that you give to It. In that Instant, you allow your Memory of God to offer you all of Its Treasures, Which have been kept for you. How gladly the Holy Spirit offers them to you, for whom the Holy Spirit has kept them! God shares the Holy Spirit's Thanks to you, because God does not want to be deprived of Its Effect. The Instant of Silence that you accept into your mind welcomes God and Eternity and lets them enter where they want to abide, because in that Instant, you do nothing that makes you afraid.

13. The Memory of God arises in your mind the Instant that you have no fear to keep the Memory away. In that Instant, the personal mind's remembering is gone; there is no fearful image of the past to stand in the way of your awakening to the Presence of Peace. Eternity extends throughout the Stillness of your mind, and What you remember now is not fear, but God, Which fear was made to undo and make you forget. The Stillness speaks of Love that you remember from before the personal mind's remembering of the past came between you and the present to shut out Love.

14. Now you are at last aware of your Present Cause and Its Benign Effect. Now you understand that what you made has no cause and no effects at all. You have done nothing, and you have never had any need to do anything. God the Cause is Its Own Effect, and there is no other cause that can generate a past or future. God's Effect is Changeless, Eternal, beyond fear, and entirely past a world of separation.

15. What do you lose by no longer seeing what has never existed?

Where is your sacrifice when your Memory of God has come to take the place of loss? There is no better way for you to close the gap between illusions and Reality than to allow your Memory of God to flow across it and make a Bridge that it will take you only an Instant to cross. God has closed the gap with God. Your Memory of God has not passed you by to leave you stranded with no way to reach God. God wills that you be gently carried over the Bridge to God. God is the Bridge, God built the Bridge, and It is God that will carry you over the Bridge. Do not fear that God will fail in What It wills, or that you will be excluded from a Will that is for you.

2. Reversing Effect and Cause

1. There can be no effects without a cause, and every cause has effects. A cause is *made* a cause by its effects; God is your Creator *because* you are God's Creation. Effects do not cause their cause, but they do establish their cause's causation. So God's Effect makes God a Cause, and God's Effect must receive the Gift of causation that God's Effect has given to God. It is *because* you are God's Effect that you must also be a cause yourself and extend God as God extends God to you. Creation is Boundless and One; without beginning and without ending.

2. God's Extension is Creation. Love must be extended; Purity is not confined. It is the nature of Innocence to be Forever uncontained, without barriers, and without limitations. So your Purity is not of the body, and you cannot find It where there is limitation. The body can be healed by the Effects of your Purity, Which are as Limitless as Purity. But all healing must come about because you recognize that your mind is not within a body, and your mind's healing and Innocence are apart from a body. Healing, then, is only where its Cause is given Its Effects. Your sickness is a meaningless attempt to give effects to an unreal cause to make it seem real.

3. In sickness, you are always trying to be your own cause and to not allow yourself to be God's Effect. For this impossible desire, you must not believe that you are Love's Effect, and you must cause yourself because of what you think you are. The Cause of healing

is the only Cause of Everything, and It has only One Effect. In recognizing this, you recognize that what is not of God has no cause and no effects, and you can't see its supposed effects. A mind within a body within a world of other bodies, each with its separate mind, are the 'creations' of your split mind, causing effects that are unlike you in Reality. But as their 'creator', you must think that you are like them.

4. Nothing at all has happened, except that you have denied God, which has resulted in an illusion in which you are an alien to yourself and supposedly a part of someone or something else's mind. Your experience of the miracle does not return you to God, but it shows you that you make the illusion. It teaches you that there is a choice of illusions while you still want them, depending on what you see as the purpose for them. Do you wish for illusions of healing or for illusions of death? An illusion is like a memory in that it pictures what you want shown to you.

5. All of the personal mind's shreds of memories and illusions are held in a place in your mind that is empty of Reality. But since you are the maker of the illusion, you can perceive that you have caused the illusion, and you can accept another illusion in its place. To change the content of the illusion that you do not like, you have to realize that it is you who make it. It is only an effect that *you* have caused, and you must choose to not be the cause of this effect. In your illusions, where you project your guilt for separating from God onto an attacking and murderous world, you see yourself as a victim in a dying body, but in your forgiving illusions, no one is the victim and sufferer. These are the happy illusions that the miracle exchanges for your own. It does not ask you to make another illusion, only that you see that you made the one that you want to exchange for a happy one.

6. The world that you perceive is causeless, as is every illusion that you make in your perception that you are in the world. None of your plans there is really possible, and no design exists for your 'life' in it that you can truly understand. What else can you expect from a thing that has no real cause? Since it has no cause, it has no purpose. You may cause an *illusion*, but you will never give it real

effects, because that would change its cause, you, and it is this that you cannot do. As a maker of illusions, you are not aware of God, but you also do not know that you are in denial. You see illusions of yourself as sick or well, depressed or happy, but without a stable cause with guaranteed effects.

7.   Your experience of a miracle establishes for you that you make illusions, and that their content is not true. This is a crucial step for you in dealing with illusions. You will not be afraid of illusions when you realize that you make them up. Your fear is held in place, because you do not see that you are the author of the illusion and not a figure in the illusion. You give yourself the consequences that you gave to another to cause. And it is this that the illusion puts together and offers you to show you that your wishes have been done. So you really fear your own attack, but you see it at another's hand. If you see yourself as a victim, you suffer from the effects of the attack, but not its cause. You do not want to see that you caused the attack, so that you can see yourself innocent of it. But underneath you know you did this to yourself, and your experience of the miracle only shows you that you have done nothing real. What you fear is a cause that is without real effects that would make it a cause, and so it never was.

8.   Your perception of separation from God started with your illusion that you deprived God of Its Effect, and that God was powerless to keep you, since God was no longer your Cause. In this illusion you, who made the illusion, also made yourself into the personal self. But the personal self that you made has turned against you, taking on the role of its own creator, just as you as the maker of illusion think that you made yourself. And as you as the maker of illusion hate God, so the figures in your illusion hate you. The body is their slave, which they abuse, because the motives that you have given to them they have adopted as their own. They hate the body for the vengeance that it offers to them. It is their vengeance on the body that appears to prove to you that you could not be the maker of the illusion. First, you split off effect from its cause, then you reverse them so that the effect becomes the cause and the cause becomes the effect.

9. This is separation's final step, the one with which salvation begins because it proceeds the other way. This final step is an effect of what has gone before, appearing as a cause. Your experience of the miracle is your first step in giving back to Cause the function of causation, not effect. Your confusion of cause and effect produced your illusion, and while it lasts, you will fear becoming aware of God again. Nor will you hear God's Call, because It will seem to be to you the call to fear.

10. Like every lesson that the Holy Spirit requests that you learn, the miracle is clear. It demonstrates what the Holy Spirit wants you to learn, and it shows you Its effects are what you want. The effects of your illusion of separation from God are undone in the Holy Spirit's forgiving Perceptions, and the figures in your illusion that were your hated enemies you will perceive as benign. You will see their enmity as without cause, because they did not make it, and you will accept the role of maker of their hate, because you will see it has no effects. Now you will be free from this much of the illusion. The world that you perceive is neutral, and you do not need to fear the bodies that seem to move around in it as separate things, so they are not sick.

11. Your experience of the miracle returns the cause of fear to you, who made it. But it also shows that, having no effects, fear is not caused, because the function of causation is to have effects. Where effects are gone, there is no cause. The body is healed by miracles, because they show you that the mind made sickness and employed the body to be victim, or effect, of what it made. But this is only half of the lesson. The miracle is useless if you learn only that the body can be healed, for this is not the lesson it was sent to teach. The lesson is always that the *mind* was sick that thought that the body could be sick. Projecting the mind's guilt onto the body caused nothing and had no real effects.

12. The world in your mind is full of miracles, which stand in silence next to every illusion of pain and suffering, of sin and guilt. They are the alternative to your illusion of separation, your choice to be the maker of the illusion rather than to deny your active role in making up the illusion. They are the happy effects of you taking

back the consequences of sickness to their cause – you. The body is released when your mind acknowledges: *This is not done to me, but I am doing this.* Then your mind is free to make another choice. Beginning here, your salvation will proceed to change the course of every step in your descent to separation, until all of your steps have been retraced, the ladder has been removed, and the illusion of a world is undone.

3. The Agreement to Join

1. What waits for you in Perfect Certainty beyond salvation is not the concern of this course. You have barely started to allow your first uncertain steps to be directed up the ladder that your perception of separation from God has led you down. The miracle alone is your present concern; this is where you must begin. Having started, your way will be made Serene and simple as your illusion of separation from God ends, and you become aware of Reality again. When you accept the experience of a miracle, you do not add to your illusion of fear. Without support, your illusion will fade away without effects, because it is your support that strengthens it.

2. You cannot perceive a sick mind until you agree that there are separate minds, and you decide to be sick and to perceive sickness. If you withdraw agreement from a perception of sickness, and you accept that it is your part that makes sickness real to you, you undo separation, and your projection of guilt onto another in the world that you perceive. Then, you do not perceive the body as separate from your mind, therefore it cannot be sick. Uniting in your mind what seems like 'you' and your perception of a world outside of you prevents the cause of sickness – separation – and its perceived effects. Healing is the effect of your united mind, as sickness comes from your split mind.

3. Your experience of the miracle does nothing just *because* your Mind is One and cannot separate. But in your illusion, you have reversed this, and it seems as though your mind has been separated into many bodies which cannot join. Do not perceive sickness as real anywhere, or you participate in your illusion of separation. You will not see that the cause of sickness is your own belief in it, and

you will be looking on the separation where sickness is bred. You will join with sickness to preserve unhealed the little gap in your mind where sickness is carefully protected, cherished, and upheld as real to keep God from bridging the gap. Do not use illusions to fight God's coming into your awareness, because It is God that you want above all things in your illusion.

4.   The end of your illusion of separation from God is the end of your fear. Love has never been in the world that you perceive. The gap in your mind is little, but it holds the seeds of pestilence and every form of illness, because it is your wish to keep your mind separated. So this gap seems to be the cause of sickness, but it is not sickness' cause. The *purpose* of the gap is all the cause that sickness has. The purpose of the gap is to keep your mind separated and in a body that you see as if it were the cause of your pain.

5.   The cause of your pain is your perceived separation from God, not the body, which is also only an effect of the separation. But the separation is only an empty place in your mind, enclosing nothing, doing nothing; an insubstantial gap that is easily closed over. You have no grounds for sickness when your mind joins itself to close the little gap that seemed to exist between you and what you perceive, where the seeds of sickness seemed to grow.

6.   God builds the bridge over the gap in your mind in the space left clean and vacant by your experience of the miracle. God cannot bridge sickness and guilt, because God cannot destroy a will that God did not create. Let the effects of this alien will be gone, and do not clutch them with eager hands to keep them for yourself. Your experience of the miracle will brush them all aside to make room for God, Which wills to come and bridge your returning to your True Self.

7.   Count your experiences of miracles and your illusions of True Happiness as all the treasures that you want to keep in your perception that you are in a world, and bring your perceptions of separation to them for correction when you confuse illusions with Truth. The world is nothing but a little gap in your mind where you believe that you tore apart Eternity and broke It into days and months and years. And within the world, *you* seem to be a picture

666

of a Mind that has been broken into many pieces, each concealed within a separate insecure body.

8. Do not be afraid, but let your perception be lit by your experience of miracles. Join your mind where you saw a gap between 'you' and a world that seemed outside of you, and you will see that all sickness is without a cause. The illusion of healing lies in your forgiving your perception of separation, which gently shows you that you never sinned. Your experience of the miracle will leave you no proof of guilt to bring you a witness to what never was. And, in your perception, the miracle will make a place of welcome for God and your True Self. Your Loving Perceptions will replace with Oneness all of your perceptions of separation.

9. Your Loving Perceptions are unlike what you perceive in your illusion of a world of separation. Unlike in the world of lack, the more Love that you extend the more you are aware that you have Love. God's Love is Limitless, and you cannot be deprived of It. What God extends to you, you share in equally with God. There is no gap between you and God. Time does not wait for Love, Which has no end, and Love has bridged the space in your mind that seemed to keep you apart from God.

4. The Greater Joining

1. Accepting correction of your perception that you are separate from God means that you do not give support to illusions of sickness or death, no matter where they seem to arise in the world that you perceive. It means that you do not wish your mind to be separated into 'you' and a world outside of you and to turn illusions on yourself. So illusions will have no effect on you, and you will be free of perceptions of pain. Unless you overlook illusions of pain in the world that you perceive, you will suffer pain, because pain will be your wish, and you will become a figure in illusions of pain. So both 'you' and your mind's perceptions will be illusions and without your Real Identity. You will be anything or anyone, depending on your illusion, but you will think that you are evil, because your illusions are frightening.

2. There is a way for you to find certainty right here and now: Refuse

to be part of fearful illusions, whatever form they take, or you will lose your Identity in them. You find your Self by *not* accepting them as causing you and making you their effect. You stand apart from illusions, but not apart from the mind which makes them. Separate the illusion from its maker, and identify with the maker while letting the illusion go. The illusion is *in* your mind and the mind is you; the illusion is not you. It is the illusion that you fear, not the mind that makes it. You think that they are the same, because you think that you are a figure in your illusion. What is Real in you and what is illusion in you, you do not know, and you cannot yet tell apart.

3. The figures in your illusion think that they are real, but do not participate in this, because your Identity depends on the Reality in your mind, Which encompasses them. Your Oneness is not with the body/personal selves of 'others', but with your mind, where they seem to be. The Reality in this part of your mind is your Reality. The body/personal selves of others only seem to make a little gap in your mind between a 'you' and a 'them'.

4. And yet, there is no gap between 'your' mind and what your mind perceives 'out there' as a world. For you to believe in the illusion of other selves is for you to *not* unite your mind, because the illusion of others as real and separate is meant to separate *your* mind. Release your mind by acknowledging your Oneness with your mind where you perceive a world, but not with frightening illusions in it. If you support your illusions of others as really separate from you, you will believe that you are a separate self, and you will be bound to illusions. Illusions of fear will haunt this little gap in your mind, which is inhabited by illusions that you support in your mind within, and that you project outward onto a world.

5. Be certain that if you do your part in forgiving illusions your mind will join in Oneness. Do not call on your illusions of others to meet you in separation, or you will believe that you are an illusion of a separate self. You do not do your part when you are passively a part of an illusion instead of accepting yourself as maker of the illusion. Your identity in an illusion is meaningless, because, as effect and cause, an illusion and its maker are one. You must be

your own illusion, because, by making it, you are cause and it is effect.

6. You are confused, and you perceive confusion, because in the gap in your mind, you do not have a stable self. Your mind, which is all the same, seems to have differences. Your perception of others' illusions is your illusion, because you let it be. But if you take away your part in making illusions, you free your mind of all illusions. Others' illusions seem to attest to yours, and yours to theirs, but if you see that Truth is not part of making any illusions, all illusions will go from your mind.

7. The Holy Spirit is in you and in your perception, and the Holy Spirit is One, because there is no gap that separates Oneness from Itself. The gap that seems to be between bodies in the world that you perceive does not matter, because a mind that is One in the Holy Spirit is always One. There is no sickness when you perceive Oneness. Your desire to be a sick and split mind cannot remain without a witness or a cause, and sickness and separation are gone when you will to unite your mind. You have an illusion that your mind is separated, but by not participating in it, you leave the split in your mind empty for God to join your Mind, Which the Holy Spirit *has* joined.

8. The Holy Spirit's Function is to take the image of disconnected things that is the world that you perceive and replace it with a Perception of Oneness. The Holy Spirit extends Oneness in place of every disconnected thing that you thought was whole unto itself. To each thing the Holy Spirit extends Its Identity, Which is Oneness, to replace an image of separation. When you see Oneness, you will recognize your True Self. If you do not participate in any illusion of separation, Oneness is What your experience of the miracle will place in the little gap in your mind left clean of sickness and your belief in separation. Here, God will receive you who are One with God, because you are gracious to yourself.

9. *Thank you, God, for coming to close each little gap that seems to lie between the disconnected images in my mind. Your Holiness, Complete and Perfect, encompasses every image, and they are all joined, because*

What surrounds one surrounds all of them. How Holy is the smallest grain of sand when I recognize that it is part of my Complete Mind! The forms the images take mean nothing, because my Whole Mind encompasses each one, and every aspect of my Mind is the same as every other aspect.[1]

10. Do not join with illusions, but join the Mind where the illusions occur. God is where you join Part of God. You will not seek for substitutes to God when you perceive that you have not lost God. You will not want the 'benefits' of sickness when you have received the simple happiness of health. What God extends to you cannot be lacking, and what is not of God has no effects. What, then, do you want to perceive in the gap in your mind where separation seems to be? Sickness comes from your belief that there is joy in separation, and that giving it up would be a sacrifice for you. But the experience of miracles is the result for you when you do not insist on seeing what is not there in the gap in your mind. Your willingness to let go of illusions is all that the Holy Spirit requires of you. The Holy Spirit will place healing where sickness seemed to be, and you will not experience loss, only gain.

5. The Alternative to Dreams of Fear

1. Sickness is a sense of limitation, a splitting *off*, and a separating *from*. It is a gap that you perceive between you and what you see as 'health'. When you are sick, you see the good outside and the evil within, so sickness is separating yourself off from good to keep the evil within. God is the Alternative to your illusions of fear. When you participate in illusions of fear, you cannot extend God, but withdraw your mind from illusions, and you *will* extend God. There is no other choice. Unless you participate in something, it cannot exist. And you exist because God extends Its Will to you so that you can extend God.

2. It is your participation in perceptions of hate and malice, bitterness and death, separation and suffering, and pain and loss that makes them real to you. If you do not participate in them, they will be meaningless to you, and you will not fear them, because you will not give them your support. Where fear is gone, Love must come,

because there are only these two alternatives in your mind. Where one appears, the other disappears, and the one which you participate in becomes the only one that you have. You have the one that you accept, because it is the only one that you wish to have.

3. You are not participating in illusions of separation if you forgive their maker, and you perceive that you are not the illusion that you made. Your forgiving separates you from your illusion of separation and releases you from it. Remember, if you participate in an illusion of separation, you will believe that you are the illusion that you think you are in. And fearing it, you will not want to know your own Identity, because you will think that It is frightening. You will deny your True Self and walk in illusions that are alien to God, because God did not make them, and, in them, you seem to be something that you are not. You will attack your True Self, Which will seem to be your enemy, and you will attack your mind's perceptions as part of What you hate. There is no compromise: you are your True Self or an illusion. There is no middle ground between Truth and illusion, because if you are a thing that is not you, you must be an illusion and not the Truth.

4. You have made a little gap between illusions and Truth to be a 'safe' place where your True Self is hidden by what you have made. Here, you have established a sick world for the body's eyes to perceive. Here are the sounds and the voices that its ears were made to hear. Yet the sights and sounds that the body perceives are meaningless. The body cannot see or hear; it does not know what seeing is or what listening is for. It cannot perceive or judge or understand or know. Its eyes and ears are blind and deaf to Truth. It cannot think, so it cannot have effects.

5. Nothing God created can be sick, and what God has not created cannot be. Do not behold an illusion or hear what bears witness to illusions. You made the body to look on a world that is not here, and to hear voices that make no real sound. But there are other sights and sounds that you can perceive and understand. The body's eyes and ears are senses without sense, and they can only report what they see and hear. It is not they that perceive, but your mind perceives, and it puts together every senseless bit of

separation as witness to the world that you want. Do not let the body's eyes and ears perceive these countless fragments within the gap that you imagine is there in your mind and persuade you that your imaginings are real.

6. Creation is Reality, because it shares the Function of Oneness throughout Itself. Reality does not depend on unconnected bits and fragments that are put together to make it Truth. There is no gap within Truth for illusions of place and time, because Truth fills Everywhere and Everything and makes them Wholly One.

7. You who believe there is a little gap in your mind do not see that you are a prisoner in a world that you perceive exists there. The world that you perceive does not exist, because the gap in your mind where you perceive it is not there. The gap is carefully concealed by an illusion of a world that is no more substantial than a shifting fog but the gap is nothing. There are no secrets there where terror rises from your belief in death. Look at the little gap in your mind, and behold your Innocence in the emptiness of your belief in separation from God, which you will see when you have lost your fear of recognizing Love.

6. The Secret Vows

1. It is insane for you to punish the body. The body represents the gap in your mind, but it is not responsible for it. The body does not judge itself or make itself what it is not. It does not seek to make pain into joy or seek for pleasure in nothingness. It does not tell you what its purpose is, and it cannot understand what it is for. It cannot victimize, because it has no will, no preferences, and no doubts. It does not wonder what it is, so it has no need to be competitive. It can be victimized, but it cannot feel it is a victim. It does not accept a role but does what you tell it to do, without attack.

2. It is indeed senseless for you to hold the body responsible for sights that it cannot see and to blame it for sounds that it cannot hear. The body has no feelings to suffer your punishment of it. It behaves in the ways that you want it to, but it never makes the choice of behavior. It is not born, and it does not die. It aimlessly follows the

path that you set for it, and if you change your mind, it easily goes the other way. It takes no sides and makes no judgment of the road it travels. It does not hate, so it sees no gap in your mind. You can use it for hate, but you cannot make it hateful.

3. The body does not know the separation that you hate and fear and loathe and want. You make it to seek for separation and to be a separate thing, then you hate it, not for what it is, but for the use that you have made of it. You shrink from what it sees and from what it hears, and you hate its frailty and littleness. You despise its acts, but not as your own, though it sees and acts for you. It hears what you want it to hear, and it is frail and little by your wish. It seems to punish you, so you think that it deserves your hatred for the limitations that it brings to you. But *you* have made it a symbol for the limitations that you want your mind to have, to see, and to keep.

4. The body represents the little bit of mind that you call your own apart from God, which is kept separate from all the rest of your Mind. You hate it, but you think it is your *self*, and that without it you will lose yourself. You make a secret vow with your perception of every other 'self' that seems to walk apart from you to preserve the separateness of this 'self'. This is the secret oath that you take whenever you perceive yourself attacked. You cannot suffer, unless you see yourself attacked and losing by the attack. Your every pledge to sickness is unstated and unconscious, but it is your promise to be hurt by something or someone outside of you, and then to attack back at it or them to preserve your separation from God.

5. Sickness is anger that you take out on the body so that it will suffer pain. It is the obvious effect of the vow that you make in secret to maintain a separate self with a world outside. It can have no effects if you recognize that the separation is only in your mind. When you say, 'All that I perceive is in my mind' you keep God's Promise of Oneness, not a tiny oath to be faithful to death. Heal your mind, and you heal all that is in your mind.

6. Look on all that you perceive as a part of your mind, not as something separate, and you keep God's Promise of Oneness, as

God keeps this Promise with you. In your Oneness with God, God says, 'You are beloved of Me and I of you, Forever. Be you as Perfect as Me, because you can never be apart from Me.' You do not remember that in your Christ Mind you say, 'I will', though in that Promise God extends God to you. God reminds you of this every time that you do not participate in a perception of sickness, but you let your mind be healed and unified. Your secret vows are powerless before the Will of God, and you share God's Promises. What you substitute for God's Will is not your Will, because you have promised yourself to God.

7. The Ark of Safety

1. God does not ask for anything and neither does your Christ Mind, Which is One with God. There is no lack in your Mind. An empty space or a little gap would be a lack. It is only there that you could want something that you seem to not have. A space in your Mind where God is not, a gap between God and your Christ Mind, is not the Will of Either, because They are One. God's Promise is a Promise to God's Self, and there is no Part of God that can be untrue to What God Wills. The Promise that there is no gap in God cannot be false. What can come between What is One?

2. The beautiful relationship that you have with your mind's percep-tions is a part of you, because it is a Part of God. You are sick if you deny yourself your Wholeness and your Health, the Source of Help and the Call to heal. Your Christ Mind waits for your healing, as does everything your mind perceives. You are not apart from what your mind perceives, because healing for your mind is One or not at all, since Oneness is Where healing is. The Opposite of separation is what heals separation. There is no middle ground in any aspect of salvation; you accept it wholly or not at all. What is not separated must be One, and what is One cannot be separated.

3. Either there is a gap between you and your mind's perceptions, or your mind is One. There is no in between, no other choice, and no allegiance that you can split between the two. A split allegiance means that you lack faith in both and merely sends you spinning and grasping at anything that seems to hold some promise of relief.

You cannot count on just anything for stability. A body is a home like this, because its foundation is not the Truth. But, because it has no foundation, you can see it is not your home, but merely an aid to help you reach your Home, Where God abides.

4.   With *this* as its purpose, the body is healed, because you do not use it to witness to your illusion of separation and disease, nor do you blame it for what it did not do. It serves to help your healing, and for this purpose, it cannot be sick. Because it is in your mind, it cannot join a purpose that is not yours, and you have chosen that it not be sick. All miracles that you experience are based on this choice, and they are given to you the instant that you make it. No forms of sickness are immune, because your choice cannot be made in terms of form. Your choice of sickness seems to be of form, but sickness is one, as is its opposite. You are sick or you are well.

5.   But sickness or wellness are never limited to you in a personal identity. In your perception that you are in a world , you have an illusion of yourself as an isolated self whose thoughts do not affect what seems outside of you. When you identify with a personal self, it means that you believe that you are separate from the rest of your mind, which you project outside of you as a world, and then of course you are sick. And your sickness seems to prove that you must be separate. But all it really means is that you are committed to lacking faith that only God is Real, and this *is* sickness. The world that you perceive seems to be quite solid and substantial, but a structure's stability cannot be judged apart from its foundation. If its foundation is not solid, it does not matter how much you secure the building; it will fall under the slightest pressure.

6.   There is no sense in you seeking for security in a world that you made for danger and fear. The world's weakness lies not in itself, but in the frailty of the little gap in your mind where it stands. The world rests on a shadow, so why would you build your home on what will fall under the slightest weight?

7.   Your Home is built on your mind's perception of Health, Happiness, Innocence, and Everything that God has promised to you. No secret promise for separation that you have made has shaken the Foundation of your Home. Nothing can affect It, and,

though the world will fade from your mind, this Home will stand Forever, because Its Strength is not within Itself alone. It is a Haven of Safety resting on God's Promise that you are Safe in God Forever. No gap in your mind can interpose itself between this Shelter and Its Source. From here, you can see the body as the learning aid that it is, its worthiness determined by the extent to which you use it to liberate your Mind from the limits of the personal self. With this Holy Purpose, the body is made a home of Holiness a little while, because it shares God's Will with you.

Chapter 29

The Awakening

1. The Closing of the Gap

1. There is no time, no place, no state where God is absent from you. There is nothing for you to fear. There is no way in which you can conceive of a gap in the Wholeness of God. The least little gap would be a compromise in God's Eternal Love, and this is quite impossible, because it would mean that sometimes God's Love is hate, sometimes God's Gentleness is attack, and sometimes God's Eternal Patience fails. But this is what you *do* believe when you perceive a gap in your mind between you and your mind's perception. How can you trust God if sometimes God is not-God? God's Love is deceptive to you then, so you are justified in being wary and in not letting God come too close. So you leave a gap between you and God through which you can escape if you need to.

2. Here you plainly see your fear of God. If you hate your own perceptions, you are afraid of Love, and you perceive Love as a threat to you. And if you are afraid of Love, you are afraid of God, and it is certain that you don't know what Love means. You fear to love and you love to hate, so you think that Love is fearful and hate is Love. This is the consequence when you cherish the little gap between you and God, and you think that it is your salvation and your hope.

3. Your fear of God, the greatest obstacle that Peace must flow across, is not yet gone from your mind. The other obstacles are past, but this one remains to block your path, and to make the way to Love seem frightening, perilous, and bleak to you. You have decided that part of your mind is outside of you and is your 'enemy'. Sometimes you make friendships in the world that you perceive as long as your separate interests make friendship possible for a while. But a gap must remain between you and others, because they may turn into an 'enemy' again. You make agreements for

limited relationships in which maintaining separation is agreed upon by all the parties involved. Violating this is a breach of the agreement and not to be allowed.

4. The gap between you and the rest of your mind is not the space between bodies. Bodies only *seem* to divide up your Mind into many separate minds. Through the body/personal self, your joining with others in the world that you perceive substitutes for True Oneness. You can meet with other personal selves when you prefer, and separate until you agree to meet again. Then you seem to get in touch with them again, but it is always possible for each of you to go your separate ways. Conditional on the 'right' to separate, you will agree to meet from time to time with others, making sure that there are intervals of separation that protect you from the 'sacrifice' of love. The body 'saves' you, because it spares you total sacrifice, and it gives you time in which to build the personal self away from other personal selves, because you believe it is diminished when you meet with others.

5. The body/personal self cannot separate your mind from the rest of itself, unless you want it to be a cause of separation. Your desire for separation is how you endow the body/personal self with a power that it does not have, and you give it power over you. You think that it determines when you meet with other bodies/personal selves, and that it limits your Mind's Oneness. You think that it tells you where to go and how to go there; what it is feasible for you to undertake and what you cannot do. It dictates what the body's health can tolerate, what will tire it, and what will make it sick. And the body's 'inherent weaknesses' set up limitations on what you can do and keep your purpose limited and weak.

6. The body/personal self will do all of this if you want to have it so. It will allow you limited indulgences in 'love', with intervals of hatred in between. It will take command of when you 'love', and when you should shrink into the 'safety' of fear. The body will be sick, because you do not know that Love means Oneness. And you will misuse each circumstance and relationship in the world, and see in them a purpose that is not your True Purpose.

7. Love does not ask you for sacrifice, but fear demands that you

sacrifice Love, because fear cannot abide in Love's Presence. To maintain hate, you must fear Love, Which you allow to be sometimes present and sometimes gone. You see Love, then, as treacherous, because It seems to come and go uncertainly, and It never offers you stability. You do not see how limited and weak your allegiance to Love is, and how frequently you demand that Love go away and leave you in 'peace'.

8.   The body, which has no goal of its own, is your excuse for your own variable goals, which you force it to maintain. You do not fear the body's weakness; you fear its nothingness. Do you want to recognize that nothing stands between you and your perceptions, and that there is no gap in your mind behind which you can hide? There is a shock that comes to you when you see Christ instead of an 'enemy' in your perception of another. You feel wary when you learn that the body is not real. And you hear overtones of fear around the happy message 'God is Love'.

9.   Eternal Peace is all that happens when the gap in your mind is gone. Nothing more and nothing less. Only your fear of God can induce you to abandon God, because what does the world that you perceive offer that seems to hold you back an instant from God's Love? You allow the body/personal self to say 'no' to God's Call, because you are afraid that you will lose yourself in God. But can your Self be lost by being found?

2. The Coming of the Guest

1.   Why don't you perceive learning that you are free of the limitations of the personal mind as relief from suffering? Why do you look on the Truth as your enemy instead of welcoming It? Why does an easy path, so clearly marked it is impossible for you to lose your way, seem thorny, rough, and far too difficult for you to follow? It is because you see the road to God as the road to hell instead of as a simple way that asks no sacrifice or loss of you. You will have some regrets about the way to God that you have chosen until you realize that you give up nothing for it, and that you lose nothing on it. You do not see the many Gains that your choice offers to you, but though you do not see Them, They are here. Their Cause has

been Effected, and They must be present where Their Cause has entered.

2.   You have accepted the Cause of healing, so it must be that you are healed. Being healed, you have the power to extend healing. Your experience of the miracle is not a separate thing that happens suddenly to you as an effect without a cause. Nor is it a cause in itself. But a miracle's Cause must be where you experience a miracle. A miracle is caused now, though you do not yet perceive it. Look inward now, and you will not see reason for regret, but Cause indeed for glad rejoicing and for hope of Peace.

3.   It has been hopeless for you to try to find Peace in conflict. It has been futile for you to demand escape from separation and pain from the body that you made to serve the function of maintaining separation and pain. Pain and separation are one illusion, as are hate and fear, and attack and guilt. Where they are without cause, they are gone, and Love must come where they are not. Why aren't you rejoicing? You are free of pain and sickness, misery and loss, and all effects of hatred and attack. Pain is no longer your friend, and separation is no longer your god, and you should welcome the Effects of Love.

4.   The Holy Spirit *has* come. You asked the Holy Spirit to come, and the Holy Spirit is here. You are not wholly aware of the Holy Spirit, because you do not wholly welcome the Holy Spirit. Yet, the Holy Spirit's Gifts of Love come with It. The Holy Spirit offers Them to you, and asks that you accept Them as your own. The Holy Spirit needs your help in extending Them to be all that you perceive. Your mind will be healed when you accept your Gifts, because the Holy Spirit will extend them to all that you perceive.

5.   You do not see how much you can extend in your awareness because of Everything that you have received. But the Holy Spirit, Which you invited into your awareness, waits for you to look on It. There is no place other than your mind where the Holy Spirit can find you, or where you can meet the Holy Spirit. There is nowhere but your mind where you can obtain the Holy Spirit's Gifts of Peace and Joy and all the Happiness Its Presence brings. The Holy Spirit's Gifts are within you with the Holy Spirit. You cannot see the Holy Spirit, but you can

see in your perception the Gifts that the Holy Spirit brings. When you perceive Them, you will believe in the Holy Spirit's Presence within your mind. What you can do now, you could not do without the Love and Grace of the Holy Spirit's Presence.

6. Such is the Promise of the Living God: that you have Life, and that all of Life be a part of you. Nothing else *has* Life. The body and the world that you have given 'life' are not alive, and they symbolize your wish to be 'alive' apart from Life; alive in death, where you perceive death as 'life' and Life as death. Confusion follows on confusion here, because the world that you perceive is based on confusion alone. Its base does not change, although it seems to be in constant change. And what is constant change but a state of confusion? When you are confused, stability is meaningless to you, and shift and change are the law on which you base your 'life'.

7. The body does not change, but it represents your larger illusion that change is possible. To change is to attain a state unlike the one in which you found yourself before. There is no change in Immortality; Heaven does not know of change. But in your perception that you are in a world, change can be used by the personal mind or the Holy Spirit to teach you opposing things, and what you teach reflects the teacher that is teaching you. The body can appear to change with time, with sickness or health, and with events that seem to alter it. But this means only that the mind remains unchanged in the purpose that it has given to the body.

8. Your sickness is your demand that the body be what it is *not*, because its nothingness is a guarantee that it cannot be sick. It is your demand that the body be more than it is, because your sickness asks that God be less than All that God is. You are asked to sacrifice, then, and what becomes of you? God is told that Part of God is no longer Part of God. God must sacrifice you, and in God's sacrifice, you are made more and God is lessened by the loss of you. What is gone from God becomes your god, protecting you from being Part of God.

9. Your asking the body to be your god is your attack on it, because you are not recognizing its inherent nothingness. The body then seems to be a thing with power in itself. As *something*, you perceive

it as feeling and acting, and you think it holds you as a prisoner to itself. It can fail to be what you demanded it be, and you hate it for its littleness, not realizing that its failure does not lie in that it is not more than it should be, but only in your failure to perceive it is nothing. But its nothingness is your salvation, from which you want to flee.

10. As *something*, you ask the body to be God's enemy, replacing God with littleness, limit, and despair. When you look on the body as something to love or to hate, you celebrate your loss of God. God is the Sum of Everything, and what is not of God does not exist. So God's Completion lies in the nothingness of the body. Your Christ Mind is not dead, nor does It dwell in a body that is a temple to death. Christ lives in God, and it is this, and only this, that makes your Christ Mind your Savior. Look on the bodies that you perceive in a world as nothing, and release from sickness and death the body with which you identify. The body with which you identify cannot be more or less than the other bodies that your mind perceives.

3. God's Witnesses

1. Do not condemn yourself because the other in your Holy relationship looks on their self as a body. Beyond *all* illusions is your Reality. You must learn to perceive your Christ Mind in place of any personal mind's perceptions to remember What you are. Thus, the purpose of your relationship with the other becomes salvation as you use it to correct your perception. By extending Christ, you learn that you have Christ, because extending is your proof of having. Only if you believe that God is lessened by your strength can you fail to understand this. You cannot extend Christ unless you have It, and you cannot lose What is increased by your extending It.

2. Do you think that God loses Itself when God extends God to you? Is God made weak because God shares Love with you? Is God made incomplete by your Perfection? As God's Extension, you are the *proof* that God is Perfect and Complete. Do not deny God's Witnesses in the illusion that you prefer to your Reality. To be free from the illusion that you made, you must be your own Savior. You

must see your Christ Mind in your perception of another in what seems to be a world outside of your mind to learn that your Mind is One.

3.   There is one theme of Truth within the world of bodies and death: The personal mind cannot awaken you to God, but you can let your Christ Mind awaken you. You can overlook all forms of the illusion of separation, no matter from whose mind it seems to come. So perfectly can you forgive the illusions that others seem to perceive that they become your Saviors. As you see Christ in place of any personal mind's illusions of separation, you will see God where once you saw bodies. Bodies will disappear for you, just as heavy shadows give way to light. Where you see God, bodies are gone. In Glory, you will see your Christ Mind, and understand What really fills the gap that seems to keep your mind separated. God's Witness sets forth the Gentle Way of Kindness for you. When you forgive any illusion, your illusions are forgiven. By extending Freedom, you are given Freedom.

4.   Make way for Love, Which you did not create, but Which you can extend. In your perception that you are in a world, this means that you forgive all illusions of separation, wherever they seem to occur, so that all illusions may be lifted from *your* mind. *You* will be saved as you extend forgiveness.

5.   How Holy you are that you can perceive Christ in the midst of illusions of desolation and disaster! See how eagerly Christ, in Gratitude and Love, comes to your mind when you look away from illusions. Christ is not outside of you; It encompasses you. Just as God did not lose part of Itself in your creation, so your Christ Mind is made stronger because you extend It to overcome illusions. Christ in your mind must be equally strong in the part of your mind where you perceive a world. This is the theme of Truth in the illusion: As you extend Christ in your perception, you can be sure of Christ in you. In glad salvation you are saved.

4. Dream Roles

1.   Do you believe that some of your illusions of separation from God can be the Truth? They are all illusions *because* they are *not true*.

Their lack of Truth is the basis for the miracle, which you experience because you have understood that an illusion of separation from God *is* an illusion, and that your escape from separation depends on this awareness. You cannot escape some forms of separation and deny others. Your choice is not between which forms of separation you want to keep, but whether you want to live in separation or in God. So the miracle does not leave some of your illusions of separation untouched by its beneficence. You cannot hold onto some forms of separation while becoming aware that other forms of separation are illusions, because your being aware that separation is an illusion is total or not at all. All of your illusions will disappear when you no longer want to be separate from God.

2. In your identification with a personal self, the forms of separation from God that you like hold you back as much as the forms that make you afraid. Every form of separation is an illusion of fear, no matter what the form is. You may see fear within you, outside of you, or both. Fear can be disguised in a pleasant form, but it is never absent from your illusion of separation, because fear is the material from which the illusion is made. The form of separation can change, but it cannot be made of something other than fear. The miracle would indeed be treacherous to you if your experience of it allowed you to still be afraid because you did not recognize the source of your fear. You would not then be willing to become aware of God again, which is what your experiences of miracles prepare you for.

3. Simply stated, it can be said that the personal mind attacks when it perceives a function is unfulfilled as it wants it fulfilled. This can be in you or in someone else, but, where the personal mind sees this unfulfilled function, it will attack. Depression or attack must be the theme of every illusion of separation, because they are made of fear. They may be wrapped in a thin disguise of pleasure and joy, but this only slightly veils the heavy lump of fear at their core. In the miracle, you perceive the fear, not the wrapping in which fear is bound.

4. When you are angry, isn't it because someone has failed to fulfill the

function that, in your identification with a personal self, you have given to them? Isn't this the 'reason' that your attack is justified? The illusions of separation that the personal mind likes are those in which the functions that it has given have been fulfilled, and the needs that it thinks you have, have been met. But your fear actually arises from your belief that you have needs, and it doesn't matter whether they have been met or not. You do not want the illusion of separation more or less; you either want it, or you don't want it. Each form of separation represents some function that you have assigned from the personal mind, a goal which an event or a body or a thing should achieve for you. If it or they succeed, you like the illusion; if it or they don't succeed, then you think that the illusion is sad. But whether your needs are met or not met is not the illusion's core, but its flimsy covering.

5. Your illusions would become Happy Illusions if the personal mind were not the one to assign roles to everyone in them. Everyone *must* fail the personal mind's idea of them, and this is the only betrayal that there is. The core of the illusions that the Holy Spirit gives is never fear. The illusions may not appear to change, but what they mean changes for you, because they stand for Something Else. Your perceptions are determined by their purpose, in that perceptions seem to be what they are for. If your forgiving is the function of your illusions, then someone in your illusions who seems to attack you is really giving you a chance to forgive your perception of separation. And then your illusion of sadness is turned to an Illusion of Joy.

6. What are others for in the world that you perceive? You do not know, because in your identification with a personal self, your function is obscure to you. Do not ascribe roles to others that the personal mind tells you will bring happiness to you. And do not try to hurt others when they fail the part that the personal mind assigned to them in the illusion of your 'life'. Every illusion of separation is your call to you to heal your mind, and you have healing to extend when you see the purpose of illusions as the Holy Spirit sees them. Because the Holy Spirit loves you and not your illusions, each illusion can become for you an opportunity for

you to extend Love. As the Holy Spirit sees it, at the core of every illusion is the Holy Spirit's Love for you, Which fills whatever form it takes with Love.

5. The Changeless Dwelling Place

1. There is a Place in you Where you forget the world, and Where you have no memory of separation or illusions. There is a Place in you Where time has left, and you can hear Echoes of Eternity. There is a Resting Place in you so Still, that no sound except your praise of Heaven rises up to gladden God. Where God abides, you remember God. And Where God is, is Heaven and Peace.

2. Do not think that you can change God's Dwelling Place, because your Identity is in God, and Where God is, you must be Forever. The Changelessness of Heaven is so deep within you, that the world that you perceive just passes It by, unnoticed and unseen. The Still Infinity of Endless Peace surrounds you Gently in Its soft embrace, so Strong and Quiet and Tranquil in the Might of God that nothing can intrude on your sacred Oneness with God.

3. Perceive Christ and be glad, because this is the role that the Holy Spirit gives to you who wait for Christ. The Christ that you perceive is of your Mind, as your Mind is reflected in the Christ that you perceive, because your Mind is One in God, and It is not what the personal mind wants It to be. You are asked only to accept the Changeless and Eternal that abide in your mind where you perceive a world,, because your Identity is there. The Peace in you can only be found in your entire mind. Every Thought of Love that you extend brings you nearer to your own full awareness of your Eternal Peace and Endless Joy.

4. Your perception of your Sacred Christ Mind is the Mirror of God's Love for you. It is the Soft Reminder of God's Love by Which your Whole Mind was created, and Which still dwells in your Mind and in Its Perception. Be very still and hear God's Voice in your perception, and let It tell you the function of the world that you perceive. Your Mind was created Whole, because only the Complete can be part of God's Completion, Which created you.

5. The only gift that God asks of you is that you perceive everywhere

What God has given to you. Behold Christ, God's Perfect Gift, in Which God dwells Forever and in Which is all of Creation. Because your Christ Mind has all of Creation, all of Creation is given to you, and Where Creation lies in your Christ Mind, you can behold your Peace. The Quiet that surrounds you dwells in your Christ Mind, and, from this Quiet, your Happy Perceptions extend to unite your mind in Innocence. There is no pain or attack in these Perceptions, because in Them you leave behind your every vain illusion of separation that is the world. And being open, your mind receives the Perceptions in Which its Completion lies.

6. If you only knew of the Glorious Goal that lies beyond your forgiving you would not keep hold of any thought of separation, no matter how light the touch of evil on it seems to be. You would understand that the cost of holding onto anything God did not give to you is great, when your mind can be directed to bless and to lead you Home to God instead. Wouldn't you rather perceive God's Home in place of a world of separation? God esteems your mind as worthy of God, so why do you attack your mind where you perceive a world with hate? Others in the world that you perceive seem to perceive death in you, too, but do not believe this. Learn instead how blessed you are, because you can release your mind by extending Christ in your perception.

7. A Perception is given to you in Which your relationship with one other in the world that you perceive is your salvation. A Perception is given to you in Which you forgive all of your illusions of death, no matter in what mind they seem to happen, and you extend Hope instead of projecting separate illusions of hate. Why does it seem so hard for you to extend this Perception? Unless the Holy Spirit gives your perception its function, it is for hate, and it will continue in death's service. Each form an illusion of separation takes calls for your death in some way. When you serve the lord of death, you worship in a world of separation, using all of your defenses to keep your promise to die.

8. This is the core of fear in every illusion of separation that you keep from the Holy Spirit, Which sees a different function for the illusions that you perceive. When you use an illusion to extend

Oneness, it is no longer about attack and separation, even though this is what you initially made illusions for. Your mind where you perceive a world of separation is not without the hope of change and betterment, because it is not in the world that you find Changelessness. Be glad that this is so, and do not seek for the Eternal in the world. Your illusions of forgiving are your means for detaching from illusions of a world outside of yourself, and they lead you beyond all illusions to the Peace of Everlasting Life.

6. Forgiveness and the End of Time

1. How willing are you to forgive the personal mind's perceptions? How much do you desire Peace over endless strife, misery, and pain? These questions ask the same thing in a different way. Your forgiving is your Peace, because in it lies the end of your perception of separation and your illusions of danger and destruction, sin and death, madness and murder, grief and loss. Salvation asks that you 'sacrifice' all of this, and it gladly offers you Peace instead.

2. You who are One with God, swear not to die! You make a bargain that you cannot keep, because What is One with Life cannot be killed. You are as Immortal as God, and What you are cannot be changed. You are the only Thing in Reality that is One. What *seems* eternal in your illusions will end: the stars will disappear and night and day will no longer be. The tides, the seasons, the 'lives' of countless personal selves, what blooms and fades, and all the things that change with time will not return. The Eternal is not where time has set an end. You cannot be changed by what the personal mind has made of you. You are One with God as you have always been, and time has not appointed your destiny, nor set the hour of your birth and death. Your forgiving will not change you, but time waits on your forgiving so that the things of time can disappear, because you have no use for them.

3. Nothing survives its purpose. If you conceive of it to die, then it will die, unless you change its purpose. Change is the only thing that you made that can be made into a blessing in your perception that you are in a world, because purpose is not fixed in the world, however changeless it seems to be. Do not think that you can set a

goal unlike God's purpose for you and make it as Changeless and Eternal as God. You can give yourself a purpose that you do not have, but you cannot remove your power to change your mind and to see another purpose.

4. God gave you the ability to change what you have tried to make eternal to ensure that Heaven will not pass away from you. God does not extend God to you so that you can die. You cannot change, because your Function of Extension is fixed by God. But all your other goals are set in time and change to preserve time except for one: your forgiving, which does not aim at preserving time but at ending time. Time is gone for you when its purpose has ended. Where time once filled your mind, your mind will be restored to full awareness of the Function of extending God that God establishes for it. Time cannot end your Function's Fulfillment, nor Its Changelessness. There is no death, because you share your Function with God and Life's Function cannot be to die. Life's Function must be Life's extension, so that It may be One Forever without end.

5. The world that you perceive will bind your feet and tie your hands and kill your body only if you think that it was made to crucify you. Even though the world is an illusion of death, you do not need to let it stand for this to you. Change its purpose and everything in it will be changed as well. Everything in the world is defined for you by what you perceive it is for.

6. How lovely is the world when you perceive its purpose is your extension of forgiveness! How free from fear, and how filled with blessing and Happiness! What a Joyous thing it is for you to dwell a little while in such a Happy place. And, in such a world, you cannot forget that it *is* a little while until Timelessness comes Quietly to take the place of time.

7. Seek Not Outside Yourself

1. Do not seek outside yourself, because you will fail to find Happiness there and you will weep each time an idol falls. Heaven cannot be found where It is *not*, and your only Peace is the Peace of Heaven. Every idol that you worship in place of God will never

fulfill you. There is nothing you can substitute to find the Happiness that God brings to you. Do not seek outside yourself. All of your pain comes from your searching for Happiness where you insist that It must be. It is not there. Do you prefer to be right or Happy? Be glad that you have been told Where Happiness abides, and do not seek any longer for It elsewhere, because you will fail. It is given to you to know the Truth, and do not seek outside yourself for It.

2. You go into the world with the hopeful illusion that something outside of yourself will bring you Happiness and Peace. But Everything is in you, so this cannot be so. By looking in the world, you deny the Truth about yourself, and you look for something to be more than Everything. It is as if you think that a Part of Everything is separated off and can be found where all the rest of It is not. You give to the body/personal self the purpose of seeking for what you lack and finding what you think you need to make yourself complete. So you wander about aimlessly in search of something that you cannot find, believing that you are what you are *not*.

3. Your lingering belief that you can find wholeness outside of yourself will compel you to seek out a thousand idols. And all will fail you but one: death. You do not understand that the idol that you seek is death. Its form seems to be outside of you, but in your identification with a personal self, you seek to kill the Christ within you and prove that you are victor over It. This is the purpose that you have assigned to every idol, and this is the role that they cannot fulfill.

4. Whenever you attempt to reach a goal in which the body/personal self will gain, you try to bring about your death, because you believe that you can suffer lack and lack *is* death. To sacrifice is to give up, and therefore to suffer loss, and this is how you renounce Life. Do not seek outside yourself. For you to search outside of yourself implies that you are not Whole within, and that you are afraid to look within on your devastation, so you must look outside yourself for what you are.

5. Idols must fall *because* they have no life, and what is lifeless is a sign

of death. You perceive yourself in a world to die, so what do you expect but to find the signs of death that you seek? Your sadness and suffering proclaim the message that you found an idol that in its lifelessness is death, but which you conceive of as real and give a 'living' form. Yet each idol must fail and crumble and decay, because a form of death cannot be Life, and what is for sacrifice cannot be Whole.

6. You made all idols in the world that you perceive to keep yourself from being aware of the Truth within you, and to maintain your allegiance to the illusion that you must find completion and happiness outside of yourself. It is vain for you to worship idols in the hope of Peace. God dwells within you, and your Completion lies in God. No idol can take God's Place. Do not look to idols; do not seek outside yourself.

7. Forget the purpose that the personal self's past has given to the world that you perceive. Otherwise, the future will be like the past: a series of depressing illusions in which your idols fail you one by one, and you see disappointment and death everywhere.

8. To change all this and to open up a road of hope and release in what appears to be an endless circle of despair, all that you need to do is decide that you don't know what the world is for. You split your mind between within you and outside of you, and in the world outside you perceive idols that are supposed to have the power to make you complete within. You choose your illusions of separation, and they are what you wish, but you perceive them as though they have been given to you. Your idols do what you want them to do, and they have the power that you ascribe to them. You pursue them vainly in your illusion of separation, because you want their power as your own.

9. Illusions of separation are only in your mind through your denial. You cannot succeed in making real the illusions that you project outside of yourself. Save time by learning what time is for. Speed the end of idols in your mind, which is made sad and sick by seeing idols as real. Your Holy Mind is God's Home, and no idols can abide Where God is. Your fear of God is your fear of loss of your idols, not your fear of loss of your Reality. But you have made

a false reality that is an idol, which you feel you must protect against the Truth. The world that you perceive is the means that you use to save this idol, and salvation seems to threaten your 'life' and to offer you death.

10. It is not so. Your salvation would prove to you that there is no death and only Life exists. In 'sacrificing' death, you lose nothing. An idol cannot take the place of God. Let God remind you of God's Love for you, and do not seek to drown out God's Voice with chants of deep despair to idols of yourself. Do not seek outside of God for your Hope, because you will not find Hope of Happiness in despair.

8. The Anti-Christ

1. Do you think that you know what an idol is? You never recognize idols as what they really are. That is the only power that they have. Their purpose is obscure to you, and you both fear and worship them *because* you do not know what they are for, and why they have been made. An idol is someone or something that you value more than God. No matter their form, they are made to replace your Christ Mind in your awareness, and it is this that you never perceive and recognize. A body, a thing, a place, a situation, something that you own or want, a right that you demand or have achieved – all these are idols.

2. Do not let their form deceive you; idols are your substitutes for your Reality. In some way, you think that they will complete your little self. You want them for safety in a dangerous world where forces are massed against your confidence and peace of mind. You believe that they have the power to supply your lacks and to add the value that you feel that you do not have. You only believe in idols because you have limited and sacrificed yourself to a personal self. You seek beyond this little self for strength and for a means to stand apart from all of the misery of the world that you perceive. But your misery is the consequence of your not looking within for the Certainty and Quiet Calm that frees you from the world and lets you stand apart in Peace.

3. An idol is a false belief, a form of anti-Christ that constitutes a gap between your Christ Mind and your mind where you perceive a

world. An idol is your wish given tangible form, perceived as real, and projected outside of your mind. But it is still your thought, and it cannot leave the mind of its thinker. Nor is its form apart from the idea that it represents. All forms that oppose your Christ Mind are anti-Christ, and, if you want, they can all fall away before Christ like a dark veil that seems to shut you off from Christ. Christ is here. A veil cannot banish or undo What it seems to separate off from you.

4. The world of idols that you perceive is like a veil across your awareness of your Christ Mind, because its purpose is to separate your Mind from Itself. It has a dark and frightening purpose, but it has no power to change Life into death. The world that you perceive is nothing but a thought in your mind where God is not. Where is this place in your mind where What is Everywhere has been excluded? What can block God's Way? Whose voice can demand that God not enter your mind? The 'more-than-Everything' that you have tried to make is not something to make you tremble in fear. Christ's 'enemy' cannot take a form that will ever be real.

5. An idol is nothing! You must believe in it before it seems to come to life, and you must give it power before you fear it. Its life and power are your gifts to it, and your awareness of this is what your experience of the miracle restores to you, who have Life and Power worthy of the Gift of Heaven and Eternal Peace. Your experience of the miracle does not restore the Truth to you. It merely lifts the veil from your mind so that Truth can be What It is. Truth does not need your belief to be Itself, because, being of God, It merely *is*.

6. An idol is established by your belief, and when you withdraw your belief in it, it falls away. The anti-Christ is your strange idea that there is a power past Omnipotence, a place beyond the Infinite, and a time that transcends Eternity. This power, place, and time have taken form as the world of idols that you perceive. In this impossible world, the Deathless comes to die, the All-encompassing comes to suffer loss, the Timeless is made a slave to time, the Changeless changes, and the Peace of God gives way to chaos. And you who are One with God, and who are as Perfect, Innocent,

and Loving as God, come to hate yourself a little while, to suffer pain, and finally to die.

7. An idol is nowhere. There cannot be a gap in Infinity, an interval of time to interrupt Eternity, denial Where All is Known, or a dismal corner that is separated off from the Endless. An idol is outside Where God has set All Things Forever, and Where God has left no room for anything but God's Will. An idol must be nothing and nowhere, since God is Everything and Everywhere.

8. What is an idol for? This question has many answers in the world of separation that you perceive, because your world is peopled with idolaters. In your identification with a personal self, you worship idols, and you seek for one that might yet offer you a gift that Reality does not contain. You harbor the hope that your special deities will give you more than others possess. It must be *more*. It does not matter more of what: beauty, intelligence, wealth; even affliction and pain. An idol is always for more of *something*. When one idol falls, you find another to give you hope of finding more of something else. Do not be deceived by the many forms that 'something' takes. An idol is for you to get something more, and it is this that is against God's Will.

9. God is One, not many. What Part of God can have more, and what Part can have less? The Holy Spirit speaks for God, and It tells you that your idols have no purpose. You can never have more than Heaven. Heaven is within you, so why seek for idols that make Heaven seem like less than It is, so that you can have more than God has given you in your Oneness with God? God has given you All that there is. To be sure that you could not lose Everything, God extends Everything Everywhere. All of Life is a Part of You, as It is a Part of God. No idol can establish you as more than God, and you will never be content with less than God.

9. The Forgiving Dream

1. You are a willing slave of idols. You must be, to bow down in worship of what has no life, and to seek for power in the powerless. What happened to you who are One with God that it is your wish to fall lower than the stones on the ground and to look for idols to

raise you up? Here is your story in the illusion of separation that you have made; ask yourself if it isn't true that you do not believe that it is an illusion:

2. An idea of judgment against yourself came into your Mind, Which was created by God as Perfect as God. In that illusion, Heaven was changed to hell, and God was made into your enemy. But you can undo your illusion of judgment by not judging, because your illusion will seem to last for you only while you are a part of it. Do not judge, because, if you do, you will need idols on which to project your judgment, so that your judgment does not rest on you. Do not judge, or you will not know the Self that you have judged against. Do not judge, because to do so is to make yourself a part of illusions of separation, where idols are your true 'identity' and are your 'salvation' from the judgment of guilt and fear that you have laid on yourself.

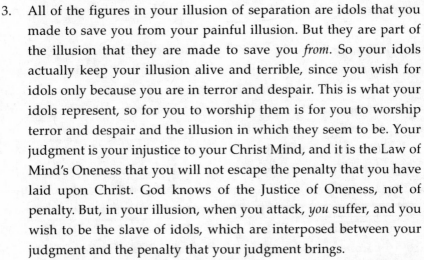

3. All of the figures in your illusion of separation are idols that you made to save you from your painful illusion. But they are part of the illusion that they are made to save you *from*. So your idols actually keep your illusion alive and terrible, since you wish for idols only because you are in terror and despair. This is what your idols represent, so for you to worship them is for you to worship terror and despair and the illusion in which they seem to be. Your judgment is your injustice to your Christ Mind, and it is the Law of Mind's Oneness that you will not escape the penalty that you have laid upon Christ. God knows of the Justice of Oneness, not of penalty. But, in your illusion, when you attack, *you* suffer, and you wish to be the slave of idols, which are interposed between your judgment and the penalty that your judgment brings.

4. There can be no salvation for you in your illusion in the way that you maintain it with a personal mind. Idols must be a part of your illusion, then, to save you from the separation from God that you believe you have accomplished, and that you think has resulted in Love being put out of you. But Love is always within you. You only have an *illusion* of separation from God, and idols are the toys that you think that you play with. Only children have need of toys. They pretend that they rule the world, and they give their toys the

power to move about, talk, think, feel, and speak to them. But everything their toys appear to do is only in the mind of the child playing with them. And children are eager to forget that they made up the daydream in which their toys are real, and to deny that their toys' wishes are their own.

5. Nightmares are childish dreams. A child's toys turn against the child who thought that he had made them real. But a dream cannot attack, and a toy cannot grow large and dangerous. A child believes this can happen, because he fears his own thoughts and gives them to the toys instead. The toys' 'reality' becomes the child's own, because they seem to save him from his thoughts. But really, they keep his thoughts alive and real, though seen outside of him, where they can turn against him for his treachery to them. The child thinks he needs the toys to escape his own thoughts, because he thinks his own thoughts are real. So he makes anything a toy to make a world outside of himself, and plays as though he is part of it.

6. There is a time when childhood should be past and gone forever. Do not seek to retain the toys of children and put them all away, because you don't need them anymore. Your illusion of judgment against yourself is a child's game in which you become your own powerful maker, but with the little wisdom of a child. What hurts you, you destroy; what helps you, you bless. But you judge as a child does, and you do not know what really hurts you and what really heals you. Bad things seem to happen, and you are afraid of the chaos in a world that is governed by laws that you think you made. But your Real Perception is unaffected by the world of separation that you think is real. And Its Law has not been changed because you do not understand It.

7. Your Real Perception is also an illusion, but the figures in it have been changed. They are not idols that betray, because they are not used by you to substitute for God, nor are they interposed between your mind and its Wholeness. You do not use them for something that they are not, because you have put away childish things. Your illusion of judgment is changed into an illusion of Joy, because that is its purpose. Your Real Perception sees only forgiving illusions,

because time is almost over. You now perceive the figures in your illusion as part of your mind, not in judgment, but in Love.

8. Your forgiving illusions do not need to last long. You do not make them to separate your mind from what it thinks. They do not seek to prove that your illusion is made by someone else. And in these illusions, you see the Reflection of Something familiar, though you have not seen It since before time began. Once your forgiving is complete, Timelessness is so close that you can perceive a Reflection of Heaven, not with the body's eyes, but with your Holy Mind, which has never left you. When you see this Reflection, you will realize that you have always known It. And time is over when you have put away illusions of judgment.

9. Whenever you feel fear in any form – and you *are* afraid if you do not feel a deep content, a certainty of help, and a calm assurance that Heaven is with you – you can be sure that you have made an idol that you believe will betray you. Beneath your hope that it will save you lie the guilt and pain of self-betrayal and uncertainty, so deep and bitter that your illusion cannot completely conceal your sense of doom. Your self-betrayal must result in fear, because fear is your judgment, leading to your frantic search for idols and for death.

10. Your forgiving illusions remind you that you live in Safety, and that you have not attacked yourself. Your childish terrors will melt away, and new illusions will come as a sign that you have made a new beginning, not another attempt to worship idols and keep attack. Your forgiving illusions are kind to every figure in your illusion, so they bring you full release from your illusions of fear. When you stop judging the world that you perceive, you will stop fearing your own judgment. And you will stop using judgment to bring release from the limitations that judgment imposes. You will remember What you forgot when judgment seemed to be the way to save you from its own penalty.

Chapter 30

The New Beginning

1. Now your new beginning becomes the focus of this lesson plan. Your Goal is clear, but now you need specific methods for attaining It. How quickly you reach It depends only on your willingness to practice every step. Each step will help a little every time you attempt it. Together, these steps lead you from illusions of judgment to forgiving illusions and out of pain and fear. They are not new to you, but they are more ideas than rules of thought to you yet. Now you need to practice them awhile until they are the rules by which you live. The goal is for you to make them habits, so that you will have them ready for whatever need arises.

1. Rules for Decision

1. In your perception that you are in a world, you continuously need to make decisions, although you do not always know that you are making them. But, with a little practice with the ones that you do recognize, a system will begin to form in your mind which will see you through the other unconscious decisions. It is not wise for you to become preoccupied with every step that you have to take. But the proper system, adopted each time you wake in the morning, will put you well ahead. If you find your resistance strong and your dedication weak, you are not ready. *Do not fight yourself.* Instead, think about the Peace that you want throughout the day, and tell yourself that there is a way in which this day can happen. Then try to have the Peaceful day that you want.

2. (1) The day's outlook starts with this:

    'Today, I will make no decisions with the personal mind.'

    This means that you are choosing to not let the personal mind be the judge of what you do. It also means that you will not listen to the personal mind's judgments of the situations where you are called upon to make a response. If you do judge these situations with the personal mind, you will have set the rules for how you should react to them. Then, an answer from the Holy Spirit will only produce confusion, uncertainty, and fear in your mind.

3. This is your major problem now: You make a decision with the personal mind first, *then* you decide to ask the Holy Spirit what to do. And what you hear from the Holy Spirit may not resolve the problem as you first saw it, which makes you afraid, because it contradicts your perception. So you feel attacked and therefore angry. There are rules by which this will not happen, but this will occur at first while you are learning how to hear the Holy Spirit.

4. (2) Throughout the day, at any time that you think of it and have a quiet moment of reflection, remind yourself of the Peace that you want. Think of the experience of Peace and say:

    'If I make no decisions with the personal mind, this is the day that I will have.'

    These two procedures practiced well will serve to let you be directed by the Holy Spirit without fear, because the personal mind's opposition will not first arise and then become a problem in itself.

5. But there will still be times when you have already let the personal mind judge what will bring you Peace. Now an answer from the Holy Spirit will provoke an attack from you, unless you quickly straighten out your mind to want an answer that will really work. You can be certain that this is what has happened if you feel unwilling to have the Holy Spirit's answer. You have let the personal mind make a decision for you, and you cannot see that your request was for Real Peace. Now you need a quick restorative before you ask the Holy Spirit again.

6. (3) Remember once again the Peaceful day that you want, and recognize that something has occurred that is not part of it. Then, realize that you have made a request of the personal mind, and that it set an answer in its terms. Then say:

'I forgot what to ask for, and I forgot to ask it of the Holy Spirit.'

This cancels out the terms that the personal mind has set and lets the answer from the Holy Spirit show you that your request was for Real Peace.[1]

7. Despite your opposition, try to observe this rule without delay, because you have already gotten angry. Your fear of your request being answered in a way that is different from what the personal mind has decided it should be will gain momentum until you believe that the day that you want is the one where the personal mind gets *its* answers on *its* terms. This will destroy your day by robbing you of the Peace that you really want. This can be very hard for you to realize when you have already decided the rules that will promise you a happy day. But this decision can still be undone by simple methods that you can accept.

8. (4) If you are so unwilling to receive the Holy Spirit's answer that you cannot even let go of your request, you can begin to change your mind with this:

'At least I can decide that I do not like what I feel now.'

This much is obvious, and it paves the way for the next easy step.

9. (5) Having decided that you do not like what you feel, nothing is easier than for you to continue with:

'And so I hope I have been wrong.'

This works against your sense of opposition, and it reminds you that Help is not being forced on you, but that It is something that you want, because you do not like the way that you feel. This tiny opening will be enough for you to go ahead with just a few more steps that you need to let yourself be helped by the Holy Spirit.

10. Now you have reached the turning point, because it has occurred to you that you will gain if what you have decided with the personal mind is a mistake. Until you reach this point, you will believe that your happiness depends on the personal mind being right. Now

you have attained enough sense to see that you will be better off if it is wrong.

11.   (6) This tiny grain of wisdom will be enough to take you further. You can see that you are not being coerced, but that you merely hope to get the Peace that you want. And you can say with perfect honesty:

'I want another way to look at this situation.'

Now you have changed your mind about the day by remembering the Peace that you really want. Your day's purpose of Peace is no longer obscured by your insane belief that you want it for the goal of making the personal self be right when it is wrong. So you are made aware that you are ready to ask the Holy Spirit, because you cannot be in conflict when you ask for the Peace that you want, and you see that it *is* Peace for Which you ask.

12.   (7) This final step is your acknowledgment that you are no longer opposed to the Holy Spirit's Help. It is a statement of an open mind, maybe not yet certain, but willing to be shown:

'Perhaps there is another way to look at this situation. I cannot lose anything by asking.'

Now you can make a request of the Holy Spirit that makes sense, so the answer will make sense to you as well. You also will not fight against the answer, because you see that it is you who will be helped by it.

13.   It must be clear that it is easier for you to have a happy day if you prevent unhappiness from entering your mind at all. But this takes practice of the rules that will protect you from the ravages of fear. When this has been achieved, your sorry illusion of judgment will be forever undone. In the meantime, you have need for practicing the rules for its undoing. Consider again the very first of the decisions which are offered here:

14.   You can begin a happy day with the determination to not make decisions with the personal mind. This seems to be a decision in

itself, but you cannot make decisions without either the personal mind or the Holy Spirit, and the only real question is with which one you will choose to make them. This is not coercion but a simple statement of a simple fact. Whatever you decide, you make decisions with an idol or with God. You ask help of the anti-Christ or Christ in your mind, and which you choose will tell you what to do.

15. Your day is not random. It is set by your choice to live it with the personal mind or with the Holy Spirit, and by how the counselor that you choose perceives your happiness. You *always* ask advice of the personal mind or of the Holy Spirit before you decide anything. Understand this and you can see that you are not being coerced, and that you have no grounds for opposing the Holy Spirit so that you can be free. There is no freedom for you from the consequences of the counselor you choose, and if you think that there is, you must be wrong.

16. The second rule is also a fact, because you and your counselor must agree on what you want before it can occur. It is this agreement that permits all things to happen. Everything is caused by you uniting your mind with either an illusion of judgment or with the Truth. Your decisions cause results *because* they are made by you and the counselor in your mind that you choose, for yourself and for the world that you perceive in your mind. What you want for your day you extend in your perception, which will be what you want it to be, and it will reinforce the role of the counselor you choose.

17. Your mind is never split in two, but it seems to be. So it takes uniting your mind with the Holy Spirit for Happiness to promise that Happiness will be all that you perceive. And it takes uniting your mind with the Holy Spirit to understand that you are not an isolated personal self, and to guarantee that the Joy that you want will be wholly extended in your mind where you perceive a world. You will understand the basic Law of Mind's Oneness that makes your decision-making powerful, and gives it all the effects that it will ever have. Your mind must be united in the Holy Spirit before you can make a decision for Peace. Let this be the one reminder that you keep in mind, and you will have the day of Peace that you

want, and you will extend It in your perception, because you have It. The personal mind's judgment is lifted from the world of separation that you perceive by your decision for a Happy day. And as you receive It, so you must extend It.

2. Freedom of Will

1. Don't you understand that to oppose the Holy Spirit is to fight *yourself*? The Holy Spirit only tells you *your* Will; the Holy Spirit speaks for *you*. In the Holy Spirit's Divinity is your Divinity, and all that the Holy Spirit knows is your Knowledge, saved for you by the Holy Spirit, so that you may do your Will through the Holy Spirit. God asks you to do your Will, and God joins with you in doing It. God's Oneness is not divided. Heaven Itself, Where Everything is One with you, represents your Will. All of Life is One with your Glad Consent. Every Thought God has waits for your blessing to *be*. God is not your enemy, and God asks only that you call God 'Friend'.

2. How wonderful it is for you to do your Will! *That* is Freedom. There is nothing else that can be called Freedom. You are not Free, unless you do your Will. God cannot leave you, who are One with God, without What God has chosen for Itself. God ensured that you will never lose your Will when God extended the Holy Spirit to you as God's Perfect Answer to your perception of separation from God. Hear the Holy Spirit now, so that you will be reminded of God's Love, and you will learn *your* Will. God will not have you made a prisoner to what you don't really want, because God wills your Freedom with you. For you to oppose God is for you to make a choice against yourself and to choose limitation.

3. Look again on your 'enemy': your Christ Mind, Which you chose to hate instead of to Love. This is how hatred and a world ruled by fear arose in your perception. Now hear God speak to you through the Holy Spirit, Which is God's Voice and your Voice, reminding you that it is not your Will to be a prisoner to fear, a slave to death, and a little creature with a little 'life'. Your Will is Limitless; it is not your Will that your Will be limited. The Holy Spirit in you is One with God in Creation. Remember God, Which created you,

and Which through you created Everything. Everything in Creation gives you thanks, because it is by your Will that It exists. Heaven is filled with Love by your Will.

4. You have no cause for anger over a world that only waits for your blessing to be set free from your mind. If you are limited, then God is limited, because what you do to What is One with God you do to God. Do not think that God wants to limit you, who are co-Creator of Reality with God. God keeps your Will Eternally Limitless. Your mind awaits the Freedom that you will extend through it when you recognize that you are Free. You will not forgive the world that you perceive until you have forgiven God, Which gave your Will to you. It is by your Will that your mind where you perceive a world is set free, and you cannot be Free apart from God, because you share God's Holy Will.

5. God turns to you to ask you to save your mind where you perceive a world, because your Mind is One, and It is healed and saved as One. Your Freedom and your Will extend in perception, and this is how you learn that death has no power over you. It is your Will to heal your mind, and because you extend your Will in your perception, your mind is healed. Now you have forgiven God, because you have looked on what your mind perceives as part of you.

3. Beyond All Idols

1. Idols take specific form, but your Will, being Limitless, is Everywhere. Your Will has no form, and It is not content being expressed in form. Idols are limits. They are your belief that there are forms that will bring you happiness, and that by limiting yourself, you attain everything. It is as if you say, 'I have no need of Everything. I want just this little thing, and it will be like everything to me.' This must fail to satisfy you, because it is your Will that Everything be yours. Choose idols and you ask for loss; choose Truth and Everything is yours.

2. It is not form that you seek. There is no form that can substitute for God's Love or for all the Love within your Divinity. No idol has the power to substitute for Oneness or to make the Limitless limited.

You do not want an idol; it is not your Will to have one. When you decide on the form of what you want, you reduce your Will to a specific form and see It in an idol. But this can never be your Will, because what is One with Everything cannot be content with small ideas and little things.

3. Behind your search for idols is your yearning for Completion. Wholeness does not have a form, because It is Limitless. When you seek for a special person or thing, it means that you believe that you are lacking, and that you need some form to add to you and to make you complete in a way that you like. The purpose of an idol is for you to not look beyond it to the true source of your sense that you are incomplete: Your belief that you have made your separation from God real. Only if this were true would you be alone and lacking, and then it *would* be necessary for you to search for wholeness outside of yourself.

4. It is never the idol that you really want. The experience of Wholeness that you think that an idol offers to you is What you want, and you have the right to ask for It. It is not possible that Wholeness can be denied to you, because your Will to be Complete is God's Will, and this is given to you by *you* being God's Will. God does not know form, and God cannot answer you in terms that do not have any meaning. Your Will will not be satisfied with empty forms that are made to fill a gap that is not there. This is not what you want. God's Oneness does not give power to separate people or things to make Itself Whole. There is no idol that you can call on to give you What you already have in your Oneness with God.

5. Completion is your *Function* in your Oneness with God. You do not have to seek for It at all. Beyond your idols is your Holy Will to be What you are. 'More than whole' is a meaningless idea. If you could be changed or reduced to form and limited to what you are *not*, then you would not be One with God. But you cannot give part of yourself away, and you don't need any idol to be yourself. An idol is not Whole, and it cannot make Whole. But what you really ask for cannot be denied to you. Your Will is granted, not in a form that will never content you, but in the Whole, Complete, and Lovely Thought of God that you are.

6. What God doesn't know does not exist, and What God does know exists Forever, Changelessly. A thought endures for as long as the mind that thinks it, and in the Mind of God there is no ending, nor a time in which you, God's Thought, are absent or can suffer and change. God's Thought is not born, and It cannot die. It shares the attributes of Its Thinker, and It has no life apart from Its Thinker. The thoughts that you think, even in seeming separation, are in your mind, as you are in the Mind of God, Which thinks of you. There are no separate parts in God's Mind; It is Forever One, Eternally United, and at Peace.

7. Your Thoughts of God seem to come and go for you, but all this means is that you are sometimes aware of Them and sometimes unaware of Them. A Thought of God you forget is born again to you when It returns to your awareness, but It did not die when you forgot It. It was always there, only you were unaware of It. God's Thought of you is Perfectly Unchanged by your forgetting God. It will always be exactly the same as It was before the time when you forgot It, It is unchanged in the interval of time when you forget It, and It will be just the same when you remember It.

8. Your Thoughts of God are far beyond all change, and They exist Forever. They do not wait for birth, but for your remembering and your welcome. God's Thought of you is Unchangeable and Eternal, set in Heaven, but unknown to you when you think that you are outside of Heaven. God's Thought of you is Still and Lovely through all Eternity. There is no time in Which It is not here; no instant when It fades or is less Perfect.

9. Know God and know God's Thought of you, because God is the Eternity that holds you Safe. The Perfect Purity of God's Thought of you does not depend on whether or not you are aware of It. God's Mind encompasses Its Thought of you and Softly holds It within. It is as far from the world as the world is from Heaven. Your idols, not distance or time, keep God's Thought invisible to you.

10. Beyond all of your idols is God's Thought of you, completely unaffected by the turmoil and terror of the world that you perceive, your illusion of birth and death, and the myriad forms that fear takes for you. Undisturbed, God's Thought of you remains exactly

as It has always been, surrounded by a Stillness so Complete that no conflict comes even remotely near. It rests in Certainty and Perfect Peace. Here, your One Reality is kept Safe, completely unaware of the world of idol worship that you made, and which does not know God. In Perfect Sureness of Its Changelessness and of Its Rest in Its Eternal Home, God's Thought of you has never left God's Mind. God's Thought of you knows God, as God knows It is in God.

11. Where could God's Thought of you exist but in you? Your Reality is not separate from you, nor is It in a world that Reality cannot know. Outside of you there is no Eternity, Changelessness, or Reality. Your Mind is in Heaven, because There your Mind is One with God, without end. You do not have two realities, only One, and you cannot be aware of more than one. An idol or God's Thought of you is your reality. Do not forget that idols hide What you are, not from God's Mind, but from yours. Your Reality still exists; God has never changed. But you who are One with God are unaware of your Reality.

4. The Truth Behind Illusions

1. In your identification with a personal self, you attack what does not satisfy you, so you do not see that you made it up. When you fight, you always fight your illusions, because the Truth beyond them in your mind is so Lovely, Still, and Gentle that, if you were aware of It, you would entirely forget defensiveness and rush to Truth's Embrace. The Truth can never be attacked, and you knew this when you made idols, because you made idols so that you could deny this. You only attack false ideas, never the Truth. All idols are the false ideas that you made to fill the gap that you think is there between yourself and Truth. You attack idols for the things that you think that they represent, but the Truth that lies beyond them you cannot attack.

2. The wearying, dissatisfying gods that you make are like children's toys. A child is frightened when a jack-in-the-box springs open, or when a soft, silent stuffed bear squeaks when she grabs it. The 'rules' that the child has made for boxes and stuffed bears have

failed her and have broken her 'control' of her environment. The child is afraid, because she thought that her rules protected her. Now she must learn that boxes and stuffed bears did not deceive her or break any rules or make her world chaotic and unsafe. She was mistaken about what made her safe, and she thought that it had left her.

3.   The gap that you perceive in your mind between you and Truth is filled with 'toys' in countless forms, and each one seems to break the rules that you set for it. But they never were what you thought they were. They may appear to break your 'rules' for safety, because your rules were wrong. *You* are never endangered. You can laugh at the 'frightening' things of the world that you perceive, just as a child learns that her toys are not a threat to her. But, just like the child who likes to play with her toys, you still perceive that the world obeys rules that you made for your enjoyment. So there are still rules of yours that can be broken, and when they are, they frighten you. But are you at the mercy of the world that you made? Can it represent a threat to you?

4.   Reality observes God's Law of Oneness, not the rules that you set. It is God's Law that guarantees your Safety. All the illusions that you believe about yourself and your world do not obey any laws. For a little while, they seem to dance according to the rules that you set for them, but then they fall and cannot rise again. They are only toys, so do not grieve for them. Their dancing never brought you Joy, but neither were they things to frighten you or to make you 'safe' when they obeyed your rules. You do not need to cherish them or to attack them, but merely to perceive them as meaningless. See meaning in any one of them, and you give meaning to them all. See no meaning in any of them, and they cannot touch you.

5.   Appearances deceive *because* they are appearances and not Reality. Do not dwell on them in any form. They only obscure Reality for you, and they frighten you, because they hide the Truth. Do not attack what you made to deceive yourself, because then you prove that you have been deceived. Your attacking has the power to make illusions seem real to you, but what it makes is nothing. You cannot

be made afraid by a power that has no real effects at all. Only your illusion of yourself is frightened by your illusions. Look calmly at your 'toys' of attack, and understand that they are idols that dance to your vain desire to make the illusions that you attack real to you. Do not worship them, because they are not here. But you forget this when you attack. In your Oneness with God, you do not need to defend yourself against your illusions. Your idols do not threaten you at all. Your only mistake is that you think that they are real. What can the power of illusion do to you?

6. Appearances deceive you only when you want to be deceived. But you can make a simple choice that will forever place you far beyond deception. You do not need to be concerned with how this will be done, because this is far beyond what you can understand yet. But you will understand that mighty changes have come about when you decide one very simple thing: The Completion that you want will not come from an idol. This is how you are freed of idols.

7. Your salvation is a paradox indeed! It can only be a Happy Illusion. It asks you to forgive all the things that no one ever did, to overlook what is not there, and to not look on the unreal as Reality. You are only asked to let your Will be done, and to no longer seek for what you do not want. You are asked to let yourself be free of illusions of what you never were, and to no longer seek to substitute idle wishes for the Will of God.

8. Here, your illusion of separation from God starts to fade and disappear from your mind, because here you begin to perceive the gap that is not there between you and God without the toys of terror that you made. This is all that is asked of you. Be glad you're your salvation asks so little; it asks for nothing in Reality. Even in illusions, It asks only that your forgiving be your substitute for fear. This is the only rule for you to have Happy Illusions. The gap is emptied of your toys of fear, then you see illusions for the unreality that they are. Illusions are for nothing, and you who are One with God can have no real need of them. They do not offer you a single thing that you can really want. You are delivered from illusions by your Will and restored to What you are. God's plan for your salvation is only a means to extend God to you.

5. The Only Purpose

1. Your True Perception is the state of mind in which you see your forgiving your perception of separation from God as the only purpose for the world that you perceive. Fear is then no longer your goal for the world, because escape from guilt is your aim. You perceive the value of forgiving, and it takes the place of idols, which you no longer seek, because you do not value their 'gifts'. You do not set rules with the personal mind, and you do not make demands of anyone or anything to twist and fit into your illusion of fear. Instead, you wish to understand everything as it is, and you recognize that you must first forgive the personal mind's perception of everything, *then* you will understand it.

2. In your world of separation, your 'understanding' is acquired through separation, but your True Perception makes it clear to you that your understanding is *lost* through separation. Through your True Perception, you see it is folly to pursue separation as a goal. You do not want idols, because you understand that separation is the only cause of your pain in any form. You are not tempted by separation's vain appeal, because you perceive that you do not want suffering and death. You have grasped the possibility of Freedom, and you welcome It, and you understand the means to gain It. The world that you perceive becomes a place of hope for you, because its only purpose is to be a place where your hope of Happiness is fulfilled. And nothing that you perceive in the world stands outside of your hope, because your mind is united in the belief that your purpose of forgiving your perception of separation from God is one in which everything that you perceive in the world must share if your hope be more than an illusion.

3. At this point, you do not remember Heaven quite yet, because your forgiving still has a purpose. Yet, you are certain that you will go beyond forgiving, and you remain in the perception that you are in a world until your forgiving is made perfect. You have no wish for anything but this, and fear has dropped away from you, because you are united in your purpose within yourself. There is a hope of Happiness in you so sure and constant that you can barely stay a little longer in your perception that you are in a world. But you are

glad to stay until Oneness is all that you perceive and your entire mind is healed and ready to rise up to God with you. This is how you are made ready for the step taken by God, in which all forgiveness is left behind.

4.	The final step is God's, because after your forgiving is complete, only your Oneness with God remains. You cannot understand this outside of Heaven, because understanding this is Heaven Itself. Even your True Perception's purpose is outside of Oneness and Eternity, but fear is gone from It, because Its purpose is forgiveness, not idolatry. So you are prepared to be yourself, and to remember that you who are One with God know Everything that God understands, and you understand It Perfectly with God.

5.	Your True Perception falls short of Perfect Understanding, because Perfect Understanding is God's Own Purpose, completely extended to you and Perfectly Fulfilled. But your True Perception is a state of mind in which you have learned how easily idols go when you still perceive them but you do not want them. Your mind willingly lets idols go when you understand that they are nothing, nowhere, and without a purpose. Only then can you see that your perception of separation from God, and the guilt that it inspires, is without a purpose and is meaningless.

6.	So your True Perception gently brings the world's real purpose of your forgiving your perception of separation from God into your awareness to replace the goal of separation and guilt. And all that stood between your image of yourself and What you really are is Joyfully washed away by your forgiving. But God does not need to extend God to you again for you to be One with God. The gap between you and the part of your mind that you perceive as outside of you was never there. And What you know in your Oneness with God, you still know.

7.	When you forgave your perception of separation by extending your Identity to your perception of another in the world that seems outside of you, you brought yourself to the edge of your True Perception. You might still look back at the world of separation and think that you see an idol that you want, but your path has been set surely away from idols and toward Reality. When you joined your mind you joined in Christ, and you will see your Christ Mind fully reflected in your perception before you wholly remember God. You will not remember God until you have reached beyond forgiving to the Love of God. You will accept the Love of your Christ Mind first, and then your Knowledge that Christ and God are One will come.

8. How light and easy is your step across the narrow boundaries of the world of fear when you have recognized your Christ Mind! With you is Everything that you need to walk away from fear forever with perfect confidence, and to go straight to the outskirts of Heaven Itself. Your Christ Mind has been waiting for your acknowledgement. Now that it has come, It will not delay in showing you the way. Christ's Blessing lies on you as surely as God's Blessing lies on your Christ Mind. Christ's gratitude toward you is beyond your understanding, because you have lifted the limitations that you imposed on It, and with Christ in your awareness you can go Home to God.

9. An ancient Self-hate is passing from your perception, and with it goes all hatred and fear from your mind. Do not look back any longer, because What lies ahead is all that you have ever really wanted in your heart. Give up the world of separation, but not in sacrifice, because you never really wanted it. All the happiness that you have sought in the world has only brought you pain, and you have bought every moment of contentment with suffering. Joy has no cost. It is your Sacred Right, and you never pay for Happiness. Speed on your way to God in honesty, and do not let your experiences in the world that you perceive deceive you in retrospect. They were not free from bitter cost and joyless consequences.

10. Look back in honesty, and when you are tempted to believe in an idol, think of this:

'There was never a time when an idol brought me anything except guilt. All were bought at the cost of pain, and the price was paid by my entire mind.'

Be merciful in your perceptions, then, and do not choose an idol thoughtlessly, because you will pay the price with your entire mind. You will be delayed when you look back, and you will not perceive that Christ is here. Look forward, and walk with confidence and with a happy heart that beats in hope, instead of pounds with fear.

11. The Will of God lies Forever in your joined mind. Until you joined your mind, you thought that God was your enemy. But, by joining your mind with its own perceptions, which seemed outside of it, you learned that your Will is One. The Will of God must reach to your awareness, and you cannot forget for long that It is your own.

6. The Justification for Forgiveness

1. Your anger is *never* justified; attack does *not* have a foundation. It is with these ideas that your escape from fear begins and will be made complete. Here, you find True Perception in place of illusions of terror. It is in these ideas that your forgiving rests and you find it to be natural. You are not asked to offer pardon where attack is justified. That would mean that separation from God is real, and that you are being asked to overlook reality. That is not pardon. You would be assuming that, by responding in a way that is not justified, your pardon is the answer to an attack that is real. But your pardon would actually be inappropriate by being granted where it is not due.

2. Your pardon is *always* justified; it has a sure Foundation. You are not asked to forgive the unforgivable, or to overlook a real attack that calls for punishment. Your salvation does not ask that you make unnatural responses, which are inappropriate in light of What is Real. It asks that you respond appropriately to what is *not* real by not perceiving it as though it *is* real. If attack were real, and you forgave it, you would be giving unjustified pardon, and you would be sacrificing your rights. But you are only asked to see forgiving as your natural reaction to 'attack' that comes from your error of perceiving separation as real, which is therefore your call for help. Your forgiving your perceptions of separation is your only sane response to them; it *keeps* your Rights from being attacked.

3. This understanding is the only change of your mind that lets your Real Perception take the place of your illusions of terror. Fear arises

713

when you think that attack is justified, and if attack had a real foundation, your pardon would *not* have a real foundation. You achieve your Real Perception when you perceive that the basis for your forgiving is quite real and is fully justified. While you regard your forgiving as an unwarranted gift, it upholds the guilt that it is supposed to 'forgive'. Your unjustified forgiving is another form of attack, and this is all that you ever can give in your identification with a personal self. Sometimes the personal mind pardons 'sinners', but it upholds their 'sin' as real, so they do not really merit the forgiveness that it gives.

4.   This is the false forgiving that the personal mind employs to keep your sense of separation from God alive. If unmerited pardon is what forgiving is, then it means that you are guilty of separating from God, and you then can't help but fear God. But you are saved from this dilemma by forgiving your perception of separation and learning that it has not occurred. Your mind believes Its Source is like itself. If you can look out at the world that you perceive and forgive it, you teach yourself that God's forgiveness of you is your right. And if you do not think that what you perceive merit a frightening judgment, then you will not think that you do. You will believe that you merit as little or as much punishment as you think what you perceive merits.

5.   Recognize that your forgiving is merited, and it will heal you. Your forgiving gives your miracles the strength to overlook your illusions, and this is how you learn that you are forgiven, too. You can overlook every appearance. If there was even one that you could not overlook, it would mean that some forms of separation are beyond forgiving, and that some errors are unchangeable and Eternal and beyond correction or escape. There would be at least one mistake that had the power to undo Creation and to make a world that could replace It and destroy the Will of God. Only if this was possible could there be some appearances that could withstand the miracle and not be healed by it.

6.   Your belief that some forms of sickness and joylessness cannot be healed by your forgiving them is sure proof that you wish for idolatry. This belief means that you are not yet prepared to let go of

all idols, because you prefer to keep some. You will think that some appearances are not appearances, but real. Do not be deceived by the meaning of your fixed belief that some appearances are harder for you to look past than others. It always means that you think that your own forgiving of yourself must be limited. You will have set yourself a goal of partial pardon and limited escape from guilt. This can only be false forgiving of yourself and the world.

7.   Either the miracle can heal all forms of sickness, or it cannot heal at all. Its purpose cannot be to judge which forms of sickness are real and which appearances are true, because if one appearance cannot be healed, then one illusion must be a part of Truth. And you will not be able to escape all guilt, but only some of it. You must entirely forgive all of your mind's illusions, or you keep an image of yourself that is not Whole, and you remain afraid to look within and find escape from every idol there. Your salvation rests on your faith that there cannot be some forms of guilt that you cannot forgive, so there cannot be some appearances that have replaced the Truth about you.

8.   Look on your relationship with another who seems outside of you with a willingness to see it as it is. Do not keep any part of your perception of the other outside of your willingness that it be healed. For you to heal is for you to be made Whole in your awareness again, and Wholeness can have no missing parts that are left outside. Your own forgiving of yourself rests on recognizing this and on your being glad that there are not some forms of sickness which miracles must lack the power to heal.

9.   Your Christ Mind is Perfect, or It couldn't be One with God. You will not know Christ if you think that you do not merit escape from guilt and all of its forms and consequences that you perceive. To know the Truth about yourself, there is only this way to think of your mind and all that it perceives:

Thank you, God, for my Christ Mind's Perfection.
In Christ's Glory, I see my own.[1]

Here is your Joyful statement that there are no forms of separation that can overcome the Will of God, and your glad acknowledgment that you have not succeeded in making illusions real by your wish. This is only a simple statement of the Truth.

10. Look on your Holy relationship with hope, and you will understand that you cannot make an error that can change the Truth in your mind. It is not difficult for you to overlook mistakes that do not have effects, but when you see an idol, you are not forgiving. In specialness, you have made an idol of your relationship, and it is a sign of death. Then it cannot be your salvation, and it seems as though God is wrong about you, rather than that you have been wrong about the relationship that has been given to you for your salvation and deliverance.

7. The New Interpretation

1. God has not left the meaning of the world that you perceive to the personal mind's interpretation, because, if God did, it would have no meaning. Meaning that reflects Truth cannot constantly change. The Holy Spirit looks on the world as having the one unchanging purpose of your forgiving it, and every situation that you perceive in the world is in accord with this. Only if the world's goal could change with each situation could each situation be open to an interpretation which is different each time you think of it. Then, you would add a new element into the 'script' that you write for every minute in your day, and everything that happens now would mean something else later.

2. In your identification with a personal self, this is how you write your 'scripts'. They only reflect your plans for what the day *should* mean according to the personal mind's goal. So, you judge disaster and success, advance and retreat, gain and loss according to the personal mind's script of the moment. The fact that the events have no meaning in themselves is demonstrated by the ease with which you can change your judgment of a situation based on your ongoing experience. Looking back, you see a different meaning for a situation than you saw at the time it occurred. But, what you are really doing is showing yourself that there was no real meaning there at all. You assigned meaning according to your present goal,

which can change, and which will shift meaning for the situation when it does.

3. Only a constant purpose can endow events with stable meaning, but it must accord *one* meaning to *all* events. If each event is given a different meaning, it must mean that each has a different purpose, and your confusion then becomes their meaning. Your perception cannot be in constant flux and allow for stability of meaning anywhere. Fear is a judgment that is never justified. Its presence means that you wrote a fearful script, but not that what you fear has a fearful meaning in itself.

4. Your perception can only be stabilized through a common purpose for all that you perceive, with one interpretation being given to the entire world and to your experiences in the world. In the common purpose of your forgiving, you extend one judgment to everyone and everything that you perceive. In fact, you do not have to judge, because you realize that everything has the same meaning, and you are glad to see it everywhere. The purpose of your forgiving cannot change *because* you want to perceive it everywhere, unchanged by circumstances, so you extend it to all events to perceive stability.

5. To escape from judgment yourself, you only need to realize that all things have the one purpose of being forgiven, which you share with them. Nothing in the world can be opposed to this purpose, because it belongs to everything as it belongs to you. In a single purpose, your idea of sacrifice ends, because there cannot be different purposes where some things gain and other things lose. There is no sacrifice apart from the idea that gain and loss are possible, and this is the idea that makes for different goals and shifting perceptions and meanings. In one united goal of being forgiven, loss is impossible, because your willingness to forgive all that you perceive makes your interpretation stabilize and last.

6. True Communication cannot be established in your mind while you perceive things in the world as symbols that mean different things. The Holy Spirit's goal of forgiveness gives one interpretation that is meaningful for your mind *and* for all that it perceives, so that you can join in True Communication with everything in your perception and it with you. When you see everything as a

symbol of one meaning, there is no sacrifice of meaning for you. Your sacrifice of Oneness has resulted in your loss of the ability to see relationships among events in your perception. Looked at separately, events have no meaning or purpose in themselves, because they can only be understood in relationship with other events. In any thought of separation, there is no meaning, and events are part of a distorted script that is forever unintelligible. This is not True Communication. Your illusions are but the senseless, isolated scripts that you write with a personal mind. Do not look to illusions of separation for meaning. You can only extend illusions of forgiving, which mean the same thing for your mind and for all that it perceives.

7.   Do not interpret from the personal mind, because the separation it sees means nothing. Everything will shift in what it stands for, and you will believe that the world that you perceive is unstable and dangerous. But it is only your interpretations that are lacking in stability, because they are not in line with the Truth in you. This is a state that seems so unsafe that you *must* be afraid. Do not continue this way. The Holy Spirit is your one Interpreter, and through the Holy Spirit's use of everything that you perceive as a symbol for your forgiving, your mind is joined again in True Communication.

8. Changeless Reality

1.   Appearances deceive, because they can change. Reality is Changeless, so It does not deceive at all. If you fail to see beyond appearances, then you *are* deceived. Everything that the body sees will change, yet you think that it is real, and after it changes, you will still think that it is real. So 'reality' *seems* to you to be form and changeability, but actually Reality is Changeless. It is this that makes It Real and separates It off from appearances. Reality must transcend all form to be Itself. It cannot change.

2.   Your experience of miracles is your salvation from appearances, because it demonstrates that all appearances can change because they *are* appearances, and they do not have the Changelessness of Reality. Changelessness is in your mind, beyond appearances and

deception. It is obscured by the changing perceptions that you think are reality. Your Happy Illusion takes the form of perfect health, freedom from all lack, and safety from disaster. Your experience of miracles is proof that you are not bound by loss or suffering in any form, because they can be so easily changed. This demonstrates that they were never real, and that they could not stem from Reality. Reality is Changeless, and Its Effects cannot be altered. Appearances are shown to be unreal *because* they change.

3. When you are tempted by anything in the world, it is only your wish to make illusions real. It does not seem to be this, but it is your assertion that some idols have a powerful appeal that makes them harder for you to resist than those that you do not want to be real. When you are tempted by the world, it is nothing more than your prayer that your experience of the miracle not touch some of your illusions to keep their unreality obscure to you, and to make them real to you. Heaven does not answer this prayer, and a miracle cannot be given to you to heal only the appearances that you do not like. Then you will have established limits, and what you ask for will be given to you, but not by God, Which does not know limits. You will have limited yourself.

4. Reality is Changeless. Your experience of miracles shows you only that the illusions that you have interposed between Reality and your awareness of Reality are unreal, and that they do not interfere with Reality at all. Your belief that some appearances are beyond the hope of change means that you do not consistently perceive miracles, because you have asked that miracles not heal *all* of your illusions. You will be given a miracle when you want healing, but no miracle can be given to you unless you want it. Choose what the personal mind wants to heal, and the Holy Spirit is not free to bestow healing on you. When you are tempted by illusions, you deny Reality, and you become the willing slave of what you chose instead.

5. Reality is Changeless, so a miracle is here for you to heal all things that change to a happy form that is devoid of fear. This Perception will be given to you for your relationship with another who seems outside of you, but not while you still want it otherwise in some

respects. This means that you do not want your relationship healed and whole. The Christ in your Real Perception is Perfect. Is it This that you want to look on? Then do not hold onto any illusions of the other that you prefer to see instead of Christ. You will see Christ when you let Christ come to you. And when you see Christ, you will be certain that you are like It, because your Christ Mind is the Changelessness in you and in your mind mind where you perceive a world.

6.   Christ is What you will look upon when you decide that there is not one appearance that you want to hold onto in place of What your Mind is. Do not let any temptation to prefer an illusion allow uncertainty to enter your mind. Do not be guilty or afraid when you are tempted by illusions, and do not give illusions the power to replace the Changeless in your perception. Every appearance will fade if you request a miracle instead. There is no pain from which you will not be free if you let your Christ Mind be What It is. Why do you fear to see Christ? You only behold your True Self when you see It. As your perceptions are healed, you will be freed of guilt, because the Appearance of Christ is your own.

Chapter 31

The Final Vision

1. The Simplicity of Salvation

1. Your salvation is so simple! All you need to recognize is that what was never True is not True and never will be True. The impossible has not occurred, and it can have no effects, and that is all. This cannot be hard for you to learn, if you want it to be true. Only your unwillingness to learn it can make such an easy lesson seem difficult. How hard can it be for you to see that what is false is not true, and what is true cannot be false? You can no longer say that you cannot perceive the difference between the false and the True. You have been told exactly how to tell one from the other, and just what to do if you become confused. Why, then, do you persist in not learning such a simple thing?

2. There is a reason, but do not think it is because the simple things that you need to learn for your salvation are difficult. For your salvation, you only learn the very obvious. You only go from one obvious lesson to the next, in easy steps that lead you gently from one to the next, with no strain at all. This cannot be confusing, but you *are* confused, because somehow you believe that what is totally confusing is easier to learn and understand. What your split mind has taught you is such a giant learning feat that it is indeed incredible. But you have accomplished it only because you wanted to, and, in your diligence, you did not judge it as too hard to learn or as too complex to grasp.

3. You cannot doubt the power of your learning skill if you under-stand how carefully you have learned separation from God, and the pains to which you have gone to practice and repeat its lessons endlessly, in every form of which you can conceive. There is no greater power in your perception that you are in a world than your learning, because the world was made by it, and even now depends on it alone. You have so over-learned the lessons that your

split mind has taught you, that they are fixed in your mind like a heavy curtain to obscure the Simple and Obvious. Don't say that you cannot learn the Simple and Obvious, because your power to learn is strong enough to teach you that your will is not your own, your thoughts do not belong to you, and even that you are something other than What you are.

4.   You cannot maintain that these lessons of separation are easy. But you have learned more than this. You have continued taking every step, no matter how difficult, and without complaint, to build a world that suits you. Every lesson that makes up your world arises from your first lesson, which was that you successfully attacked and separated yourself from God. This lesson is so enormous, that for you the Holy Spirit's Voice seems still and small before it. The world began with this one strange lesson, which is powerful enough to make you forget God, to make your True Self an alien to you, and to place you in seeming exile from the Home Where God establishes you. You who are One with God have taught yourself that you are guilty of separating from God, so do not say that you cannot learn the simple things that you need for your salvation!

5.   Learning is an ability that your split mind made and that it gave to you. It was not made to do the Will of God, but to uphold your split mind's wish to oppose God's Will, and to make a will apart from God's Will more real to you than God's Will. This is what your learning has sought to demonstrate, and you have learned this. Now your ancient over-learning stands seemingly immovable before the Holy Spirit, to teach you that the Holy Spirit's Lessons are not true, that they are too hard for you to learn, too difficult for you to perceive, and too opposed to what is 'real'. But you will learn them, because learning them is the only purpose that the Holy Spirit has for your learning skill. The Holy Spirit's lessons in forgiving have a Power that is mightier than your split mind's purpose, because they call to you from God and from your True Self.

6.   The Holy Spirit's Voice is not so still and small that It cannot rise above the senseless noise of meaningless sounds. God does not will that you forget God, and the Power of God's Will is in the Holy

Spirit's Voice, Which speaks for God. Which lessons will you learn? What outcome is as inevitable as God, and as far beyond doubt and question? Your little learning, which is incredibly difficult, and has resulted in a strange outcome, cannot withstand the simple lessons being taught to you by the Holy Spirit every moment of every day, since time began and learning was made.

7. There are only two lessons for you to learn, and each has its outcome in a different perception for you. Each perception follows surely from its source. The certain outcome of the lesson that you are guilty of separating from God is the world that the personal mind perceives. It is a world of terror and despair. There is no hope of happiness in it, there is no plan of safety in it that will ever succeed, and there is no joy that you can hope to find in it. But this is not the only outcome that your learning can produce. However much you have over-learned your chosen task of separation, the lesson that reflects God's Love is still stronger. You *will* learn that you are Innocent, and you *will* experience a different perception.

8. The outcome for you in the lesson that you are Innocent is a Perception in which there is no fear, and in which everything that you perceive is lit with Hope and Gentle Friendliness, because you recognize that everything is in your mind. You perceive everything appealing to you for Love and to be One with you. You recognize that every call for Love is from a part of your mind to you, and you do not misunderstand, or leave unanswered with Love, any call for Love. You understand that this call for Love is everywhere, because your mind is everywhere, and that it always has been, but that you had not perceived this. Now you see that you were mistaken, because you were deceived by forms that seemed to hide your mind's call for Love. You did not hear the call, and you appeared to have lost a Loving part of yourself. The other lesson that you can learn is the soft, Eternal calling for Love to your Whole Mind from every part of your mind that you perceive.

9. Your mind longs for Wholeness and for you to hear its call for Wholeness. Without your Loving answer, everything that your mind perceives seems to represent death, but you can perceive the call for Life instead, and understand that it is your own. Your

Christ Mind remembers God with all the Certainty that your Christ Mind knows God's Love. But only in Innocence are you Love, because God *would* be fear if you could be guilty. Your Christ Mind remembers your Oneness with God, but in guilt you forget What you really are.

10. The lesson that you are guilty results in your fear of God, as surely as you remember God's Love when you learn that you are Innocent. Your hate fosters fear and looks on its source as itself. You are wrong when you fail to hear the call for Love that is behind your every perception of seeming death and murderous attack, which are only your mind's pleading to be restored to Love. You do not understand Who calls to you behind every seeming form of hate and call to conflict. But you will recognize Christ when you answer in the Love with Which your Christ Mind calls to you. Christ will appear when you have answered, and you will know that God is Love.

11. Your temptation to choose illusions is only your wish to make the wrong decision about what you want to learn, and to have an outcome that you do not really want. But you can recognize your unwanted state of mind as a motivation to reassess your choice because you prefer another outcome. You are deceived if you think that you want disaster, chaos, and pain. Do not hear this call within yourself, but listen deeper for your call for Peace and Joy, and all that you perceive will give you Peace and Joy. As you hear, you will answer, and your answer will be the proof of what you learned. And what you perceive will be the outcome of your learning.

12. Be still an instant and forget all that you ever learned through the personal mind, all that you ever thought through it, and every preconception that it has of what things mean and what their purpose is. Let go of the personal mind's ideas of what the world is for. It does not know. Let every image that it holds onto be loosened from your mind and swept away.

13. Be innocent of any judgment, and unaware of any thought of evil or good that has ever crossed your mind about anyone or anything in the world that you perceive. Now you do not know what they are for, and you are free to learn. Now, the part of your mind where

you perceive a world is born again to you, and you to it, without your sentence of death upon it or on you. Now, your entire mind is freed from an ancient lesson, and Truth has been left a place to be reborn in your awareness.

2. Walking with Christ

1. Your old lesson of separation from God is not overcome by your new lesson of Oneness with God opposing it. Your old lesson does not need to be fought or vanquished for you to know the Truth. There is no battle to prepare, no time to expend, and no plans that you need to make for you to learn the lesson of Oneness. There *is* an old battle being waged within you against the Truth, but Truth does not respond. You cannot be hurt in such a war, unless you hurt yourself. You have no enemy in Truth, and you cannot be assailed by illusions.

2. It is time to review again what seems to stand between you and the Truth of What you are. There are steps in your relinquishment of your perception of separation from God, and the first is your decision for Truth. After that, the Truth is revealed to you. In your split mind, you wish to establish what is true, and, by your wish, you made two choices that you think you must choose between whenever you must decide on anything. Neither choice is true, nor are they different from each other. You must see them both before you can look past them to the one Alternative that really *is* a different choice. This Alternative is not an illusion that you made to obscure What It represents.

3. What you want to choose between is not a choice, and it is an illusion that it is a free choice, because either will have the same outcome for you. The choice that you think that you have to make in any situation is whether you are going to be a leader or a follower, with someone else taking the role that you did not choose. You think each role has different advantages, and that in their fusion you can find satisfaction and peace. You see yourself forever divided between these two roles, and every relationship that you make in your perception that you are in a world, whether you have made them with 'enemies' or 'friends', is supposed to be

a means to help you save yourself from this split.

4. Sometimes you call the relationship 'love'; sometimes you think that your wanting the other dead is justified. You hate the one to whom you give the leader's role when you want to lead, and you hate the one who does *not* take the leader's role when you want to follow. These separate roles are what you made 'others' for, and this is what you have learned their purpose is. Only if they serve this purpose are they fulfilling the function that you have given to them, and if they don't serve this purpose, you hate them because they have no purpose or usefulness to you.

5. You will think that others want from you what you want from your relationship with them. You choose Life or death for yourself, and you perceive your choice in your relationships with others. There are two calls that you can hear in every relationship, and they do offer you different outcomes. If you hear in your relationships a call for either a leader or a follower, then you have chosen death. But if you perceive that the call is for either hate or forgiveness, then you are hearing truly different calls. Hear the call for hate, and your mind is separated and lost. But hear in your relationships with others your own call for forgiveness, and your mind is joined and saved. What do others ask you for? Listen well, because in others you will hear what you want to come to you, because it is your own mind that you are hearing.

6. Before you react to a call that you think you hear in a relationship with another, think of this:

    'I will respond in my relationship with this other with what I want. And what I learn of this relationship is what I want to learn about myself.'

Then wait an instant and be still. Forget everything that you thought you heard in the personal mind, and remember how much it does not know. Your relationships with others are not for playing leader or follower, but for your recognizing that what your mind perceives is a part of your mind. They can represent the forgiveness that you really want to the extent that you will let them. Your advance toward or retreat from Peace is made in your choice of how you look on your relationships with others. See Love in place of the personal mind's perceptions, and you progress toward Peace. Your mind remains split unless you keep Christ in your awareness by seeing Christ reflected in your perceptions of others.

7.   Your Whole Mind is One in God's Love, so you will be saved from all appearances, and you will answer your Christ Mind, Which calls to you from everything that your mind perceives. Do not think the old thoughts of separation; forget the dismal lessons that the personal mind teaches you about yourself. Your Christ Mind calls to you from everything that you perceive, and It does not see leaders or followers, but It answers every call with Love. Because your Christ Mind hears One Voice, It cannot hear an answer that is different from the one that It gave to God when God extended God to It.

8.   Be very still an Instant. Come to this Instant without any of the lessons that you learned from the personal mind, and put aside all of the images that it has made. Your old thoughts of separation will fall away before your new thoughts of Oneness, without opposition or intent. There will not be an attack on the things that, in separation, you thought were precious and in need of care. There will not be an attack on your wish to hear a call that has never been made. Nothing will hurt you in this Holy Instant to Which you come to listen silently, and to learn of the Truth that you really want. You will not be asked to learn more than This. As you hear It, you will understand that you only need to come away without the thoughts that you do not really want and that were never true.

9.   Forgive your relationships with others all the appearances that are only the old lessons that you have taught yourself about the reality of separation in you. Hear in your relationships your own call for mercy and release from all the fearful images of what you think you are. You think that it is safer to play a role of leader or follower in your relationships, but you cannot make progress toward Peace when you think that any role in a world of separation is the way to attain It. Your journey's goal is the re-uniting of your mind, so the

way for you to attain Peace is in your recognizing that all that you perceive is in your mind. In this choice, the outcome of your learning is changed because your Christ Mind is reborn in your awareness.

10. To let this happen, it is enough for you to spend an Instant without your old ideas of what your relationships with others are for, and of what others are asking of you. You will perceive your purpose in your perceptions of others. You can perceive in them a request for the forgiving that *you* want. Everything that your mind perceives needs forgiveness as you do. The request may take many different forms, but it is not the form that you answer to. If you see your request for forgiveness in your perceptions, you receive forgiveness as you answer, because you will perceive one purpose in every-thing, and that is that your mind unite in Love. As part of your mind, your perceptions of others are Part of God.

11. Uniting your mind is how you remember and accept your mind's Oneness. Alone in the personal mind, you deny your mind's Oneness with what your mind perceives. While you insist that your relationships with others are for playing the role of leader or follower, you are lost, because Love cannot be given to you in the personal self. You are confused, and in your endless doubting you stagger back and forth between roles. But these roles are only appearances of what the journey is and how it must be made. Christ is here to be sure that every step that you take to God you make in certainty. Your denial can obscure your perception and make your path seem obscure, but your Christ Mind makes it all clear.

3. The Self-Accused

1. You condemn others for their guilt only when you believe that *you* are guilty. As you prepare to make a choice that will result in a different outcome from all that has gone before, there is one thing that you first must over-learn. Being aware of this must become a habit of response so typical of everything that you do, that it becomes your first response to all temptation to choose illusions and to every situation that occurs. Learn this well, because it is here

that you can shorten your unhappiness by a span of time that you cannot realize: You never hate others for their sins, but only for what you believe is your own sin of separating from God. Whatever you see as another's form of separation obscures the fact that you are seeing your own separation from God, and that is why you think it merits attack.

2. You would not see another's form of separation as a sin if you did not believe that *you* cannot be forgiven for separating from God. To you, separation from God is real in another *because* you believe it is real in you. You attack sin everywhere else so that you don't have to hate yourself for 'sinning' by separating from God. Whenever you attack, it is because you believe that you are sin, and by attacking, you assert that you are guilty of separating from God, and you must give as you deserve. Your mind always perceives itself. If you did not believe that you deserve attack it would not occur to you to give attack. There would be nothing to gain for you in attacking, and you would not see any benefit in destroying another.

3. You always perceive sins in bodies, not in your mind. You don't see sins as purposes, but as actions, and bodies act; your mind does not act. So you think that the body must be at fault for what it does. You do not see it as a passive thing that is only obeying your mind's commands. If you are sin, then you are a body, because your mind does not act, and purpose must be of the body, not of your mind. So you think the body acts on its own and is self-motivating. If you are sin, you lock your mind in a body, and you give your mind's purpose to the body, which acts instead of your mind.

4. But the body *obeys* your mind. It cannot think, and it does not have the power to learn, to pardon, or to limit. It does not give your mind orders or set conditions your mind must obey. It only limits your mind when you are willing for it to be limited. It sickens at the bidding of your mind when you want to be restricted to it, and it grows old and dies when your mind is sick. Your learning is all that causes change, so the body, which cannot learn, cannot change, unless you prefer that the body change to suit your mind's purpose. Your mind can learn, and it is only in your mind that

change is made.

5. When you prefer to think that you are sin, your mind has one purpose for you: that it see the body as the source of sin to keep itself limited, and to deny that *it* is the source of hate, evil, sickness, attack, pain, age, grief, and suffering. When you see yourself in a body, your mind preserves the idea of sacrifice, because in a body, separation and guilt rule. Then the mind orders that the world that it perceives be like what it is in the body: a place where there is no mercy, and where fear is overcome only through death. In the body, you are made into sin, and sin cannot abide in the Joyous and Free, because these are the enemies that sin must kill. Sin is preserved in death, and if you believe that you are sin, you must die for what you think that you are.

6. Be glad that you recognize what you believe, because you have the means to change what you believe. The body will only follow your mind, and it cannot lead you where you do not want to go. The body does not guard your denial of God, and it cannot interfere with you becoming aware of God. Release the body, and you will no longer see any body as limitation on your mind. You will not want to hold onto guilt and limitation by perceiving them in others.

7. In Innocence, you release what you perceive in gratitude for your own release. Then What you perceive will uphold your freedom from limitations and death. Open your mind to change, and there will be no punishment for you or in your perception. God has not asked you for sacrifice, so there is no sacrifice for you to make.

4. The Real Alternative

1. You have a tendency to think that the world that you perceive can offer you consolation and escape from the problems that it is its purpose to keep in your awareness. This is because the world is a place where your only choices are among illusions, and you seem to be in control of the outcomes that you choose. So you think that the narrow band of time between birth and death is given to you to use for you alone; a time when everyone conflicts with you, but you can choose which road leads you out of the conflict and difficulties that you've decided do not concern you. But they are in your mind,

so they *are* your concern. You cannot escape your mind's perceptions by leaving them behind. Whatever road you choose to take, what is in your mind must go with you.

2. You have a Real Choice that is not an illusion, but the world that you perceive does not offer you This. All its roads lead you to disappointment, nothingness, and death. It offers you no other alternative. Do not seek within the world for escape from your problems, because you made the world so that you could not escape your problems. Do not be deceived by all the different names that you have given its roads, because they have only one end – death. Each is your means to gain death, however different they seem to be. You may travel happily on some a while before the bleakness enters; on others you suffer from the start. Your choice, then, is not what the ending will be, but when it will come.

3. You have no real choice when whatever road you choose ends the same. You may prefer to try them all before you learn that they are all one. The world that you perceive seems to offer you a large number of roads to take, but the time must come when you learn that they are all the same. You may be tempted to despair and lose hope when you see that they all lead nowhere, but with this realization you can learn your greatest lesson. You must reach this point, and then go beyond it. It is true that there is no choice at all within the world, but this is not the whole lesson. This is only the first part of the lesson.

4. Do not try another road, another person, or another place, because you have learned the way the lesson starts, but you do not yet perceive what it is for. The purpose of the lesson is the Answer to the search that you undertook when you came to believe that there is an Alternative to be found beyond the world that you perceive. Learn without despair that there is no hope of real answer in the world, but do not judge the lesson that only begins with this. Understand that you waste time if you do not go beyond this part of the lesson. From this lowest point, your learning will lead you to the Heights of Happiness, in Which you will see that the purpose of the lesson is perfectly within your grasp.

5. In order for you to turn away from them, you must understand the

futility of the many paths that you can take in the world that you perceive. This is where you begin to seek Another Way. While you see a choice where there is none, you cannot make a real decision. The power of your decision-making begins with your learning where it has real use.

6.   Your learning that the world that you perceive offers you only one choice, no matter what form it seems to take, is the beginning of your accepting that there is a Real Alternative to choose. For you to fight against this step is for you to defeat your true purpose in your perception that you are in a world. In your split mind, you do not perceive yourself in a world to find Truth, but to make your perception of separation from God real to you. And your searching among many different paths in the world is your attempt to decide for yourself what is true, and this keeps you from reaching the Truth.

7.   Do not think that your Happiness can ever be found by your taking a road away from Happiness. This does not make sense. To you who seem to find this course too difficult to learn, let it be repeated that to achieve a goal you must proceed in its direction, not away from it. And every road that leads away from your goal will not advance your purpose. If this is difficult for you to understand, then this course is impossible for you to learn. Otherwise, it is a simple teaching in the obvious.

8.   When you have seen the Real Alternative, It presents you with a choice that you have the power to make. Until you have reached this point, you have no choice and can only choose how to continue to deceive yourself. This course attempts to teach you that the power of your decision-making cannot lie in your choosing among different forms of the same illusion. In your perception that you are in a world. you see your only choice as whether you are going to perceive lack within you, or to project it onto what you perceive. This is utterly opposed to Truth, because all real lessons teach you that what your mind perceives is what you believe about yourself.

9.   God has not left Its Thought! But you have forgotten God, and you do not remember God's Love. No path in the world that you perceive can lead to God, nor can any worldly goal be one with

God. No road in the world leads you within, because, unless your purpose is futile wandering, every road in the world was made to separate your journey from your True Purpose of God. All roads that lead you away from your Oneness with God will lead you to confusion and despair. But God has not left you to die or to be without God within you.

10. God has not left Its Thought! God can no more depart from you than you can keep God out. You abide with God in Oneness, Which keeps you Both complete. There is no road that really leads you away from God; a journey away from yourself does not exist. It is foolish and insane for you to think that there could be a road with this aim. Where would it go, and how could you travel on it without your own Reality?

11. Forgive yourself your madness, and forget all the senseless journeys and goal-less aims that you have undertaken. They have no meaning. You cannot escape from your Oneness with God, because God is Merciful and did not let you abandon God. Be thankful for What you are, because in That is your escape from madness and death. You can only find yourself in God, and every real path leads you to God.

5. Self-Concept versus Self

1. Your learning in your perception that you are in a world is built on your concept of a 'self' that is adjusted to the 'reality' of the world. This image of a 'self' suits well a world of shadows and illusions, because it walks at home where what it sees is like itself. Building a concept of a 'self' is the purpose that the personal mind has for your learning in the world. You come to the world without a self, and you make a self as you go along. By the time you reach 'maturity', you have perfected this self to meet the world on equal terms, and to be at one with its demands.

2. You have made a concept of a self, but it bears no resemblance to your Real Self at all. It is an idol that you make to replace the Reality of your Oneness with God. This concept of a self that the personal mind teaches you is not what it appears to be, because it serves two purposes, only one of which your mind can recognize.

The first aspect of this self presents a face of innocence, and it is this you act on. This aspect smiles, charms, and even seems to 'love'. It searches for companions, and it sometimes looks on suffering with pity and an offering of solace. It believes that it is good in an evil world.

3.   This aspect grows angry at the world, which is wicked and unable to provide the love and shelter that its innocence deserves. It is often wet with tears over the injustices that the world accords those who are generous and good. It never makes the first attack, but every day a hundred little things make small assaults on its innocence, provoking its irritation, and, at last, its open insult and abuse.

4.   This aspect, with the face of innocence that your 'self' proudly wears, can tolerate attack in self-defense, because it is a well-known fact that the world deals harshly with defenseless innocence. The personal mind never omits this aspect, because you need it, and the other aspect is the one that the personal mind does not want you to see. It is this other aspect on which the personal mind looks, because it is here that its 'reality' is set in your mind to see that it lasts.

5.   Beneath your face of innocence is the lesson that you made a concept of a self to teach yourself: Someone else is responsible for your separation from God. This is a terrible lesson in displacement, and it causes you fear so devastating that your face smiling above it must look away, so that you do not perceive the self-treachery it hides. This lesson teaches: 'I am the thing that *you* have made of me, and, as you look on me, *you* stand condemned because of what I am.'[1] The personal mind smiles with approval on this concept of you as someone else's responsibility, because it guarantees that you will not look within, so it and its world will be safe, because you will never escape them.

6.   Here is your central lesson, in which someone else is eternally condemned in your place, because what you are is now *their* sin. It is not possible for you to forgive this. It does not matter what another actually does, because your accusing finger points at them, unwavering and deadly in its aim. Your finger also points at you,

but the personal mind keeps this buried even deeper below your face of innocence. You keep all of your and the other's 'sins' hidden, so that you do not perceive them as only errors, which you would clearly see if you looked honestly at them. Now you cannot be blamed for what you are, because you cannot change what others make of you. You and others are symbols of separation and sin to each other, and you condemn others for the thing that you think that you are and that you hate.

7.   A self-concept is not natural to you; you learn it. It does not exist apart from your learning. It is not given to you by God, so you must make it. Not one self-concept that you make for yourself or for others is true, and many are distortions of your fear. A concept is a thought to which its maker gives meaning. Self-concepts maintain the world that you perceive, but they cannot be used to demonstrate that the world is real. You make all of them within the world, where they are born in its shadow, grow in the world's ways, and finally 'mature'. They are ideas of idols, painted with brushes of separation, that cannot make a single picture representing Truth to you.

8.   A concept of a self is meaningless, because it is really for your separation from God. Yet, all of your learning, as the personal mind directs, begins and ends with the single aim of teaching you a concept of yourself, so that you will choose to follow the 'laws' of the world of separation, and never seek to go beyond its paths, nor realize the real way to see yourself. So the Holy Spirit must find a way to help you see that if you want Peace, your self-concept must be undone. It can only be unlearned through lessons that teach you that you are Something Else. Otherwise, you will think that you are being asked to be without a self, and a greater terror will arise in you.

9.   The Holy Spirit's lesson plans are arranged in easy steps. Though you may experience some discomfort, and even distress at times, there is no shattering of the self that you have taught yourself, only a re-translation of what seems to be the evidence on its behalf. Consider, then, what proof there is that you are what others have made of you. Even though you may not yet perceive that this is

what you think, you certainly see that you behave as though it were true. Do others react for you, see your future, and ordain beforehand what you should do in every circumstance? They must've made the world as well as you to have such prescience of things to come!

10. That you are what others have made of you seems most unlikely. Even if they did, who gave you the face of innocence? Is this your contribution? Then who is the 'you' who made it? And who is deceived by your goodness and attacks it? Forget the foolishness of the concept that others make you, and think about the two aspects of the self that you think that you are. If one is made by others, who made the other? And from whom are you hiding the awareness that others make you? Even if the world is evil, there is still no reason for you to hide that others make you. Who is there to care? Only what is attacked needs to be hidden in defense.

11. Maybe the reason the concept that others make you must be kept hidden is that *you* are the one who would not think it was true. What would happen to the world that you perceive if all of its underpinnings were removed? Your concept of the world depends on your concept that others make you. Both would go if you raised either concept to doubt. But the Holy Spirit does not seek to throw you into panic; It only asks if just a little question might be raised.

12. There is an alternative way for you to look at what you must be. You might, for instance, be the thing that you choose others to be. This shifts your concept of the self from something that is totally passive to make way for your active choice and some acknowledgment that your own interaction must enter into your self-concept. There is some understanding that you choose for both you and others, and that what others represent to you is your choice. This shows a glimmer of perception's law that what you see reflects your mind. But who did the choosing first? If you are what you choose others to be, then there must be alternatives for you to choose among, and someone must have made the choice.

13. This step has some gains for you, but it does not yet approach a basic question: What did the learning that gave rise to your concepts of a self? There must be something that came before. The

main advantage of shifting to the second point of view from the first point of view is that you acknowledge that you have entered into the choice of your self-concept. But your pay for this gain in almost equal loss, because now you stand accused for others' separation from God. You must share in guilt, because you chose it for others in the image of your own separation from God. Before, only others were treacherous; now you must be condemned as well.

14. The great preoccupation of the personal mind is a self-concept for you. In your identification with it, you believe that you must find the answer to the riddle of yourself. So your salvation is nothing more than your escape from concepts. It does not concern itself with the content of your mind, but with the simple fact that it thinks, and that what can think can choose and can be shown that different thoughts have different consequences. Your mind can learn that everything that it thinks in separation from God reflects the deep confusion that you feel about how you were made and what you are. Only vaguely does a concept of a self appear to answer what you do not know.

15. Do not seek your Self in symbols. There is no concept that stands for What you are. It doesn't matter what concept you accept while you perceive a self in separation from God. It is meaningless, and you do not perceive that you interact only with your own perceptions. For you to see a world of separation is for you to be guided by the personal mind, and you see the world as you see yourself. Your self-concept embraces all that you look on, and nothing is outside of this perception. If you are hurt by anything, you are seeing a picture of your secret wish to be hurt. In your suffering, you see your own desire to kill the Christ Mind in you.

16. As your learning goes along, you will make many self-concepts. As you change your perception of yourself, each change will show up in your relationship with your mind where you perceive a world. You will experience some confusion with each shift, but be grateful that what you have learned through the personal mind is loosening its grip on your mind. Be happy in the confidence that all self-concepts will go at last and leave your mind in Peace. The role of

the accuser will appear in many places and in many forms, and each will seem to be accusing you. But you can trust it will all be undone.

17. The personal mind cannot teach you images of yourself, unless you want to learn them. There will come a time when images have all gone by you, and you will see that you do not know what you are. It is to your open mind that Truth returns without limits. Where you lay aside self-concepts, Truth is revealed to you exactly as It is. When you have raised every self-concept to doubt and question, and you have recognized that they cannot stand before the Truth in you, then the Truth will be free to enter your guilt-free mind. There is no statement that the personal mind is more afraid to hear from you than this:

'I do not know what I am, so I do not know what I am doing, where I am, or how to look on the world or myself.'

In this lesson, your salvation is born. And What you are will tell you of Itself.

6. Recognizing the Spirit

1. You see the body or you recognize your Spirit; there is no compromise between these two perceptions for you. If one is real, then the other must be false, because reality denies its opposite. You have no choice in perception but this, and what you decide to perceive determines what is real and true for you. Your whole world depends on this one choice, because you believe that you can establish what you are. If you choose the body, you will never escape it as your reality, because you want it to be so. But choose your Spirit, and all of Heaven will bless your perceptions, and you will see a world only for the purpose of extending healing and blessing in your awareness.

2. Your salvation is the undoing of your perception of separation from God. If you choose to see the body, you will behold a world of unrelated things and events that make no sense at all. This person appears and then disappears in death; that one is doomed to

suffering and loss. No one is exactly as they were an instant before, and they will not be the same an instant from now. You cannot trust where change is constant, and who is worthy of your trust if they are only dust? Your salvation is the undoing of all of this, because Constancy arises in your perception when you release yourself from perceiving the cost of separation from God by letting it go.

3. To be saved, you do not have to perceive only your Spirit and not perceive the body at all; you only have to want this to be your choice. You can see the body without help, but you do not yet understand how to perceive Truly. Your salvation is the undoing of the world of separation in your mind, and this brings you a Perception that the body's eyes can never find. Do not be concerned with how this can be, because you do not even understand how you see the world that you made. If you did, it would be gone. You must let go of all perceptions of good and evil so that both may disappear, and you cannot hide your Real Perception behind them. How is this done? It is not done at all. There is nothing left to be done in God's Creation.

4. Only in arrogance do you think that *you* must make the way to Heaven plain to yourself. The means are given to you for your Real Perception to replace the world of separation in your mind. Your Will be done! In Heaven and in the world, this is forever true. It does not matter where you believe you are, or what you think is the truth about you. It makes no difference what you perceive, or what you choose to feel, think, or wish. Gods says, 'Your Will be done' and It is done to you accordingly.

5. You who are One with God, but who believe that you can choose to perceive yourself as your split mind wants you to be, do not forget that there isn't a concept of yourself that will stand against the Truth of What you are. Truth cannot be undone, but concepts are not difficult to change. One True Perception that does not fit your picture of your world will change your perception of the world, because it will change your concept of yourself.

6. If you know that you are invulnerable, then you will perceive a world that is harmless. If you are forgiving, then the world that

739

you perceive will be forgiving, because you will have forgiven it your misperceptions. If you think that you are a body, then you will perceive a world that is treacherous and out to kill you. And if you know that you are Spirit, then you know that you are deathless and without the promise of corruption or the stain of 'sin'. From Spirit, you will perceive a world that is stable and worthy of your trust; a happy place to rest a while, where you don't need to fear anything, and you only love. You will welcome everyone and everything to your Kind heart, and in your True Innocence, you will not be hurt.

7.   Holy Part of God, your Will be done! It does not matter if you are in Heaven, or if you think that you are in a world. What God Wills for you can never change. The Truth in you is as Pure and Innocent as Love Itself. You *are* worthy that your Will be done!

7. The Savior's Vision

1.   Learning is change, and your salvation does not require that you use a means that is still too alien to your thought system to be helpful, or that you make changes that you cannot yet recognize. While you still perceive yourself in a world, you need concepts, but your salvation requires that your concepts change. For your salvation, you must learn through contrasts, not through Truth, Which has no opposite and cannot change. In the personal mind's concept, the guilty are 'bad' and the innocent are 'good', and you hold a concept of yourself in which you are both, and you count the good in you to pardon the bad in you. You do not trust the 'good' in anyone else, because you believe that the 'bad' in them is lurking behind it. This concept emphasizes treachery, and it makes it impossible for you to trust. It cannot change while you perceive the 'bad' in you.

2.   As long as you value separation from God, you will not reveal to yourself all of the thoughts that you consider 'evil', and you will not see that those that you are aware of are meaningless. So they will come to you in fearful forms to shake your sorry concept of yourself, and to darken it with yet another 'crime'. You are too confused about yourself to see your Innocence. But, if you find that your projections of the personal mind on one other who seems

outside of you are wholly worthy of forgiveness, then your concept of yourself will change. You forgive your 'evil' thoughts when you forgive the personal mind's projections on another, because you do not let them affect you. You choose to no longer make the other a symbol of your evil and guilt, and as you give your trust to the Innocence in your perception, you give it to the Good in you.

3. In terms of concepts, this is how you look on more than a body when you look on another, because a body never seems to you to be the 'good'. You perceive the actions of a body to come from the 'baser' parts of a person. By focusing on the Innocence in your perception of another, their body decreases in importance in your sight, and you eventually see their body as little more than a frame around the Good in you. And when you have reached the Perception of Innocence that is beyond what the body's eyes alone can see, this will then become your concept of yourself. You will interpret what you see with the Holy Spirit that God has given you as Aid, and in the Holy Spirit's Perception there *is* another way to see.

4. You can live in the Holy Spirit's Perception as much as in your perception of a world of separation, because both are concepts of yourself, which you can alternate, but you can never hold at the same time. The contrast between these concepts of yourself is far greater than you think, and you will love this new Concept of yourself because It will not limit you to a personal self. By extending forgiveness in your perception of someone that you once perceived as separate and outside of you, you will recognize that your mind is not limited to a personal self, and you will accept forgiveness for your entire mind.

5. Have faith in the Innocence in your perception of the other in your Holy relationship, so that your fearful concept of yourself may change. Look on your perception of Good in the other, so that you are not frightened by your 'evil' thoughts. All this happy shift requires is that you be willing to let it occur. Remember the Concept of yourself that this shift brings, and welcome the contrast to your former self-concept that it offers. Extend the kind gift of forgiveness, so that you can have forgiveness in your awareness,

and let your cruel concept of yourself be changed to one that brings you the Peace of God.

6.   The concept of yourself that you have before this shift means to guarantee that your real function in your perception that you are in a world remains forever unaccomplished. It dooms you to bitter depression and to a sense of futility. But this does not have to be, unless you choose to conceal your self-concept in your mind, and hold it beyond the hope of change. Give this concept to the Holy Spirit, Which understands the changes that your mind needs to let it serve the function of Peace by extending Peace. You *can* see yourself in another way. Wouldn't you rather see yourself as necessary to your salvation than as the enemy of your salvation?

7.   Your concept of your self stands like a barricade before the Truth in you and hides It from your sight. Everything that you perceive is merely an image, because you look at it through a barrier that dims and warps your Spiritual Perception, so that you see nothing with Real Clarity. At best, you see a shadow of the Truth beyond, and at worst, you see frightening images that come from your guilt and fear. What you see is hell, because fear *is* hell. But your True Perception, Which is your Spiritual Perception, and the Holy Spirit within you, lead you out of hell, with all the Love that your mind perceives.

8.   Behold your role in your perception that you are in a world! God has entrusted your salvation from the misery of hell to your entire mind. Your extension of God's Grace makes everyone and every-thing that you perceive your Savior. You first learn this when you look on your perception of one other in the world that seems outside of you, and you see your True Self. You then lay aside your personal self-concept, because nothing stands between your mind and What it perceives, so there is no separation in it. In this Perception, you see Christ, and you realize that you can look on everything as you look on this one other. The veil is lifted from your Real Perception, and you are aware where you were once in denial.

9.   The veil across your Christ Mind, your fear of God and salvation, and your love of guilt and death are all different descriptions for the error of separation that seems to split your mind between 'you'

and a world that you perceive outside of you. Judgment is the weapon that you give to your illusion of yourself to maintain without Love the space between your mind and what it perceives. While you hold the weapon of judgment, you perceive yourself in separation as a body/personal self, because you perceive others as a reflection of what you believe that you are.

10. All of your temptation to choose illusions is only your wish to stay in hell and misery. This gives rise to an image of yourself that can be miserable and remain in hell. Overlook one other body/personal self as real, and you save yourself, and you become a Savior to your entire mind as your forgiveness extends to all that it perceives. God entrusts you with your entire mind, because if you were only a partial Savior, you would be only partially saved. God has given you to forgive your perception of everyone you meet or look upon, everyone you see an instant and forget, everyone you have known long, those you knew but have forgotten, and those you will meet. God gives you your Whole Mind, and your part in your salvation is to forgive your mind every concept of separation it ever had.

11. You cannot save yourself while you wish to stay in hell. You see Holiness through your Holy Mind, Which looks on the Innocence within, so expects to see It everywhere. Your Holy Mind calls on Innocence in your perception of everyone and everything, so that they can be What you expect. With your Savior's Perception, you see Innocence in everything, and your own salvation everywhere. You hold no self-concept between your Calm Mind and What It sees. You bring Love to what you perceive, so that you can see your Mind as It really is.

12. Whatever forms the temptation to choose illusions takes for you, they reflect your wish to be a self that you are not. From this wish, a concept of yourself rises to teach you that you are the thing that you wish to be. It will remain your concept of yourself, until you no longer cherish the wish to be not-yourself. But while you cherish being not-yourself, you will perceive others in the likeness of the self that you made. Your perception can only represent your wishes, because it does not have the power to create. It can look with Love or it can look with hate, depending on whether you

743

want to see your mind is One or to keep your mind separated.

13. Your Savior's Perception is innocent of any of the personal mind's judgments on you or others. It does not see a past anywhere, so It serves your open mind, which is unclouded by old concepts and is prepared to look only on the present. It does not judge, because it does not know, and recognizing this, it asks: 'What is the meaning of what I behold?' Then the answer is given as Christ enters your open mind, because you asked, in innocence, to see beyond the veil of old ideas.

14. Be vigilant against your temptation to choose illusions, remembering that it is only your insane and meaningless wish to make yourself a thing that you are not. Then think well on the thing that you want to be, because it is a thing of madness, pain, treachery, despair, and failing dreams, whose only hope is to die to end its illusion of fear. This, and only this, is what tempts you. Is it difficult for you to choose *against* this? Consider what your temptation to choose between illusions is, and see the real alternatives that you have to choose between. There are only two, so do not be deceived by what seems like many choices. Your choice is Heaven or hell, and you can only choose one.

15. Do not deny to all that you perceive the Love that has been given to you. You need to perceive the Love in you, because you despair when you withhold your Savior's Perception,, and all you see is death. You do not know that your salvation is here when you deny it, and you will not see it until you look on everything with forgiveness. Can you to whom God says, 'Release yourself!' be tempted to not listen? This is what this course teaches you, and this is all there is for you to learn.

8. Choose Once Again

1. In all of its many forms, your temptation to choose illusions has only one lesson that it teaches: You, who are One with God, are a body, born in what must die, unable to escape its frailty, and bound by what it orders you to feel. The body sets the limits on what you can do, its power is the only strength that you have, and your grasp cannot exceed its tiny reach. Ask yourself if this is what you want

to be, when your Christ Mind is asking you to:

> 'Choose once again if you want to be your own Savior, or if you want to hold your mind in hell.'

2. How do you make this choice? This is easily explained, because you always choose between the weakness of the personal self and the Strength of your Christ Mind. What you choose is what you think is real. By simply not using the personal mind to direct you, you withhold your power from it, and the Love of Christ in you takes charge of everything that you do. Give the weakness of the personal mind to your Christ Mind, and Christ will give you Christ's Strength in its place.

3. Those situations that you judge as 'trials' are lessons in forgiveness that you did not learn before. They are presented again, so that where you made a faulty choice before, you can now make a better one, and escape the pain you chose before. In every difficult, distressful, or perplexing situation, Christ gently says, 'Choose again.' Christ will not leave you with one source of pain unhealed or any image to veil the Truth in you. Christ will not leave you comfortless and alone in an illusion of hell, but will release your mind from everything that hides your Christ Mind from your awareness. Christ's Holiness is yours, because your Christ Mind is the only Power that is Real in you. Christ's Strength is yours, because Christ is the One Self that God created.

4. The images that you make cannot prevail against What God wants you to be. Never fear your temptation to choose illusions, then, but see it as another chance to choose again, and let Christ's Strength prevail in every situation where you raised an image of yourself before. What appears to hide your Christ Mind is powerless before your Christ Mind's Majesty, and disappears in your Christ Mind's Holy Perception. You are your Savior when you see as your Christ Mind sees, and when you choose Christ's Strength instead of the personal mind's weakness. You *will* correct your perception, because your mind is One with all the Power of God's Will. You Will only What God wills.

5. Make these words your happy habit of response to all temptation to perceive yourself as weak and miserable:

'I am One with God. I cannot suffer.'

Thus you invite Christ's Strength to prevail, replacing the personal mind's weakness with the Strength of God, Which cannot fail. You will see that your experience of miracles is as natural as fear and agony appeared to you to be before you chose Holiness. In that choice, all false differences are gone from your perception, you lay aside all illusory alternatives, and nothing is left to interfere with the Truth in you.

6. You *are* One with God, so is your mind where you perceive a world, despite the images that you see. What you see as sickness, pain, weakness, suffering, and loss is only your temptation to perceive yourself as defenseless and in hell. Do not yield to this, and you will see all pain in every form disappear like mist before the sun. A miracle has come to heal you, and to close the door on your illusions of weakness, so that the way to salvation is open for you. Choose once again what you want to perceive, remembering that every choice establishes what you will believe is your own identity.

7. Do not deny your Christ Mind the little gift It asks of you when in exchange your Christ Mind lays the Peace of God before you, and the power to extend Peace in place of the personal mind's uncertain, lonely, and fearful perceptions. It is given you through your Christ Mind to perceive your Oneness.

8. Do not fail to hear the Voice of Christ or to listen to Its Words. Your Christ Mind asks you only for your own release. There is no place for hell in your mind's perception, which can still be so intensely Lovely and One that it is only a step for you from it to Heaven. To your tired mind, Christ brings a new Perception, so clean and fresh that you will forget the pain and sorrow that you perceived before. But you must extend this Perception everywhere, otherwise you will not see It. For you to extend this Gift is for you to make It yours. God has ordained, in Loving Kindness, that It be for you.

9. Be glad that you can walk the world that you perceive aware of

Christ and find so many situations in which to extend God's Gift of Real Perception, and so receive It as your own. This is how every trace of hell, secret sins, and hidden hates are undone in your mind. All the Loveliness that they conceal are like Lawns of Heaven that lift you high above the thorny roads that you traveled before you remembered Christ. Hear your Christ Mind, and join with It. God has ordained that your Christ Mind cannot call to you in vain, and in God's Certainty, your Christ Mind rests content. You *will* hear, and you *will* choose again. In this choice, your entire mind is set free.

10. *Thank you, God, for the Holiness that I can perceive in place of every misperception of separation. My faith in my Holiness is Your Faith in It. I am as sure of the Holiness of my Mind as You are sure that It will always be Holy. I will extend this Gift of Holiness to all that my mind perceives, because you gave It to me for my entire mind, and as I want to do Your Holy Will, so will I perceive It. I give thanks for every Perception of Holiness. My salvation will echo through my mind with every choice to perceive Holiness that I make, because my mind is One in Purpose, and the end of hell is near.*

11. *In joyous welcome, I extend my Mind to all that I perceive, reaching past my every temptation to make separation from You real to me, and looking with fixed determination toward Your Constant Love beyond. You give me my Whole Mind, because It belongs to You, and You cannot fail in Your Will. I give You thanks for What my Mind is, and every time that I extend Love, Heaven is brought closer to being all that I perceive, and I give thanks to You.*

12. *And now I say 'Amen' because my Christ Mind dwells in my awareness, where You set Christ in Calm Eternity before I imagined time. My journey ends Where it began. No trace of it remains, I do not believe in illusions, and not one spot of denial remains to hide Christ from me. Your Will is done, Completely and Perfectly, and your Creation recognizes You, and I know that You are my only Source. Clear in Your Likeness does Love extend from Everything that Lives in You. I have reached Where my Mind is One and I am Home, Where You want me to be.*[1]

Notes

Chapter 1
Part 1:
[1] The Principles are summarized here, and the paragraphs do not correspond with the original.
Part 7:
[1] This is offered for clarity and does not appear in the original.

Chapter 2
Part 6:
[1] For example, you perceive yourself as being attacked, and you want to extend Love instead. The personal mind is advising you that this is weak, and that you should attack back to appear strong. Your behavior vacillates between both motivations.

Chapter 4
Part 5:
[1] See Chapter 1, Part 7.

Chapter 13
Part 1:
[1] 'atoning' here means 'payment', not 'correction'.
Part 10:
[1] Italicized to represent a prayer.

Chapter 15
Part 7:
[1] This is elaborated on in Chapter 16, Part 5.

Chapter 16
Part 5:
[1] Specifically, Chapter 15, Part 7.
Part 7:
[1] 'atonement' here means 'payment', not 'correction'.

2   Italicized to represent a prayer.

Chapter 17
Part 6:

1   For example, instead of giving a whole relationship to the Holy
     Spirit, you only call on the Holy Spirit when the relationship is
     particularly conflicted. This is your attempt to forge a compromise
     where you get to keep separation from God, but you benefit from
     the Holy Spirit's occasional guidance. You do not achieve total Peace
     in the relationship, because you are living in two 'realities': the
     world and God. But, if you acknowledge that only God is Real, and
     you see extending this awareness to the relationship as a means for
     remembering God, then you will give the whole relationship to the
     Holy Spirit and experience it in total Peace.

Chapter 18
Part 6:

1   You want the illusion of separation from God, but the body does not
     do this for you. The body cannot do anything. The illusion of
     separation is a decision and perception of your mind.

Chapter 19
Part 3:

1   For example, let's say you have an addiction. If you believe that you
     are truly the personal self (separate from God; a 'sinner'), then you
     might believe that you can change your behavior, but not the actual
     addiction (the 'sin'). However, if you realize that you are not
     separate from God, that in God you have Everything, and that
     seeking for salvation (happiness, peace, wholeness, etc.) in your
     substance of choice is only the result of your error of identifying
     with a limited personal self, you can let go of the addiction. But if
     you still hold onto guilt by identifying with a personal self, you may
     overcome a specific addiction, but switch to another form of seeking
     outside yourself for relief from the pain of perceiving yourself
     separate from God. Nothing will really have changed; you will still
     anticipate punishment.

Part 4:

1   In the original, this part is written for two who are supporting each
    other in a Holy relationship, of which both are aware. Since many
    students do not share this experience simultaneously with another,
    this translation is written from the perspective of only one party. But
    two who are experiencing the Holy relationship together would each
    practice extending Love and forgiveness in the same way to support
    each other.

Chapter 21
Part 1:

1   Paragraphs 6–9 in this part mix auditory (song) and visual (light)
    metaphors for God. In this translation, the metaphor in the original
    paragraph 10 has been omitted for clarity.

Chapter 23
Part 2:

1   Love is Oneness with God, so the 'substitute for Love' is separation
    from God, or specialness. In essence, since the absence of Love is
    fear, the 'substitute for Love' is fear. But the personal mind will never
    tell you this. Instead, it has you seek endlessly for this valuable
    elusive 'substitute' in others without ever clearly defining what it is.
    In this way, it keeps you pursuing further separation, and this is why
    your seeking for wholeness and meaning is never over when you
    identify with a personal self.

Chapter 25
Part 4:

1   This is figurative, not literal. There is no form in God's Oneness.

Chapter 27
Part 1:

1   In the original, some parts of this chapter deal specifically with how
    Dr Schucman used a sick body to make another feel guilty, and how
    she could help him undo his sense of guilt by accepting healing for
    her body. This would seem to imply that Dr Schucman was respon-

sible for another's perceptions, but the dynamics of their specific relationship were under the guidance of Jesus, Who understood how each of their minds worked, and what they could understand in their experience of their relationship. Where possible, these references have been generalized here.

2 Much of this chapter is about using physical illness as an accusation against the world. This is only one of many uses to which the personal mind puts physical illness.

Part 4:

1 For example, 'What happens when I die?' This question has no real answer, because there is no such thing as a body, birth, or death. It is actually a statement that you are a body, and that death is real, and any possible answer then reinforces their reality. A real question would be: 'Do I die?'

Chapter 28

Part 1:

1 'Present memory' is remembering what you know but have denied, rather than remembering the past.

Part 4:

1 Italicized to represent a prayer.

Chapter 30

Part 1:

1 For example, you perceive that someone is treating you unfairly. You ask the Holy Spirit to show you how to 'handle' this person, and the Holy Spirit reminds you that it is not the person who needs to be corrected, but it is your perception of the situation that needs to be corrected. Since the Holy Spirit is not answering you on the personal mind's terms (how to handle the 'unfair' person) you get angry, until you recognize that your request was designed to set a limit on the response that you would accept. The Holy Spirit's answer, in turn, shows you that your real request was 'Show me how I can be at Peace again.'

Part 6:

1 Italicized to represent a prayer.

Chapter 31

Part 5:

1 Consider your feelings toward others that are reflected in these statements: 'You make me feel...'; 'If only you would...then I would be happy'; 'I have a headache because you...' These feelings imply that others are the cause of your experience; they make you.

Part 8:

1 Italicized to represent a prayer.

Glossary

Original Text	Translation
altar	your mind
atone	to correct your perception of separation from God
(the) Atonement	the full correction of your perception of separation from God
Attack	separation from God; separation from your mind's perceptions
awaken, reawaken	remember God; become fully aware of God
brother(s)	other(s); what is appearing; perceptions of the world; perceptions of others; personal mind's projections; perception of other(s); the world that you perceive
communication (world)	relationship; joining; healing; union
communication (God)	Oneness with God
communion	communion; Oneness; joining
condemnation	guilt; condemnation; separation
consciousness	personal mind
(to) create (mind)	the power of the mind
(to) create (Mind)	to extend God's Being; to extend God; God's extension (verb); your extension (verb) of God
creation (yours)	Your Extension (noun) of God
Creation (God's)	you; God's Being; God's Oneness; the Extension of God's Being; God's Extension (noun); Reality
dark(ness)	denial; illusions; thoughts of separation
dissociation	denial; separation
dream (not sleeping)	illusion

ego (individual)	personal mind; personal self
ego (neutral; universal)	split mind
faithlessness	faith in the personal mind/self
Father	God; the Whole
fear	being afraid; your perception of separation from God
give	extend
Grandeur	Limitlessness
grandiosity	personal self-inflation
Great Rays	Limitless Love
guilt	guilt; separation from God
host to God	God is within you
hostage to the ego	limited by the personal mind
(your) inheritance	God's Oneness
injustice	injustice of separation
Innocence	Oneness with God, Christ Mind
judge/judgment	to think with the personal mind; judge the separation as real
justice (God's)	the Justice of Oneness; God's Justice; the Holy Spirit's Justice; True Justice
Kingdom of God	Oneness with God
lack	your perception of separation from God
Law of Mind	the mind can only see itself; in God, Oneness, the extension of God everywhere, always; in the personal mind, projection
Light	awareness, Love, Truth
littleness	limitedness
loss	your perception of separation from God
magnitude	Limitlessness
Mind (healed)	Mind; Christ Mind; God's Mind
mind (separated)	mind, personal mind, split mind
miracle	an extension of God's Love
miracle worker	accept miracles (God's Love) for yourself
miscreate	perceive separation from God; reject

	God; reject Reality
no order of difficulty in miracles	God's Love can be extended every where, without exception
perceive/perception	the split mind; the level of the personal mind; a world separate from God; interpretation; evaluation; choice; judgment
real world	Real Perception
reason	True Reasoning
redeemed/redemption	corrected; the correction of your perception that you are separate from God
right-mind(edness)	corrected personal mind, miracle-minded, awareness of your Oneness with God
savior	your Christ Mind; your perception of Christ in another
share	extend
sin(s)	separation; the belief that separation from God is real; forms of separation
sinlessness	Innocence
Son of God	you; One with God; Part of God; God's Extension (noun)
sons of God	others; the world that you perceive
Sonship	your entire mind (in the world); your Whole Mind (in God); your Christ Mind; God's Extension (noun)
special function	special function of forgiveness
Spiritual Sight	Spiritual Perception; Real Perception
time and space	the world that you perceive
universe (non-material)	Oneness; Reality; All
universe (material)	the world that you perceive; all that you perceive
vigilance	awareness; make an effort to be aware of

world	the world that you perceive; your perception; your entire mind
world (real)	Real Perception
Wrong-mind(edness)	perception of separation from God, personal mind

Waiting for a Partner:

* God is getting things ready...
You never go wrong waiting for God to 'move'!...
Wait - it is for our good....

* He is purifying our motive concerning what we desire?...

* He is teaching us to trust Him ...
If I trust Him, I will wait.

* He is protecting us from 'something'.

* God can use this as a testimony in the end.

Have a
Faith / trust
Be patient
Humility
Courage and stand still ⟵ Resist the temptation to do it
Resist the pressure of other people.
Resist the fear of failure

* He saves the best for those who are
willing to wait on Him.
He acts in behalf of those who wait for Him.

756

About the Translator

Liz Cronkhite has been a student of *A Course in Miracles* since 1984 and a life-coach since 2000. From her home in Las Vegas, Nevada she mentors students of the *Course* from around the world. You can learn more about her and what she offers at www.acimmentor.com.

Wait, weigh + watch

★ Our willingness to wait shows ★
the value of what it means to us.
we place on the object we are
waiting for.

any way

BOOKS

O is a symbol of the world, of oneness and unity. In different cultures it also means the "eye," symbolizing knowledge and insight. We aim to publish books that are accessible, constructive and that challenge accepted opinion, both that of academia and the "moral majority."

Our books are available in all good English language bookstores worldwide. If you don't see the book on the shelves ask the bookstore to order it for you, quoting the ISBN number and title. Alternatively you can order online (all major online retail sites carry our titles) or contact the distributor in the relevant country, listed on the copyright page.

See our website www.o-books.net for a full list of over 500 titles, growing by 100 a year.

And tune in to myspiritradio.com for our book review radio show, hosted by June-Elleni Laine, where you can listen to the authors discussing their books.

MySpiritRadio